OTTO KAISER

ISAIAH 13–39

OTTO KAISER

ISAIAH 13-39

A Commentary

SCM PRESS LTD
BLOOMSBURY STREET LONDON

Translated by R. A. Wilson from the German
Der Prophet Jesaja/Kap. 13–39
(Das Alte Testament Deutsch 18)
published 1973 by Vandenhoeck and Ruprecht,
Göttingen

Translation © SCM Press Ltd 1974

334 00727 5
First published in English 1974
by SCM Press Ltd
58 Bloomsbury Street, London ₁WC1
Second impression 1978
Printed and bound in Great Britain by
REDWOOD BURN LIMITED
Trowbridge & Esher

CONTENTS

v

While Rabbi Menahem was living in the Land of Israel, a foolish man climbed the Mount of Olives unobserved. When he got to the top, he blew the ram's horn. The people were startled and soon a rumor sprang up that this was the blowing of the ram's horn which was to precede redemption. When this was reported to Rabbi Menahem, he opened his window, looked out into the world, and said: 'This is no renewal!'

Martin Buber, *Tales of the Hasidim: The Early Masters*, on Rabbi Menahem Mendel of Vitebsk.

IN PLACE OF A PREFACE

Anyone trying to discern the plan underlying the structure of the second and larger half of the book of Isaiah must stand well back and survey it as a whole. Otherwise he will lose his way in the details, the considerable number of problems of literary criticism which occur, and the apparent stumbling blocks, if not contradictions, in the composition. Such a survey must accept, as an established conclusion of scholarship, that the previous history of two blocks of tradition, chs. 24–27 and 36–39, is distinct and separate.

Thus chs. 36–39 form an appendix taken from the books of Kings at a time which can hardly be earlier than the fourth century BC, together with some stories in which the prophet Isaiah appears as a plenipotentiary mediating between Hezekiah and Yahweh, and even as a healer and miracle worker. These stories are of no importance for the knowledge of the historical activity of the prophet. The picture they present is in conflict to the relationship between Isaiah and the men in power during the crisis of the year 701, which we can reconstruct from the sayings of this period which unquestionably go back to Isaiah. Instead, they give us an insight into the kind of narrative current in late pre-exilic circles, and into the faith of post-exilic circles by whom the prophet was venerated, and for whom Hezekiah's purchase of the freedom of Jerusalem had become the classic example of confidence in God and a complete contrast to the events of the year 587.[a]

The eschatological and apocalyptic compositions drawn together in chs. 24–27 are known throughout modern literature on the Old Testament as the Apocalypse of Isaiah. The period in which they were composed lies between the second half of the fourth century and the first third of the second century BC. Its themes are the successive catastrophies of the final age which come upon the whole earth, the conquest of the powers in heaven, on earth and in the sea who are hostile to God, the distress and redemption of the people of God, and the final glorification of Zion, to whose heavenly king the nations come in pilgrimage, and even the resurrection of the dead.

[a] For a full discussion see below pp. 367ff.

They form a self-contained eschatological cycle. In part, its ideas and topics have in common with other comparable texts the feature of being comprehensible only when compared with similar passages. This is a characteristic which also creates a problem for the reader in other passages of the book of Isaiah. Often only isolated features are selected from the conceptions of the events of the world catastrophe which form the background to these passages. It could obviously be assumed that their original hearers or readers were able to interpret them aright and understand them in their context. For us, however, these passages often present us with insoluble problems, because we are faced with several possible ways of fitting them into the drama of the final age, each of which alters the total picture. For the moment, the best we can do is to make the various possibilities clear without attempting an exact interpretation but merely drawing attention to the problem. Perhaps when a synopsis is one day drawn up of the use of eschatological material in the prophetic books the matter may be clearer.[a]

The use of the title 'Apocalypse of Isaiah' for Isa. 24–27 usually gives commentators the opportunity of criticizing it or at least of setting out their own understanding of the term. In this commentary the usage I follow distinguishes between eschatological, proto-apocalyptic and apocalyptic. I use the term 'eschatological' for expectations which look forward to a decisive crisis in the destiny of Israel and of the nations, but which do not depart from the sphere of history. I describe them as apocalyptic when they look forward to a crisis brought about by supernatural or cosmic intervention, the connection with concrete historical forces has become confused or appears fantastic, and there are calculations concerning the beginning the events of the end. The extensive intermediate stratum which comprises most of the text of the second half of the book of Isaiah is described as proto-apocalyptic, a term which is intended to cover the transitional stage between eschatological expectations within history and apocalyptic expectations on a cosmic scale. I admit, of course, that opinions can differ in any case about which is the right category; this is obvious from the ambiguity of the prophecies, which I have already mentioned. From the point of view of the categorizations of apocalyptic used by scholars of Judaism and the New Testament, the conceptions described here as apocalyptic would probably still be termed eschatological. My only concern in the terminology that I

[a] For a full discussion of the composition of chs. 24–27 see below pp. 173ff.

propose is to create a suitable instrument for the classification of Old Testament texts. Finally, I would point out that I have repeatedly used the concept of eschatology in a general sense to describe the whole complex of conceptions, without risk of adding to the reader's confusion, because the context provides sufficient guard against mis-understandings. It must also be recalled here that we should not simply take for granted that Jewish thought evolved in a straight line from eschatology through proto-apocalyptic to apocalyptic. It would be more realistic not only to assume a conflict between a theocratic Israel which was content with the existence of Judaism as a cultic community, and eschatological Israel,[a] but also to presume the co-existence of eschatological, apocalyptic and even genuinely prophetic tendencies, even though it is not possible for us to identify the section of society which sustained these groups. Only the future can show whether a critical study of these tendencies on a sociological basis may achieve better results. In this respect, the historical obscurity surrounding post-exilic and early Hellenistic Judaism creates difficulties for everyone who tackles the problem.

Apart from chs. 24–27 and 36–39, an approximate plan at least can be discerned for what remains. The oracles upon foreign nations in chs. 13–23 are introduced by a saying against the capital of the world empire, as the embodiment of world power, ch. 13, and against the world ruler, 14.4ff., and are concluded by a saying against the trading city of Tyre, ch. 23. The introduction which results is certainly not the product of accident, and bears witness to the way in which Judaism's eschatological theology of history took shape in the interpretation of the events leading to the exile.[b] One might therefore suspect that the same is true of the conclusion of the collection. It is a mistake to imagine too great a break after ch. 23.[c] This misrepresents the structure of the work, which consciously passes from the judgment upon the nations in the final age to the eschatological judgment on Jerusalem in the tempest of the nations, in ch. 28. There are numerous previous references to this event (cf. 14.24ff.; 17.12ff. and 22.1ff.). This theme is maintained up to and including ch. 33, in which we find a kind of compendium of the eschatological conceptions associ-

[a] Cf. O. Plöger, *Theokratie und Eschatologie*, WMANT 2, 1959 (³1968), ET *Theocracy and Eschatology*, Oxford and Richmond, Va., 1968, to which I owe a great deal in the present commentary, even where I do not follow him.

[b] Cf. also P. R. Ackroyd, *Exile and Restoration*, OTL, 1968, pp. 232ff.

[c] For the composition of chs. 13–23 cf. below pp. 1ff.

ated with the fate of Jerusalem. By contrast, the two following chapters, 34 and 35, stand somewhat on their own, but by their contrast between the fate of Edom and the transformation of the desert for the homecoming of the exiles form an adequate conclusion. Thus it is very questionable whether chs. 28–32 should be treated as a separate 'Assyrian cycle' as is usually done.[a] The supposed justification for this is the implication that in 32.9–14 we once again have the words of the prophet Isaiah. Since in my view this is a false judgment from the point of view of literary criticism, there are no adequate reasons other than convention for making a division here.

A present-day reader will normally open the book of Isaiah in order to learn something about the activity and preaching of the prophet who lived in the eighth century. He will, of course, find what he is looking for in this commentary, in so far as it endeavours to identify the primary material from the prophet, particularly in chs. 28–31. But what a modern reader seeks and the purpose of the men to whom we owe the book of Isaiah in the form in which it has been handed down are fundamentally different. The redactors, as we call these anonymous persons for want of a better term, were not concerned to preserve sayings actually uttered by the prophet as faithfully and as unchanged as possible. Nor did they regard the word of Yahweh once uttered as exhausted in the great catastrophe of Judah in 587, but also as pointing on to the coming final judgment upon the people of God and the city of God. Thus our exposition will have the task, which we have no more than indicated here, of interpreting the sayings which we attribute to the prophet Isaiah not only on the basis of their own period, but in addition against the eschatological context in which they have been handed down. If this attempt is made, for example, with 28.14ff., the result is at first so astonishing that one begins to doubt whether there is any Isaianic basis at all. Whenever any distinct, independent unit is identified this question requires an answer. In view of the fact that alterations were made to the Isaiah roll down to the Hellenistic period, there is bound to be a demand to deny on principle that any saying derives from the prophet himself, if it can be explained on the basis of a different period.[b] It is obvious that this principle raises difficulties, since Judah's external relationships followed an almost regularly recurring pattern, as can be

[a] For the literary criticism of chs. 28–32 cf. below pp. 234ff.

[b] Cf. W. Schottroff, 'Jeremia 2.1–3. Erwägungen zur Methode der Propheten-exegese', *ZThK* 67, 1970, pp. 293f.

seen by examining, for example, 30.1ff. and 31.1ff. If we are not to come to the embarrassing conclusion that the whole tradition concerning Isaiah must be relegated to the level of legends about him, we must claim the reverse, that at least a basic stratum must be shown to derive from the prophet whose name the book bears. Here, starting with individual texts, one can go on to associate with them others which are related in spirit. If the result of this examination is the likelihood of a relatively early redaction, which for want of a better term must be ascribed to a circle of disciples, the question finally arises, to what degree the sayings were written down by the prophet himself and to what degree this happened only after a period or oral tradition. Within the framework of the task on which we have set out, the problem can be formulated, but not yet answered. The fact that a solution is urgent may hasten the new study of the first twelve chapters of the book of Isaiah which is so badly needed.

Cappel, Near Marburg-Lahn   OTTO KAISER
Summer 1972

GENERAL ABBREVIATIONS

AHW	*Akkadisches Handwörterbuch*, W.v.Soden, Wiesbaden, 1965ff.
ANEP	*Ancient Near East – in Pictures Relating to the Old Testament*, ed. J. B. Pritchard, Princeton N.J. 1954
ANET²	*Ancient Near Eastern Texts Relating to the Old Testament*, ed. J. B. Pritchard, Princeton N.J. ²1955
AnOr	*Analecta Orientalia*, Rom
AO	Der Alte Orient, Leipzig
AOAT	Alter Orient und Altes Testament, Kevelaer und Neukirchen-Vluyn
AOB²	*Altorientalische Bilder zum Alten Testament*, ed. H. Gressmann, Berlin und Leipzig, ²1927
AOT²	*Altorientalische Texte zum Alten Testament*, ed. H. Gressmann, Leipzig und Berlin ²1926
AR	D. D. Luckenbill, *Ancient Records of Assyria and Babylonia* I–II, Chicago 1926 (=New York 1968)
ArOr	*Archiv Orientální*, Prague
ASThI	*Annual of the Swedish Theological Institute*, Leiden
ATD	Das Alte Testament Deutsch, Göttingen
ATh	Arbeiten zur Theologie, Stuttgart
AThANT	Abhandlungen zur Theologie des Alten und Neuen Testaments, Zurich
ATAO⁴	Alfred Jeremias, *Das Alte Testament im Lichte des Alten Orients*, Leipzig ⁴1930
BA	*The Biblical Archaeologist*, (New Haven) Cambridge, Mass.
BASOR	*Bulletin of the American Schools of Oriental Research*, (South Hadley, Mass.), Baltimore, Maryland
BAT	Die Botschaft des Alten Testaments, Stuttgart
BBB	Bonner Biblische Beiträge, Bonn
BevTh	Beiträge zur evangelischen Theologie, Munich
BH	=*Biblia Hebraica* ed. R. Kittel, Stuttgart (³1937) ¹⁰1962
BHS	=*Biblia Hebraica Stuttgartensia* ed. K. Elliger et W. Rudolph: 7 *Liber Jesaiae* praep. D. Winton Thomas, Stuttgart 1968
BhTh	Beiträge zur historischen Theologie, Tübingen
BHW	*Biblisch-Historisches Handwörterbuch*, Göttingen
BJRL	*Bulletin of the John Rylands Library*, Manchester
Bib	*Biblica*, Rom

BK	Biblischer Kommentar, Neukirchen
B–L	H. Bauer und P. Leander, *Historische Grammatik der Hebräischen Sprache des Alten Testaments*, Halle 1922 = Hildesheim 1962
BRL	K. Galling, *Biblisches Reallexikon*, HAT I. 1, Tübingen, 1937
BSt	Biblische Studien, Neukirchen
BWANT	Beiträge zur Wissenschaft vom Alten und Neuen Testament, Stuttgart
BZAW	Beihefte zur *Zeitschrift fur die alttestamentliche Wissenschaft*, Giessen till 1934, then Berlin
CAH	The Cambridge Ancient History
CTA	A. Herdner, *Corpus des tablettes en cunéiformes alphabétiques découvertes à Ras Shamra-Ugarit de 1929 à 1939*, Paris, 1963
EH	Exegetisches Handbuch zum Alten Testament, Münster
ET	English translation
EvTh	*Evangelische Theologie*, Munich
FRLANT	Forschungen zur Religion und Literatur des Alten und Neuen Testaments, Göttingen
FzB	Forschungen zur Bibel, Würzburg
G-K	Gesenius-Kautzsch, *Hebräische Grammatik*, ed. E. Kautzsch, Leipzig ²⁸1909 = *Gesenius' Hebrew Grammar*, ed. E. Kautzsch, Second English Edition ed. A. E. Cowley, Oxford 1910 (1960)
HAL	*Hebräisches und Aramäisches Lexikon zum Alten Testament*, ed. W. Baumgartner, Lieferung I, Leiden, 1967
HAT	Handbuch zum Alten Testament, Tübingen
HAW	Handbuch der Altertums-Wissenschaft, Munich
HK	Handkommentar zum Alten Testament, Göttingen
HNT	Handbuch zum Neuen Testament, Tübingen
HO	Handbuch der Orientalistik, Leiden
HUCA	*Hebrew Union College Annual*, Cincinnati
ICC	International Critical Commentary, Edinburgh
IEJ	*Israel Exploration Journal*, Jerusalem
JAOS	*Journal of the American Oriental Society*, New Haven
IB	*Interpreter's Bible*, New York
JBL	*Journal of Biblical Literature*, (New Haven; Philadelphia) Montana, Miss.
JCS	*Journal of Cuneiform Studies*, Cambridge, Mass.
JNES	*Journal of Near Eastern Studies*, Chicago
JSS	*Journal of Semitic Studies*, Manchester
KAI	H. Donner und W. Röllig, *Kanaanäische und Aramäische Inschriften* I–III, Wiesbaden, ²1968–69
KAT	Kommentar zum Alten Testament, ¹Leipzig, ²Gütersloh
KBL	L. Koehler und W. Baumgartner, *Lexicon in Veteris Testamenti Libros*, Leiden 1953

KC	Kamper Cahiers, Kampen
KHC	Kurzer Hand-Commentar zum Alten Testament, Freiburg, Leipzig und Tübingen
KP	*Der Kleine Pauly. Lexicon der Antike*, Stuttgart
KuD	*Kerygma und Dogma*, Göttingen
LUÅ	Lund Universitets Årsskrift, Lund
MIO	*Mitteilungen des Instituts für Orientforschung*, Berlin
MeyerK	*Kritisch-exegetischer Kommentar über das Neue Testament* founded by H. A. W. Meyer, Göttingen
NTD	Das Neue Testament Deutsch, Göttingen
NTL	New Testament Library, London and Philadelphia
NZSTh	*Neue Zeitschrift für Systematische Theologie und Religionsphilosophie*, Berlin
OIP	Oriental Institute Publications, Chicago
OrAnt	*Oriens Antiquus*, Rome
OTL	Old Testament Library, London and Philadelphia
PEQ	*Palestine Exploration Quarterly*, London
PhB	*Philosophische Bibliothek* (Meiner)
PJB	*Palästinajahrbuch*, Berlin
POS	Pretoria Oriental Series, Leiden
PRU	*Le Palais Royal d'Ugarit*. Mission de Ras Shamra, Paris
RB	*Revue Biblique*, Paris
RGG	*Die Religion in Geschichte und Gegenwart*, Tübingen
RHR	*Revue de l'Histoire des Religions*, Paris
RLA	*Reallexikon der Assyrologie*, Berlin (and Leipzig)
RM	Die Religionen der Menschheit, Stuttgart
RVV	*Religionsgeschichtliche Versuche und Vorarbeiten*, Berlin
SAB	Sitzungsberichte der Preussischen Akademie der Wissenschaften zu Berlin
SAL	Berichte über die Verhandlungen der Sächsischen Akademie der Wissenschaften zu Leipzig, Berlin
SAW	Sitzungsberichte der Österreichische Akademie der Wissenschaften, Vienna
SNVAO	Skrifter utgitt av det Norske Videnskaps-Akademi i Oslo
StBTh	Studies in Biblical Theology, London and Naperville, Ill.
StTh	*Studia Theologica* (Lund), Oslo
SVT	Supplements to *Vetus Testamentum*, Leiden
TDNT	*Theological Dictionary of the New Testament* (ET of *ThWBNT*), Grand Rapids, Michigan
TGI²	K. Galling, *Textbuch zur Geschichte Israels*, Tübingen, ²1968
THAT	*Theologisches Handwörterbuch zum Alten Testament*, edd. E. Jenni and G. Westermann, Munich
ThB	Theologische Bücherei, Munich

ThLZ	*Theologische Literaturzeitung*, Berlin
ThQ	*Tübinger Theologische Quartalschrift*
ThStKr	*Theologische Studien und Kritiken*, Hamburg, Gothe
ThWAT	*Theologisches Wörterbuch zum Alten Testament*, Stuttgart
ThWBNT	*Theologisches Wörterbuch zum Neuen Testament*, Stuttgart
ThZ	*Theologische Zeitschrift*, Basel
UF	*Ugarit Forschungen*, Kevelaer und Neukirchen-Vluyn
VT	*Vetus Testamentum*, Leiden
WMANT	Wissenschaftliche Monographien zum Alten und Neuen Testament, Neukirchen-Vluyn
WUNT	Wissenschaftliche Untersuchungen zum Neuen Testament, Tübingen
ZA	*Zeitschrift für Assyrologie*, Berlin
ZAW	*Zeitschrift für die alttestamentliche Wissenschaft*, (Giessen) Berlin
ZDMG	*Zeitschrift der Deutschen Morgenländischen Gesellschaft*, (Leipzig) Wiesbaden
ZDPV	*Zeitschrift des Deutschen Palästina Vereins*, (Leipzig) Wiesbaden
ZThK	*Zeitschrift für Theologie und Kirche*, Tübingen

DEAD SEA SCROLLS

1QH	=Cave 1 Qumran, Psalms of Praise
1QIsa	=Cave 1 Qumran, Great Isaiah Roll
1Qs	=1 Qumran

WITNESSES TO THE TEXT

LXX	=Septuagint (Greek), quoted from *Septuaginta auct. soc. litt. Göttingensis editum* Vol. XIV *Isaias*, ed. J. Ziegler, Göttingen 1939
LXX[L]	=Lucianic recension of the LXX
Targ	=Targum (Aramaic), quoted from *The Targum of Isaiah*, ed. J. F. Stenning, Oxford 1953
Vg	=Vulgate (Latin)
Aq	=Aquila
M	=Massoretic Text (Hebrew)
Th	=Theodotion

COMMENTARIES
usually cited by author's name only

A. Bentzen, 1943; J. A. Bewer, 1950; C. J. Bredenkamp, 1887; A. Condamin, 1905; F. Delitzsch, 1866, ⁴1889; C. F. A. Dillmann, 1890; C. F. A. Dillmann and R. Kittel, ⁶1898; B. Duhm, HAT III.1, 1892, ⁴1922; W. Eichrodt, 1960; F. Feldmann, 1925/26; J. Fischer, 1937; G. Fohrer, 1960; G. B. Gray, ICC, 1912; H. Guthe and O. Eissfeldt, 1922; V. Herntrich, 1950; H. W. Hertzberg, 1936, ²1952; E. J. Kissane, 1941; E. König, 1926; K. Marti, KHC 10, 1900; C. von Orelli, 1887, ³1904; O. Procksch, 1930; H. Schmidt, ²1923; R. B. Y. Scott and G. D. Kilpatrick, IB 5, 1951, pp. 149–773; J. Steinmann, 1950; J. Ziegler, 1948.

TRANSLATOR'S NOTE

Where chapter and verse divisions of the Hebrew (and German) Bible differ from those of the English versions, the former have been retained.

COMMENTARY

CHAPTERS 13–23

THE ORACLES OF THE NATIONS

CHAPTER 13.1

Heading

1 Oracle concerning Babylon which Isaiah the son of Amoz saw.

[1] The heading in 13.1, like the two preceding headings in 1.1 and 2.1, marks a more significant break. Unlike the headings which follow elsewhere in chs. 13–30, it explicitly names as the author the prophet Isaiah who is additionally described as the son of Amoz. The redactor is no doubt claiming in it that the oracles concerning foreign nations which follow also derive from the prophet. It is notable that this heading, like those that follow, speak not of the 'word' but of the 'oracle'. There is so far no agreement about the meaning of the Hebrew word *maśśā'* which is so translated. Whereas some follow the Vulgate, Luther and the AV and translate 'burden', others seek an explanation in the phrase 'raise the voice' which frequently occurs in the Old Testament, and derive from it the word *maśśā'* with the meaning 'raising (of the voice), oracle'.[a] In the following chapters these headings fall into two main groups. The first adds to 'oracle' the name of the country or city at which it is directed, while the second takes up a particularly characteristic key-word from the oracle which follows. Apart from the heading in 13.1 the first type includes 15.1 (Moab), 17.1 (Damascus), 19.1 (Egypt) and 23.1 (Tyre), while the second group consists of 21.1 ('from the desert'), 21.13 ('in the desert'), 22.1 ('the valley of vision') and 30.6 ('beasts of the Negeb'), while the

[a] See the recent study by S. Erlandsson, *The Burden of Babylon*, Coniectanea Biblica, Old Testament Series 4, Lund 1970, pp. 64f., where the debate that has taken place in recent decades is referred to.

heading in 21.11 ('Dumah') remains doubtful. 14.28 was formed in imitation of the headings. Finally, the heading in 22.15b stands on its own.

If chs. 13–23 are considered as a whole, it is clear that there are also individual units with no heading, although they can scarcely be regarded as mere additions to one of the oracles which possess a heading. Thus there are no such headings for the short oracle against Assyria in 14.24ff. and the saying against Ethiopia in ch. 18. On the other hand, the introduction to ch. 20 may be regarded as describing it sufficiently. Perhaps one may conclude from the present situation that 14.24ff., 14.28ff. and 18.1ff. were not brought into the collection until after the other oracles against the nations had already received their headings.

The order of the sayings within the collection tells us little at first sight. The prophecies against Babylon in 13.1–14.23 are followed in 14.24–27 by a saying against Assyria. But a further difference is immediately obvious: whereas Babylon is to be annihilated in its own country, the Assyrians are to fall in the Holy Land. Thus the Babylonians are not included in the army of the nations which is to surge against the city of God. On the other hand, 14.28ff. prophesies the extermination of the Philistines by the enemy from the north whom we are to associated with the tempest of the nations. An older, late pre-exilic or more probably exilic prophecy may lie behind 13.2–22. In its present form it is post-exilic, and its outlook allows us to describe it as proto-apocalyptic. The taunt on the fall of the tyrant in 14.4b–21 is also likely to be a product of the post-exilic period. Interest in the fate of Babylon did not come to an end with the conquest of the city by Cyrus in the year 539. Because Babylon was responsible for the fate of Jerusalem and of the Jews, it became the symbol of the world power hostile to God, and its king became the world ruler who was equally hostile to God. Thus at the beginning of the prophecy we have the promise that on the day of Yahweh the world power and the world ruler which are God's enemies will be destroyed. The link between the prophecy against Babylon and that against the world ruler is provided by the passage from a later period of tradition, which gives the impression of being composed by a learned scribe, 14.1–4a; it seems to be later than the postscript in 14.22–23 to the taunt concerning the world ruler. The prophecy against the Philistines in 14.28–32 may come from the year 333, but may be even more recent. The section 14.24ff. must be dated in the

Seleucid period. Assyria had come to be the name used for the Hellenistic kingdom.

The extensive oracle concerning Moab which forms chs. 15 and 16 could, like 13.2ff., have been edited from one or two earlier compositions, but in its present form it likewise refers to the final events which are to bring about the decisive turning point in history. In 16.4b–5 we have a later Messianic addition, and in 16.13–14 a calculation, approaching the style of apocalyptic, of the fulfilment of the prophecy, which may come from the same hand as 21.16f. In spite of what the heading suggests, ch. 17 is directed not only against Damascus, but also against the northern kingdom of Israel, or rather, what was left of it in the post-exilic period. It is understandable that there should have been a desire for the fall of the Aramaean metropolis in the north, which had survived all political storms. There are no indications which enable us to date it more exactly. 17.7 and 8 show that the redactors sought to understand the sayings against Damascus and Israel in an eschatological sense. 17.9–11 also look forward to the visitation in the final age, though the short prophecy of warning, containing the reason for the condemnation, against the inhabitants of Jerusalem who took part in the cult of Adonis in 17.10–11 may be an Isaianic fragment. 17.12–14 once again recalls the coming tempest of the nations.

Chapters 18–20 are directed against Ethiopia and Egypt. As we have mentioned, ch. 18 may not have been introduced until relatively late, because it lacks a heading. The proto-apocalyptic prophecy of the conquest of Ethiopia in the final age (18.1–6) is followed in 18.7 by postscript in prose which describes the conquered bringing gifts to Yahweh. The oracle against Egypt in 19.1–15 may have been composed in several stages. Its political background is either the collapse of the internal order of the country before its reconquest by Artaxerxes III Ochos round the middle of the fourth century, or else the battle of Raphia in 217 BC. The additions in 19.16ff. which look forward first to a conversion of the Egyptians and then to the actual establishment of a threefold people of God, consisting of Egypt, Assyria and Israel, were composed at the earliest in the third century BC, and at the latest before the middle of the second century BC. By contrast to the xenophobic spirit of the other oracles concerning the nations they bear witness to tendencies towards a universalist concept of salvation which were developed in association with, if not by, the Jewish diaspora in Ptolemaic Egypt.

Just as the movement in ch. 17 proceeds from Damascus in the north towards Israel, so in chs. 18 and 19 it moves northwards from the furthest regions in the south which were known at that time, so that Jerusalem remains the centre of the movement. Egypt and Ethiopia were both mentioned in the narrative about the prophet in ch. 20, an isolated account of a sign enacted by Isaiah from the years 713–711. In content it seems to draw together uncritically reminiscences from the first two decades of the eighth century and the first two thirds of the seventh century. In the form in which it now exists it cannot be earlier than the sixth century.

To the astonishment of the reader, 21.1–10 brings us back to the moment of the conquest of Babylon. It does not seem impossible that an older poem has been used, but this is not absolutely certain. If so, it would have to be dated in the period before 539. It is possible that in its present form it refers to the further march of the victors against Jerusalem. 21.11–12 is a total enigma. The oracle seems to raise the question when the end of the distress (for Edom?) will come. 21.13–15 sketches for us the fate of the caravans of the Dedanites fleeing before their pursuers, and 21.16–17 calculates the time of the fall of the sons of Kedar. But the onrush of enemies does not leave Jerusalem untouched. 22.1–14 preserves what may be the final saying of the prophet Isaiah after the campaign of the Assyrians against Jerusalem in 701. Two fulfilments at the time of the exile in 22.7–11, and finally, in vv. 5 and 6, the explicit reinterpretation of the prophetic threat, refer the passage to the attack of the nations upon Jerusalem. In 22.15–18 there is a threat proclaimed against an unknown steward (comptroller of the household), only later identified with the Shebna of II Kings 18.18 (= Isa. 36.3), which must derive from Isaiah. It is followed in vv. 20–23 by a prophecy of salvation, originally eschatological in intention, of the installation of a faithful royal officer in the period of salvation. This was later interpreted to refer to Eliakim the son of Hilkiah, who likewise occurs in II Kings 18.18 (= Isa. 36.3) and elsewhere. It is supplemented by a prophetic threat in 22.24f., but the historical reference of this prophecy can no longer be discerned.

The cycle of oracles against the nations opens with sayings against the great capital city as the seat of world power, and against the world ruler; and in ch. 23 it is concluded by a similar oracle against the leading merchant city of the ancient world. According to its heading it is directed against Tyre. But it can be shown that it was originally written on the occasion of the destruction of Sidon by Artaxerxes III Ochos in the year 343. It was then reinterpreted to refer to the conquest of Tyre by Alexander the Great in the year 332, by the addition of part of 23.15 and v. 16. Finally, the poem seems to have received a final addition after 274 BC, in the form of part of 23.15 and 23.17–18. These verses prophesy that the city will once again rise as a commercial power in the service of the people of God.

Unless ch. 23 was added later to the Isaiah roll, 19.1ff. may provide, in spite of the uncertainty about its dating, an indication that the oracles against the nations were first gathered together towards the end of the fourth century or the beginning of the third century, and supplied with headings either then or later.

If we look back over the compilation, we can discern the outline of the eschatological events which it described. The army coming from the ends of the earth gathers at Yahweh's bidding before the gates of Babylon, in order to bring about the end of the world power and the world ruler, with that of the capital city. The oracle against Assyria in 14.2ff. affirms that the army will storm on and finally reach Judaea. 14.28ff. and chs. 15–16 imply that the army will overwhelm the East and the West. That the Holy Land and the city of God will not be spared can be seen from the movement from north to south in ch. 17 and from south to north in the two following chapters; in each case the movement ends at Jerusalem. 14.24ff. and 17.12ff. also show that it was thought the attack on the city of God would bring about the complete destruction of the enemy. Rather oddly, the recommencement of the movement in 21.1ff. refers to Babylon. Perhaps the redactor thought that after the fall of the city other forces would be released which might proceed to attack Jerusalem. Whereas the Arabs take flight against the attackers (21.13ff., 16f.) so that the army of the nations presses on even into the Arabian peninsular, Jerusalem is not spared (22.1ff.). The army from afar will carry out Yahweh's judgment against a people which has ceased to care. How great the danger will be is shown by the fact that even the mighty Tyre will be unable to resist the enemy.

CHAPTER 13.2–22

The Days of the Great City Will not be Prolonged

2   'On a bare hill raise the signal,
       cry aloud to them;
    wave the hand for them to enter
       the gates of the nobles.[a]

3   I myself have commanded ⟨for my anger⟩[b]
       ⟨the army of my consecrated⟩,[b]
    yes, have summoned my heroes ⟨   ⟩[b]
       who proudly exult.'[c]

4   Hark, a tumult on the mountains,
       ⟨the roaring⟩[d] of a great multitude.
    Hark, an uproar of kingdoms,
       of nations gathering together!
    Yahweh of hosts is mustering
       a host for battle.

5   They come from a distant land,
       from the end of the heavens,
    Yahweh and the weapons of his indignation,
       to destroy the whole earth.[e]

6   'Wail, for the day of Yahweh is near;
       as might from the Almighty[f] it will come!'

7   Therefore all hands will be feeble,
       and every man's heart will melt.

8   . . . .
    . . . and they will be dismayed.[g]

[a] LXX reads here, 'Open, rulers!' and Vg: . . . *et ingrediantur portas duces*. The variants do not seem to reflect a different original text, but to have each rendered the meaning in their own way. Objections are certainly possible to M, but any proposed improvement can be no more than a guess.

[b] See *BHS*.   [c] For the construction cf. G-K, § 135n.

[d] Read with K. Budde, 'Jesaja 13', in *Abhandlungen zur Semitischen Religionskunde und Sprachwissenschaft. Festschrift W. W. Graf von Baudissin*. BZAW 33, 1916, pp. 65 etc., *hᵃmōt* instead of *dᵉmūt*, cf. 17.12. Contrary to what is stated in Dillmann-Kittel, Ezek. 23.15 cannot be taken as evidence for the use of *dᵉmūt* in the sense 'like'. The traditional reading is no doubt the result of a conscious change, with the intention of removing the divine command from the human sphere.

[e] Or: 'the whole country'.   [f] M literally 'from *šaddai*'.

[g] Building up from 'and they will be dismayed', which is now completely isolated, and taking into account II Sam. 4.1; Jer. 6.24 and especially 50.43, we may reconstruct: 'The men of Babylon shall hear and they will be dismayed.' But *wᵉnibhālū* may be simply a marginal gloss, and it is impossible to be certain.

Pangs and agony will seize them,[a] [b]
  they will be in anguish[b] like a woman in travail.
They will look aghast at one another;
  their faces will be aflame.

9 Behold, the day of Yahweh comes, cruel,
  with[c] wrath and fierce anger,
to make the earth a desolation
  and to destroy its sinners from it.

10 'When the stars of the heavens and their constellations
  do not give their light;
the sun is dark at its rising
  and the moon does not shed its light,

11 I will punish the world for its evil,[d]
  and the wicked for their iniquity;
I will put an end to the pride of the arrogant,
  and lay low the haughtiness of the ruthless.

12 I will make men more rare than fine gold,
  and mankind than the gold of Ophir.'

13 Therefore the heavens ⟨will tremble⟩[e]
  so that the earth is shaken out of its place,
at the wrath of Yahweh Sebaoth
  in the day of his fierce anger.

14 It will come about: like a gazelle cut off from its fellows
  or like sheep with none to gather them,
every man will turn to his own people,
  and every man will flee to his own land.

15 Whoever is found will be thrust through,
  and whoever is caught will fall by the sword.

16 Their infants will be dashed to pieces
  before their eyes;
their houses will be plundered
  and their wives ravished.

17 'Behold, I am stirring up the Medes against them,
  who have no regard for silver
  and do not delight in gold.

. . . .

[a] Cf. with Delitzsch Job 18.20 and 21.6; also G. Fohrer, KAT² 16, 1964, p. 298.
[b] For this form cf. G-K, § 47m.
[c] For the *waw concomitantiae* cf. G-K § 154 note b.
[d] Cf. S. Erlandsson, *The Burden of Babylon*, Coniectanea Biblica, Old Testament Series 4, Lund 1970, p. 23.
[e] See *BHS*.

18   and bows, young men will shatter them[a]
          their eyes will not pity children;
      they will have no mercy on the fruit of the womb.[b]

19   And Babylon, the glory of kingdoms,
          the splendour and pride of the Chaldeans,
      will be as when God overthrew
          Sodom and Gomorrah.

20   It will never be inhabited
          or dwelt in from generation to generation,
      no Arab will pitch his tent there[c]
          no shepherds will pasture there.[d]

21   But demons will lie down there,[e]
          and its houses will be full of owls;
      there ostriches will dwell,
          and there hairy ones will dance.

22   Jackals will cry in his towers,[f]
          and wild dogs in the palaces of pleasure.
      Its time is close at hand,
          and its days will not be prolonged.

In 13.2–22 the prophecy of the judgment of the world that is to take place on the day of Yahweh, and that of the conquest and destruction of Babylon, are remarkably intermingled. We first witness an unknown person summoning together an army, and learn from him that he is preparing a punitive expedition (vv. 2–3). And then the prophet describes for us the tumult of the nations which are gathering together, and confirms our suspicion that it is none other than Yahweh who is mustering his hosts (vv. 4–5). If the received text of v.2b is correct,[g] the attack that is imminent is directed against a capital city.[h] But according to v. 5b it is either a whole country or a

---

   [a] A literal translation of M. *BHS* proposes: 'And the bows of the young men are shattered.' The variants do not help. Cf. Erlandsson, p. 25. The numerous proposed emendations in the commentaries attempt to present as a series: young men, maidens, children, the unborn. It is not possible to be certain.

   [b] The order of v. 18b *a* and *β* is reversed, following Duhm and Marti.

   [c] For this form cf. G-K, § 68k.   [d] Literally 'will make to lie down'.

   [e] *KBL* follows Torrey (*The Second Isaiah*, Edinburgh 1928, pp. 289f.) in translating *ṣiyyīm* as a derivative of *ṣiyyā*, dry land, steppe, with the sense 'demons'.

   [f] The suffix presumably refers to the king. For the possibility of the substitution for each other of *r* and *l* cf. Erlandsson, p. 28.

   [g] Cf. above p. 6 note a.

   [h] Cf. below *ad loc*.

whole earth which is to be destroyed – the Hebrew text permits both translations. The latter interpretation is supported by the proclamation in vv. 6–13 that the day of Yahweh is near, will bring terror to all men (v. 7) and will involve the punishment of the evil throughout the world and the destruction of the mighty (v. 11). Verse 14 turns from this universal event, involving both heaven and earth, and returns to one located in a particular place: we learn that a panic-stricken flight will proceed from a centre which is not actually named. Those who have been attacked have clearly suffered a complete defeat which breaks the power of their people for ever (vv. 15–16). Finally we hear in v. 17 that the pitiless Medes are being summoned by Yahweh as the attackers. In v. 18 we find out for the first time that this attack is to be on Babylon which is to be destroyed for ever.

Obviously the person responsible for the chapter as we have it was prepared to tolerate the tension which results from the interweaving of prophecies of a local and a universal future event. The present-day reader is tempted to separate the two and to ask whether there may not be, underlying the present text, separate units on which the proto-apocalyptic redactor drew. In the attempt to identify them, the observation that the substance of vv. 16 and 18 overlaps might lead one to suppose that whoever composed the chapter was able to make use of an older prophecy of a disaster to a city which is not named, and another prophecy of the conquest of Assur or Babylon by the Medes or Persians. Since vv. 2–5 are in the 2:3 *qīnā* metre, while the rest of the chapter is a mixture of 3:3, 2:3 and 2:2 couplets,[a] one might go on to attempt to distinguish fragments of an older original, within the prophecy of the day of Yahweh in vv. 6–13, by means of a literary criticism based upon rhythmical considerations, and to treat them as fragments of the supposed earlier prophecy of the conquest of a city. But such attempts are necessarily subjective, and we shall therefore refrain from them here. We shall content ourselves in our exposition with making clear the intention of the composition as we possess it, and so explaining the remarkable intermingling of the prophecy of the judgment of the world and of the imminent conquest and destruction of Babylon.

In this task, the fact that not only in the book of Joel, but also in numerous passages in the great prophecy against Babylon in

[a] For the problems of Hebrew metre cf. O. Kaiser, *Einleitung in das Alte Testament*, Gütersloh ²1970, pp. 256ff.

Jeremiah 50.1–51.58 there are parallels or even in some cases quotations from the present passage,[a] causes us, in the present state of study, more difficulty than help; in particular, because the prophecy in the book of Jeremiah, which in substance concentrates wholly upon the fall of Babylon, seems to be dependent upon the present text, it is easy to jump to the conclusion that our text can be explained on the basis of the situation of the exile.[b] The fact that in the book of Joel the reverse situation is the case, and we find only the eschatological features associated with the day of Yahweh,[c] shows how complex the situation is. It would only be possible to explain it finally with the aid of a synoptic study of the redactions of all the prophetic books.

The question of the date of the proto-apocalyptic composition which we possess, as well as that of the original which may have been used in some passages in it, cannot be answered without considering the history of Babylon. But we need to look too at the history of eschatological belief in post-exilic Judaism. The kingdom of Judah seems to have become a vassal state of the neo-Babylonian emperor Nebuchadnezzar at the beginning of 603 BC. The fall of the king of Jerusalem and Judah, Jehoiakim, which took place at the latest at the turn of the year 601/600, set the catastrophe slowly but remorselessly into motion. On the 16 March 597 Jerusalem was conquered for the first time by Nebuchadnezzar. Jehoiakim's successor, the young king Jehoiachin, was deported to Babylon with part of the governing class of the country. Because the new king Zedekiah, who was installed by Nebuchadnezzar, was also unwise enough to rebel, the emperor led a new campaign against the unruly kingdom of Judah, which ended in July 587[d] with the conquest of the city and the subsequent destruction of the Temple, the palaces and the city wall, together with the

---

[a] Cf. 13.2 with Jer. 51.27f.; 5ba with 50.25aβ; 8a with 50.43b; 9ba with 50.23b (?); 13a with 50.34b and 51.29a; 14b with 50.16bβ; 17 with 51.1aβ, 11aa 2; 18a with 51.3 (?) and 50.30a (?); 18b with 50.42aa; 19b with 50.40a; 20 with 50.39b; 21aa ba with 50.39a.

[b] W. Rudolph, HAT I.12, ³1968, p. 299, and A. Weiser, ATD 20/21, ⁵1965, p. 427, are among those who take Jer. 50f. to be written during the exile. F. Giesebrecht, HK III.2.1, 1894, p. 248, and B. Duhm, KHC 11, 1901, p. 360, and also J. P. Hyatt, IB 5, 1956, pp. 790 and 1124, consider it was composed later.

[c] Cf. 13.6 with Joel 1.15; 2.1b; 7 with 2.6; 10 with 21.10b; 13a with 2.10a; 3.4 and 4.15.

[d] Cf. M. Noth, Geschichte Israels, Göttingen ³1956, § 23; ET History of Israel, London and New York ²1960, § 23.

deportation of Zedekiah and further groups from the governing class. After the failure of the attempt to place the country under a Jewish governor, Gedaliah, the country was probably incorporated into the neighbouring province of Samaria. But the neo-Babylonian kingdom was also not destined to last for long.

The Indo-Germanic Medes, closely related to the Persians, had settled in the north-west of the Iranian plateau, and with the fall of the new Assyrian kingdom had rapidly grown into one of the great powers of western Asia. In 614 Kyaxares, king of the Medes, succeeded in conquering Assur. In 612, in league with the Babylonian Nabopolassar he was also able to occupy Nineveh. During the whole period of Nebuchadnezzar's reign (604–562) there was peace between the two kingdoms. Admittedly the building of a wall and numerous fortifications shows that Nebuchadnezzar regarded Media as a potential danger. When Cyrus II of Persia (559–529) threw off his vassalage to Astyages, king of the Medes (585–553), in the year 553, took him prisoner and assumed the rule of Media, the last king of Babylon, Nabonidus (555–538), may still have regarded him as a welcome counterbalancing force against the danger from the Medes, particularly as he had already allied himself with Nabonidus. Not until the Persian attack upon the Lydian kingdom of Croesus did the whole of the ancient world realize what they had to expect from the young empire which had risen with such unexpected rapidity. After the fall of the Lydian capital Sardis in 546, the Babylonian kingdom moved irresistibly towards its collapse. Step by step Cyrus was able to enlarge his own kingdom at the expense of Babylonia, until Babylon finally fell into his hands without a struggle in 539. After the disturbances which followed the death of the Persian king Cambyses in 522, and extended to Babylonia, two revolts followed each other in quick succession, one by Nidintu-Bel, the son of Nabonidus, and the other by an Armenian, Aracha. But as early as November 521 the successor of Cambyses, Darius I, once again had Babylon firmly in his hands. There was a final revolt in the early years of the reign of Xerxes the I, led first by Bel-Shimanni, which was suppressed with great violence, and ended not only with the razing of the fortifications set up by Nebuchadnezzar, the destruction of the Esagila temple and the melting down of the golden statue of Marduk, but also with the incorporation of the country into the satrapy of Assyria. Although the city remained the true trading metropolis of the Near East, it never really recovered from this blow (482). Right until the conquest of the country after the battle of Gaugamela in 332 by Alexander the Great, Babylon remained firmly in Persian hands. Alexander stayed there in 324 and intended to make the city, if not the capital of his mighty empire, at least the principal city of Asia. But his sudden death brought all these plans to an end. When the eastern royal residence of the Seleucid kingdom was moved to Seleucia-Ctesiphon by Seleucus I, Babylon fell into an uninterrupted decline and decay, and was described by the Hellenistic historian and biographer Strabo as a wilderness (cf. XVI. 15).[a]

If we attempt to date the text as we now possess it, we must first take into account the remarkable fact that the unknown prophet whom scholars call Deutero-Isaiah, and who speaks to us in chs. 40–55, hoped that the defeat of Babylon by Cyrus would bring about the liberation of his people and the great crisis in the affairs of the world, but never once speaks of the Medes, who for a considerable time had no doubt been coupled with the Persians by the Jews and by the Greeks.[b] It must also be noted that the group of conceptions associated with the day of Yahweh, which are typical of post-exilic eschatology, are not yet to be found in Deutero-Isaiah. Although there are risks in drawing conclusions from the silence of the sources, these facts make it doubtful whether the composition in its present form can be dated in the period of the conquest of Babylon by Cyrus in the year 539. On the other hand we must ask whether some basic elements in it may have been composed on the occasion of the campaign of the Medes against Assyria or of Cyrus against Babylon. The description of the Medes in v. 17 may point to a time in which the attacks of the Persians had not yet been experienced. Of course it could just as well be understood as a statement made in isolation on a particular occasion. We must also remember that the city to which the Jews owed the loss of their existence as an independent state became increasingly the symbol of the great city and world power which was hostile to God. This explains why there was still a lively concern with its fate long after it had ceased to play an active role in

---

[a] Cf. H. S. Nyberg, 'Das Reich der Achämeniden', *Historia Mundi* 3, Munich 1954, pp. 77ff. and 98f.; and also E. Kornemann, *Weltgeschichte des Mittelmeerraumes von Philipp II von Makedonien bis Muhammad*, ed. H. Bengtson, Munich 1967, pp. 148ff. and 211. For an argument against the view that Alexander wanted to make Babylon the capital of his empire, cf. F. Schachermeyer, *Alexander in Babylon und die Reichsordnung nach seinem Tode*, SAW 268.3, 1970, pp. 74ff.

[b] Cf. e.g. Dan. 9.1 and J. Duschesne-Guillemin in *KP* 3, 1969, col. 1128.

world politics. The use of the name of the city in the Revelation of John in the New Testament shows that it ultimately developed into a pure symbol separable and transferable from the concrete entity.[a] The introduction into the imagery of the future and final judgment of God upon the world power and the great capital city, features of the former enemy whose power had now vanished, fortified belief in the certainty of the coming day of Yahweh.

[2–5] *The Summoning by Yahweh Sebaoth.* The poet makes us eye-witnesses of the issuing of a military command.[b] Who the commander is, where he is situated and to whom he is issuing his instructions is in part obscure at the beginning, and in part remains obscure. On a bare hill, so that it is visible at a distance, a signal post is set up, perhaps nothing more than a smooth pole without any emblem.[c] A comparison with 5.26; Jer. 51.27 and 51.12 shows that such a sign could be used as a signal for mobilization, for assembling or for attack. The additional confirmation of the visual sign by cries and hand signals emphasizes the urgency of the action: it is the will of the commander that no time should be lost in preparing for the attack.[d] If the sections which are being assembled do not immediately recognize the signal post or advance too slowly, the cries and hand signals draw their attention to the signpost or urge them to hurry. In the extant Hebrew text the goal of the attack is described as 'the gates of the nobles'. This expression is a poetic metaphor either for one or several capital cities or for their most important gates.[e] The expression has sometimes been read as an allusion to the name of Babylon as *bābilu*, 'gates of God' or *bābilāni*, 'gates of the gods'.[f] But the allusion would have been an inept one if only because there is a qualitative distinction between gods and nobles. In any case it cannot be assumed that the author would have understood the Akkadian name of the city at all (cf. Gen. 11.9). Finally, it has not yet been certainly established that vv. 2–5 originally referred to an

[a] Cf. P. R. Ackroyd, *Exile and Restoration*, OTL, 1968, pp. 222f., and also Rev. 14.8; 16.19; 17.1ff. and 18.2ff.

[b] For the category of the call to flight and to battle cf. R. Bach, *Die Aufforderung zur Flucht und zum Kampf*, WMANT 9, 1962.

[c] Cf. R. de Vaux, *Les institutions de l'Ancien Testament* II, Paris 1960, p. 28; ET *Ancient Israel. Its Life and Institutions*, London and New York, 1961, p. 227; but also K. Galling, *BRL*, col. 16off., and Isa. 5.26; 11.10, 12; 18.3; Jer. 4.6; 50.2; 51.12, 27.

[d] Delitzsch, *ad loc.*

[e] Following Dillmann-Kittel, against Duhm, *et al.*

[f] Cf. *RLA* I, pp. 333 and 366.

attack upon Babylon. Even in the present context it is possible to regard it as directed against a number of cities.

[3] Verse 3 lifts the veil somewhat from the original mystery and suggests to the hearer or reader that he is witnessing the issuing of a command by a very unusual commander: for who would so exalt himself in his speech and at the same time describe those whom he is commanding in so natural a way as the instruments of his anger and as the army of his consecrated, except Yahweh? The consecration of the warrior[a] is in accordance with the nature of the campaign as a holy war. According to a widespread conception, the consecration of warriors consisted of abstinence from sexual intercourse and perhaps also from alcoholic drinks.[b] Deuteronomy 23.10f. at all events shows that within the army camp certain sexual practices were taboo. Similarly II Sam. 11.10 shows that sexual continence was required from an army in the field.[c] Verse 16b does not contradict this, because in some circumstances a distinction could be made between behaviour before and after victory. Finally, Num. 31.19ff. shows that at the conclusion of the campaign certain rites of purification are once again to be carried out.

At the words of the heavenly commander, the army proceeds, with its forces assembled and in undisturbed self-confidence, to carry out the order to execute his anger upon his enemies.

[4] The scene changes. We have just witnessed the issuing of God's command and the declaration of his purpose; now our attention is drawn to the tumult, uproar and raging of the nations who are gathering on the mountains in accordance with the order.[d] We cannot tell whether the poet had any precise geographical idea of the situation of the city being attacked, and whether he was thinking of the Elamite mountains as the place where the nations coming from the Iranian plateau were gathering.[e] Perhaps the poet simply had in mind the natural circumstances of his own mountainous homeland. In v. 4b he no longer calls his audience to listen and passes on to an

[a] Cf. Micah 3.5; Jer. 6.4; 22.7; 51.27f. and Joel 4.9, also Zeph. 1.7.

[b] Cf. F. Scwally, *Der heilige Krieg im alten Israel*, Leipzig 1901, p. 60 and G. von Rad, *Der heilige Krieg im alten Israel*, Göttingen ²1952, p. 7. M. Weiss, 'The Origin of the "Day of the Lord" Reconsidered', *HUCA* 37, 1966, pp. 32ff., disagrees.

[c] A distinction must be made, against Weiss, between soldiers on leave and those at the front.

[d] For a later interpretation cf. above p. 6 note d.

[e] This view has been repeated in commentaries at least since Delitzsch.

interpretative description. Our suspicion that the commander is Yahweh is here explicitly confirmed: it is none other than Yahweh Sebaoth, the almighty God of Israel who rules over the armies of heaven and earth,[a] who is mustering his forces for the battle.[b]

[5] Verse 5 once again emphasizes the weirdness of what is taking place: the attackers are not familiar neighbouring nation but hosts who come from the uttermost ends of the earth,[c] from the unknown distance, in order to carry out the anger of Yahweh.[d]

[6-13] *The horrors of the imminent day of Yahweh.* We may have supposed so far that the war described is one being waged in a particular place and affecting a single city and a single country. But we now learn in a dramatic climax that in reality it is the day of Yahweh and therefore the judgment of the world which is at hand. [6] Therefore the proto-apocalyptic writer gives a general call to raise the cry of lamentation. He declares the imminence of the day of Yahweh in the same words as Zeph. 1.14aα.

It is generally held nowadays that belief in the day of Yahweh as a day of judgment can be traced back in the Old Testament as far as the eighth century, where the earliest evidence of it is in Amos 5.18–20, and then in Isa. 2.6–22. Whether both passages in fact go back to the two prophets themselves, or whether the whole conception did not rather arise later in association with post-exilic hopes, needs to be clarified in connection with a thorough examination of the history of the redaction of the prophetic books. The derivation of the concept of the day of Yahweh is a matter of dispute in present-day scholarship. Whereas a number of scholars would follow Mowinckel in deriving it from the complex of ideas of the pre-exilic harvest festival and its 'day of the feast of Yahweh' (Hos. 9.5),[e] von Rad would locate it among the concepts associated with the holy

[a] Cf. our comment on 6.3, Kaiser, *Isaiah 1–12*, OTL, 1972, pp. 77f., and for the most recent discussions, G. Fohrer, *Geschichte der israelitischen Religion*, Berlin 1969, pp. 159f.

[b] For the muster before setting out to battle cf. Josh. 8.10; I Sam. 11.8; I Kings 20.15 and II Chron. 25.5.

[c] For this expression cf. Deut. 30.4 and Neh. 1.9.

[d] Cf. 10.5; 30.27; 10.25 and 26.10.

[e] Cf. S. Mowinckel, *The Psalms in Israel's Worship* I, Oxford and New York 1962, pp. 116ff.; A. R. Johnson in *The Old Testament and Modern Study*, ed. H. H. Rowley, Oxford and New York 1951 (1961), pp. 191ff.; and in *Myth, Ritual and Kingship*, Oxford 1958, pp. 219ff., esp. p. 235; A. Weiser, ATD 24, [5]1967, pp. 170f.; H. Ringgren, in *Tradition und Situation. Festschrift A. Weiser*, Göttingen 1963, p. 110.

war.[a] Weiss offers yet another explanation, regarding it as an innova-
tion by the prophet Amos, and is certainly correct in emphasizing its
association with the concept of theophany.[b] For the understanding of
the present text it is sufficient to affirm that the day of Yahweh was
the moment of his mighty manifestation and intervention. The
destructive power with which he will come is described in the same
play of words as in Joel 1.15: on this day will come the God who is
referred to by the ancient name *šaddai*,[c] in whom the proto-apocalyptic writer heard an echo of the Hebrew word *šdd* 'ravage, lay
waste, be violent'. Faced with the coming of this terrible day, mankind will be seized with complete inner and outer paralysis.[d] The
trembling fear and shaking terror of men is compared to the anguish
of a woman in labour.[e] But whereas a woman in labour cries, men
will still only stare at each other aghast in horror[f] and begin to
sweat from fear.[g] If the day of Yahweh is to come, then God himself
will appear[h] in order to pour out his anger remorselessly over the
earth.[i] The purpose of his coming is not the devastation of the earth
as such,[j] but the destruction of the sinners who dwell on it.[k]

[a] 'The Origin of the Concept of the Day of Jahwe', *JSS* 4, 1959, pp. 97ff., and
also *Old Testament Theology* II, London and New York, 1965, pp. 119ff. He is
followed by H. W. Wolff, BK 14.5, 1963, pp. 38f. and J. Jeremias, *Theophanie*,
WMANT 10, 1965. Cf. also W. Eichrodt, *Theology of the Old Testament* I, OTL, 1961,
p. 267.

[b] Cf. above, p. 14 note b.

[c] Cf. W. F. Albright, 'The Names Shaddai and Abram', *JBL* 54, 1935, pp. 180ff.,
but also M. Weippert, *ZDMG*, 1961, pp. 42ff.

[d] Cf. Ezek. 21.12.

[e] Cf. Hos. 13.13; Micah 4.9f.; Jer. 6.24; 49.22, 24; 50.43; Isa. 21.3; Joel 2.6;
Isa. 26.17; Ps. 48.10, etc.

[f] Cf. Gen. 43.33; Isa. 29.9; Jer. 4.9; Hab. 1.5; Ps. 48.6.

[g] Cf. also Nahum 2.11 and Joel 2.6; but see Jer. 30.6.

[h] Cf. Pss. 50.3; 96.13; Isa. 35.4; 40.10; 59.19; 63.1ff.; 66.15; Mal. 3.2; and also
Ex. 19.9; 20.24; Deut. 33.2; Judg. 5.4; Ps. 68.8 and Hab. 3.3.

[i] Cf. Zeph. 1.15; Nah. 1.2ff.; Ezek. 7.19; Lam. 1.12; 2.21f.; Isa. 30.27ff. and
34.6ff.; and H. Ringgren, 'Einige Schilderungen des göttlichen Zorns', *Tradition
und Situation*, pp. 107ff.

[j] For the play on words, which is not reproduced, cf. also Jer. 4.7; 18.16 and
51.29.

[k] 'Sinners' can be taken here, in accordance with the basic meaning of the verb
ḥṭ', cf. e.g. Prov. 8.36; Job 5.24 and Judg. 20.16, to mean those within and outside
Israel who offend against the world order established by God. Cf. R. Knierim,
Die Hauptbegriffe für Sünde im Alten Testament, Gütersloh 1965, pp. 66f., and H. H.
Schmid, *Gerechtigkeit als Weltordnung*, BhTh 40, 1968, pp. 166ff.

[10] In vv. 10–12 Yahweh speaks again.[a] The onset of his day will be announced by the darkening of the stars of the night and of the sun, which is a consequence of God's approach in the darkness of the clouds;[b] for he remains concealed, and purposes to remain concealed, from the eyes of men.[c] As a result the inhabitants of the earth are at once cast into a chaotic situation (cf. Gen. 1.2; Amos 5.8) which brings every activity to a halt. Thus the absolute darkness is itself a part of the judgment.[d] If we look behind the ancient imagery, the verse states that when the hidden God carries out his manifest judgment, mankind is forced back into pure passivity, from which there is no refuge back into the world. Mankind is deprived of the world as an open field for the exercise of man's own potentialities.

[11] God appears and calls the earth and its guilty inhabitants to account.[e] The arrogant and the violent,[f] who in their haughtiness care neither for divine nor human right, are seized upon and shattered by the day of judgment which breaks over the earth. [12] The way in which the proto-apocalyptic author judges the prospects of man in the sight of God is shown by v. 12: the survivors of this day will be

[a] God is the speaker at most down to v. 13a.

[b] Cf. Ps. 18.10ff.; Ex. 19.16; 24.15; Deut. 4.11; 5.20. J. Koenig, *RHR* 169, 1966, pp. 24f., sees here a reminiscence to the ancient volcanic tradition of Sinai, or more exactly to the phenomenon of the cloud of smoke and dust pouring out of the centre of the volcanic eruption. In my opinion he has not taken sufficient account of the history of the conception of the theophany at Sinai, though this does not detract from the value of his convincing demonstration that the volcanic hypothesis still bears consideration.

[c] Cf. I Kings 8.12.

[d] Cf. Amos 5.18ff.; 8.9; Micah 3.6; Zeph. 1.15; Jer. 4.23; Ezek. 30.3; 32.7; Joel 2.2, 10; 3.4; 4.15; Isa. 24.23 and 30.26.

[e] In the Old Testament *rāšāʿ* means primarily someone who 'because of his acts must expect to be found guilty by a court . . .', L. Rost, 'Erwägungen zu Sacharajas 7. Nachtgesicht', *ZAW* NF 17, p. 226 (repr. *Das kleine Credo und andere Studien zum Alten Testament*, Heidelberg 1965, p. 73). For the basic meaning of the verb *ʿwh*, 'deviate', cf. Ps. 38.7; Lam. 3.9 and Isa. 24.1; see Knierim, pp. 237ff. Cf. also Amos 3.2 and Ex. 20.5.

[f] The Old Testament *zēd*, cf. Prov. 21.24, etc. is no doubt equivalent to the 'hot one' of the Egyptian wisdom texts, 'who gives free rein to his feelings, begins a quarrel, is discontented and creates discontent, has no morals and so comes into conflict with everyone' (H. Brunner, *Altägyptische Erziehung*, Wiesbaden, 1957, pp. 4f.). The *ʿārîṣ*, the violent man, is a person who produces terror when he comes on the scene. Cf. for the root J. Aistleitner, *Wörterbuch der ugaritischen Sprache*, SAL 106.3, 1963, p. 243, no. 2103.

even more rare than fine gold.[a] There is no clear answer to the
question whether the proto-apocalyptic writer conceives of a universal judgment or a selected judgment which overtakes only the
godless. Verse 11 suggests a selection, while v. 12 suggests a universal
action of God which comes upon the whole of mankind without
distinction. Thus the prophecy makes it impossible for the hearer or
reader to imagine that he is unaffected by the coming day of Yahweh.

[13] Just as God, coming in the darkness of the clouds, obscures the
stars, his thundering voice[b] makes the heavens tremble (they are
thought of as a firm vault resting upon the edges of the earth)[c] and
shakes the earth, so that – according to this conception – it breaks
away from its foundations on which it was thought to rest mysteriously
over the sea of the abyss.[d]

[14–16] *The hopeless flight.* At first there seems to be no connection
between the prophetic account of the experience of Yahweh's
mustering of his army and the proclamation of the terrible day of
Yahweh. But in what follows the two sections are linked; for we must
now consider the situation as described in vv. 14–16 in association
with the day of Yahweh. We can conclude from vv. 15f. that the
mighty summoning together of the host was intended for this very
day. [14] Regardless of the universal character of the visitation in the
preceding vv. 6–13, v. 14 clearly portrays a single place. The flight
proceeds from a centre which is not specified more closely, but in
view of what follows it ought most probably to be regarded as a
capital city, for only in such a place can we suppose that people
from different nations would be present as courtiers, merchants,
warriors and slaves. The vagueness of the statement makes it very
difficult to give a more exact interpretation. The passage portrays
not some arbitrary situation, but the consequences of the day of
Yahweh for the inhabitants of the capital city. It is still possible to see
in this city every city which is not inhabited solely by its own native
population.

[a] Gold of Ophir is also mentioned in Ps. 45.10 and Job 28.16. I Kings 9.28 tells
of the import of gold from Ophir by Solomon. The country is usually located in
south-western Arabia, cf. R. Bach, *RGG*[3], IV, col. 1658f. and L. Rost, *BHW* II,
col. 1353.

[b] Cf. Pss. 18.8; 68.9; 77.19; 104.32; I Kings 19.11; Isa. 6.4; Nahum 1.5; Jer.
4.24; 10.10; Hag. 2.6, 21; Joel 2.10; 4.16; Isa. 29.6 and 24.18, together with Jer.
51.29.

[c] Cf. Gen. 1.6ff.

[d] Cf. Ps. 24.1f.; Job 38.4ff.

The comparison between those who are taking flight and a gazelle cut off from its followers emphasizes not only its speed but also its isolation,[a] while the next simile of the sheep without a shepherd stresses their defencelessness and helplessness.[b] Flight is virtually hopeless. [15] Anyone on whom the attackers lay their hands must die.[c] The fate of the city, which is already defenceless through its terror alone (cf. v. 7), is sealed. Once the men capable of bearing arms have been put to flight and largely mastered (cf. vv. 11 and 12), the city is open to the depredations of the victors. Before the eyes of the helpless parents their children are dashed in pieces,[d] their houses plundered[e] and, as the scene can be reconstructed, their wives, dragged from their hiding places, are ravished. [16] In a few bold strokes the poet draws a picture of total defeat and complete abandonment to the conqueror, describing the conquest of the city only indirectly, as it is reflected in what happens to its defenders and its inhabitants.

[17-18] *The ruthless Medes.* The form of the rest of the chapter can be regarded as a continuous utterance by God. The clearly fragmentary character of v. 18, however, makes it difficult to reach a firm conclusion about the original length of the utterance of God, which in view of the later insertion in v. 19 should perhaps best be regarded as concluding with v. 18. [17] We now finally learn who are the warriors summoned by Yahweh to attack the great city which still has not been named: they are the cruel Medes who remorselessly reject every offer of ransom (cf. Zeph. 1.18)[f] and ruthlessly hew down whatever gets in their way (cf. v. 15). [18] The received text of v. 18a presents insuperable difficulties.[g] But it is clear that the victors are destroying the hopes of the defeated for all time by pitilessly destroying the growing and future generations, the young people and the children and even the unborn. The 'fruit of the womb' may, though need not necessarily, mean the foetus, since there is evidence in the Old Testament of the ripping open of the womb of

[a] Cf. Prov. 6.5; II Sam. 2.18 and I Chron. 12.9.
[b] Cf. Ezek. 34.12; Jes. 53.6 and especially Nahum 3.18 and Jer. 50.17.
[c] Cf. Jer. 50.30 and 51.3f.
[d] Cf. Hosea 14.1; Nahum 3.10; II Kings 8.12 and Ps. 137.9.
[e] Cf. Jer. 50.10, 26f.
[f] According to Ibn Ezra in Procksch, *ad loc.* Delitzsch's explanation, that the Medes came to exact vengeance and not for booty, contradicts v. 16b, in this context at least.
[g] Cf. above p. 8 note a.

pregnant women as a particularly remorseless form of cruelty (cf. Amos 1.13; Hos. 14.1; II Kings 8.12 and 15.16).

[**19–22**] *The everlasting devastation of Babylon.* The city which by its splendour and might surpassed, or surpasses, all cities and kingdoms of the earth, and so forms the justified pride of those who live in and around it, here described as Chaldeans,[a] is to be destroyed for ever like the 'classical example of divine punishment',[b] Sodom and Gomorrah.[c] The reference to the cities which according to the testimony of scripture were destroyed in the legendary primal age is meant to strengthen the assurance of the hearer or reader that the same God who once carried out his vengeance will ultimately destroy this great city and world power, and every other which is hostile to him. Just as these cities disappeared in the earthquake, so too this city will fall for ever into ruin. People will avoid its accursed sight for all time. Nomadic Arabs[d] or wandering shepherds will not even be persuaded to make a short stay there. [**21–22a**] So the place will become the refuge of the desert animals, which occupy a curious position between the world of animals and that of demons,[e] and whose presence helps to increase the uncanny nature of the ruins.[f] Owls and ostriches[g] will dwell there. Among them will leap the 'hairy ones', the satyrs or goat demons, whose cult, probably deriving from Canaanite popular belief, seems to have had a location in

___

[a] The biblical term 'Chaldeans' for the Babylonians goes back to the name of eastern Aramaean tribes, who after settling in south-west Mesopotamia formed the basic population of the neo-Babylonian kingdom, cf. R. Borger, *BHW* I, col. 296f.

[b] H. Haag, *Bibel-Lexicon*, Einsiedeln, Zürich and Cologne 1951, col. 1532.

[c] Cf. Gen. 19; Deut. 29.22; Isa. 1.9; Amos 4.11; Jer. 49.18 and 50.40a, and also Matt. 10.15 and 11.23, as well as the Koran, Sura 69.9. An overthrowing of God is a very powerful overthrowing. For the superlative use of *'lhym*, God, cf. Gen. 1.2; 23.6; 30.8 and Isa. 14.13.

[d] From the time of Jer. 3.2 this can be demonstrated to be a term for the nomads of the Syrian–Arabian desert; cf. also Jer. 25.23f., Procksch *ad loc.* and H. P. Rüger, *BHW* I, col. 118f.

[e] Cf. Isa. 34.12 and Jer. 50.39.

[f] Cf. J. Wellhausen, *Reste arabischen Heidentums*, Berlin 1897, ³1961, pp. 149ff.; H. Duhm, *Die bösen Geister im Alten Testament*, Tübingen and Leipzig 1904, p. 48 and J. Henninger, 'Geisterglaube bei den vorislamischen Arabern', in *Festschrift P. Schebesta*, Studia Instituti Anthropos 18, Vienna-Mödling 1963, pp. 313ff.; and also A. Musil, *The Manners and Customs of the Rwala Bedouins*, New York 1928, pp. 414ff., and also Tobit 8.3; Bar. 4.35 and Matt. 4.1; 12.43. On the subject as a whole cf. also O. Böcher, *Dämonenfurcht und Dämonenabwehr*, BWANT 90, 1970, pp. 65ff. and pp. 86ff.

[g] Y. Aharoni, *Osiris* 5, 1938, pp. 469f., identifies it with *bubo bubo ascalaphus*.

Jerusalem itself before the time of Josiah.[a] The riotous activity in tower dwellings and royal palaces is silent.[b] Only jackals[c] and wild dogs sing their horrible song there.

Zephaniah 2.14f. describes the judgment upon Nineveh, and Isa. 34.10ff. that over Edom in a similar way. The prophecy of vv. 19–22 is clearly echoed in Rev. 18.2f. [22b] The poet concludes his prophecy with a kind of formula which affirms that the time of terror destined for Babylon.is imminent and will not delay (cf. Deut. 32.35; Zeph. 1.7, 14; Obad. 15; Ezek. 7.7; 30.3; Jer. 48.16; Joel 1.15; 2.1 and 4.14).

Looking back over this prophetic poem, we see that it foretells the conquest and destruction of Babylon by the Medes on the day of Yahweh. What is described in vv. 6–13 as the direct intervention of Yahweh, with all kinds of accompanying cosmic phenomena, is experienced upon earth as a historical catastrophe. Future historical events are interpreted as the action of God by means of the features of the concept of theophany. Just as he is not known in the framework of the theophany directly, but only by the cosmic effects of his presence, so in history the presence and action of God are recognized by the effects he brings about. Obviously the assumption is always present that he lives and is the final force behind everything that happens. The man who is here revealing to us part of his vision of history already held this belief as an Israelite. For him, this God and the fate of Israel were inseparable. Because God has involved himself in the history of this people, the powers which are offending against Israel must fall. Since Israel had lost its freedom because of Babylon, Babylon would one day fall. God uses the nations as his instruments, but this does not mean that he relaxes his demand to be recognized alone as God, a demand which also includes moral obedience. The fate which Babylon had brought upon Israel also explains why the prophecy of the everlasting destruction of Babylon occurs at the beginning of the oracles against the nations in ch. 13–23. The reason for God's coming intervention is not given in the poem in a specific rebuke which names the concrete faults of Babylon, but in two

[a] Cf. II Kings 23.8; and also Lev. 17.7; Isa. 34.12, 14; 53.9 conj. and II Chron. 11.15; and see G. Fohrer, *BHW* I, col. 315f.

[b] For the palace arrangements from the period of Nebuchadnezzar to that of Alexander the Great cf. Schachermeyr, *Alexander in Babylon*, SAW 268.3, 1970, pp. 49ff.

[c] But cf. *KBL* sub voce and Delitzsch *ad loc.*

different passages, where it is given very general expression in theological terms. In v. 3 we learn that the consecrated of Yahweh are gathered together to execute his anger. In vv. 9 and 11 we also learn that his terrible wrath will fall upon the sinners, the proud and the arrogantly violent. No concrete reason is given why this anger should be directed particularly against Babylon, among all the violent people of this earth. In the light of Israel's experience, it obviously needed no further justification for those whom this Jewish thinker was addressing. This distinctive association of a universal and a particular expectation of judgment, together with the lack of any concrete reason, resulted in the prophecy of the punishment of Babylon becoming a transparent medium, such that this city and the fate prophesied for it came to be a symbol of the godless city in general and its fate.

This text does not concern itself with the fact that the power which yesterday was the instrument of God's anger tomorrow falls victim to it, though the point is dealt with in 10.5–15. Anyone who considers the history of the nations seems to see a diabolical game in which one nation destroys another and one power another, and what has just been imposed by force is always declared to be justified,[a] so that might is right.[b] The constant tendency to declare that might is right shows that something is out of order here.

The Jewish thinker interprets the feelings of men and nations towards each other as failings with regard to God. But if history is understood as a series of failings with regard to God, there is still hope. For because God remains the Lord of history in a hidden way, then history does not ultimately possess the character of a fate leading to doom. It loses this character the moment man recognizes God's deity and then acts according to his will. When the disasters men bring upon each other are proclaimed to be a disaster in their relationship to God, the diagnosis breaks through the veil of fate, and through the moral level on which ethical demands are valid, to the deeper level at which man is dependent upon God. If he looks for security to the faithfulness of God and not to the mutual love of men and to the world, he will also of course have the power to satisfy the demand made upon him by his fellow man as his brother, that he should take him into his care and exist for him and with him. The loss of God is the sin which underlies all the failures of men with regard to

---

[a] Cf. Plato, *Laws* 890a.
[b] Cf. the speech of the Athenians to the Melians, Thucydides v. 89.

each other. Consequently the New Testament couples together the commandment to love God and that to love one's neighbour (cf. Mark 12.28ff.; Luke 10.25ff.). Since our existence as men is determined, in so far as experience permits such an assertion, by distance from God rather than by closeness to God, our history is a disaster with regard to God, who cannot be replaced as the basis and counterpart of our being. We fall victims to his anger which is executed in our being abandoned to each other. If we allow the declaration that the catastrophies of the world, and with them the catastrophies of our own life, are a disaster and a failure with regard to God, to bring us face to face with God, then, in the actual passive recognition of the power of sin at work in us, reconciliation takes place. Only in the recognition that we are in truth godless do we come to possess the truth. The Christian would be ill advised if, in the face of the urgent reforms required in human society, he were to cease to press for a revolution in human hearts, which gives hope and therefore means that there is more to be hoped for even for this world. But this revolution is brought about only through the word which makes us capable of perceiving ourselves as sinners and calls us to be God's partners in history.

CHAPTER 14.1–4a

The Great Turning-point

1 For Yahweh will have compassion on Jacob and will again choose Israel, and will set them in their own land. Aliens will join them and will cleave to the house of Jacob. 2And the peoples will take them[a] and bring them to their place, but the house of Israel will possess them in Yahweh's land as male and female slaves; they will take captive their captors, and rule their oppressors. 3And it will come about, when Yahweh has given you rest from your pain and turmoil and the hard service with which you were made to serve, 4you will take up this taunt against the king of Babylon:

[a] I.e. the Israelites. Cf. the 'house of Jacob' which follows.

The late editor, whom one might almost term a scribe, no doubt already had available to him in his Isaiah roll the prophecy of the destruction of the great city of Babylon in 13.2–22, edited in an eschatological sense, and probably also the taunt song 14.4b–21, which 14.22–23 referred to the king of Babylon. He felt the absence, behind the prophecy of the destruction of the great capital city, of an explicit affirmation that its ruin had been decided by Yahweh for the sake of Israel, and that its fall would introduce the decisive turning point in the destiny of the people of God. His words, drawn from his study of scripture, were meant to assure those who heard them[a] when the book was read in public worship that the sufferings of Israel in the past and the present were leading on to a glorious future, in which it could sing its song of mockery at the fallen world power. Though his words are artless, and there are difficulties in the syntax,[b] they give us a valuable insight into the way in which the prophetic writing, which was not yet regarded as unalterable, was kept alive in the Jewish community of late Old Testament times. They give us an impression of the tense expectations of this later period, and the dependence of its ideas upon the literary tradition of Israel, which was at that time becoming scripture in the strict sense.

[1] The beginning, with the 'for' of explanation,[c] shows that vv. 1 and 2 were understood as the continuation and climax of the preceding prophecy of the day of Yahweh and the destruction of Babylon for ever, which would then take place. From the first, the purpose of the judgment of Yahweh's anger upon the world, and upon the great capital city as the symbol of world power, lies in the turning point in the destiny of Israel, the house of Jacob. The period of punishment in which the people is enslaved and might feel itself rejected (cf. Lam. 5.22; Isa. 41.8f.; 54.7f.) is followed by the period of divine mercy in which Israel is once again chosen by its God. In v. 1a, the scribe can be seen to be dependent first of all upon Isa. 49.13b, and then, even more closely, upon Zech. 1.7 and 2.16. In his ideas he looks back to the first calling of Israel from slavery in Egypt (cf. Ex. 19.5 and Hos. 11.1). The oppression by Pharaoh at that time corresponds to the present oppression by the world empire. And just as that choosing

---

[a] Cf. the direct address in vv. 3 and 4a.

[b] Cf. the suffixes, which in 2aα refer to the Israelites, and at the beginning of 2aβ to the gentile nations.

[c] A different interpretation in G. Quell, 'Jesaja 14.1–23', in *Festschrift F. Baumgärtel*, Erlangen 1959, pp. 131ff.

and liberation was followed by the giving of the Promised Land, so it will be followed on this occasion by the return of the scattered Israelites to the *'aḏāmā*, their own soil. Since the redactor prophesies the return home in almost the same words as Ezek. 37.14, we may perhaps suggest that this word, which originally referred to the red-brown arable land suitable for cultivation, possessed through its contrast with dismal, uncultivated land the emotive associations of our word 'home',[a] reflecting as in Ezekiel the splendour of the Promised Land.[b] The gathering together of the scattered Israelites is paralleled by the increase of the people of God through the proselytes. But the *gēr*, the alien, does not refer merely to the Canaanites who lived among the Israelites. It can also refer at least to the non-Israelites who in the diaspora felt themselves drawn to Judaism.[c] This hope, to which there is virtually no parallel from the age in which it was uttered, is similar to Zech. 2.15; Isa. 56.3 and 6, cf. also 55.5. Since v. 1b interrupts the continuity between v. 1a and v. 2a, it is not impossible that v. 1b represents a later addition to the portrait of the age of salvation.[d] But the idea of non-Jews joining the people of God may have been moved forward, in order to allow v. 2 to conclude more effectively with the description of the coming reversal of the relationship between the oppressors and the oppressed. This is the more probable, in that the latter theme reoccurs in v. 3.

[2] Verse 2 gives an extravagant answer, drawn from Isa. 49.22ff.; 60.4ff.; 61.5 and 66.18ff. to the question of how the return of the scattered Israelites is to take place: the peoples in whose midst they are forced to live will bring them back themselves into their ancestral home. Of course this service shown to those who were hitherto despised and without rights assumes the judgment of God over the whole earth, proclaimed in 13.9–13.[e] This is the only explanation for the expectation that those who return home are to transform their helpers into servants and handmaids whom they possess as slaves.[f] On the land which Yahweh possesses, which of course includes the whole

---

[a] Cf. L. Rost, 'Die Bezeichnungen für Land und Volk im Alten Testament', in *Festschrift O. Procksch*, Leipzig 1934, repr. in *Das kleine Credo und andere Studien zum Alten Testament*, Heidelberg 1965, pp. 77ff.

[b] W. Zimmerli, BK 13.1, 1969, p. 169.

[c] Cf. what seems to be a technical use of the niphal participle of *lwh* in Esth. 9.27, and also the translation of *gēr* in this passage by *prosḗlytos* in A, *Σ* and *Θ*.

[d] Cf. Procksch *ad loc.*

[e] Cf. also O. Kaiser, *Isaiah 1–12*, OTL, 1972, pp. 28ff.

[f] For *hitnaḥēl* as a technical term of law cf. Lev. 25.44ff. and Num. 32.18.

of the earth (Ps. 24.1; I Cor. 10, 26) but consists in particular of the land of Canaan (cf. Hos. 9.3 and Lev. 25.23),[a] the peoples who have escaped the catastrophe have come into the possession of Israel. With an allusion to Judg. 5.1, and perhaps also with a reminiscence of Ex. 3.7; 5.6, 10, 13, there is an explicit affirmation of the reversal of the present relationship between Israel and the nations: those who hold Israel captive will then be taken captive by Israel, and the oppressors will be ruled by Israel.[b]

[3] The day in which Yahweh gives rest to the suffering community must be understood on the basis of 13.6 and 9 as the day of Yahweh. It brings an end to weary toil (cf. Gen. 5.29), to the restless turmoil and forced labour (Ex. 4.14; 6.9 [P]) which is now imposed upon the community that is being directly addressed. When the people are set free the *naḥ{a}lā* will become *m{e}nūḥā*; the land of their inheritance will be a place of rest, a place where they will remain undisturbed (cf. Deut. 12.9f. and 25.19).

[4] The liberated people will take up its taunt against the world power at which people now tremble:[c] the danger is past for ever. When this has been achieved, the community that is being addressed can look calmly back upon the afflictions of the present time. Because even now they hear the taunt, as in 12.1ff. they hear its song of thanksgiving of the age of salvation, they are called out of the trials of the present time, and as a community in expectation already participate in the coming salvation. To the scribe, who clearly had access to the Pentateuch, the 'former' and the 'latter' prophets – the present historical books from Genesis to II Kings and the prophetical books (without Daniel) – it was certain that his promise, based upon the testimony of the fathers, would soon be fulfilled (cf. 13.22b).

Anyone whose starting point is the Christian universalism of salvation as found in Paul, and for whom there can be no distinctions of nation or race in the church (cf. Gal. 3.38), may regard 14.1–4a as a 'revoltingly arrogant expectation' (Duhm) or the testimony of 'the

---

[a] For the tension introduced by the idea 'of a choosing of a particular people (and country) by the God who rules the whole world' cf. P. Altmann, *Erwählungstheologie und Universalismus im Alten Testament*, BZAW 92, 1964, p. 9.

[b] This seems to be the basic meaning of *rdh* in Hebrew.

[c] *māšāl*, really 'the same' and then 'a comparing saying, a proverb'. For the nuance here cf. O. Eissfeldt, *Einleitung in das AT*, Tübingen [3]1964, p. 123; ET *The Old Testament: an Introduction*, Oxford and New York 1965, p. 92: ' "To become a proverb", i.e. "to become a by-word", means the same thing as to become the object of men's mockery.' Cf. also Deut. 28.37 and Ps. 69.12.

unseemly piety of a late period' (Fohrer). While one cannot go as far as Delitzsch in saying that 'to be ruled by the people of God, is in the mind of the prophet the good fortune of the nations, and to allow themselves to be governed by that people is their liberty', one must at least agree with him that it was not possible for the Old Testament hope to be identical with that of the New Testament, if only 'because for the time and the outlook of the Old Testament the church could not be manifested in any other form than that of a nation'.ᵃ Nevertheless the scribe envisages the possibility of others joining the Jewish nation and faith, so that his purpose is perhaps well described by saying that he regards the time of the judgment of the world as also a time of decision. Here the imminence of the expectation means that present time, and the proselytes with it, are drawn in. In the short book of Zephaniah, we see that the expectation expressed here could be surpassed by yet another, 'to him shall bow down, each in its place, all the islands of the nations' (Zeph. 2.10f.; 3.9b–10; cf. also Isa. 19.23ff.). Not until the judgment of God upon the world is taken so seriously and sin is acknowledged at so profound a level that even one of the elect must confess: 'There is no distinction; since all have sinned and fall short of the glory of God, they are justified by his grace as a gift, through the redemption which is in Christ Jesus' (Rom. 3.22ff.) has the point been reached at which it is possible to recognize and bear witness on the basis of faith that 'God has consigned all men to disobedience, that he may have mercy upon all' (Rom. 11.32).

CHAPTER 14.4b–21

How you are Fallen from Heaven, Shining Star . . .

4b How the oppressor has ceased,
    the ⟨fury⟩ᵇ ceased!

ᵃ It is not improbable that for this Jew servitude to other human beings seem more worthy of human dignity than idolatry.

ᵇ Cf. BHS; but cf. H. M. Orlinsky, VT 7, 1957, pp. 202f.

5   ⟨Broken is⟩ᵃ the staff of the wicked,
       the sceptre of the tyrants,
6   that smote the peoples in wrath
       with unceasing blows,
    that trampled the nations in anger
       ⟨trampling without mercy⟩ᵇ
7   The whole earth is at rest and quiet;
       they break forth into singing.
8   The junipers rejoice at you,
       the cedars of Lebanon, saying,
    'Since you were laid low, against us
       no hewer comes up.'

9   The Waste Land beneath is stirred up
       to meetᶜ you when you come;
    it rousesᶜ the shades to greet you,
       all the leaders of the earth;
    it ⟨starts up⟩ᵇ from their thrones
       the kings of the nations.
10 All of them will speak
       and say to you:
    'Have you too become as weak as we,
       become like us'?
11 Your pomp is brought down to the Waste Land,
       the sound of your harps;
    maggots are the bed beneath you,
       and worms are your covering.

12 How you are fallen from heaven,
       Shining Star, son of the Dawn!
    ⟨How⟩ᵇ you are cut down to the ground,
       you who laid the nations low!
13 You said in your heart,
       'I will ascend to heaven;
    above the stars of Godᵈ
       I will set my throne on high;
    I will sit on the mount of assembly
       in the far north;

ᵃ Following Guthe, *ad loc.*, H. Jahnow, *Das hebräische Leichnamslied im Rahmen der Völkerdichtung*, BZAW 36, 1923, p. 239, etc., read *nišbar*, and delete 'Yahweh' as a secondary interpolation.

ᵇ Cf. *BHS*.

ᶜ Cf. *BHS*. Since *še'ōl* is feminine, *ʿwrr* and *hqym* should be regarded as infinitives: GK 145t.

ᵈ 'Stars of El (God)' means 'the highest stars', cf. Gen. 1.2; 23.6; 30.8.

14 I will ascend above the heights of the clouds,
   I will be like the Most High.'

15 But you are brought down to the Waste Land,
   to the depths of the Pit.

16 Those who see you will stare at you,
      and ponder over you:
   'Is this the man who made the earth tremble,
      who shook kingdoms,

17 who made the world like a desert
      and overthrew ⟨its⟩[a] cities,

18b who did not let his prisoners go,
      each ⟨to⟩[b] his home?'

18 ⟨   ⟩[c] The kings of the nations
      lie in glory,

19 but you are cast out, away from your sepulchre
      like a loathed ⟨untimely birth⟩,[d]
   clothed with the slain, those pierced by the sword, ⟨   ⟩[e]
      like carrion trodden under foot.

19b Those who go down into the stony Pit, ⟨   ⟩[e]

20   You will not be joined with them ⟨   ⟩[e]
   because you have destroyed your land,
      you have slain your people.
   Nevermore be named
      the seed of ⟨the evildoer⟩![f]

21 Prepare slaughter for his sons
      because of the guilt of ⟨their father⟩,[f]
   lest they rise and possess the earth,
      and fill the face of the world ⟨   ⟩![a]

This taunt, in the form of a lament, upon the death of a world ruler
and the fall of his empire, is one of the most powerful poems not only
of the Old Testament, but of the whole literature of the world. It is
meant to refer in its present context to the end of the king of Babylon,
as is clear from the framework, apparently going back to two different

[a] Cf. *BHS*.
[b] With Budde, delete *bāyᵉtā*, bring v. 18b forward and read *'iš lᵉbētō*.
[c] With Budde, *et al.*, delete *kol*.
[d] With Schwally, *ZAW* 1891, p. 258, *et al.*, read *kᵉnepel*. – M: 'branch'.
[e] Cf. *BH*.
[f] Cf. *BHS*. If vv. 20b and 21 are not simply to be regarded as redactional additions, which according to the context refer to the Babylonians (cf. 14.22), we must
accept that the original singulars were changed into plurals when 14.22f. was
interpolated.

hands, which is provided by 14.1–4a and 14.22f.[a] But since the poem itself mentions neither the name of the ruler nor of his country, there is no guarantee that the interpretation by the redactor is in accordance with the intention of the poet. Thus it is not surprising that critical Old Testament scholarship in the last two centuries has proposed many different interpretations. There have been attempts to understand the song as a poem which was in fact composed after the death of one of the rulers of the ancient Near East who are known to us. But these cannot stand up to a comparison between the poem and the date of their lives, and especially the circumstances of their deaths.[b] Of course, the possibility always remains that the first news, on some unknown occasion, of the death of an emperor stimulated the imagination of the poet.[c] But this interpretation borders on another, which has largely been preferred to it, that in his song the poet is expressing the certain hope of the end of a hated ruler. In this case it is impossible to decide whether the emperor intended is an Assyrian,

[a] Cf. below, p. 43.

[b] The Assyrian emperor Sargon II was murdered, but his son Sennacherib ascended the throne only a few days later, so that it is doubtful whether the news of the former event could have reached Jerusalem before that of the latter. Sennacherib himself was murdered by his sons, but the struggle for the throne, from which Esạrhaddon emerged victor, remained in the family. Sinshariskun was killed in 612 at the conquest of Nineveh, but was hardly an exceptional ruler. He is said to have plunged with his family into the flames of the burning palace. Of the Babylonian kings, the successor of the great Nebuchadnezzar, Amel-marduk, was murdered by Neriglissar, who immediately succeeded him, however, on the throne. Nabonidus was not killed when Cyrus took Babylon in 539. The rise and end of the ephemeral Nebuchadnezzar III, after the death of the Persian king Cambyses, would hardly have interested the Jews in the manner of the present poem. When we examine the murders of Persian kings, and the confusion which followed them, it is easier to find an occasion for eschatological expectations than for the composition of this song as an echo of their death. Of course there were ample grounds for eschatological hopes during the Persian period. The troubles which followed the death of Cambyses in 522, the murder of Xerxes I in 465 and the more or less successful revolts during the reigns of Artaxerxes I, Darius II, Artaxerxes II, and finally during the early years of the reign of Artaxerxes III provide adequate occasions. If we look for a murdered king whose sons died with him, we find only the ephemeral Arses (337/36) who however was followed by an Achaemenid in Darius III. When he was murdered in 330 by Bessos, Judaea and Babylonia already formed part of the empire of Alexander, so that a song of triumph would hardly have been sung. The situation with regard to Alexander's children is well-known.

[c] Cf. the pertinent considerations of W. Staerk, *Das assyrische Weltreich im Urteil der Propheten*, Göttingen 1908, p. 144, who regards the song as an echo of the death of Sennacherib in 681.

Babylonian or Persian king, or even Alexander the Great, since there are no criteria to be found within the poem for its dating. For basically there are no limits to the poetic imagination. And a detail which contradicts our historical knowledge might present no objection to the identification of the ruler, because we cannot necessarily assume that the poet possessed the knowledge which we have from our study of the sources. Finally, we must consider whether he may not have been anticipating the moment in which God was to bring about the end of the final world ruler in the long chain of empires which had destroyed each other and yet remained essentially the same. The fact that the name of the ruler is not given, the jubilation throughout the liberated world at his fall, and the explicit statement that the staff of the wicked and of tyrants has been broken, point in this direction. But perhaps the poet's understanding of the poem was the same as that of the redactor's. Since the king of Babylon played so fateful a role in the history of the kingdom of Judah and was the primary cause of the subsequent enslavement of Judah, which survived the fall of his kingdom, it is easy to understand why in post-exilic Judaism it was he who became the symbol of the power hostile to God. The oracles against Babylon (13.2ff. and 21.1ff.), and the similar passages in Jeremiah and Ezekiel, are sufficient evidence of this. The contradictions which are present with regard to what we now know about the end of the Babylonian kingdom may be explained in part by the legends (cf. Dan. 5)[a] and partly by the attempt to give an idealized and typical picture. Thinking back to the fall of the Assyrian and particularly of the Babylonian kingdom, people came to realize the transitoriness of every world power and every tyrant, to the last of whom the true Lord of the world would deliver the final blow. The eschatological consciousness of post-exilic Judaism was formed by theology coming to terms with the catastrophies in the history of Judaism itself, and those which had overtaken the world powers that had been its enemies.[b] The absence from the original of the divine name Yahweh, which was only introduced later by a redactor in v. 5, is indeed surprising, but does not provide sufficient reason to justify the view that the composition was originally non-

[a] Whether Belshazzar, who for a time acted as the regent of his father Nabonidus in Babylon, died when the city was taken, is unknown. Cf. O. Plöger, KAT² 18, 1965, p. 90.

[b] On these two points cf. H. Schulz, *Das Buch Nahum. Eine redaktionskritische Untersuchung*, shortly to appear in the series BZAW.

Israelite.[a] A glance at Ezek. 28.12ff. shows how Judaism itself could take up Canaanite myth and make use of it in its own theology of history.[b] In addition, the mythical allusions in vv. 12ff. were also enough to show contemporaries that the tyrant had offended against the deity of the highest God and was the cause of his own fall. The identity of this God with Yahweh was not a matter of doubt for the Jews. In view of these considerations, the balance is in favour of regarding this poem as composed in the post-exilic period, well after the events of the sixth century.

The statement at the beginning of our exposition, that this poem is a taunt in the form of a lament, calls for some explanation of this literary category. It has almost without exception three stressed syllables in the first, longer hemistich and two in the shorter second hemistich which follows. This means that its metric form is that of the qīnā, the lament for the dead. Most of its themes are also drawn from this form. But by reversing its intention, it becomes a parody, a taunt in the form of a lament. Just as the leader of the singing in the rite of lamentation intones each individual chorus, so the poet as it were quotes individual 'laments', which have now become songs of triumph. In v. 8b we hear the rejoicing of the cedars of Lebanon, which delight in the end of him who felled them; in v. 10b we perceive the astonishment and at the same time the malicious pleasure in the question of the kings in the abode of the shades; for he who was once beyond compare has now shared their fate and suffered death. In vv. 16b–17.18b we hear the equally astonished but already answered question of those who discover the body of the tyrant in the slaughterer's yard. The death of a just and wise king may be lamented, but the tyrant's end elicits nothing but rejoicing and malicious pleasure on earth and in the underworld. This basic feeling explains the transformation of the themes of the funeral song into its opposite: the lament for the dead emphasizes the incomparability of the dead person in order to arouse sorrow at his loss and to placate his shade; but this song does so only in order to celebrate the liberation that has come with his death. Nothing is left of him but an insubstantial shade cast down into the lowest depths of the underworld. The participles in the lament expressing praise, which are a device in a hymn to glorify the dead king, have been turned into accusations (cf. vv. 6, 12

[a] See above p. 31 note b.
[b] On the literary problem of the book of Ezekiel, cf. J. Garscha, *Studien zum Ezechielbuch* (shortly to appear).

and 16b). The conciliatory and comforting theme of the king's honourable burial among his fathers, the assurance of a good name and of a life continued in his children, is pitilessly transformed into the opposite in vv. 18–20a and 20b–21.[a]

The effectiveness of the song is due on the one hand to the objectivity, to which there seems to be hardly any exception, with which the poet makes his statements or quotes his 'witnesses'. But there is no doubt about his real purpose, which is suddenly revealed in all its passion in the concluding demand to slaughter the dead king's sons. In the second place it is due to the variation of scene. Whereas in the first stanza, extending from v. 4b to v. 8, we are on the earth, which together with its trees celebrates its liberation, the second stanza in vv. 9–11 carries us down to the shades of the underworld. The third stanza, vv. 12–15, reflects in the language of myth the disastrous failure of the attempts to climb up into the highest heaven, an attempt which has ended in the uttermost depths of the underworld. Then, in the fourth stanza, vv. 16–19, we are once again on earth among the onlookers at the slaughterer's yard gazing at the disgraced body. The final stanza, consisting of vv. 19b, 20–21, keeps in the first instance to the theme of the lack of burial in a tomb, in order to assert the complete comfortlessness and utter ruin of the tyrant. Then, in the demand for the slaughter of his sons, it once again comes to a climax, and with it reaches the end of the poem.[b] That tyranny is in conflict with the divine ordering of the world (cf. 10.5ff. and 14.24–27). The prophet is inspired by a firm certainty that the man of self-confidence and hybris, who arrogantly and in contempt for other men reaches out for the rule over the world which is reserved for God alone, will suddenly fall victim to the judgment of God and bring down his empire and his progeny with him into the depths. This certainly enables him to speak not only to his contemporaries, but to all who look forward to a kingdom of righteousness, peace and brotherhood. But perhaps one does not need to be a king or a tyrant to heed a warning against arrogantly over-vaunting oneself.

[4b–8] *The rejoicing of the earth at the death of the tyrant.* In the style of a lament for the dead, the song begins with an *'ēk*, 'Ah, how . . .' (v. 4b). If the continuation is compared with the lament for Saul and

---

[a] Cf. Jahnow, pp. 242ff.

[b] The fact that the last stanza is deficient by two successive lines, and the text in vv. 18 and 19 is seriously corrupt, suggests that there have been redactional changes and additions, cf. also above p. 29 note f.

Jonathan (II Sam. 1.19, 25 and 27) the parodying of the form is obvious at once. A people will lament at the death of its heroes, but hardly for the end of an oppressor and the affliction he has caused.[a]

[5–6] In terms which are possibly borrowed from 9.3 and which find a parallel at least in 10.5f., 24 and 14.29, the end of the rule of violence is compared to a broken staff. It is difficult to decide whether the 'wicked tyrants' refer to the subordinates of the ruler, who as his instruments carry out his infuriated commands and judgments, or whether the genitives are attributive and descriptive, so that the translation ought to read: 'the wicked staff, the tyrannical sceptre'.[b] Perhaps their main purpose is to hint that the dead king is regarded as the last in the long chain of oppressive rulers on this earth (cf. also vv. 20ff.) and that his fall has brought an end to oppression upon earth for ever. The description of them as *rešāʿîm*, wicked men, contains in itself a judgment upon them, for a *rāšāʿ* is in fact really a person 'who by reason of his acts must expect to be found guilty by a court, if . . . he can be brought before a court.'[c] The Hebrew word translated 'tyrant' has in reality the neutral sense of a ruler, but readily takes on a negative tone. Nothing more glorious can be said of the dead king in this panegyric lament than that he exercised a merciless rule of violence and terror over the nations (cf. Jer. 20.23).

[7–8] Consequently there is no lamentation after his death: the whole earth has at last found rest and is no longer devastated by the tyrant's campaigns. Even nature joins in the chorus of joy. The poet portrays the Syrian juniper tree, similar to the cypress, and the proverbial cedars of Lebanon breaking into song: their arch enemy who demanded their wood is dead! Behind this statement by the trees of Lebanon in the poem there lies the long history of the exploitation of the forests of Lebanon by the rulers of Syria at that period (cf. Isa. 37.24; Hab. 2.17a and Ezek. 31.16).[d]

[9–11] *The reception of the dead king in the underworld.* As in 5.14 and 28.15 the underworld, Sheol, is personified here. Although it is obvious that in their descriptions of the realm of the dead the poets drew upon popular conceptions, it must also be pointed out that they developed them in their own way and thus influenced the form they

---

[a] For *nōgēš*, oppressor, cf. 14.2.

[b] Cf. 9.3; 10.5, 24; 14.29.

[c] L. Rost, *ZAW* 1940/41, p. 226, repr. *Das kleine Credo und andere Studien zum Alten Testament*, Heidelberg 1965, p. 73.

[d] Cf. e.g. Luckenbill, *AR* I, § 804; II, § 697; *ANET²*, p. 307 and Curtius, X.I.19.

took in the future. The question of how far this is merely poetic imagery, and where the seriously intended representation begins, can in the nature of things hardly be answered. Primitive conceptions seem first to have thought only of an attenuated survival, growing constantly weaker, in association with the remains of the former self; the bones in the grave (cf. II Kings 13.20ff., Amos 2.1), the blood (cf. Gen. 4.10; 37.26; Job 16.18; Isa. 26.21) and the name (cf. Deut. 25.5f. and II Sam. 18.18). But in the course of centuries, if not of millennia, these views developed into the conception that the dead were gathered together in a particular place in the utmost depths. There they led a shadow-like existence in forgetfulness of their former selves (cf. Ps. 88.13; Eccles. 9.5). By means of a spirit of the dead one could force them to come back on to earth and to ask them questions (cf. I Sam. 28). It was perhaps also thought that before certain catastrophies upon earth the lamentation of the forefathers disturbed in their rest could be heard (cf. Jer. 31.15). But otherwise the dead were just r°pā'îm, 'the weakened.' Sheol was thought of by the Israelites, as by other peoples of antiquity, not only as under the surface of the earth, but still more as deep beneath the cosmic sea upon which the earth rested like a disc.[a] The frequent comparison of Sheol with a pit, a cistern, leads to the conclusion that this underworld was conceived of as a great cistern beneath the earth, beneath the waters of which men sank down in death.[b] For present-day thought the relationship between the grave and the underworld presents a special problem. Every cult of the dead associated with the body and the grave proceeds originally from the conviction that what is done to the dead person is of decisive importance for his continued existence. To tear him from his grave, to scatter his bones, to burn his body and to cast away the ashes of the bones into the wind

---

[a] Cf. A. R. Johnson, *The Vitality of the Individual in the Thought of Ancient Israel*, Cardiff and Mystic, Conn., ²1964, pp. 88ff.; L. Wächter, *Der Tod im Alten Testament*, ATh II.8, 1967, pp. 181ff.; N. J. Tromp, *Primitive Conceptions of Death and Nether World in the Old Testament*, Biblica et Orientalia 21, Rome 1969. – On the location of Sheol, cf. Gen. 7.11; 8.2; 49.25 etc., with Job 38.16f.; Pss. 69.16; 71.20 and esp. 88.5ff. and Jonah 2.3ff. Cf. also P. Reymond, *Lo'eau, sa vie et sa signification dans l'Ancien Testament*, SVT 4, 1958, p. 212. – For similar concepts outside Israel cf. B. Meissner, *Babylonien und Assyrien* II, Heidelberg 1925, pp. 110ff. and fig. 27 on p. 109; H. Kees, *Totenglaube und Jenseitsvorstellungen der alten Ägypter*, Berlin ³1972, pp. 59ff. and H. J. Rose, *A Handbook of Greek Mythology*, London and New York ³1945, pp. 19 and 78ff.

[b] Cf. with Johnson Pss. 30.4; 88.4f.; Prov. 1.12; Isa. 38.18 and Ezek. 31.16.

or the river meant to continue the dissolution of his person which had
begun with death, and to take it to the point of complete annihilation.
Between the conception of a shadowy survival associated with the
remains of the dead person, and the other idea of his sinking down
into the underworld, there is a tension which as time went on was
bound to lead to the conception of the underworld taking on an
independent form. But the literary record of the conclusion of this
process, as far as Judaism is concerned, lies beyond the limits of the
Old Testament, whereas the Greeks, in accordance with their more
intensive and extensive experience of the world, reached this point
sooner. As in fact is shown by the conceptions associated with the
death and burial of abortions, the uncircumcised, the murdered and
the executed, the tension was not at first felt between the conceptions
of the grave and the house of the dead, and of the underworld as their
permanent dwelling place. The grave and Sheol remained parallel
conceptions for the same thing. There was a correspondence with
what happened to the dead person in the grave or outside the grave
and what took place in the underworld. Anyone who remained unburied or was cast carelessly into a pit or into the slaughterer's yard,
as was the case with the groups mentioned above,[a] also rotted away
in the realm of the shades outside the community which protected
him, which as a rule was the community of his forefathers. It is
against the background of these conceptions that we must also understand the poetic elaboration of them which we have here and which is
adapted to a particular case.

[9] Sheol waits in restless expectation to receive the mighty king. It
arouses the leaders[b] and the kings of the past from their shadowy
conditions and starts them from their thrones. The dead take with
them into the underworld nothing of what they have acquired during
their lives (Eccles. 5.14). But they nevertheless seem to possess certain
attributes of their former position even in the shadowy other world
(cf. I Sam. 28.14). We can perhaps conclude from Ezek. 32.22ff. that
dead kings were thought of as surrounded by their courtiers even in

---

[a] Cf. Ezek. 28.8, 10; 31.18; 32.19ff.; Jer. 26.23; II Kings 26.3; Isa. 53.12 (conj.);
Tob. 1.17ff., and O. Eissfeldt, 'Schwerterschlagene bei Hesekiel', *Studies in Old
Testament Prophecy, Festschrift for T. H. Robinson*, ed. H. H. Rowley, New York and
London 1950, pp. 78ff.; repr. *Kleine Schriften* III, Tübingen 1966, pp. 6ff.; O.
Kaiser, *Der königliche Knecht*, FRLANT 70, ²1962, pp. 113f.

[b] Actually 'leading goat' of the flock, cf. Jer. 50.8 and Zech. 10.3, and also P. D.
Miller, 'Animal Names as Designations in Ugaritic and Hebrew', *UF* 2, 1970, pp.
177ff. and p. 184.

the underworld. In order to make sure of this, appropriate sacrifices used to be offered to them.[a] The reader ought to visualize for himself the grandiose and terrible scene: in the darkness and half-light of the great cistern of the underworld, the shades of the kings, surrounded by their shadowy armies, sit motionless upon their thrones. Then the gate of the underworld opens (cf. 38.10). The underworld shakes and the shadows spring up from their thrones. When Babylonian, Egyptian or Greek descriptions of such scenes are recalled, the reticence of the Hebrew author is clearly felt. In particular, he makes no personification of the God of the dead, unambiguously distinguished from the underworld itself. Here Sheol is a personified, living realm, comparable in this to the earth, rather than a real God of the dead, whose cries and blows could awake the shades. The poem comes close to the limits of such a conception, without however going beyond them (cf. also 38.18). For even though the dead do not praise God, and their dialogue with God is ended (Ps. 115.17),[b] yet Yahweh remains the first and the last, apart from whom there is no God (Isa. 44.6).

[10] The kings of the realm of shadows give the newcomer, whose glory and reputation has reached the underworld through those who were killed by him, or about whom they had learnt through the special knowledge they have as dead beings, a welcome which is full of astonishment and yet of malicious pleasure. He whose power surpassed that of all the kings and mighty ones of the earth is now an insubstantial shade like them. This affirmation, in the form of a question, cannot but drive the new arrival, ashamed and silent, into the uttermost corner (cf. v. 15).

[11] In v. 11, on the analogy of the very short speech of the trees in v. 8, the poet once again takes up the word himself. He sharply stresses the difference between the former glory and the present loathsome existence of the dead king. All the former pomp of the great lord, and everything, such as music, which once distinguished the way of life, the dwelling and the pleasures of the king, are gone. For him too, the sign over the realm of the dead is Dante's 'Abandon

---

[a] Cf. e.g. C. L. Woolley, *Ur of the Chaldees*, London 1929, pp. 33ff. and esp. 57ff., and for the survival of the practice of offering at least horses to the dead, cf. G. E. Mylonas, *Mycenae and the Mycenean Age*, Princeton 1966, pp. 116f., and V. Karageorghis, *Cyprus*, London, 1969, pp. 150ff.

[b] Cf. G. Schunack, *Das hermeneutische Problem des Todes im Horizont von Römer 5 untersucht*, Tübingen 1967, pp. 63ff., where the development is traced into the New Testament.

hope, all ye who enter here!' There is a gruesome identification of existence in the grave and in Sheol in the second line: Instead of the king's magnificent bed there are maggots and worms, which crawl horribly over the body, as his couch and covering. Whereas other kings sit on their shadowy thrones even in the underworld, the tyrant, cast out without a grave, lacks even this feeble reflection of his former greatness and glory.

[12–15] *The failure of the attempt to climb into heaven.* By the use of an old Canaanite myth, the arrogant intentions of the world ruler are contrasted with his ultimate fall into the underworld. The proper name *hēlēl*,[a] translated 'Shining Star', is derived from a Semitic root which means 'to be (become) pure and bright, to shine'.[b] The Greek Bible translates it *eōsphoros*, 'bringer of the morning light, morning star' and with this translation certainly gives the right starting point for a reconstruction of the underlying myth. The morning star had intended to climb high up above the clouds and the highest star in order to set up his throne upon the mountain of the assembly of the gods in the uttermost north, and so to take away from the highest god, *'ēl 'elyōn*, the rulership of the world. But the attempted usurpation ended lamentably with his fall into the underworld.

'ēl 'elyōn seems to have been the highest god, venerated in Jerusalem in pre-Israelite times (cf. Gen. 14.19),[c] and the mention of *ṣāpōn* as the mountain of God in v. 13 points in its turn to the assimilation in Jerusalem of a theme from Canaanite mythology (cf. Ps. 48.3).[d] This does not exclude the possibility that the poet here was borrowing directly from Canaanite mythology, although we cannot at the moment identify more closely the process of transmission. In the present state of the sources the most obvious thing seems to be to look for parallels first in the most extensive source for ancient Canaanite religion, the texts from Ugarit in Northern Syria. Although they

[a] See also *BHS* and J. C. de Moor, *UF* 2, 1970, p. 225, § 10q.

[b] Cf. Accadian *elēlu*, 'be, become pure', Syriac *ḥallel*, 'purify' and arabic *halla*, 'appear, show oneself', as well as *hilāl*, 'new moon'. Cf. also P. Grelot, 'Isaïe 14.12–15 et son arrière-plan mythologique', *RHR* 148, 1955, pp. 22f., and J. W. McKay, 'Helel and the Dawn-Goddess', *VT* 20, 1970, p. 452.

[c] Cf. H. Gese, *Die Religionen Altsyriens*, in Religionen der Menschheit, ed. C. M. Schröder, 10.2, Stuttgart, 1970, pp. 116f., and F. Stolz, 'Strukturen un Figuren im Kult von Jerusalem', *ZAW* 67, 1955, pp. 168ff.

[d] Cf. H. J. Kraus, BK 15.1, 1960, pp. 342ff.; O. Kaiser, *Die mythische Bedeutung des Meeres in Ägypten, Ugarit und Israel*, BZAW 78, ²1962, pp. 53f. and Gese, pp. 56f. and 123f.

have not so far provided any direct parallel to the present passage,[a] they illuminate some of its individual features. Thus the Ugaritic epics also contain the conception of an assembly of the gods upon a mountain, which is probably familiar to most readers only from Greek mythology.[b] But unlike the present text, they do not identify the mountain with *sāpōn* which is reserved for the god Baal.[c] A similar conception exists in the Old Testament, as is shown by the passages which mention the council of '*ēl* (cf. Ps. 82.1),[d] the assembly of the heavenly beings (cf. Ps. 89.6) and the gathering of the spirits who serve Yahweh (cf. Job 1.6ff., II Kings 22.19ff. and Isa. 6).[e]

There is also from Ugarit a ritual narrative of the birth of the gods Shachar and Shalim, the morning and the evening twilight, or morning and evening stars.[f] Finally, there is an occasional mention of a god *hll*, but we do not know for certain what conceptions were associated with him.[g] But perhaps we can reconstruct more exactly the myth presupposed by the composer of the present text by going back to the Greek tradition of Phaethon, which in its turn seems to derive from a Phoenician or Canaanite original. Thus in a lost tragedy Euripides tells how Phaeton, the son of the sun god Helios and the heroine Klymene, one day begged permission, in spite of his father's warning, to drive the chariot of the sun. But he was not capable of the task; the horses ran away with him, so that he threatened to set the earth on fire. When the earth cried for help Zeus struck Phaethon with a thunderbolt, so that he fell down into the

[a] For the vain attempt of the goddess Athtar to ascend the throne of Baal with the approval of El, cf. A. Caquot, 'Le dieu Athtar et les textes de Ras Shamra', *Syria* 35, 1958, pp. 45ff., and Gese, pp. 137ff. Against the attempt to identify with each other the Athtar myth and the Helel myth, recently made by U. Oldenburg, 'Above the Stars of El', *ZAW* 82, 1970, pp. 187ff., cf. McKay, pp. 455ff. and 461ff.

[b] Cf. Kaiser, *Mythische Bedeutung*, pp. 60ff. and Gese, pp. 100ff. For the Greek assembly of the gods on Olympus cf. M. P. Nilsson, *Greek Piety*, Oxford 1948, p. 2, and for the corresponding Babylonian conception, Miessner, *op. cit.*, p. 111.

[c] Cf. Kaiser, *ibid.*, pp. 53f. and Gese, p. 57.

[d] For the range of possible interpretations of Ps. 82 cf. O. Eissfeldt, *JSS* 1, 1956, pp. 29f., repr. *Kleine Schriften* III, p. 390, and M. Tsevat, *HUCA* 50/51, 1969/70, pp. 123ff.; and especially, for the present context, J. Morgenstern, *HUCA* 14, 1939, pp. 106ff.

[e] On this topic cf. also F. M. Cross, *JNES* 12, 1952, pp. 274ff.

[f] Cf. Gese, pp. 8off.

[g] Cf. J. C. de Moor, 'The Semitic Pentheon of Ugarit', *UF* 2, 1970, p. 192, no. 101 and p. 225, § 10q, and Gese, pp. 8of. De Moor discusses the half-moon, and Gese both morning star and half-moon.

(legendary) stream Eridanos.[a] Hesiod alludes to an older form of the
Greek myth when he states that Phaethon was the son of the dawn,
Eos, and of a certain Kephalos, who does not interest us here.[b] Since
the fate and name of Phaethon (derived from the Greek *phaetho*, 'to
shine') is ultimately the same as that of our mythical hero,[c] we can
postulate that the origin of *hēlēl* myth, as Gunkel already recognized,
lay in a natural observation: as it rises, the shining morning star
grows feebler because of the rays of the rising sun.[d] And so the
Canaanites too may have told how the morning star, the son of
Shachar, the god of the morning light, was so arrogant as to try to cast
down from his throne the highest god, who lived far above the clouds
and stars. But then the sun-god Shamash or the sun-goddess Shapsu
came and cast him into the sea and into the depths of the underworld.[e]
And every time he tries to break out again and renew his rebellion
against the highest god, he is forced back into his subterranean
dungeon.[f]

In a similar way, Ezek. 28.11ff. describes the fall of the king of
Tyre with the aid of the myth of the primal man, who once lived
upon the mountain of the gods and was cast down on to the earth
because of his iniquity.[g] Lamentations 2.1 describes the destruction
of Jerusalem by the Babylonians as a fall from heaven to earth. The
continuing influence of such conceptions is shown by Matt. 11.23 and
Orac. Sibyll. 5.72. Jewish conceptions of Satan were particularly
influenced by them (cf. Enoch 86; Life of Adam and Eve 11ff.;
Luke 10.18, cf. also II Cor. 11.14 and Rev. 20.1ff.).

[12–13] The mythical archetype as it were comes to life in the fall

[a] Cf. Rose, p. 262; H. Gunkel, *Schöpfung und Chaos in Urzeit und Endzeit*, Göttingen
1895, pp. 133f., and Grelot, pp. 30f.

[b] *Theogony* 986ff.

[c] Cf. M. C. Astour, *Hellenosemitica*, Leiden ²1967, p. 269: 'The name Phaeton,
"the shining, glittering", is an exact translation of *Hēlēl*. The suggestion by McKay,
p. 463, that the Greek myth of Phaethon found its way to Syria and Palestine and
was there assimilated with the Athtar myth seems unlikely to me.

[d] P. 133.

[e] Cf. Gese, pp. 166f.

[f] Cf. also the myth of Ishtar's descent into the underworld, *AOT*², pp. 206ff., and
*ANET*², pp. 106ff., which likewise, though probably in a different way, are
concerned with the temporary disappearance of Venus; and cf. E. Dhorme, *Les
religions de Babylonie et d'Assyrie*, Mana I. II: Les anciennes religions orientales,
Paris 1949, p. 321.

[g] Cf. K. H. Bernhardt, *Das Problem der altorientalischen Königsideologie im Alten
Testament*, SVT 8, 1961, p. 86, and W. Zimmerli, BK 13.2, 1969, *ad loc.*

of the world ruler. His dishonoured end forms the sharpest contrast with his plans to conquer the world, or, in mythical terms, his attempt to seize the throne beyond the stars (cf. Life of Adam and Eve 15) which stands upon the mountain of God, and upon which the destinies of the whole of the world are decided. [14–15] This attempt transgresses the limits laid down for both mortal and heavenly beings, for he is trying to take the place reserved for the highest God alone, and is consequently punished by a fall into the deepest and darkest depths of the underworld.

[16–19] *His dishonoured end*. The catalogue of the misdeeds of the fallen tyrant, whose desecrated body is found in the rubbish pit by the passers-by, corresponds to the praise of the deeds of a dead king in a genuine lament. The man before whom the earth trembled and kingdoms shook, who devastated the earth and its cities, and whose prisoners languished in his dungeons to the end of their lives, the terror of the world, now lies among the bodies of the rabble. The astonished and at the same time mocking calls of the passers-by remind us that the people of antiquity (and they are not alone in this) did not on principle treat those smitten by fate with sympathy and pity, but with derision and mockery, in order to be seen to be avoiding those struck by the anger and punishment of God or of the gods.[a] We shall not consider here whether and how far sympathy is appropriate even towards someone who has slaughtered people. We understand that here the poet is trying to bring before our eyes how the tyrant has fallen to the uttermost depths, and we shall not discuss whether human dignity is preserved when scorn is poured over someone after he has been judged.

[18–19] The emphasis upon the honourable burial of the kings of the world in general presents the refusal of any burial to the tyrant as an even more severe punishment than his death alone. For the people of the ancient world there was no more terrible fate than to remain unburied, and no more sacred duty than that of giving burial to relatives or comrades in arms.[b] For someone who remained unburied lacked even the little bit of peace which death can bring men. As grave goods show, the dead were regarded even as needing food, at least at first. Those unburied were condemned not to rest until the last remnants of their body decayed, and their shadowy existence came to an end with it. Thus we read in a Babylonian text that the

[a] Cf. Kaiser, *Knecht*, p. 92.
[b] Cf. e.g. Sophocles, *Antigone*, 450ff.

dead person 'whose body is cast upon the field . . . whose dead spirit does not rest in the earth and has none to care for it' must wander restlessly about in order to seek nourishment, 'from the dregs left in the pot and the scraps thrown upon the street'.[a] The battle for the body of Patroclus, the ransoming of Hector's body and the burial of Polyneices by Antigone show how much importance the Greeks attributed to proper burial.[b] The Egyptian cult of the dead in general demonstrates the stifling power, casting fear over the whole of life, of such conceptions among Israel's southern neighbours.[c] According to the tradition, a prophet such as Amos could not prophesy anything more terrible against the priest of Bethel than death in an unclean land (Amos 7.17). In the book of Tobit, on the other hand, the burial of the Jews and non-Jews executed by the Assyrian king is seen as a particularly pious act (cf. Tobit 1.17ff.; 2.3ff.).

The fallen tyrant is cast on to the slaughterer's dump, where abortions, that is, those who have not existed (cf. Eccles. 6.3ff.), and those who have been murdered and executed await dissolution. We cannot tell whether he has fallen in battle or has been executed and quartered after being taken prisoner (cf. v. 12); for in antiquity all sorts of mutilations could be practised upon the body of a fallen enemy, until it was left for the vultures and the dogs to eat (cf. Homer, *Iliad* XXII 330ff. and II Kings 9.33ff.).

[19b–21] *The absolute end.* Anyone who rested united with his fathers in the family grave still as it were enjoyed in the underworld the protection and security of his family.[d] Someone who is without a grave lacks even this. Thus even in the most attenuated form of the shadowy existence in the underworld his life is threatened. He who has brought ruin not only upon himself but upon his country and his people by his excessive urge for power now finds no one to show mercy and carry out the duty of burial for him. Even the continuance of his name, and his flesh and blood, in his children and children's children is denied him. Since from the seed of the criminal one could expect further crimes, and a renewed attempt to seize world power

[a] Meissner, p. 147.

[b] Cf. *Iliad* XVII; XXIV and Sophocles, *Antigone*, 69ff. – For the burial rites of archaic and classical times cf. D. C. Kurtz and J. Boardman, *Greek Burial Customs*, London 1971, pp. 142ff.

[c] Cf. H. Kees, *Totenglaube und Jenseitsvorstellungen*.

[d] Cf. Gen. 25.8; I Kings 2.10; 15.24; etc., and R. de Vaux, *Les Institutions de l'Ancien Testament* I, Paris 1958, p. 97; ET *Ancient Israel: Its Life and Institutions*. London and New York 1961, p. 59.

with all its terrible consequences for the inhabitants of the earth, his sons too have to be slaughtered. In accordance with early legal ideas, which were unaware of the individual personality, sons had to atone for the guilt of their fathers.[a] We have here, however, in addition to the idea of kinship, the further conception that the rule of the tyrant might be continued through his sons. How close the poet is with his final demand to the political realities of antiquity can clearly be seen by recalling the fate of the last king of Judah, Zedekiah: Nebuchadnezzar had him dragged before him at Riblah. There his sons were slain before his eyes. Then the wretched king was blinded and carried off in chains to Babylon, to the deepest dungeon (cf. II Kings 25.6ff.). It may be that the poet had this in mind when he was writing the last lines of this poem.

CHAPTER 14.22–23

The Total Annihilation of Babylon

22 'And I will rise up against them,' saying of Yahweh Sebaoth, 'and cut off from Babylon reputation and remnant, progeny and posterity,'[b] saying of Yahweh. 23'And I will make it a possession of the hedgehog, and pools of water, and I will ram it down with the ram[c] of destruction,' saying of Yahweh Sebaoth.

The same hand as can be detected in 14.20 and 21[d] has added in these verses a concluding comment upon the prophecy concerning Babylon in chs. 13 and 14. In v. 22 the redactor takes up the theme of the extermination of the mighty ruler's progeny from the two final verses of the taunt song upon his fall, and interprets them unambiguously, as he had attempted to do in the previous brief interpolations, as referring to the total annihilation of the Babylonians. With two alliterative pairs of words, which we can render in English 'reputa-

---

[a] Cf. II Kings 14.5f.; Deut. 24.16, and Josh. 7.24f.; I Sam. 22.16ff.; II Sam. 3.29 and 21.1ff.; but also Ezek. 18.4, cf. vv. 5ff. with vv. 14ff.

[b] The reproduction of the play on words is largely based on G. B. Gray, *Isaiah I–XXVII*, ICC, ⁴1956, p. 262 [Translator].

[c] For the meaning of *ṭ'ṭ'* and *maṭ'aṭē* cf. L. Knopf, *VT* 8, 1958, pp. 178f.

[d] Cf. above p. 29 note f and p. 33 note b.

tion (literally 'name') and remnant' and 'progeny and posterity'[a] he presents Yahweh himself as emphasizing that no single Babylonian will survive the final catastrophe which is expected to fall upon the city. None of them will survive to keep alive the name of the people (cf. Josh. 7.9; II Sam. 14.7 and Zeph. 1.4). No 'remnant' will escape the expected massacre (cf. 13.15ff.).[b] Not only the adults but also the children will be exterminated (cf. Gen. 21.23; Job 18.19; Eccles. 41.5; 47.22) so that the nation will never be able to recover from the blow it has suffered. Verse 23, on the other hand, takes up the idea in 13.19ff. of the total destruction of the city, which after its conquest will become a marsh, the preserve of animals which roll themselves up, presumably hedgehogs.[c] The completeness of the destruction is impressively compared with the image of ramming down, borrowed from the world of work: just as the workers ram flat the last remnants of demolished houses in order to prepare the ground for new building, so Yahweh will bring about the destruction of the city, except that here the destruction will not be followed by a rebuilding.

Although the political role of Babylon in history may have long been over, for post-exilic Judaism the city, which had played so ominous a role in its own history, remained a symbol of all the forces on this earth which are hostile to God. It was consequently not possible to imagine any change which would bring the salvation of Israel unless the hated former oppressor was first annihilated. The formula of revelation which is repeated three times in the short passage, 'saying of Yahweh Sebaoth' or 'saying of Yahweh', is meant to assure the redactor's community, and all future readers of the Isaiah roll, that the complete destruction of Babylon and its inhabitants is the will of God, who as Lord over all powers in heaven and on earth[d] also possesses the power to bring about the end of the great capital city of the world.

The concentration upon the fate which it was expected and hoped would come upon Babylon, and the language, which is less traditional in its usage, in so far as it is possible to say this of so short a fragment, suggests that the redactor of 14.22f. wrote earlier than the learned scribe of 14.1–4a. If it is to him that we owe the incorporation of the preceding poem, he deserves our thanks.

[a] See above p. 43 note b.
[b] Cf. Josh. 13.12; II Sam. 21.2; Amos 9.12; Isa. 14.30.
[c] Others prefer the rendering 'bittern'; but cf. 34.11.
[d] Cf. the comment on 6.3 and 13.4.

CHAPTER 14.24–27

Yahweh's Plan against Assyria and against the Nations of the Earth

24 Yahweh Sebaoth has sworn:
    Surely,[a] as I plan[b] so ⟨it shall happen⟩[c]
    and as I purpose, so shall it stand.
25 I will break Assyria in my land,
    and upon my mountains trample her underfoot;
    and her yoke shall depart from them,
    and her burden from his[d] shoulder.
26 This is the purpose that is purposed[e] concerning the whole
    earth;
    and this is the hand that is stretched out over all the nations.
27 For Yahweh Sebaoth has purposed, and who will annul it?
    His hand is stretched out, and who will turn it back?

[24–27] The prophecy of the destruction of Assyria upon the mountains of the Holy Land is introduced not by a formula of revelation to an envoy or messenger, but by means of the brief statement in v. 24a that an oath has been taken. It is uncertain whether the oath and the words spoken by God, which begin in v. 24b, finish in v. 25, or not until v. 26 or v. 27; for it is quite possible that the statement of confirmation in v. 26 could be meant to be spoken by Yahweh, and the passage to a sentence which speaks about him in the questions in the following verse may also, if meant to be spoken by him, have had the function of emphasizing the validity of the message. But it is striking that the certainty that what is announced in v. 25 will be realized, a certainty which the oath in itself supplies, is replaced by a reflection upon the irrevocability of God's purpose. The dominating idea of the divine plan, which because it is divine cannot be diverted,

---

[a] For the oath formula, cf. G-K, § 149b.

[b] For the rendering of the perfects cf. Grether, § 79h.

[c] Read with 1Q Isa *thyh*, cf. also LXX, Vg and Targ. The intention of the Massoretes is explained by H. Donner, *Israel unter den Völkern*, SVT 11, 1964, p. 145, though he prefers M. The fact that *BHS* does not even note the variant readings is one of its deficiencies.

[d] One is tempted to amend with *BHS*, but in view of 9.3 and 10.27 it is perhaps better not to do so.

[e] For the *dagesh forte* cf. G-K, § 35b.

becomes the central theme as early as v. 24b and is therefore additionally confirmed by the account of the oath in v. 24a and the oath formula in v. 24b, in order to create in the reader a firm certainty that the prophecy will be fulfilled. The blurred form suggests that the *Sitz im Leben* of the prophecy is the study of a devout redactor, and not the direct proclamation of a prophet. In fact a study of the ideas and turns of phrase which occur in the poem show that as in 10.16–19 and 10.20–23 we have the work of a scribe from a later period, and not a saying by the prophet Isaiah.

The fact that the opposite view is nowadays almost universally accepted requires us to enlarge upon what is to be found in this passage.[a] The idea of an oath by God as the most solemn form of assurance is found in prophecies of judgment by Amos[b] and Isaiah,[c] and is taken up by the Deuteronomic redactor of the book of Jeremiah,[d] who draws elsewhere on the conception which his school held of the promise of the land of Israel as an oath to the fathers.[e] A similar idea is also found in the book of Ezekiel.[f] On the other hand it is possible to trace how from the time of Deutero-Isaiah this usage became more frequent in prophecies of salvation and in oracles against foreign nations which are similar in function.[g] That Yahweh's thoughts are carried out is stated in Num. 33.56 in almost the same terms as in v. 24.[h] Just as this passage states that God's plans cannot be diverted, so the redactional passage 8.9ff. (cf. v. 10) describes the failure of the attacks of the nations. The basic idea, with a slight change in the wording to suit the context, derives from Prov. 19.21 (cf. Pss. 33.11 and 73.24) but is already adopted by Deutero-Isaiah (cf. 46.10). On the other hand, there is not much evidence of the conception of Yahweh's plan in the first Isaiah, since the isolation of

[a] B. Stade, *ZAW* 3, 1883, p. 16; H. Hackmann, *Die Zukunftserwartung des Jesaja*, Göttingen 1893, pp. 106f., note 3, and Marti *ad loc.*, all argued against Isaiah as the author.

[b] Cf. Amos 4.2; 6.8; 8.7.

[c] Cf. Isa. 5.9; 22.14.

[d] Cf. Jer. 22.5; and see W. Thiel, Die deuteronomische Redaktion des Buches Jeremia, typed thesis, Berlin, 1970, pp. 394ff., shortly to appear in WMANT; cf. also Jer. 44.26.

[e] Cf. e.g. Gen. 15.18; 22.16; 26.3; Ex. 13.5, 11; Deut. 1.8; 4.31; 8.1; 9.5 and *passim*; Jer. 11.5.

[f] Cf. Ezek. 5.11; 17.16 and 19.

[g] Cf. Isa. 45.23; 54.9; 62.8; Ezek. 20.33; 33.11, 27; 34.8; 35.6; 36.5 and 7.

[h] For the late character of this passage cf. M. Noth, ATD 7, 1966, *ad loc.*; ET *Numbers*, OTL, 1968, *ad loc.*

5.19 raises justifiable doubts, while 19.12, 17; 23.8f. and 28.29 are secondary.[a] The same is true of Micah 4.12. On the other hand, the idea of a divine plan directed against the nations also plays a part in the late oracles against the nations in the book of Jeremiah.[b] The idea which occurs in v. 25 that Yahweh will destroy the Assyrians in his own land[c] is, as we show below, not a prophetic hope expressed by Isaiah but one which first occurs in proto-apocalyptic passages. 29.5ff. and 31.4ff. are no more Isaianic passages than 10.16ff.; 10.24ff. or 17.12ff.[d] The conception of the protection of Zion against approaching enemies (the Assyrians, as here), which is also to be found in the popular prophetic legend of Isa. 37.33ff., was drawn from the theme of the battle of the nations in the Zion psalms (cf. Pss. 46.7ff.; 48.5ff.; 76.3ff. and 87) and it became widespread in post-exilic, proto-apocalyptic circles, which looked forward to the attack of a powerful army of the nations upon the Holy Land and its destruction by Yahweh before the gates of Jerusalem (cf. especially Zeph. 3.8; Joel 4; Ezek. 38f. and Zech. 14). On the basis of this conception it is easy to understand that the divine plan should be thought of as extending to the whole earth in v. 26 (cf. 10.23; 12.5; 13.5; 25.8 and 22.22). The paraphrasing of the Holy Land in terms of its mountains, and the corresponding expression 'my mountains' is also very late.[e]

That v. 25b is taken from 10.27 has long been recognized and has led almost all commentators since Duhm to exclude this couplet from the poem, particularly as the possessive and pronominal suffixes 'his', 'them' and 'their' have no antecedent.[f] Verse 26 continues with the phrase describing the outstretched hand of Yahweh from 5.25; 9.11, 16, 20 and 10.4. The application of this anthropomorphic image to the enemy seems to be influenced by the Deuteronomic set phrase of the mighty hand and outstretched arm of Yahweh.[g]

[a] But cf. J. Fichtner, 'Jahwes Plan in der Botschaft Jesajas', *ZAW* 63, 1951, pp. 16ff., repr. in *Gottes Weisheit*, ATh II.3, 1965, pp. 27ff.; and G. von Rad, *Theologie des Alten Testaments* II, Munich 1960, pp. 172f.; ET, *Old Testament Theology* II, London and New York 1965, pp. 154f.

[b] Cf. Jer. 49.20, 30 and 50.45.

[c] Cf. Jer. 2.7; 16.18; Ezek. 36.5; 38.16; Jonah 1.6 and 4.2.

[d] Cf. above and below on the passages mentioned.

[e] Cf. Ezek. 6.2f.; 19.9; 33.28; 34.13; 39.17 and *passim*; Ezek. 38.21 and Zech. 14.5.

[f] But cf. Hackmann, p. 107, note 3.

[g] Cf. Deut. 4.34; 5.15; 7.19; 26.8; Jer. 21.5 and also Jer. 32.21.

Finally, the first question which occurs in v. 27 goes back to the corresponding negative phrase in 8.10a, while the second, concluding question seems also to go back to 43.13 and 5.25; 9.11, 16, 20 and 10.4. To ignore these facts would be to dispute the validity as a whole of the study of linguistic usage as a tool of literary criticism. It would also lead to an unfortunate distortion of the preaching of Isaiah which would ultimately repeat the view of him found in the legends that were current about him, by making him the father of apocalyptic.[a]

It has often been emphasized that the situation of this poem in its present place, following a prophecy about Babylon, is secondary. If this had been its original position, it would have had its own heading: *maśśā' 'aśśūr*. Its content, however, places it in the context of 10.4ff. We must consider the possibility that it once formed the conclusion of 10.4–14 and that later, when it was displaced, 10.15 was interpolated.[b] Obviously the redactor of the book who is responsible for placing the oracle in its present position felt the lack of a prophecy against Assyria within the collection in chs. 13–23.

[24–25a] The short poem shows that in spite of his entire dependence, discernible throughout, upon phrases and ideas derived from his study of scripture, the scribe who was enlarging the Isaiah roll was able to create a well composed and impressive whole. Although the world power disguised by the pseudonym Assyria was able in his age to determine the course of history and the fate of the people of God, yet he was certain that Yahweh could calmly observe this, and that Israel could take comfort in the midst of its trials, because Yahweh's irrevocable plan would ultimately bring an end to this world power. When the new Assyria or one might almost say, the eternal Assyria, repeatedly manifested in a new form, set out with the nations of the world to storm Zion, it would suffer the same fate as that undergone,

[a] Stade, *ZAW* 3, 1883, p. 16, called this poem 'a passage pasted together from Isaianic phrases'. Duhm, 4th ed., pp. 122f., took the opposite view that Stade had failed to demonstrate the origin and purpose of the compilation, and held: 'There is not a word in the whole passage that could not have come from Isaiah.' We trust we have supplied Stade with the detailed arguments he needed.

[b] J. Vermeylen, *La composition littéraire du livre d'Isaïe, I–XXXIX*, Louvain 1970 (hectographed), p. 43 and p. 37. Cf. also Cheyne, *Introduction to the Book of Isaiah*, London 1895, p. 79; Dillmann-Kittel *ad loc.*; but also Marti, p. 130, and for an argument from form criticism, B. S. Childs, *Isaiah and the Assyrian Crisis*, StBTh II.3, 1967, pp. 38f. Because of his own personal literary criticism of ch. 10, Procksch would place the passage following 10.32.

according to the stories which circulated among the devout, by Sennacherib's attack upon Hezekiah's Jerusalem (cf. 36f.) and would suffer total annihilation (cf. 30.27ff. as well as Pss. 60.14 [=108.14]; 44.6; Isa. 63.6, and also Jer. 12.10). The great preoccupation of devout Jews with this hope, which ultimately derives from the Zion psalms, is equally demonstrated by the apocalyptic prophet in Dan. 11.45, according to which Antiochus Epiphanes would meet his end between the Mediterranean Sea and the holy mountain of Zion.[a]

[26–27] Just as Yahweh once stretched out his hand against his own people in order to strike them again and again, he will now raise it for the last, final and irrevocable blow against the world power, the second Assyria (cf. also 5.20). Thus the scribe reveals for us his hopes, but also the considerations which lead him to them, the results of which to him are a matter of such conviction that he even dares to present them as the oath and reflection of Yahweh himself.

[25b] Since v. 25b lacks the coherence found elsewhere in the poem, we must regard this couplet as an even later addition. The interpolator who speaks here felt the lack of an explicit statement that the conquest of Assyria would bring the moment of freedom for his own people, as he read in 10.27a. Since the background to 10.27a is 9.3, he seemed to have expected, at the same time as the liberation of his people from the yoke of foreign rule, the beginning of the rule of the king upon the throne of David, whose kingdom and peace will never end (cf. 9.6).

CHAPTER 14.28–32

Against the Philistines

28 In the year that King Ahaz died came this oracle:
29 Rejoice not, all Philistia,
    that the rod of him who smote you[b] is broken!
    For from the serpent's root comes forth an adder
    and its fruit is a flying dragon.

[a] Cf. N. Porteous, *Daniel*, OTL, 1965, *ad loc.*

[b] This translation is, in view of 9.12; 10.20, 24 and 30.31, more probable than 'the staff which smote you' (literally: 'the staff striking you'), which is just as possible in principle.

30 But the very lowliest[a] will feed,
     and the poor lie down in safety;
     but I will[b] kill your root with famine,
     and your remnant he[b] will slay.
31 Wail, O gate; cry, O city;
     Quail, all Philistia![c]
     For smoke comes out of the north,
     and there is no straggler[d] in his ranks.[e]
32 What will one answer[f] the messengers of the nation?[g]
     For Yahweh has founded Zion,
     and in her the wretched of his people find refuge.

Our translation does not attempt to resolve in advance the tensions present in the text; the reader is thus given some idea of the difficulties which the commentator faces. If we follow the Hebrew text, we have a word of Yahweh. For the 'I' who speaks in v. 30b is certainly none other than Yahweh, who is here addressing the Philistines directly. But to our astonishment the discourse immediately drops the style of direct address, and the first person is replaced by the third person. The great Hebrew Isaiah manuscript from Qumran Cave I in fact uses the first person in both cases, while the Greek translation has the third person in both cases. It almost seems as though both attempted in their own way to deal with the difficulty they felt in v. 30b. The classical Massoretic Hebrew text, followed in our translation, was presumably trying to distinguish between God's direct intervention in the form of hunger and the slaying of the remnant by the conqueror. There are other oddities concealed in the oracle. The metaphor of the root fits the context of v. 29 much better

a Literally: 'the first-born of the lowly', cf. Job 18.13. The suggestion that instead of $b^e k \bar{o} r \bar{e}$, first-born we should read $b^e k \bar{a} r \bar{\iota}$ or $b^e k \bar{a} r \bar{a} y$, on my meadow(s), or $b^e h^a r \bar{a} r \bar{a} y$, on my mountains, is based on justifiable doubts about the placing of the very lowliest with the poor. But the late character of the passage and the tradition of the text indicate caution.

b LXX and Targ. read $w^e h \bar{e} m \bar{\iota} t$, he will kill, and 1QIsa and Vg $'eh^e r \bar{o} g$, I will slay.

c Inf. abs. in an imperative sense.

d 1QIsa reads $m \bar{o} d \bar{e} d$, 'and no one misses'.

e Hapax legomenon.

f But the preceding verb in the 3rd sing. masc. can in theory also have the messengers as its subject, cf. G-K § 145 o, so that LXX and Targ (see n. g) offer a possible interpretation. The messengers or kings would in astonishment spread the news that Zion had been spared.

g 1QIsa: 'kings of the people'; LXX: 'and what will the kings of the peoples reply?'; Targ: 'And what good messages will be messengers of the peoples bring?'

than that of v. 30b. In addition, the threat in v. 30b anticipates in an awkward way the dramatic proclamation in v. 31, so that one might suspect that it was an interpolation. The way in which v. 30a comes between v. 29 and v. 31, without any apparent connection, is also odd. If we look at the concluding verse, we notice the absence of a sentence giving the reason for its second half. Thus if v. 30b is moved to precede v. 32b, a double difficulty is removed. It remains curious that v. 32a consists of only a single line, whereas elsewhere – apart from the heading – we always have two lines which are complementary or which have the same meaning. Thus it may be that v. 32a was the work of a later redactor who understood the introductory *kî* of v. 32b to mean not 'for' but 'indeed'. This immediately suggests that perhaps the saying concerning Philistia in vv. 29 and 31 existed independently and was only later enlarged by the addition of the promise to the poor in Zion. Finally, we must ask whether any part of the oracle goes back to Isaiah. With regard to vv. 30a and 32, it can rightly be objected that Isaiah did not usually mean by the lowly and poor the people of Jerusalem in general, or the devout among them, but those of his people who were actually poor and oppressed (cf. 3.15; 10.2; also 3.5; 1.23 and 9.16).[a]

[28] Since the *heading* is at first sight sufficient guarantee of the Isaianic origin of the original basis of the prophecy, we must first check this. Its opening words are clearly based upon 6.1, where we read: 'In the year that King Uzziah died . . .' The continuation of the sentence is based upon the headings of the oracles which recur from 13.1 to 23.1 and again in 30.6. If it had originally read 'came this word of Yahweh to Isaiah' it would hardly have been altered. Since it neither names the foreign nation to which the oracle refers, nor takes up a key-word from it, it is probably more recent than the other oracle headings, and is consequently of no value in deciding the author and the occasion of the saying. Perhaps the heading is a product of the history of the Messianic interpretation of the oracle, as illustrated by the Greek translation of v. 30. According to the Greeks, the seed of the serpent will feed the poor; thus v. 29 is understood in a Messianic sense. The Targum, the Aramaic paraphrase, interpreted the text in exactly the same sense. This interpretation has also found favour in recent times. But v. 31 quite clearly requires an enemy from the north. This makes the Messianic interpretation impossible. Once the secondary nature of the heading is realized, there

[a] Cf. Duhm and Marti, *ad loc.*

is no longer any need to suppose that the death of the oppressor of the Philistines and that of King Ahaz took place at the same time. This theory is put forward in only one of the various competing attempts to resolve the difficult problems of the chronology of the kings of Judah in the second half of the eighth century, that of Begrich, who dates the death of Ahaz in the year 727/26. For Tiglath-pileser III died in that year. If one follows Albright and Andersen, who appeal to II Kings 18.13 (= Isa. 36.1), the year of Ahaz' death is 715/14. In this case there is no corresponding Assyrian date.[a]

By far the greatest difficulty, however, lies in the lack of clarity found in the text, and reflected in the translation, as to whether the poet is describing as successive generations the snake, the adder and the flying fiery dragon, or whether he calls the offspring of the snake first an adder and then a dragon. In the first case, the Isaianic authorship of vv. 29 and 31 is also excluded, because oracles containing omens and fragments of calculation of this kind are entirely in the spirit of apocalyptic, but not in that of the pre-exilic prophet (cf. Dan. 2 and 11). In the second case, the saying can be dated on the occasion of the death of Tiglath-pilesar, or alternatively, on that of the death of Sargon II in 705. In 734 Tiglath-pileser defeated Hanno of Gaza. Sargon II finally overthrew Hanno, while in 711 he took action against the revolt of Ashdod.[b] His successor Sennacherib had once again to undertake a campaign against the Philistines in 701, for Ashkelon and Ekron had allied themselves with Hezekiah of Judah against him.[c] If the prophecy is dated in the year of the death of Sargon it would be composed in anticipation of the great Palestinian revolt of the year 703–701, and would show us the joy of the oppressed nations and the prophet's forecast, a gloomy one in spite of its vigour, and meant in fact not to warn the Philistines but his own people. But it would be surprising in this case if the prophet had not supplied any

---

[a] Cf. J. Begrich, 'Jesaja 14.28–32', *ZDMG* 86, 1933, p. 73. repr. *Gesammelte Studien zum Alten Testament*, ThB 21, 1964, p. 128; A. Jepsen, 'Zur Chronologie der Könige von Israel und Juda', in Jepsen and R. Hanhart, BZAW 88, 1964, pp. 36ff.; W. F. Albright, 'The Chronology of the Divided Monarchy of Israel', BASOR 100, 1945, pp. 20ff. and K. T. Andersen, 'Die Chronologie der Könige von Israel und Juda', *StTh* 23, 1969, pp. 102ff.

[b] Cf. also pp. 112f. below.

[c] Cf. *AR* I, § 815; *ANET*[2] p. 283; *TGI*[2], pp. 58f.; *AR* II, § 55; *ANET*[2], pp. 284f.; *TGI*[2], p. 62; *AOT*[2], pp. 350f.; *AR* II, § 62f.; *ANET*[2], p. 286; *TGI*[2], pp. 63f.; *AOT*[2], pp. 352ff.; *AR* II, § 239ff.; *ANET*[2] pp. 287ff. and *TGI*[2], pp. 67ff. Cf. also H. Donner, *Israel unter den Völkern*, SVT 11, 1964, pp. 4f., 106ff. and 117ff.

reason for his saying, such as Amos, for example, had thought proper in the case of his oracles concerning foreign nations (cf. Amos 1.3ff.). In the late oracles concerning foreign nations, such reasons are not found. Finally, our commentary will show that v. 29 certainly and v. 30 possibly can be understood as echoes of earlier texts. In this case the mixture of images which we observe in v. 29 can be taken as evidence against the hypothesis of Isaianic authorship that is accepted by the majority of commentators in the present century.[a] Verse 29 seems to be evidence against the view that the poem was composed without an immediate historical reference, and had in mind the final enemy who would come from the north, overrun the nations and yet meet his end before the walls of Zion – unless we assume that this eschatological idea has been given a frivolous form, and that snake-adder-dragon form a succession of generations. If this second possibility is excluded, we may seek the historical reference in the year during the reign of Alexander, when there may have been rejoicing in the Philistine cities and in Gaza, which by this time had long been settled by the Arabs, at the defeat of the Persian King at Issos, in ignorance of what Tyre and Gaza, who dared to resist the Macedonian, were to face[b]. The question of course arises whether the poet saw Alexander as the enemy from the north and was anticipating his campaign against Zion. In this text, as in almost all such passages, it is unfortunately true that we should like to know much more about its origins and the ideas behind it than we shall ever be able to find out. Thus we shall content ourselves with giving a brief exposition of the text in its original order and refrain from all further speculation.

[29 +31] *The warning to the Philistines.* Without giving any reason, and adapting himself to the style of most of the oracles found in chs. 13–23, the prophet-poet addresses the whole land of the Philistines, in order to call a halt to its untimely joy at the death or defeat of a ruler under which it has suffered severely. The metaphor of the broken rod seems to go back to 9.3, and the expression 'of him who smote you' to 9.12, although 30.31 and perhaps even 10.20 and 24

[a] Apart from the authors mentioned in the following note, the only exception is Kissane; he regards the oracle as by Isaiah, and does not doubt that the heading is too, but identifies the flying seraphs with the renewed Davidic monarchy of the Messianic age. For the other customary identification with one of the Assyrian kings of the eighth century cf. e.g. F. Wilke, *Jesaja und Assur*, Leipzig 1905, pp. 39ff. and most recently S. Erlandsson, *The Burden of Babylon*, Lund 1970, pp. 68f.

[b] Cf. Duhm and Marti, *ad loc.*

probably also influenced the choice of words (cf. also Obad. 12; Micah 7.8 and Jer. 48.17). The mixture of the imagery of plants and animals in v. 29b is also odd. One immediately suspects that the use of the expression 'root' was inspired by 11.1, 10 and 37.31, and that of the fiery dragon (*sārāp*) by 30.6. The idea as such loses nothing from the mixture of metaphors. It is clear that a ruler of the next or next but one generation will bring about an oppression far overshadowing what has been suffered at the hands of the previous generation. The snake is followed by the adder which is feared because of its fatal bite (cf. Ex. 4.2ff.; 7.8ff.; Isa. 11.8) while the adder is followed by the fabulous winged, fiery serpent, the dragon, which according to popular tales was supposed to appear in the desert (cf. 30.6; Num. 21.6ff.; Deut. 8.15 and Herodotus III 109).[a] Whereas the Philistines regard the danger as past, they and – as we can say when we look at the stanza which follows – the whole world of the nations are in fact faced with an intensification of the threat from which there is no escape.

What is one day to happen is as though present to the seer. Thus he already calls upon the gates and city to raise the cry of lamentation because they will be overpowered by the imminent attack.[b] Here the gate is addressed not as the place where the inhabitants gather,[c] but as the crucial point in the conquest of the city. It must wail, because the savage mob of the enemy will pour through it into the conquered city. A greater horror will seize the whole land of the Philistines, and not merely some of the cities, when it perceives the signs of the advancing army. We cannot tell whether the seer was thinking of the watch-fires, signal fires, or, what would certainly have produced the most terrifying impression, the clouds of smoke billowing high into the sky from the burning of conquered cities. The fact that the smoke comes from the north is in accordance with the usual route of attack from the empires of Asia Minor and Mesopotamia, but must have reminded the readers, who were no doubt familiar with the book of Jeremiah, of the enemy from the north who had become a typical figure (cf. Jer. 1.14f.; 4.6; 6.1; 13.20; 46.20; 47.2; 50.3, 41; 51.48 and

---

[a] Cf. also O. Kaiser, *Isaiah 1–12*, OTL, 1972, p. 76 (on Isa. 6.2) and also T. H. Gaster, *Myth, Legend and Custom in the Old Testament*, New York and London 1969, pp. 573 and 655.

[b] For the parallel use of wailing and crying cf. also Jer. 25.34 and 48.20.

[c] Against Fohrer, *ad loc.*

Ezek. 26.7). If in the last phrase of v. 31 we retain the traditional Hebrew text, it clearly states that the hope of a sudden weakening of the hostile army through disobedience or desertion is in vain. A powerful, disciplined and therefore doubly dangerous army is approaching! The sense of the Hebrew text of the great Qumran manuscript is that the army is so numerous that no one can count it.[a]

[30a + 32b] *The refuge of the devout on Zion.* With an adversative 'but',[b] the seer transfers his gaze in the second stanza from the Philistines to the quite different fate of the devout in Jerusalem. Just as Jerusalem, according to the tradition that was current in the intervening years, had been saved from Sennacherib's attack by its trust in God,[c] so it would not fall to the final enemy with his powerful army. The people of God, described in the language of the psalm as the lowly and the poor,[d] have therefore no need to despair. Like a flock protected by a good shepherd it can feed and lie down in safety.[e] Because Yahweh has himself laid the unshakeable foundation walls of Zion (cf. 28.16; Ps. 87.1) those among his people who know that they are dependent upon his help and put their trust in it will find refuge and safety here in all the storms that are to come (cf. Zeph. 3.13; Isa. 10.2).[f] The background is clearly formed by the tradition of Zion, the mountain of God, which remains unshaken in the rising up of the nations, as it did in that of the primaeval sea, and before which the enemy will meet their end.[g]

[32a] The redactor wanted to make the picture of the nations gathered before the walls of Zion even clearer. He therefore describes the giving of the calm answer of the certainty of faith to the messenger

[a] *mdd* is used elsewhere with *b* only to refer to the measuring vessel used, cf. Ex. 16.18 and Isa. 65.7.

[b] Cf. G-K, § 163a-b.

[c] Cf. also 36.1ff.; 37.9bff., 22ff.

[d] Cf. Pss. 72.13; 82.4; Amos 4.1; Isa. 10.2; 11.4 and 26.6; and G. Botterweck, *ThWAT* I, cols. 38ff., or E. Gerstenberger, *THAT* I, col. 23ff.

[e] Cf. Pss. 23; 77.21; 78.52; 80.2; 95.7; 100.3; Isa. 40.11 and Ezek. 34.15; 28.26; 34.25 *et passim*.

[f] Cf. Ezek. 38.8, 11, 14.

[g] Cf. Pss. 46; 48; 76; Hab. 2; Zech. 14 and also Ezek. 38f. and on the last passage H. M. Lutz, *Jahwe, Jerusalem und die Völker*, WMANT 27, 1968, pp. 157ff. and pp. 200ff., and also F. Stolz, *Strukturen und Figuren im Kult von Jerusalem*, BZAW 118, 1970, pp. 72ff. and esp. pp. 92f.; and for a different view, G. Wanke, *Die Zionstheologie der Korachiten*, BZAW 97, 1966, pp. 74ff.

of the army brought up by King Dragon,[a] or to all the kings of the nations gathered there,[b] who would demand the surrender of the city as Sennacherib's Rabshakeh and Sennacherib himself once did (cf. 36.1ff. and 37.9bff.). **[30b]** Since he also felt it important that there should be no doubt about the annihilation of the Philistines, he also interpolated v. 30b, which in the text which we possess gives the impression that Yahweh intended first of all to strike the Philistines himself with a famine, in order then to hand them over to the enemy to be massacred. But he was probably thinking simply of the two stages, investment and starving out, and then of the subsequent conquest of the city. That the root is to be starved out is not a very happy metaphor (cf. for a more apt image Hos. 9.16). The 'remnant' means the Philistines who have survived the siege. What is meant is clear enough: none of the Philistines will escape the last enemy! If we ask why there was such a burning expectation in Judah of the fall of the Philistines, with whom Judah would soon have lived as neighbours for almost a thousand years, we must recall not only the ancient struggles for dominance in the case of Saul and David, but particularly the part the descendents of the Philistines played in the trade in Jewish slaves (cf. Amos 1.6f.; Ezek. 25.15; Zeph. 2.4f. and Jer. 47).

In conclusion we give a translation of the basic text in the order which underlies our exposition:[c]

29 Rejoice not, all Philistia,
    that the rod of him who smote you is broken.
    For from the serpent's root comes forth an adder
    and its fruit is a flying dragon.
31 Wail, O gate, cry, O city;
    Quail, all Philistia!
    For smoke comes out of the north,
    and there is no straggler in his ranks.
30a But the very lowliest will feed,
    and the poor lie down in safety.
32b For Yahweh has founded Zion,
    and in her the wretched of his people find refuge.

[a] In the context of a historical interpretation the messengers are seen as the ambassadors of the Philistines, whose attempt to obtain participation in the coalition against Assyria ought in the prophet's opinion to be rejected.

[b] Cf. above p. 50 note g.

[c] Cf. also Begrich, pp. 69ff., repr. pp. 124ff.

Chapters 15.1–16.14

Moab

1   An oracle concerning Moab.[a]
    Truly, laid waste in a night,
        undone is Ar-Moab.
    Truly, laid waste in a night,
        undone is Kir-Moab.[b]

2   ⟨The daughter of Dibon has gone up⟩[c]
        to the high places to weep;
    over Nebo and over Medeba
    Moab wails. On every head of his is baldness,
        every beard is shorn;

3   in his streets they gird on sackcloth;
        on ⟨his⟩[c] housetops they lament;[d]
    in ⟨his⟩[c] squares everyone wails,
        melting in tears.[e]

4   Heshbon and Elealeh cried out,
        their voice was heard as far as Jahaz;
    therefore ⟨the loins⟩[c] of Moab ⟨shook⟩,[f]
        his will failed.

5   My heart cries out for Moab;[g]
    ⟨whose fugitive⟩[c] [came] to Zoar. ⟨   ⟩[h]
    For the ascent of Luhith
        they climb up weeping;
    on the road to Horonaim
        ⟨they raise⟩[i] a cry of destruction;

6   the waters of Nimrim
        are a desolation;
    the grass is withered,
        the new growth fails. ⟨   ⟩[j]

---

[a] Cf. on 13.1, above p. 1.

[b] For another possible translation see below, *ad loc.*

[c] Cf. *BHS.*

[d] Following W. Rudolph, 'Jessaja 15–16', in *Hebrew and Semitic Studies presented to G. R. Driver*, ed. D. Winton Thomas and W. D. McHardy, Oxford and New York 1963, p. 134, add *yinhū*.

[e] For this forceful expression cf. Rudolph, *ibid.,* and *KBL* sub voce.

[f] Read *rā'ᵃdū.*   [g] Cf. Jer. 48.31.

[h] 'The third Eglath' is a gloss.   [i] Read *jeᶜarᶜērū*, pilpel of *'wr.*

[j] 'The verdure is no more' is metrically superfluous and should be regarded as a gloss.

7   Therefore the abundance they have gained
          and what they have laid up
     over the Brook of the Poplars
          they carry away with them.[a]

8   Truly, a cry
          went round the land of Moab;
     ⟨its⟩[a] wailing reached to Eglaim,
          ⟨as far as⟩[a] Beer-elim. ⟨   ⟩[a]
     Truly, the waters of Dimon
          are full of blood.
     Yet I will bring upon Dimon something more
     a lion for those of Moab who escape,
     and for the remnant of Adama![b]

16.1 Send a ram
          to the ruler of the land,[c]
     from the rock in the desert,[d]
          to the mount of the daughter of Zion.

2   *It shall come about: like fluttering birds,*
          like scattered nestlings,
     the daughters of Moab shall be
          at the fords of the Arnon.

3   'Give (*sing.*)[a] counsel,
          grant (*sing.*)[a] justice;
     make your shade like night
          at the height of noon;
     hide the outcasts,
          betray not the fugitive.

4   Give sojourn among you to
          ⟨the outcasts⟩[e] of Moab
     be a refuge to them from the destroyer.
     When ⟨the oppressor⟩[f] *is no more,*
          and ⟨the destroyer⟩[g] *has ceased,*
     and the trampler has vanished[h]
          from the land,

---

[a] Cf. *BHS.*
[b] But cf. the proposed emendation in *BHS, ad loc.*
[c] For the translation cf. below, *ad loc.*
[d] Cf. G-K, § 145d.
[e] 'My outcasts, Moab' is the result of an eschatological interpretation.
[f] Read *ḥōmēṣ.*
[g] Read *šōdēd.*
[h] Cf. G-K, § 145d.

5   *then a throne will be established in steadfast love*
     and on it will sit constantly
     *in the tent of David*ᵃ
     a judge who seeks justice
     and is swift to do righteousness.

6   We have heard of the pride of Moab,
        how ⟨proud⟩ᵇ he was;
     of his arrogance, his pride, and his insolence –
        his false boasts.

7   Therefore let Moab wail,
        let every one wail,
     For the raisin-cakes of Kir- ⟨hadash⟩ᶜ
        ⟨they⟩ᵇ mourn, utterly stricken.

8   For ⟨   ⟩ᵈ Heshbon languishes,
        and the vine of Sibmah;
     the lords of the nations
        have struck down its branches,
     which reached to Jazer
        and strayed to the desert;
     its shoots spread abroad
        and passed over the sea.

9   Therefore I weep with Jazerᵉ
        for the vine of Sibmah;
     I drench you with my tears,
        O Heshbon and Elealeh:
     for upon your summer and your harvest
        the shout has fallen.

10   And joy and gladness are taken away
        from the fruitful field;
     and in the vineyards no songs are sung,
        ⟨and⟩ᵇ no shouts are raised:
     no one ⟨   ⟩ᵇ treads out wine in the presses;
        the shout ⟨is hushed⟩ᵇ

11   Therefore my soul moans for Moab
        like a lyre,
     and my heart for Kir-⟨hadash⟩ᶜ
        ⟨like a flute⟩ᶠ

ᵃ An important interpretative addition, though metrically is evidently secondary.
ᵇ Cf. *BHS*.   ᶜ Instead of *ḥāreś* read *ḥādāš*. For the argument see below on 15.1.
ᵈ *śadmōt* is most likely an interpretative gloss. Otherwise read with 1Q Isa
'*umlālā* and cf. G-K, § 145k.
ᵉ Literally 'weep with the weeping of Jazer'.
ᶠ Add *keḥālīl jeʰemē*, cf. Jer. 48.36, and Procksch and Fischer, *ad loc.*

12   *And when Moab presents himself,*
        when he wearies himself upon the high place,
      When he comes to his sanctuary to pray,
        he will not prevail.

13 This is the word which Yahweh spoke concerning Moab in the past. [14]But now the Lord says, 'In three years, like the years of a hireling, the glory of Moab will be brought into contempt, in spite of all his great multitude, and the remnant will be very few and feeble.'

Procksch has rightly described this oracle on Moab as the problem child of exegesis.[a] The wording in important passages in the poem is ambiguous, while in others it is doubtful. In addition, apart from 16.13f. which themselves make it clear that they are additions, there are many traces of later interpolations. Opinions have differed as to whether at least a coherent original basis exists within 15.1–16.12, or whether there are several originally independent poems. The attempt to relate a single underlying unit, or at least essential parts of it, to a particular historical situation have been as controversial as the equally fundamental issue, whether it is a prophecy looking forward to the future or a poem of lamentation which is meant to be understood as a taunt. The fact that parts of the poem have been incorporated into Jer. 48.29–38 unfortunately does not permit even a relative degree of certainty about the *terminus ad quem* for the origin of the present composition. For in the form in which we possess it, Jer. 48 is certainly later than Jeremiah himself, although there is no agreement about its date.[b] It is notable, however, that there is nothing that corresponds to 16.1–6 in the book of Jeremiah. But to conclude from this that these verses at least were not incorporated into the content of the book of Isaiah until after the composition of Jer. 48.29ff. is equally difficult, since the tendency displayed by the compiler of Jeremiah provides sufficient reason for their omission. Nor can a firm starting point be found in the deliberate reapplication of the present oracle in 16.13f. It cannot be assumed, moreover, that when these verses were added, 15.1–16.12 had already reached the form in which we find them.

---

[a] P. 208.
[b] Cf. W. Schottroff, 'Horonaim, Nimrim, Luhith und der Westrand des "Landes Ataroth" ', *ZDPV* 82, 1966, pp. 184ff., and esp. the comparison of identifications, p. 184.

In this situation it is not surprising that commentators hold widely differing views. Ultimately, there is agreement only that 16.13f. do not belong to the original form of the oracle. The suggestion has often been made that 16.2, which breaks the train of thought between 16.1 and 3, should be placed behind 15.9aα. Whether 16.4b–5 are a later addition or a genuine original part of a unity consisting at least of 16.1–4a or 16.1–6 is disputed. Attempts to divide 15.1–16.12, or 15.1–9; 16.1–5 (or 6) or 16.5–12 (or 16.7–12) into stanzas differ equally among themselves.

A few examples will show the confusion into which the attempt to relate the composition to historical facts has led commentators. König ascribed the poem to a Judaean prophet living in the last third of the ninth century and concluded that a Bedouin attack upon Moab had taken place in his time. Hitzig regarded the prophet Jonah the son of Amittai, the prophet mentioned in II Kings 14.25, as the author, though no one agreed with him. More recently, Rudolph connected the poem with an attack by Jeroboam II of Israel upon Moab.[a] But he ascribed it to a Judaean author whose sayings were then incorporated into 16.13f. by Isaiah. Van Zyl regards 15.1–9a and 16.6–11 as a taunt song derived from Bedouin circles, which was composed on the occasion of their attack upon Moab, became known in Judah and was extended by Isaiah by the addition of 15.9b–16.5 and 16.12. But since they had not accepted its invitation to come to Zion, he himself added 16.13f.[b] Procksch regarded 15.1–16.5 as composed by Isaiah: the prophet gives a Messianic prophecy of salvation to the Moabite refugees. On the other hand, he thought that 16.6–12 were more recent, but pre-exilic rather than post-exilic, and therefore possibly composed by Jeremiah. Kissane regarded 15.1–16.12 as an Isaianic prophecy which the prophet re-issued before Sargon's attack in 720 or 715, with the addition of 16.13f. Marti regarded 15.1–9a and 16.7–10 as an elegy from the fifth century composed on the occasion of an attack by Arab nomads upon Moab, which was quickly extended by the prophecy 15.9aαb; 16.4a, 6 and 12; then finally, in the second century, the gloss 16.4b, 5 and the conclusion 16.13f. were added. In 15.1–9a +16.2 Fohrer sees the lament of a Judaean poet on the

---

[a] *Loc. cit.*; cf. his summary pp. 141ff., and following him Eichrodt, *ad loc.* H. Ewald, *Die Propheten des Alten Bundes* I, Stuttgart 1840, pp. 229f., supposed that Isaiah had adapted an older prophecy.

[b] H. Van Zyl, *The Moabites*, POS 3, 1960, pp. 20ff.

occasion of actual events which it is no longer possible to identify precisely, and probably deriving from post-exilic times. He regards 16.1, 3–5 as yet another post-exilic composition, in which the war song of a neighbouring people was reinterpreted in the light of eschatological theology. He makes no further suggestions about the date of 16.6–12, but he no doubt also regards it as post-exilic. Finally, Duhm, after some doubts at first, regarded 15.1–16.12, with the exception only of 15.9aβb; 6.2 and 13f., as a unity, the whole of which he dated in the second century. He considered that the basic text came from the days of Alexander Hyrcanus, and the redaction from the time of Alexander Jannaeus. He considered the occasion of the poem to have been an attack by the Nabataeans.

Our knowledge of the *history of Moab* in the pre-exilic period is patchy, and in the post-exilic and Hellenistic period depends upon incidental references.[a] After the conquest of the country by David, the Arnon seems to have formed the border between Israel and the Moabite vassal state (cf. II Sam. 24.5; 8.2). The Moabites seemed to have become independent again immediately upon the death of Solomon, and thereafter they extended their territory step by step back towards the north, as far as the heights of Medeba. King Omri of Israel drove them back again and made them once more vassals, but left them Dibon and Aroer. However, after the death of Ahab, King Mesha of Moab was able to throw off the yoke (cf. II Kings 3.5 and the Mesha inscription, lines 5ff.) and once again extended his boundary as far as the northern point of the Dead Sea (cf. the Mesha inscription lines 9ff.). A joint attack upon Mesha by Israel, Judah and Edom, under the leadership of Jehoram, failed after considerable success at first (cf. II Kings 3.4ff., 21ff.). It is, to say the least, uncertain whether we may conclude from II Kings 10.32f, that the area as far as the Arnon was reconquered by Jehu.[b] Whether or not the Aramaeans succeeded later in the ninth century in bringing Moab under their control, Jeroboam II of Israel was able to extend the north-eastern boundary of his kingdom at least as far as the northern point of the Dead Sea (II Kings 14.25; Amos 6.14).[c] At the end of the

[a] Cf. also van Zyl, pp. 133ff., though in my view he uses the sayings concerning Moab in the prophetic books too uncritically in his historical evaluation.

[b] But cf. van Zyl, pp. 145f.

[c] Cf. H. W. Wolff, BK 14.2, 1969, pp. 335, and W. Rudolph, KAT² 18.2, 1971, p. 226; but also Y. Aharoni, *The Land of the Bible*, London 1966 and Philadelphia 1967, p. 313.

war against Syria and Ephraim the Moabite king Salamanu appears among the tributaries of the Assyrian emperor Tiglath-pileser III.[a] As long as Assyrian hegemony lasted, Moab remained a faithful vassal, with one apparent exception. We learn by chance that in the last third of the eighth century there was an attack upon Edom by the Gidiraya, presumably a Bedouin tribe coming from the east.[b] Like Judah, Moab extricated itself by a timely submission from the revolt against Sargon II stirred up by Ashdod and suppressed in 711[c]. When Sennacherib came to Palestine in 701, he found king Kammusunadbi of Moab among those who voluntarily paid him tribute.[d] Under Esarhaddon, king Musurri of Moab, like his Judaean counterpart Manasseh, appears as one of the many kings who were obliged to support his building programme.[e] We also find Musurri among the kings who have to supply auxiliary troops to the emperor Asshurbanipal during his first campaign against Egypt.[f] In the course of the war between Asshurbanipal and Shamash-shum-ukin, Arabs who had attacked Moab succeeded in killing king Kamashaltā of Moab and capturing the survivors, including their king Ammuladi of Qadri.[g] Because of the weakness of Assyria during the final years of Asshurbanipal and his successors, king Josiah of Judah was certainly able to extend his kingdom towards the west and north. There is no evidence, however, of the annexation of Moabite territory; but because of the energy and strength displayed by Kamashaltā himself, this is improbable.[h] In 603 at the latest Moab recognized the hegemony of the neo-Babylonian emperor Nebuchadnezzar.[i] According to II Kings 24.1, the emperor mobilized 'Edomites', Moabites and Ammonites against the rebellious Judah. If we take into account what the Babylonian chronicle tells us concerning the fourth year of Nebuchadnezzar and what Josephus recounts (*Ant.* X. 88), the revolt of Jehoiakim of Judah must have taken place in the late autumn of 601, or perhaps not until the beginning of the year 600.

[a] Cf. *AR* I, § 801; *AOT*[2], p. 348; *TGI*[2], p. 59.

[b] Cf. H. Donner, 'Neue Quellen zur Geschichte des Staates Moab in der zweiten Hälfte des 8. Jahrhundert v. Chr.', MIO 5, 1957, pp. 173ff.

[c] *AR* II, § 195, cf. also §§ 30 and 62, and *AOT*[2], pp. 350f.

[d] *AR* II, § 239 and *AOT*[2], p. 352.

[e] *AR* II, § 690.

[f] *AR* II, § 876 and *ANET*[2], p. 294.

[g] *AR* II, § 870.

[h] Cf. van Zyl, p. 154 and Y. Aharoni, *The Land of the Bible*, p. 350.

[i] Cf. D. J. Wiseman, *Chronicles of Chaldean Kings*, London 1956, p. 350.

According to Jer. 27.3 Moab took part in a conspiracy against
Babylon in 595/4,[a] but this does not seem to have had any practical
consequences. However, the flight of Judaeans to Moab and Ammon
when the conquest of Jerusalem took place in 587[b] assumes that both
of these kingdoms still existed at that time (cf. Jer. 40.11). According
to Josephus (*Ant.* X. 181ff.) Nebuchadnezzar conquered Ammon and
Moab in the twenty-third year of his reign (582), while according to
Jer. 52.30 there was a fresh deportation of Jews to Babylon in this
year, so that we cannot exclude the possibility of an extensive revolt
in the same year. The information given by Josephus is suspect, since
it associates this campaign with another campaign against Egypt for
which there is no historical evidence.[c] The gaps in our knowledge
may be filled by postulating, as Noth does, that Moab succumbed to
the attacks of nomads in the course of the sixth century.[d]

The later fortunes of the country are obscure until the Hellenistic
period. One may assume that though the country no longer formed
part of the Babylonian province Babili and Ebirnari, it was ultimately incorporated into the Persian satrapy of Abarnahara, with
which it later formed part of Alexander's province of Syria. The
early history of the Nabataeans is equally obscure, and only systematic study and evaluation of further archaeological sources will
cast any further light upon it. They first appear in history on the
occasion of a campaign undertaken by Antigonus Monophthalmos in
312 BC, apparently against Petra (cf. Diodorus Siculus XIX. 94.1–
100.2).[e] The Nabataeans had also brought Edom under their control
by the fourth century at the latest. There is evidence of their further
advance into the country east of the Jordan in the second century:
Judas Maccabaeus encountered them as he advanced three days
journey beyond the Jordan (I Macc. 5.25, cf. also II Macc. 5.8).
According to Trogus, quoted by Justin, king Erotimus, who is
probably to be identified with Ḥaretat II, took advantage of the

a Cf. W. Rudolph, HAT I, 12, [3]1968, *ad loc.*

b But cf. the dating of the fall of Jerusalem in 586 by A. Malamat, 'The Last
Kings of Judah and the Fall of Jerusalem', *IEJ* 18, 1968, pp. 137ff.

c Van Zyl, p. 157, disagrees.

d *RGG*[3] IV, col. 1066.

e Cf. A. Droysen, *Geschichte des Hellenismus* II, ed. E. Bayer, Tübingen 1952, pp.
246ff., and E. Schürer, *Geschichte des jüdischen Volkes* I, Appendix II, Leipzig
[3-4]1901, pp. 729f.; ET *History of the Jewish People in the Time of Jesus Christ* I.2,
Edinburgh 1900, p. 349.

weakness of the Seleucid and Ptolemaic kingdoms around 110BC to trouble them both by his raids. An attack by Alexander Jannaeus against the Nabataean king Obedas ('obodat I) ended in a defeat east of the lake of Gennesaret, and this also brought to naught the successes he had only recently over the 'Arabs' in Moab and Gilead (cf. Josephus *Ant.* XIII. 374).[a]

This survey of the nine-hundred-year history of Moab, brief as it is, shows how little we know, and how risky it is to associate even parts of the present text with any particular historical situation, either the attack by the Gidiraya, the invasion of the Nabataeans, or even an entirely hypothetical campaign by Jeroboam II into the Moabite heartland.[b] The task of our exposition must rather be to illustrate the various possibilities of interpretation offered by the obscurities of the poem itself, and to make clear the theological conception of the redactors.

[15.1–9] *The night raid upon Moab and its consequences.* The poet begins a funeral lament upon Moab, the victim of a night raid by enemies who are not named. The typical metre with three stressed syllables in the first, longer hemistich and two in the shorter second hemistich clearly dominates the whole poem, apart from a few exceptions. The poet does not name the enemies – only in 16.8, which cannot be said with any certainty to have belonged originally to 15.1ff., mentions the 'lords of the nations' in general terms – and merely describes the consequences of their attack. This makes two interpretations possible. Either he was referring to an event which had just taken place, the principal facts of which were known to his hearers, or else he had in mind a future event, was concerned only with the fact of Moab's sudden destruction, and did not possess or think it necessary to work out a more detailed conception of how it was to take place.

[1] Unfortunately the difficulties of interpretation begin with v. 1. There is controversy as to whether Ar and Kir are concrete places or general terms. It is clear from Deut. 2.18, however, that Ar-moab could be identified with the country of Moab in general.[c] But it is questionable whether one can follow the Targum in identifying Kir

---

[a] Cf. Schürer, pp. 731ff. (ET p. 352), and J. Cantineau, *Le Nabatéen* I, Paris, 1930, pp. 6ff.

[b] Cf. the view of Noth, *RGG*[3], col. 1066.

[c] Cf. Schottroff, *ZDPV* 82, p. 180f.

with the present-day *el-kerak*, as is usually done.[a] The expression may refer not to a particular city but to the cities of Moab in general. If it does in fact refer to a particular place which is simply called the 'city of Moab', it seems likely that the capital of the country is meant. A process of deduction may perhaps permit us to conclude that its real name was *qīr ḥādāš*, 'new town'.[b] On the assumption that Ar is not the name of a city, but a term for the whole country of Moab, it is preferable to retain the translation given above and not to choose the other possible rendering: 'Yes, in the night in which Ar was destroyed, Moab was wiped out . . .'[c] The poet seems to have had in mind night raids against the whole country of Moab, but in the first instance and in particular against its capital, which lay south of the Arnon.

[**15.2–3**] In v. 2 we are in the district just north of Arnon, at Dibon, and then we move further north to Nebo and Medeba. Dibon, the present-day *dhībān*, is about 5km (three miles) north of the Arnon. All the inhabitants of the city, referred to in the poetic term 'daughters of Dibon',[d] went up to the sanctuary in order to hold a service of lamentation. We know from the Mesha inscription that King Mesha founded a high place as a sanctuary for the Moabite national god Kemosh in his royal residence *qeriḥō* near Dibon.[e] High places consisted of an open space with an altar and certain cult emblems.[f] The high places mentioned here were dedicated both to Kemosh and his warrior manifestation Astar-Kemosh.[g] Since the high places lay outside the city, the poet seems to be thinking of Dibon itself as not yet affected by the enemy attack. Or is he perhaps thinking of the survivors going up to lament in the sanctuary after the attack?

---

[a] Cf. F. M. Abel, *Géographie de la Palestine* II, Paris 1938, p. 418; J. Simons, *The Geographical and Topographical Texts of the Old Testament*, Leiden 1959, § 1246f. and van Zyl, p. 70.

[b] In 16.11 *qīr ḥareś* occurs similarly in conjunction with Moab, so that the two can be identified. While it is found in Jer. 48.31 and 36 in the same form, in II Kings 3.25 and Isa. 16.7 it occurs as *qīr ḥᵃreśet*. LXX gives a form in 16.7 and Jer. 48 (LXX ch. 31) which shows that it read in the original *qīr ḥādāš*, 'new town'. Cf. the references in n. a above.

[c] This interpretation is supported by G. R. Driver, *JSS* 13, 1968, p. 44, and he is followed by Eichrodt. For the construction, in this case, see G-K, § 130d.

[d] Cf. e.g. 1.8.

[e] Cf. lines 3f. in H. Donner and W. Röllig, *KAI* I, 1962, no. 182, and II, 1964, pp. 168 and 171f.; *AOT²*, p. 440; *ANET²*, p. 320 and *TGI²*, p. 52.

[f] Cf. *BHW* II, col. 736.

[g] Cf. the Mesha inscription, line 17.

Verse 3 suggests the former possibility. Thus we are given the impression that the terror aroused by the rampaging attack of the enemy upon the Moabite heartland south of the Arnon spread across the river northwards from city to city.

Verse 2b is once again ambiguous. It can be translated either 'For Nebo and for Medeba Moab wails' or 'Upon Nebo and upon Medeba Moab wails'. In the first case both cities would have been destroyed, while in the second case they would have been terrified by the dreadful news of the attack. Unfortunately v. 4 is equally uncertain in meaning, so that the picture relapses into vagueness. Nebo, now known as *khirbet el-muhayyit*, lies just 2km (one mile and a quarter) south of the present-day Mt Nebo, while Medeba, now *mādabā*, famed for its Byzantine mosaic map of Palestine,[a] is about 5km (three miles) to the south-east.[b]

Throughout the country there is terror, with public mourning to invoke the aid of the gods. Apart from the cries of lamentation, this is expressed by shaving the head, cutting off the beard and putting on a rough hair shirt (sackcloth).[c] Wherever the Moabites show themselves outside their houses, whether upon their flat roofs (cf. 22.1), in the streets or in the town square, they present a lamentable sight. Since the Hebrew word for baldness, *qorḥā*, is reminiscent of the name of king Mesha's royal residence *qeriḥō*, some commentators have suspected a mocking allusion to the northern capital.[d] Of course there can be no certainty in such a matter.

[15.4] Verse 4 at once raises the question whether Heshbon and Elealeh are crying out because they have heard the dreadful news of the devastation of the heartland south of the Arnon, or because they themselves have suffered attack. 16.8 and 9 assume, however, that the enemy's attack has fallen upon the north of the country as well. But it is not certain that 16.7ff. were composed at the same time as 15.1ff. It is notable, however, that v. 4 begins with a consecutive imperfect and then continues with a perfect; thus it is possible to connect the terror that has broken out in Nebo and Medeba with an

---

[a] Cf. H. Donner and H. Cüppers, 'Die Restauration und Konservierung der Mosiakkarte von Madeba', *ZDPV* 83, 1967, pp. 1ff.

[b] Abel, vol. II, pp. 397 and 381f.; Simons, § 1249f.

[c] Cf. Amos 8.10; Micah 1.16; Isa. 22.12; Jer. 41.5; and O. Kaiser, *Isaiah 1–12*, OTL, 1972, p. 50, on Isa. 3.24. For a discussion of the sack, cf. I. P. Seierstad, *Die Offenbarungserlebnisse der Propheten*, SNVAO 1946, (²1965), p. 166.

[d] Cf. Abel vol. II, p. 418 with Donner and Röllig, *KAI* II, p. 172.

attack against the north. Heshbon, the present-day *ḥisbān*, is approximately 9km (five and a half miles) north of Medeba, while Elealeh, the present-day *el-ʿāl* is just 3km (almost two miles) to the north.[a] That the outcry is audible from the northern boundary of Moab as far as Jahaz, which if it can be identified with *khirbet iskander* is a good 30km (eighteen miles) to the south,[b] is of course poetic exaggeration, meant to emphasize the size of the catastrophe. At the same time this permits the poet to move back to the events in the south with which he is once again concerned. The people, identified with the man Moab, lose heart at what has fallen upon them or is to fall upon them. There is clearly no question of resistance. We can come to the provisional conclusion that the poet has in mind an attack upon the heartland of Moab south of the Arnon, but possibly also upon the north of the country at the same time.

(**15.5–7**) The poet assures us that he is deeply moved by the fate of the Moabites. We must regard this as a stylistic device to re-emphasize the severity of the blow which has struck Moab, rather than an expression of genuine feeling (cf. 21.3f. and Jer. 48.17, 31ff. and especially v. 36). The country is seized by general flight. The fact that the course of the flight is traced only towards the south-west may be merely a stylistic device to give the equal weight to the lines mentioning the north and the south, either because of an actual or imagined fact of an attack upon the area south of the Arnon alone, or because of the idea that the way to the north was also blocked by an enemy. The first refugees have already reached Zoar, a city which must certainly be looked for near the south-eastern point of the Dead Sea, probably in the region of the *ghōr eṣ-ṣāfiye*.[c] It is probably mentioned in order to indicate that the route of the flight is through the Arabah into Judaean territory (cf. 16.1, 3f.). The refugees travelled by way of the ascent of Luhith, the road to Horonaim and the waters of Nimrim. Horonaim can possibly be identified with *ḥawronān*, mentioned in lines 31f. of the Mesha inscription, which would be a further indication that the places of refuge lie to the south-west. If Horonaim is to be identified with *khirbet el-medān* and Luhith with *khirbet edh-dhubāb*,[d] the refugees would be travelling by different routes, the enemy close behind them, to the lower course of

---

[a] Abel, vol. II, pp. 348f. and 312; Simons, § 1251f.

[b] Cf. K. H. Bernhardt, *ZDPV* 76, 1960, pp. 155ff.

[c] Cf. Schottroff, *ZDPV* 82, p. 182.

[d] Cf. Schottroff, pp. 202ff.

the *wādī en-numēra* where the waters of Nimrim must have been.[a] The devastation extends to all these places, even to the famous waters of Nimrim, an area clearly famed for the particular luxuriance of its vegetation. Bundling together their possessions, some provisions and perhaps some silver, the refugees hurry away.[b] If we have so far correctly identified the place names, or even if we have only traced the direction of the flight accurately, on the basis that it is towards Zoar, we must identify the Brook of the Poplars with the *wādī el ḥesa* where the refugees reach the border of Edom.[c]

[15.8] Verse 8 recalls our attention to the country of Moab, where meanwhile the enemies are still raging. Eglaim should be identified according to Byzantine tradition with *rujm el-jimilē*, unless a different place name in its vicinity is preferred. We are back here in the *el-kerak* district (cf. v. 1).[d] Beer-elim which has been tentatively identified with *wādī eth-themed*, a tributary of the *wādī el-wāle*, would once again bring us a few miles back across the Arnon towards the north-east.[e] Thus the contemporary listener, familiar with certain basic geographical features of the country, is given the impression that the whole region of Moab is seized with terror in the face of an overwhelming enemy.

[9] At best only the first sentence of v. 9 is likely to have belonged to the original poem. But even if this is the case, it is difficult to follow what is implied. The name Dimon is widely regarded as a corruption or modification of Dibon, intended to refer to the word *dām*, blood, which follows. Jerome tells us that in his days both forms of the name were in use for Dibon. As v. 2 does not seem to assume that the city has been destroyed, the conclusion has been drawn that the northern capital was also overtaken by the disaster. But it is still possible that Dimon may be a different city, to be identified with *khirbet dimnē*, which lies 4km (two and a half miles) north-west of *er-rabba*,[f] This would bring us back again across the Arnon towards the south. The rest of v. 9 is an old *crux interpretum*. The poem passes

---

[a] Cf. Schottroff, pp. 200f.

[b] Cf. Ps. 17.4 and Gen. 41.36.

[c] Cf. K. Elliger, *PJB* 32, 1936, pp. 42ff.; Abel vol. II, p. 94; Simons § 266 and § 1256ff., and Schottroff, p. 183.

[d] Cf. Abel vol. II, pp. 310f.; Simons § 1259 and van Zyl, p. 69.

[e] Cf. Abel vol. I, p. 461; Simons, § 441 and van Zyl, pp. 85f.

[f] For the material in Jerome, cf. Dillmann-Kittel *ad loc.* and van Zyl, p. 80; for the identification of the Waters of Dimon with *ʿain el-megheisil*, cf. Abel vol. II, p. 372 and Simons, § 1261.

straight into the first person, and God is speaking; and this shows at once that v. 9aβ b is either completely corrupt or forms a gloss. The content of the statement is also far from clear. 'Something additional' is a very abstract expression for further blows of fate. There is some doubt whether 'lion' is the object, and therefore a rather curious description of the coming enemy, or is in apposition, although out of place, and describes Moab, who otherwise is so heroic and like a lion. Finally, it is not clear whether *'ᵃdāmā* is a place name here, or simply means 'arable land'. To change 'lion' into 'Ariel' (LXX) and 'Adama' into 'Edom', thus understanding the whole sentence as an ironic affirmation that the lands belonging to Moab would consist from now on of no more than its places of refuge in Judah and Edom, seems far fetched[a]. Other attempts to reconstruct the text, which keep closer to the context, seem highly tentative.[b] We must continue to affirm that a later writer is here recording, in words which are either extremely cryptic or have been corrupted by still later transcribers, his expectation that an even greater disaster will come upon Moab.

[**16.1–5**] *The answer to the request for a place of refuge.* That 16.1ff. are not by the same hand can be seen immediately from the fact that v. 2 is out of context; and its most likely position seems to be after 15.9aα. If this is so, it must have been put in its present position when the addition mentioned above was made to that verse. Perhaps this is no more than another example of a later reader giving utterance to his feelings. A marginal comment describing the refugees, who were dependent upon their pleas for protection in Jerusalem, was finally incorporated, appropriately enough, into the text. Curiously, not only the daughters of Moab, female Moabites, but also the fords of the Arnon are compared to birds driven from their nests and fluttering aimlessly about (cf. also 10.14). Even if 'the daughters of Moab' is taken to refer to the cities, it is no more appropriate to the context. In any event the glossator, who understood the poem as referring solely to future events, intended to emphasize the bewilderment and helplessness of the Moabites upon whom the catastrophe was to come.

[**4b–5**] The problems faced by the passage are not solved simply

---

[a] E. Power, *Bib* 13, 1932, pp. 435ff., disagrees.

[b] This Kissane proposed to read *kī ša'ōt ʿal-dīmōn nispōt liplēṭat mōʾābᵃnīyā ʾ wᵉliš'erīt 'ēmā*: 'Because disasters are multiplied over Dimon. For the escaped of Moab there is sorrow, for the remnant terror ...' Cf. also Rudolph, *Studies*, pp. 132 and 135.

by making clear the secondary character of v. 2. The main question is
whether vv. 4b–5 form an original or a secondary part of the poem. It
seems very strange that the request to give asylum to the refugees in
Jerusalem is followed by the promise that when the catastrophe is
concluded a righteous king will rule and judge in the tent of David.
The attempt has repeatedly been made to resolve the difficulty by
suggesting that the verses should be understood as part of the message
to the daughters of Zion which the Moabites are described as
uttering, that the tent means the kingdom of the descendants of
David, and that the righteous ruler is actually the king of Moab who
will maintain a vassal relationship towards Jerusalem. But there are
considerable objections to this.[a] On the one hand, it is improbable
that the 'tent of David' means more than David's dwelling place.[b]
Secondly, it would be strange for the setting up of a permanent and
righteous rule by a Moabite to be described in the colours of the ideal
king of Judah, with not·a single mention being made of his subjection.
This proposal in fact fails to recognize the eschatological conception
which is reflected in these verses. If the statements are related to the
future king of salvation in Jerusalem, their exposition presents no
difficulties requiring a forced interpretation. Of course one has then
to seek a solution of the problem of their relationship to the context.
They cannot meaningfully be interpreted as a promise to the
Moabites.[c] On the other hand the difficulties are removed when it is
recognized that they give an answer to the question of when there
will once again be a ruler in Jerusalem to whom the Moabites can
turn for help. Between the time in which the author of vv. 4b and 5
wrote, and the devastation of Moab which is to result in their petition
for help, there were still to come the tempests that were to fall upon
Jerusalem after which the everlasting Davidic kingdom was to arise.
From this point of view, one might be inclined to regard vv. 1–5 as a
unity. But the awkward transition from v. 4a to v. 4b suggests rather
that vv. 4b–5 are a secondary addition. This makes more probable
Marti's view that 16.6 was the original reply to the request of the
Moabites. In view of the ambiguity of the statements in 15.1–8 and
our scanty knowledge of Moabite history, it is hardly possible to
answer the question which still remains open, whether the laments

[a] I disagree here with W. W. Graf Baudissin, *ThStKr* 61, 1888, pp. 519f.;
Rudolph, *Studies*, p. 140 and Eichrodt, *ad loc.*

[b] Cf. also H. W. Wolff, BK 14.2, 1969, on Amos 9.11.

[c] Procksch and Fohrer, *ad loc.*, though their dating is different.

upon Moab derive from a period in which there was still a king of Judah, or whether from the first they described eschatological woes.

[16.1] The terse wording of v. 1 leaves some questions open. It is possible on the one hand, by a very slight change in the vowel signs which were later incorporated into the Hebrew text, to read 'they send' instead of 'send' (imperative). Secondly, the expression 'ram of the ruler of the land' is ambiguous. It may be a technical term for a gift handed over on the occasion of submission (cf. II Kings 3.4) or a request for protection; it is uncertain whether it is a subjective or objective genitive, i.e. whether the ram is to be sent *from* the Moabite ruler of the land or *to* the Judaean ruler of the land. The place-name which follows 'from the rock in the desert' is no further help, whether it is to be understood as a general poetic term or with a concrete meaning (*sela'* = Petra),ª for the Moabite ruler himself may have fled. If our understanding of vv. 4b and 5 is the right one, the redactor always supposed that the ruler was in Jerusalem. In any case the embassy is going to the mountain of the daughters of Zion, Jerusalem (cf. 10.32).

[3–4a] Verses 3 and 4a reveal the task given to the ambassadors. On Zion they are to ask counsel and obtain a decision. It is not possible to be certain whether the original reference was to political or military measures on behalf of the invaded neighbouring country, or merely to a favourable decision about its refugees. But the continuation rather suggests the second possibility. Just as men need shade under the hot southern midday sun, those who have been driven from their home country need protection in the country that receives them (cf. 32.2). In legal terms, they are seeking the status of a *gēr*, a protected person, which was associated with permission to reside in a foreign country (cf. e.g. Gen. 15.13; Ruth 1.1 and II Sam. 4.3).ᵇ

[4b–5] Whereas v. 6 was originally intended as a mocking rejection of the plea, vv. 4b–5, which now follow the announcement of the petition for help to Zion, it now explains the situation in Jerusalem during the attack upon Moab, which is thought of as taking place in the future: the siege of the city by the nations will already be over (cf. 29.1ff.; 33, but also 28.14ff.). Thanks to God's love and faithfulness the throne will already have been set up there again (cf. Isa. 55.3). On it descendants of David will sit for all time (cf. II Sam.

ª Cf. Simons, § 1262.
ᵇ See *KBL* sub voce.

7.13; Ps. 89.3ff. and Isa. 9.6). As the king of the age of salvation, he will seek justice and be swift to bring about the triumph of righteousness (cf. Pss. 72; 101; Isa. 11.1ff. and 32.1ff.). This hope is really of comfort only to the Jews. They can look beyond the distress which is coming upon them (cf. 14.24ff.) to the age of salvation. It is of no benefit to the Moabites who beg for protection in their need.

[16.6–12] *A lament upon the destruction of the vineyard of Moab.*

[6] As a result of the redaction, v. 6 has lost its previous function as a negative answer to the boastful Moabites, so that it has become the introduction to the taunt in the form of a lament which now concludes the poem and elaborates upon the theme of the vineyards of Moab, which were clearly famous in their time. The emptiness of the Moabites' confidence in themselves has been demonstrated by the collapse of their country. Moab's pride ended with a fall. And the poet goes to great lengths to describe a mocking lament. [7] Both in the south and in the north of the country, the basic conditions for wine production which permitted the preparation from the grapes of raisin cakes, a particular delicacy (cf. II Sam. 6.19 and S. of S. 2.5), has now been destroyed.

[8] Sibmah, which is mentioned here for the first time in the poem, is near Heshbon,[a] while Jazer is probably to be identified with *tell ʿarēme*, approximately 5km (three miles) north-west of *nāʿūr*.[b] The extent of the destruction of the wine-growing areas gives a further indication of the wide extent of Moabite territory, which stretched to the north and to the east as far as the edge of the desert. One inevitably wonders whether the vines and grapes are not meant here as a symbol of the Moabite population. A strangely vague description of the destroyers as 'lords of the people', which occurs elsewhere in the Old Testament only in Ps. 68.31,[c] is in its very imprecision quite appropriate in the context of the conception of an eschatological threat.

[9–11] In this stanza the poet appears to be emphasizing his profound distress at what he has experienced, or rather observed.[d] Verse 6 does not suggest that he played a very honourable part in it. Deeply moved, he wishes to mourn with Jazer for the vines of the

[a] Abel, vol. II, p. 458; Simons, § 298 and van Zyl, p. 91.

[b] Cf. R. Rendtorff, *ZDPV* 76, 1960, pp. 124ff.

[c] The former widespread rendering of 8aαα2 as 'whose grapes once forced (i.e. intoxicated) the lords of the nations' (most recently in Procksch) seems more recently to have been generally abandoned.

[d] Cf. Seierstad, pp. 149f.

neighbouring Sibmah, and even water Heshbon and Elealeh with his tears. The essential point in this rhetoric is found in the contrast between the anticipated joy of the harvest and the echoing shouts of the enemy, followed by silence in the vineyards.

[**12**] In v. 12 we once·again have an interpolation, intended to supply the lack of an explicit affirmation that the lamentations of the Moabites mentioned in 15.2 are fruitless.

[**16.13–14**] *The end of Moab will come soon!* In the last two verses, which are recognizable as a later addition both by their introduction and also by the fact that they are in prose, we have the words of someone who believed that he possessed a more exact knowledge of God's plan for history, a belief that had been current in apocalyptic circles since the second century (cf. Dan. 12.11f.). The condemnation of Moab uttered by Yahweh sometime in the past will now be carried out, with the certainty which it possesses as a word of Yahweh, within the next three years, and so too will the new glorification of Zion prophesied in 16.4bf., although the latter is not explicitly mentioned. The years are compared with those of a *šākîr*, a day labourer (cf. Lev. 25.53) or a mercenary (cf. Jer. 46.21). In the first case the allusion is to the labourer's heavy toil, and in the second case either to the many battles that would take place during these years (cf. Job 7.1) or perhaps to the three-year-period for which a mercenary is taken on. The association of this comparison with the mention of a remnant[a] shows that the apocalyptic writer was here, too, thinking of the devastation of Moab in battle. The Hebrew expression rendered 'very few' is also found in 10.25. It should be particularly emphasized that 16.13f. finds an almost literal parallel in 21.16f. It is possible that both additions come from the same apocalyptic writer.

[**15.1–16.14**] Looking back upon the whole section, we can state with certainty that 15.9aβ b; 16.2 and 12 are explanatory additions, that 16.4b–5 is very probably an eschatological redaction, and that 16.13f. is clearly an apocalyptic addition; and all these passages can be excluded from the original content of the chapter. In 16.7–11 the mention in v. 8 of the 'lords of the people' was at least an indication that the final lament refers to an eschatological destruction of Moab. Whereas the devastation of the region south of the Arnon is mentioned only briefly in v. 7, the final lament explicitly emphasizes the destruction of the Moabite borderlands in the north. It was not

[a] Cf. *BHW* III, col. 1592f.

possible to say for certain whether the introductory lament 15.1–8 (9aα) refers to an attack upon both the south *and also* upon the north of the country. It was clear, however, that v. 4 can be related to an attack upon the north. The deficiencies in our historical knowledge make it very difficult to decide whether at least 15.1–8 (9a) refer to a concrete historical event or are already eschatological in intention. 16.1 implies that 15.1–8 (9aα) and 16.1, 3–4a and 6 were composed before the exile, though this is not absolutely certain; for the understanding expressed in 16.4bf. that the poem is eschatological in conception may be correct.

If the poem is non-eschatological, its message would be that of pride comes before a fall, and that self-assurance and arrogance towards a neighbouring people can be transformed only too quickly into a pathetic need for help. If it is eschatological, its message would be, in spite of what seems to us an equivocal attitude to a neighbouring people, that the God who in this age has set apart the community of his elect, and yet has destined their humiliation, has not abandoned his promises and will make the mockers realize this. With his impatient arithmetic, the apocalyptic writer has miscalculated. But we still must acknowledge that he took seriously the power of God.

CHAPTER 17.1–3

Against Damascus and Israel

1   Oracle concerning Damascus.
    Behold, Damascus ⟨will cease⟩[a] to be a city,[b]
    and will become ⟨   ⟩[c] a heap of ruins.
2   ⟨Her cities will be forever⟩[d] deserted,
        they will be for flocks,
            which will lie down, and none will make them afraid.
3   The fortress will disappear from Ephraim,
        and the kingdom from Damascus;

---

[a] Read with *BH mūsārā*.
[b] Cf. G-K, § 119x.
[c] Cf. *BHS*.
[d] Read with *BH ʿārēhā ʿadē-ʿad*.

and the remnant of Syria will be like the glory
of the children of Israel.
says Yahweh Sebaoth.

The above threat, which attempts to reproduce the metre of the
funeral lament and is without any reason for the threat, is directed
against Damascus and Israel, and is attributed by modern commentators to the prophet Isaiah. They date it at the opening of the
war with Syria and Ephraim,[a] when king Pekah of Israel and king
Razon of Damascus joined together to drive out their Judaean
colleague Ahaz, in order to replace him by a prince who would lead
Judah into battle alongside them against the Assyrian emperor
Tiglath-pileser III.[b] In 732 Damascus was conquered and thus
became the capital of an Assyrian province, while the kingdom of
Israel, whose territory was considerably reduced in 734 and 732,
suffered the same fate, together with its capital, in 722-21.[c] In ch. 17,
vv. 4-6 and 10-11 are claimed in whole or in part to be of Isaianic
authorship, apparently being regarded as the continuation of 17.1-3.
We must ask whether there are really any grounds for dating these
stanzas in the eighth century. Even if v. 2b is regarded as a gloss taken
from Zeph. 3.13 (cf. Job 11.19) the linguistic form and the content
arouse suspicions. Verse 3 can be understood as a prophecy predicting
the same fate for both Syria and Israel. But it is also possible, and
indeed seems probable to me, that the verse has in mind the relatively
pitiful later existence of Samaria, and desires the same fate for
Damascus, which was flourishing. The systematic structure of the
oracles against the nations characteristically ignores Edom, which
had become obsolete in the course of the fourth century.[d] In its place
they speak of the rich oases of northern Arabia. But they do include
a prophecy against the old enemy in the north and against Samaria,
which from the religious point of view was becoming more and more
open to suspicion. Unfortunately, the history of Damascus from the
time of its last mention by Asshurbanipal, who travelled through it,
until the entry of Parmenion in 333 BC lies in total obscurity, for the
city clearly passed from one overlord to another without any further

---

[a] Cf. e.g. H. Donner, *Israel unter den Völkern*, SVT 11, 1964, pp. 38ff.

[b] Cf. on 7.1ff.

[c] Cf. A. Alt, 'Tiglatpilesars III erster Feldzug nach Palästina', *Kleine Schriften* II,
pp. 150ff. and *ibid.* pp. 195ff. and 210f.; H. Tadmor, 'The Campaigns of Sargon
II of Assur', *JCS* 12, 1958, pp. 22ff. and 77ff.

[d] Ch. 39 is a late composition.

occurrence. Its last attempt to regain its independence was as early as 720, when Samaria too once again revolted against Sargon. In the period of the successors of Alexander, Antiochus I forced Ptolemy II to withdraw from Damascus, and Seleucus II did the same to an army sent by Ptolemy III. In the Seleucid period Damascus had become, after Antioch, the second administrative headquarters of the western half of the kingdom.[a] The expectation that, in spite of having continued to flourish against all the storms of the centuries, the former Aramaean metropolis (cf. Ezek. 27.18) would suffer its final fall before the beginning of the age of salvation fits perfectly well into the total picture built up in the oracles against the nations (cf. also Jer. 49.23–27). The feelings of the inhabitants of Jerusalem and Judah towards their former brother-nation to the north were, to say the least, ambivalent. This can be explained when we recall the incorporation of Judaea into the province of Samaria by Nebuchadnezzar, the resistance in Samaria to the rebuilding of Jerusalem under Nehemiah, the hellenizing of Samaria towards the end of the fourth century and the simultaneous rebuilding of Shechem and the building of the temple upon Gerizim. In spite of the confused state of the sources, we can assume that the hellenization of Samaria was preceded by disturbances directed against the Macedonian rulers, leading to a conquest of the city either by Alexander or by Perdiccas.[b]

The flourishing city of Damascus is to become a place of ruins (cf. 23.13; 25.2, and also Ezek. 26.15, 18; 27.27; 33.13, 16; 32.10) and is never again to be rebuilt. The same fate is to befall not only the cities belonging to Damascus, in the ruins of which the shepherds will pasture their sheep (cf. 13.19ff.; 27.10; 32.14 and Zeph. 2.14),[c] but also Ephraim, the Samaritan heartland of the ancient northern kingdom.[d] In prophesying the end of the *kingdom* of Damascus,[e] either the poet was taking upon himself the mantle of Isaiah, from whom ultimately the whole poem is derived by way of the tradition in

---

[a] Cf. A. Barrois, *Dictionnaire de la Bible: Supplément*, II, Paris, 1934, col. 283 and E. Bevan, *The House of Ptolemy*, Chicago 1968 (1927), pp. 62 and 204, and also F. M. Abel, *Histoire de la Palestine* I, Paris 1952, pp. 45 and 48.

[b] Cf. H. G. Kippenberg, 'Garizim und Synagoge', *RVV* 30, 1971, pp. 33ff.

[c] For 'lying down' see, in spite of the borrowing from Zeph. 3.13, also 11.6, 7; 13.20f.: 14.30; 27.10 and 25.7, all of which are non-Isaianic passages.

[d] For *nšbt*, cease, disappear, cf. 14.4; 33.8; Ezek. 30.18 and 33.28; for *mibṣār*, fortified city, cf. 25.12 and 34.13.

[e] *mamlākā* only in the secondary passages 9.6; 10.10; 13.19; 14.16; 19.2; 23.11, 17; 37.16 and 20.

7.1–16 (cf. also 5.17),[a] or else he had in mind the later favours shown to the city by foreign overlords. What is left after the devastation of the Aramaeans possesses no more importance and honour than what the storms of history have left behind of the former flourishing northern kingdom of Israel, which from the political point of view was virtually nothing.[b]

CHAPTER 17.4–6

The Remnant of Israel –
The Unpicked Fruit on an Olive Tree

4 And in that day it will come about:
      the glory of Jacob will be brought low,
      and the fat of his flesh will grow lean.
5 And it shall be as when ⟨a reaper⟩[c] gathers together the stalks,
      and his arm harvests the ears,
      and as when one gleans the ears of grain
      in the Valley of Rephaim.
6 Gleanings will be left in it,
      as when an olive tree is beaten –
   two or three ripe berries
      in the top of the highest bough,
      four or five ⟨on the branches of a fruit tree⟩,[d]
      says Yahweh God of Israel.

It is certain that vv. 4–6 in their present form were not the original continuation of 17.1–3. Attempts to isolate an original nucleus which in content and above all in form could have belonged to the previous

[a] For the literary character of Isa. 7 E. G. Kraeling, 'The Immanuel Prophecy', *JBL* 50, 1931, pp. 277ff. ought in my view to be taken into account in the future. In my exposition I passed too quickly over the fact that it is a narrative in the third person.

[b] In spite of the name of Isaiah's son, *šeʾar yašūb*, 7.3, the remnant, *šeʾār*, is mentioned in the book of Isaiah only in secondary passages, 10.19f., 21f.; 11.11; 14.22; 16.14 and 21.16f. For the succession 'remnant' and 'glory' cf. 10.18f.; 16.14 and 21.16f.

[c] Read *qōṣēr* with *BH*.

[d] See *BHS*.

prophecy of warning differ greatly.[a] That the verses are in fact intended to follow 17.1–3 is clear from the opening words alone, 'and in that day it will come about', which usually point to a later addition. Thus v. 4 is meant to emphasize the fate prophesied for Israel in v. 3. Verses 5a, 5b and 6 continue the process of exposition, v. 5 bringing a change of image from v. 4, and v. 6 a less violent change from v. 5. It is not possible to tell whether the series of additions is the work of one hand or several.

[4] *Jacob grows lean*. The prophet retains the personification in order to foretell that the northern kingdom, or its posterity,. here referred to as Jacob, will lose its *kābōd*, everything which brings it power and respect, subjective and objective honour. It is likened to a man who has grown thin, and whose outward appearance proclaims his fate.[b]

[5] *Next to nothing is left to Israel*. The two similes in v. 5 are taken from the corn harvest, which was familiar to everyone in the pre-industrial age. When the reaper gathers together the standing stalks of corn with his left arm (cf. Ps. 129.7), and with his sickle in his right hand (cf. Jer. 50.16) cuts off the ears (cf. Job 24.24), he naturally takes care that as few as possible remain standing.[c] Anything he overlooks or loses when he is tying the sheaf together is gathered by the gleaners. The location of the field in the valley of Rephaim, the present day *al-baqʿa*, immediately in front of the gates of Jerusalem,[d] implies that because the city contained many landless poor, what was left would naturally be very small.[e]

[6] *The fruit left on the olive tree*. The final addition develops the idea of the minute remnant. Whereas v. 5 emphasizes how little chance of survival there is, v. 6 stresses the very small number which remains.

[a] Procksch deletes v. 4. Donner, SVT 11, pp. 39f., emends 4aα, 5a and 6b, but treats vv. 10 and 11, as is very usual, as belonging to 17.1–11. Without any literary criticism Eichrodt believes that 17.1–11 can be attributed to Isaiah.

[b] For *dll*, to be low, and *mšmn*, fat, cf. 10.16, and for *bśr*, flesh, also 10.18. The argument against Isaianic authorship lies not in the fact that these words are used, but in the way they are used.

[c] For this topic cf. G. Dalman, *Arbeit und Sitte in Palästina* III, Gütersloh 1933, pp. 41f. and 44ff. For *qṣr*, to harvest, cf. 37.30; for *qāṣīr*, the harvest time, also 9.2, 16.8; 17.11; 18.4., 5 and 23.3. For the figurative use (harvest = judgment) cf. also Hosea 6.11; Jer. 50.16; 51.33 and Joel 4.13. *šblym*, ears, occurs in 27.12, where *lqṭ* is also found.

[d] Cf. J. Simons, *Geographical and Topographical Texts of the Old Testament*, Leiden 1959, § 1267 and § 211; G. Sauer, *BHW* III, col. 1590f.

[e] Cf. also Ruth 2. Dalman, pp. 64f. and Deut. 24.19.

The *fate* of those left is not considered.[a] During the olive harvest men climb into the trees in order to beat down with sticks or rods the fruit that cannot be reached by hand.[b] Anything that remains out of reach on the highest branches is next to nothing by comparison with what a tree bears in a good year. What is to survive of Ephraim? The answer is, next to nothing.

CHAPTER 17.9–11

Punishment for Apostasy

9 In that day his cities of refuge[c] will be ⟨like the deserted (cities) of the Hivites and the Amorites⟩[d] which they deserted because of the children of Israel, and there will be no desolation (there).
   10 For you have forgotten the God of your salvation,
        and have not remembered the rock of your refuge;
     therefore, though you must plant anemones[e]
        and ⟨sow⟩[f] the cuttings of an alien (god), ⟨and⟩[f]
   11 on the day that you plant them, you grow them
        and make them sprout in the morning that you sow;
     ⟨Gone⟩[g] is the harvest in the day of sickness[h]
        and incurable pain.

The short section above presents the reader with some puzzles. He will know that v. 9 differs from vv. 10 and 11 not only because the

---

[a] It is in 24.13.

[b] Cf. Dalman, IV, 1935, pp. 193ff.; Deut. 24.20. For *nqp*, beat down, cf. 10.34; for the whole phrase 24.13. For the leaving of last fruits, cf. also Jer. 49.9. For *saʿîp*, branch, cf. 2.12; 10.33 and 27.10; for *poriyyā*, fruit tree, 32.12.

[c] M, which is supported by 1QIsa, ought not to be assimilated to vv. 10f., in order to remove the tension, which can only be resolved by literary criticism.

[d] Following LXX, read *kaʿᵃzūbōt haḥiwwî wᵉhāʾᵉmōrî*.

[e] Literally 'plants (or 'plantings') of the beloved' (masc. pl.!) which can be seen as a double plural, following G-K, § 124q, and translated 'plants (or 'plantings') of the beloved' (masc. sing.). But it can also refer to anemones, which in fact were particularly associated among the Greeks and Romans with the God Adonis. Cf. W. W. Graf Baudissin, *Adonis und Esmun*, Leipzig 1911, p. 88.

[f] Read with Marti *tizrāʿîn ūbᵉyōm* and cf. G-K, § 470.

[g] Cf. *BHS.*

[h] Cf. G-K, § 122q.

former is in prose and the latter in verse, but also because they are differently addressed. Verse 9 gives information to the reader, while vv. 10 and 11 are addressed directly, as can be seen from the Hebrew text, to a female person or to an entity conceived as such. In its context, v. 9, which from its introductory words can be clearly recognized as an interpolation, refers either to the men mentioned in vv. 7 and 8, or looks back beyond vv. 7 and 8 to Jacob in vv. 4–6, in other words to the northern kingdom of Israel or whatever had survived from it. It is difficult to tell whether vv. 7f. were added to vv. 4–6 earlier than v. 9, or the other way round. Unfortunately, it is also impossible to tell whether vv. 10 and 11 ever directly followed vv. 4–6. Thus we cannot assume in our exposition that the accusation and threat in vv. 10 and 11 were originally spoken against the northern kingdom, in which case the female figure addressed would be either the virgin Israel (cf. Amos 5.2) or the city of Samaria. The redactor may have supposed this. But we may doubt whether in so doing he correctly interpreted the original meaning of the warning, for which a reason is provided, and which if the 'for' at the beginning of v. 10 is deleted can quite well stand on its own.

[9] In spite of the uncertainty about which of the previous verses it originally referred to, the meaning of v. 9 is clear. In that eschatological day of Yahweh the tempest of the nations or of God which roars over the land (cf. 14.22ff.; 17.12ff. and 2.6ff.) will leave its cities lying as abandoned as those of the population which preceded Israel, the Hivites[a] and the Amorites,[b] who had either been driven out or killed when the Israelites entered Palestine. The idea that a godless Israel must share the fate of its predecessors in the country is not a new one, but is derived from Deuteronomic writing (cf. Deut. 8.19ff.; 9.4f.; Josh. 23.15ff.; cf. 24.20; Lev. 18.28 and also Amos 9.7). Of course in this case there is no further population to take Israel's place, and all that will be left is the uninhabited waste (cf. 5.9; 1.7 and 6.11, and also, for the phrasing, Ex. 23.29; Lev. 26.33; Jer. 4.27 or Ezek. 12.20). Because of the proclamation of judgment which follows, the redactor did not go on to speak of the resettlement of the country by the growing remnant (cf. 37.31f.) and the returning diaspora (cf. 14.1f. and 35.10). Looking back, we can realize that it is not basically important whether he primarily had in mind the area of

---

[a] For the Hivites cf. e.g. Num. 13.24; Josh. 11.13; Judg. 3.3; II Sam. 24.7 and F. M. Abel, *Géographie de la Palestine* I, Paris ²1933, pp. 321f.

[b] For the Amorites cf. e.g. Jos. 5.1; 7.7; Judg. 6.10 and R. Bach, *BHW* I, col. 84f.

the former northern kingdom or, in general terms, the people in the country as a whole, or even Judah, because the prophecy concerns an event which will not stop at the borders of either one country or another.

[10–11] The persons addressed, the origin and date of the warning and reason in vv. 10 and 11 are quite uncertain. The context does not even exclude the possibility that it was originally uttered against Jerusalem and should be understood in this sense. Moreover, in spite of the clear use of the language of the Psalms, it is not impossible that it is an isolated saying of the prophet Isaiah, who for example in 30.2 and 31.1 uses language reminiscent of that familiar to us from the Psalms.[a] Of course nothing is certain from the content, since a considerable later composition is not ruled out. We must recall, however, that only a few years ago an obviously heathen sanctuary was discovered no more than 300 yards south of the precinct of the Jerusalem Temple. It has not yet been finally dated, but can be cautiously placed in the period round 700 BC.[b] Literary evidence for pre-exilic foreign cults can be found for certain in 57.3–13a,[c] even if the relevance of Isa. 1.29ff. is questionable,[d] and no certain conclusions have been reached by the recent intensive literary criticism of the book of Jeremiah.[e] Its adoption into a post-exilic collection is evidence for the continuing relevance of this theme, which on consideration is not surprising. Until Judaism had achieved complete internal consolidation as a cultic community, the loss of political independence must have brought with it a growing temptation from the surrounding cults. In our view, this is reflected in Deuteronomy and in the Deuteronomic history.[f] But Ezek. 8 is sufficient evidence of the seductive power of heathen vegetation cults in post-exilic Jerusalem. Thus it is clear that we cannot hope to identify the author and the date of composition.

[a] In disagreement with Fohrer, ad loc.

[b] Cf. esp. with some certainty K. M. Kenyon, *Royal Cities of the Old Testament*, London and New York 1971, pp. 114ff.

[c] Cf. C. Westermann, ATD 19, 1966, p. 259; ET *Isaiah 40–66*, OTL, 1969, p. 324.

[d] H. Wildberger, BK 11.1; ad loc., once again argues that it is genuine.

[e] Cf. e.g. W. Thiel, Die deuteronomistische Redaktion des Buches Jeremia, thesis, Berlin 1970, shortly to appear in WMANT; E. W. Nicholson, *Preaching to the Exiles*, Oxford 1970 and W. Schottroff, 'Jeremia 2.1–3. Erwägungen zur Methode der Prophetenexegese', *ZThK* 67, 1970, pp. 263ff.

[f] Cf. O. Kaiser, *Einleitung in das Alte Testament*, Gütersloh ²1970, pp. 110ff. and 144.

The city (or population of a country) personified as a virgin, or at least as a female figure, is acting as though she had forgotten that she possesses in Yahweh her salvation[a] and the rock of her refuge[b] which cannot be shaken in any distress. This she shows by her practice of Canaanite cults, in association with the lament for Adon, the Adonis of Greek and Latin sources, the lord who is present in the spring flowers and who dies with them at the first heat of summer. In Greece a rapidly growing and equally rapidly withering seed was sown in small dishes made from broken jars at the appropriate season, in order to give a visual representation of the death of the god.[c] The prophet avoids naming the foreign god, but may well be referring to his nickname 'the beloved' in the name of the flowers, and goes on to apply the significance of the action to the people who are carrying them out: Just as no harvest is anticipated for these gardens, but only withering and dying away, so the people in the day of visitation will find no salvation, but only death.

CHAPTER 17.7–8

The Eschatological Conversion

7 In that day men will regard their Maker, and their eyes will look to the Holy One of Israel. [8]They will not have regard for ⟨ ⟩[d] the work of their hands, and they will not look to what their own fingers have made. ⟨ ⟩[d]

[a] Cf. Pss. 18.47; 24.5; 25.5; 27.9; 62.8; 65.6 and *passim*.

[b] Cf. Pss. 18.3; 19.15; 31.3; 62.3; 71.3; 89.27 and *passim*.

[c] For the gardens of Adonis cf. Baudissin, p. 141 and R. de Vaux, 'The Cults of Adonis and Osiris', *The Bible and the Ancient Near East*, London and New York 1971, pp. 210ff. = *RB* 42, 1933, pp. 3ff., and with the qualifications given there also L. Deubner, *Attische Feste*, Berlin 1932, repr. Darmstadt ³1969, pp. 220ff., with pl. 25. Since the passage also speaks of the cuttings of an alien (god), Fohrer suggests that here as in Ezek. 8.17 we have an allusion to the practice in connection with the Egyptian sun-god, in which in Canaan bunches of grapes instead of flowers were held up to the rising sun, in order to give it new life. Cf. G. Fohrer, *ad loc.*, and HAT 1.13, 1955, pp. 52f.; but also W. Zimmerli, BK 13.1, 1969, pp. 222f. For Marti's suggestion that 18.5f. should follow 17.11, see below on 18.1–7.

[d] Cf. *BHS*. Presumably a glossator was inspired by 17.10f. to introduce here the altars, Asheroth and incense altars as symbols of false religion.

A later redactor felt the lack, in the context of a prophecy of judgment against the related people of Israel to the north, of an explicit affirmation that people would repent when faced with the creator's act of judgment (cf. also 20.20; 5.15 and especially 10.20–23; 30.22 and 29.18). In the details of his phraseology and ideas he is clearly dependent upon the Isaianic literature.[a] For him, 'that day' is of course the great day of Yahweh, which is described so impressively in 2.6ff. and in this context is of course the basic assumption in oracles concerning foreign nations.[b] While people may still seek refuge in the idols they have manufactured themselves, in the utter distress of the coming event which is to shake the whole earth they will look for salvation to the one true God who alone, as the creator, can claim man's worship, and who as the Holy One of Israel[c] has manifested himself as the true Lord of the nations in his miraculous guiding of the people of God through the turmoils of history to the final glorification of Jerusalem.

CHAPTER 17.12–14

The Tempest of the Nations

12 Ah, the thunder of many peoples
  they thunder like the thundering of the sea!
 Ah, the roar of nations, like the roaring
  of mighty waters[d] they roar.

13 ⟨ ⟩[e]
 He rebukes them,
  and they flee away,[f]

---

[a] For ʿōśē, creator, maker, cf. 44.2; 51.13; 54.5; for the 'Holy One of Israel' cf. 1.4; 30.11, 12, 15; 31.1; 37.23; 41.14; 43.3; 47.4 and *passim*. For the 'work of hands' as a term for idols cf. 2.8; I Kings 16.7; II Kings 19.18; 22.17; Jer. 25.6f.; 32.30. For polemic against idols as human products cf. 40.19; 41.6f.; 40.20; 44.9–17.

[b] Cf. above, on 13.9.

[c] Cf. my comment on 1.4 in *Isaiah 1–12*, OTL, 1972.

[d] In view of 28.2 the moving of *kabbīrīm*, which is often proposed, seems ill advised.

[e] V. 13a contains an alternative reading for v. 12b with the more usual *mayim rabbīm*.

[f] Cf. G-K, § 119z.

chased like chaff on the mountains before the wind
and thistle balls before the storm.
14   At evening time, behold terror!
Before morning, it is over!
This is the portion of those who despoil us,
and ⟨the lot⟩ᵃ of those who plunder us.

The meaning of this short, poetically intense prophecy is revealed
only against the background of the conception of an eschatological
tempest of the nations raging against Zion, a conception in which an
older background in nature-myth can still be perceived in the first
verse and a half. But modern commentators, with few exceptions,
attribute it to the prophet Isaiah, mostly. dating it in the period of the
final revolt against Assyria led by Hezekiah about the year 701.ᵇ A
feeling that the statements in 18.4–6 are incomplete has sometimes
led to the present oracle being regarded as an introduction to 18.1–6.ᶜ
We believe this is a correct, though not fully worked out, understanding of the conceptions in 18.4–6. On the other hand, it has been rightly
objected that 17.14 provides our oracle with a satisfactory conclusion,
while 18.1 provides a suitable opening for what follows.ᵈ Recent
objections to Isaianic authorship have presumably failed to convince
because they have not been carried through logically and have overlooked the redactional character of 14.24–27; 29.1–8; 30.27–33 and

---

ᵃ Cf. *BHS*.

ᵇ Thus e.g. Cheyne dates it in the year 723, Procksch, Fischer, Kissane and
G. von Rad, *Theologie* II, Munich, ¹1960, pp. 167f. (ET *Old Testament Theology* II,
London and New York 1965, pp. 156f.), date it between 721 and 710. Duhm,
Dillmann-Kittel, F. Wilke, *Jesaja und Assur*, Leipzig 1905, pp. 85ff., Hans Schmidt,
Feldmann, Eichrodt and B. S. Childs, *Isaiah and the Assyrian Crisis*, StBTa II, 3,
1967, pp. 50ff., dated in 701. Gray, H. Wildberger, *VT* 7, 1957, p. 69, O. Eissfeldt,
Einleitung in das Alte Testament, Tübingen, ³1964, p. 421 (ET *The Old Testament: an
Introduction*, Oxford and New York 1965, p. 313), H. M. Lutz, *Jahwe, Jerusalem und
die Völker*, WMANT 27, 1968, pp. 47ff., H. P. Müller, *Ursprünge und Strukturen
alttestamentlicher Eschatologie*, BZAW 109, 1969, p. 86, cf. note 239, and F. Stolz,
Strukturen und Figuren im Kult von Jerusalem, BZAW 118, 1970, pp. 86ff., all argue for
Isaiah as the author. The fact that W. Staerk, *Das assyrische Weltreich im Urteil der
Propheten*, Göttingen 1908, pp. 92ff. has difficulties, in view of 22.1ff., in dating the
oracle in 701 is to his credit, in spite of his conjecture of a second campaign undertaken by Sennacherib against Hezekiah in 701, which he associates with the
present poem.

ᶜ Cf. Duhm and Kissane, but also Dillmann-Kittel, *ad loc.*, who is more cautious.

ᵈ Cf. Wilke, p. 86.

31.4-9.[a] If these passages are regarded as deriving in part or in whole from the prophet, it is necessary to regard him as the true father of Jewish eschatology and apocalyptic, and to accept that the kings of Judah were right to ignore its fantastic conceptions. For a king who bears a real responsibility for his people cannot indulge in the luxury of waiting for a besieged Jerusalem to be saved by the theophany of Yahweh in a storm and an earthquake. Nor are such ideas possible for a prophet who still lives in the midst of a people capable of an active part in shaping its own history. When, almost two hundred years later, Deutero-Isaiah took up the cultic conceptions of Jerusalem and used their images to proclaim the coming redemption, he was still firmly rooted in history, in that he regarded the Persian King Cyrus as the real instrument of liberation. Later the Jews were excluded as a political factor from history; under the pressure of foreign overlords who repeatedly destroyed and replaced each other, and of their own political impotence, they seemed to lack any chance at all of achieving their own freedom. Only then did they turn their ancient cultic conceptions into a myth which looked to the future, a myth possessing a characteristic charm and intensity of faith which even a critical commentator cannot overlook.[b] About the same time legend took over the recollection of the salvation of Jerusalem by the capitulation (meanwhile forgotten or suppressed) of Hezekiah in the year 701 and created the figure of the prophet Isaiah, who prophesied

[a] Fohrer *ad loc.* Cf. Müller, p. 86, note 239. B. Stade, *ZAW* 3, 1883, p. 16, Marti, Guthe, E. Balla, *Die Botschaft der Propheten*, ed. G. Fohrer, Tübingen 1958, pp. 470f., and G. Wanke, *Die Zionstheologie der Korachiten*, BZAW 97, 1966, pp. 116ff., all regard the oracle as post-exilic. It is no accident that G. Hölscher, *Geschichte der israelitischen und jüdischen Religion*, Giessen 1922, and R. H. Pfeiffer, *Introduction to the Old Testament*, New York [2]1948, London 1952, do not mention the passage in the chapters which they devote to the prophet Isaiah. S. Mowinckel, *Jesajadisiplene*, Oslo 1926, cf. id. *He That Cometh*, Oxford and New York 1956, p. 135, regarded it as the work of the disciples of Isaiah, but presented a different view in *Psalmenstudien* II, Kristiania, 1922, p. 255.

[b] It is not possible here to express a view on the recent dispute about the origin of the theme of the battle of the nations. Cf. Wanke, pp. 70ff., with Lutz, pp. 213ff., and Stolz, pp. 72ff., though Wanke's hypothesis that the theme is post-exilic in origin is not the last word on the subject. A study of Deutero-Isaiah from the point of view of tradition history, taking it as a complete unit and seeing it in the light of the different hypotheses about the cult at Jerusalem before and after the exile is perhaps the most likely approach to resolve some of the questions that have been raised. In fact since the appearance of H. J. Kraus, *Die Königsherrschaft Gottes im Alten Testament*, BhTh 13, 1951, this has been one of the most urgent needs in Old Testament study.

the miraculous sparing of the city to the devout king and ultimately looked forward himself to the destiny of Jerusalem in the final age (cf. 37.31f.).

If we ask how these late expectations of a tempest of the nations and the glorification of Jerusalem in the final age concern us, we must first affirm that even today faith must take into account the fact that God is the ultimate lord of history. With respect to him our plans and the success of our actions remain ultimately undecided, and the future is beyond our control. But even faith does not possess the guarantee that God will spare his own in this age from distress and persecution, suffering and death. Nor has the believer any right, by trusting in the help of God, to relinquish his own responsibility for history. Thus it is easy for us to understand the ideas which express the faith of a cultic community isolated from history. But we cannot simply accept that faith as it stands. We must ask on what it was based, and by so doing understand it better than it could understand itself. It is certain that not only individual human beings, but nations themselves fail with regard to God in the course of history; that violence and the absence of peace are the consequences of an unbelieving egoism, and that the true peace of the nations is impossible without humble brotherly love. Whether hope must ultimately look beyond this finite life is something which only one's own faith can decide.

[12] With the introductory *hōy*, 'Ah, woe!', a passionate exclamation, the poet draws our attention to the images which follow.[a] The 'many peoples' are as in Micah 4.13 (cf. 4.11) the army of the 'final age' raging forward to attack Zion; the destruction of this army is to inaugurate the age of salvation for Israel and peace for the whole world. Its tumultuous roaring and thundering is as it were a repetition of the rebellion of the sea against its creator (cf. Ps. 46.4, 7),[b] but by contrast to Pss. 46 and 65.8 (v. 12b in fact does no more than paraphrase the latter) the succession or juxtaposition of these two rebellious powers of nature and history here represents a comparison between the two, in which the roaring and thundering of the sea is reduced to an image for the tempest of the nations.[c]

[a] Cf. also Procksch, *ad loc.*, and Lutz, p. 48, who sees an echo of the tradition of the funeral lament here.

[b] Cf. Isa. 51.15; and also Ps. 93.2; Jer. 5.22; 31.35, and Pss. 83.3; 65.8 and Isa. 13.4.

[c] Cf. also Jer. 6.23; 50.42 and 51.55. Lutz, p. 48, talks of an identity of the two powers, which in my view is too strong.

[13] Verse 13a remains within the conceptual world of the ancient mythical tradition of the victory of Yahweh over the sea, which we know in an older version from the Ugaritic epic of the battle of Baal against the sea-god Yam:[a] just as, according to Ps. 104.6, Yahweh put to flight the waters by his thunderous voice at the founding of the earth, he would one day, in the decisive battle before the gates of Jerusalem, drive away the nations by his mere rebuke.[b] The word 'rebuke', however, does not very well reflect the characteristic dynamic significance of the Hebrew equivalent; for the latter refers to language which comes very close to a curse, and 'curse' might perhaps be a better translation.[c] The coming of the nations *out of* the distance, or from the ends of the earth, which is found elsewhere,[d] is paralleled here by their being driven by the curse *into* the distance (cf. 8.9, and also 31.9). The object of the rebuking or cursing, represented in the original by the preposition and suffix *bō*, is either the roaring and thundering of the nations (cf. 5.13f.) or, in a conception which would be closer to that of myth, the sea (of the nations).[e] The two following images which describe the scattering of the enemy in a panic are taken from a different setting, the everyday life of the farmer. When the thresher has ground up the sheaves of corn with the ears, the mixture is thrown against the wind with a winnowing shovel, the threshing floors being mostly upon the heights before the city, so that the chaff flies away and the heavier grains of corn fall to the ground.[f] Similarly the wind blows across the harvested fields the thistle-balls which are formed from the withered and tangled plants.[g]

[14] Verse 14 takes up the conception of the divine redemption during the night, before the breaking of the dawn, which is to be

---

[a] Cf. O. Kaiser, *Die mythische Bedeutung des Meeres*, BZAW 78, [2]1962, pp. 140ff.; H. W. Schmidt, *Alttestamentlicher Glaube und seine Umwelt*, Neukirchen 1968, pp. 126ff.; and of course also Gunkel, pp. 100ff. and Mowinckel, *Psalmenstudien* II, p. 255.

[b] Cf. Ps. 18.16; Job 26.7ff.; 38.8ff.; Nahum 1.4; Isa. 50.2; Pss. 106.9; 9.6; 68.31; 80.17; Isa. 66.15; Ps. 76.7 and 33.3

[c] Cf. Lutz, p. 49.

[d] Cf. 5.26; Jer. 4.16; 5.15; Isa. 13.5; Ezek. 39.2; and also Isa. 46.11.

[e] Cf. Lutz, p. 49, n. 7.

[f] Cf. 29.5; 51.15f.; Hosea 13.3; Zeph. 2.2; Pss. 1.4; 35.5f.; and 83.14ff.; for *rdp*, chase, pursue, cf. Pss. 35.6 and 83.16; for the image itself, cf. G. Dalman, *Arbeit und Sitte in Palästina* III, Gütersloh 1933, pp. 126 and 139.

[g] Cf. Dalman, *Arbeit und Sitte* I, 1928, p. 53. I owe to Pastor Dieter Völker of Boostadt the attractive German rendering *Rollkraut* for *galgal*, 'thistle balls'; it reflects the meaning of the Hebrew root.

found in association with the conception of the tempest of the
nations in Ps. 46.6 (cf. also Isa. 30.29ff.). The question whether we
have here a mythological element which derives from the pre-exilic
festival cult of Jerusalem, or with one which is post-exilic, is at the
present-day a matter of dispute.[a] Ultimately, however, it does not
affect the understanding of the present verse, which proclaims the
utterly astonishing annihilation of the nations. Whereas stark terror
and aimless confusion prevail in the besieged city in the evening, by
the morning the billowing tempest has disappeared like a phantom
(cf. 27.9). Without losing sight of the enemy and as it were dwelling
upon the joy of the redeemed, as happens in 31.29, the proto-
apocalyptic poet concludes by contrasting the hope of the nations,
here portrayed as plunderers and robbers, and their actual portion,
which consists at best in the saving of their lives.[b] It is not difficult
to perceive behind these concluding lines the longing of the poet and
his community to be relieved of foreign domination, to be free in a
liberated country and to enjoy without restrictions what their own
hands have produced.[c]

CHAPTER 18.1–7

Yahweh Can Bide his Time

1   Ah, land of whirring wings[d]
     which is beyond the rivers of Cush,

[a] Cf. also 37.36; 9.1; Ps. 110.3, and also Pss. 30.6; 59.7, 15, 17; Ex. 14.27, and
the comment of J. Ziegler, 'Die Hilfe Gottes "am Morgen" ', *Alttestamentliche
Studien. Festschrift F. Nötscher*, BBB 1, 1950, pp. 281ff. For the cultic interpretation cf.
S. Mowinckel, *Psalmenstudien* II, p. 64 and pp. 126f.; H. Schmidt, HAT I. 13, 1934,
p. 89; H. J. Kraus, BK 15.1, Neukirchen 1960, pp. 340f.; A. Weiser, ATD 14/15,
[7]1966 (ET *The Psalms*, OTL, 1962), on Ps. 46; A. R. Johnson, *Sacral Kingship in
Ancient Israel*, Cardiff and Mystic, Conn. [2]1967, pp. 92ff. and H. P. Müller, p. 43.
Cf. also above, p. 86 note a.
[b] For the corresponding meaning 'share' and 'lot' cf. Gen. 14.24; Num. 31.36;
I Sam. 30.24 and Obad. 11; Nahum 3.10; Joel 4.3
[c] That v. 14b is not to be regarded as a later programmatic addition is rightly
emphasized by Lutz, p. 50.
[d] Cf. Arab. ṣalla and ṣalṣalla, to whirr, to rattle, but for a different rendering,
KBL, *sub voce*. G. R. Driver, *JSS* 13, 1968, p. 45, refers to the Aramaic ṣlṣl and

2   which sends ambassadors by the Sea,
      in vessels of papyrus upon the waters!
    Depart, you swift messengers,
      to a nation, tall and smooth,
    to a people feared near and far,
      a nation mighty and conquering,[a]
    whose land the rivers wash.[b]

3   All you inhabitants of the world, you who dwell on earth,
      when a signal is raised on the mountains, look!
    When a trumpet is blown, hear!

4   For thus Yahweh said to me:
    I will be quiet and look from my dwelling
      like the heat of Zach[c] above the light,
      like a cloud of dew in the heat[d] of harvest.

5   For before the harvest, when the blossom is over,
      and the flower ripens into a grape,
    the shoots will be cut off with pruning hooks,
      and the spreading branches will be hewn off and cleared.

6   They shall all be left to the birds of prey[e] of the mountains,
      and to the beasts of the earth.
    And the birds of prey will summer upon them,
      and the beasts of the earth will winter upon them.

7 At that time gifts will be brought to Yahweh Sebaoth from a people tall and smooth, from a people feared near and far, a nation mighty and conquering,[a] whose land the rivers wash,[b] to Mount Zion, the place of the name of Yahweh Sebaoth.

Modern scholarship unanimously attributes the present oracle to the prophet Isaiah and places it either in the period of the Philistine revolt in the year 713–711,[f] or in the year after the death of Sargon in

---

Arabic *ḍulḍulu* (?) and postulates the meaning 'ship', altering *kᵉnāpáyim* into *kᵉnāpīm*, 'sails' in order to retain 'land of sailing ships'.

[a] Literally 'of vigour and of treading down'. H. Donner, *Israel unter den Völkern*, SVT 11, 1964, p. 122, refers to 28.10f. and takes the *qaw-qāw* as an onomatopoeic stammered form to characterize a strange, incomprehensible language. Similarly, Fischer interpreted it as an imitative sound for the marching of an army. Driver, p. 46, understands *qaw-qāw* as a reduplicated adjective with a superlative meaning. He proposes to emend *mᵉbūsā* into *mᵉbasseh*, despicable.

[b] Cf. *KBL sub voce*, but also Driver, p. 46.

[c] Cf. Y. Ahoroni in *PEQ* 95, 1963, pp. 3f., and below, *ad loc*.

[d] But see *BHS*.   [e] Cf. *BHS*.

[f] Following e.g. Procksch, Fischer, Kissane, Fohrer and Vermeylen. Marti followed E. Meyer in thinking of the year 728.

705 in which Hezekiah played the decisive role in southern Palestine in the movement of revolt against Assyria.[a] The implication is that the ambassadors mentioned in v. 2 are in Jerusalem at the behest of the Ethiopian Pharaoh Shabako in order to discuss common action against the Assyrians with Hezekiah. Accordingly, the majority of commentators see vv. 5f. as a prophecy that Yahweh himself will destroy the Assyrians, so that political measures against them will be unnecessary. The background to this interpretation is the conviction that Isaiah, according to 29.1ff.; 30.27ff. and 31.4ff., shared such an expectation towards the ends of his active life. From the point of view of literary criticism, this interpretation sees 18.1–6 either as directly linked to 17.12–14[b] or else treats it as an independent unit. Fohrer follows a line of his own by regarding vv. 5 as a prophecy not of a fall of Assyria, but on the contrary of the destruction by the Assyrians of the coalition against them. It is this which leads him to place the oracle in the period of the Philistine revolt. Finally, Marti regarded only vv. 1–2 and 4 as belonging to the prophecy concerning Ethiopia, and deleted v. 3 as a later interpretation, regarding vv. 5 and 6 as the original conclusion of 17.1–11. The former deletion commanded some agreement in the opposite camp, the latter quite rightly none at all; for the gardens of Adonis in 17.10f. and the metaphor of the vineyard in 18.5ff. are quite distinct.

If one does not share the traditional view that the prophet looked forward to a direct intervention of Yahweh and the destruction of the Assyrians before the gates of Jerusalem during the revolt of the concluding years of the eighth century,[c] a fundamentally new interpretation of the poem is required. Such an interpretation will agree, however, with most commentators in accepting that the *hōy*, 'Ah, woe, ha!' in 18.1 is the beginning of a new unit, while v. 7 is a secondary addition in both form and content. Verse 4 forms the best starting point. Yahweh is still waiting but has not yet intervened. But, vv. 5 and 6 continue, when the right moment has come, 'the shoots will be cut off', and enemy power will be destroyed. According to v. 3 the event deserves the attention of all the inhabitants of the earth, that is, it is of world-wide significance. The problem is how the first two verses are connected with this event. Even if they were to be

[a] With e.g. Cheyne, Dillmann-Kittel, Duhm, Gray, Feldmann, Donner and Eichrodt.
[b] With Duhm and Kissane.
[c] Cf. the passages referred to below.

regarded as a fragment which was originally independent, they must now be understood in the context of the whole poem. The difficulty lies in the fact that the introductory *hōy*, 'Ah!' can be understood either as threatening (cf. 10.5) or as merely an exclamation to draw attention to what is being said (cf. 55.1). Consequently the basic question is whether the Ethiopians are the subject or the object of the events referred to in v. 5. Are they the destroyers or those destroyed? Or do their ambassadors, whether real or present in the imagination, function merely as witnesses? The last possibility can be excluded, because otherwise there would be no point in emphasizing the military power of that nation.[a]

It is strange that Ezek. 30.9 understands the present passage to mean that Yahweh himself was sending the ambassadors to Ethiopia in order to proclaim the imminent destruction of that country.[b] The fact that this oracle has been included among the prophecies against the nations does imply that this interpretation, the earliest known to us, is correct, in so far as the passage in fact refers to the destruction of a powerful military nation. Its greatness and power is emphasized solely in order to give the most powerful possible impression of the fall that awaits it, the time of which is known to Yahweh alone and which he is keeping to himself. Not only Assyria and Babylon, but Ethiopia and Egypt must also fall before the harvest is ripe (cf. 13f., 21.1ff. and 14.24ff.). The lack of precision in the poem, together with the appeal to the inhabitants of the earth, argues against an interpretation in terms of contemporary history and suggests that an eschatological understanding is appropriate to the text. For the power of Ethiopia to be broken is a necessary part of the great drama of the breaking of the power of the nations which is to precede the age of salvation. The only necessary exegetical assumption in this understanding is that v. 2 is an ideal and not a real scene. Yet it has a considerable advantage over the traditional interpretation, for it has neither to pass over in silence the presence of the ambassadors in Jerusalem nor to concern itself with the Assyrians, who are nowhere mentioned, in order to get some meaning out of the text. Likewise, it does not have to transpose or emend the text. On the other hand, this interpretation makes the later addition in v. 7 more comprehensible, for that verse simply adds a further detail to the eschatological scene.

[a] That the prophet Isaiah had not so high a view of Egypt, is shown by a glance at 30.4f. and 31.3.
[b] Cf. Eichrodt, ATD 22.2, 1966; ET *Ezekiel*, OTL, 1970, *ad loc.*

Of course we must remember that because the allusions are so brief, much in the portrait we possess remains obscure and ambiguous.

[1] With the introductory 'Ah!' or 'Woe!' upon the 'land of whirring wings' the prophet-poet hints that a great disaster is being prepared for Ethiopia (*kūš*). That we are correct in identifying the country with the land to the south of Egypt is shown by the geographical information, which is also found in Zeph. 3.10, and which refers to the fact that the country extends beyond the White Nile, the Blue Nile and the Atabara. The profusion of insects in Egypt, observed by Herodotus (II.95), is also regarded by the poet as a particular characteristic of this country, the furthest to the south known to the ancient world.[a] [2] Of course the poet also knows that the Nile, referred to as in 19.5 and Nahum 3.8 as *yām*, 'sea', forms with its tributaries the sole traffic artery in the country,[b] which even ambassadors have to use on their journeys. He is also able to mention the light boats made of bundles of papyrus, which must have been regarded, especially by people from Palestine, as very characteristic of Egypt. They could be carried easily round rapids and were particularly popular for hunting in the papyrus thickets. The description of this exotic scene, however, goes beyond the bounds of probability, because these boats were not suitable, due to their limited durability, for lengthy journeys.[c] The use of the Nile rafts outside the Delta is unthinkable. Nor are the details given by the prophet intended to describe the route of the ambassadors as such, but merely to give an impression of the great skill of the distant nation. The same tendency is also responsible for the description of the ambassadors as 'swift'. In fact, against the background of the much admired qualities attributed to the Ethiopians in what precedes and follows, the paradox of the demand to the ambassadors to depart, for which for the moment no reason is given, is all the more striking. It arouses a curiosity to know the cause. Just as Herodotus described the Ethiopians as 'the tallest and most beautiful people of the world'[d] the proto-apocalyptic poet also emphasizes their height and their smooth, hairless skin, though he did not think it worth while to mention that their skins were dark.

---

[a] Cf. W. Helck, KeP I, col. 201ff. or K.-H. Bernhardt, *Die Umwelt des Altes Testaments* I, Berlin 1967, p. 126.

[b] Thus even today Arabic still speaks of *baḥru-'n-nīli*; *baḥrun*, sea, lake, great river, stream is exactly equivalent to the Hebrew *yām*.

[c] Cf. H. Kees, *Kulturgeschichte des Alten Orients. Ägypten*, HAW III.1, 1933, p. 111.

[d] III. 20 and 114.

Once highly regarded as Pharaoh's mercenaries, they had impressively and lastingly demonstrated their military ability to the Palestinians by the conquest of Egypt under the kings of the twenty-fifth dynasty, which they set up.[a]

[3] The hope aroused by the enigmatic demand to the Nubian ambassadors is intensified by v. 3, although the meaning of the statement is not immediately clear. The inhabitants of all the land in the world[b] are to look when the banner is set up and the signal horn blown. As is shown, for example, by Jer. 51.27, both signs can serve to give a command to soldiers. As late as the end of the nineteenth century Schumacher observed during his survey work in Transjordan a similar involuntary effect from signal flags which he had set up: the tribes of the area at once armed and assembled in order to learn what danger was threatening.[c] Thus it looks at first sight as though these signals were meant to call the inhabitants of the earth together for battle. In this case one could assume that, as in 13.2, Yahweh is implicitly the commander. The aim of the attack could well be Zion, if the background of the expectation is the tempest of the nations against Jerusalem and the people of God, as would be suggested by 17.12ff. But it may be that the proto-apocalyptic prophet understood the military signs in a more general sense as indications of the onset of the day of Yahweh, as in Joel 2.1 (cf. also Isa. 27.13). This day is not to come only upon all who are lofty and proud among the people of God (cf. 2.1–12ff.) but also upon their enemies and the nations of the whole earth, to bring a terrifying end upon them and at the same time to prepare the way for the untramelled rule of God over the earth (cf. 13.6; Jer. 46.10 and Ezek. 30.20ff.). If we assume this latter interpretation here, the saying presents a good deal more inner coherence. The expectation that the Ethiopians will be affected by this event, which brings to end the confused course of human history, is also found not only in Ezek. 30.2ff. but also in Isa. 45.14.[d] Thus we may regard this passage as a very early form of the New Testament hope of the signs of the end, which according to Matt. 24.6f. were also to include wars between the nations.

[a] See also below, p. 112.
[b] Cf. Ps. 33.8; Lam. 4.12; Isa. 26.9, 18. Marti has rightly pointed out that *tēbēl*, dry land, *terra firma*, never occurs in Isaianic sayings; but cf. 13.11; 24.2 and 34.1
[c] C. Schumacher's 'Der Dscholan', *ZDPV* 9, 1886, p. 232.
[d] Cf. C. Westermann, ATD 19, 1966; ET *Isaiah 40–66*, OTL, 1969, *ad loc.*

[4] Ultimately, even the New Testament statement in Mark 13.32 that 'of that day or that hour no one knows, not even the angels in heaven, nor the Son, but only the Father' is shared by our proto-apocalyptic prophet. Whatever seem to be the prospects upon earth, whatever the nations may do or plan, Yahweh stands apart from it all and has no purpose of his own in it. The prophet-poet claims to have learnt from him that he remains calmly and quietly in a suitable place of his own, which is not described in any further detail, in order to observe carefully what is going on upon earth (cf. Ps. 33.13). Just as the shimmering of the summer month *zach*, named after its heat (its name has been discovered on an *ostrakon* from Arad dating from the sixth century BC), seems to stand over the light, and as the mist rising from the Mediterranean and then moving east climbs high over the land, while the people below long for the night time dew to prevent the husks of the grain from opening too soon,[a] Yahweh looks calmly down from above, because he knows when his time has come.

[5–6] The next image, a paraphrase for the right moment for the destruction of the Ethiopians, may have been suggested by the song of the vineyard, 5.1ff. It brings with it a slight shift in time from v. 4 to the period of the harvest: In order to understand it a few practical details are required. In Palestine the vines flower in May. The grapes begin to ripen in August. September is the normal month for gathering them. At the first pruning before the flowers bloom the bunches which did not bear any fruit in the previous year are removed (cf. also John 15.2,6) while at the second pruning, after flowering and when the fruit is setting, the shoots and leaves which cover the grapes are cut away to increase the yield. In view of the lack of heating material in Palestine it is usual to dry the shoots that have been cut off and to use them for fires.[b] Verse 6 shows that the poet is interested not in the fruit-bearing branches which remain on the vine but with the shoots which have been cut off. Just as the farmer knows when he has to take up his pruning hook and cut the surplus shoots off, Yahweh knows when the hour has come for the visitation of the nations and

[a] Cf. G. Dalman, *Arbeit und Sitte in Palästina* I.2, Gütersloh 1928, pp. 310f., who takes the phrase to refer not to the eastward moving clouds which keep the dew from the land, but to the clouds which pile up in the west and bring the land their dew in the night. This preference is no doubt related to his whole understanding of 18.1ff. For the average temperatures in the hottest month, August, now cf. E. Orni and E. Efrat, *Geographie Israels*, Jerusalem 1966, p. 119, who give 22–26°C for the mountains and 24–26°C for the coastal plain.

[b] Cf. Dalman, *Arbeit und Sitte in Pälastina* IV, pp. 330f.

therefore of the Ethiopians. It is difficult to tell how far the interpretation of the final element in the metaphor should be pressed, the
abandonment of the pruned shoots to the birds of prey as a summer
dwelling and the beasts of the earth as a winter dwelling. Since an
allegorical interpretation like that of Dan. 4.7ff., 17ff. is as impossible
as a realistic one like that of Ezek. 39.17ff., one must refer back to
Isa. 5.5f. and see in the image no more than the powerlessness which
follows the catastrophe. An interpretation which takes into account
the grapes which remain and ripen on the vine is not possible in the
case of this image, which is concerned only with the fate of the
surplus growth.

[1–6] If we now look back, we can say what message is given to the
ambassadors who are addressed in an ideal scene, the time and place
of which is not specified. They are intended to announce to a proud,
beautiful and mighty nation that at the hour of the army of the
nations determined by Yahweh it will be overrun and annihilated.
From his scholarly-sounding knowledge of a distant nation, Isaiah's
metaphor of the vineyard and his own acute observation of nature the
proto-apocalyptic prophet has created an oracle which, in spite of its
partial obscurity and its changes of imagery, is unquestionably
coherent. The fact that it has no heading of its own and is placed
immediately before the following oracle against Egypt leads first of all
to the conclusion that it was included very late in the Isaiah roll, and
secondly to the likelihood that its author, to whom 20.3ff. was already
available, felt that a particular saying against Ethiopia ought to be
included in the collection of oracles against foreign nations.[a]

[7] Finally, a later reader of the oracle expressed his certainty that
after the judgment of Yahweh has been executed upon them, the
proud, beautiful and powerful people of Ethiopia will be subjected to
his rule and as a sign of their acknowledgement of his power will bring
gifts to Zion, cf. also 19.21. 'That time' means to him the time, foretold in vv. 5f. and known only to Yahweh, of destruction. The
solemn 'gifts will be brought' goes back to Ps. 68.30 (cf. also 76.12).
The title Yahweh Sebaoth recalls the universal power of God over
the nations.[b] The repetition of the epithets applied to the Ethiopians
in v. 2 serves the same purpose of emphasizing their power: however

[a] In this context it should be noted that the south of Egypt was in the hands of
Nubian kings from 206–185 BC; cf. H. Bengtson, *Griechische Geschichte* HAW III. 4,
³1965, p. 414.
[b] Cf. my comments on 6.3 and 13.4.

mighty and terrible this people may be, Yahweh is still more powerful and more terrible (cf. Ps. 93.4). The goal of the pilgrimage of the conquered is the holy place^a 'of the name of Yahweh Sebaoth', Mount Zion. This paraphrase for the Jerusalem Temple shows the influence of the Deuteronomic theology of the *šem*, the name, which distinguishes between Yahweh's dwelling in heaven and the terrestrial site of his revelation and above all of his worship, associated with his name.^b The background to the whole addition is the expectation of the pilgrimage of the nations to Zion, which we find in 2.2–5; 45.14; 60.3ff., as well as in 66.18, 19, 21, cf. also Zeph. 3.8ff.

CHAPTER 19.1–15

The Judgment upon Egypt

1 Oracle concerning Egypt.
 Behold, Yahweh is riding on a swift cloud
  and comes to Egypt;
 and the idols of Egypt will tremble at his presence,
  and the heart of Egypt will melt in his breast.^c

2 And I will spur Egypt against Egypt,
 and they will fight, brother against brother and neighbour
  against neighbour,
 city against city, kingdom against kingdom;

3 and the spirit of Egypt in his breast will be emptied out,^d
  and I will confound his plans;
 and they will consult the idols and the sorcerers,
  and those who return^e and the wizards;

4 and I will give over Egypt into the hand of a hard master;^f
  and a fierce king will rule over them,
 says the Lord, Yahweh Sebaoth.

---

^a For *māqōm* in this sense cf. e.g. Gen. 12.3; 22.3f.; Jer. 7.3.
^b Cf. e.g. Deut. 12.5; 14.23; I Kings 8.27, 29; 9.3, 7; II Kings 21.7; 23.27; Ps. 102. 16–23 and H. Bietenhard, *ThWBNT* V, p. 256, 14ff.; *TDNT* V, p. 257.
^c 'In his breast' may have become transposed into this verse from v. 3.
^d For the verbal form cf. also *BHS*.
^e See my comment on 8.19, *Isaiah 1–12*, OTL, 1972, p. 122, note a.
^f For the *pluralis excellentiae* cf. G-K, § 124i and 132k.

5 And the waters of the Sea will be dried up,
   and the River will be parched and dry;
6 and its canals will ⟨stink⟩[a]
   and the Niles of Masor[b] will diminish and dry up,
   reeds and papyrus will rot away,
7 the rushes ⟨   ⟩[a] on the brink of the Nile,
   and all sown land by the Nile will dry up,
   be driven away, and be no more.
8 The fishermen will mourn, and all will lament
   who cast hook in the Nile;
   and they who spread nets
   upon the water will languish.
9 The workers in flax will be in despair,
   ⟨the combers⟩[a] and weavers ⟨grow pale⟩[c]
10 ⟨Those who serve it⟩[a] will be crushed,
   and all who work for hire will be grieved.

11 The princes of Zoan are fools
   the wise counsellors of Pharaoh ⟨counsel⟩[a] stupid counsel.
   How can you say to Pharaoh,
   I am a son of the wise, a son of ancient kings?
12 Where then are your wise men?
   Let them tell you and make known
   what Yahweh Sebaoth has purposed against Egypt.
13 The princes of Zoan have become fools,
   and the princes of Noph[d] are deluded;
   ⟨The princes⟩[a] of her tribes
   have led Egypt astray.
14 Yahweh has mingled within ⟨their⟩[a] breast a spirit of
   confusion;[e]
   and they have made Egypt stagger in all his doings
   as a drunken man staggers in his vomit.
15 And there will be nothing for Egypt
   which head or tail, palm branch or reed may do.

[a] Cf. *BHS.*

[b] The name *māṣōr* for Egypt, which is found also, for example, in 37.25 and Micah 7.12, should be noted. Since the usual *miṣrayim* is a dual form, the author may intend to show that he is thinking of one Egypt, and more precisely of Lower Egypt. Cf. the Akkadian *muṣur* and also Dillmann-Kittel, *ad loc.*

[c] See *BHS.* Kittel has already noted that there is no evidence for this division of combing to women and weaving to men in Egypt. The certainty of the tradition of the text in vv. 9 and 10 is particularly clear here.

[d] Memphis.

[e] See also *BHS.*

[1-15] This prophecy against Egypt, to which five additions were later made (vv. 16-25) was not composed by Isaiah. The numerous verbal similarities to other passages in the book are evidence not that Isaiah was the author, but that it is the work of a devout writer who drew all his ideas from the book. As is shown by the recurrence of the word Egypt, six times in vv. 1-4 and four times in vv. 12-15, his poetic ability was not that of the great prophets of the eighth century. The continuity of ideas between the three stanzas, vv. 1-4, 5-10 and 11-15, is so loose, and the transition of ideas from the first to the second so great, that the close connection between contents of the first and third stanzas has suggested to some commentators that vv. 5-10 are a later interpolation. But since the third stanza itself does not simply follow smoothly from the first, but takes up and develops the theme of v. 3a, it would in this case be necessary to regard it too as an addition.[a] But since even the first stanza was written at a late period, and the prophecies are dependent upon earlier prophetic themes, it is perhaps better not to attempt literary criticism of this kind, particularly as a certain developing train of thought can be identified in the whole poem. The first stanza announces the collapse of the religious and civil order of the country, the second describes the destruction of its economic basis and the third the helplessness of the king and his officials in the face of the disasters that are sweeping over them.

The very general nature of the political allusions makes it difficult to date the prophecy with any certainty. Verse 4 assumes that Egypt is politically independent, and v. 2 that it lacks inner stability. Since the literary characteristics of the prophecy make it impossible to accept that it was composed in the seventh century, we cannot relate it to the campaigns of the Assyrian emperors Esarhaddon or Asshurbanipal which led ultimately to the conquest of Egypt.[b] Thus we must look for a date at the earliest in the Persian period, within which the period between the revolt of Amyrtaios, 404 BC, and the final reconquest of Egypt by Artaxerxes III Ochos, 343 BC, fulfils both conditions. The reconquest of the country and the instability of the kingdom were both constant political themes throughout these decades; the Persians did not succeed in reconquering Egypt until their fifth attempt, but during the same period there were five

---

[a] For the literary criticism cf. especially T. K. Cheyne, *Introduction to the Book of Isaiah*, London 1895, pp. 112ff.; Marti, p. 155 and Procksch, p. 244.

[b] Cf. Cheyne, pp. 114ff.

changes of monarch, revolutions or open revolts.[a] Whether this
prophecy is to be dated in the reign of Artaxerxes II (404–359/8) or
Artaxerxes III (359/8–338/7)[b] or even in the closing years of the
third century, when an attack upon Egypt by Antiochus III might
have been expected,[c] it is not important for its interpretation. Its real
significance lies not in its scanty historical content, but in the insight
which it gives us into the faith and thought of a Jew who did not
allow the political impotence of his people to shake his belief that
Yahweh remained the lord of the nations and the guide of their fate.

[1–4] *The collapse of the civil order.* Drawing upon an ancient
conception, rooted in Canaanite mythology, of the passing by of the
god on his chariot of clouds (cf. Pss. 68.5, 34; 104.3; 18.10f.; 99.1;
Deut. 23.26),[d] the prophet foretells the coming of Yahweh to Egypt.[e]
Where he comes from is not stated. If the poet had been asked, he
might perhaps have referred to Yahweh's heavenly dwelling.[e] As at
his theophany of judgment[f] his mere appearance is sufficient to
destroy the false gods, the idols (cf. 2.8, 18, 20; 10.10f.; 31.7; Ps.
96.5), so that the judgment upon the gods of Egypt once carried out
at the exodus and later foretold by the prophets will be exercised
upon them.[g] As a result the Egyptians will lose their courage and
power of decision.[h]

[2] In v. 2 Yahweh begins to explain why he is setting out against
Egypt, and his words continue until v. 4bα. He 'spurs' the Egyptians
against each other so much (cf. 9.10) that all order collapses as everyone struggles against everyone else. The human bonds between
relations and neighbours will break down just as rapidly as the civil
order to which the terms city and kingdom refer. In the case of the
cities and kingdoms the author was no doubt thinking of the pro-

[a] Cf. O. Kaiser, 'Der geknickte Rohrstab', *Wort und Geschichte. Festschrift K.
Elliger*, AOAT 18, Neukirchen, 1972, pp. 99ff.; 'Zwischen den Fronten', *Wort,
Lied und Gottesspruch II, Festschrift J. Ziegler*, Würzburg 1972, pp. 197ff.

[b] Cf. also E. G. Kraeling, *The Brooklyn Museum Papyri. New Documents of the Fifth
Century BC from the Jewish Colony at Elephantine*, New Haven 1953, p. 116.

[c] J. H. Bengtson, *Griechische Geschichte*, HAW III. 4, ²1965, pp. 414f.

[d] Cf. H. J. Kraus, BK 15.1, 1960, p. 472.

[e] Cf. also Jer. 49.38.

[f] Cf. A. Weiser, ATD 14/15, ⁷1966, pp. 33 and 43; ET *The Psalms*, OTL 1962,
pp. 50 and 64.

[g] Cf. Weiser, pp. 34 and 41; ET pp. 51 and 61.

[h] For the Old Testament understanding of the heart, cf. my commentary on
6.10, *Isaiah 1–12*, p. 83 and now to H. L. Jansen, *BHW* II, col. 708 and F. Stolz,
THAT I, col. 861ff.

vincial capitals and provinces with their princely families, which
were rivals in the later period. He is obviously influenced by 3.5f. If
the prophecy was not written until the late third century, the background may be the revolts by native Egyptians against the Ptolemies,
which broke out after the battle of Raphia in 217 and went on continuously.[a] [3] There is no way out of this situation for the Egyptians,
since their 'spirit', the vital force given to men by God, and regarded
like the heart as the seat of the sensations, intellectual faculties and
will,[b] is thrown into confusion, and their ability to make and carry
out[c] clear decisions is paralysed by Yahweh. In short, his presence
deprives the Egyptians of their reason. The general helplessness is
reflected in the questioning of idols and mediums. It is interesting
that the author, whose judgment is of course based upon the standard
of his own faith and pays no attention to what the Egyptians themselves believed,[d] uses features from 8.19 to portray their superstition.
We cannot tell whether this was because of his ignorance of Egyptian
belief and superstition, or whether his purpose was merely to stick as
closely as possible to expressions elsewhere in the book.

[4] Not until v. 4 do we learn the purpose of Yahweh's intervention, the handing over of the country to a hard and violent foreign
ruler (cf. 37.25). That a foreign ruler is meant, and not a particularly
powerful and cruel Egyptian king, is most likely in view of the argument of vv. 2–4, where the situation of Egypt's internal politics,
reaching almost the point of civil war, and the inability of the Egyptians to undertake concerted operations, prevent the crisis from
being resolved internally, so that the helpless country falls into the
hands of a foreign ruler.[e] In any case it is questionable whether the
Egyptians or any other oriental people would have seen any particular punishment in severe rule by a king of their own.[f] The solemn
formula of attribution (cf. 1.24, and also 3.1; 10.16, 33) emphasizes
the unlimited power of the God who is here proclaiming his will, and
who as 'the Lord' controls all heavenly and earthly powers.[g]

[a] Cf. Bengtson, p. 414.
[b] Cf. Ps. 104.29f.; II Kings 19.7; Job 32.8; Ex. 35.21 and F. Baumgärtel,
ThWBNT VI, pp. 359, 6ff. and B. Reicke, *BHW* I, col. 534f.
[c] Cf. my comment on 9.5, *Isaiah 1–12*, p. 127.
[d] Cf. my comment on 10.7, *Isaiah 1–12*, p. 142.
[e] Cf. with Fohrer also Ezek. 30.12.
[f] Cf. Duhm, Dillmann-Kittel and Marti, *ad loc.*
[g] For the divine name Yahweh Sebaoth, cf. my comment on 6.3, *Isaiah 1–12*,
pp. 76f. and above, 13.4, 15.

[5-10] *The destruction of the basis of life in Egypt.* The second stanza announces an intensification of the disaster in the form of a great drought. We have discussed above the possibility that this passage may be regarded as a later interpolation. In any case its content looks beyond the foreign ruler mentioned above (cf. v. 4) to the period of internal demoralization which is to come. Its content gives almost the impression that it is a midrash on Ezek. 30.12a. The more exact knowledge of Egyptian circumstances displayed here, by contrast with the first stanza, have given rise to the suggestion that the author lived in Egypt.[a] The drought caused by the drying up of the Nile, the canals that run beside it and its tributaries is not meant to be understood as a consequence of a breakdown of the irrigation system in connection with the previously mentioned collapse of internal order in the country, but as a consequence of the coming and intervention of Yahweh.[b] It is to bring an end to the proverbial fertility of Egypt (cf. Gen. 13.10; Num. 11.5, 18). If the Nile summer floods, whose natural causes were still a mystery to Herodotus,[c] did not take place, not only would it mean the end of the reeds, papyrus and rushes, the plants which grow wild on the banks, but also of agriculture.[d] With the simultaneous collapse of the fisheries and the production of linen, which was an important export, the economic catastrophe would be complete. Fish formed part of the main nourishment of ordinary people.[e] Their importance as food for the peasants in Egypt was noted by Herodotus (cf. II. 91, also II. 77). As Num. 11.5 and Ezek. 29.4 show, the rich fisheries of Egypt were also known in Israel. That apart from fishing for pleasure, the fish were caught with rod and line and with all kinds of small and larger nets, including stake nets, is shown by pictures in Egyptian tombs.[f] We mention only briefly that the Egyptians were particularly skilled in preparing flax as well as in weaving.[g] Herodotus observed that in Egypt it was not the women but the men who sat at the loom (cf. 2.35). The inclusion after that

[a] Cf. Fohrer, *ad loc.*
[b] Cf. Dillmann-Kittel, *ad loc.*
[c] Cf. II. 19ff.
[d] Cf. Gen. 41; *AOT*², p. 79; *ANET*², pp. 31f.; and for the layout of the fields, Herodotus II. 14f.
[e] Cf. A. Erman and H. Ranke, *Aegypten und aegyptisches Leben im Altertum*, Tübingen 1923, p. 140.
[f] Cf. A. Erman and H. Ranke, pp. 268ff., with figs. 109-111.
[g] Cf. A. Erman and H. Ranke, pp. 535ff., and R. J. Forbes, *Studies in Ancient Technology* IV, Leiden 1964, pp. 27ff. and 196ff.

of the fishermen and the various persons involved in the preparation
and working of flax, of the generalizing term 'all who work for hire'
among those particularly affected, shows the author's sense of
reality. He knew that in an economic crisis it is above all the poorer
people who bear the burden.ᵃ

[11–15] *The helplessness of Egypt and its inability to act.* The third
stanza takes up the ideas of helplessness and inability to act from v. 3
and develops them further. But one cannot perceive any clear link
with the situation described in the first stanza. Rather, these verses go
back behind the first stanza. In spite of its famous wise men (cf.
I Kings 5.10) Egypt is cast without preparation into the catastrophe
brought upon it by Yahweh, since as before (cf. Gen. 41) they are
unable to work out what God has in mind. Both on the border, in the
region in which Yahweh's power was once demonstrated against
Egypt, in Zoan, the Tanis of the Greeks, now *ṣan el-hagar* in the north-
eastern Nile Deltaᵇ and in the ancient capital of Lower Egypt,
Memphis,ᶜ the possession of which also controlled access to Upper
Egypt, the royal officials are seen to be incapable and stupid. These
two cities are picked out not only on geographical grounds, and, as
one might suppose from Ezek. 30.13f., on traditional grounds; their
choice also reflects the fact that the political centre of gravity in the
country lay during the author's time in Lower Egypt.

[11] The status claimed by the Egyptian court officials, who
represent themselves to their king as heirs of their nation's great
tradition of wisdom and as members of ancient royal families,ᵈ is in
complete contrast to their actual ability. [12] The test proposed to
reveal their inability, however, goes far beyond what it was fair to
expect of them, and can hardly have any purpose other than that of
emphasizing the superiority of the Jewish prophets over the wise men
of Egypt, and so of glorifying the God of the Jews (cf. Gen. 41; Isa.
43.8ff.; 44.6ff.; 45.20ff. and also Dan. 2). [13–15] But their passive
inability to discern the will of Yahweh is not all; as in 3.12, they lead

ᵃ For the lot of the Egyptian worker cf. A. Erman and H. Ranke, pp. 138ff.

ᵇ Cf. M. Krause, *BHW* III, col. 2244f., and for a detailed discussion H. Kees,
Das alte Ägypten. Eine kleine Landeskunde, Berlin 1955, pp. 109ff.

ᶜ Known in Egyptian since the time of the new kingdom as *mnf*, and therefore
in the Old Testament sometimes as *mop*, Hos. 9.6 and sometimes *nop*, Jer. 2.16;
44.1; 46.14, 19; Ezek. 30.13. Cf. S. Morenz, *BHW* II, col. 1236f. and Kees,
pp. 8off.

ᵈ Cf. also H. H. Schmid, *Wesen und Geschichte der Weisheit*, BZAW 101, 1966,
pp. 36ff., and Herodotus II. 77.

their people astray, because by sending a particular spirit (cf. I Kings 22.20ff.; II Kings 19.7; Job 12.24f.) Yahweh has cast confusion into their minds (cf. 29.9f.). As a result their proposals paralyse the will of their people, who thus become completely incapable of action. In an apparent echo of 28.7ff. the aimlessness of their action is dramatically compared with the behaviour of a drunken man who staggers round helplessly in his vomit. Verse 15 briefly sums up what has been said in the statement that Egypt will consequently no longer be capable of any common action which includes the whole nation; the comparison of the high and low in the nation with head and tail, palm branch and reed derives from 9.13.

CHAPTER 19.16–24

The Conversion of Egypt

16 In that day the Egyptians will be like women and shudder and tremble with fear before the shaking hand which the Yahweh Sebaoth shakes over them. [17]And the land of Judah will become a terror to the Egyptians; every one to whom it is mentioned will fear because of the plan which Yahweh Sebaoth has planned against them.

18 In that day there will be five cities in the land of Egypt which speak the language of Canaan and swear allegiance to Yahweh Sebaoth. One [of these][a] will be called the City of ⟨Righteousness⟩.[b]

19 In that day there will be an altar to Yahweh in the midst of the land of Egypt, and a pillar to Yahweh at its border. [20]It will be a sign and a witness to Yahweh Sebaoth in the land of Egypt; when they cry to Yahweh because of oppressors he will send them a saviour, and will ⟨fight [for them]⟩[c] and deliver them. [21]And Yahweh will make himself known to the Egyptians; and the Egyptians will know Yahweh in that day and worship with sacrifice and burnt offering, and they will make vows to Yahweh and perform them. [22]And Yahweh will smite Egypt, ⟨with healing blows⟩[d] and they will return to Yahweh, and he will heed their supplications and heal them.

[a] Cf. below on v. 18.
[b] Read *haṣṣedeq* with LXX and cf. for the other readings A. van Hoonacker, *Revue Bénédictine* 36, 1924, pp. 303ff.
[c] Cf. *BHS*.
[d] For the construction cf. G-K, § 113a.

23 In that day there will be a highway from Egypt to Assyria, and the Assyrian will come into Egypt, and the Egyptian into Assyria, and the Egyptians will worship Yahweh with the Assyrians.[a]

24 In that day Israel will be the third with Egypt and Assyria, a blessing in the midst of the earth, [25]whom[b] Yahweh Sebaoth has blessed, saying, 'Blessed be Egypt my people, and Assyria the work of my hands, and Israel my heritage.'

The prophecy of judgment against Egypt, 19.1–15, written at the earliest in the course of the fourth century, was later added to five times. The final result of this was a decisive change in its import. The first redactor, who speaks in vv. 16 and 17, seems to have felt the lack in the prophecy which he read of any connection with his own people. He filled this gap in a way which for us at least is extremely enigmatic. A further redactor directs his attention to the Jewish diaspora which existed in Egypt. What he added in v. 18 is ultimately no less puzzling than the comment of his predecessor. He seems, however, to have had the intention of naming certain signs of the time, by which the imminence of the prophesied visitation upon Egypt could be recognized. The third addition, extending from v. 19 to v. 22, changes the whole application of the warning. A mere punishment of Egypt is changed into a visitation which brings about its conversion to Yahweh. The conversion is brought about by the salvation of the Jewish diaspora by a saviour whom Yahweh has sent. The fourth addition in v. 23 was not content with this, and states that in the future there will be relations between Egypt and Assyria, who will worship Yahweh in common. A final hand in vv. 24–25 adds the attractive thought of a people of God which now includes Israel, Egypt and Assyria. 19.16–24 should be dated in the third or early second century BC.

[16–17] *Egypt under the terror of God*. With the favourite formula of introduction for eschatological interpolations, 'in that day', which is used by all the additions in this chapter, the redactor loosely attaches his message to vv. 1–15. Here 'that day' is meant to be the day in which Yahweh will come to Egypt and which will bring the beginning of everything proclaimed in the foregoing prophecy. Under the pressure of the blows from Yahweh which fall upon the

[a] But cf. LXX, Targ and Vg, which see this passage as a prophecy of a war between the two nations, which ends with a victory of the Assyrians over the Egyptians.

[b] I.e. Israel. Cf. Dillmann-Kittel, *ad loc.*

land and the people,[a] the Egyptians will be completely demoralized. Verse 17 shows that it is automatically assumed that the Egyptians will recognize Yahweh as the cause of the blows that strike them; for only this can explain why, at the bare mention of the land of Judah, they will be terrified at the plan which the almighty Yahweh[b] has prepared against them. Unfortunately there is no explanation of how they come to know this, and of what Yahweh's plan consists. Perhaps it is this obscurity which inspired the interpolator of vv. 19ff. with his more philanthropic ideas, and retrospectively makes us grateful to his terse predecessor. Possibly the author of vv. 16–17 supposed that at the sight of the drying up of the Nile waters the Egyptians would be reminded of the plagues of Egypt in the past or even of the miracle of the exodus (cf. 11.15; Zech. 10.11; Ex. 14f.; Isa. 51.10)[c] and would conclude that Yahweh was also at work in the visitations they were now suffering. Thus they might anxiously ask whether they were to face another Passover night. Accordingly the terror at the mention of the land of Judah would be a consequence of the occupation of the country by the Egyptians, and in fact by the Ptolemies, the first of whom, with Antigonus Monopthalamos, made use of the conflicts between Cassander, Lysimachus and Seleucus and occupied southern Syria, though without complying with the request, after the decisive battle at Ipsos in 301 BC, to vacate the country once again in favour of Seleucus.[d] Just as Yahweh had once brought to an end the slavery in Egypt, he would once again severely chastise and remove the occupiers.

[18] *Five cities subject to Yahweh in Egypt.* Verse 18 faces the commentator with a whole series of problems to which many widely divergent solutions have been proposed. Is the mention of five as the number of cities in Egypt in which Hebrew is spoken meant to refer to exactly five cities,[e] or to be merely a round figure?[f] Are the inhabitants who speak the 'language of Canaan' adherents of the Jewish diaspora in Egypt[g] or Egyptians who have adopted the sacred

---

[a] Cf. also 11.15; and in addition 30.32.

[b] Cf. my comment on 6.3, *Isaiah, 1–12*, OTL, 1972, pp. 76f. and above p. 15.

[c] Cf. also König, *ad loc.*

[d] Cf. H. Bengtson, *Griechische Geschichte*, HAW III.4, ³1965, pp. 369f. and M. Hengel, *Judentum und Hellenismus*, WUNT 10, 1969, pp. 8ff.;

[e] With e.g. van Hoonacker, p. 306.

[f] With most modern commentators.

[g] With e.g. Duhm, Marti, Gray, Procksch, Scott, Fohrer and Eichrodt, *ad loc.*

cultic language of the Jews?[a] Is a horrific title given to all five cities[b] or is only a single city in fact named and emphasized?[c] And which of the names found in the various witnesses to the text should be preferred? Should we follow one and read '*ir haheres*, 'city of the sun', and identify it with Heliopolis[d] or even with the Jewish settlement dating from the second century upon *tell el-yehūdīye*?[e] Or should we follow most Hebrew manuscripts in reading '*ir haheres*, and once again read into this nickname, 'city of destruction', an identification with Leontopolis/*tell el-yehūdīye*?[f] Or again, should we follow the reading given in most LXX manuscripts, which imply a reading '*ir haṣṣedeq* 'city of righteousness' (cf. 1.26)?[g] The variety of readings shows that the text of v. 18b has undergone a distinctive interpretative history.

Verses 19ff. imply that the five cities in Egypt should be regarded as Jewish settlements. In the style of apocalyptic *vaticinia ex eventu* they are so described in mysterious terms: as speaking the language of Canaan[h] and paying allegiance to Yahweh. One might suspect from Jer. 44.1 that besides the fifth city explicitly distinguished here, the reference is to the cities of Migdol, Tahpanhes, Noph (Memphis) and Pathros, though of course Pathros refers to upper Egypt as a whole.[i] Which of the Jewish communities is then called the 'city of righteousness' may remain undecided. There is certainly a possibility that this may refer to Alexandria, as the intellectual centre of Egyptian Judaism. Of course it is also possible that the apocalyptic

---

[a] With e.g. Delitzsch, Dillmann-Kittel, Feldmann and Kissane, *ad loc.*

[b] With van Hoonacker.

[c] With most modern commentators.

[d] Fohrer. – For ancient Heliopolis cf. H. Kees, *Das alte Ägypten*, Berlin 1955, pp. 93ff.

[e] Cheyne und Scott; cf. E. Naville, 'The City of Onias and the Mound of the Jew', *Memoir of the Egypt Exploration Fund* 7, London 1890, p. 20; also K. H. Bernhardt, *Die Umwelt des Alten Testaments* I, Berlin 1967, p. 80.

[f] With König, *ad loc.* Whether the Hebrew word can be taken as a direct reference to Leontopolis, cf. Hitzig, Duhm and Marti, *ad loc.*, is very doubtful, cf. *KBL sub voce.* Referring to Jer. 43.13, Delitzsch, Feldmann and Fischer *ad loc.* interpreted the name as City of the Destruction of the breaking down of the idols.

[g] I agree with Gray that a later alteration, dogmatic in purpose, of an original 'City of Righteousness' into 'City of Destruction' is more probable than the reverse.

[h] Note that this is the origin of an expression which became proverbial. For the matter itself cf. M. Noth, *Die Welt des Alten Testaments*, Berlin [4]1962, p. 46, n. 2 and p. 202.

[i] Cf. *BHW* III, col. 1400.

writer has in mind circumstances in Egypt quite unknown to us, in which only five of the Jewish communities in Egypt were considered by him as orthodox. But he sees the existence of the Jewish communities in Egypt, whether they are to be identified in this or some other way, as a sign that the visitation upon Egypt is imminent. Perhaps there had already been pressures upon these communities, which in his eyes called for an intervention of Yahweh. This is assumed in the following addition.

[19–22] *The conversion of Egypt.* The assumption on which the third and longest addition is based is the existence of oppressed Jewish communities. The universal expectations in this passage are reminiscent of Zeph. 2.11 and 3.9b–10.[a] The theologian who speaks here is answering the question posed to him by v. 17: How can the Egyptians recognize that Yahweh on behalf of his people is at work in the blows which come upon them? He seems to understand the plan of Yahweh differently from v. 17, as a plan of salvation which also includes the Egyptians. By sending to his faithful, oppressed by the Egyptians, as it were a second Moses to be a saviour and to conquer the oppressors, he will impart to the Egyptians the certainty that Yahweh is God, so that they are converted to him.[b] But while this may be the correct interpretation of the central idea, it remains uncertain whether the cult objects mentioned in v. 19 are thought of as being set up by the Jews, by Jews and Egyptians in common, or only by Egyptians. A more basic question is whether vv. 19–20a are describing the result of the prophecy that follows, or one of the conditions for its coming about. Since the memorial pillar and altar are meant to serve as signs to remind Yahweh of his community living there, and probably also as signs to manifest Yahweh to the Egyptians, they must have been set up by the Jews who lived in Egypt. Like v. 18, v. 19 must be understood as a *vaticinium ex eventu.* In other words, it is most probable that the apocalyptic writer had in mind a massebah and an altar to Yahweh set up in Egypt during the time in which he lived. Where this altar and the massebah set up near the border actually stood, we no longer know. The Jewish sanctuary in Elephantine can have survived Persian rule over Egypt for only a short time.[c] The setting up of the Jewish Temple in Leontopolis by the high priest Onias IV during the rule of Antiochus V Eupator (164?–162) (cf. Josephus,

a Cf. K. Elliger, ATD 25, [6]1967, *ad loc.*
b Cf. Judg. 2.10ff.; 3.9, 15; 6.6, 36.
c Cf. E. G. Kraeling, *The Brooklyn Aramaic Papyri*, New Haven 1953, pp. 111ff.

Ant. XIII. 65ff. and *War* VII. 420ff.) took place at almost the latest possible date for any redaction of the book of Isaiah. According to Josephus, Onias appealed to the present passage for his extraordinary actions, but this is not necessarily historical. It is worth noting, however, that it was possible for a Jewish temple cult to continue there until it was closed down by the Romans after the destruction of Jerusalem, in 73 AD.[a] The intellectual attitude of the texts suggests that the earliest possible date for its composition is the period of Ptolemy III, who according to the Letter of Aristeas 12–14 deported thousands of Jews to Egypt, some as military colonists and some as slaves.[b] The relatively friendly attitude to the Egyptians reflected in v. 22, however, requires a period in which there were not merely negative but also positive relationships between the Jews who lived in Egypt and their environment, and perhaps even Egyptian proselytes who encouraged more far-reaching expectations. For the blows which are to fall upon the Egyptians are seen as leading not as formerly to their death, but to their conversion and therefore to their life (cf. for various attitudes expressed in Ex. 14.4, and also Deut. 32.39; Hos. 1 and Isa. 57.17f.). For the present apocalyptic writer, Yahweh is the God who listens not only to the lamentations of the people but also to those addressed to him by other nations. An idea which is not developed here, but is implicitly present, is that the sufferings of those who are faithful to God are the sufferings of martyrs for the salvation of the world.[c]

[23] *The highway from Egypt to Syria.* It is hardly possible to tell whether it is the same hand or another which is responsible for the next addition. In any case the theologian who speaks here has developed the ideas of the immediately preceding verse and has also included the Seleucid kingdom, which he here names Assyria, in the hope of salvation. The importance of this idea is not reduced by the fact that in the third century, and of course in the second century too, there was an extensive Jewish diaspora in Mesopotamia and in all

[a] Cf. E. Schürer, *Geschichte des jüdischen Volkes* § 31.4, vol. III, Leipzig [4]1909, pp. 144ff.; ET, *History of the Jewish People in the Time of Jesus Christ* II.2, Edinburgh 1898, pp. 286ff.; V. Tcherikover, *Hellenistic Civilization and the Jews*, Jerusalem and Philadelphia 1959, pp. 276ff. J. Jeremias, *Jerusalem zur Zeit Jesu*, Göttingen [3]1962, pp. 209f., ET, *Jerusalem in the Time of Jesus*, London and Philadelphia, 1969, p. 186; also Hengel, p. 499.

[b] Cf. Tcherikover, pp. 272ff. and Hengel, pp. 27ff.

[c] Cf. also O. Kaiser, *Der Königliche Knecht*, FRLANT 70, [2]1962, pp. 136f.

probability also in Syria.[a] If we are to accept that there is a concrete historical background for the hope uttered here, this may possibly be sought either in the Syrian wars of Ptolemy II Philadelphos (285–246) and Ptolemy III Euergetes (246–221), the most likely being the Laodike war in the reign of the latter, in the course of which Euergetes crossed the Euphrates, though with only brief success.[b] Or else it may be sought in an attitude favourable to the Ptolemies spreading among the Jews after the peace of Apamea in 118 BC.[c] The free passage between the kingdoms of the Ptolemies and the Seleucids seems to arouse the hope of the union of the two kingdoms, the initiative apparently coming from the south. Thus when the 'Assyrians', that is, the inhabitants of the Seleucid kingdom, are to come to believe in Yahweh, the condition for this seems to be contained in the previous prophecy: the spark of faith springs from the Jews living in Egypt to the Egyptians, and from them to the Syrians. On the other hand there seems to be no connection with 14.24ff. or 30.27ff.

[24–25] *The blessed community of nations.* In these verses the hope contained in the faith of the Old Testament reaches a height and range which puts it on the level of 2.2ff. and Zeph. 2.11, 3.9b, 10, cf. also Isa. 45.20ff. There is no longer a narrowly exclusive hope of salvation which can conceive of the freedom and salvation of Israel only when other nations are enslaved and put to shame. Of course the primacy of Israel in the history of salvation, as the original recipient and instrument of Yahweh's revelation, is not altogether absent. It remains the fact without which the revelation of God would lapse back into obscurity. But within this fact, our theologian is concerned not with Israel as one earthly entity among others, or at the expense of others, but with the Israel which owes its existence, and the justification for its existence, in its previous isolation from the nations solely to its answer to God's call,[d] and is called to be God's instrument for the salvation of the world. The ancient enmity between the people of God who were once called out of Egypt and the nations and powers along the Nile and in the region of northern Syria and Mesopotamia comes to an end when they turn to Yahweh. Their former enmity

[a] Cf. Schürer § 31.1, vol. III, pp. 6ff. (ET II.2, pp. 223ff.), and Tcherikover, pp. 287ff.

[b] Cf. F. M. Abel, *Histoire de la Palestine depuis la conquête d'Alexandre jusqu' à l'invasion arabe* I, Paris 1952, pp. 44ff.; Bengston, pp. 394ff.

[c] Cf. Hengel, p. 17, but also pp. 55ff.

[d] Cf. also F. Mildenberger, *Gottes Tat im Wort*, Gütersloh 1964, pp. 26ff. and pp. 52ff.

now becomes a unity in which the people blessed by Yahweh become at the same time a blessing for the nations (cf. Gen. 12.2ff.; and also Ex. 19.5f.). Thus God's blessing no longer applies solely to Israel; the nations are also blessed through Israel. In the threefold formula of blessing uttered over Israel, the Egyptians are described as Yahweh's people (cf. such passages as Hos. 2.25; Lev. 26.12; Jer. 7.23; 11.4; Ezek. 36.28) while the Syrians are the 'work of his hands' (cf. Isa. 60.21; 64.8; Deut. 32.6); and they are joined with Israel, whose title recalls the divine history that lies behind it and its continuous association with God (cf. Pss. 28.9; 94.5; Micah 7.14 and Deut. 4.20). Together they form a *single* new and permanent people of God.

Of course such hopes would not have been possible without human contacts between the Jews in Egypt, to whom the theologians of the prophecies in 19.19ff., with their early form of apocalyptic, most probably belonged, and their increasingly hellenized environment. To the extent to which people of different nations and religions are forced to become acquainted with each other and to live together, human relationships are set up which cannot and ought not to be ignored by an understanding of faith which is honest with itself. There are various reasons why the universalist tendencies of Judaism expressed in Jewish propaganda and missionary activity in the Hellenistic and Roman period finally died out, and gave way to a new defensiveness towards everything alien. These reasons were perhaps not so much persecution of the Jews which repeatedly broke out during the Hellenistic period and the early Roman Empire, but rather the consequences of the total collapse of the Jewish state and the passionate struggles during the Bar Kochba revolt, which forced Judaism to isolate itself once again from the outside world, and brought about the victory of the traditions which as early as the Maccabaean period had passionately advocated a clear break with Hellenistic civilization.[a] Finally, a considerable place must be accorded to Jewish reactions to the recognition of Christianity as the state religion and the ensuing prohibition of conversion to Judaism.[b] Christianity understands itself as having entered into the heritage of the synagogue; it must therefore regard itself as responsible for

[a] Cf. N. N. Glatzer, *Geschichte der talmudischen Zeit*, Berlin 1937, pp. 66ff.; *Anfänge des Judentums*, Gütersloh 1966, pp. 92f.

[b] Cf. Glatzer, *Geschichte*, pp. 71f.; also A. Harnack, *Die Mission und Ausbreitung des Christentums in den ersten drei Jahrhunderten* I, Leipzig ²1906, p. 11 n. 5; ET *The Expansion of Christianity in the First Three Centuries* I, London 1904, p. 11 n. 1.

winning the nations to the obedience of faith and love, and must
constantly try to find out how it is guilty for the failure of the nations
yet to be convinced by its testimony of love and suffering. It must ask
why God has allowed the synagogue to endure and Islam, which in
its own time was nourished by the heritage of Judaism, as of Christianity, to spread, and why he has allowed all three to become en-
tangled in hostility, suffering and guilt.[a] Perhaps Christianity has
often lacked any sign of the testimony of suffering which it is obliged
to give and which is given here by a devout and nameless Jew; and
has perhaps thought itself justified by the sacrifice of Christ, without
being ready, may we suggest, to sacrifice itself in imitation of him.

CHAPTER 20.1–6

He who Places his Hope in Egypt

1 In the year that the Tartan, who was sent by Sargon the king of
Assyria, came to Ashdod and fought against it and took it – ²at that
time Yahweh had spoken by Isaiah the son of Amoz, saying 'Go, and
loose the sackcloth from your loins and take off ⟨your sandals⟩[b] from
your feet', and he had done so, walking naked and barefoot – ³Yahweh
said, 'As my servant Isaiah has walked naked and barefoot for three
years as a sign and a portent against Egypt and Cush, ⁴so shall the king
of Assyria lead away the Egyptians captives and the Cushite exiles, both
the young and the old, naked and barefoot, with buttocks ⟨bared⟩,[c]
to the shame of Egypt. ⁵Then they shall be dismayed and confounded because of Cush their hope and of Egypt their boast. ⁶And the inhabitants
of this coastland will say in that day, "Behold, this is what happened to
those in whom we hoped and to whom we fled for help to be delivered
from the king of Assyria! And we, how shall we escape?" '

[1–6] Round about 715 BC the Ethiopian Pharaoh Shabako conquered the whole of Egypt and gave the princes of Palestine fresh
hope of liberation from the yoke of the Assyrian emperor Sargon II.

[a] Cf. e.g. O. Kaiser, 'Christlich-islamische Begegnungen. Ein Versuch in
Rückblick und Ausblick', *Die Karawane* 12.3 (Ludwigsburg), 1971, pp. 38ff.
[b] Cf. *BHS.*
[c] Cf. *BHS* and B-L, 61e.

The centre of resistance in the years 713–711 was Ashdod, the most northerly of the Philistine cities.[a] When its king Azuri withheld his tribute payments from Sargon and at the same time sent envoys to stir the kings of the neighbouring kingdoms to rebellion, the emperor succeeded in replacing him by his younger brother Achimiti.[b] But this measure failed, because the Philistines revolted against the new lord who had been imposed upon them, drove him out and made a certain *jamani*, an Ionian, king in his place. He succeeded in arousing the interest not only of the other Philistine cities, but also of Edom, Moab and Judah in a coalition against Assyria, which of course based its hopes upon support from the newly founded Ethiopian-Egyptian empire. But once again the expectations of Egyptian help were not fulfilled. Shabako clearly felt that a conflict with his more powerful Assyrian neighbour was of no value to him. When the Ionian fled to Egypt as the Assyrian army drew nearer, Pharaoh handed him over, bound hand and foot, to the emperor. With the conquest of Ashdod, Gath and Asdudimmu, the port of Ashdod,[c] the revolt had been crushed, and no Egyptian army had been sent. We do not know how far the Davidic king reigning in Jerusalem, Hezekiah, had become involved in the movement for revolt. Since we know nothing of the Assyrian campaign of the year 711 going as far as Judah and its eastern neighbours, we may assume that he went no further than conspiracy, or else submitted in good time.

Verse 1 dates the word of God contained in vv. 3–6 in the situation of the year 711. Verses 3f. give the explanation of a striking sign carried out by the prophet, while vv. 5 and 6 describe the consequences for the Judaeans and the Philistines. Between v. 1, which is in the style of annals, and the prophecy of judgment in vv. 3–6, v. 2 is inserted as a parenthesis. It begins by giving the time of the prophecy in a general phrase and records the divine command to carry out the sign.[d] In form it is an account by someone else of a prophetic sign, for it speaks of Isaiah only in the third person.

[1] The date given for the word of God in v. 1 differs from the statements of Assyrian inscriptions in stating that it was not Sargon himself, but the Tartan, literally 'second', or in modern terms the

[a] Cf. K. Elliger, *BHW* I, col. 138.

[b] Cf. *AOT²*, p. 350; *ANET²*, pp. 286f. and *TGI²*, pp. 63f.

[c] For Asdudimmu cf. Honigmann, *RLA* I, p. 167.

[d] V. 2 is regarded as a secondary interpolation by Duhm, Cheyne, Marti, Fohrer and Eichrodt.

'commander-in-chief',[a] who was in charge of the punitive expedition against the rebellious Philistine city. The records state that on a sudden decision the emperor set out with only his bodyguard.[b] We cannot tell whether the difference is to be explained by a confused recollection on the part of the bearers of the Judaean tradition (cf. also II Kings 18.17) or the custom of monarchs of ascribing to themselves the acts of their subordinates.

[2] If v. 2 is not to be deleted as a later addition, it must be placed in parenthesis, and the general phrase 'at that time' taken to refer to a period before v. 1. Otherwise it conflicts with the statement in the verse that follows, that the prophet went about naked and barefoot for three years. The language of v. 2, opening oddly with the introduction to a prophetic saying, emphasizing that the action enjoined was a revelation and describing a statement addressed to Isaiah as something Yahweh says through him, shows that it is relatively late in composition.[c] The entire content can be found in the following verse. When it goes beyond this to speak explicitly of the loosening of the sackcloth tied to the prophet's back, it is presumably doing no more than repeating the conceptions of the prophet's clothing current at the time it was written.[d] As in the popular stories of the prophet in chs. 36–39[e] and in the headings 1.1; 2.1 and 13.1, Isaiah is explicitly called the son of Amoz. There is disagreement as to whether in accordance with the command the prophet remained stark naked or wore a loin cloth. Whereas in Israel nakedness was regarded as a scandal (cf. Gen. 9.22; also Gen. 3.7 and 10) there was no contradiction to this in its being the mark of prisoners and fugitives (cf. II Chron. 28.5, Amos 2.16 and Micah 1.8).[f] This was assumed by the interpretation in the verses that follow.

[a] Cf. A. Ungnad, *ZAW* 41, 1923, pp. 205f., and O. Rössler, *BHW* III, col. 1965.

[b] *ANET*[2], p. 286. The fact that the mobilization was limited to the bodyguard shows how urgent the campaign was in Sargon's eyes. For normally the guard and the standing army were supported by contingents gathered from the whole kingdom. Cf. W. Manitius, 'Das stehende Heer der Assyrerkönige', *ZA* 24, 1910, p. 112; and also H. W. F. Saggs, 'Assyrian Warfare in the Sargonic Period', *Iraq* 25, 1963, pp. 145ff.

[c] Cf. e.g. Ex. 9.35; Lev. 10.11; I Sam. 28.17; I Kings 12.15; Jer. 37.2 and Hag. 1.1 and 3.

[d] Cf. II Kings 1.8; Zech. 13.3 and Matt. 3.4. Cf. also G. Fohrer, 'Die Gattung der Berichte über symbolische Handlungen der Propheten', *Studien zur alttestamentlichen Prophetie*, BZAW 99, 1967, p. 97; and *idem*, *BHW* III, col. 1638.

[e] Cf. 37.2, 21; 38.1.

[f] Cf. the portraits of completely naked male prisoners in G. Loud, *Megiddo*

[3–4] The thread of the narrative, interrupted by the interpolation of v. 2, is taken up again. The relationship between v. 3 and v. 4 is that of picture and caption. The impression they give, which has been much debated, is that the meaning of Isaiah's extraordinary behaviour was only revealed to him after three years, i.e. after at least fourteen months, by a special inspiration. It has, however, been pointed out that the prophet's strange attire could have been understood in part at least by his contemporaries, as by Isaiah himself, before the full meaning of the action was made clear: 'A great misfortune is coming, so that many exalted persons will have to go about without top clothes, and barefooted.'[a] In psychological terms the behaviour of the prophet has been interpreted as a compulsive act, in which he was impelled by a compulsion which he could not explain, but which he experienced as caused by God.[b] If an action is to be regarded as meaningful when its significance is completely clear neither to the prophet nor to those who witness it, the obvious assumption is that it has a particular effective force of its own. What Levy-Bruhl said of omens within magical cultures applies to such an action: 'What they reveal would not take place without them.'[c] The difference between a magical action and the symbols or signs enacted by the Israelite prophets consists in the fact that the latter are based 'not upon human acts which contain in themselves the power to produce an effect, but upon the power of Yahweh whose activity extends into human reality'.[d] Verses 2 and 3 certainly mean us to understand the sign as brought about by God, and in no way as deriving from the personal initiative, let alone the abnormality, of the prophet.

The description of Isaiah, presented as uttered by Yahweh, as 'my servant' itself emphasizes that the sign is an act of obedience. This strange act also forms part of the carrying out of the task for which the prophet had declared himself ready (cf. 6.8).[e] It is a sign ('ōt)

Ivories, OIP 52, 1939, plate 4. 2a–b; *AOB*², plate 57, fig. 128 and *ANEP*, p. 124 fig. 385.

[a] Fr. Haeussermann, *Wortempfang und Symbol in der alttestamentlichen Prophetie*, BZAW 58, 1932, p. 109.

[b] Cf. G. Hölscher, *Die Profeten*, Leipzig 1914, p. 30.

[c] *La mentalité primitive*, Paris ⁴1925, p. 128; ET *Primitive Mentality*, London and New York 1923, p. 125. For the reality of magical abilities, cf. A. E. Jensen, *Mythos und Kult bei den Naturvölkern*, Wiesbaden ²1960, pp. 272ff.

[d] G. Fohrer, 'Prophetie und Magie', *Studien zur alttestamentlichen Prophetie*, p. 251.

[e] Cf. also O. Kaiser, *Der Königliche Knecht*, FRLANT 70, ²1962, pp. 18ff.

and portent (*mōpēt*)ᵃ of what is to happen to the Egyptians and the
Ethiopians. For both are going to be carried off into captivity and
exile by the Assyrian emperor, naked not only to the heat and cold,
but also to the mocking eyes of those who gaze at them from the edge
of the road.ᵇ

[5] Since the inhabitants of the Philistine coast are not explicitly
mentioned until v. 6, those who are dismayed and disappointed in
v. 5, but are not named, must be another group, consisting of all who
looked with hope to Egypt and thought that it could be a source of
self-confidence to them when faced with the emperor. Naturally the
narrator regards the inhabitants of Jerusalem and Judaea as included
in this group (cf. 30.1ff., 6f.; 31.1ff. and 36.9f.). Crushed and confounded in their hope, they remain behind,ᶜ [6] whereas the Philistine
who took part directly in the events look forward anxiously to the
future: for how shall their cities be able to face an attacker to whom
Pharaoh has succumbed?

[1–6] The concluding verse seems to place the narrative in the
period before the fall of Ashdod, when that city was still able to
entertain hopes of a relieving army from Egypt.ᵈ Since there was no
Assyrian attack upon Egypt in 711, the prophet, to whom according
to the whole narrative the word of God goes back in substance, was
disappointed in his hopes, even though Ashdod and its allies in fact
fell to the Assyrian attack. In conclusion, however, we must ask
whether the narrative we possess is really that of an event preserved
for posterity by, for example, a circle of disciples close to Isaiah (cf.
8.16) or whether it is a more popular tradition from a later period,
such as we find in chs. 36–39. The idea that Isaiah in fact walked
naked and barefoot for three years, or even for only fourteen months,
through Jerusalem seems inconceivable to us in view of the climate
there. In this attire, the prophet would have been considerably
limited in the occasions on which he could leave the house. But as a
purely narrative theme it is impressive even at the present day. Even

---

ᵃ The same two terms are found together in Deut. 13.2, 3; 28.46; 29.2; 34.11;
and in the plural also 6.22; 7.19; 4.34; 26.8; Isa. 8.18; Jer. 32.20f.; Neh. 9.10 and
Ps. 135.9. For these terms cf. also F. Stolz, *THAT* I, col. 91ff.
ᵇ 'To the shame of Egypt' is generally regarded as a gloss.
ᶜ The same term is also found in 37.27. Some forms of *ḥtt* are found within Isa.
1–39 in 7.8; 30.31 and 31.4; Job 9.3; and of *bwš* in 1.29; 19.9; 23.4; 26.11; 29.22;
Job 30.5.
ᵈ Cf. H. Donner, *Israel unter den Völkern*, SVT 11, 1964, p. 115.

though Isaiah is not yet described here as a potential or actual miracle worker, as in 7.11 and 38.4–9, cf. also 37.36, he is already being portrayed with superhuman features. On consideration, v. 6 also sounds strange, because it assumes not merely the military defeat of the Egyptians but also an invasion of Egyptian territory followed by a deportation which is not limited to prisoners of war in the true sense.[a] The statement that the inhabitants of the coast fled to the Egyptians for help in order to be delivered from the emperor is certainly ambiguous, but in any case conflicts with the concluding question, how they are to escape. For if they had in fact fled to Egypt, they would automatically have been affected by the occupation of Egyptian territory. But if they had done no more than to send petitions to Egypt, as hastily as if they were fleeing, it is strange that the Assyrians should attack first Egypt and then the Philistine cities. All these difficulties are resolved if we take seriously the view that we have here a narrative composed long after the events of the year 711, and which is ultimately of interest to us not because it is historically reliable, but because of its theological content. We must also take into account the fact that the events of the intervening years had overlaid the memory of Sargon's campaign against Ashdod, and in view of the well-known attack by the prophet upon the hopes placed in 701 in help from Pharaoh Shabako[b] (cf. 30.1ff., 6f.; 31.1ff. and 39.6), may well have distorted it. An intervention on the part of Isaiah in the year 711, which has not been preserved, may of course lie in the background. Let us note briefly here that the hopes Hezekiah placed in 701 in Egyptian help were confounded, the relieving Egyptian army was defeated at Eltekeh, and Jerusalem was forced to capitulate by Sennacherib.[c] More important, Esarhaddon (680–669) and Asshurbanipal (668–632?) in fact attacked Egypt and for a time incorporated it into their kingdom. In 671 Esarhaddon succeeded in conquering Memphis.[d] In 665 Asshurbanipal pene

[a] For *gālūt* as a technical term for the deportation cf. all the passages where it occurs, and especially in addition to 20.4, II Kings 25.27 (= Jer. 52.31; Isa. 45.13; Jer. 24.5; 28.4; 29.22; Jer. 40.1; Ezek. 1.2; 33.21; 40.1; Amos 1.6, 9; Obad. 20.) For the terms 'young' and 'old' together cf. Deut. 28.50; Josh. 6.21; Jer. 51.22 and Esth. 3.13.

[b] The mention of Tirhakah in II Kings 19.9 is based on an error, as is shown by an examination of the chronology by J. M. A. Janssen, 'Que sait-on actuellement du Pharaon Taharqa?', *Bib* 34, 1953, pp. 26ff.

[c] Cf. below on vv. 36f.

[d] Cf. Luckenbill, *AR* II, § 580; *ANET*², p. 293 and F. K. Kienitz, *Die politische*

trated as far as Thebes, where he captured rich booty and seems in
fact to have carried out some deportations.[a] It is perhaps possible
that Hezekiah's successor Manasseh revolted against Asshurbanipal
on the occasion of a campaign in Palestine undertaken by the
Pharaoh Psammetichos I, but had very quickly to submit once again,
according to II Chron. 33.11.[b] By this time, of course, the Ethiopians
had long lost their hegemony over Egypt. Finally, though still not
going as far forward as post-exilic times,[c] we must also recall the
hopes of help from Pharaoh Hophras (Apries) during the final years
of the kingdom of Judah under Zedekiah (597–587), hopes which
ended with the fall of the kingdom of Judah (cf. Jer. 46.2ff.; 37.1ff.
and Ezek. 29ff.).[d] It is easy to understand that among devout Jews,
who had kept alive the memory of the prophet Isaiah, there were
stories current in the years before and after the catastrophe of 587
concerning what God had prophesied through him and how his
prophecies were fulfilled. Before the catastrophe there would have
been the hope of warning and restraining those who, in spite of all
the warnings by the prophets and the experiences undergone since,
still hoped for deliverance by the Egyptians from the power of
Babylon. After the collapse of the kingdom, the destruction of the
Temple, the exile of the king and of large numbers of the ruling class,
such stories may have served to remind people that the God who had
once warned against the vanity of hope in Egypt was at work in the
catastrophe itself, and would continue to accompany his people
throughout their history, so long as they sought their help not from man
but from him. That these considerations are not merely speculations
is demonstrated by ch. 39. And we believe that the linguistic form of
the present narrative does nothing to contradict this interpretation.[e]

Geschichte Agyptens vom 7. bis zum 4. Jahrhundert vor der Zeitwende, Berlin 1953, p. 8
and A. Gardiner, *Egypt of the Pharaohs*, Oxford and New York 1961, p. 346.

[a] Cf. Luckenbill, *AR* II, § 776ff.; *ANET*[2], p. 295, and cf. Kienitz, pp. 8f. and
Gardiner, pp. 346ff.

[b] Cf. K. Galling, ATD 12, Göttingen 1954, and W. Rudolph, HAT I. 21,
Tübingen 1955, *ad loc.*

[c] Cf. above p. 100, note a.

[d] Cf. also the Lachish *Ostrakon* no. 3 in H. Donner and W. Röllig, *KAI* No. 193,
with commentary, II. pp. 191ff., *ANET*[2], p. 322, and *TGI*[2], pp. 75f.

[e] We ought perhaps to mention specifically that this excludes any direct statements about the religious psychology of Isaiah as he is described here. The most
recent description of the problem is to be found in I. P. Seierstad, *Die Offenbarungserlebnisse der Propheten*, Oslo [2]1965, pp. 162ff.

CHAPTER 21.1–10

Fallen, Fallen is Babylon!

1   *Oracle From the Desert*[a]
    As whirlwinds in the south sweep on,[b]
       it comes from the desert,
       from a terrible land.
2   A hard vision is told to me,[c]
       the false one acts falsely,
       and the destroyer destroys,
    'Go up, O Elam!
    Lay siege, O Media!
    All the sighing
       I bring to an end.
3   Therefore my loins are filled with shaking,
       pangs have seized me,
       like the pangs of a woman in travail;
    I am bowed down so that I cannot hear,
    I am dismayed so that I cannot see.[d]

[a] Commentators differ in their view of the originality and meaning of the reading 'wilderness of the sea', found or assumed in all witnesses to the text other than LXX. Those who retain it, understand it to refer either to the Babylonian lowland (Delitzsch), the desert south-east of Babylonia on the Persian Gulf (Dillmann-Kittel), or the Syrian-Arabian desert west of the lower Euphrates (Fohrer). But it is very unlikely that the original intention of the heading was one of such scholarly geographical precision and was not rather, as in 21.13 and 22.1, cf. v. 5, a keyword which seemed appropriate as a mnemonic quotation. For *yām*, sea, is either a secondary addition or a scribal error. The proposed emendation *midbārîm*, deserts, is not found in the Old Testament. It would be technically possible to follow R. B. Y. Scott, *VT* 12, 1952, pp. 278ff., in reading *midbār d^ebārîm*, altering *bā'* to *bā'îm* but is not likely, since the verb *bw'* in conjunction with *dābār* elsewhere does not refer to a beginning of the receiving of a revelation, as the context would require here in this case, but the beginning of what is foretold, cf. e.g. Deut. 18.22; Judg. 13.17; Jer. 17.15; 28.9; Ps. 105.19. – Marti regarded *yām* as the relic of *hemyā*, to roar, or *hāmā*, there is roaring, cf. also *BHS*. But since the metrical structure is not completely clear, there are problems in attempting to complete the first lines. If we accept that the keyword was a heading taken from the text, then we should probably reconstruct *mimmidbār*. It is not clear what the interpolator had in mind; presumably after the haplography of the first *m* he found simply *mdbr*.

[b] For the construction cf. G-K, § 114 o.
[c] For the construction cf. G-K, § 121 a–b.
[d] According to Marti this is a *min-privativum*.

4 My mind[a] reels,
   horror has appalled me;
the cool of the evening that I longed for
   has been turned for me into trembling.

5 'They prepare the table ⟨   ⟩[b]
   they eat, they drink.
Arise, O princes,
   oil the shield!'

6 For thus the Lord
   said to me:
'Go, set a watchman,
   let him announce what he sees.

7 When he sees carts,
   horsemen in pairs,
trains of asses,
   trains of camels
let him listen diligently,
   very diligently.'

8 Then ⟨the seer⟩[b] cried:
'Upon a watchtower, O Lord,
   I stand
   continually by day;
and at my post
   I keep watch
   whole nights.'

9 And, behold, here come
   carts with men,
   horsemen in pairs.
And he answered,
   'Fallen, fallen is Babylon;
and all the images of her gods
   are shattered to the ground.'

10 O my threshed one,
   child of the threshing floor,
what have I heard
   from Yahweh Sebaoth
the God of Israel,
   I announce to you.

It is not merely on the first reading that the reader has to struggle
with the different impressions given by this oracle. Whereas on the

---

[a] Literally: 'my heart'.
[b] See *BHS*.

one hand he is impressed by the mysterious and gloomy atmosphere
of the first five verses, and the quite different dream-like scene of the
second five verses, he is also faced by a whole series of obscurities and
tensions which ultimately arouse the suspicion that he has perhaps
failed to understand the prophecy properly. What is it in fact that
comes roaring out of the desert like a whirlwind in the south? Is it
the revelation which rushes upon the poet in a violent but only
fragmentary form, or the powerful army of the Elamites and Medes?
Who is the false one and the destroyer, the attacker and the attacked?
Or are these terms a cypher understandable only to the poet's
contemporaries, and indicating to them the coming of the day of
Yahweh and the shattering event which it was to bring to the nations?
It is presumably God himself who gives the Elamites and the Medes
the order to attack. But whose sighing will he bring to an end, and
who has caused it? For whom is the table spread? Are those who are
attacked sitting down unconcerned to their meal, while the attackers
are already making the final preparations for their onslaught? Or is
the object of this attack laying before them like a table that has been
spread? Does the scene with the watchman give us an insight into a
characteristic example of the split personality of a visionary, or does
it describe to us a visionary dream-image? What is the meaning of
the carts, riders and beasts? Are they parts of the conqueror's army?
Are the victors carrying away their booty? Or do they perhaps
represent the return home of those who were sighing under the rule
imposed by Babylon? And who is it who finally utters the cry of
jubilation at the fall of Babylon, the watchman, or God giving an
interpretation? And why is the prophet-poet so horrified at what he
sees in so fragmentary a form, although it is quite clearly an event
bringing the salvation for which his people have longed for so many
years? – When one looks for internal coherence in the text, there are
some difficulties in v. 6. To what does the introductory 'for' relate?
For between the first and second halves of the poem the causal
relationship is rather the reverse of that suggested by this opening
word. Because Babylon has been attacked by the Elamites and Medes,
it has finally fallen! Or, if we recall the prophetic character of the
whole poem, the fall of Babylon is to follow the attack of these
enemies! Does the horror and agitation of the poet, so movingly
described in vv. 3 and 4, therefore represent the consequence of the
vision described in vv. 6–9?

Here we seem to have a clue, leading to the suggestion that the original form of the poem consisted of vv. 2a, 3–4 and 6–9. This in fact provides a logical continuity. If we then gather together vv. 1b, 2bβa, 3 and 5, we have another fragmentary but equally coherent unity. We appreciate the work done, however, by the man who wove the two poems together into so impressive a whole. For in the form in which we have them, not only is the opening in v. 1b more impressive than if the poem had begun with the elegiac v. 2a, but the alternation between the orders for battle[a] and the painful descriptions of visionary horrors are more dramatic than if each of our hypothetical units were taken on their own. Thus we must hesitate once again, and are obliged either not to take the poet so literally in the opening words of v. 6, or to suppose that he invented the whole of the first scene after the revelation of the second scene had been given to him in a dream or a vision. This makes it even more difficult, however, to know why the news of the fall of Babylon so horrified him. We would understand his horror much better if it had been the consequence of his participation, in his ecstasy, in the catastrophe which was being prepared for Babylon.

What seems at first to be a direct description of an experience has finally been shown to be a deliberate work of art which we have no right to reduce to its component parts. This raises the question, whether it is an ancient prophecy from the period of the Babylonian empire or a late prophecy composed in the study or temple cell of a devout Jew.

[1b–5] *The enemy is coming!* The poem begins with the mysterious but stirring announcement of what is to come. Like one of the much feared sandstorms, which our poet knows from experience in the steppe and desert south of the mountains of Judah, or of which he has heard tell,[b] a power which is not named at first whirls out of the

---

[a] For the literary category cf. R. Bach, *Die Aufforderungen zur Flucht und zum Kampf im alttestamentlichen Prophetenspruch*, WMANT 9, 1962, pp. 51ff.

[b] For sandstorms where there is a south-west wind in Babylonia, cf. S. A. Pallis, *The Antiquity of Iraq*, Copenhagen 1956, p. 14. An impressive account of a sandstorm is given by C. R. Raswan, *The Black Tents of Arabia*, London and Boston 1935, pp. 77ff.: 'Two days afterwards we . . . felt the wind more stifling and driving dense dust-clouds before it. We weathered the first day of it, though it blew with unremitting fierceness and perseverance. But on the next day it developed into a veritable sandstorm of such violence, that one could barely keep one's seat in the saddle. . . . The third day was a repetition of the second, a howling gale, clouds, whirling sand, and no visibility beyond ten paces. . . . Our hands and faces were chapped; . . . the lips became parched; . . . the breath came in pants;

desert, the terrible land (cf. 30.6; Deut. 1.19). As in 5.28 and Jer. 4.13 it seems to mean not a revelation coming with violence upon the prophet, but the rushing advance of a mighty attacker. Whether the poet possessed concrete knowledge of the deserts which stretched east of the Tigris and beyond the well-watered arable country of Babylon, we cannot tell.[a]

[2] The poet at once changes the theme and tells us of the revelation he has received, in order to let us know that he is not speaking of an actual event, but one seen in a vision. The Hebrew ḥāzūt, 'vision, manifestation' can have, as in 29.7, the very neutral meaning of a revelation taking place in one of many ways. Just as we speak of 'hard words', the poet speaks of a hard revelation. The composite nature of the poem does not permit us to tell whether this was directly imparted to him, or whether he is already alluding here to the scene beginning in v. 6. The first sentence of v. 2b, 'The false one acts falsely and the destroyer destroys', has the effect of an outcry which can most easily be applied to Babylonian rule, unless the poet held a complicated eschatological conception in which the fall of Babylon was the signal for world-wide revolt and conspiracy on the part of the nations. 33.1 suggests the possibility of a similar complex of ideas associated with the key-word 'destroyer' (cf. also Jer. 6.26). If this can be assumed, it explains why the poet is horrified at the revelation he has received of the fall of Babylon, instead of rejoicing at it (cf. 47; 49.13 with Zech. 14.1ff. and Isa. 29.1ff.); the woes of the final age which precedes the rule of God over this earth are now beginning!

Like one pursued the poet once again changes his theme and records the order which, in view of the concluding 'All the sighing I bring to an end', can only be spoken by God (cf. 13.2f.). The Elamites are to draw near and the Medes to begin the siege.[b] The reader is

---

the blood hammered heavily in the heart and the temples. Our camels dragged themselves along only with the utmost effort, groaning and complaining. In one of the sadle-bags we carried one of our slaves, who had collapsed from exhaustion on the second day. . . . On the fourth day the storm took on fresh fury. The wind howled more fiercely than ever. Our lungs were choked with dust. Worn out by the constant buffeting and sleepless nights, with aching joints, dead-tired, at the end of our strength, we groped our way forward.'

[a] Cf. Pallis, ibid.

[b] For the use of the verbs ʿlh and ṣwr in the call to battle, cf. with Bach, p. 62, Jer. 46.9; 49.31; 51.27; Joel 4.9, 12 and Jer. 6.6; 50.14f., 29; 51.11; and for the verb ʿlh in connection with a verb describing a typical military action, Jer. 5.10: 6.4–6; 49.28; 50.21, 26, 29; Joel 4.13; Micah 4.13.

kept even more in suspense, because he still does not know who is to
be attacked. But contemporary readers would guess this at once from
the name of the nations to whom the order is given.

The mention of the Elamites, particularly as they come first, is of
course at first sight astonishing. For this country, lying east of
Babylonia, ceased to be a serious opponent of the Mesopotamian
empires as early as 639 BC, when the Assyrian emperor Asshurbanipal
conquered Susa. For the period between 625, when the Babylonian
general Nabopolassar sent the exiled Elamite gods back to Susa, and
540, when the Elamites threatened Uruk, we have perhaps only one
single mention of difficulties between Elam and Babylon, from the
year 596/95.[a] As the result of the Elamite defeat in 639, Cyrus I, a
king belonging to the Persian tribes which from the eighth century on
had penetrated into Elam, succeeded in extending his power. When
the empire of the Medes was founded shortly afterwards, the districts
subject to Cyrus I became dependent upon Medea, and this situation
was not brought to an end until Cyrus II, the later conqueror of
Babylon, crushed the king of the Medes, Astyages, in 553.[b] The
possibility that the Elamite attack upon Uruk in 540 was ordered by
Cyrus should certainly be taken into consideration.[c] Since it is not
likely that the present passage is a quotation from an older prophecy
of warning addressed to the Assyrians – at that period the Medes and
the Babylonians were allied – the likely conclusion here is that Elam
and Medea are paraphrases for the Persian kingdom. For Elam to be
mentioned first gives an old fashioned ring to the verse, but emphasizes the primacy of the Persians over the Medes.

The sentence that follows sounds as though it is giving a reason:
God is calling up these nations because it is his intention to bring all
sighing to an end. It is not clear whether he proposes to remove the
reason for the lamentation of the exiles, the Jews living in the
diaspora (cf. 51.11 [35.10]) at their slavery in Babylon, or more
generally for the sighing of the whole creation (cf. Rom. 8.19ff.).[d]
In view of v. 10, the first possibility is the most likely. But if we are

a Cf. D. J. Wiseman, *Chronicles of the Chaldaean Kings*, London, 1956, p. 36.

b Cf. also below, pp. 139ff. and also G. B. Gray, 'The Foundation and Extension
of the Persian Empire', in *The Persian Empire and the West*, edd. J. B. Bury, S. A.
Cook and F. E. Adcock, CAH IV (1926), 1969, pp. 2ff. and H. H. von der Osten,
Die Welt der Perser, Stuttgart 1956, pp. 59ff.

c S. Smith, *Isaiah Chapters XL–LV*, London 1944, p. 135.

d Cf. Ps. 6.7; 31.11; 38.10; 102.6; Jer. 45.3; Job 3.24.

not to dismiss the two following verses as pure rhetoric, by which the poet is seeking to impress upon us the immensity of the disaster which is to fall upon Babylon, the other interpretation is not out of the question.

[3–4] A glance at 15.5; 16.9, 11 and Ezek. 21.11 shows that assertions that the author is involved or affected may serve simply to emphasize the severity of the events foretold. But it is notable that the horror of the poet described here, which has a profound physical effect, the shaking of his loins and an anguish like that of the pangs of a woman in labour, are also attributed elsewhere to persons struck by disaster (cf. 13.8; Jer. 6.24; 30.6; Ezek. 30.4, 9; Nahum 2.11). It should also be noted that descriptions of the horror overcoming a prophet because of the future revealed to him become prominent in the late period (cf. Dan. 10.16). It becomes a stylistic device which is intended to make us believe that the experiences are genuine. Now the prophet here claims that he has literally heard and seen what he describes. Even the evening hour, when the winds coming from the sea bring people in Syria and Palestine relief from the heat of the day, has lost its joy for someone who has received such baleful knowledge. It is possible, though not certain, that the poet is here referring to the time of day in which he claims to have received the vision. Certainly the vision of vv. 6ff. is very appropriate to the period between the day and the time when one dreams.

[5] But we have not yet finished with the poet's direct participation in the visionary event. Once again he hears something. We would have been grateful to him for expressing himself less cryptically. For we can do no more than guess at the interpretation of v. 5. The first half of the verse is usually regarded as a description of the nobles of Babylon unsuspectingly sitting down to their banquet, and suddenly interrupted as they carouse by the cry 'To arms!' In fact according to the description in Herodotus I, 191, people were still celebrating unconcerned in the centre of Babylon when it was captured almost without a battle in 539, even though the outer suburbs had already fallen. But a prophet could hardly have known anything about this beforehand. Nor do we know whether the circumstances of the conquest had later become known as far as Judah. In looking for another solution, one certainly does not need to go straight to Ezek. 39.17ff.; Zech. 9.14f. and *Pirqe Aboth* III. XX, and treat v. 5a as a reference to an eschatological meal of judgment.[a] It may be that this

a Cf. Marti, *ad loc.*

verse, like vv. 2b, 3, must be understood as a renewed challenge to the attackers. Just as when a table is set and one needs only to sit down and reach out, so Babylon lies before its enemies. The concluding instructions to the leaders support this. The testing and necessary care of weapons are part of the immediate preparations for battle. The oiling of leather shields, which is also mentioned in II Sam. 1.21, is presumably meant to increase their elasticity, in order to avoid their being split when struck by a stone, spear or other missiles.[a]

[6–9] *The prophecy of the fall of Babylon.* No less a scholar than Gustav Hölscher has interpreted the scene described here as auto-suggestion: the prophet's ego felt itself so possessed by an outside force that it became virtually 'an entity outside the human visionary, acting on its own, and appearing as the instrument of the visionary faculty'. So it has become the 'watchman' whom the prophet can instruct and whom he expects to bring him supernatural information.[b]

Since according to the wording the watchman is instructed by the poet and his reply is heard at once, whereas according to v. 8 the process must have lasted several days, one ought to regard it not as an auto-suggestive experience of dual personality but rather as a dream or a *visio interna*, an auditive and visionary experience unrelated to external reality, which in technical medical language is called a 'pseudo-hallucination'.[c] The conclusion that while the prophet speaks of a watchman as of a third person, he in fact means himself, goes beyond what the passage actually states. It could of course be emended accordingly, as has been in fact proposed.[d] In attempting to come to a conclusion, we must realize that on principle it is hardly possible to submit a poet writing thousands of years ago to a psycho-

---

[a] Cf. Aristophanes, *Acharnians*, 1128.

[b] *Die Profeten*, Leipzig 1914, p. 70. Cf. also Fr. Haeussermann, *Wortempfang und Symbol in der alttestamentlichen Prophetic*, BZAW 58, 1932, p. 18; I. P. Seierstad, *Die Offenbarungserlebnisse der Propheten Amos, Jesaja und Jeremia*, Oslo [2]1965, pp. 146ff. My attention was also drawn by Seierstad to the fact that F. Giesebrecht, *Die Berufsbegabung der alttestamentlichen Propheten*, Göttingen 1897, pp. 55ff. had already recognized, rightly in my view, that the passage really clothes a prophecy in a poetic form.

[c] Cf. K. Jaspers, *Allgemeine Psychopathologie*, Berlin, Göttingen, Heidelberg 1953, p. 59; ET *General Psychopathology*, Manchester 1962, p. 68; C. Weinschenk, 'Illusionen, Halluzinationen und Wahnwahrnehmungen', *Archiv für Psychiatrie und Zeitschrift für Neurologie*, 189, 1952, pp. 463f.; Seierstad, pp. 57f.

[d] F. Buhl, *ZAW* 8, 1888, pp. 157ff.

logical diagnosis without possessing very exact details of the circumstances in which he lived and composed. The possibility which we
have mentioned several times in the course of our interpretation, that
the text as we possess it is a purely literary composition, means that
we shall make no attempt here at a psychological interpretation. To
understand the passage, it is sufficient to state that the poet is describing to us a dream-like vision. Any psychological interpretation
which goes beyond this is pure speculation.

[7] The Lord – the poet reverently avoids the name of God – has
commanded him to set a watchman who will tell him his observations. So that he, and especially the reader, can know what the
purpose of this is, more exact instructions for the watchman follow:
when a train of carts, pairs of riders, and caravans of donkeys and
camels come into sight, he must pay very great attention! It is not at
all clear whether these expressions refer to parts of an army – possibly
the conqueror's baggage train carrying away booty – the caravans of
liberated exiles returning home, or the setting out of a great army to
perpetrate new outrages. Once again, one may ask whether the
destroyer in v. 2 is identical with the Medes and Elamites, as the
conquerors of the final age. This observation in any case depends
upon later interpretations. It is superfluous to ask whether the
watchman took his post upon a tower or upon a high mountain,[a] for
the scene is an imaginary one.

[8] It can be taken for granted that the prophet is carrying out
God's command, so that this is not mentioned (cf. 7.3ff.; 20.2ff.).
Instead, we are witnesses of the impatient suspense of the watchman,
remaining uninterruptedly at his post (cf. also Hab. 2.1). This
suspense is finally relieved in a cry addressed directly to God, which
can best be described as a declaration of readiness. The purpose of
this short episode within the narrative is to introduce a delay between
the foretelling and the occurrence of the event, which not only
increases the suspense but also gives a more natural form to the
course of the action. [9] The watchman has hardly finished when the
expected train of riders and horsemen comes in sight. The description
of them varies slightly from that given in v. 7: the trains of donkeys
and camels are no longer mentioned. Instead we learn that the carts
are drawn by men – or should we translate 'by human beings'? In the
logic of the scene the statement that follows is a word of God which is

---

[a] Cf. II Sam. 13.34; Jer. 6.1; Isa. 40.9.

addressed to the prophet, and through him to the readers of the poem.[a] As far as the form is concerned, the triumphant 'Fallen, fallen is Babylon . . .' is an imitation of the secular funeral lament (cf. II Sam. 1.8; Amos 5.2 and Lam. 1.15). The time of the hated world power is over. Its idols, the essence of its hostility to God, lie shattered on the ground (cf. Jer. 51.8 and Isa. 46.1f.). (Revelation 18.2 takes up this cry of triumph and relates it to the fall of the world capital of the final age, Rome.) Did the watchman see the returning exiles? Did he see the victors hastening to further conquests? We cannot break down the obscurity that lies over the poem.

[10] *The conclusion.* Even the poet's concluding words do not remove the doubt as to whether he is foretelling merely the fall of Babylon or going beyond it to the subsequent horrors. Full of compassion, he addresses himself to his people, so often put to shame and mistreated in the course of history. If *mᵉdušātī* is not to be understood as a neuter expression ('my threshed one') it is likely that the female person addressed is the daughter of Zion, the city of Jerusalem, which the Babylonians treated so cruelly when they conquered it in 587 (cf. Lamentations and II Kings 14.18–25.21). But perhaps the poet had in mind not only all the sufferings associated with this, but also the sufferings which Zion was to face in the final age, when he goes on to speak of the 'child of the threshing-floor' and so develops a comparison which elsewhere was applied to the enemies of Israel (cf. Isa. 41.15; Jer. 51.33; Micah 4.12f. and Hab. 3.12).

The strange obscurity which envelops this poem, the artificiality, in our view, of its prophetic features, the transitions which can be observed in the use of traditional themes and its deliberate but by no means naïve dramatic construction make it doubtful whether it can really be understood as a prophecy composed before the conquest of Babylon in 539 BC.[b] It seems rather to draw upon these events in order to portray the imminent fall of the world city, and to see in it the onset of the woes of the final age which precede salvation. This assumption explains why the conclusion of the poem is not the jubilation of the prophet and the explicit proclamation of liberation, but a compassionate address to Zion as a child constantly flayed on

[a] Cf. Amos 7.8; 8.2; 9.1; Jer. 1.12, 14; Zech. 1.14f., 19, 21; 2.5; 4.14; 5.3f., 6, 8, 11; 6.8; and also Ezek. 8.17f.; 9.9ff.; 11.7; 37.12 and Zech. 3.1ff.

[b] But cf. K. Galling, 'Jesaja 21 im Lichte der neuen Nabonidtexte', *Tradition und Situation. Festschrift A. Weiser*, Göttingen 1963, pp. 49ff. and P. R. Ackroyd, *Exile and Restoration*, OTL 1968, p. 223.

the threshing floor of history, but to whom the poet is bound to impart what has been told him with certainty as the word of God. And since he is no longer able to speak, like the prophets of the past, to a living community in the Temple, he presents his message disguised as one of theirs, in order to impress upon his hearers what he had added to the ancient book.

CHAPTER 21.11–12

'Dumah' Oracle

11 *Dumah*[a] *Oracle*
One is calling[b] to me from Seir,
  'Watchman, when will the night end?
  Watchman, when will the night end?'
12 The watchman says:
  'Morning is coming,
    though it is still night!
  If you want[c] to inquire, inquire;
    come back again.'[d]

This short passage is one of the most enigmatic in the whole book of Isaiah, which is not without its obscurities. A British churchman of the last century stated that for all its practical significance for his contemporaries and for later generations it might just as well not have been written.[e] But since the person who incorporated it into the oracles against foreign nations in the book of Isaiah and must have had some purpose in mind, such a statement shows only that we lack the key to its understanding. We shall see whether the last hundred years has really advanced its interpretation at all. The ancient translators already had difficulties with this oracle.

The problems begin with the heading itself. Does Dumah refer to the oasis *dumāt al-jandal* or to *al-jauf* at the edge of the *nafūd* desert in

---

  [a] For the problems cf. the commentary.
  [b] For the construction cf. G-K, § 116 w.
  [c] For the forms cf. B-L, § 57h and z.
  [d] For the asyndetic construction cf. G-K, § 120g.
  [e] Cf. T. K. Cheyne, *Introduction to the Book of Isaiah*, London 1895, p. 128.

inner Arabia?[a] Or was the redactor referring to a Dumah in the area of ancient Edom, which was still known in post-Christian times?[b] Since there is an immediate mention of someone calling from Seir, the mountains south-east of the Dead Sea (cf. Gen. 33.14; Num. 24.18; Deut. 2.1ff.; Judg. 5.4), a reference to Edom is certainly likely. Thus the LXX replaced Dumah by Seir.[c] The possibility that the reading Dumah is derived through a copyist's error from Edom (cf. Gen. 25.13-15) is therefore worth considering.[d] Finally, however, *dūmā* can also be simply and straightforwardly translated 'silence'. Was the scribe responsible for the redaction perhaps expressing his own failure to understand the oracle in this way?[e]

Anyone who works through the commentaries will find in them not only considerable caution[f] but also definite references to particular historical situations. Because of the enmity which existed between the Jews and the Edomites after the destruction of the Temple in 587, some commentators believe that the oracle cannot have been composed during or after the exile, and affirm its Isaianic authorship.[g] In the search for an appropriate historical situation, Procksch suggested Sargon's campaign against the Arabs in 715. Duhm attributes the passage to the same author as 21.1-10, and believed that it was the answer to the Edomites' question, whether they would not soon enjoy better times, since the Babylonians, their overlords and trading partners, were involved in battles with the barbarians from the East. Finally, Galling attempted to find a definite place in history for the oracle. After the withdrawal of the last neo-Babylonian emperor, Nabonidus, from Arabia,[h] the freedom-loving Arabs had come from Edom to a prophet in Judah to inquire from him whether their

---

[a] Cf. J. Simons, *The Geographical and Topographical Texts of the Old Testament*, Leiden 1959, § 1279.

[b] Jerome, cf. Dillmann-Kittel and Procksch, *ad loc.*

[c] It should be noted, however, that LXX also translates *dūmāh* by Idumaea in Gen. 25.14, cf. K. Elliger, *BHW* I, col. 357.

[d] If we assume a technical haplography we should read the concluding ' of the preceding *maśśā*' as the first letter of the following word *'edōm*. The intrusive *h* would be a consequence of a misinterpretation based on 21.13ff., or else a miscopying of *m* assimilating it with the *mh* which follows twice.

[e] Some commentators, e.g. Dillmann-Kittel and Eichrodt, *ad loc.*, relate the 'silence' to the evasive answer.

[f] Cf. e.g. Fohrer, *ad loc.*

[g] Cf. e.g. Fischer, *ad loc.*

[h] Cf. below, p. 135.

servitude under the Babylonians was coming to an end.[a] Finally, the present text, like that which precedes it, has attracted the attention of religious psychologists who believed that they could see in the watchman a symbol of the prophetic faculty.[b]

If we ignore the introduction in v. 11bα, the short poem recounts a perfectly everyday episode.[c] A number of unnamed persons ask a watchman how much of the night has passed, i.e. whether it will soon be morning. The double question betrays the impatience with which the questioners await the dawn. The watchman replies that morning is coming, but that now it is still night.[d] His reference to the coming of the dawn – which might in fact be paraphrased: 'The morning will soon come!' is an answer to the impatience of those who are questioning him. But since it is still dark, he can ultimately only console them by asking them to repeat their question. So far so good.

Now the introduction in v. 11bα undoubtedly implies that the episode is more than an everyday occurrence, quite apart from the fact that so ordinary an episode would be out of place within a book of prophecy. The 'watchman', however, is clearly a Judaean, either in Jerusalem or elsewhere in Judaea. Who would be inquiring all the way from Edom whether the night was ending soon? For a start, the sun rises in the east, and secondly a cry coming from Edom would be heard by a Judaean watchman only if he lived right on the border. Thus we must understand the whole scene in a symbolical, metaphorical sense. In the Old Testament night and the darkness usually symbolize misery, distress or disaster (cf. Job 35.10; 30.26; Isa. 8.29; 9.1; Amos 5.18.20; Nahum 1.8; Eccles. 5.16) while light and dawn symbolize redemption and salvation (cf. Pss. 27.1; 97.11; 90.14; Isa. 9.1). Consequently, to ask when the night will end must be under-

[a] K. Galling 'Jesaja 21 im Lichte der neuen Nabonidtexte', *Tradition und Situation, Festschrift A. Weiser*, Göttingen 1963, pp. 58ff.

[b] Cf. F. Haeussermann, *Wortempfang und Symbol in der alttestamentlichen Prophetie*, BZAW 58, 1932, p. 21. It is not advisable to draw profound psychological conclusions from the poetic dialogue of question and answer with the watchman, cf. also S. of S. 3.3.

[c] In disagreement with P. Lohmann, 'Das Wächterlied Jes. 21. 11–12', *ZAW* 33, 1913, pp. 23ff.; cf. also the brief but telling criticism by Galling, p. 59.

[d] This interpretation of *wᵉgam lāyᵉlā*, similar to that by F. Buhl, *Geschichte der Edomiter*, Leipzig 1893, pp. 68f. is in accordance with the logic of the scene with its reference to the coming of the morning and the proposal that the question should be put again and in my view is definitely to be preferred to the more usual interpretation, that the watchman is foretelling the coming of both morning and night.

stood as a question about the end of the distress, and the reply as an indication that while the distress will certainly end, the time is not yet known.

If the brief introduction were not there, this word of consolation could be regarded without further ado as an addition to 21.1–10, a short episode from everyday life replying to the question of the faithful as to when the news of the fall of the world capital will at last reach the oppressed and harried people of God, and the age of salvation will dawn. This interpretation is perhaps the least artificial; for it avoids all speculation as to why a prophet or writer of Judaea should suddenly be interrogated by Edomites or be concerned with what happens to them. But it is conceivable that a redactor of the book of Isaiah felt the lack among the oracles against foreign nations in chs. 13–23 of an oracle against the Edomites, particularly as there were prophecies against the Moabites and some Arab tribes (cf. 15f. and 21.13ff.),[a] and found reasons in contemporary events unknown to us to treat the present verses as such. If this is too speculative, then in view of the Aramaisms in v. 12,[b] which rule out a date of composition before the exile, and probably also during the exile, one must be content to conclude that our knowledge of Edomite history in post-exilic times is too sparse to provide a historical setting for the oracle. In particular, it is not known whether at the time it was composed the Edomites still lived in the hills of Seir, or whether the Arabs who in the early Hellenistic period were known as Nabataeans had not long ago replaced them.[c] If it is regarded as the saying of a genuine prophet, it remains strange that he did not go beyond his fundamental certainty of the coming of an age of salvation or the end of a period of oppression or distress; and all kind of speculation remains possible as to why a Judaean should give an oracle upon Edom.

[a] In this case of course ch. 35 would also have been lacking.

[b] For '*th* cf. M. Wagner, *Die lexikalischen und grammatikalischen Aramäismen im alttestamentlichen Hebräisch*, BZAW 96, 1966, p. 31, no. 31. His examples, Deut. 33.2; Jer. 3.22 and 12.9 (conj.) can hardly be maintained as pre-exilic. For *b'h* cf. Gray, *ad loc.*

[c] Cf. also most recently J. R. Bartlett, *PEQ* 104, 1972, pp. 35ff.

CHAPTER 21.13–15

Caravans in Flight

13   *Oracle: In the Desert*
     Pass the night off the track[a] in the desert,
     O caravans of the Dedanites.[b]
14   To the thirsty
       bring[c] water,
     O inhabitants of the land of Tema.
     ⟨Meet⟩[d] the fugitive with his bread.
15   For they have fled from the swords,
       from the drawn sword,
    from the bent[e] bow,
       and from the press of battle.

Without any introduction to explain the situation, the poet plunges us into a dramatic action which reveals, line by line, the outlines of a genre painting. The caravans of the Dedanites, who are found in the Old Testament both as the inhabitants of the oasis city of Tema and also as merchants travelling long distances (cf. Ezek. 27.20; 38.13 and Job 6.19), are told to seek their night quarters away from the caravan route out in the trackless desert terrain. This command makes clear the extraordinary danger to which they are exposed, for after a strenuous day's travel under a burning sun, through desolate, waterless ravines and baking plains, sometimes covered with sand and sometimes with stones, a caravan urgently needs to find a waterhole in the evening if the men and animals are not to die of thirst. Without outside help the thirsting travellers would soon be doomed. The poet consequently calls upon the Temanites to bring water and bread to the fugitives who are hungry and almost dead with thirst. The fact that the Dedanites are described as fugitives makes it clear that on their journey they have encountered an overwhelmingly strong enemy. The last verse confirms this, though it does not explain the

---

   [a] *yaʿar* is rough, uneven and difficult terrain, with or without vegetation, cf. Arabic *waʿara* and its derivatives.
   [b] For the construction cf. G-K, § 146a.
   [c] For the hiphil of *'th* cf. G-K, § 76a or B-L, § 59g.
   [d] Cf. *BHS*.
   [e] Literally: 'trodden'.

circumstances: faced with drawn swords, drawn bows and a violent attack, the caravans have had to take flight.

Looking at the geographical situation of Dedan and Tema, we can work out with considerable probability the direction from which the caravans were coming; Tema, the present-day *taimā*, was an oasis city with plentiful supplies of water, and lay at the point where the caravan route to the Persian Gulf crossed the ancient incense route leading from southern Arabia to the north. Dedan, which was still known in the Middle Ages as *ad-daidān*, was close to the present-day *al-'ulā*, south-west of *taimā*. Here a route forks off from the incense route to the port of *al-ḥaura*, the Leukēkōme of antiquity, on the Red Sea.[a] Since the passage speaks of the caravans of the Dedanites, not of the Dedanites as such, we can certainly exclude an attack upon Dedan itself. Thus the caravans were coming either from the Persian Gulf, or more probably, from the north. In any case their flight homewards would have taken them through the region of Tema.

It is hardly likely that this intensely poetic account, consisting in all of three demands and the reason for them, is intended to make a past event known to the poet's own people. In view of the lack of concrete statements concerning the pursuers, it is more likely that it is a prophecy. But there is some doubt as to what occasioned it.

We do not know very much about the history of northern Arabia in pre-Christian times. In 738 BC the priestess of the tribe of the Kedar, in whose country Dedan lay, paid tribute to Tiglathpileser III. Tema was one of the Arabian cities which became obliged to pay tribute to the same emperor at the end of the war with Syria and Ephraim.[b] In 715 Sargon II had to undertake a campaign against Arab tribes living between the Gulf of Aqaba and *taimā*. In 703 the Arabs took part in the movement of revolt against Assyria stirred up by the Babylonian Marduk-aplu-iddina (Merodach-Baladan) but were ultimately defeated by Sennacherib, like the Judaeans. In 689 Sennacherib had once again to pacify the Arabs, suppressing a revolt led by the Kedar. When Shamash-shum-ukin later revolted against Asshurbanipal, the Kedar attacked the region between *hamā* and Edom, but were defeated once again. The independence which they gained after the death of Asshurbanipal was of short duration; in 599 the Babylonian emperor Nebuchadnezzar sent an expeditionary force

---

[a] Cf. A. Grohmann, *Kulturgeschichte des Alten Orients. Arabien*, HAW III. 1; III. 4, 1963, pp. 42ff.

[b] Cf. ATD 17¹⁻³, p. 3; ET, O. Kaiser, *Isaiah 1-12*, OTL, 1972, p. 4.

against the Arabs, and according to Jer. 49.28 against the Kedar as well.[a] In 580 the same tribe appears among the vassals of Nebuchadnezzar. Finally, the last neo-Babylonian emperor Nabonidus moved his royal residence for ten years to Tema.[b] It may be that he was forced to withdraw from the country by the Arabs, for a year later they are said to have taken part in the conquest of Babylon by Cyrus. In fifth and sixth centuries a state seems to have been set up under the leadership of the Kedar, and its boundaries may have extended from the southern border of Judaea as far south as Dedan. Tema, however, until it came to form part of the Nabataean kingdom, seems to have formed the centre of another state.[c]

It has been suggested that the poem belongs in the period of the Arab revolt against Sargon, and that Isaiah was its author[d]. Others point to its similarity with 21.1–10, and date both prophecies in the years before the capture of Babylon by Cyrus. The suggestion is that in the present poem the Dedanites are being described as witnesses of the attack upon Babylon.[e] The idea that the threat to the caravans extends as far as Arabia, however, makes this unlikely. The same argument can be advanced against a dating in the years of the Babylonian occupation under Nabonidus.[f] If we are not satisfied with the conclusion that we can no longer know anything about the situation envisaged in the poem, we must consider the possibility that the eschatological threat from unnamed enemies coming from the north, to which the poem is taken to refer in its present context in the oracles against foreign nations, was in fact already intended by the poet who composed it. As in 21.1 and 22.1 the later heading takes up a keyword from the prophecy (cf. v. 13b) in order to give it a name.

[a] Cf. A. Weiser, ATD 20/21, [5]1966, *ad loc.*; ET *Psalms*, OTL, 1962, *ad loc.*

[b] W. Röllig, 'Erwägungen zu neuen Stelen Nabonids', *ZA* 56, 1964, pp. 243ff. places the return of Nabonidus in 540.

[c] Cf. Grohmann, pp. 21ff. and J. Cantineau, *Le Nabatéen* I, Paris 1930, p. 3.

[d] E.g. Procksch and Kissane, and with some reservations also Fischer.

[e] Duhm and Marti.

[f] This dating is given by K. Galling, 'Jesaja 21 im Lichte der neuen Nabonidtexte', *Tradition und Situation, Festschrift A. Weiser*, Göttingen 1963, pp. 49ff.

CHAPTER 21.16–17

The Destruction of the Benē Kedar

16 For thus the Lord[a] said to me, 'Within ⟨three⟩[b] years, according to the years of a mercenary, all[c] the glory of Kedar will come to an end; [17]and the remainder of the archers of the mighty men of the Benē[d] Kedar will be few;[e] for Yahweh, the God of Israel has spoken.'

Perhaps the author of this passage is the same apocalyptic writer, claiming to know God's plan for history, who speaks in 16.13f. and who correctly understood that Dedan lay in the country of the Benē Kedar.[f] Thus he enlarges the preceding prophetic warning, on the basis of what was certainly a burning expectation of God's decisive intervention in history. Within three years the prophecy which he already found located among the oracles against foreign nations will be fulfilled against the Benē Kedar.[g] Then the power of this Arab tribe, which was clearly well known not only for its merchants but also for its archers, would be broken, and its numbers reduced.

CHAPTER 22.1–14

The Unforgivable Guilt of Jerusalem

1   *Oracle: The Valley of Vision*
    What do you mean that you have gone up,[h]
    all of you, to the housetops,

[a] 1QIsa: Yahweh.

[b] The figure, which it has long been noticed is missing, cf. Marti, *ad loc.*, has now been found in 1QIsa. Read *šālōš šānīm*. Cf. 16.13.

[c] *kol* is lacking in 1QIsa, LXX and Aq. But cf. the preceding *wklh* which is perhaps responsible for the omission.

[d] For the unusual succession of genitives cf. G-K, § 128a.

[e] For the construction cf. G-K, § 146a.

[f] Cf. above p. 134.

[g] Cf. above on 16.13f., p. 74.

[h] In the text 2nd. fem. sing.

2 you who are full of shoutings, tumultuous city,
    exultant town?
   Your slain are not slain with the sword
    or dead in battle.

3 All your rulers have fled together,
    without the bow they were captured.[a]
   All of you who were found[b] were captured,
    though they had fled far away.

4 Therefore I said: Look away from me,
    Let me weep bitter tears;
   do not labour to comfort me
    for the destruction of the daughter of my people.

5[c] *For a day of tumult and trampling and turbulence[d]*
    is the Lord's, Yahweh Sebaoth!
   In the valley of vision an outcry rings out,[e]
    and shouting for help to the mountains.

6 *And Elam bore the quiver*
    – on the chariots men, riders –
   and Kir uncovered[f] the shield.

7[g] *It came about; your choicest valleys*
    were full of chariots,
   and the horsemen took their stand at the gates.

8 *He took away the covering of Judah,*

9[h] *In that day you looked*
    to the weapons of the house of the forest,
   and you saw the breaches of the city of David
    for they were many,
   and you collected the waters of the lower pool,

[a] LXX forms an uncertain basis for the alteration of the text of the verse which has become almost the rule since Duhm, the transposition of vv. 3a and 3b, and at least the replacement of *nimṣā'yik* by *'āmmīṣayik*, 'your strong ones'.

[b] Cf. 13.15.   [c] An eschatological redaction is in the background here.

[d] The alliteration is also found in the Hebrew.

[e] The meaning of *meqarqar qīr* is disputed. Traditionally *meqarqar* has been derived from *qir*, wall. Thus Eichrodt translates: 'the wall-breaker attacked'. H. Ewald, *Lehrbuch der Hebräischen Sprache*, Göttingen [8]1970, p. 809 n. 3, however, translates with reference to v. 6: 'Qīr will be shattered and Shōa is on the mountain.' Cf. also Ezek. 23.23. Our translation derives *meqarqar* and *qir*, following G. R. Driver, *JSS* 13, 1968, pp. 47f. and M. Weippert, *ZAW* 73, 1961, pp. 98f. from the Arabic *qarqara*, which can refer to various noises, and the Ugaritic *qr*, noise, sound, tumult, taking *meqarqar* as a participle *pa'lēl* cf. G-K, § 55d and *šō'a* as the verbal noun of *šw'*, to call for help.

[f] Literally, 'made naked'.   [g] An early exilic redaction. Cf. below.

[h] A historicizing redaction. Cf. below.

10   *and you counted the houses of Jerusalem,*
     and you broke[a] *down the houses to fortify the wall.*[b]

11   *You made a reservoir between the two walls*
     for the water of the old pool.

     [c]*But you did not look to him who did it,*[d]
     nor did you have regard[e] *for him who planned it long ago.*

12   The Lord Yahweh Sebaoth called
     in that day
     to weeping and mourning,
     to baldness and girding with the sack.

13   And behold, joy and gladness,
     slaying oxen and killing sheep,
     eating flesh and drinking wine.
     'Let us eat and drink,[f]
     for tomorrow we die.'

14   Yahweh Sebaoth has revealed himself in my ears;
     'Surely this iniquity will not be forgiven you
     till you die',[g]
     says the Lord, Yahweh Sebaoth.

The present passage is a unit in itself, distinguishable by its heading in v. 1a and its concluding formula in v. 14b, as well as by its content, from what precedes and follows it. In its present form it poses a number of questions concerning its inner coherence, which it is difficult to answer with certainty. In vv. 2–5 and 12–14 it assumes a situation in which the inhabitants of Jerusalem can breathe freely once again after a very recent military defeat. Their enemies are named in v. 6 as Elam and Kir. The geographical situation of the Elamites, east of Babylonia, means that they can be conceived of as attacking Judah only either in alliance with other Mesopotamian troops or else as a fabulous distant nation. According to Amos 9.7, Kir was the original home of the Aramaeans, while according to Amos 1.5 it was a place to which they might be exiled, but its identification can only be a matter of conjecture.[h] It must also be

---

[a] For the form cf. G-K, 20m.

[b] Literally: 'to make inaccessible'.

[c] Again due to early exilic redaction.

[d] Cf. G-K, 93ss and 124k.

[e] A. Sperber, *A Historical Grammar of Biblical Hebrew*, Leiden 1966, p. 647, translates 'neither . . . did ye fear (r'$h = yr$')'.

[f] For the construction cf. G-K, § 113dd.

[g] For the construction cf. G-K, § 149b.

[h] Cf. W. Rudolph, KAT² 18.2, 1971, pp. 131f.

pointed out that in Isaiah's day the Elamites could have been neither the enemies of the Judaean kingdom on their own account nor the allies of the Assyrians, since they did not forfeit their independence until 647/46, and in any case were the allies of Merodach-Baladan in his struggle against the Assyrians.[a] If v. 6 envisages a previous campaign against Judah with Elamites taking part, it would have to be dated in the period of the neo-Babylonian kingdom. Assuming the unity of the oracle, the only possible occasion would be Nebuchadnezzar's campaign against Jerusalem in the year 597, since vv. 1f. are quite inappropriate to the situation following the fall of the city in 587. But there are considerable objections to any connection with the events of 597. After the king and his court had handed themselves over, and even if the deportation of the ruling class had not yet begun, nothing like the sentiments expressed here could have been expected. It seems impossible to adopt the other solution and interpret the whole poem as an eschatological prophecy, since the additions in vv. 9–11a must be treated as an early testimony to the fact that the oracle goes back to actual events. Thus we must accept that at least the basic substance of the text relates to the only possible remaining situation, that which existed after the siege of Jerusalem by the Assyrian King Sennacherib in the year 701, and to attribute it to Isaiah as its author.[b]

Even when vv. 9–11a have been excluded, it is extremely difficult to elucidate the growth of the oracle. Since v. 5 contains no indication of time, it is possible to understand it in a wholly eschatological sense. That it ought in fact to be so interpreted can be seen from the

[a] Cf. W. Hinz, *Das Reich Elam*, Stuttgart 1964, pp. 115ff., and J. A. Brinkman, 'Elamite Military Aid to Merodach-Baladan', *JNES* 24, 1965, pp. 161ff. Cf. also p. 124.

[b] It is not possible here to discuss the very different views of the unity and purpose of 22.1–14, but we should note that e.g. Duhm, Marti, Gray, Feldmann, Procksch, Fischer and Kissane regard 2bf. as referring to a future event, whereas e.g. Guthe, Ziegler, Fohrer, Donner, SVT 11, 1964, pp. 128f., and Eichrodt believe that it refers to a past event. Likewise, commentators differ as to whether vv. 5–7 look forward or back. B. S. Childs, *Isaiah and the Assyrian Crisis*, StBTh II, 3, 1967, p. 26, takes the statements as referring to the past, but considers it impossible to date them historically, although he recognizes that they assume a siege of Jerusalem and regards the whole poem as being by Isaiah. Note finally that H. L. Ginsberg, *M. M. Kaplan Jubilee Volume*, New York 1953, English Section, pp. 251f. and *JAOS* 88, 1968, p. 47, regards vv. 1–3 as a sarcastic word of comfort by Isaiah for an anticipated lament, and also sees v. 4 as a lament for what is to come.

gloss in v. 6a, which is borrowed from 21.9a. It is unlikely that vv. 7–8 and 11b were composed by Isaiah, particularly in view of v. 11b with its comment that the events which had come about were planned long ago by Yahweh. So vv. 7–11 represent a later exegesis carried out in the early post-exilic period, consisting of at least two steps, the second of which is to be found not only in vv. 9b–11a, but is already present in v. 9a, which should be regarded as an introduction to what follows. Although it is still impossible to be certain whether or not troops from Elam and Kir could have taken part in the siege of Jerusalem in 588/87, I hesitate to attribute vv. 5b and 6 to the same redactional stratum. Neither in v. 8 nor in v. 12 ought 'in that day' to be excluded from its context. On the other hand v. 14b is superfluous in its position following v. 14a and is certainly redactional. Thus the basic text going back to Isaiah is vv. 1b–4 and 12–14.

The first half is largely in the metre of the funeral lament (3+2), while the metrical form of the second half is more free. That this is no reason to subdivide the text further is clear from a single glance at 5.1–7. Note that the heading v. 1a, as in 21.1 and 13, takes a key-word from the oracle which follows, the expression 'valley of vision' in v. 5.

[1–4] *The untimely rejoicing of the inhabitants of Jerusalem.* The defeat of the great revolt against Assyria, which in the year 703 spread from the south to the south-west of the Assyrian empire,[a] reached a climax in 701 with the capitulation of Hezekiah in Jerusalem, which was besieged by the emperor's troops. We learn of this through II Kings 18.13ff. and especially from the annals of the Assyrian emperor Sennacherib.[b] Hezekiah lost a considerable part of his kingdom, which was divided between the kings of Ashdod, Ekron and Gaza.[c] He had to hand over his elite troops and also make large payments of money and goods from the temple treasury and the royal privy purse. Even princesses, women of the court, and male and female singers had to be handed over to Sennacherib and were carried off to Nineveh. But as often happens in history, the city, liberated from the rigours of war and the siege, was seized not by a serious attitude

---

[a] For the chronology of the events between 705 and 701 cf. S. Smith in *The Assyrian Empire*, CAH III, 1929 (1960), pp. 61ff. and 71ff., and J. Lewy, 'The Chronology of Sennacherib's Accession', *AnOr* 12, 1935, pp. 225f.

[b] *AOT*², pp. 352ff.; *AR* II, § 239f. cf. § 309ff., 326f. and 347; *ANET*², pp. 287f. and *TGI*², pp. 67ff.

[c] Cf. K. Elliger, *Kleine Schriften zum Alten Testament*, ThB 32, 1966, pp. 61ff.

of self-examination and repentance, but by the abandoned delight of those who had once again escaped. (There have been objections to the interpretation proposed here, but it is an attitude which from a psychological point of view is entirely comprehensible.)

One person stood aside from the universal joy, the prophet Isaiah. In the public hearing he sounded the notes of the lament for the dead, and reproachfully asked Jerusalem, personified as a virgin, the reason for this abandoned joy. For the inhabitants of Jerusalem, perhaps still ignorant of the full extent of the conditions of surrender, had climbed up on to the flat roofs of their houses, not in order to lament (cf. 15.3; Jer. 48.38 and II Sam. 16.22) but in order to express their joy at the withdrawal of the enemy and their own survival. Anyone who has ever experienced the activity in the evening in the streets of an oriental or Mediterranean city would realize that Isaiah is not exaggerating when in v. 2a he describes Jerusalem as a city full of shouting (cf. Zech. 4.7), tumult and exultation (cf. also 5.14; 32.13 and Zeph. 2.15; Isa. 23.7).

The description which follows in vv. 2b and 3 is not of a future catastrophe, which is not prophesied until v. 14, but looks back upon events during the siege. The mention of the siege is meant to remind Isaiah's hearers how inappropriate their attitude is. Are they rejoicing because of the shameful death of the soldiers and the cowardly flight of their leaders? Anyone who had met his death in the previous weeks of fighting around Jerusalem had not fallen in battle but had been seized while fleeing from the besieged city and executed, to the horror of those who remained, and with the intention of making them realize that surrender was the only way out (cf. Num. 19.17; Lam. 4.9 and Ezek. 32. 17ff.).[a] No one who tried to flee, whether across the Jordan to the Ammonites and Moabites or through the hills of Judah and the Arabah to the Edomites (cf. II Kings 25.5; Jer. 40.11), succeeded in escaping: the officers and other dignitaries[b] who tried to flee had to surrender without a struggle.[c] However far anyone had

---

[a] Cf. O. Eissfeldt, *Kl. Schriften* III, Tübingen 1966, pp. 6ff.

[b] The concrete meaning of *qāṣîn*, leader, depends upon the context. In Josh. 10.24 it means e.g. a military leader, in Isa. 1.10; 3.6f. the magistrates, cf. H. Wildberger, BK 10.1, 1965, p. 37. Here it may refer to leaders from both spheres.

[c] The word *miqqešet*, 'without a bow' has often been regarded as difficult and has led to proposed emendations. It may be, as Feldmann thinks, that the leaders allowed themselves to be taken captive without those who captured them needing to shoot a single arrow.

gone, he was taken by his pursuers and brought back in chains, either to die by the executioner's sword or to be deported to Assyria. In other words, the military defeat in the besieged city was complete. The situation was in fact as Sennacherib describes it, 'himself (Hezekiah) I shut in like a caged bird in his capital Jerusalem. I threw up entrenchments against him. I made it hard for him to go out of the gate of his city.'[a]

[4] The prophet's demand that they should look away from him (cf. Job 7.19; 14.6) and leave him undisturbed to his bitter sorrow, for which the reasons were deeper than those around him could yet know, and to abandon any attempt to comfort him, is not meant to be realistic but must be understood against the background of the formal language of the funeral lament. It is not a real rejection of people who are trying to comfort the distressed prophet, but a way of emphasizing the vastness of the misfortune, the full extent of which he does not believe the inhabitants of Jerusalem can yet understand. In place of the assurance in a lament that no one is there to comfort the mourner (cf. Lam. 1.2, 16, 21; 2.9) we have here the rejection of potential comforters. The attention of the hearers is drawn even more firmly to what Isaiah still has to say about the fate of the people of the southern kingdom, who are poetically described as 'the daughter of my people' (cf. Jer. 8.11; Lam. 2.11; 3.48; Isa. 47.1; also Amos 5.2 and Micah 1.8).

[12–14] *The unforgivable guilt.* The real depth of the prophet's grief was brought about not so much by what had just happened, but by his knowledge of what was irrevocably destined for his people, because they had failed to hear the voice of their almighty God who had spoken to them in the defeat they had just suffered.[b] By these blows God sought to call them to repentance, but instead they gave themselves up to the joys of the moment. They were not expressing by weeping, mourning, shaving the hair upon their head and girding themselves with the sack, a coarse skirt woven of goat or camel hair,[c] their grief and penitence[d] at their dismissal of the warnings of judgment which Yahweh had given them previously through Isaiah (cf. 30.1ff.; 30.15ff.; 31.1ff.; 30.8ff.; 28.7ff.). Instead of seeking God's

---

[a] Translation based on R. Borger, *TGI*[2], p. 69.

[b] For Yahweh Sebaoth, cf. my commentary on 6.3 (*Isaiah 1–12*, OTL, 1972, *ad loc.*) and 13.4.

[c] Cf. G. Fohrer, *BHW* III, col. 1638.

[d] Cf. F. Nötscher, *Biblische Altertumskunde*, Bonn 1940, pp. 93ff.

pardon in this way, they were giving themselves up to abandoned joy, had slaughtered cattle, goats and sheep, and were eating and drinking as at a joyful festival (cf. Deut. 16.2; Luke 15.23ff.; Job 1.13). By contrast to our own dining customs, the unusual feature is not the drinking of wine but the eating of meat (cf. Lam. 2.12). The words placed in the mouth of the carousers, 'Let us eat and drink, for tomorrow we die,' which the apostle Paul takes up in I Cor. 15.32, may be a quotation from a drinking song like those known to us from Egyptian tombs. Thus one of these harper's songs reads:

> Celebrate a joyful day, noble one!
> Forget all evil and think of joy,
> Until the day comes [when you disembark
> In the country which loves silence.][a]

The idea of enjoying life to the full because death is coming for certain is common to all mankind. The following verse of Alcaeus had been preserved:

> It is ill yielding the heart to mischance, for we shall make no advance if we weary of thee, O Bacchus, and the best medicine is to call for wine and drink deep.[b]

But Isaiah is of a different opinion. For him the attitude of the inhabitants of Jerusalem is iniquitous, because it does not take account of God as the lord of history, who is seeking to guide men by the blows which strike them to repent and to remember him and his demands. If they do not remember him, and fail to hear the call of God which comes to them in the disaster, he will strike them once again for the last time. Thus the words of Yahweh, the lord of reality, ring in Isaiah's ears (cf. 5.9) and he hears the solemn oath that the wickedness of their unwillingness to repent, and the guilt that results, will only be atoned for by death; that is, it will be objectively wiped out.[c] In other words, for Isaiah the events of the year 701 are no more than a preliminary to the final catastrophe which is to fall upon the southern kingdom, because its people have not seized their last chance of turning to him who has smitten them (cf. 9.12).

---

[a] S. Schott, *Altägyptische Liebeslieder*, Zürich 1950, p. 134.

[b] Alcaeus, no. 158 in J. Edmonds (ed.), *Lyra Graeca* I (Loeb Classical Library), London 1922, p. 416. Cf. also Horace *Carm.* II. 3, and the often quoted '*Carpe diem*', I. 11.

[c] For *kpr*, cover, atone, cf. F. Maass, *THAT* I, col. 845.

[1–4 +12–14] Formally, the oracle consists of a prophecy of judgment on a similar pattern, in which vv. 1–4 and 12–13 form the reproach or accusation and v. 14 the warning or judgment.

[7–8 +11b] *Preoccupation with the present moment.* As we begin our exposition, let us recall once again the difficulty of an analysis of vv. 5–11 by literary criticism. We cautiously accepted that in substance there are three post-Isaianic additions. In our view, the words 'And it came about' begin the contribution of the first interpolator. In the spirit of his great predecessor, he affirms that the people of Jerusalem, faced with the approaching Babylonians, have not thought of Yahweh and the destruction of the city which Isaiah prophesied, and repented accordingly, but are relying upon its fortifications. After the fall of the city in the midsummer of 587, he hoped to bring the survivors to recognize the hand of Yahweh in the catastrophe that had come upon them.

By the choice, fruitful valleys he is presumably referring to the eastern end of the valley of Hinnom (cf. Josh. 15.8; II Kings 23.10; Neh. 11.30; also II Kings 25.4)[a] and the plains of Rephaim (cf. Josh. 15.8; II Sam. 5.18; Isa. 17.5).[b] While the chariots and baggage vehicles of the Babylonians were drawing near, the cavalry vanguard was already establishing positions at the gate, in order to make sure that the besiegers could advance unhindered. In the hour of danger the eyes of the people of Jerusalem turned to the palace, which is called here only the 'House of the Forest of Lebanon'. It covered a greater area than the Temple of Solomon, and seems in fact to have been an audience building for the public activities of the king.[c] Since the golden shields placed there by Solomon were either used for the purposes of public audience or were specially reserved as part of the royal treasure (cf. I Kings 10.17 and 14.26f.) the House of the Forest should not be thought of as originally an arsenal. It is possible that king Jehoiakim replaced the palace of Solomon by another and used the former palace for a different purpose (cf. Jer. 22.13f.). Or again, at the same time as Zedekiah renounced his vassalege to Nebuchadnezzar he may have set up an arsenal there. Be this as it may, the people of Jerusalem relied upon their king's armaments instead of recognizing the hand of Yahweh behind the encroaching danger.

[a] Cf. J. Simons, *The Geographical and Topographical Texts of the Old Testament*, Leiden 1959, § 36, and H. Kosmala, *BHW* II, col. 723.

[b] Cf. Simons, § 211 and G. Sauer, *BHW* III, col. 1590.

[c] Cf. I Kings 7.2ff. and M. Noth, BK 9.1, 1968, pp. 137f.

They did not recall that long ago, through Isaiah, he had given a warning of the coming catastrophe which had power to bring it about (cf. 5.1ff.; 5.8f., 11ff. and Micah 3.12).[a]

[8a] Verse 8a is somewhat enigmatic and may be a gloss by a later reader. It is not clear who took away the covering of Judah and what is meant by this expression. Because the verb is in the singular, the subject is more likely to be Yahweh than the enemy. The covering presumably means the protection which he had previously given to the southern kingdom (cf. Ps. 105.39 and Isa. 4.5f.) or else the covering of the nakedness of the virgin Judah which has been removed, so that she is now the object of open contempt.[b]

[9–11a] *The defence measures taken by the people of Jerusalem.* Either on the basis of his own experience or of oral tradition, the reader, probably still living in the sixth century, has added a list of the measures taken to strengthen the defences as the Babylonian army approached in the year 588. Because of the long siege that was expected, not only had the walls to be firm but a sufficient water supply had to be ensured. On the inspection of the walls of the city of David, which seems to have lain on the south-eastern hill (cf. II Sam. 5.7, 9; I Kings 2.10),[c] breaches were found. This may be associated with the prohibition made by Nebuchadnezzar round about 597 of any repairs to the walls or the restoration of the defences of the city to a state in which they could be used against him. As an emergency measure, the houses of Jerusalem were counted, and then, in spite of the expected arrival of refugees from the countryside and the suburbs of Jerusalem that lay outside the walls, all that could be dispensed with were torn down. This was the quickest way to obtain the stones which were then used to repair and strengthen the walls. Considerable remains of the eastern wall of Jerusalem from the days of Zedekiah have recently been discovered.[d]

---

[a] Cf. my comment on 9.7, *Isaiah 1–12*, p. 130.

[b] Feldmann rightly points out that 'covering' never refers to clothing. But cf. nevertheless Gen. 20.16. Though Eichrodt, referring to 25.7, sees it as the averting of danger, we must note with Feldmann that in spite of its skilful measures Judah remained blind to Yahweh.

[c] Cf. Noth, p. 32. The frequent assertion that Jerusalem was of 'minimal size' in the period of the kings, cf. H. Kosmala, *BHW* II, col. 839, can no longer be maintained in this form since the excavations by N. Avigad, *IEJ* 20, 1970, pp. 1ff. and 129ff.

[d] Cf. K. M. Kenyon, *Royal Cities of the Old Testament,* London and New York

The fact that both v. 9b and v. 11a speak of ensuring the water supply does not indicate the work of different editors, for there seems to be an attempt to produce a parallel structure: 'Walls – water – walls – water'. The 'Lower Pool' is now generally identified with the *birket el-ḥamra* about 200 metres (218 yards) below the pool of Siloah.[a] Its name clearly contrasts it with the 'Upper Pool' mentioned in II Kings 18.17 (Isa. 36.7) and Isa. 7.3, which some have sought in north of the city,[b] and others in the immediate neighbourhood of the spring Gihon,[c] but which in any case cannot be identified with the predecessor of the present pool at the outlet of the Siloah channel constructed by Hezekiah.[d] If the 'old pool' can be identified with the Lower Pool,[e] we must suppose that an additional cistern was constructed below the *birket el-ḥamra*.[f] If, however, it is to be sought in the north of the city and identified with the Upper Pool, then we must think of it as a cistern constructed at the end of the central valley, between the two walls which are also mentioned in II Kings 25.4.[g] It is quite possible that vv. 9b and 11a referred to an associated operation, as appears at first sight, since the same procedure is observed in strengthening the walls. In this addition, almost scholarly in the impression it gives, the redactor was trying to make even more evident the distance between what the inhabitants of Jerusalem were doing and what according to v. 11b they ought to have been doing.

[5–6] *The coming day of Yahweh.* While we repeat our reminder that the literary criticism of vv. 5–11 is extremely difficult, and that there is particular uncertainty about where v. 6 belongs, we conclude our exposition of this difficult passage with a commentary on what in our view is its most recent stratum. If our arguments above are correct, vv. 5 and 6 are the attempt of a proto-apocalyptic writer to make the ancient prophecy of Isaiah a reality to his own community, by an

---

1971, p. 147; but it is essential to consult Avigad for the extension of the city west of the temple precinct, pp. 129ff.

  [a] Cf. M. Burrows, *ZAW* 70, 1958, pp. 222f.

  [b] Cf. J. Simons, *Jerusalem in the Old Testament*, Leiden 1952, pp. 334ff. and Donner, SVT 11, pp. 10f.

  [c] Cf. L.-H. Vincent and M.-A. Steve, *Jérusalem de l'Ancien Testament* I, Paris 1954, p. 295.

  [d] Cf. also Kenyon, pp. 137ff. and PEQ 97, 1965, p. 15.

  [e] Vincent and Steve, p. 295.

  [f] Unfortunately the position concerning the tunnel system south-east of the *birket el-ḥamra*, cf. PEQ 97, 1965, pp. 16f., is still not clear.

  [g] Cf. Avi-Yonah in Burrows, p. 223.

eschatological interpretation, in spite of the historicizing additions to it which relate it to the events of the year 587. The judgment of Yahweh upon Jerusalem first proclaimed by Isaiah and fulfilled in 587, will not be the last. In the final defeat of all the powers on this earth which are hostile to God there will once again be a visitation of Jerusalem, which, in spite of the final liberation which is not mentioned here (cf. 29.1ff.; 30.27ff.), will be no less terrible than that in the past (cf. also 28.14ff. and Zech. 14.1ff.). In the expected day of Yahweh, which will decide the fate of Jerusalem and of the nations,[a] the army of the nations will gather before its gates (cf. v. 7), and by contrast to the present careless rejoicing in the city (cf. v. 2) there will be a violent tumultuous confusion (cf. Ezek. 7.7; Isa. 17.12 and Ps. 46.7), consisting of nations which trample everything down (cf. 18.2), making the inhabitants helpless with dismay (cf. Micah 7.4). In the valley mysteriously referred to as the 'valley of vision', presumably to be identified with that of the Benē Hinnom,[b] the startling cry of the attackers (or the pursued?) rings out, so that the cries for help of the inhabitants, so suddenly overpowered, are carried up to the hill on which the city is built. The Babylonians who by this time have been destroyed themselves (cf. 13–14 and 21.1ff.) are replaced by the distant Elamites and people of Kir, the former with the quiver in their hands to send a rain of arrows upon everything visible before the city and upon its walls, and the latter advancing to the attack with the protective covers removed from their shields.[c] It is the intention of the proto-apocalyptic writer to understand vv. 1–3 also as a prophecy of this final day of judgment which is to come. Since its coming is certain, it is now time for the people of Jerusalem to repent and humbly trust in Yahweh's help.[d]

[1–14] The inclusion of 22.1–14 among the oracles against foreign nations assumes that the proto-apocalyptic redaction has already taken place. With its intermingling of recollections of the events of 587 and the anticipation of the coming day of Yahweh, this text is further evidence of the way in which, in the post-exilic period, the eschatological expectations of Judaism were created in the process of coming to terms with the catastrophic experience of the fall of Jerusalem.

[a] Cf. my commentary on 13.6.
[b] Cf. above on v. 7.
[c] Cf. Aristophanes, *Acharnians* 582 and 1136.
[d] Cf. Ezek. 9.

CHAPTER 22.15–25

Sayings against Individual Court Officials

15bβ Against Shebna, the chamberlain.

15   Thus says ⟨   ⟩ᵃ Yahweh Sebaoth;
      Come, go to this steward!

16   What have you here and whom have you here,
      that you have hewn a tomb for yourself,
      you who hew a tomb on the height,
      and carve a habitation for yourself in the rock?ᵇ

17   Behold, Yahweh will shake you out,
      ⟨as one shakes out a garment⟩ᶜ
      and rids oneself vigorously of lice!

18   He will roll you up into a little ball,
      like a ball
      into a wide and broad land.
      Die there!
      Away there with your ceremonial chariots,
      You shame of your master's house!

19   *I will thrust you from your office,*
      and ⟨cast you down⟩ᵈ from your station.

20   In that day it will come about;
      I will call my servant,
      Eliakim, the son of Hilkiah,

21   and clothe him with your robe,
      and bind round him your girdle,
      and commit your authority into his hand;
      and he shall be a father
      to the inhabitants of Jerusalem
      and to the house of Judah.

ᵃ Cf. *BHS.*

ᵇ For the *yod-compaginis* cf. G-K, § 90m; for the construction cf. G-K, § 144p.

ᶜ Read with H. L. Ginsberg, *JBL* 69, 1950, pp. 55f. and G. R. Driver, *JSS* 23, 1968, pp. 48f. *kᵉṭalṭēlā beged.* M arose by a haplography of the *k*, a metathesis of *g* and *b*, and the confusion of *d* and *r*. For the meaning of *ṭwl*, pilpel, we must accept 'shake out' by analogy with Jewish-Aramaic. Otherwise Marti's objection to the present text remains unanswered: if *ṭalṭēl* means 'to throw far away' or the like, we must pass straight from v. 17a to v. 18a and delete what comes between as a disruptive addition. To justify the confusion by the prophet's excitement would be to overlook both the distance in time between the receiving of the word and its utterance, and between utterance and commitment to writing.

ᵈ Cf. *BHS.*

22 And I will place the key
   of the house of David on his shoulder.
   He shall open, and none shall shut,
   he shall close, and none shall open,
23 I shall fasten him like a tent-peg,
   in a firm place,
   and he will be a throne of honour
   to his father's house.

24 And they will hang on him the whole weight of his father's house, the shoots and the leaves, every small vessel, from the cups to all the flagons. [25]In that day, is the saying of Yahweh Sebaoth, the peg that was fastened in a sure place will give way; and it will break and fall, and the burden that was upon it will be cut off, for Yahweh has spoken.

This text too faces the reader with a whole series of problems. Should he regard the whole of it, or at least vv. 15–23, as composed by Isaiah?[a] Or should he accept that it was composed in at least three stages, of which only the first, to be found in vv. 15–18, goes back to Isaiah, whereas vv. 19–23, and particularly the last two prose verses, 24–25 are later additions?[b] Does the heading now occurring awkwardly at the end of v. 15 and giving the impression of being originally a marginal gloss, correctly name the person to whom vv. 15–18 are addressed, or is it the result of a láter speculation based on II Kings 18.18 and its parallel in Isa. 36.3, either interpreting vv. 19–23 or perhaps even giving rise to them? And why did the prophet so passionately attack the court official? Was it simply his desire for status, expressed in the carving out of a tomb in the rock, and regarded by the prophet as so unseemly, or were there reasons of internal and external politics? Our exposition will show that the text gives rise to even more questions. Our reasons for regarding the whole passage as having come into being over a lengthy period are these. Verse 19 goes back behind v. 18b, and whereas throughout vv. 17 and 18 Yahweh is spoken of in the third person, in vv. 19–23 he is

---

[a] 22.15–25 are regarded as Isaianic by e.g. Dillmann-Kittel, Hans Schmidt, Kissane and perhaps also Eichrodt; 22.15–23 at least are ascribed to the prophet by Feldmann, Procksch, Hertzberg, Fischer, E. Jenni, *Die politischen Voraussagen der Propheten*, AThANT 29, 1956, pp. 42ff. (assuming that 22.20–23 was first an anonymous eschatological prophecy in contrast to 22.15–18), Steinmann and R. Martin-Achard, 'L'oracle contre Shebna et le pouvoir des clefs', *ThZ* 24, 1968, pp. 241ff.

[b] Cf. Duhm, Cheyne, Marti, Gray, Guthe and Fohrer, *ad loc.*

always the subject, in the first person; for it would not have been possible for the prophet to speak of Eliakim as his servant or to take it upon himself to intervene directly in the staffing of the royal court. Thus it will be clear that we regard vv. 19–23 as the first addition, which was then followed by the prose of vv. 24–25.

[15–18] *Against the arrogance of a court official.* In vv. 15–18 we have a prophecy of warning and judgment, together with a reason, which is extraordinarily dramatic in its language, and directed against a Jerusalem court official who is not named. In strict formal terms it must be described as the commissioning of a messenger. It is possible that it originally began with v. 15b ('Come, go to this steward. . . .'), with the words 'and say to him' following immediately. The formula of the prophetic message, 'Thus says Yahweh Sebaoth' would then have formed the direct introduction to the reproach or accusation which states the reason for the warning or judgment in the two verses that follow.[a] We can assume that the prophet carried out the task given to him and met the high official face to face. The word 'here' in v. 16 suggests that the encounter took place outside the city beside the grave, which was perhaps not yet finished, on one of the slopes east of the valley of Kidron, though we cannot be quite certain about this. Of course the question at once arises, whether we should follow the gloss in identifying the owner of the grave with Shebna, who according to II Kings 18.18 and the parallel passage in Isa. 36.3 is described as a *sōpēr*, a 'scribe'. That is, his office as the head of the royal chancellery had a position similar to that of a present-day secretary of state.[b] In these passages, however, he is listed in the second position after Eliakim, the son of Hilkiah, who is there given the title ascribed here to Shebna, that of the *'ašer 'al-habbajit*, one 'who is over the house', the chamberlain, who in addition to the administration of the palace and the royal domains seems to have taken on in the course of time a position comparable at least to that of the Egyptian vizier.[c] Assuming as correct the identification of the

[a] For the literary form cf. also C. Westermann, *Grundformen prophetischer Rede*, BevTh 31, 1960, pp. 101f.

[b] Cf. R. de Vaux, 'Titres et fonctionnaires égyptiens à la cour de David et de Salomon', *RB* 48, 1939, pp. 397ff.; J. Begrich, '*Sōfēr* and *Mazkir*' (1940): *Gesammelte Studien zum Alten Testament*, ThB 21, 1964, pp. 67ff.

[c] Cf. M. Noth, *ZDPV* 50, 1927, p. 217, repr. *Aufsätze zur biblischen Landes-und Altertumskunde* I, Neukirchen 1971, p. 163; de Vaux, pp. 400ff. and H. J. Katzenstein, 'The Royal Steward', *IEJ* 10, 1960, pp. 149ff.

sōkēn, 'steward', here with Shebna as chamberlain, attributing it to a disciple of Isaiah, and with the aid of conjectural harmonizations of II Kings 18.18 and the present text, some commentators have concluded that Shebna first replaced Eliakim and then, perhaps in fact under the influence of the prophet, was reduced from the first to the second position at court. In order to explain this, it is further necessary to assume that the two officials adopted a different approach to the foreign policy of Judah. Shebna, it is suggested, was in favour of a pro-Egyptian and anti-Assyrian policy, while Eliakim followed the prophet in favouring a more cautious policy, looking forward to a change brought about by Yahweh, in the fortunes of the Assyrian vassal state of Judah. Against this is the fact that we in fact meet Eliakim in the office of chamberlain during the revolt against Assyria in the year 703–701, if we can assume that II Kings 18.18 is reliable in this respect. Finally, it is assumed in support of this hypothesis that to address the official as *sōkēn*, 'steward', itself expresses contempt. But although the word 'this' which follows it in Hebrew seems to be perjorative in intention, as in 7.4 and 8.6, this is not sufficient in itself to show that the title, which is not found elsewhere in the Old Testament, but for which there is direct evidence not only in its Accadian equivalent, but also in Ugaritic, Phoenician and Punic texts, and which is usually translated 'governor',[a] is to be taken in a derogatory sense here. If it is possible to conclude, from the fact that it was possible to speak in Ugarit of the *skn* without naming him, that there was only one person who bore that title at any one time,[b] the same could be true of Jerusalem. We must remember that the information which we have in the Old Testament about positions at court and those who occupied them has reached us very much by chance. Thus it is quite possible that in Isaiah's time, to which we attribute 22.15–18 for lack of sufficient reason to the contrary, there may also have been a 'governor' who had certain particular duties in the administration of Jerusalem or Judah. On the other hand, it is

[a] Cf. the occurrences in J. Hoftijzer, *Dictionnaire des inscriptions sémitiques de l'ouest*, Leiden 1965, p. 193, sub voce *skn*; the inscriptions *KAI* no. 1.2; 31.1, 2 and the arguments in J. Aistleitner, *Wörterbuch der ugaritischen Sprache*, SAL 106. 3, 1963, p. 220 no. 1909, and also in *PRU* III, 1955, p. 235; IV, 1956, p. 262; VI, 1970, p. 151; II, 1957, p. 212; V, 1965, p. 161 and p. 202. – For *sokenet* in I Kings 1.2. and 4 now cf. M. J. Mulder, *VT* 22, 1972, who rejects the usual translation 'nurse' and regards it as a female equivalent of *skn*, so that it would have to be translated 'deputy' (i.e. of the aged king).

[b] A. Alt, 'Hohe Beamte in Ugarit', *Kl. Schriften* III, Munich 1959, p. 194.

possible that a later reader applied this word to Shebna, and at the same time found in the following passage an allusion to Eliakim, being inspired in both cases by their mention in II Kings 18.18 and the parallel in Isa. 36.3.[a]

Since an inscription has been found on a grave in *silwān* (now on display in the British Museum) which describes as the owner of the grave a chamberlain, of whose name unfortunately only the final element, containing the divine name Yahweh, has been preserved, and since an attempt has been made to identify with him the Shebna of this passage,[b] we must add a further comment. The assumption in the identification of this unknown chamberlain with Shebna is that the name Shebna was a short form, e.g. for the *šᵉbanyāh(ū)* found in Neh. 9.4 and 10.5. In theory this is possible.[c] But the proposal has also been made to fill the gap in the inscription by *hilq* and to read *hilqiyyāhū*, so that it would be the grave of the father of Eliakim.[d] But the inscription cannot be dated with certainty to the period round about 700. It may be later, so that the grave may have belonged to a later chamberlain of the king of Judah, completely unknown to us.[e] Finally, as we have shown, it is far from certain that the *sōkēn* here was a chamberlain. Thus the grave in *silwān*, which was carefully marked out from the surrounding rocks, and consisted of a chamber hewn into the stone and a rectangular doorway, no doubt originally fitted with a fine stone door, and possessed a false window with a small rectangular hole for light and air, gives us only an impression of how we are to think of the official's grave.[f]

When all these hypotheses have been dealt with, the interpretation of the prophecy of warning is no easier. [15] It is clearly important to

[a] Cf. below on vv. 19–23.

[b] Published by N. Avigad, 'The Epitaph of a Royal Steward', *IEJ* 3, 1953, pp. 137ff. (cf. *KAI* no. 191), who on pp. 150f. recalls and discusses a similar proposed addition by Y. Yadin. Is this the gravestone from the time of Uzziah near Jerusalem with the name Shebaniah, mentioned by Eichrodt, p. 100? Martin-Achard, p. 247, advises caution.

[c] See for an argument in this direction M. Noth, *Die israelitischen Personennamen*, Stuttgart 1928, no. 1302 and 1303, with a comment on p. 38. – De Vaux, p. 400, admits that this is undoubtedly possible, but argues for the derivation from the Egyptian name *šbnw* (H. Ranke, *Die aegyptischen Personennamen*, 1938, p. 325 notes 11 and 12).

[d] Katzenstein, p. 153.

[e] Cf. H. Donner, *KAI* II, Wiesbaden, 1964, p. 189.

[f] Cf. the plans in Avigad, pp. 138f. and plate 11; for the type of grave at this period cf. also D. Ussishkin, *PEQ* 103, 1971, pp. 101f. with fig. 4.

Isaiah that his readers, like the steward, should be in no doubt that he has come out to meet the powerful official not on his own initiative and because of his own antipathy to him, but because he is carrying out a direct command from God.[a] If, as we have suggested above, he spoke his words to the official in the name of Yahweh Sebaoth, he no doubt intended to remind him that over him who was powerful there was one more powerful still.[b] The command rather gives the impression that it came upon the prophet with great suddenness. It breathes a passion which is maintained to the end of the prophecy. The word *bō'*, which we translate 'go', can be more accurately rendered 'go in'. Thus we must assume that Isaiah sought out the official either in his palace or in fact up the hillside in his tomb, where he would have wished to supervise the work.

[16] The reproach contained in v. 16 is not immediately comprehensible to us. Why should a man who possesses the means not prepare a fine grave on the rocky slopes outside the city, and indeed allow himself at the last to be cast into the pit for common people (cf. II Kings 23.6 and Jer. 26.23)? The prophet's angry double question challenges the official's right to such a grave in the rock. The suggestion that the cause lies only in the man's humble origin, and in his being regarded as a mere parvenu, does not really seem to do justice to the angry tone of the question and the concluding charge that he is shaming his master (cf. v. 18b). Even if it were considered possible that the prophet, who elsewhere takes a stand on behalf of the rights of the poor and oppressed, also possessed certain class prejudices, a more thoroughgoing interpretation is necessary. Perhaps the most likely is that the double question is posed to a foreigner who had no real claim on the people and the country.[c] But it is also necessary to assume that for Isaiah the news of the construction of the grave is only the final act on the part of a man whose attitude and conduct in office he rejected. A word of God came to the prophet, probably like lightning, as far as his subjective

---

[a] But cf. below and, for the associated theological problem O. Kaiser, 'Wort des Propheten and Wort Gottes', *Tradition und Situation. Festschrift A. Weiser*, Göttingen 1963, pp. 83ff.

[b] For Yahweh Sebaoth cf. my commentary on 6.3 (*Isaiah 1–12*, OTL, 1972, *ad loc.*) and 13.4.

[c] So too de Vaux, p. 400. The possibility that the reference throughout may be to a Persian resident in Jerusalem, in which case the prophecy as a whole would be post-exilic, should at least be discussed. But in view of v. 18aγ pre-exilic composition seems more likely.

experience was concerned, but we must assume that his mind was in
some way prepared for it. What was it in the foreigner which had
disturbed Isaiah? Was it merely his ostentation, his liking for showing
himself to the inhabitants of Jerusalem in a ceremonial chariot, or
were there more serious charges in the background? If we examine
the text itself once again, the most we can discover is that according
to v. 17 Isaiah regarded the 'governor' as a louse on his people's skin.
Was he then one of those who by 'iniquitous degrees' and 'regulations
of suffering' (cf. 10.1), perhaps by the introduction of a new land
law which was to the disadvantage of the poor,ᵃ was dishonestly
lining his own pocket? The text itself gives no indication which part
of Isaiah's career it belongs to. We cannot be sure, from its insertion
after 22.1–14, that it comes from the period around 701. Isaiah's
passionate feeling can be detected, but the reason for it is lost in the
mists of time.

[17] Whereas the 'governor' feels himself extraordinarily secure
in Jerusalem and unassailable in his office, Isaiah regards him as in
Yahweh's eyes no more than a louse, which one tries to shake out of
one's clothes. Yahweh will seize him like a little ball quickly rolled
together from scraps of cloth, and hurl him far out of Jerusalem into
a 'doubly wide' land, that is, a country spreading out in both directions, by which perhaps Assyria may be intended. The official who
imagines himself so secure here will one day have to go into exile, to
die there far from his honoured grave. And the same will be true of
the things of which he is now so proud. They too will be carried off
into the far country as the victor's booty. What Isaiah thinks of the
man who drives about in the ceremonial chariot he tells him once
again to his face, directly insulting him: he is in fact a shame upon
the house of his master. He does not bring his king honour, as one
ought to expect of a reliable minister, but shame.

It may be that as far as its content is concerned the oracle has little
to offer us. But we must be thankful for the fact that the tradition has
preserved it for us, because it further enriches our picture of the

---

ᵃ Cf. my commentary on 10.4 (*Isaiah 1–12*, OTL, *ad loc.*) and for the problem,
which was particularly pressing at that time, see later H. Donner, 'Die soziale
Botschaft der Propheten im Lichte der Gesellschaftsordnung in Israel', *OrAnt* 2,
1963, pp. 229ff.; O. Kaiser, 'Gerechtigkeit und Heil bei den israelitischen Propheten und griechischen Denkern des 8.–6. Jahrhunderts', *NZSTh* 11, 1969, pp.
312ff. and K. Koch, 'Die Entstehung der sozialen Kritik bei den Profeten',
Probleme biblischer Theologie. Festschrift G. von Rad, Neukirchen 1971, pp. 236ff.

career of the prophet Isaiah. The prophet did not appear only before his people as a whole, gathered in the sanctuary, or, as the secondary tradition tells us, before their kings, but also before individuals, in order to hold up to them the mirror of the truth of God, in which man is bound to see himself very poorly reflected. It is only natural that we should not only like to have more exact details of the reasons for this severe condemnation of the official, but also to learn how he received the prophecy, whether he laughed at the fanatic, had him whipped or left him unmolested as God's fool. But we would have to go on from exposition to free invention, which no doubt has a right to fill the gap.

[19–23] *The servant of Yahweh.* Verse 19 clearly forms a literary link between the prophecy of warning (vv. 15–18) and the investiture oracle (vv. 20–23). The question of its origin is linked with our view of the true meaning of vv. 20–23. According to v. 20b it refers to the chamberlain Eliakim, the son of Hilkiah, whom we know from II Kings 18.18 (Isa. 36.3) and II Kings 19.2 (Isa. 37.2). If we assume that v. 20b is original, then it is necessary to date the oracle in a time in which the office of chamberlain was filled, if not by Eliakim himself, at least by his progeny. In this case the identification of the *sōkēn*, the steward or deputy, in v. 16 with Shebna would then have led, at the latest in a second stage, to this oracle emphasizing God's approval of the exercise of the office by Eliakim's descendants. Although it is not certain, it is probable that what according to our other sources was the highest office at the court of Jerusalem was to some extent hereditary. One piece of evidence in support of this is the fact that the governor Gedaliah, appointed by Nebuchadnezzar after the conquest of Jerusalem in 587 (cf. II Kings 25.22 and Jer. 40f.), is identical with the chamberlain Gedaliah to whom a seal found in Lachish, and attributable to the late period of the kings, bears witness; his grandfather was the *sōpēr*, the secretary of state Shaphan (cf. II Kings 22.8), and his father was Ahikam who, since he is mentioned before *his* father Shaphan in II Kings 22.12 may very well have been chamberlain.[a] Finally, it is also interesting in this context that Eliakim, whose name we find on an impression taken from a seal, seems to have administered the properties of King Johoiachin even after the latter had been deported.[b]

[a] Cf. Katzenstein, pp. 135f.

[b] Cf. W. F. Albright, 'The Seal of Eliakim and the Latest Pre-exilic History of Judah', *JBL* 51, 1932, pp. 71ff.

However, to suppose that a prophecy in favour of a long dead contemporary of Isaiah and another against him should have been first composed in post-exilic times is a conclusion of despair, and highly improbable from a historical point of view, unless it were meant to refer to an Eliakim *redivivus*, a chamberlain who would return in the time of salvation. On the other hand, if the oracle in vv. 20–23 originally referred to an anonymous figure, it is quite comprehensible that in the course of the identification of the *sōkēn*, the steward, with Shebna and the servant with Eliakim, a procedure which is reminiscent of the composition of the headings to the Psalms, the length of time the office had been obsolete and perhaps certain rivalries about which we know nothing among the ancient families of Jerusalem should have led to the addition of vv. 24–25, so completing the chapter. This would also mean that v. 19 was a product of this historicizing redaction, because it also reads the replacement of Shebna by Eliakim into the text that follows. In our view, Jenni rightly recognized that in vv. 20–23 we have an eschatological figure, but he was unable to make full use of his realization because he accepted that Isaiah was the author of the passage.[a] In spite of the connections between the investiture oracle and the figure of a vizier such as is portrayed in the story of Joseph, we must not overlook the similarity between the ideas it contains and messianic prophecies such as Isa. 9.1–6 and Zech. 3.1ff.; 6.9ff., and even the servant songs, Isa. 42.1ff. and 49.1ff.

[20] With the favourite formula of introduction for additions with an eschatological content, a devout writer living well into the post-exilic period, or even in the Hellenistic period, and looking forward to the coming of the Messianic age after the fall of the foreign nations, begins his prophecy of salvation. Because of its content it can best be described as an investiture or inauguration oracle. The 'steward' or 'deputy' in v. 15 is presumably for him the representative of the foreign power.[b] When he is driven out of Jerusalem by Yahweh, and the kingdom of peace of the king from the line of David is set up there, this king, like his predecessors in the past and all the great ones

---

[a] *Ibid.*, pp. 43ff.

[b] For the Persian province of Judah cf. U. Kellermann, *Nehemia. Quellen, Überlieferüng und Geschichte*, BZAW 102, 1967, pp. 159ff. During the Ptolemaic period of hyparchy of Judaea would have had a *hyparchos* or *oikonomos*, cf. M. Hengel, *Judentum und Hellenismus*, WUNT 10, 1969, pp. 36f.

of the earth, will have a court, headed by a deputy or vizier, whose qualities must correspond to those of the coming prince of peace. Thus 'in that day' (cf. 10.27; 11.11; 24.21; 27.12, 13),[a] after the fall of the governor imposed by the foreign king (cf. 9.1ff. and Zech. 12.7),[b] Yahweh will himself call to this office a man submissive and obedient to him, his servant (cf. Num. 12.7 and Isa. 42.1).[c] [21] He will bestow upon him the signs of his dignity: the long tunic with half sleeves[d] and the girdle which gathers it about the waist, a garment[e] similar to that worn by the priests (cf. Lev. 8.13). For him to bind the girdle firmly round the man he has chosen expresses the fact that he is permanently investing him and his descendants with the office.[f] The investiture precedes the formal handing over of the power of office,[g] which presumably took place by means of a formula of institution (cf. Zech. 3.7). Just like the king in the age of salvation, his deputy is also to be a father to the administrative district of Jerusalem and Judah which is subject to him (cf. 9.5, and also Gen. 45.8).[h] It is one of the features of a father that he guides his children, depending upon their behaviour, with kindness or sternness,[i] and ensures that they lack nothing.[j] Note that the prophet Isaiah used to speak of the inhabitants of Jerusalem, but not of the house of Judah (cf. 5.3, 7).[k] [22] As a sign of his exercise of office, the key of the

[a] Cf. also the simple 'on that day', 2.20; 4.2 and *passim*.

[b] Cf. 9.9f.; 11.1ff.; 32.1ff.; Micah 5.1ff.; Jer. 23.5f.; 33.15ff.; Zech. 9.9; 13.1 and Ezek. 34.23ff.

[c] Cf. also O. Kaiser, *Der Königliche Knecht*, FRLANT 70, ²1962, pp. 19f.

[d] Cf. Ex. 28.4, 39, 40; 29.5, 8; 39.27; 40.14; Lev. 8.7, 13; 16.4.

[e] Cf. Ex. 28.4, 39, 40; 39.9; 39.29; Lev. 8.7, 13; 16.4, and K. Elliger, HAT I. 4, 1966, p. 116.

[f] Cf. Gen. 41.41–44; Esth. 6.7–9; Zech. 3.3–5.

[g] *memšālā* refers here and in Micah 4.8 and Jer. 34.1 to the authority of the office, in I Kings 9.19 (para. II Chron. 8.6); II Kings 20.13 (para. Isa. 39.2); Pss. 103.22; 114.2; 145.13; Gen. 1.16; Ps. 136.8f. to what is governed and in II Chron 32.9 a military force. The fact that the passages where it occurs are almost all post-exilic must be taken into account in the literary criticism of the present oracle.

[h] The expression *jōšēb jerūšālayim*, the inhabitants of Jerusalem, occurs not only in 5.3 and 8.14, but also in Zech. 12.8, 10. Apart from II Sam. 2.4, 10, 11 we read of the *bēt yᵉhūdā*, the house of Judah, only in post-exilic texts. Cf. II Kings 19.30 (para. Isa. 37.31); Jer. 3.18; 13.11; 31.27; 33.14; 36.3; Ezek. 4.6; Hos. 1.7; Zeph. 2.7; Zech. 8.13, 15, 19; 10.3, 6 and 12.4.

[i] Cf. Ps. 103.13 and Prov. 13.1.

[j] Cf. Job 29.16 and 31.18.

[k] But cf. 37.31.

royal palace in Jerusalem, the house of David (cf. Neh. 12.37 and
II Sam. 20.3) is laid over the shoulder of him whom Yahweh has
chosen. The locks and keys of palace doors in those days were not like
the tiny devices which we often find nowadays, but were of an
appropriate size.[a] To commit to him the exclusive power of opening
and closing the palace expresses his control over all the government
offices set up there.[b] In the New Testament the concept of the power
of the keys is taken up again in the promise and authority given to
Peter (Matt. 16.18f.),[c] and also in Rev. 3.7, where this passage is
directly quoted and presented as uttered by the exalted Lord, who as
the David of the final age opens the way to the heavenly palace to his
followers.[d]

[23] Just as a tent peg supports the whole tent (cf. 33.20) the
servant of Yahweh will support the kingdom of his king by his
righteous and fatherly rule. And in order for him to be able to do this,
he will as it were be hammered by Yahweh into firm, reliable ground,
or, to interpret the metaphor, be installed in office for life.[e] Verse 23b
abandons the metaphor. The honoured seat, or throne of honour,
does not mean the honoured place in a Bedouin·tent near the peg
that holds it,[f] but in very general terms the honoured position which
his family is to have by virtue of his office, and which in part will be
handed on to his descendants. Whereas the prophecy of warning
against the arrogant steward concluded with the statement that he
shamed his master, so this prophecy of salvation tells of the honour
which will be accorded to the deputy of the king in the final age. (It
may be that the devout writer who gave us these words was inspired
to this prophecy by 1.26f.).

[24-25] *The burden of his father's house.* The historicizing redactor
who related vv. 15-18 to Shebna and vv. 20-22 to Eliakim, the son
of Hilkiah, felt the need to affirm that the status of Eliakim, or that of
the successors who would be drawn from his family, would not

---

[a] Cf. Judg. 3.25 and I Chron. 9.27, with R. Knierim and B. Reicke, *BHW* III,
col. 1703f. or I. Benzinger, *Hebräische Archäologie*, Tübingen 1907, pp. 93f.; P.
Volz, *Die biblischen Altertümer*, Stuttgart 1925, p. 292, and K. Galling, *BRL*, col. 460.

[b] Cf. de Vaux, p. 379 and Martin-Achard, p. 252.

[c] Cf. R. Bultmann, *Theologie des Neuen Testaments* I, Tübingen 1953, p. 63; ET
Theology of the New Testament I, London and New York 1951, § 8.4, and the works
given in Martin-Achard, p. 25.

[d] Cf. E. Lohse, NTD 11.10, 1971, *ad loc.*

[e] Cf. also Zech. 10.4.

[f] Here I disagree with Procksch, and other commentators.

remain unshaken, because it would be eroded by the hereditary oriental evil of nepotism and the abuse of a relation's standing by the members of his clan. Transforming the image of the tent peg hammered into the ground to that of a peg in the wall (cf. Ezek. 15.3), he describes in dramatic terms, and with a play upon the significance of the word *kābōd* which means not only honour as in v. 23 but according to its derivation can also mean weight, how the whole clan will hang like a weight upon the peg represented by their exalted member, just as if one were to hang all the vessels to be found in a house upon a single wooden peg on the wall. There can only be one result; the peg will fall out of the wall and all the pots will shatter.

One may well ask what were the interests expressed behind this historicizing revision, and why the writer took upon himself the mantle of Isaiah in order to prophecy in his person the fall of Eliakim and his father's house. One immediately suspects that he was holding up the mirror to a hated contemporary, perhaps a Jewish tax official working on behalf of the Ptolemies and responsible for the finances of Judaea and the Temple,[a] thus seeking to prophesy his fall with impunity. By associating vv. 15ff. and vv. 18ff. with II Kings 18.18 (Isa. 36.3) he implied that Shebna would have to be followed by Eliakim in his office. But we may have here simply a straightforward and scholarly historicization by a reader steeped in the teaching of the wisdom schools, who was expressing his conviction that one great man follows another, but that everyone eventually falls if he does not conduct his office incorruptibly and without regard for the interests of his family. One cannot say that his warning and threat is limited in its application to the ancient or the modern East.

CHAPTER 23.1–14

The Destruction of Sidon

1   *Oracle concerning Tyre.*
     Wail, O ships of Tarshish,
       for ⟨your stronghold⟩[b] is laid waste.

[a] Cf. Hengel, p. 46.
[b] Read with v. 14 *mā'uzzeken*.

As they return from[a] the land of the Kittim
it is revealed to them.

2 ⟨Be still⟩,[b] O inhabitants of the coast,
⟨merchants⟩[c] of Sidon,
⟨whose messengers pass over the sea,
over many waters⟩[d]

3 Her revenue was ⟨   ⟩[e] the grain of the Nile,
⟨   ⟩[f] the chandler of the nations.

4 Be ashamed, O Sidon ⟨you who are saying⟩,[g]
I have neither travailed nor given birth,
I have neither reared young men
nor brought up virgins.

5 *When the report comes to Egypt*
they will be in anguish, the report about Tyre.

6 Travel to Tarshish, wail.
O inhabitants of the coast!

7 Is this your exultant city
whose origin is from days of old,
whose feet carried her
to settle afar?

8 Who has purposed this against ⟨Sidon⟩[h]
who wears crowns,[i]
⟨   ⟩[j] whose traders
were the honoured of the earth?

[a] For *mbw'*, cf. W. Rudolph, 'Jesaja 23.1–14': *Festschrift F. Baumgärtel*, ed. J. Herrmann, Erlanger Forschungen A 10, Erlangen 1959, p. 168.

[b] Read *nidmū*.

[c] Read *soḥªrē* with LXX, Vg and Targ.

[d] Read *'ōbªrīm yām mal'ªkēhā mayyim rabbīm* as required by the sense and the metre.

[e] Delete *qªṣīr yªōr* as an interpretive gloss which does not fit the metre.

[f] Delete *wattªhī* as a gloss.

[g] The text of v. 4a is seriously corrupt. The mere deletion of αβ, 'the stronghold of the sea, saying' makes no improvement. The phrase 'for the sea has spoken' is equally out of place, for the sea is masculine, whereas the lament of v. 4b is only possible from a woman. Thus between 'be ashamed, O Sidon' and the beginning of the lament we should assume only an introduction to the words of Sidon. I propose to read, largely maintaining the existing consonants, *hā'ōmeret*.

[h] Text: *ṣōr*, Tyre. But read *ṣīdōn*, according to Duhm's suggestion. For the arguments in favour of this see the introduction below.

[i] Basically the translation 'who bestows crowns' is also possible. For the intransitive meaning of the hiphil in the case of a denominative verb cf. J. Lindblom, 'Der Ausspruch über Tyrus in Jes. 23', *ASThI* 4, 1965, p. 66.

[j] Delete *'ªšer* on metrical grounds.

9 Yahweh Sebaoth has purposed it,
   to defile ⟨pride⟩ᵃ
   ⟨to destroy glory, to dishonour
   the honoured of the earth⟩ᵇ

10 ⟨Build over⟩ᶜ your land, ⟨   ⟩ᵈ O daughter of
   Tarshish;
   there is no wharf any more.

11a Yahweh has given command concerning Canaan
   to destroy ⟨its stronghold⟩.ᵉ

11b He has stretched out his hand over the sea,
   he has shaken the kingdoms;

12 ⟨   ⟩ᶠ You will no more exult
   O oppressed ⟨   ⟩ᵍ daughter of Sidon;
   arise, pass over to the Kittim,
   even there you will have no rest.

13 Behold! The land ⟨of the Kittim he has destroyed,
   laid in ruins.⟩ʰ

14 Wail, O ships of Tarshish,
   for your stronghold is laid waste.

ᵃ Read *gā'ōn*.

ᵇ Read *lᵉkallōt ṣᵉbī lᵉhāqēl nikbaddē 'ereṣ*, and for *nikbaddē* cf. p. 692

ᶜ Read *'ibᵉdī* with 1Q Isa, LXX and A. The corruption is due to the confusion of *d* and *r*.

ᵈ Delete *kayᵉ'ōr* as a gloss.

ᵉ Read *ma'uzzēhā*, cf. 1Q Isa.

ᶠ Delete *wayyō'mer* as a gloss, which wrongly interprets the demand that follows as uttered by Yayweh, and is betrayed by the fact that it interrupts the metre.

ᵍ Delete *bᵉtūlat* as a gloss.

ʰ V. 13 is so corrupted by a series of glosses that a reconstruction depends upon conjecture. In view of the structure of the stanzas it ought probably not to be completely deleted. As far as content is concerned, we would expect a reason for v. 12b. We should follow Duhm and Marti in looking for the conclusion of the original text in the last two words of the verse. The repetition of the object *'ereṣ* in *šāmāh* suggests that a verb has been lost. One may very cautiously follow Marti in conjecturing that it was *hišmīd*, instead of *kaśdīm*. In order to preserve the metre, *'ereṣ* should then lose its tone through the addition of a *maqqēp*. Thus we read: *hēn 'ereṣ-kittīm hišmīd šāmā lᵉmappēlā*. The origin of the confusion in the traditional text may perhaps be explained as follows. We should follow Marti in supposing that to the basic text of v. 13a as reconstructed above, there was first added the gloss 'this is the people which (*'ašer*) established an anchorage for ships (or sailors: *lᵉṣiyyīm*) with its look-out towers (?), cities (*'ārāw*) and dwelling towers', The mis-reading of *'šr* as *'aššūr* lead to the deletion of the Kittim, the alteration of the original *hišmīd* into *kaśdīm* and the conjectural *'ārāw* into *'orᵉrū*. When Babylon came to be incorporated into the Seleucid kingdom, identified with Assyria, *lo' hāyā* was then interpolated. For the historical situation cf. Lindblom, pp. 69f.

The final oracle against a foreign nation in the collection of chs. 13–23 has provoked the greatest disagreement about its meaning. Exegetes disagree about whether it is a prophecy of the future or a prophetic lament about something in the past, and also about whether it was originally addressed to Sidon and Tyre, or to only one of these two cities. The reason for the latter problem is that the heading in v. 1a, the obvious gloss in v. 5 and the more recent addition in vv. 15–18, as well as the traditional text in v. 8, right in the middle of the poem, all speak of Tyre; but vv. 2, 4 and 12 refer to Sidon. If the poem is regarded as a prophecy of the future, this can be ignored, because it is not then necessary to relate it to the actual course of history; for we do not know of any occasion when both cities were conquered and destroyed at the same time. Thus there are many commentators who date it in the last third of the eighth century and attribute it to the prophet Isaiah, believing that in the days of the Assyrian emperor Sennacherib he foresaw the conquest of Sidon, from which king Luli later fled to Cyprus.[a] The fact that an attempt was later made to relate the whole poem to Tyre suggests that it originally referred solely to the fall of Sidon, but was later reinterpreted following the impression made by the catastrophe that came upon Tyre. This disaster can be identified only with the conquest of the island fortress by Alexander the Great in the summer of the year 332. The immense impression this made upon contemporaries is reflected in the testimonies of ancient historians.[b] However, a study of the linguistic usage of the poem against Sidon argues against any early dating.[c] This makes it probable, as has often been suggested, that the song can be associated with the conquest and destruction of Sidon by Artaxerxes III Ochus in the year 343.[d] Since the emperor had suppressed the rebel king Pnytagoras of Salamis at the latest in the spring of 344,[e]

[a] Cf. e.g. Cheyne (Salmaneser/Sargon); Dillmann-Kittel (Salmaneser/Sargon); Feldmann; Procksch; Fischer; Kissane; Rudolph, pp. 166ff.; Eichrodt, ad loc. and S. Erlandsson, The Burden of Babylon, Lund 1970, p. 100. E. G. Kraeling, BHW III, col. 1784, has in mind the period of Esarhaddon.

[b] Cf. Arrian, Anabasis II. 15.6–24.6; Diodorus, XVII. 40.2–46.6 and Curtius, IV.II.1–IV.21.

[c] I eventually hope to discuss this material in another context.

[d] Cf. Duhm, Marti, Steinmann, ad loc. Fohrer considers that the song was not composed until after the fall of Tyre, so that it looks back upon the catastrophes that overtook both cities. Lindblom, pp. 62f. regards Sidon as the terrified witness of the conquest of Tyre.

[e] For the dating of the fall of Sidon cf. E. Bickermann, 'Notes sur la chronologie

there is some difficulty with regard to v. 1, because it seems to assume unhampered travel between Cyprus and Sidon. Yet v. 13 seems to assume that Cyprus has also been reduced to subjection. Thus the tension between v. 1 and the historical facts known to us may be ignored, particularly as we do not know to what extent sea traffic between the Phoenician cities and Cyprus was in fact restricted. The fact that in vv. 8 and 9 the event is interpreted as the consequence of a divine decree is in accordance with the understanding of the song as a prophetic comment on a past event.[a] The song is formed of three stanzas, each consisting of seven couplets, vv. 1b–4; 6–9 and 10–14. The dominant metre is that of the *qīnā* or funeral lament, as in most of the oracles against foreign nations. Since it is not a serious lament, we can regard it as a taunt song upon the destruction of Sidon. The repetition of the first line at the conclusion gives the poem considerable formal unity. As a whole, it is evidence that the Judaism of the fourth century had by no means lost its poetic power. The fact that it has been placed after the oracle against Jerusalem in ch. 22 may perhaps be a further indication that it was composed at a late period and inserted subsequently into the Isaiah roll.

[1b–4] *The destruction of Sidon.* Instead of describing the destruction of Sidon in straightforward terms, the poet addresses in dramatic language the ships of Tarshish, or their crews, returning from their trading voyages. Apparently sharing their feelings, he calls upon them to raise the cry of lamentation, because on their return from Cyprus they have received the terrible news of the destruction of their home port. As is shown in particular by I Kings 22.49, 'ships of Tarshish' means merchant ships suitable for journeys across the open sea.[b] Since v. 6 seems to regard it as possible that the inhabitants of the Phoenician coast should flee to Tarshish, while v. 10 directly addresses the city, it is not out of the question that the poet, like the Chronicler, directly associated the name with the place of origin of the ships (cf. II Chron. 9.21; 20.36f.). Thus we cannot necessarily assume that he had a real understanding of the location of the city. As in the case

---

de la XXXe dynastie', *Mélanges Maspero I, Mémoires publiés par les membres de l'institut français d'archéologie orientale du Caïre* 66, Cairo 1934, pp. 80f. For the crushing of the revolt in Cyprus cf. F. K. Kienitz, *Die politische Geschichte Ägyptens vom 7. bis zum 4. Jahrhundert vor der Zeitwende*, Berlin 1953, p. 103.

   [a] Cf. Lindblom, pp. 56f.
   [b] Cf. also I Kings 10.22; Isq. 2.16: 60.9 and Ezek. 27.25.

of its mention in the book of Jonah, the poet may simply have understood by it the most westerly city that he knew by name. According to Gen. 10.4 it was known at an early date that it lay far in the west. According to Ezek. 27.12 silver, iron, tin and lead were imported from it. Tarshish is usually identified even today with the Tartessos of the ancient writers, which lay on the Atlantic southern coast of Spain, and was probably founded by the Tyrseni of Asia Minor. It has recently been powerfully argued that it should be sought in the region of Huelva, where both the mineralogical conditions and the archaeological data are present.[a] After the destruction of Tartessos by the Cathaginians towards the end of the sixth century, the name of the city persisted as the designation of an area. Our sources do not indicate whether the trade of the region with the mother country, Phoenicia, came to an end with the destruction of the city. South of Tartessos, Tyre seems to have found it as early as the eleventh century the trading depot of Gadir, the present-day Cadiz.[b] Kition, the present-day Larnaka, was colonized by Tyre about 800 BC, but then attained its independence under Phoenician kings, and last of whom was executed by Ptolemy I in 312.[c] The city gave the inhabitants of Cyprus the name of Kittim, which the Jews also used later to refer to the Greeks and Romans.

[2–3] Instead of the former cheerful bustle in the trading metropolis there is now a lifeless silence. The inhabitants of the coast, by whom according to v. 2b the poet principally means the merchants

---

[a] Cf. J. Mª. Blázquez, *Tartessos y los orígenes de la Colonización fenicia en Occidente*, Acta Salmanticensia 58, Salamanca 1968; cf. the review by M. Lambert, *Syria* 47, 1970, p. 198, and also K. Galling 'Der Weg der Phoniker nach Tarsis in literarischer und archäologischer Sicht', *ZDPV* 88, 1972, pp. 2ff.

[b] Cf. A. Schulten, *Tartessos. Ein Beitrag zur ältesten Geschichte des Westens*, Universität Hamburg. Abhandlungen aus dem Gebiet der Auslandskunde 54, Hamburg ²1950; W. F. Albright, 'New Light on the Early History of Phoenician Colonization', *BASOR* 83, 1941, pp. 14ff., who argues for the derivation of the name from the Akkadian **taršišu*, ultimately from *rašāšu*, 'to melt' so that in the first instance ships of Tarshish would have been ore carriers. But cf. also B. H. Warmington, *Carthage*, London 1960, pp. 25f., and 68: D. Harden, *The Phoenicians*, Ancient Peoples and Places 26, London 1962, p. 160, and with reservations J. Simons, *The Geographical and Topographical Texts of the Old Testament*, Leiden 1959, § 25. The traditional location on the Atlantic coast of Spain has been opposed by A. Herrmann, 'Die Tartessosfrage und Weissafrika', *Petermanns Geographische Mitteilungen* 88, 1942, pp. 353ff. He considers that the city lay in the region of the lake Tritonis, the present-day *shott el-jerid* on the Tunisian coast.

[c] Cf. Ernst Meyer, *KP* III, col. 404ff.

of Sidon, have been silenced, that is, killed. The attributes listed in
the lines that follow emphasize the difference between their former
prosperity and their present misery: the agents and messengers of
Sidon were for a long time familiar figures on every sea. The corn
trade of Egypt passed through the hands of Sidon, which was also
enriched by the products of other nations. The city lived on what the
efforts of other nations produced. [4] Adopting the common Old
Testament personification of a city as a woman, the poet calls upon
Sidon to be ashamed of itself. The Hebrew verb signifies both the
subjective and objective loss of *kābōd*, honour, that which brings a
person dignity, respect and well being (cf. II Kings 19.26 [Isa.
37.27]).[a] For the Israelites a woman's shame consisted either in her
being violated or in her childlessness (cf. Gen. 29.31ff.; I Sam. 1.6ff.
and Isa. 54.5f.). Accordingly the poet reminds Sidon of her own
lamentations at her childlessness, that is, at the loss of her sons and
daughters in the conquest.[b] There is no reference here to daughter
cities.

[5] *A double interpolation.* Verse 5 seems to have come into being in
two stages, as can be seen from the phrase 'the report about Tyre'
tagged on at the end. The first glossator clearly had in mind the
connection between the conquest of Sidon by Artaxerxes III at the
beginning of the year 343 and his victorious attack upon Egypt in
the autumn of the same year. This brought an end to the independence
of Egypt which had been regained by the revolt of Amyrtaios in 404
and which since then had been repeatedly defended against all
Persian attempts to reconquer the country.[c] The second glossator
connects the whole song with the conquest of Tyre by Alexander, the
last stage but one upon his route into the kingdom of the Pharaohs.

[6–9] *The disaster to Sidon as an act of Yahweh.* In order to emphasize
the hopeless situation of the survivors, the poet calls upon them to flee
lamenting to Tarshish. That this destination is not to be taken
literally is shown by v. 12, which ironically proposes flight to Cyprus.
[7] The renewed call to lament is emphasized by the question which
follows, which, pointing to the former prosperity and commercial
importance of the city, is meant to increase its sorrow at the blow it
has suffered. Before the city's destruction, its life was characterized

---

[a] Cf. also Lindblom, pp. 6of.
[b] For the expressions of lamentation cf. 26.17 and 66.7, and also the verbs *gdl*
and *rwm* in the same order in 1.2.
[c] Cf. Kienitz, pp. 104ff.

by uninhibited rejoicing,[a] for it claimed to be the oldest of the Phoenician cities (cf. Strabo, XVI. 2.22) and controlled a far-flung network of trading depots.

[8] Within the structure of the poem the second question is addressed to those spoken to previously, but in fact serves to enlighten and assure the poet's Jewish audience that it was none other than their own God who had brought about the fall of Sidon. This also makes it clear to whom the song is really addressed. The answer makes clear the rhetorical nature of the question as far as the Sidonians are concerned, for it could hardly have occurred to them that Yahweh was at work here. For the Jews, of course, it must have been a comforting assurance that in spite of his apparent passivity in the history of the nations during the past two hundred years, Yahweh had not abdicated from his rule over the world. Thus at the very beginning of the question we find the decisive keyword *yāʿaṣ*, which denotes not only plans but also decision and the carrying out of plans.[b] As in 14.24ff. we are given an indirect insight into the poet's deliberations.[c] But before the answer is given in v. 9, the question emphasizes the former royal status of the city, reflected in the princely rank accorded to its merchants and purple sellers throughout the world. This was necessary in order to show the strength and power required to bring about the fall of such a city. [9] In his answer the poet consciously uses the ancient throne name of his God, Yahweh Sebaoth, for this emphasizes his universal power and authority.[d] His decision to destroy Sidon (cf. 14.27 and 19.12) was directed against a pride to which only he had any right and a glory which was his alone, and against the proud arrogance and ostentation of its inhabitants.[e] The background to this reason for Yahweh's intervention is perhaps not only the view that honour and deference in the world is due exclusively to Yahweh (cf. Ps. 24.10; Rev. 4.12) but also to the way the poet and his circle, if not the whole Jewish community of the late fourth century, understood itself as the lowly and humble (cf. 14.30). Since no charge is made against Sidon except its pride and ostentation, there do not seem to have been at that time any

[a] Cf. 5.14; 22.2; 32.13 and Zeph. 2.15.
[b] Cf. my commentary on 9.5, *Isaiah 1–12*, OTL, 1972, *ad loc.*
[c] Cf. above, pp. 45ff.
[d] Cf. my commentary on 6.3, *op. cit.*, and 13.4.
[e] Cf. 16.6; Zech. 9.6; 10.11 and Ezek. 7.20. For the two ideas together, cf. Isa. 4.2 and 13.19.

more specific tensions between the Jews and the Phoenicians.

[10–14] *The hopeless situation of the survivors.* In the third and final stanza the poet turns to the consequences of the fall of the great trading metropolis, in order to emphasize once again the greatness of its fall and the irresistible power of his God. For the trading partners of the city, represented by the most westerly, Tarshish, the only way of scraping a living left after the fall of their main customer is, as far as the poet can see, a return to agriculture, to self-sufficiency. After the destruction of the wharfs of Sidon the hope of setting up new merchant fleets would be as foolish as that of setting up other commercial relationships, since Yahweh had destroyed not only Sidon but the other Phoenician coastal fortresses. According to the scanty information in Diodorus concerning the attitude and fate of the other Phoenician cities during the revolt, the poet is exaggerating the extent of the Persian reprisals.[a] That Tyre was the first to profit from the fall of Sidon, as Sidon was later to do from the fall of Tyre, lay far beyond his economic understanding, just as his geographical knowledge did not extend to the fact that it was Punic and Greek merchants who would gain from the fall of both Tyre and Sidon.

[11a] Verse 11a, taking up again the metaphor of Yahweh's outstretched hand, stresses in general terms that the command of Yahweh which was fulfilled in the destruction of Sidon is irresistible. There is absolutely no escape from his grasp! This anthropomorphic image, which occurs in Isaiah and especially in Ezekiel, is derived from the ancient conception of Yahweh as a warrior.[b] The connection between this threatening gesture and the sea can be explained perhaps not only by the situation of the Phoenician cities, but also by the memory of the myth of Baal's battle against the sea-god Yam, which in the Old Testament is transferred to Yahweh.[c] **[12–14]** In the concluding verses the poet once again turns directly to Sidon in order to affirm to the crushed city that its former happiness can never return, and to make clear that there is no hope in the situation of the survivors. The irony of the call to flee to Cyprus is immediately revealed, for the poet is of the opinion – far exaggerating the actual

[a] Cf. XVI. 45.6.

[b] Cf. 9.11, 16, 20; 5.25; 14.26f.; Ezek. 6.14; 15.13; 16.27 and *passim*, and especially Ezek. 14.9; also Ex. 6.6; 7.5; Deut. 4.34; 5.15 and *passim*.

[c] Cf. Pss. 29.3; 89.10ff.; 93.3f.; Job 9.6; 38.11; Isa. 13.13 and 14.16; and O. Kaiser, *Die mythische Bedeutung des Meeres in Ägypten, Ugarit und Israel*, BZAW 78, [2]1962, pp. 44ff. and 140ff. and more recently J. C. de Moor, *The Seasonal Pattern in the Ugaritic Myth of Ba'lu*, AOAT 16, 1971, pp. 116ff.

situation – that Yahweh had also destroyed the cities of this island. Repeating the call to lamentation from v. 1, made to the ships returning from a long journey, the poet brings his taunt song to an effective conclusion. There is a parallel between the hopeless flight *from* Sidon and the pointless return *to* Sidon.

Perhaps some additional historical information will be useful to the reader. The failure of the attempt by Artaxerxes III in 351–50 to regain Egypt for Persia was the signal for a revolt on the part of the Phoenician cities and the princes of the Cypriot city states who paid tribute to the Persians. In Phoenicia King Tennes of Sidon was the inspiration of the revolt. The first Persian attempt to reconquer Phoenicia, led by the satraps of Syria and Cilicia, failed after some success at first, for in the meanwhile Tennes had obtained from Pharaoh Nektanebos II military reinforcements in the form of a contingent of four thousand Greek mercenaries, commanded by Mentor of Rhodes. However, the emperor succeeded in suppressing resistance on Cyprus after 345, and conquered his last and most determined opponent, Pytagoras of Salamis, after a long siege and investment of his city, at the latest at the beginning of the year 343. When Artaxerxes appeared personally in Phoenicia, with a new army, King Tennes tried to save himself in an abominable fashion by the betrayal of his city. By agreement the Persian army was admitted by Mentor into the city, and its unfortunate inhabitants, who as a sign of their willingness to fight to the last had already destroyed their ships and thereby deprived themselves of the possibility of flight, now sought death in the flames which consumed their houses. Artaxerxes executed the traitor Tennes and took Mentor into Persian service. The example made of Sidon had the expected effect upon the remaining Phoenician cities. They immediately capitulated.[a]

Remote from the tensions and the distinctive hopes of the fourth century BC, we cannot but feel compassion with a people which fought for its freedom and was defeated by a despicable betrayal. It is understandable that the faith of another oppressed people should have regarded them with hatred and scorn, but one would hope it could no longer serve as an example to us after more than two thousand years. We can share only the faith which forms the unexpressed background to the poem, that on this earth there is no freedom and no peace worthy of the name as long as God has not conquered the hearts of men and made them capable of fellowship.

[a] Cf. Diodorus, XVI. 40.3–45.6 and the comment of Kienitz, pp. 100ff.

CHAPTER 23.15–18

The Fall and the Visitation of Tyre

15 In that day *it will come about: Tyre will be forgotten for seventy years.* ⟨*In the days of another king*⟩ᵃ *at the end of seventy years*, it will happen to Tyre as in the song of the harlot:
  16 Take a harp,
      go about the city,
      O forgotten harlot!
  Make sweet melody,
      sing many songs,
      that you may be remembered.
17 At the end of seventy years, it will come about: Yahweh will visit Tyre, and she will return to ⟨her⟩ᵇ hire, and will play the harlot with all the kingdoms of the world upon the face of the earth. 18Her merchandise and her hire will be holy to Yahweh; it will not be stored or hoarded, but her merchandise will supply abundant food and fine clothing for those who dwell before Yahweh.

About midsummer 332 BC, Alexander the Great succeeded after a siege lasting seven months in conquering the island fortress. Its defenders had fought boldly and with ingenuity, and their courage had not failed them even when the Macedonians constructed a mole to join the island to the mainland. After the city had been captured by an attack from the sea, those inhabitants of Tyre who were capable of bearing arms, in so far as they had not already been killed in battle, are said to have been crucified and their wives and children, not all of whom had been evacuated to Carthage, sold into slavery.ᶜ These

---

ᵃ The received text, 'like the days of a king' is meaningless, because kings were not distinguished by a particularly long life. And even if they lived to seventy they were not basically superior to an ordinary mortal. This was noticed by LXX, which adds behind its rendering 'like the time of a king' a phrase 'like the time of a man', cf. Ps. 90.10. Seventy years is of course far from normal for the reign of a king. Thus it seems probable that we should follow Procksch in reading *bīmē melek* *'aḥēr*, accepting a confusion between *b* and *k* and between *r* and *d*. 1QIsa has omitted everything between *whyh bywm hhw'* and *lṣy*, though this does not mean that it can claim to be original.

ᵇ Cf. *BHS*.

ᶜ Cf. Arrian, *Anabasis* II.15.6–24.6, Diodorus, XVII. 40.2–46.6 and Curtius, IV.II. 1–IV.21. For the alleged crucifixion of 2000 people after the conquest of Tyre by Alexander in Diodorus XVII.46.4 cf. W. W. Tarn, *Alexander the Great* II,

events naturally made a powerful impression upon the neighbouring peoples, including the Jews. In addition to Zech. 9.1–8,[a] the redaction and extension of the taunt song on the destruction of Sidon in 343 BC (23.1b–14) is evidence of this. The heading in v. 1b, the interpolation in v. 5 and the alteration of the name in v. 8, all show that the song was now understood as a fulfilled prophecy of the conquest of Tyre. At the same time an appendix was added to it which, according to Fohrer, consisted at first of no more than a shorter version of v. 15 introducing the taunt song in v. 16. It was a later redactor who added the eschatological prophecy in the two following verses, 17 and 18. But it is not likely that the addition to v. 15 was composed by the same hand. It should be regarded as an even later gloss, since it makes an awkward attempt to resolve the differences in content and chronology between vv. 15–16 and 17–18. It may be the work of the same glossator who is responsible for the various clumsy interpolations in 23.1b–14.

[15–16] With the typical formula of introduction for later additions, 'in that day', a redactor in the period of Alexander begins his appendix to the song against Sidon, which he had reinterpreted. By so doing he gave his own words the appearance of an ancient prophecy, a procedure which we find continued in the pseudepigraphic apocalypses. In order still further to mock the city of Tyre, which a short time ago had been so powerful, he makes use of a street song such as might have been heard in a seaport town. It calls upon a prostitute, despised because of her age, to go out on to the street and draw attention to herself by singing, in order to attract new custom.[b] He thereby created a simile to which there are previous parallels,[c] and which by way of the second addition to this passage was to influence the conceptual material used in the religious criticism of society: the comparison between commercial power and a

---

Cambridge 1948 (1950), p. 82, who considers it probable that Cleitarchus was a witness of this. For an account of the latter cf. *ibid.* pp. 54f. Against Diodorus XVII. 46.6–47.6 cf. Arrian, II.24 and Curtius, IV.1. 15ff. and Justin, XI. 10. 8f. and e.g. J. Kaerst, *Geschichte des Hellenismus* I, Berlin and Leipzig [3]1927, p. 373 note 2 – For the military aspect of the siege of Tyre by Alexander cf. E. Schramm in J. Kromayer and G. Veith, *Heerwesen und Kriegführung der Griechen und Römer*, HAW IV. 3.2, 1928 (1963), p. 218 and p. 236, with figs. 72–74.

[a] Cf. K. Elliger, 'Ein Zeugnis der jüdischen Gemeinde im Alexanderjahr 332 v. Chr.', *ZAW* 62, 1949/50, pp. 63ff., and ATD 25, [6]1967, *ad loc.*

[b] Cf. also Horace, *Carm* I. 25 and *Epod.* 8.

[c] Cf. Hos. 2.4ff.; Jer. 3.6ff.; Ezek. 16 and Nahum 3.4.

prostitute (cf. Rev. 18.1ff.). For commerce takes up any contact which it hopes will bring in money. The immediate concern of the author of this addition, however, was the sudden fall of the ancient trading metropolis. Its position was now of course taken over by Sidon.

[17–18] By contrast, the eschatological redactor prophesies that the city will return to prosperity for the benefit of his own religious community. It is quite likely that at least v. 17 is a *vaticinium ex eventu*, because in the year 274 the autonomy of Tyre was restored by Ptolemy II Philadelphos.[a] The period of seventy years laid down by Yahweh before fulfilment is taken, as is the verb, from Jer. 25.11 and 29.10 (cf. II Chron. 36.21 and Ezra 1.1). There is no indication that they should be interpreted, as in Dan. 9.2, 24ff., as weeks of years. The primary meaning of the number, as is shown by Ps. 90.10, is the whole length of a human life. If we are correct in supposing that the redactor was working later than 274 BC, then he provides valuable evidence of the intensified eschatological expectations to be found in Judaism during the third century. For the particular hope which he expresses, that the trade of Tyre with all the kingdoms of the earth will be protected by Yahweh, and carried out for the benefit of the people of Jerusalem, is comprehensible only in the framework of the much wider conception of the transformation of the fortunes of Jerusalem. When Yahweh casts down the nations of the earth, the survivors will voluntarily make pilgrimage to Jerusalem in order to hand over their treasures there (cf. Pss. 72.10; 96.8; Isa. 45.14; 49.22f.; 60.9–11 ; Hag. 2.7; Zech. 14.21, and particularly Isa. 18.7).

Referring back to the simile introduced in vv. 15f., he calls the highly profitable trade 'playing the harlot'. The appositional phrase 'upon the face of the earth' is not meant to indicate where the rendezvous takes place, but emphasizes that the trading relationships are on a world-wide scale (cf. Jer. 25.26; Ezek. 38.20 and Zeph 1.2). The goods and profit that will come into the city will not belong to it, but to Yahweh. The word *qōdeš* which we translate 'holy' still possesses its original meaning here: something is holy when it has been removed from secular use and dedicated to the deity or to his sanctuary (cf. Lev. 27.10). Since the profits of trade are only referred to metaphorically as the rewards of prostitution, Deut. 23.18 does not

---

[a] Cf. E. Schürer, *Geschichte des jüdischen Volkes im Zeitalter Jesu Christi* § 23, vol. II, Leipzig ⁴1907, p. 98 (not in ET), and F. -M. Abel, *Histoire de la Palestine depuis la conquête d'Alexandre jusqu' à l'invasion arabe* I, Paris 1952, p. 52.

apply to them. Those who dwell before Yahweh must be taken to mean not only the priests (cf. Ps. 134.1) but all the inhabitants of Jerusalem.[a] When the proceeds of the trade of Tyre are handed over, they will enjoy in the future a life of luxury. They will thus be taking on the role of the priestly kingdom and holy people (cf. Ex. 19.6) from whom the nations of the earth will receive instruction (cf. Isa. 2.2ff.).

[15] The glossator has connected the resurgence of Tyre with the rule of someone other than the conquering king, either expressing in cryptic form his knowledge of the restoration of the autonomy of Tyre by Ptolemy II, or referring to another favour shown to the city of which we are ignorant – unless he was simply speculating. He transforms the taunt upon the prostitute to a description of the newly developed activity of Tyre in foreign trade.

[a] Cf. Dillmann-Kittel, *ad loc.*

CHAPTERS 24–27

THE APOCALYPSE OF ISAIAH

As scholars became aware of the gradual growth of the book of Isaiah, they could not fail to realize that it was impossible for chs. 24–27 to have been composed by the eighth-century prophet.[a] To mention only a few of the most obvious arguments which occur to a reader familiar with the history of Israel's faith, it is clear that the disaster to Jerusalem in the year 587 lies behind these chapters (cf. 27.3). Unlike the genuine sayings of Isaiah, they are concerned not with the judgment of Yahweh brought down upon Jerusalem by the people's disobedience, but with a future visitation on a world-wide scale (24.1ff.), which no one can escape (24.16aff.) and in the course of which all innocent blood will be avenged (26.1), though the possibility of being spared seems to exist for the oppressed people of God (26.10). The emphasis on a disaster falling upon a city in 24.7ff.; 25.1ff. and 26.1ff., which will give the community cause for joy and thankfulness (24.14ff.; 25.1ff.; 26.1ff.), makes it clear that the catastrophe is not to fall upon Jerusalem but upon some other entity, although the mention of Moab in 25.10bff. is not the key for its interpretation. The expectation of a cosmic judgment including in its scope the powers of heaven and of the underworld (24.21ff.; 27.1), the beginning of the reign of Yahweh on Zion, where he gives the nations a feast of rejoicing (24.23; 25.6ff.), the abolition of death itself (25.8a; 26.19) and a new song of the vineyard which is clearly meant to provide a contrast with the earlier song (cf. 5.1ff. with 27.2ff.), all show that it is impossible to date the chapters in the eighth century, and that they ought all to be regarded as composed in the late post-exilic period or even as late as the Hellenistic period.

In the history of the exegesis of these chapters, an early dating in the exilic period, to which Marie-Louise Henry has somewhat oddly

[a] Cf. e.g. W.M.L. de Wette, *Lehrbuch der historisch-kritischen Einleitung in die kanonischen und apokryphischen Bücher des Alten Testaments*, Berlin [6]1845, § 209b, pp. 314f.

returned,[a] was followed by an extremely late dating on the part of
Duhm and Marti. It was Duhm who first posed the question of the
original unity of the composition, however questionable his own
results may have been, and (in my view at least) his attempts to
identify the city mentioned in some of the songs. Duhm regarded 24;
25.6–8; 26.20–27.1, 12, 13 as the original material, and related
24.7ff. to the condition of Jerusalem after the departure of Antiochus
VII Sidetes (138–129) in 135 BC and 24.14ff. to the defeat of the
Seleucids by the Parthians in 130/129. As far as the later additions are
concerned, he proposed to relate 25.1ff. to the destruction of Samaria
by John Hyrcanus (between 113 and 105), regarded 25.3 as an
allusion to Rome and 26.1–9 as composed in the same period, and
considered that 25.9–11 were not added until the period of Alexander
Jannaeus (103–76 BC). This is not the place to trace the often tangled
history of the exegesis of these chapters during the present century.
Instead we shall outline the results of three important studies, and
then, before setting out our own position, we shall briefly survey the
attempts to identify the city in the songs.

We owe to Rudolph a vigorous emphasis upon the eschatological
nature of the poem. However, he believed that he had identified in
24.10–16 a comment upon the conquest of Babylon by Alexander the
Great in 331 and that this provided a starting point for dating the
basic material of the apocalypse, from which he excluded 25.10b–11;
26.14a, 18bβ, 19 and 27.2–11. Note that he emphasized the prophetic
character of the songs in 25.1ff. and 26.1ff., and also, having regard
to the conclusion of the Old Testament canon, argued against a
dating in the Maccabaean period.[b] Here we must also add that the
coming into being of the Qumran community and its scripture
tradition seems absolutely to exclude the dating even of tiny interpolations later than 140 BC. Indeed, a consideration of the origins of the
movement suggests that a safety factor of at least twenty years earlier
should be allowed for,[c] though it is not impossible that further textual
discoveries, perhaps even of the Greek Bible, may still bring surprises.

After Hylmö's attempt in 1929 to use the idea of a prophetic

[a] M.-L. Henry, *Glaubenskrise und Glaubensbewährung in den Dichtungen der Jesajaapokalypse*, BWANT 86, 1967.

[b] W. Rudolph, *Jesaja 24–27*, BWANT 62, 1933, p. 64.

[c] Cf. F. M. Cross, *The Ancient Library of Qumran and Modern Biblical Studies*,
New York ²1961, pp. 70ff., 118ff., 164ff., and H. Stegemann, Die Entstehung der
Qumrangemeinde, thesis, Bonn (1965) 1971, pp. 247ff.

liturgy to interpret the chapters, Lindblom sought to show that it was more properly a cantata referring to the destruction of Babylon in 485. He believed that 24.21–23; 25.8a,[a] 10b–12; 26.15–19 and 27.1 should be excluded from the original poem. He dated 26.15–19 in the period of Demetrius II and the enlargement of Judaean territory which took place in 145 BC.[b] Though he explained his views in full, it is questionable whether his literary criticism led him to the right conclusions, and his datings are untenable. Thus, for example, even if the city walls of Jerusalem had been renewed before the time of Nehemiah, they would have presumably been destroyed once again in 585/84.[c] The fact that he was obliged to reject the eschatological interpretation of the city songs makes one sceptical of his interpretation. The attempt to fit the accursed city into history led him to take a step backwards from the position achieved by Rudolph.

On the other hand, Plöger was quite correct in vigorously restoring the eschatological nature of the poem to the centre of the argument. Basically he regarded 24.1–20 and 26.20–21 as the older stratum, to which at the same time, or not much later, a second was added, consisting of 24.21–23; 25.6–8, 9–10a; 26.7–11 and 12–19, both of which he dated in the Ptolemaic period (and, in view of the explicit expectation of the resurrection of the dead found in the second stratum, towards the end of it, though before 200 BC.)[d] It is surprising that he regarded ch. 27 as a collection dating from the fifth century, dealing with the theme of the reunion of the northern and southern kingdoms, and added later. It is also strange that appealing, one may presume correctly, to Rudolph,[e] and certainly in agreement with Lindblom,[f] he related 25.1–5 and 26.1–6 to a historical event in the past and excluded them as later additions. In taking 25.1ff. to refer to Babylon, he follows Lindblom and others. The background to his view that 26.1ff. reflects the fate of a Moabite city can be found in Eissfeldt[g] and ultimately in 25.10bff. In my view the special treatment he accords to these two songs is odd, because in discussing

---

[a] And previously Duhm and Marti.

[b] *Die Jesaja-Apokalypse Jes. 24–27*, LUÅ, N.S. I. 34, 3, Lund and Leipzig, 1938.

[c] Cf. 26.1, and for this topic O. Kaiser in *Wort und Geschichte. Festschrift K. Elliger*, AOAT 18, 1972, p. 102. Cf. also Neh. 1.3.

[d] O. Plöger, *Theokratie und Eschatologie*, WMANT 2, 1959, p. 96; ET, *Theocracy and Eschatology*, Oxford and Richmond, Va., 1968, p. 77.

[e] Cf. Rudolph, pp. 56 and 64 with Plöger, p. 87; ET, p. 69.

[f] Cf. Lindblom, pp. 72ff.

[g] O. Eissfeldt, *Einleitung in das Alte Testament*, Tübingen [2]1956, p. 394; [3]1964,

24.8ff. itself Plöger emphatically and correctly insisted, in spite of his view that they were originally independent, that in their present context these verses are not meant to refer at all to the destruction of a particular city, but to the eschatological end of city life altogether. This in my view is an improvement upon Rudolph. Fohrer rightly followed Plöger in his approach to 24.7ff., and just as rightly followed the lines laid down by Rudolph with regard to 25.1ff.; while in 26.1ff. he ultimately comes to the same conclusion as Plöger, though without attempting to identify the city.[a] We shall return to this problem in connection with our survey of attempts to interpret the meaning of the city. Meanwhile, it is important for Plöger's whole view of the passage to observe that he follows Rudolph in regarding 24.14–18a as the relic of a conflicting interpretation of the eschatological *kairos* within Judaism, and sees 26.7–11 as reflecting a conflict between eschatological circles and their opponents. It is essentially on this basis that he treats the poem in its basic form, or at the latest in its enlarged form, as a 'handbook' for strengthening their own (eschatological) faith in all its distinctive forms and as a work of apologetic against their opponents.[b]

The unnamed city in 24.8ff.; 25.1ff.; 26.1ff. and finally also in 27.10f. has greatly exercised the imagination of commentators, since it seemed to offer a starting point for the dating of the poem. This can be shown by a brief and by no means exhaustive summary.[c] Marie-Louise Henry has recently attempted to associate the city songs with the conquest of Babylon by Cyrus,[d] while Lindblom preferred to connect it with the occupation by Xerxes in 485. In this he received the partial approbation of Kessler[e] and also the basic agreement of Anderson, especially with regard to the probable date of composition.[f] Rudolph related the passage to the capture of Babylon by Alexander the Great in 331. Within the present century, however, Procksch has proposed the fall of Carthage in 146 BC and Eissfeldt,

---

pp. 438f.; ET *The Old Testament: an Introduction*, Oxford and New York 1965, p. 326; Plöger, p. 87; ET, p. 69.

[a] Cf. Fohrer, *ad loc.*

[b] Pp. 83f.; ET p. 66.

[c] Cf. also O. Ludwig, Die Stadt in der Jesaja-Apokalypse. Zur Datierung von Jes. 24–27, thesis, Bonn 1961, pp. 51ff.

[d] Cf. above, p. 174, note a.

[e] W. Kessler, *Gott geht es um das Ganze. Jesaja 56–66 und Jesaja 24–27*, BAT 29, 1960, *ad loc.*

[f] G. W. Anderson, *Isaiah XXIV–XXVII Reconsidered*, SVT 9, 1963, pp. 118ff.

like Smend and Oort before him, a Moabite city, and like Mulders[a] after him a destruction of Dibon round about 250 BC. Duhm, Marti and Guthe connected it with the destruction of Samaria in 107 BC, and Ludwig with the fall of the Jerusalem citadel achieved by Simon Maccabaeus in 147 BC.[b] There are various reasons for our own reservations with regard to all these attempts. In the first place, we would argue that the question of the previous history of individual sections is of no significance for the understanding of the composition as we possess it, for in every case they are given a fresh significance within it. Our second and perhaps most convincing reason is that we believe we shall be able to show in our exposition that 24.7ff.; 25.1ff. and 26.1ff. at least have no previous history as independent units, and no other *Sitz im Leben* than that which they possess in this book. They were composed for their present context. The completely obscure text 27.10f. does not alter this conclusion.

Our task now, therefore, is to set out our own understanding of the origin of the composition and the date we propose. We must, however, draw attention to the fact that with texts of this kind an explanation of their origins and an attempt to date them can only be approximate. Moreover, we cannot assume in an eschatological or apocalyptic composition that either as a whole, or within its separate parts, its order exactly corresponds to the chronological order of the events which it was thought would take place in the *eschaton*. Such compositions clearly claim freedom to make use of the most disparate aspects, depending upon the particular concern in each case, and upon whether the intention was to arouse a proper degree of fear of what was to come, to nourish a lively future hope or to strengthen failing courage at the present day. It is immediately obvious that this is a severe hindrance to any analysis which attempts to trace the growth of the composition. From the prospect of judgment of the world in 24.1–13 our attention is drawn to the rejoicing in the age of salvation, in 24.15–16aα, and then back in 24.16–aββb to the judgment. But as early as 24.21–23 the prospect of judgment reached its climax with the promise of the imprisonment of the heavenly powers hostile to God, the inauguration of the reign of Yahweh upon Zion and the new fellowship of God with Israel. Thus within the chapter a twofold eschatological pattern is repeated twice. The question of

[a] E. S. Mulders, *Die Teologie van die Jesaja-Apokalipse*, Groningen and Djakarta 1954, pp. 78ff., cf. p. 91 and p. 93.
[b] Pp. 88ff.

course remains whether this is original. The fact that 24.1–13 and 24.16b–20 make a similar use of biblical tradition seems to me to make it certain that they share the same author. Whether it can be assumed that this proto-apocalyptic theologian could have rested content with the mere prospect of the judgment, and whether it was possible for him to have done so in view of the assumptions which his community took for granted, is a question which it is no longer possible to answer with certainty. I should like, however, to draw attention to the possibility that he is also responsible for the composition of 26.1–18, 20–21, which otherwise would have to be regarded as a second stratum. It begins with a prophetic song of thanksgiving in 26.1–6, which clearly reveals its edificatory purpose of comforting the community in their present time of trial, goes on to a broadly based, meditative 'lamentation of the people' in 26.7–18, which stresses the necessity of the divine judgment and so makes what is to come acceptable to the worshipping congregation, and concludes with an injunction concerning their attitude in the final wrath in 26.20–21. All this is perfectly compatible with the original material in ch. 24. I would regard 24.14–16aα, the short eschatological song of thanksgiving with its introduction, together with v. 16aβ as a literary transitional message, and the further eschatological song of thanksgiving at the fall of the world city in 25.1–5, as a second stratum, together with 25.9–10a, which is also an eschatological song of thanksgiving for Yahweh's help and immediate presence. We might call this the stratum of the eschatological songs of thanksgiving. The reason why this redaction did not touch ch. 26 is probably to be sought in the songs which already formed part of the original content of this chapter, and secondly to its rigid form, unified by the linking together of sections. I would attribute 24.21–23 and 25.6–8 to a third stratum which clearly displays more advanced apocalyptic speculation, and in view of the awkwardness of 25.8aα in its context, and of 26.19, I would attribute them to a fourth redaction, which expressed a faith in the resurrection of the dead. The formation of ch. 27 may have taken a different course, but in respect of 27.1 and 27.12f. at least it can be regarded as an additional stratum to 24.21–23 and 25.6–8, whatever conclusions we come to with regard to the rest of the chapter and 25.10b–12.

The most difficult task of all is to translate the relative chronology of these strata into an absolute one corresponding to the course of Israelite history. Since the relationship between 26.19 and Dan.

12.2a remains uncertain, the date of the book of Daniel can be used, only with some caution as a guide to the dating of the additions concerning the resurrection; this would give the period between 167 and 164 BC as *terminus ad quem*.[a] Working back from this, the stratum which can be identified in 24.21ff. and 25.6ff. can be placed in the first third of the second century. With regard to the rest, in view of the little we know about the history of the eschatological hope in the late exilic and Hellenistic periods, I would advise caution. It seems to me more or less certain that hopes such as are represented by Haggai and the oldest portions of the book of Zechariah[b] would have failed, by the time of Xerxes at the latest, to stand up to sober examination.[c] On the other hand the convulsions undergone by the Persian kingdom during the twenty years or more following 370 BC would have nourished them afresh, if earlier events had not already done so. If we take into account the familiarity with the biblical writings which in our view can already be discerned in the oldest stratum, they cannot be dated before a certain degree of scholasticism had become established. This may well have been possible as the fourth century BC proceeded, and then remained in force, until the redaction of the traditional books of the Bible gave way, presumably under the influence of the check imposed by sectarian groups such as the Qumran community and the Samaritans, to the production of the newer works which we refer to as Apocrypha and Pseudepigrapha.

CHAPTER 24.1–13

The Judgment upon the World

1   Behold, Yahweh will lay waste the earth
      and make it desolate.
    And he will twist its surface
      and scatter its inhabitants.

[a] Cf. N. Porteous, *Daniel*, OTL 1965, p. 142, and also O. Plöger, KAT[2] 18, 1965, pp. 28ff.

[b] Cf. my observation in O. Kaiser, *Einleitung in das Alten Testament*, Gütersloh [2]1970, pp. 11f.

[c] Cf. O. Kaiser, 'Der geknickte Rohrstab', *Wort und Geschichte. Festschrift K. E. Elliger*, AOAT 18, 1972.

2   And it shall be, as with the people, so with the priests;
     as with the slave, so with his master;
     as with the maid, so with her mistress;
     as with the buyer, so with the seller;
     as with the lender, so with the borrower;
     as with the creditor, so with the debtor.

3   The earth shall be utterly laid waste
          and utterly despoiled:
     for Yahweh has spoken
          this word.

4   The earth shrivels and withers,
          the world[a] languishes and withers;
     ⟨the height languishes together⟩[b] with the earth.

5   For the earth lies polluted
          under its inhabitants;
     for they *have transgressed the laws*,
          ⟨*altered*⟩[c] *the statute*[d]
          broken the everlasting covenant.

6   Therefore a curse devours the earth,
          and its inhabitants must atone.
     Therefore the inhabitants of the earth wither away,[e]
          and few men are left.

7   The wine shrivels, the vine languishes,
          all the merry-hearted sigh.

8   The mirth of the timbrels will be stilled,
          the noise of the jubilant will cease,
          the mirth of the lyre will be stilled.

9   No more will they drink wine with singing;
          the beer will be bitter to those who drink it.

10   The city of chaos[f] will be broken down,
          every house shut up so that none can enter.

11   An outcry in the streets for wine!
          all joy will fade away,
          the gladness of the earth will be banished.

12   Desolation will be left in the city,
          the gates will be battered into ruins.

ᵃ Literally: *terra firma*.
ᵇ Cf. *BHS*.
ᶜ Read ḥilleᵖū.
ᵈ The later gloss refers more specifically to the guilt of the Jews.
ᵉ 1QIsa: 'grow pale'.
ᶠ The Hebrew word is *tōhū*.

13   For thus it shall be in the midst of the earth
        among the nations,
     as when an olive tree is beaten, as at the gleaning,
        when the vintage is done.

Whatever the previous history of 24.1–13, the prophecy in it of a
world-wide catastrophe which affects men of all classes and all
places should be regarded as a unity.[a] The quotation formula in v. 3b
clearly separates the previous verses, vv. 1–3a, from the rest. But in
content there is no significant division. Thus the first three verses as it
were sound the keynote for all the rest of the prophecy, and for the
whole of the composition which follows. Verses 4–6 can be recognized
as a second stanza: the keyword with which they open is taken up
once again in v. 7. In content they supply the reason for the prophecy,
but in formal terms they constitute a complete prophecy of warning.
Verses 7–13 prophesy and describe the effects of the coming catastrophe. The dominant feature is the end of all joy, while the background is that of the unnamed, destroyed city. Finally, the virtually
total destruction is affirmed in a similar way to 17.6. The possibility
of the destruction of a real city having formed the background to
vv. 8–12 can only arise if one overlooks the future sense of the verbs in
the perfect tense which stand at the beginning of every sentence.
Once this is perceived, no reason remains for regarding it as an
independent song, originally sung on the occasion of the destruction
of a city. The whole passage is pure prophecy, concerned with the
fact of the coming world-wide catastrophe and its effects. The way in
which it will come about is a secondary matter.

   In spite of a delight in repetitions, the passage does not succeed in
giving the reader a clear picture of the visitations which it foretells.
The fact that the surface of the earth is to be distorted may suggest
that an earthquake is meant. But this too, is obviously meant to be
understood as the consequence of an immense drought which is to
fall upon heaven and earth (cf. v. 4). And while the plundering of the
earth in v. 3 may suggest the wild onrush of soldiers, further consideration shows that it ultimately refers to nothing more than an
objective effect of the cosmic catastrophe. This casts light on the
statements about the destroyed city: its collapse seems to be the
consequence of the extermination of its population, not of a military

---

[a] O. Plöger, *Theokratie und Eschatologie*, WMANT 2, 1959, p. 73, ET *Theocracy
and Eschatology*, 1968, p. 57.

conquest. The fact that people cry in their distress for wine instead of for water is associated with the fact that the poet has become confused by his theme of the disappearance of all joy. As in 32.9ff., however, it is worthy of note, and is also reminiscent of 16.7ff. and 9ff. Anyone who does not share the emotion evoked by the apocalyptic prophet may consider it to his discredit that his imagination, with the images of distress which it has conjured up, cannot encompass the real distress of people who are starving and dying of thirst. Perhaps we may conclude from this either that he considered it necessary to base his own portrait on previous imagery, or else that he lived at a time which was relatively secure from such catastrophes.

[1–3] *The universal judgment upon the earth.* The poet's success in creating an atmosphere of gloom with his opening statement will be acknowledged, even if v. 1 is felt to be richer in words than in ideas. It is clear that Yahweh is to afflict the earth in a hitherto unparalleled way, and within the clearly foreseeable future.[a] There is nothing to explain at first how we are to understand in concrete terms the laying waste and desolation of the earth (cf. Nahum 2.11) or the twisting of its surface. It is equally unclear what is to bring about the scattering of the inhabitants of the earth, an event which recalls Gen. 11.8f. One can scarcely ignore the possibility that the poet is ultimately thinking only of the small band of survivors scattered across the whole earth. That the poet is concerned less about how the catastrophe is to take place than about its consequences for mankind is shown by the six contrasting sets of two words in v. 2 which cover cultic, domestic and economic life. The first appears to be taken from Hos. 4.9 and may have inspired the whole list.[b] The content of the verse offers no problems of understanding: the imminent catastrophe will destroy all religious and social privileges. It will come upon people without regard for their social standing, their riches or their poverty (cf. also Enoch 52.7). No one can hope to escape it because of religious or political influence, authority to command, or riches, nor indeed because of their unimportance, dependence or poverty. The contrast between priest and lay people emphasized at the beginning of the list gives an indication of the society in which the poet lived. It is clear that the priestly aristocracy was distinguished as such from the rest of the people.

Verse 3a scarcely introduces any new element into the image,

---

[a] For 'Behold, Yahweh . . .', cf. 10.33; 19.1; 22.17; 26.21; 30.27; 39.6; 40.10.
[b] Cf. H. W. Wolff, BK 14, 1, 1961, *ad loc.*

when it anticipates that the earth will not only be laid waste but also plundered. What now fills with life will disappear. No one can escape this visitation from God. This is the message which the apocalyptic poet places at the head of his poem, and for which he claims divine authority by referring to what Yahweh has already said (cf. 1.20 and 40.5). If he had been asked to authenticate this claim, he would presumably have pointed not so much to his own private experiences as to the words of the prophet, for he understood himself to be the legitimate interpreter of this message. He is presumably referring to it in the expression 'this word', which is frequently deleted.[a]

[4-6] *The judgment as a punishment.* In v. 4 the second stanza continues the prophecy of the catastrophe, and in so doing answers the fearful question aroused by the previous verses. What do they mean? There will be a drought, comes the reply, on a vast scale, and affecting not only the earth but also the heavens, described here as in v. 21 as 'the height'.[b] The meaning has to be understood within the framework of the contemporary picture of the world as the drying up of the ocean which lies above the earth, in heaven, and below the earth (cf. Gen. 1.6f., 9; 7.11 and Amos 7.4f.). The apocalyptic poet draws the idea from Hos. 4.2 as a prophetic utterance. Isaiah 33.9, on the other hand, should be regarded as an echo of the present text. The reason for Yahweh's act of judgment is given in v. 5a as the pollution of the earth by its inhabitants, which according to Num. 35.33 (cf. Ps. 106.38) is brought about by blood-guilt, according to Jer. 3.2 by the adultery of a woman, and according to Jer. 3.9 by idolatry. Number 35.33 in fact lays down that land polluted by blood can only be atoned for by the person who spilt it. The continuation shows that it is blood-guilt which is intended here. Since it must be a covenant which takes in the whole of mankind, the only possible basis is the covenant with Noah in Gen. 9.1ff., which includes the legal ordinance followed by Num. 35.33 (cf. Gen. 9.6) and which is explicitly described as an everlasting covenant (Gen. 9.16). The breaking of the covenant (cf. Lev. 26.15; Deut. 31.16; Jer. 33.20; Ezek. 17.15) brings into force the curse which the apocalyptic writer naturally assumes is linked with the making of this covenant (cf. Deut. 27.15ff., 24; 28.15ff., 23 and also Deut. 29.19). While in v. 6 the curse appears as a 'malign force acting on its own'[c] (cf. Lev. 5.1) we must not over-

---

[a] Cf. Plöger, p. 71; ET p. 55.

[b] Cf. also below, on 32.15.

[c] W. Schottroff, *Der altisraelitische Fluchspruch*, WMANT 30, 1969, p. 29.

look the fact that it ultimately derives its power from Yahweh as the
sole guarantor of the covenant (cf. Zech. 5.1ff.). Any one who has
brought guilt upon himself falls victim to the consequence of guilt,
punishment, unless his sins have been pardoned (cf. Ps. 34.22). Here
it falls upon men by a roundabout route. The earth polluted by the
spilling of guiltless blood no longer receives rain or spring water (cf.
Deut. 28.23) and becomes unfertile. In this way the human population is wiped out in large numbers. It is certainly no accident that
our search for parallels within the prophetic books brings us once
again to Hos. 4, this time to 4.2 (cf. also Hos. 2.23ff.). It looks in fact
as though the apocalyptic poet felt that Hos. 4.1–10 gave him the
authority for the present prophecy, and that he had found there
the answer to his question concerning God's plans for mankind and
the earth. This, however, is evidence against the suggestion we made
at the beginning, that he lived in a specially peaceful period. One
must at least assume that he so frequently received news of wars and
rumours of war that he considered the hour had come in which the
prophecy of the book of Hosea, which he regarded as referring to the
whole earth, would be fulfilled.[a] If we feel that this led him away
from the prophet's message, it brings him nearer to the reader who is
searching the bible for an answer to the problems of his life, and the
preacher who is seeking guidance for his congregation.

[7–13] *The consequences of the judgment.* If we ignore v. 13, which is
clearly based upon 17.16, there is no link with an underlying prophetic text comparable to that in the previous stanzas, although there
are many expressions reminiscent of passages in scripture. The
repetition in v. 7 of the theme of the drought from v. 4, which
artistically links the two final stanzas, seems to echo Joel 1.10 and 13
(cf. also Hag. 1.11): on the thirsty earth the juice dries up in the
grapes and the branches of the vine. The close connection, obvious to
anyone living in Mediterranean regions, between wine and joy (cf.
Judg. 9.13) brings into the foreground the theme of the end of joy,
v. 8 echoing Lam. 5.15 and the content of v. 9 being reminiscent of
Isa. 5.11f. and Amos 6.3ff., but also of Joel 1.5 and 16. Verse 11 is
remotely reminiscent of Jer. 14.2. A comparison with Joel 1 shows
how much more concrete the description of the drought is there than
in the present passage. But one could scarcely venture to treat Joel 1
as the basic text on which the present stanza is based. Finally, it is
surprising that the prophecy of the desolation and ultimate decay of

[a] Isa. 33.8 takes up the ideas of the breach of the covenant in a different way.

the city, which is given here as an example of the fate of all cities, should be followed by a recurrence of the theme of the end of wine and joy (cf. also 32.12) when in view of the general distress and many deaths, leading to the desolation and ultimately to the decay of the cities, we would expect to find a reference to funeral laments. This may well be related to the fact that the apocalyptic writer lived in a society which was itself unaffected by the wars of the time, and in which the upper classes at least could devote themselves undisturbed to a life of enjoyment. The preacher seeks to impress upon them that the time is not far off in which their survivors, and all whose main aim is pleasure and the enjoyment of life, will long for the golden days of the past and go wailing through the streets. In accordance with the whole context, v. 12 can hardly be regarded as an allusion to military attacks leading to the destruction of the city. In a city empty of human beings everything decays, even the gates. Similarly, v. 10 also assumes only the decay of a dying city, in which the dwellings are either kept locked by the few survivors or which are collapsing so that their entrance is blocked. Joy will come to an end; the present life of the cities will cease! Verse 13 correctly summarizes the meaning of the stanza, that only a minute number upon the whole earth will survive the catastrophe. It recalls the beating of the olive trees, when, as explained in regard to 17.6, only a few olives are left hanging on the tree, and extends the simile of 17.6 to the grape harvest, when only a few grapes are left for the gleaners in the vineyard.

CHAPTER 24.14–16a

The Rejoicing of the Time of Salvation

14 They lift up
    their voices, and rejoice
  at the majesty of Yahweh,
    they shout (louder) than at the Sea.[a]

[a] For the construction cf. G-K, § 133e and Kessler, *ad loc.*

15 Therefore in the lands of light[a]
   honour Yahweh
   in the islands of the sea,
      the name of Yahweh
      the God of Israel.
16 From the end of the earth
      we hear songs of praise,
      splendour to the righteous!

This short prophecy has been treated by modern commentators in a number of different ways. Whereas some regard it as purely a future prophecy, others regard it as a description of premature joy on the actual occasion of an act of salvation which was supposed at the time to have brought the turning point of history. The reasons for the latter view have first of all been that the new departure in v. 16b seems to assume a contradiction of this sort, and sometimes also that the origin of the rejoicing seems to be the sea.[b] Of course there are reasons for rejecting both of these arguments. In the first place, there is nothing to suggest that the tense of the verbs should be regarded as anything other than future, as in the preceding passage 24.1-13. The third verb in v. 14, as a perfect at the beginning of a sentence, must of course be taken in the same sense as the imperfects. It is also clear that in exactly the same way as Ps. 113.3, v. 15 addresses its call to rejoicing first to the east and then to the islands lying in the west. There is also a possibility, however, that the end of v. 14 is not an indication of direction at all, but is, as implied in the above translation, an allusion to the miracle at the Red Sea. Of course it is not possible to be absolutely sure of this.

[a] Since M. Jastrow, *Dictionary of the Targum* I, New York ²1950, p. 32, recognizes an 'ôr II with the meaning 'break of day' there is no need to follow Procksch in referring to the interpretation which has become usual since the time of Ewald, where *bā'ûrîm* is understood as a form of 'ûryā I, the evening horizon, the place where the sun goes down, the west.
[b] Cf. W. Rudolph, *Jesaja 24-27*, BWANT 62, 1933, pp. 31f. and pp. 61f.; O. Plöger, pp. 74f.; ET, pp. 57f.; O. Ludwig, Die Stadt in der Jesaja-Apokalypse, thesis, Bonn 1961, pp. 98f. and pp. 102ff. and also M.-L. Henry, *Glaubenskrise und Glaubensbewährung in der Dichtung der Jesajaapokalypse*, BWANT 86, 1967, p. 62 and pp. 54f. Henry thinks that the rejoicing is at the conquest of Babylon by Cyrus in 539, Rudolph to that associated with the conquest of Babylon by Alexander the Great in 331, and Ludwig in the battle at Emmaus in 165 BC which is decisive in I Macc. 3.37-4.25, and in which the Maccabees achieved their first great victory. Plöger does not commit himself.

Following the prophecy of the world-wide catastrophe, we are introduced to a new group of persons, distinguished by an emphatic pronoun from the rest of mankind, which was treated as a whole in the previous prophecy. This group is to rejoice at the majesty of Yahweh, and in the conceptual world of Jewish eschatology it is obvious to suppose that they are members of the people of God. For according to this mode of thought the judgment upon the world ultimately means salvation for Israel, even though Israel and its spiritual centre at Jerusalem are first of all to share in the suffering (cf. e.g. 29.1ff.; 30.27ff.; 33 and 34f.). We find the same introduction of Israel, interrupting the general argument, in 35.2b. The things that are going to bring Israel's salvation in the future will surpass the miracle of the exodus at the first, and will call forth from those who are redeemed an even greater rejoicing (cf. Ex. 15.1f. 20f. and Isa. 41.17ff.; 43.16ff.). No consideration is given to the concrete events, to the way in which Yahweh's majesty is to be demonstrated so that Israel shall have reason to rejoice. The apocalyptic writer also does not attempt to establish any connection with the preceding prophecy of world-wide catastrophe. If he had been asked how the two could be reconciled, the drought falling upon the whole world and the vast slaughter among mankind that it brings, and the subsequent glorification of Israel, and whether the former would not bring with it a similar loss of life among the Israelites at home and throughout the world, he would perhaps have pointed to the miracle of the Passover night or even to that of the darkness over Egypt (cf. Ex. 12.29, 22f.; 10.22f.). We must remember, however, that apocalyptic thought is still conducted entirely within the myth and does not have to construct the unity of its world, but finds it ready made in the mythical consciousness,[a] and also that the basic principle of this kind of thought is that of a multiplicity of approaches,[b] which makes it possible for statements to follow each other which according to our conceptions would be contradictory; whereas the only concern of ancient man in any particular case was to bring to prominence the aspect which concerned him at that moment. First the judgment; then the salvation of Israel! It was the purpose of the apocalyptic writer who introduced not only this song of thanksgiving but also the

[a] Cf. E. Cassirer, *Philosophie der Symbolischen Formen II. Das Mythische Denken,* Darmstadt 1953, pp. 78ff.

[b] Cf. H. Frankfort, *Ancient Egyptian Religion,* New York ²1949, p. 13, and O. Kaiser, *Die mythische Bedeutung des Meeres,* BZAW 78, ²1962, pp. 5ff.

song in 25.1f., that both should be emphasized. It is not clear who are the speakers in vv. 15 and 16a. The most likely possibility is the redeemed Jews in the Holy Land, who are now putting out a call to the nations of the world to give their God Yahweh the honour due to him, and hear their call echoed by the choirs at the ends of the earth. That this interpretation is not pure imagination is shown not only by the emphasis upon Yahweh as the God of Israel, but also the fact that in passages such as Ps. 76.11; 97.1, 6; 98.2ff.; Isa. 42.10, 12 and 51.5, we learn that the nations and islands are waiting upon Yahweh and giving him honour. Thus the nations set forth, singing, upon their journey to Zion, and the great pilgrimage of the nations begins,[a] which had been awaited since the days of Deutero-Isaiah and which had been ceremoniously anticipated previously in the cult of the first temple. The word which we translate 'splendour' can mean actual jewels (cf. Ezek. 7.20), the land of Israel (Dan. 8.9; 11.16) or in more general terms anything which adorns and beautifies (cf. 4.2; 28.1ff.). In later apocalyptic the 'righteous one' is the Son of Man (cf. Enoch 38.2; 53.6). But this figure still lies beyond the horizon of the present apocalyptic writer. Since Yahweh is never called 'the righteous' without some addition (cf. Ex. 9.27)[b] we shall interpret the phrase as referring not to the Holy Land[c] but as in 26.2 to the devout Jews who, in the sense of the addition to 24.5 have not broken the covenant with Yahweh and have kept his commandments. It remains obscure how we are to understand the splendour promised to them. We may think either of the jewels which the Gentile pilgrims are to bring to Jerusalem (cf. Pss. 96.7f.; 76.11f.; Isa. 60.3ff., 9; 45.14) or else of the return of the diaspora (cf. 43.5ff.; 49.2ff.; 60.3ff.). But the poet may have been thinking of the renewal of the country, serving the Jews as an adornment (cf. 30.23ff.; 29.17; 4.2). The expression offers scope to the reader to read into it whatever seems particularly fitting and desirable to him in this context.

[a] Cf. my commentary on 2.2ff.; *Isaiah 1–12*, OTL, 1972, p. 26. The singular expression 'the end of the earth' occurs only here; elsewhere, 11.2; Ezek. 7.2; Job 37.3 and 38.13 we find the plural 'the ends of the earth', cf. also LXX and Vg.

[b] But cf. Henry, pp. 49f.

[c] Ludwig, p. 103.

CHAPTER 24.16b–20

No Escape from the Judgment

16b And I said,
It is my secret![a] It is my secret![a]
Woe ⟨to the false⟩[b] who deal falsely
the false who falsely work falsehood!

17 Scare, pitfall and snare
are upon you, O inhabitant of the earth!

18a He who flees at the sound of the scare
shall fall into the pit;
and he who climbs out of the pit
shall be caught in the snare.

18b For the sluices of heaven will be opened,
and the foundations of the earth will tremble.

19 ⟨Bursting⟩,[b] the earth will burst,[c]
breaking, the earth will break,
shaking, the earth will shake.

20 The earth will stagger like a drunken man,
sway like a hut;
for its criminality lies heavy upon it,
and it will fall, and will not rise again.

This passage looks back behind 24.14–16a and returns to the coming judgment. The link obtained by means of the words 'And I said' is a loose one, and it is scarcely possible to base upon it the theory that there was a disagreement within Judaism, one group seeing the onset of the time of salvation in a particular event which had already come about, and another whose spokesman insists here that the time of salvation will be preceded by the judgment of the world.[d] The way in which the apocalyptic writer in this passage works is so similar to that which we observed in 24.1–3 that it is likely that the author is the

[a] Cf. LXX and Tg, and also M. Jastrow, *Dictionary of the Targum* II, New York [2]1950, p. 1464 sub voce *rāzā᾽*, *rāz*. Since this is a lamentation concerning the false, the derivation from the Arabic *ruz᾽un*, lost, harm, misfortune, proposed by, e.g., Delitzsh, seems inappropriate. *KBL* sub voce does not attempt an interpretation.

[b] Cf. *BHS*.

[c] Delete the article.

[d] Cf. above p. 186, note b, and with Gray, Jer. 17.18; Pss. 20.8 and 120.7, and also the conjecture discussed above, p. 177 that *wā᾽ōmar* was first introduced as a transitional phrase when 24.14–16a was later interpolated.

same. The different expectations – that of a great drought in 24.1ff. and the destruction of the cosmic order here – do not represent an exclusive contradiction or disagreement between the two prophecies. This can be seen from vv. 17 and 18a, which in a threefold image emphasize that the coming catastrophes offer no hope of an escape for men. We must not overlook the fact that vv. 18b–20 not only give the reason for the warning in the first stanza, vv. 16b–18a, but in the present context also prepare the way for 21–23.

[16b–18a] *No escape from the judgment.* The devout author's study of scripture has made him certain what will happen in the future. Thus he regards himself as the bearer of the eschatological secret,[a] the content of which first of all justifies a cry of despair at those who are false, treacherous and objectively unreliable. This is a particular characteristic, within the expectations of the final age, of the mysterious destroyer and figure of falsehood, whom we encounter in 21.2 as the conqueror of Babylon and in 33.1 as the attacker of Jerusalem. The plural here seems to imply the figures and forces on earth which are hostile to God and acknowledge no human relationships (cf. also Jer. 12.1) whom we met in 24.5 as those who broke the eternal covenant.[b] This is the broadest possible interpretation; that it is correct is shown by statement which follows in vv. 17 and 18a, which refers to the fate of all the inhabitants of the earth, and recurs later in Jer. 48.43f.[c] Taking up an alliterative and possibly proverbial expression, 'the (hunter's) scare and the pitfall' (cf. Lam. 3.47), the poet continues the alliteration (all three Hebrew words start with the same letter *pē*) with the 'snare' (actually the dropnet) and gives a new version of Amos 5.19, a prophecy which in language full of associations describes the darkness of the coming day of Yahweh. The purpose is to impress upon the reader that there is no escape from the judgment that is to come (cf. 24.2).

[18b–20] *The irruption of chaos.* Whereas in 24.1ff. the apocalyptic poet presented us with the picture of a terrible drought, killing vast numbers, he now intensifies the danger that is imminent by looking forward to the dissolution of the whole cosmic order. The sluices in

---

[a] The uncertainty of the translation should be explicitly mentioned, although the usage of the Targum and the testimony of the LXX seem adequate to me.

[b] M.-L. Henry, *Glaubenskrise und Glaubensbewährung*, BWANT 86, 1967, pp. 63ff., disagrees.

[c] Cf. B. Duhm, KHC 11, 1901, p. 351; A. Weiser, ATD 20/21, [5]1966, p. 401 and W. Rudolph, HAT I. 12, [3]1968, p. 283. With these scholars I disagree with P. Volz, KAT[1] 10, 1922, p. 406.

the firmament of heaven which otherwise hold back the heavenly ocean and let through only rain in the right amount, will be opened (cf. Gen. 7.11; 8.2). This means a new flood, and the abrogation of what Yahweh had created at the beginning of the third day of creation (cf. Gen. 1.9f.). But this terror is not enough; for at the same time the earth is seized by a continuous earthquake, so that it shakes (cf. Ps. 18.8)[a] in its foundations, by which it is mysteriously established upon the deep (cf. Jer. 31.37; Job 38.4ff.), breaks into pieces, looses its fixed position[b] and staggers about aimlessly and ungovernably like a drunk man,[c] or sways like a watchman's hut[d] for temporary occupation, loosely constructed of boughs and branches. Anyone who has ever experienced the irresistible force of onrushing floods and the uncanniness of even a small earthquake will understand what terrors face mankind, according to the expectation of the apocalyptic prophet. He interpreted the drought in 24.5 as a consequence of the blood guilt which polluted the earth. He does not now rest content simply with a prophecy, but points to the cause, which he sees as its criminality,[e] which can of course only mean that of its inhabitants. This lies like a heavy burden upon the earth, causing it to fall. It is notable that in this prophecy Yahweh remains completely in the background, and also that the apocalyptic writer applies to the earth the saying which in Amos 5.2 refers to the fall of Israel. Whereas the previous prophecy of catastrophe left a slight, albeit tiny hope of escaping the divine judgment, the present prophecy portrays a situation with no escape. But we may question whether the poet intended it to be understood so literally, that there was no room for hope among his own people.

[a] Cf. also Ps. 85.2; Deut. 32.22 and Eth. Enoch 55.7f.
[b] But cf. Pss. 93.1; 96.10 and 104.5.
[c] Cf. 28.7f. and 29.9.
[d] Cf. my commentary on 1.8, *Isaiah 1-12*, OTL, 1972, p. 10, note a.
[e] For the meaning of *peša'* cf. R. Knierim, *Die Hauptbegriffe für Sünde im Alten Testament*, Gütersloh 1965, pp. 179f.

CHAPTER 24.21–23

The End of all the Kingdoms of the World and the
Beginning of the Kingdom of Yahweh

21 It will come about in that day:
Yahweh will call to account
the army of the height in the height
and the kings of the earth, on the earth.
22 They will be gathered all together
as prisoners in a cistern,[a]
they will be imprisoned in a prison,
and after many days they will be called to account.
23 Then the pale one[b] will be confounded,
and the hot one[c] ashamed;
for Yahweh Sebaoth will have become king
on Mount Zion and in Jerusalem
and (shine) splendour before his elders.

At least the unknown person who interpolated 24.21–23 in their
present position was of the opinion that even though the visitation in
24.18b–20 seems to take the form of a relapse of creation into chaos,
the world and history will not really come to an end, but will only
then have their true beginning, which will then continue throughout
the future. As a result the significance of individual prophecies in the
apocalypse becomes relative, each in turn bringing particular aspects
of the final events into prominence. No attempt is possible, of course,
to fit the different statements into a coherent total picture. The
present oracle, the bulk of which is a prophecy of warning threatening
all cosmic and earthly powers other than or in opposition to Yahweh,
is clearly intended from its conclusion to be understood as a prophecy
of salvation for Jerusalem and Israel. Some of its conceptions are very
ancient, such as that of the elders of Israel, who may look upon their
God (cf. Ex. 24.9ff.). It is remarkable that the concept of the meal
which is found in Ex. 24.9ff. is not taken up again until 25.6ff. This
has rightly caused commentators to ask what the relationship is
between these two passages, and how they came to occupy their

---

[a] For the construction cf. G-K, § 117q.
[b] The reference is to the moon, in Hebrew 'the pale one'.
[c] The sun.

present position within the Apocalypse of Isaiah.[a] No less traditional, and known to us from the Old Testament, is the other conception, associated here with that of the sight of God and the covenant meal, of the inauguration of the reign of Yahweh on the occasion of his victory over the forces of chaos and the nations who represent them in history.[b] But there are other conceptions here, of which we find only the first stages in the Old Testament, such as that of the stars which act as the angels of the nations, their conquest and their long imprisonment. With the favourite formula for interpolations, 'It will come about in that day' (cf. 4.2; 3.18; 10.23; 11.10; 12.1), the apocalyptic prophet or apocalyptic redactor loosely attaches his promise to the preceding scene of horror.[c] That the day of Yahweh is meant is already indicated by the connection between 24.17f. and the text which underlies it, Amos 5.18. The details of what is to happen on this day remain obscure. The poet is either little concerned with the circumstances or is deliberately setting out to speak only in allusions, in order to satisfy the taste of a later period by making his prophecy as mysterious as possible. Or he may have been able to assume that his hearers were familiar with the details. It may even be possible that to some extent the conceptions were not yet accepted in his community, so that it was not possible to develop them further. When the poet mentions not only the visitation upon the kings of the

---

[a] The generally accepted view is expressed by M. L. Henry, p. 162: 'It seems to be generally agreed that 26.6–8 is a continuation of the conceptions of salvation in 24.21–23.' Whereas e.g. Duhm, Marti and Procksch saw 25.6ff. as an immediate and direct continuation of 24.23, Plöger, p. 77, n. 1 (ET p. 60 n. 17), emphasized the formal independence of the two passages and argued that they should be understood as two later interpolations which were independent of each other, although they may both have had in mind a particular version of the history of salvation. But there is much to be said in favour of the view of Ludwig, pp. 113f., that the first passage at least, the form of which shows no clear line of demarcation at the beginning, was from the first the product of redaction.

[b] On the tradition underlying Ex. 24 cf. W. Beyerlin, *Herkunft und Geschichte der ältesten Sinaitradition*, Tübingen 1961, pp. 33ff., 44ff., and L. Perlitt, *Bundestheologie im Alten Testament*, WMANT 36, 1969, pp. 181ff., though the dispute about the history of these traditions is itself of no importance for the understanding of our text. The discussion provoked by the hypothesis of S. Mowinckel, *Psalmenstudien* II, Kristiania, 1922, that Israelite eschatology originated in a pre-exilic festival of Yahweh's enthronement is by no means yet resolved. Cf. above, p. 15 note e, p. 16 note a and p. 86 note b.

[c] For the secondary character of 24.21–23, cf. above, p. 178.

earth,[a] but also that of 'army of the height in the height', a reader familiar with the Old Testament quickly recognizes the expression 'the height' as a favourite paraphrase in apocalyptic writing for heaven (cf. 24.18; 32.15 and 33.5). Thus the passage is speaking of the army of heaven, by which, according to Ps. 33.6; Isa. 40.26; 45.12; Jer. 33.22 and Neh. 9.6, we are to understand the stars which obey Yahweh's command.[b] But since the visitation upon them assumes their insubordination, let us once recall that the worship of the stars was of course forbidden in Israel (cf. Zeph. 1.5; Jer. 8.12; 19.13 and Deut. 4.19). In the last of these passages we find the strange conception that Yahweh has allotted the stars to the other nations to worship. From this it was only one further step to seeing in the army of heaven, or of the height, in the present passage the astral angels of the nations which we meet in the Old Testament in Dan. 8.3ff.; 10.13, 20.f.[c]

In the Ethiopian book of Enoch, an apocalypse possibly not completed until Christian times, but certainly going back in part to the beginning of the second century BC,[d] we learn more about these angelic beings who guide the course of history from the conquest of the northern kingdom by the Assyrians to the beginning of the final age with the rise of Judas Maccabaeus (cf. Eth. Enoch 89.65ff., 59), but are then cast into the lake of fire (Eth. Enoch 90.25).[e] We also find there the conception of the stars which had left their courses and are now kept prisoner in a place beyond heaven and earth for ten thousand years (cf. Eth. Enoch 18.11ff.). In 18.14 it is implicitly stated that this is also a prison for the army of heaven. The present apocalyptic writer does not seem to have elaborated his astral angelology in such detail. That he is thinking of the angels of the nations seems likely from the parallel drawn with the kings of the

---

[a] For *pqd* in a hostile sense cf. 26.14; 27.1 and Ps. Sol. 15.14; Syr. Baruch 83.2; 20.2 and IV Esdras 5.56. That a visitation can possess a double aspect is shown by Eth. Enoch 60.6.

[b] The conception of the army of heaven at the heavenly court of Yahweh, cf. Isa. 40.3; Job 1.6 and 2.1, can be ignored in this context, although there are cross connections in tradition history.

[c] Cf. A. Bentzen, HAT I. 19, ²1952, p. 69, and M. Hengel, *Judentum und Hellenismus*, WUNT 10, 1969, pp. 341ff.

[d] For this apocalypse and the other pseudepigrapha, cf. L. Rost, *Einleitung in die alttestamentlichen Apokryphen und Pseudepigraphen*, Heidelberg 1971, pp. 84ff.

[e] Cf. Hengel, pp. 342ff.

earth. Whereas in the concept of the abyss the idea of a prison filled with fire at the edge of the world has clearly become combined with that of a dungeon under the earth (cf. Rev. 9.2, 11; 11.7; 17.8), the present poet seems in fact to be thinking only of the great cistern in the underworld (cf. 14.15), the kingdom of the dead under the earth.[a] There all who possessed cosmic and earthly power were to wait until they were brought for the final judgment, a conception which reminds us of Enoch 18.16, but also of Rev. 20.2f., and clearly envisages something like an intermediate Messianic kingdom preceding the last judgment. The extent to which this conception, which probably goes back in the end to Iranian religion, had spread in Judaism can be seen from the allusions in Eth. Enoch 91.12ff.; 93.3ff.; Syr. Bar. 29.3ff., orac. sibyll. 3.652ff. and IV Esdras 7.28ff., as well as Syr. Bar. 40; Prayer of Manasses 2ff.[b]

The further statement that the moon and the sun will be confounded seems not to refer to the terror of the two heavenly bodies which give light to the earth at the mighty appearance of God, after his victory over the powers in heaven and earth opposed to him and ultimate enthronement in triumph as king in Jerusalem and on Zion in his temple (cf. Eth. Enoch 102.2 as well as Ps. 47.9; 93.1; 98.10; 97.1; Zech. 14.9). The meaning is literally that the splendour of his light, manifesting his presence, his *kābōd* (cf. Ezek. 43.4; 10.8ff.; 1.4ff.) shines so bright that not only the holy city but the whole earth is lit by it, and the light of the sun and the moon grows pale and is superfluous (cf. Isa. 60.19; Zech. 14.7 and Rev. 21.23; 22.5). Just as Yahweh once revealed himself on Sinai before the elders of his people in the whole fulness of his light when the covenant was made (cf. Ex. 24.3ff. 9f., he will once again show himself to the elders of Israel in order, needless to say, to ratify this covenant for all time. Note that in the Apocalypse of Isaiah there is not a single word about the Messiah, king of the time of salvation. When Yahweh himself begins to reign over his people, the Messiah no longer seems to be needed, but only the elders, who represent the people before God.

[a] F. Nötscher, *Altorientalischer und alttestamentlicher Auferstehungsglaube*, Würzburg 1926, p. 210 and Ezek. 32.18ff.; Pss. 30.4; 8.4f. and Prov. 1.12.

[b] Cf. E. Lohse, NTD 11, ³1971, pp. 103f. and Nötscher, pp. 67ff.; J. Duchesne-Guillemin, *Ormazd et Ahriman. L'aventure dualiste dans l'antiquité*, Paris 1953, pp. 66ff.; F. König, 'Die Religion Zarathustras' in *Christus und die Religionen der Erde* II, Freiburg 1951, pp. 644ff. and also the articles by H. Cazelles and M. Mole in: *Le jugement des morts*, Source Orientales 4, Paris 1961, pp. 103ff. and 143ff.

It is easy nowadays to be somewhat bewildered by the certainty of the faith that lies behind these colourful religious ideas, drawn from many sources. But it is right to ask whether we can cheerfully live and grow old without the central hope of this text, that God will one day call to account all the rulers of this world, and make an end to all evil, and that nothing will any longer be able to separate man from God (cf. Rom. 8.38f.).

CHAPTER 25.1–5

The World Capital Falls

1 Yahweh, thou art my God;
      I will exalt thee, I will praise thy name;
   for thou hast done wonderful things,
      plans formed of old,[a] faithful and sure.
2 For thou has made ⟨the city⟩[b] a heap,
      the impregnable city a ruin;
   the palace of aliens is no city,
      it will not be rebuilt for ever.
3 Therefore ⟨people⟩[c] will glorify thee;
      ⟨   ⟩[d] ruthless nations will fear thee.
4 For thou hast been a refuge to the poor,
      a strong refuge to the needy in his distress,
   a shelter from the storm,
      a shade from the heat.

ᵃ For the use of *mērāḥōq* to refer to time cf. II Kings 19.25; Isa. 37.26; II Sam. 7.19 and I Chron. 17.7.

ᵇ Read *ʿîr*, with many commentators from Dillmann-Kittel to Fohrer. MT is due to the distraction of the eye by the lines that follow or the continuation.

ᶜ It is obvious that the received text of v. 3 is not in order. If it is impossible to understand the received *ʿam-ʿāz* in a collective sense or to look for an unknown contemporary illusion, perhaps to the Macedonians, the parallelism suggests an original *ʿammîm*, which after the interpretation of *qiryat* in v. 3b was changed to *ʿam-ʿāz* to strengthen the reference to the master race of the world capital.

ᵈ Delete *qiryat* as a later exegesis, which conflicts with the content of v. 2.

> For the mind of the ruthless is like a winter storm,[5] like
> heat in a dry land.[a]
> Thou dost subdue the noise of the aliens;
>   heat by the shade of a cloud,
>   so the song of the ruthless is stilled.

In 25.1–5 our attention seems to be directed away from the future, to which the prophecies in ch. 24 refer, to the past, for an anonymous worshipper seems to be uttering a song of thanksgiving upon the fall of a city. But v. 3 implies that there are no grounds for trying to fit the song into the known history of the Jews, or to look for a city, the fall of which could have inspired the poet's song.[b] A glance at Ps. 86.9 shows that the subject here is probably the conversion of the nations to Yahweh at the end of time. Finally, the song also has distinctive formal characteristics. The occasion for it, an event which is decisive not merely for an individual, but ultimately for all the nations of the world, would lead one to describe it as a collective thanksgiving, a thanksgiving of the people.[c] Against this, however, there is the fact that the song is uttered by an individual and lacks a call to his own community or nation to join in the praise. It is equally striking that the consequence drawn in v. 3 from the saving act of God is provided with a reason in v. 4 in the language of the individual psalms. Finally, one may hesitate whether to treat the original substance of v. 5 as expressing the theme of confidence, or, as we have done, to take it as the transition to a prophecy. Thus it looks as though this passage is not a psalm of thanksgiving taken from a different context, but a prophetic song of thanksgiving composed specifically for its present place.[d] The poet, thoroughly familiar with the language of the psalms, expresses in this way his firm conviction that the unknown city, which like Babylon in chs. 13 and 14 is a symbol of the whole concentration of power hostile to God, will one day be annihilated, and anticipates the thanksgiving for this. But because the event still lies in the future and very little of Yahweh's power can be observed at the present moment, he begins with a confident profession of faith

---

[a] A glossator was also at work here. By contrast to his work (or that of his predecessors and successors) in v. 3 his comment here does not introduce a disruptive element.

[b] Cf. above pp. 176f.

[c] See e.g. B. J. Lindblom, *Die Jesaja-Apokalypse Jes. 24–27*, LUÅ, NF I. 34.3, 1938, p. 30.

[d] Cf. also Rudolph, p. 35, and Fischer and Fohrer, *ad loc.*

in Yahweh (cf. Pss. 31.15; 40.6; Jer. 31.18 and especially Ps. 118.28). Yahweh will not disappoint the trust placed in him and so will give reason for thanksgiving (cf. Pss. 30.2; 145.1; Ex. 15.2 and Ps. 54.8). What Yahweh will do – we can completely abandon the fiction that the prophet is looking back on the past – is contrary to human expectations and is therefore astonishing and marvellous (cf. Pss. 9.5, 2; 40.6). But it is nevertheless in accordance with the plans which he made long ago and which of course are already known (cf. also 9.5).

It may be that here the poet is not merely giving an eschatological interpretation to oracles against foreign nations such as chs. 13, 14 and 21, but also had certain psalms in mind. It is possible that the train of ideas between v. 1b and v. 2 may have been influenced by II Kings 19.5, cf. Isa. 37.26. But we must not imagine the poet as it were reading through his rolls of the scriptures and making comments upon it. His whole life must have been so filled by the conceptions of scripture and by daily familiarity with it that its words and phrases poured from him. As in a city on which a religious curse has been imposed, the palace of the aliens, i.e. its centre of government, will no longer be rebuilt once Yahweh has turned it into a heap of ruins (cf. Deut. 13.17; Ezek. 26.14 and Isa. 23.13). This demonstration of Yahweh's power will open the eyes of the nations who now rely upon their own power, and they will become aware who the real lord of the nations is, so that in future they will recognize him, pay him due honour and fear him, abandoning for ever their own rule by force. (cf. Pss. 86.9; 67.4f.; 96.7ff.; 47.4, 10; 68.29f.; Isa. 40.4f., as well as Pss. 33.8; 67.8; 40.4 and 96.9). The destruction of the capital city of the world will produce this effect because it will clearly be to the benefit of the people of Israel, who are thought of here as needy and poor (cf. 14.30; Ps. 27.13 and 82.4) and whose God will reveal himself as a true refuge by saving them (cf. Pss. 27.1; 31.3; 90.1 and Isa. 4.6).[a] Thus the poet ends his prayer with an expression of his confidence that Yahweh will subdue the noise of the aliens, and silence the arrogant song of those who use violence (cf. 17.12f.; 13.4; Amos 2.2). At the same time, he shows that he and his companions are suffering under the rule of foreigners, which has lasted since the conquest of Jerusalem in 587 (cf. Lam. 5.2; Isa. 1.7).[b]

[a] For the similes see the comment on 32.2.
[b] For the stratum to which 25.1ff. belongs within the whole composition, cf. above p. 178.

CHAPTER 25.6–8

The Feast for the Nations

6 Yahweh Sebaoth will make
   for all people on this mountain
   a feast of fat dishes, a feast of wine on the lees,
      of fat dishes with the marrow, of strained wine on the lees.
7 He will destroy on this mountain
      the cover,[a] ⟨covering⟩[b] all peoples,
      the veil, veiling all nations.
8 *He will destroy death for ever.*[c]
   The Lord Yahweh will wipe away
      the tears from all faces,
   the shame of his people he will take away
      from all the earth.
   For Yahweh has spoken (it).

The same hand as introduced 24.21–23 seems also to be responsible for the present description of salvation, in which the nations are drawn into the salvation.[d] Whereas the preceding prophetic song of thanksgiving, 25.1–5, speaks of the recognition of Yahweh by the nations after the destruction of the capital city of the world, the eschatological prophet, learned in scripture, who writes here describes all nations as making a pilgrimage to Zion,[e] which is described in v. 6, referring back to 24.23, simply as 'this mountain'.

[6] The tradition largely regards the pilgrimage of the nations to Zion from the point of view of the gifts which the nations bring to Zion (cf. Pss. 96.7f.; 68.29ff.; 72.10; Isa. 45.14; 60.3ff. and 66.12) or even of the services which they can render to those who live in the city of God (cf. Isa. 45.23; 61.5f. and 66.12, 19f.) and who are now,

[a] Literally: 'surface of the husk'. Cf. Dillmann-Kittel and Job 41.5.
[b] Cf. *BHS*.
[c] Verse 8aα is, as is generally recognized, a later interpolation which interrupts the direct continuity of thought between v. 7 and v. 8a; the covering which a mourner has over his face is removed, and then his tears are wiped away.
[d] Cf. above p. 178.
[e] Cf. my commentary on 2.2ff., *Isaiah 1–12*, OTL, 1972, p. 26, and Zech. 8.22; Jer. 3.17; Ps. 102.19ff. and 87, and the comments of G. Fohrer, *ThWBNT* VII, p. 315 (repr. *Studien zur alttestamentlichen Theologie und Geschichte*, BZAW 115, 1969, p. 233).

as priests, contrasted with all other nations (cf. Isa. 61.6 and Ex. 19.6).[a] The idea of that the nations will be welcomed, which is given its finest expression in Isa. 2.2ff., forms a contrast to this. The prophet here, however, concentrates on the meal which Yahweh gives to the nations who have gathered together for the festival (cf. Zech. 14.16ff.). The very best is set before them, fat delicacies flavoured with the marrow (cf. Ps. 63.6 and Job 36.16) and old wine, fermented out, and still standing on its lees, though of course strained before being poured. On the occasion of Yahweh's enthronement (cf. 24.23) a share in the great sacrificial meal will be given both to foreign pilgrims to the festival as well as to the Jews themselves (cf. I Sam. 11.15; I Kings 1.25, 9ff.; II Sam. 6.18; I Kings 8.62ff. and Neh. 8.10, and also Pss. 23.6; 36.9 and Jer. 31.14.[b] This table fellowship brings the nations into fellowship with God (cf. Matt. 8.11; 2.22ff.; Luke 14.15; 22.18 and Rev. 19.9).[c] In the Old Testament, the idea of the pilgrimage of the nations to Zion occupies the same position as the idea of mission in the New Testament. The sending of messengers out into the world is the consequence of the concealed revelation of God in the crucified Christ and the proclamation of the risen Christ. Whereas in the Old Testament and in Judaism the idea of the salvation of the nations is a marginal one,[d] it can still be said that in the end both the Old and the New Testaments are in agreement in looking forward to the acceptance of all nations into fellowship with God, since otherwise the honour of God would not be maintained and peace among conflicting nations would not be conceivable (cf. 45.23f. with Phil. 2.9ff.). **[7]** For the nations, too, this will bring an

[a] Cf. also G. Fohrer, 'Priesterliches Königtum', *ThZ* 19, 1963, pp. 359ff. (repr. *Studien*, pp. 149ff.).

[b] For the background in tradition history cf. S. Mowinckel, *Psalmenstudien* II, SNVAO II, 1921, 6, Kristiania 1922, Amsterdam, [2]1961, p. 126 and pp. 296ff.; and E. S. Mulder, *Die Teologie van die Jesaja-Apokalipse*, Groningen and Djakarta 1954, pp. 29f. and J. C. de Moor, *New Year with Canaanites and Israelites*, KC 21, 1972, pp. 6, 17f. and 28.

[c] Cf. also Eth. Enoch 62.14; Slavonic Enoch 42.5. For the possible eschatological character of the common meals of the Qumran community, cf. F. M. Cross, *The Ancient Library of Qumran and Modern Biblical Studies*, New York [2]1961, pp. 83ff., 241, but also J. Jeremias, *Die Abendmahlsworte Jesu*, Göttingen, [3]1960, pp. 25ff.; ET *The Eucharistic Words of Jesus*, new ed., London and New York 1966, pp. 31f.

[d] Cf. W. Bousset and H. Gressmann, *Die Religion des Judentums im späthellenistischen Zeitalter*, HNT 21, [3]1926, pp. 234f. – For the Old Testament expectations cf. R. Martin-Achard, *Israël et les nations*, Neuchâtel 1959 and G. Fohrer, *ThWBNT* VII, p. 315 (repr. *Studien*, pp. 232f); *TDNT* VII, p. 316.

end to the time of suffering and mourning. Though they are mourning the dead who have fallen in the last great battles of history, on Zion Yahweh will as it were take away from them the veil of covering with which they have covered their faces as mourners (cf. II Sam. 15.30; 19.5; Jer. 14.3f. and Esth. 6.12).[a]

[8] A later redactor has correctly interpreted the preceding verses when he adds that God will abolish death itself, the fate which man must suffer; for as long as people die, there can be no end to mourning and suffering upon this earth. The apostle Paul and the author of the Revelation of John seem to some extent to have agreed with him by using this phrase, or the whole verse, to express the Christian hope of eternal life and the ultimate abolition of death (cf. I Cor. 15.54[b] and Rev. 21.4). If the uncovered faces still show traces of tears, Yahweh will wipe them all away and take away the cares of all who have gathered together in Jerusalem to celebrate the beginning of his reign upon this earth.[c] The rejoicing of those who in the kingdom of God partake of fellowship with God and the peace of his kingdom overcomes the sorrow which in a world without peace, failing to acknowledge the rule of God, spares no one. It is of course taken for granted that this will bring an end to the sufferings of Israel, but the preoccupations of the prophet's community call for the explicit statement that the shame of having been ruled by foreigners since the fall of Jerusalem in 587, of having to live as strangers among the nations and suffering want as the people of God (cf. Jer. 24.9; 29.18; 51.51; Ezek. 5.15; 22.4; 36.30; Neh. 1.3; 3.36; 2.17; Joel 2.17),[d] will be taken away, as is promised in Zeph. 3.18 and Joel 2.19.[e] After the conquest of the world power and the glorification of God in his people, Israel will no longer have to suffer the contradiction which has characterized its whole journey through history: that of being the people of the God who created heaven and earth, and guides the stars and the destinies of nations, and yet of being at the same time

[a] For the metaphorical relating of the action to the removal of spiritual blindness by Procksch, cf. Kessler, *Gott geht es um das Ganze. Jesaja 56–66 und Jesaja 24–27 übersetzt und ausgelegt*, BAT 19, 1960, *ad loc.*

[b] Paul follows Th, cf. also Aq, where *neṣaḥ* is taken in the meaning 'victory' which is possible in Aramaic, cf. M. Jastrow, *Dictionary of the Targum* II, p. 928, sub voce *neṣaḥ* and *neṣaḥ*.

[c] Cf. also Ps. 126.5f.; Isa. 35.10; 51.11.

[d] Cf. also Dan. 9.16.

[e] Cf. also Isa. 52.13ff.

one nation among others, and, worst of all, subject to the Gentiles and largely forced to live as pariahs among them.[a]

CHAPTER 25.9–10a

Israel's Song of Thanksgiving

9   It will be said on that day:
    Lo, here[b] is our God,
       in whom we hoped, for him to save us.
    This is Yahweh, in whom we hoped![c]
    Let us be glad and rejoice in his salvation!
10a For the hand of Yahweh will rest on this mountain.

The delivery of Israel from its shame (cf. 25.8b) inspires the prophet to a song of thanksgiving, the main theme of which is that the hope he has placed in Yahweh has not been disappointed.

There is disagreement about the length of the song. Some commentators limit it to v. 9, and regard v. 10a as the transition to a further prophecy,[d] but most regard it as ending with v. 10a, although in this case it is sometimes treated as a direct continuation of 25.6–8.[e] Others again regard vv. 9–12 as a late addition and a unity,[f] while others include v. 12 at least in the short song.[g]

Since the song of rejoicing follows 25.6ff., and, as is shown by the words 'on this mountain' in v. 10a (cf. 25.6f.; 24.23), seems to assume the preceding description of salvation, the content of the attack upon

[a] For this cf. M. Weber, *Das antike Judentum. Ges. Aufsätze zur Religionssoziologie* III, Tübingen ³1963 (1920), pp. 2ff.

[b] Cf. also 21.9.

[c] In spite of the absence of v. 9b in LXX the secondary character of the phrase is not certain. The repetition may be intentional.

[d] Cf. Dillmann-Kittel, *ad loc.*

[e] So Procksch, *ad loc.* and Lindblom, pp. 37ff. but cf. also Plöger, pp. 79f. and Fohrer *ad loc.*, as well as M.-L. Henry, pp. 184f.

[f] So Duhm, Marti, Feldmann, Fischer and Ziegler *ad loc.*; Mulders, p. 34; cf. also Kissane, p. 278, as well as Gray, who is always cautious.

[g] Cf. P. Lohmann, 'Die selbständigen lyrischen Abschnitte in Jes. 24–27', *ZAW* 37, 1917/18, pp. 30ff.; Rudolph, pp. 16f. and also Kessler, p. 147.

Moab seems to be too late for this context.[a] It must be admitted, however, that the range of eschatological expectations is so wide, and the lack of any structure which corresponds to our logic is so marked, that it is not impossible that the prophet had in mind the contrast between the fate of Israel and Moab: Israel's place is with Yahweh on Mount Zion, but that of Moab is on the dunghill.[b] Since there is still some doubt whether in the light of 26.5 v. 12 is original,[c] we may tentatively limit the song to vv. 9–10a. Although it is so short, it is questionable whether it was taken from some other context and was not rather composed for its present position, in which it is perfectly appropriate.[d]

As in the prophetic Ps. 25.1–5, there is a clear exhortatory intention in this short song of thanksgiving, that of countering all the doubts aroused by the contrast between the present situation of Judaism and the extraordinary changes anticipated, and of giving an assurance in the form of a song anticipating the thanksgiving, that the hopes placed in Yahweh will not have been in vain and the hour of their fulfilment will certainly come. Deutero-Isaiah, Isa. 40.9, called for a proclamation to the people of Jerusalem that their God was drawing near.[e] Now, in the time of salvation, the people of Jerusalem and the Jews gathered from the whole world to Zion for the enthronement of their God repeatedly cry out in triumph that the God in whom they had hoped (cf. 33.2; 26.8; 40.21; Pss. 37.9; 25.3, 5; 39.8; 130.5 and 40.2) is now in their midst. They call upon one another to rejoice (cf. Ps. 32.11; 27.12; and Isa. 66.10f.) because his hand now rests upon Zion, taking possession of it, guiding and guarding it (cf. II Chron. 30.12; Ezra 7.6, 28; 8.31).[f]

---

[a] Rudolph, p. 17.
[b] Mulders, p. 34.
[c] But cf. Lohmann, p. 37 and Rudolph, p. 17.
[d] I disagree with M.-L. Henry, p. 185. Cf. above p. 178.
[e] Cf. K. Elliger, BK 11. 1, 1970, p. 36.
[f] Mulders, op. cit.

CHAPTER 25.10b–12

Moab will End in the Dung-pit

10b But Moab will be trodden down in his place,
    as straw is trodden down in the dung-pit.
11 Even though he spreads out his hands in it,
    As a swimmer spreads (them) out to swim,
    He will lay low his efforts in spite of the skill[a]
    of his hands.
12 Your impregnable, fortified walls he will bring down,
    lay low, cast down to the ground, to the dust.

Unless 25.10b–12 were written originally as a continuation of the song of thanksgiving in 25.9–10a, and therefore belong to the original body of the prophecy,[b] they were either interpolated on a historical occasion which is unknown to us[c] or added by a redactor who thought it necessary to emphasize, following 25.6–10a, that the hated Moab would not have any part in the coming fellowship of the nations with God (cf. Deut. 23.4) and would come to a shameful end. Not content with the images which were at hand in chs. 15 and 16, he perhaps intended the dramatic picture here to be an appendix to the oracle against Edom in ch. 34; the despicable vulgarity of the present passage exceeds even the bloodthirstiness of ch. 34. While the conception of the treading down of enemies as such is taken from tradition (cf. Judg. 8.7; II Kings 13.7; Amos 1.3; Isa. 41.15 and Micah 4.13), it remained for this writer to elaborate it and give it its present remarkable setting. The implication is perfectly clear: Moab will come to a shameful end, and in spite of its despairing efforts will be unable to resist, since it will be opposed by none other than Yahweh. Verse 12, derived from 26.5, is an attempt to give the prophecy a concrete form appropriate to the context (cf. 25.2).

[a] Cf. Arabic *irbatun*, skill.
[b] Cf. above p. 202.
[c] Cf. Plöger, p. 80; ET p. 63.

CHAPTER 26.1–6

The Chorus of the Redeemed

1 In that day
this song will be sung
in the land of Judah.
We have a strong city;
salvation is set up[a]
by battlements and bulwarks.

2 Open the gates
For the entry of the righteous nation
that keeps faith.

3 For constant purpose[b]
thou dost store up well-being 〈   〉[c]
because it trusts in thee.

4 Trust in Yahweh for ever
for 〈   〉[c] Yahweh is
an everlasting rock.

5 For he has brought low
the inhabitants of the height.
He cast[d] them down,
cast them down to the ground,
threw them down to the dust.

6 Feet trampled[e] it,
the feet of the poor,
the steps of the lowly!

Like ch. 25, ch. 26 also begins with a prophetic song, which anticipates
the fall of the world power and the beginning of the time of salvation.[f]

---

  [a] For the construction cf. G-K, § 145O.
  [b] For the meaning of *yēṣer* cf. e.g. Gen. 6.5; 8.21.
  [c] Cf. *BHS*.
  [d] In spite of Lindblom, p. 47, the imperfects are completely unobjectionable. At
the beginning of a sentence they usually have the function of the perfect.
  [e] Cf. G-K, § 245k and note.
  [f] Ch. 26 is sub-divided and regarded by commentators in very different ways.
Some see the original unity as consisting of vv. 1–19, cf. e.g. Duhm, Dillmann-
Kittel, and also Marti, as well as Feldmann, Ziegler and Gray *ad loc*. Others,
however, separate vv. 1–14 from 15–19 and 20–21, such as Lindblom, pp. 40ff., or
vv. 1–6 from 7–21, as Guthe, Procksch, Plöger, pp. 84ff. (ET pp. 68ff.) and Fohrer,
or else from vv. 7–10; 11–21 like Kessler, or v. 7–27.1, like Fischer. Rudolph

This at least is the way in which the song preserved in vv. 1b–6 is intended to be understood in its present position following v. 1a. Consequently, any possible previous history of the song can be ignored as of no significance for its present context. Verses 1b–6 cannot be called a song of thanksgiving in the narrower sense. It lacks the typical themes of this category, such as an introduction calling upon people to sing, give praise or play music for Yahweh, the invocation of Yahweh, or words recalling the distress which has been endured. Instead, the song begins in v. 1b with the spontaneous rejoicing which sounds the first basic note of the poem, the security of the singers' own city. Verse 2 follows with an address to the gates, and rapidly reveals the situation envisaged, in which warriors or pilgrims (it is not certain which) are demanding entry. Verse 3 is difficult to describe. It is perhaps best to see it as an expression of confidence. Verse 4 follows with a demand to trust in Yahweh, including a reason, which is followed in vv. 5 and 6 by an account of the saving act which Yahweh has carried out, while v. 6 dwells on the activity of the poor and needy. Verse 5, with its theme of the destruction of a lofty city, provides a contrast with v. 1b. It should be particularly emphasized that within the song the call to praise and thanksgiving is replaced by a call to trust in Yahweh. This makes it doubtful whether there was ever an originally independent song of thanksgiving or victory associated with the conquest and destruction of a city.[a] It is equally questionable whether we should relate it to the consecration of the walls of Jerusalem after their reconstruction by John Hyrcanus, following the destruction of Samaria in 110 BC. Indeed, in view of the rise of the Qumran community and the associated problems of the conclusion of the main process of redaction

---

regards vv. 1–6 as a separate unity, but amends it considerably. Attention should be given to the observation by Skinner, in Gray, p. 437, that vv. 1b–19 are dominated by a 'concatenated' structure, in which a word or idea is taken up from one verse and suggests a new thought for the next.

[a] Some scholars, e.g. Plöger, pp. 86f. (ET pp. 69f.) or Fohrer ad loc., have regarded vv. 1–6 as a solemn thanksgiving, and others, e.g. Kessler, taking up a suggestion by Lohmann, ZAW 37, 1917/18, p. 40, has a song of victory. It should be noted that Lohmann sought to distinguish between an entry song in vv. 1b–3, a religious song of victory in vv. 4–5a and vv. 5b–6 as a later addition. More recently, Plöger, pp. 86f. (ET p. 69), Fohrer, ad loc. and M.-L. Henry, p. 186, have argued that the poem was originally independent and uttered on a specific occasion. For my own attribution of it to a particular stratum within the whole composition cf. above p. 178.

of the Old Testament, this is highly unlikely.[a] The poet imagines his community at the longed for moment of the fall of the world capital and the world power (cf. 25.1ff.), but at the same time keeps their present situation in mind and thereby intensifies their trust in Yahweh. Thus with vv. 3 and 4 in mind, we can summarize as follows: If only you go on trusting firmly and unshakeably in Yahweh, then it will actually come about that you will enter Jerusalem as his liberated people, because he has destroyed the world power and world capital, and you who are now defenceless will be able to destroy every trace of it.

This is all that needs to be said to understand the song. We should observe that in v. 1b the poet has used alliterations, reproduced in the translation; literally 'walls and bulwarks'. He is imagining his own city as secure and incapable of capture, because it is protected by a wall, an outer wall and an embankment.[b] Since the whole nation is unlikely to have been taking part in a battle, we can assume that the demand to open the gates is made, as in Pss. 118.19 and 24.7, 9, by pilgrims to a festival. Just as in Ps. 118.20 the righteous can enter through the gate of Yahweh, i.e. of the sanctuary,[c] the people, which is righteous because it is faithful and obedient to Yahweh, demands entry, and this of course is accorded to it. The theme of steadfastness and loyalty is taken up in v. 3, with the purpose of affirming that Yahweh is preparing salvation for those who trust in him. The verse can be compared with Ps. 112.7, and Ps. 143.8. Verse 4 also takes up this theme, with a clear call to trust in Yahweh whose reliability is described by means of a simile likening him to a rock which lasts for ever. The background to this verse seems to be formed by Ps. 62.8f. Verse 5 is in sharp contrast to what precedes, replacing the concept of the everlasting rock with the contrasting picture of the lofty city cast down to the ground and in to the dust. If we remember that the comparison is one of importance, and that the more important object is represented as greater and higher than that which is less important (cf. also 2.2),[d] there is no need to look for a royal capital set upon a

[a] Cf. H. Stegemann, Die Entstehung der Qumrangemeinde, thesis, Bonn (1965) 1971, pp. 247ff. This hypothesis was held by Duhm and Marti.

[b] Cf. e.g. E. Unger, RLA I, p. 336; E. Kirsten and W. Kraiker, Griechenlandkunde, Heidelberg [5]1967, pp. 142f., and more recently S. Runciman, The Fall of Constantinople, London 1965, p. 89.

[c] Cf. Weiser, ATD 14/15; ET, The Psalms, OTL, 1962, ad loc.

[d] Cf. e.g. W. Wolf, Die Kunst Aegyptens, Gestalt und Geschichte, Stuttgart 1957, pp. 87f.

high hill.[a] The choice of verbs is reminiscent of 2.6ff. (cf. 2.9, 11, 17). The height is emphasized in order to make the fall into the depths even more impressive. After Yahweh has taken away the power of the world capital and its inhabitants, the poor and lowly,[b] who have no power in the present world, will be able to stamp it out completely with their feet and destroy every trace of it upon the earth. We can certainly compare this verse with Ps. 37.10f., which envisages the end of the godless and which promises possession of the land to the meek and oppressed (cf. Matt. 5.5). It must be acknowledged that the poet-prophet, learned in the scripture and imbued with the language and conceptions of the Psalms, has brought the prophetic song to a successful conclusion with this threefold repetition (cf. Judg. 5.30).

CHAPTER 26.7–21

The Community in the Distress of the Final Age

7   The way of the righteous is level,
　　　smooth the path of righteousness, which thou dost lay.
8   Yes, in the path of thy judgments,
　　　Yahweh, we wait for thee;[c]
　　thy name and thy invocation[d]
　　　is the desire of the soul.
9   My soul yearns for thee in the night,
　　　Yes, my spirit within me seeks thee.[e]
　　For from thy judgments upon the earth,
　　　the inhabitants of the world[f] learn righteousness.
10 If favour is shown to the wicked,
　　　he does not learn righteousness;
　　But ⟨on the earth⟩[g] he perverts the right
　　　and does not see the majesty of Yahweh.

　　[a] E.g. Fischer *ad loc*. But for another view, cf. Ziegler, *ad loc*.
　　[b] These two words are found together elsewhere only in Zeph. 3.12. Apart from that we find *'ānī* and *'ebyōn* together, cf. e.g. Ps. 40.18.
　　[c] But cf. 1Q Isa.
　　[d] Literally 'the remembering of thee'.
　　[e] Cf. Ps. 39.4; 5.5; there is no need for the amendment proposed in *BHS*.
　　[f] *tēbēl*.
　　[g] Cf. *BHS*.

11 Yahweh, that thy hand is lifted up,
       they will not see.[a]
    Let them see the zeal for the people, and be ashamed.
    Let the fire against thy adversaries consume them.

12 Yahweh, thou wilt ordain well-being for us,
       thou hast wrought for us all our works.

13 Yahweh our God,
       other lords beside thee rule over us,
       but thy name alone we remember.

14 The dead will not live;
       the shades will not arise;
    therefore thou dost visit with destruction[b]
    and dost wipe out all remembrance of them.[c]

15 But thou wilt give more to the people, Yahweh,
       thou wilt give more to the people;[d]
          thou wilt be glorified;
       thou wilt enlarge all the borders of the land.

16 Yahweh, ⟨in the distress of thy visitation we cry out,
       in the affliction⟩[e] of thy chastening ⟨to thee⟩.[f]

17 As a woman with child, when she is near her time,
       writhes and cries out in her pangs,
       so are we because of thee, Yahweh.

18 We are with child, we writhe, we ⟨   ⟩[g] bring forth wind.
    We bring no deliverance to the country,
       and no inhabitants of the world are born.[h]

20 Come, my people, enter your chambers,
       and shut your doors[i] behind you;
    hide yourselves[g] for a little while
       until the wrath is past.

21 For behold, Yahweh is coming forth out of his place
       to punish the inhabitants of the earth for their iniquity,
    and the earth will disclose her blood
       and will no more cover her slain.

[a] For the form cf. R. Meyer, *Hebräische Grammatik* II, Berlin ³1969, § 63.5a, pp. 100f.

[b] The suffix refers to '*ᵃdōnīm* in v. 13.

[c] For the tense structure cf. Grether, § 79k and 81e.

[d] Against the usual translation 'thou wilt increase the people . . .' cf. Lindblom, pp. 48f. and e.g. Deut. 19.9; Gen. 30.24 or I Chron. 21.3; Ps. 115.14.

[e] Read *bᵉṣar pᵉqūdātᵉkā sāʿaqnū bᵉlaḥaṣ*, cf. also Ziegler *ad loc.*

[f] Read *lāk.*   [g] Cf. *BHS.*

[h] For v. 19 cf. the special section on it below. For the meaning of *npl*, to fall, cf. also the substantive *nēpel*, untimely birth, abortion, e.g. Ps. 58.9.

[i] For the punctuation cf. *BHS.*

The poet now turns away from the eschatological salvation which he has invoked in his prophetic anticipation of the future, the song in vv. 1–6. Instead, in vv. 7–18, a lamentation of the people, wordy, meditative in effect and going beyond the strict laws of this category, he speaks as though leading his people in prayer (cf. v. 9) and directs the attention back to the distress which has not yet been brought to an end. The eschatological prophet goes on in vv. 20–21 to tell his community how this time of distress has to be endured when it grows worse, when it is no longer a matter of human enemies, but of Yahweh himself carrying out his final, decisive act of judgment upon the world. Later, under the influence of the much more recent hope of resurrection, v. 19 was interpolated to provide an answer to the lamentation. It both promises the resurrection of the dead in a form appropriate to the context and at the same time gives a new interpretation to v. 20.

Because of the tightly knit structure of the song,[a] no further attempts to subdivide it are possible without doing it violence. On the basis of the classical elements of the psalm of lamentation,[b] vv. 7–9 may be described as a confession of trust, vv. 10–11 as a petition for Yahweh's intervention, v. 12 as the expression of the certainty of being heard, vv. 13–15 as a renewed expression of trust, and vv. 16–18 as a description of the distress, the lamentation proper. Note that the poet does not use the typical metre of a lamentation (3+2). The theme of trust, taking up half the song, is particularly prominent, and so is the introduction of a didactic note in vv. 7a, 9b and 10a, where the prayer takes on the form of the proverbs used in the wisdom literature. Thus a formal analysis itself points to the parenetic nature of the poem, and this becomes directly evident in the instruction given in v. 20. The poet's purpose is to show his congregation how to endure the distress of the final age, patiently trusting in Yahweh's righteous actions and in his help alone, praying and withdrawing into the privacy of home life.

[7–9] With this in mind, the prayer opens in v. 7 with a confession which comes to be the theme of all the rest of the poem, that the way of life of one who remains faithful to Yahweh and is therefore regarded

a Cf. above, p. 205 note f.
b Cf. H. Gunkel and J. Begrich, *Einleitung in die Psalmen*, HK II E, 1933, pp. 121ff., or C. Westermann, *Das Loben Gottes in den Psalmen*, Göttingen 1954, pp. 36ff., or A. Weiser, ATD 14/15[6] pp. 44ff., ET *The Psalms*, OTL, 1962, pp. 66ff., or O. Kaiser, *Einleitung in das Alte Testament*, Gütersloh [2]1970, pp. 264f.

by him as righteous (cf. 26.2) is straight and level, because Yahweh himself makes it smooth and removes obstacles from his path (Pss. 25.10; 27.11; Prov. 1.3; 2.9 and Ps. 1.6). In a time in which this principle does not seem to hold, faithfulness to Yahweh is shown (v. 8) by the refusal of the community to doubt that the confused course of history, of which man cannot make sense, is nevertheless subject to Yahweh's righteous guidance.[a] As a result they do not cease to hope in Yahweh (cf. Pss. 25.3; 69.7; Isa. 40.23 and Ps. 37.9). Thus the desire of the community must be that Yahweh should glorify his name, and should give cause to remember his acts (cf. Pss. 30.5; 135.13; 102.13 and Josh. 7.9).[b] This unshakeable confidence is shown in the constancy of the hope placed in him (cf. v. 9, cf. also Pss. 77.7; 6.7; 88.2;1 19.55); this finds its support in the experience, asserted as a matter of principle, that what Yahweh's judgments bring upon men is justice; that he does right to the righteous and ultimately destroys the godless (cf. Ps. 71.16ff.; 119.7, 71; Jer. 12.16 and Deut. 31.13).

[10–11] The confession of trust concluded with a wisdom proverb, and the petition for Yahweh's intervention in v. 10 begins in the same way, with a statement in the form of a proverb emphasizing the necessity of Yahweh's acts of judgment, as the only way the wicked man can be brought back to righteousness. No distinction is made here between Jews and non-Jews, although the context suggests that the primary reference is to the gentiles who do not acknowledge the majesty and rule of Yahweh (cf. Ps. 9.18).[c] When v. 10b states that they do not see the majesty of Yahweh, this does not mean that they will not see his glory in the final age (cf. 33.17; 40.5), but must be interpreted in accordance with the statement that follows, as referring to their present blindness with regard to Yahweh's power.[d] If they fail to recognize that he is already present and ready to strike them (cf. Ex. 14.18 and Num. 33.3), the moment of truth will come for them when they see Yahweh's zeal for his own people and are ashamed (cf. Pss. 25.3; 86.17; Zech. 1.14f.; Isa. 9.6; 37.32). The prayer of the oppressed should be that this will happen, and that the hour of their destruction by Yahweh will come. Yahweh's fire should be understood not metaphorically but in a completely realistic sense.

[a] For the expression cf. Prov. 2.8 and Isa. 40.14.
[b] Cf. also W. Schottroff, *THAT* I, col. 513 and 516.
[c] But cf. also Gray, *ad loc.* and Plöger, pp. 82f. (ET pp. 64f.).
[d] Cf. Rudolph, pp. 46f.

Even at this late period, the ancient concept of the theophany is still an active force.[a]

[12–15] The petition is followed in v. 12 by the affirmation of the certainty of being heard, which is based upon the fact that in the peoples' past history all decisive help has come from Yahweh. This is an understanding of the relationship between human and divine action which was basically formed in Israel by the event of salvation at the Red Sea (cf. Ex. 14.14). In its defencelessness, the Jewish community could expect no change to be brought about by its own power, or rather impotence (cf. vv. 17f.); but it looked forward to such a transformation from Yahweh, who can bring down even mighty kingdoms. As a sign of the close link between him and those who are praying, and of the trust placed in him, he is addressed as 'our God'. Against the background of this confessional formula the contrast between the claim it implies and the outward reality, between the fact that Israel belongs to this God and their actual state of political servitude, is particularly marked. This contradiction is of course evoked not in order to raise doubts about Yahweh's power, but to provide the occasion for an intervention (cf. Neh. 9.36f.), on the part of him on whose name alone they call and from whom alone, therefore, they look for help. While v. 14a is widely understood to apply to the fate of the enemy, the use of this theme in Pss. 6.5f.; 88.11ff.; 30.10f.; cf. Isa. 38.17ff.; Ps. 115.17f. suggests that the reminder that death is final may perhaps be one of the themes meant to be the occasion for Yahweh's intervention on behalf of those who pray to him. Because without the help of Yahweh they are lost and without salvation, he will so completely destroy the foreign overlords who have arrogated to themselves his position as the ruler over Israel, that even the memory of them will be extinguished (cf. 14.20b). When Yahweh is glorified in this way in his enemies and the enemies of his people, this will take the form not only of their destruction, but also of an unexpectedly great extension of the borders of Israel.[b] This hope is very easy to understand in view of the considerable contraction of Jewish territory after the catastrophe of 587, the break-up of the ancient Israelite settlements and the ancient promise of the possession of the land, as well as the memory of the

[a] Cf. Ps. 50.3; Deut. 4.22; I Kings 18.38; II Kings 1.10; Isa. 29.6; 30.30; 33.10f., 14; Ps. 18.13f.; 29.7; 97.3.
[b] For *gōy* referring to Israel cf. with Lindblom, p. 49, e.g. Deut. 4.6; Isa. 10.6; Jer. 7.28 and Ps. 33.12.

size of David's empire (cf. Deut. 19.8; Isa. 54.2f.; Ezek. 36.33ff.; 47.13–48.35; particular attention should be paid to 47.14).

[16–18] The poet moves on from the promise, expressed in the stylized form of a profession of trust, to a direct lamentation in vv. 16–18. This begins in v. 16 with the invocation of Yahweh (cf. Ps. 87.7; 120.1; II Chron. 30.9). The admission it contains, that the present distress is a visitation and chastening from Yahweh, leaves no doubt that he stands above the distress and can therefore avert it.[a] What it consists of is not explicitly stated, but the context suggests that it should be thought of as provoked by the foreign lords in v. 13. The poet portrays his community as confessing their inability to help themselves or to bring about the longed for time of salvation, he makes a comparison between their own efforts and those of a woman about to give birth (cf. also 59.4). But while she bears a child, they as it were bring forth only wind, that is, nothing at all. Without the imagery, this means that with all their efforts they have shown themselves incapable of bringing the country any help.[b] It is difficult to say whether behind this there lie any particular experiences in the recent past of the poet and his community, or whether the poem looks back to the whole past history of Israel since the loss of independence in 587. In particular, we are dependent upon conjectures for the date of the chapter, and there are many gaps in our knowledge of the history of post-exilic and early Hellenistic Judaism. We lose very little from this uncertainty, because even if there is a reference to particular events, the second theme would also have influenced the passage.

[20–21] The lamentation is uttered by the poet himself, as it were, in the name of his community, though it can be assumed that the actual situation for which it was composed was none other than its present context in the book of Isaiah. It is not answered by an oracle of salvation. Instead, the poet gives an instruction, to which a reason is added, concerning their attitude when the distress increases. When he calls upon the people to enter into their chambers, to close the doors behind them, to hide and wait until the wrath is passed (cf. Zeph. 3.8; Isa. 10.25; 30.27; Dan. 11.36), he does not mean that they are to face death fearlessly and lie down in the grave without terror, because they will soon be raised up by Yahweh, as one might

[a] Cf. also Micah 7.4; Ex. 3.9 and Prov. 3.11.
[b] The reference is not to real childlessness, infertility and a decrease of population (against Lindblom, pp. 49f.; cf. also Plöger, p. 85; ET, p. 67).

assume from Dan. 12.13. Against this interpretation it can be pointed out that there is no instance in the Old Testament in which the word *ḥeder*, chamber, means a grave.[a] Rather, he is advising his community to withdraw into the innermost rooms of their houses, in preparation for the expected but brief distress which is to come (cf. Ps. 30.6; Isa. 10.25), and there to await the end of the divine wrath. The passage has been compared with the visitation upon Egypt and the sparing of Israel in the Passover night (cf. Exod. 12.23)[b] and even of the saving of Noah and his family from the flood in the ark (cf. Gen. 7.1, 16).[c] But it may also be compared with Ezek. 9 which speaks of a selective act of judgment in Jerusalem itself. It has rightly been pointed out that in the call to hide from the terrible apparition of Yahweh in the rock or in the dust (cf. 2.10, 19) the poem is alluding to the day of Yahweh (cf. 2.10, 19).[d] The prophet expects, however, that the final menace from Yahweh will also affect Jerusalem and Judah. It is perhaps possible that like 29.6; 30.30 (cf. also 31.8) he is thinking of a powerful storm which will break out over Jerusalem and the nations gathering together outside its gates (cf. 14.24ff.; 17.12ff.; 28.14ff.; 29.1ff.; 30.27ff. and 31.4ff.). In this case the call to draw into the inner rooms of one's house would be meant literally and would not just be a metaphor based on behaviour during a storm. Behind this time of distress, which with its conclusion is the last to be expected, stands Yahweh himself. He intervenes even more directly than when he visited his own nation by handing it over to foreign rulers. This can be seen from the concluding v. 21. In words taken from Micah 1.3, it prophesies that Yahweh will come forth from his heavenly dwelling to what we may interpret as the last judgment upon men, whose guilt, *ʿāwōn*, is now punished. The totality and finality of his action can be seen from v. 21b which prophesies that the earth will then disclose all blood that has not been atoned for, every secret, forgotten or concealed murder (cf. Gen. 37.26; Job. 16.18, and also Lev. 17.13; Ezek. 24.7f.) so that the blood can cry out to Yahweh as its avenger (cf. Gen. 4.10; Ps. 9.13 and Rev. 6.10).[e] The last judgment is the final cleansing of both the earth and of mankind. But here

---

[a] Plöger, p. 85; ET, p. 68.

[b] Cf. Gray, Fischer and Ziegler, *ad loc.*

[c] Cf. Procksch, Kessler, Fohrer, *ad loc.* and Mulders, p. 52.

[d] Lindblom, p. 52.

[e] For this conception and its continued existence among the Bedouin, cf. G. Fohrer, KAT² 16, 1963, pp. 290f.

the scholarly prophet breaks off. Is the reader meant to go back to the beginning of the chapter and read the song of thanksgiving once again merely in order to dream of what it will be like? No, he is to do so in order to have confidence in the distresses of his own time that Yahweh will ultimately set everything to rights, even and above all where human help can do nothing. And perhaps present or future readers will be pleased that a later writer has added the promise in v. 19, opening up a vista which makes it easier to believe in the righteousness of God.

CHAPTER 26.19

The Resurrection of the Dead

19 Thy dead shall live, my bodies shall rise.
O dwellers in the dust, awake and sing for joy!
For thy dew is dew of the lights (?),
so that the earth gives birth to the shades.

One has to read this short passage several times in order to become really aware of the irritation caused by the change of possessive pronouns. The attempt to work out who is speaking and to identify the literary category is like solving a puzzle. If the profession of trust in Yahweh is uttered by the praying community (cf. the comment on 26.7ff.) or an individual leading the prayer, then the dead are departed Israelites who are particularly close to him, or perhaps even the righteous. Then the phrase that follows, if the Hebrew word $n^e b\bar{e}l\bar{a}$ is to be understood as a collective,[a] says the same thing from the point of view of the person or persons who are praying, and also emphasizes the reality of the bodily resurrection. In this case the interjection would be addressed to the dead themselves, and the prayer that follows would be addressed once again to Yahweh and would describe the dew, by means of the pronoun, as coming from him.[b] On the other hand if Yahweh is the speaker, as most modern

[a] This was already noticed by Delitzsch, to whom we should refer.
[b] Cf. Delitzsch, Dillmann-Kittel, Duhm, Marti, Gray, Feldmann, Procksch and Fohrer, *ad loc.*

commentators accept,[a] what we have is a promise in reply to the praying community, and all the subsequent relationships are simply reversed. Of course even if the passage is understood in this sense, it is still remarkable that Yahweh should speak of his bodies, and it is tempting to remove this difficulty by a minor emendation of the text.[b] Though one must realize that different interpretations are possible, the speakers can also be identified in the following way. After Yahweh has begun by giving a brief promise of the resurrection and has awakened the dead by his word, the community replies, proclaiming and marvelling that his dew has achieved the impossible. When we go through the various possible interpretations, we must also remember that a very complicated tradition of the actual text is presented by the contrast between the Massoretic Hebrew text and the Latin translation of Jerome, the Vulgate, on the one hand, and the Qumran roll and the Greek, Syriac and Aramaic traditions on the other. The main difference lies in the change of the imperatives into imperfects; and the various witnesses to the text attempt to deal with the expression 'my body (bodies)', which some of them regard as a difficulty, in various ways. Thus the harmonizing texts make us wonder whether the text has not been amended in order to reconcile the original tensions. It has also been suggested that $n^e b\bar{e}l\bar{a}t\bar{i}$, 'my body (bodies)', is perhaps a reader's gloss, giving expression to his own personal hope.[c] Finally, it is possible that the verse, which can be seen from v. 20 to be a later interpolation,[d] first stood in the margin in a rather unclear form and was later copied in different ways. On the principle of choosing the more difficult reading in cases of doubt, we have translated the texts to which the Massoretic tradition and Jerome bear witness, without change. There is some support for this in the fact that the fantastic idea of the resurrection of the dead fits particularly well into this context as a divine promise. Verse 19 would then form with v. 20 a single promise, of which v. 20 draws the conclusion – for this is how it must be reinterpreted after the inter-

---

[a] Hylmo, in Rudolph, and the latter himself, p. 44; Lindblom, p. 50; Mulders, p. 50 and Plöger, p. 81 (ET p. 67), but also Kissane and probably Ziegler, *ad loc.*
[b] Cf. *BHS*, where the proposal to read 'your (pl.) bodies' is mentioned.
[c] Cf. Duhm and Marti, *ad loc.*
[d] If v. 19 were original, it would conflict with v. 20 in its original meaning, because the hope of v. 19 would overshadow the advice on how to behave during the final distress. How much it has done this is shown by the reinterpretation of v. 20 based on v. 19. Cf. also note 7.

polation of v. 19 – that one can peacefully give oneself up to the short sleep of death in the chamber of the grave.[a] But the idea of the resurrection is mentioned so briefly that it must have been an idea familiar, if not to all the interpolator's contemporaries, at least to his narrower community. Thus the verse can also be understood as a later continuation of the prayer, a renewal of the theme of confidence following the lamentation, and a confession of the certainty of resurrection, a certainty which enabled the prayer to look beyond the end of the visitation and the final distress and anticipate the moment in which the dead will rise again. As though this moment had come he can speak to the dead and conclude by referring to the life-giving dew of heaven which calls the shades of the underworld back into existence. While the ambiguity mentioned above does not permit a definite conclusion, it should be noted that we consider the older interpretation correct. New hypotheses are not necessarily always the best!

It is obvious that this confession of faith is in apparent contradiction to v. 14 and the tradition that lies behind it.[b] That the resurrected will respond to the call to rejoice, so that future life will be characterized by joy, needs so little explanation that the great Isaiah roll from Qumran and the Greek Bible have preserved the imperatives as imperfects (with a future meaning). Following the usual comparison of death with sleep,[c] the dead are called upon to awake, a command which one cannot read without recalling not only Ps. 88.11 but also Ezek. 37.4ff., where of course it is still a metaphor.[d] When those who are asleep are called dwellers in the dust, because of their stay in their graves,[e] the whole phrase is reminiscent of Dan. 12.2a, although it is impossible to tell which came first. The concluding sentence, giving the reason for the hope and acknowledging Yahweh's life-giving activity, presents certain difficulties in the ideas it contains. The dew, which in Palestine replaces the rain in summer, and increases in quantity in the autumn,[f] is qualified by an expression which has been differently understood, and in fact was already differently rendered by the versions. Luther followed the Greek

[a] This is how Isa. 26.20 was already understood in IV Esdras 7.32, 80 and 95.
[b] Cf. above p. 212.
[c] Cf. Jer. 51.39, 57; Matt. 27.52, but also Plato, *Apology* 32.40.
[d] Cf. Fohrer, Eichrodt or Zimmerli *ad loc.*
[e] Cf. Pss. 7.6; 22.16 and Job 21.26.
[f] Cf. F. Nötscher, *Biblische Altertumskunde*, p. 171.

Bible by translating the doubtful word (*'ōrōt*) as in II Kings 4.39, by
'herbs', whereas it is more usual nowadays to take it, following the
Latin Bible, the Vulgate, as a plural of *'ōrā*, light (cf. Ps. 139.12). A
rabbinic tradition can be quoted in favour of this interpretation,[a] as
can also be seen in the connection between light and life in the
thought of the ancient world (though perhaps not of the ancient
world alone, cf. Job 3.16; 18.18; Pss. 36.10; 56.14; Eccles. 11.7;
Eth. Enoch 58.3; Syr. Bar. 48.50).[b] Thus, referring to Ps. 104.2;
Dan. 2.22 and Eth. Enoch 51.1f., it is possible to find here a conception according to which Yahweh in his world of light disposes of a
miraculous and miracle working dew,[c] which is able to bring to life
the shades in the underworld.[d] Whereas the beginning of this
profession of confidence gives the impression of referring only to a
partial awakening, affecting the devout in Israel, or the whole of
Israel, regarded as devout, the conclusion seems to point to nothing
less than the end of the power of the kingdom of death, the resurrection of all the dead, and if we connect it with 25.8aα, the abolition of
death altogether.[e]

25.8a and 26.19 are each in their own way evidence that belief in
the resurrection of the dead only appears at the very limits of the Old
Testament; for both are later interpolations. A strict and conscien-
tious examination leaves ch. 12 of the book of Daniel as the only other
evidence in the Old Testament. Ecclesiastes 3.19ff. seems to show
that by the third century at the latest the hope of resurrection was
discussed among wisdom teachers in Jerusalem, though they dis-
agreed with it.

This belief, regardless of the concrete forms it has taken in accordance with the world view of particular periods, is essential to Christian
faith (cf. I Cor. 15.13f.). But for some people it is too much to take.

[a] Cf. with Mulders, p. 51, b. Hag 12b in L. Goldschmidt, *Der babylonische
Talmud*, IV, Berlin 1966, pp. 273f.

[b] Cf. also Mulders, p. 51.

[c] That one cannot close the file on the problem of the interpretation of *'ōrōt* is
shown by J. C. de Moor, *The Seasonal Pattern in the Ugaritic Myth of Ba'lu*, AOAT 16,
1971, p. 83 and p. 244, note 8.

[d] Cf. H. Gese, *Die Religionen Altsyriens*, RM 10.2, 1970, pp. 91f.

[e] Cf. also F. König, *Zarathustras Jenseitsvorstellungen und das Alte Testament*, Vienna
1964, who on p. 38 assumes that this is restricted to the people of Israel because of
their election. I prefer the account he gives on p. 215, referring to 25.8: 'There is
no mention in the passage that this ceasing of death is restricted to the Israelites,
although it is not probable that the author took other nations into account.'

Perhaps only when the question of its origin is answered is it once again possible for them to accept it. In our comment on 14.9ff. we discussed at length the Old Testament conceptions of the existence of the shades in the underworld. We also find an affirmation of belief that death is man's final and unavoidable fate in the statements in the Psalms which underlie 26.14. In the Babylonian Gilgamesh epic the woman Siduri, the wine-bearer, says to the hero who is in despair at the death of his friend and brother Enkidu:

> You will never find that life for which you are looking.
> When the gods created man
> they allotted to him death,
> but life they retained in their own keeping.
> As for you, Gilgamesh, fill your belly with good things;
> Day and night, night and day,
> dance and be merry, feast and rejoice . . .
> Make your wife happy in your embrace;
> for this too is the lot of man![a]

In Israel too this seems to be the most that anyone could say to man, even from the point of view of the fear of God (cf. Eccles. 11.7ff.; Prov. 5.18f.).[b] Individual groups in Judaism went further than this sceptical realism, and ultimately one can regard this as being due less to external influences as to the spelling out of the meaning of faith in God's righteousness to its final conclusion.[c] The book of Job shows how comfort was sought, in the face of the contradiction between the actions and fate of the devout and godless, on the one hand by an insight into the fundamental wickedness of man (cf. Job 4.17) and on the other hand by submission to God's control over the world, which was beyond human understanding (cf. 38.1ff.)[d]. But the question and distress associated with it must have become more intense in the period of the religious persecution by Antiochus IV, because it was now quite obvious that a devout person could be killed, whereas an

---

[a] X.III. 2ff., in A. Schott and W. von Soden, *Das Gilgamesch-Epos*, Reclam 7235/35a, Stuttgart 1958, pp. 77f.; *The Epic of Gilgamesh*, ed. N. K. Sandars, London, 1960, p. 99.

[b] Cf. also O. Kaiser, 'Der. Mensch unter dem Schicksal', *NZSTh* 14, 1972, pp. 22ff.

[c] Cf. König, pp. 283ff. and M. Hengel, *Judentum und Hellenismus*, WUNT 10, 1969, p. 368 but especially p. 357.

[d] Cf. also O. Kaiser, 'Leid und Gott. Ein Beitrag zur Theologie des Buches Hiob', in *Sichtbare Kirche. Festschrift H. Laag*, Gütersloh 1972, pp. 22ff.

apostate might escape with his life. Was the God who demanded
unconditional loyalty and unconditional obedience from Israel, and
tolerated no other god beside himself, no longer keeping the promises
which he had made to the obedient (cf. I Macc. 2.31ff. with II
Macc. 7)? If experience is in radical conflict with ethical faith, but
man must still take ethical demands seriously, he must either abandon
belief in God's righteousness or accept that God's righteousness is
exercised within a horizon which goes beyond the limits of a single
life. This is conceived of within the framework of the resurrection of
the flesh and the judgment of God, first of all because it is based in an
unspeculative way on the only life that men really know, on a realism
assured by belief in creation, and because it goes back to the conception, rooted in the cult, of Yahweh's coming to judgment.[a] At the
same time the idea of creation, which grew out of the idea of cosmic
order, was able to evolve into that of creatio *ex nihil*, creation from
nothing. In this form it became an argument for what God can do for
man in regard to his death (cf. I Macc. 7.28 and Rom. 4.17).[b] When
we look for adequate grounds for belief in the future of man beyond
his own death, we find that like the Platonic myth of rebirth, it is a
postulate of practical reason,[c] an ethical faith implied is ethical
action as such.[d]

[a] Cf. A. Weiser, ATD 14/15[7], pp. 30ff.; ET *The Psalms*, OTL, 1962, pp. 49ff.
[b] Cf. *Koran*, XVII, 52–54; 100f.; XIX, 67f. XXII, 5 *et passim*.
[c] It is not disputed that within his thought its first connections are with the
doctrine of anamnesis. Cf. U. v. Wilamowitz-Moellendorff, *Platon I*, Berlin [5]1959,
p. 372.
[d] Cf. I. Kant, *Kritik der praktischen Vernunft*, ed. K. Vorländer. PhB 38, Hamburg,
1963 (Leipzig, [9]1929), pp. 163ff. and pp. 140ff.; ET *Kant's Critique of Practical
Reason*, London 1879, pp. 349ff. and 317ff.; and also O. Kaiser, 'Dike und Sedaqa',
NZSTh 7, 1965, pp. 271f.

CHAPTER 27.1

The Last Enemy

1   In that day Yahweh will punish
      with his hard and great and strong sword
    Leviathan, the fleeing[a] snake,
      Leviathan, the wriggling snake,
      and will slay the dragon in the sea.

Whereas 24.21ff. looks forward to the final conquest of the powers of heaven by Yahweh, 27.1 promises that in 'that day',[b] which Yahweh has destined for his judgment upon his enemies, the powers of the deep, the rebellious sea, will also be defeated. As we have known for some decades from the texts found in Ugarit in northern Syria, the Canaanites had for many years recounted how the weather god and lord of the earth, Baal, had to conquer the rebellious sea, the sea-god Yam, Lotan, the fleeing and wriggling seven-headed snake, the sea-dragon Tannun.[c] The Israelites took the myth over from the Canaanites, perhaps in a somewhat altered form which told not only of Yam and Leviathan,[d] but also of Rahab (cf. 30.7; 51.9f.; Ps. 89.10ff. and Job 26.12ff.). Leviathan, like his Canaanite predecessor, had seven heads (Ps. 74.13f.). In one tradition Yahweh destroyed him (cf. Ps. 74.13f.) while according to another he made a powerful toy of him (Ps. 104.26) so that he still had to be taken into account (cf. Job 3.8 and 26.13). The contradiction is only apparent, and is resolved when we recognize that the event which once took place in the primal age is constantly repeated anew in the course of the seasons.[e] As a symbol of a power hostile to God the sea could be associated, like the sea-dragon, with the earthly enemies of Yahweh,

[a] For the meaning of *bari*[a]*h* cf. also H. Gese, *Die Religionen Altsyriens*, RM 10.2, 1970, p. 59 note 44.

[b] Cf. 24.21; 25.9; 26.1; 27.12, 13; 28.5.

[c] Cf. O. Kaiser, *Mythische Bedeutung des Meeres*, BZAW 78, ²1962, pp. 74ff.; R. Hillmann, Wasser und Berg. Kosmische Verbindungslinien zwischen dem kanaanäischen Wettergott und Jahwe, thesis, Halle 1965, p. 116; J. C. de Moor, *The Seasonal Pattern in the Ugaritic myth of Ba'lu*, AOAT 16, 1971, p. 41 and p. 244 note 8. In view of the disagreement as to whether Yam and Lotan are to be identified, the basic texts must be re-examined.

[d] The biblical Leviathan of course corresponds to the Ugaritic Lotan.

[e] Cf. Kaiser, pp. 145ff. and Hillmann pp. 144ff.

the empires of the earth. Their symbolical animals climb out of the sea (cf. Dan. 7.2ff.; Rev. 13.1). But behind them stands concealed the ancient dragon (Rev. 13.2) who can himself be embodied in historical individuals (cf. Ps. Sol. 2.25). The apocalyptic writers affirm that Yahweh will destroy the dragon, (cf. Test. Asher 7.3; Ps. Sol. 2.25 and Rev. 20.2). Finally, the imagination of the devout even invented the story that a dragon would appear on earth who was a son of him who 'girds the sphere about; ... a kinsman of him who is outside the ocean, whose tail is set in his own mouth'.[a] By comparison with these ideas, the development of Ps. 106.26 and Job 40.25 into the apocalyptic conception that Yahweh has destined Leviathan, sometimes together with the legendary Behemoth, as food for the final age, sounds almost innocent (cf. Eth. Enoch 60.7, 24; IV Esdras 6.49ff.; Syr. Bar. 29.4 and Jub. 2.11). But he is thought of as being not only in the sea, but particularly in the primaeval sea beneath the earth (cf. Apoc. Abr. 21.4). Thus he is clearly a being who threatens the earth and has therefore to be annihilated if prosperity and peace are eventually to prevail upon earth. Many commentators have seen in this passage three different monsters, which represent three kingdoms. Thus the dragon in the sea is taken to be Egypt (cf. 30.7; Ezek. 29.3; 32.2),[b] the wriggling snake the Seleucid kingdom and the fleeing snake the kingdom of the Parthians.[c] Other interpretations sometimes understand the epithets allegorically: the fleeing snake means the rapidly flowing Tigris, the wriggling snake the meandering Euphrates.[d] We cannot exclude the possibility that the apocalyptic writer had to use a secret language in order to refer to the kingdoms which he really meant, because the political situation left him no other choice,[e] but it is by no means certain that his list contains three different references rather than three parallel synonyms,[f] and really refers to different beings and not to a single being described in different ways.[g]

[a] Acts of Thomas 32, quoted on the basis of G. Bornkamm's translation in: E. Hennecke and W. Schneemelcher, *New Testament Apocrypha* II, ET ed. by R. McL. Wilson, London and Philadelphia 1965, p. 460. For the idea cf. also Kaiser, p. 35.

[b] But cf. W. Zimmerli, BK 13, 2, p. 703.

[c] Cf. e.g. Duhm, and Marti, but also Kessler, *ad loc.*

[d] Cf. e.g. Feldmann and Ziegler, *ad loc.*

[e] M.-L. Henry, p. 142.

[f] Cf. O. Kaiser, *Einleitung in das Alte Testament*, Gütersloh ²1970, pp. 254f.

[g] The word *weʿal* which is used to argue the contrary, in my view, against that of

After dwelling on all these considerations, one may ask whether the passages are concerned only with the monster which lives deep in the sea, or with the world empire. Strictly speaking this is not the question that should be asked, because we are dealing with a mythical symbol which can be effective on different levels. But the apocalyptic writer, it should be noted, does not go beyond his prophecy of Yahweh's victory in the final age over the monster in the deep, a victory which he gains in a duel with his powerful sword.[a] Behind 26.20f. we saw Yahweh's judgment upon the nations; and it follows from the logic of mythical thinking that after the incarnations of evil the evil itself must be conquered, and that God has to destroy the last enemy, if 'that day' is really to bring the final turning point in history.[b]

CHAPTER 27.2–6

The Eschatological Song of the Vineyard

2   In that day (he will say):
      A pleasant vineyard, sing of it![c]
3   I, Yahweh, am its keeper;
      every moment I water it.
      Lest anyone harm[d] it.
      I guard it night and day;

Feldmann, p. 312 and M.-L. Henry, p. 145, n. 65, is insufficient. When a sentence opened with *'al* it was possible for it to continue with *we'al* even in the case of a synonymous parallelism.

[a] For the conception of the sword of Yahweh, which clearly becomes prominent in the late period, cf. Ps. 17.13; Deut. 32.41f.; Ezek. 21.8ff.; 30.24f.; 32.10; Jer. 50.35ff.; Isa. 31.8; 34.5; 66.1; Eth. Enoch 91.12 and Rev. 1.16; 2.12.

[b] With this statement I revise my explanation of the passage in *Die mythischen Bedeutung des Meeres*, [2]1962, pp. 148f.

[c] *kerem* is fem. only here.

[d] In view of Num. 16.29 and Prov. 19.23, the only one of the many emendations worth consideration that have been proposed is that of Marti, to re-point *jipqōd* into *jippāqēd*.

4   I have no wrath.
    If I had[a] thorns ⟨and⟩[b] briars
    I would set out to battle against them.
    I would burn them up together.
5   Unless[c] people lay hold of my protection
        make peace with me,
        make peace with me.
6   ⟨In days to come⟩[d] Jacob ⟨shall take root⟩.[e]
        Israel shall blossom and put forth shoots,
        and fill the whole world with fruit.

27.2–6 is the first of a whole series of additions, in some of which the text is very badly preserved, while their content is not always clear. In spite of the connection between v. 6 and vv. 7ff., vv. 1–6 should probably be regarded as separate. After an introduction which seems to be deficient[f] and which places the song of the vineyard which follows in the future anticipated in 24.1–27.1, Yahweh himself begins to speak. Verse 6 gives the effect of a postscript to the song. Whether it is to be understood as a saying of Yahweh, or a consequence drawn by the prophet from the preceding saying of Yahweh, is not clear. We must not overlook the fact that the song itself is meant to provide a contrast to the song of the vineyard in 5.1–7, and indeed to be an abrogation of it, although the poet dealt with his task in his own way, and made it more difficult by not resting content with merely reversing its message. At first sight the call, modelled on the beginning of the song of the well in Num. 21.17, to sing to the magnificent vineyard[g] (cf. Amos 5.11 and Isa. 32.12), sounds strange. What was originally something very close to a spell in a working song[h] now requires a chorus of admirers, i.e. the nations, looking upon the eschatological magnificence of the vineyard, which according to v. 6 we have to identify with Israel.[1] Whereas Yahweh

[a] For the construction cf. G-K, § 117x.
[b] Cf. *BHS*, and cf. e.g. 5.6.
[c] For the construction cf. G-K, § 162a.
[d] Cf. *BH* and also Eccles. 2.16.
[e] Cf. *BHS*.
[f] Perhaps *yōʾmar* is lost, the subject of which would be Yahweh, from v. 1.
[g] In view of the reading to which Vg. bears witness, and its support in LXX and Amos 5.1, there is no need to insist upon the *ḥemer* of some manuscripts and the *ḥwmr* of 1Q Isa.
[h] Cf. O. Kaiser, *Einleitung in das Alte Testament*, Gütersloh ²1970, p. 260.
[1] Here I explicitly disagree with the thesis of Lindblom, pp. 53f., that the song should not be understood eschatologically.

once threatened to expose the vineyard which disappointed his hopes to plunder and destruction (cf. 5.5f.), he now gives an assurance that he himself will take over the task of guarding it. This protects it from all inroads from outside and all neglect from those inside. Whereas he once threatened that he would no longer allow any rain to fall on the vineyard (cf. 5.6) he will now water it regularly, and of course no more often than necessary, giving it sufficient dew and rain at the right time (cf. 29.17, 23ff.). For now the time of his anger against his people is finally over.[a] Verse 4b faces the reader with a riddle, and no certain solution has yet been found. If we retain the traditional Massoretic text,[b] the one theory that is clear is that a possibility is being considered and rejected. But if, comparing the passage to II Sam. 23.6f., we look beyond the rather odd mixing of agricultural metaphors with the conceptions of war and peace, the question still remains whether the weeds which Yahweh may possibly find in the vineyard of Israel and which he will then burn (cf. also 10.17; 5.24) refer to enemies within or without. The language of battle and the making of peace (cf. Josh. 9.15) seems to suggest enemies from outside. On the other hand, within the framework of the eschatological drama underlying 26.20–27.1 it 'is no longer possible to speak of such external enemies. Similarly it would be very strange if they were being offered the possibility of asylum in the Temple of Jerusalem, the condition for being spared laid down in v. 5a*a* (cf. I Kings 1.50; 2.28). These observations suggest that the reference is to enemies within who really belong to the congregation of Yahweh. It is not impossible that the prophet-poet, who was certainly writing at a late period, was thinking of the Samaritans and believed that in the context of the hope of salvation for the whole of Israel they would be spared only if they return to Jerusalem.[c] This possibility, however, comes into conflict with the idea that none of the Samaritans are to survive the terrors of the final age (cf. 17.1ff., 4ff.; 28.1ff.). Thus it seems better to suppose that the prophet had future schisms in mind and was prophesying that they offered no hope of reconciliation. This is by no means a statement of eschatological rapture, but for this very reason has a less ambiguous present application. For anything

[a] A loose connection with 26.20 is not excluded, although the anger there is really against the nations.

[b] Duhm wanted to read e.g. instead of *bammilḥāmā*, in the war, *bam^eleḥā*, 'in the salt land', cf. e.g. Jer. 17.6, which can hardly be regarded as an improvement.

[c] Cf. Plöger, p. 91 (ET p. 73), and Kessler and Fohrer, *ad loc.*

for which no participation in future salvation can be expected has even now no justification for its existence. Because nothing can endure which will separate Israel from its God in time of salvation, Israel can therefore rely on the promise that it will be firmly rooted, that is, that it will be no longer driven by force out of its own country, and will blossom and put forth shoots and fill the world with its fruit. It has been suggested that the postscript goes so far as to refer to Israel's new function of spiritual mediation (cf. 2.2ff.); but this is uncertain. The context and the parallels in Ps. 80.9ff. and Hos. 14.6ff., as well as the meaning elsewhere of the word $t^e n\bar{u}b\bar{a}$, product, fruit,[a] suggests that the reference is to the untroubled increase and growth of the whole nation in the future, so that the whole world will ultimately belong to it (cf. also 37.31f.). The apocalyptic poet deliberately mentioned Israel and Jacob, because he meant the expectation to apply to the whole people of God with its twelve tribes (cf. v. 13).

Chapter 27.7–9

A Difficult Text

7   Has he smitten him as he smote those who smote him?
      Or has he been slain as ⟨his slayers⟩[b]
8   . . .[c] by driving her out thou didst contend with her
      ⟨he chased her away⟩[b] with his fierce blast in the
            day of the east wind,
9   Therefore by this the guilt of Jacob will be expiated,
      and this will be the full fruit of the removal of his sin;
   when he makes all the stones of the altars
      like chalkstones crushed to pieces,
      No Asherim or incense altars will remain standing.

[a] Cf. Deut. 32.13; Lam. 4.9; Ezek. 36.30; Judg. 9.11 and Ecclus. 11.3.
[b] Cf. *BHS*.
[c] Whereas the older translations, except LXX, connect the word with $s^e'\bar{a}$, a measuring vessel, and Delitzsch still renders it 'with measures', it is nowadays usually derived from a verb sw', which is connected with the Arabic $z\bar{a}z\bar{a}$, and the verb is assumed to have the meaning 'push away' or the like, cf. Feldmann *ad loc.* Others simply recall the *sa-sa* calls of Arab shepherds, cf. *KBL* sub voce, p. 646, which gives the approximate translation: 'by shooing away'.

A reading of 27.7–9 leaves an expression of obscurity and jerkiness. One can read these verses again and again without knowing exactly to whom they are referring and how they fit into their context. Verse 7 poses the rhetorical question, expecting a negative answer, whether Yahweh has been as strict with Israel, (cf. v. 6) as with its tormentors (cf. also 10.20). The ambiguous comparison in the first half of the verse does not become clear until one reads the second half. Looking back, Israel realizes that Yahweh has treated his people more favourably than their enemies, in spite of everything that they have suffered since the loss of their freedom in 722 and 587. Taken in isolation, this didactic question, with its concern that the nations should understand God's acts, could have been posed by looking back upon the fate of Assyria or Babylon, and therefore at a very early period. But in the present context they must be regarded as being uttered after 'that day' of 27.1, in the 'days to come' of 27.6. Verse 8a, if we ignore the difficulty of translation at the beginning, is certainly talking of a conflict which Yahweh, who is addressed as in a confession of faith, either carried out long ago in the past, is still carrying out or will carry out in the future. The tense structure of the verbs is as ambiguous as this. The opponent, however, is an entity conceived of as a female person, and the means of conflict is driving out (cf. Isa. 50.1). Note that the second half of the verse passes from direct addresses to third person narrative. The east wind is the hot sirocco which comes out of the desert and destroys vegetation (cf. Gen. 41.6; Hos. 13.15; Isa. 14.7) and which by its violence can cause great destruction both on water and on land (cf. Ps. 48.8; Ezek. 27.26) and carries everything before it (cf. Jer. 18.17; Job 27.21). Thus it is clear that v. 8b envisages extremely severe treatment. It is unlikely that the wind should be allegorically identified with the Assyrians or Babylonians coming from the east, since we have either a metaphor and not an allegory, or else a mention of an actual destructive storm sent by Yahweh, (cf. 2.12f.). The only meaningful possibility is to identify the female opponent of Yahweh with the city, for since in the previous verse Jacob and Israel were referred to as male beings, this verse can hardly still be speaking of the people as a female being. If the verse is meant to illustrate Yahweh's comparatively mild treatment of his people in the past, we must identify the city with Jerusalem and see in its 'driving out' the deportation of its population.[a] On the other hand, if the intention is to state a

[a] Cf. Rudolph, p. 54, who, however, considers that the question in v. 7 is

contrast, then in the present context the reference would be to the
world capital of 25.1ff. and 26.1ff. But the image of the driving out of
a woman argues against the latter interpretation, since it assumes that
there was once a particularly close relationship between the city and
Yahweh. If the author had been thinking of Samaria, he would be
open to the charge of expressing himself very obscurely, except in so
far as the situation at the time not made it easier for the original
readers or hearers of the passage to understand it. A destruction of
Samaria and exiling of its population which had actually taken
place,[a] or was expected, could of course form the background for the
mild penance imposed upon Jacob in v. 9, amounting to a repetition
of the measures of purification ascribed to Josiah in the southern
kingdom, and in the northern kingdom too (cf. II Kings 23.14f. and
II Chron. 34.4–7).[b] Verse 9 is certainly to be understood as a
prophecy. Thus one may accept that v. 8 also looks forward to the
future and so fits extremely awkwardly into the context. Perhaps
v. 7 and vv. 8f. were added to 27.6 in two stages. The asherim are the
standing cult objects associated with the altars (cf. Judg. 6.25ff.),
probably wooden pillars standing on the altars (cf. Deut. 12.3), and
were probably regarded originally as manifestations of the deity of
the same name.[c] The ḥammāmīm are usually taken nowadays to be
incense altars,[d] but the argument has been advanced[e] that they were
identical with the masseboth, stones set up in holy places.[f] The
cessation of idolatry and all cultic activity outside Jerusalem is a
condition of the participation of the brother nation to the north in
the coming age of salvation (cf. Deut. 12.10ff.).

---

answered in the negative, and would also relate vv. 10 and 11 to Jerusalem. Duhm,
Marti and Fohrer resolve the problem by cutting the knot: in their view, v. 8 is
simply a marginal gloss upon v. 10, interpolated in the wrong place by a copyist.

[a] Plöger, p. 91, thinks of the fate of the northern kingdom in 722; Kessler, *ad loc.*,
recalls the destruction of Samaria by Demetrius Poliorketes in 296 BC.

[b] Cf. also Plöger, p. 91; ET p. 73.

[c] Cf. most recently W. Helck, *Betrachtungen zur grossen Göttin, Religion und Kultur
der alten Mittelmeerwelt in Parallelforschungen* 2, Munich and Vienna 1971, pp. 158ff.

[d] Cf. 17.8; Ezek. 6.6; Lev. 26.30f.; II Chron. 14.4; 34.4, 7 and the comment of
K. Elliger, *ZAW* 57, 1939, pp. 256ff.; W. Zimmerli, BK 13, 1, pp. 148f. and the
references in *HAL*, pp. 315f. sub voce.

[e] Lindblom, pp. 91ff. and especially p. 100.

[f] Cf. L. Delekat, *BHW* II, col. 1169.

CHAPTER 27.10–11

An Impregnable City

10 For the impregnable city is solitary,
    a habitation deserted and forsaken, like the wilderness;
there the calves graze,[a]
    there they lie down, and strip its branches.
11 When its[a] bough is dry,[b] they are broken,
    women come
    and make a fire of them.
For this is not a people with understanding;
    therefore he who made them will not have compassion on
        them,
he that formed them will show them no favour.

A redactor who either naïvely assumed that an adequate interpretation of his words could be found in contemporary events, or was simply repeating his own ideas in a muddled way, fails here, as in the previous verses, to make clear to which city he was referring. Thus commentators have had to guess. Some regard the verses as giving a reason for asking why Yahweh still has not had pity upon the destroyed city of Jerusalem, and why the great promises of chs. 24ff. have not been fulfilled after so long a time.[c] Others believe that this is a prophecy of the future fate of Samaria,[d] while others again regard the verses as an addition made after the destruction of Samaria in 296.[e] Finally, it is not surprising that many commentators, reminded by v. 10a of 25.2, see the destroyed city as the world capital of 25.1ff.; 26.1ff.,[f] though the suggestion has also been made that the opening words are secondary, and are intended to identify the city with Samaria.[g] All this shows why one of the most cautious commentators upon the book of Isaiah stated that what city is intended is

[a] Third fem. sing.
[b] For the form cf. G-K, § 70a note 2.
[c] Rudolph, p. 54 and Fohrer, *ad loc*. Cf. also Delitzsch, Duhm and Fischer, *ad loc*.
[d] Marti *ad loc*., cf. also Plöger, pp. 92f.; ET pp. 74f.
[e] Kessler *ad loc*. Cf. also Fischer, who, however, relates the verses to 722.
[f] Cf. Dillmann-Kittel, Procksch, Feldmann, Lindblom, p. 58 and Mulders pp. 64f.
[g] Plöger, p. 93; ET pp. 74f.

altogether uncertain.[a] In fact almost every argument in favour of identification with any one city can be countered by an argument in favour of another. In the case of Jerusalem, 1.3 (cf. also Deut. 32.6), would explain the reference to a people without understanding. But following 27.2ff., this abrupt prophecy would of course occur far too late. Moreover, if the Apocalypse of Isaiah is dated later than the early fifth century, the verses could at best be regarded as a prophecy of the destruction of Jerusalem in the final age (cf. 32.9ff.). But in this case, the prophet would have been responsible for interpolating, regardless of the context, what is not even a good poem. If the city is Samaria, and the verses a prophecy, there is at least no difficulty in connecting it with vv. 8 and 9, if one is prepared to regard them as an allusion to the fate of Samaria and the northern people of Israel. This identification is supported by a statement that they lacked under-standing (Ecclus. 50.26). If this is so, we would have here a continua-tion of the prophecy in v. 8, concerned with elaborating and giving the reason for the fate of Samaria. The description of the city as solitary is reminiscent of Lam. 1.1, and the details of its abandon-ment faintly recall Hos. 2.5; Zeph. 2.13f. and Isa. 34.13. The idea of cattle grazing in the ruins of the city is found in 5.17; 17.2; cf. also 7.25. The idea of women following the grazing cattle to break off the dry branches for firewood is an original one. The attentive may have perceived a hidden allegory in this. But on the surface nothing more is stated that these women will be the only persons to visit the ruins. In order not to overstate the case for a reference to the future fate of Samaria, let us put that for identification with the world capital. The opening words in v. 10 are bound to remind the reader of 25.2. The reader's memory cannot be so poor as to fail to recognize this set expression. The condition for the salvation of all Israel is the previous destruction of the world capital, to which the attention is drawn once again. It is Yahweh certainly who created and formed Israel (cf. 43.1; 44.2; 45.11) but it is he too who has formed the whole world and all men (cf. Ps. 86.9; Isa. 42.5 and 45.18). He certainly expects Israel to have an understanding of his deity, but is not the aim of his eschato-logical action above all that of revealing his power to all men (40.5; 45.23f.; cf. 45.20!; Ps. 96.7ff.)? And in so doing, is he not simply carrying out what of his nature as the creator he can demand of all men, so that they are all guilty if they fail to recognize him (cf. Pss. 9.18; 74.18; Isa. 45.20; Rom. 1.20)? The fact remains, however, that

[a] Gray *ad loc.*

the prophet or theologian of history responsible for this addition worked too carelessly for us to arrive at any certain conclusion.

CHAPTER 27.12–13

Two Sayings for the Israel of the Final Age

12 In that day it will come about:
   When Yahweh threshes out
      〈the ears from the River〉ᵃ
   to the Brook of Egypt,
      you will be gathered
   to one anotherᵇ
      you Israelites.

13 In that day it will come about:
   When the great horn is blown
      those who were lost in the land of Assyria will come,
      and those who were dispersed in the land of Egypt,
   and will worship Yahweh
      on the holy mountain in Jerusalem.

In view of the obscurity of 27.7–11, it is easy to see why it has been suggested that vv. 12–13 are part of the original material of the apocalypse and follow 27.1. While this is not impossible, it remains uncertain, because the loose connection of both verses with their context can be regarded as a sign that they are later and separate additions. Verse 12 adds a distinctive feature to the portrait of the age of salvation, connecting it with Ezek. 42.13ff. and at the same time distinguishing it from that passage. By portraying Yahweh as threshing out the reaped ears of corn (cf. Judg. 6.11; Ruth 2.17; Job 24.24) within the boundaries of the original kingdom of David from the Euphrates to the Brook of Egypt, the *wadi al-ʿarīš* (cf. Gen. 15.18; I Kings 8.65; Ezek. 47.15ff.),ᶜ he is actually referring, as the

---

ᵃ Read with Lindblom, p. 60 *šibbōlīm mēhannāhār*, cf. also *BHS*.
ᵇ Cf. Eccles. 7.27.
ᶜ Cf. Y. Aharoni, *The Land of the Bible*, London 1966 and Philadelphia 1967, pp. 63ff. and pp. 263f. with map 21 on p. 262.

continuation shows, to the separation of Israelites and gentiles.[a]
The Israelites will be carefully picked out (cf. also 17.5 and Amos
9.9). We are not told what happens to the gentiles. Within the
metaphor the Israelites are likened to particularly valuable grains of
corn, while the gentiles are likened to the chaff and straw which is
either blown away by the wind (cf. 17.13) or thrown into the fire
(cf. Matt. 3.12). We may rightly conclude from the verse that at the
time it was composed there were both many gentiles in Palestine
and many Jews in Syria.[b] The meaning is of course that the land
within the boundaries of the kingdom of David will be returned to
Israel, for its sole use.

There is a certain logic in the addition of v. 13. It may be that the
theologian responsible for v. 12 himself thought of the idea of describing the return of the world-wide diaspora from the two Israelite
kingdoms into the Holy Land, purged of all foreigners. But it is
equally possible that someone else felt the absence of this expectation
and added an explicit expression of it. The day in which the great
ram's horn – Luther and most English translations have 'trumpet' –
is blown is of course the day of Yahweh. The horn was used in Israel
to sound the alarm and the call to attack (cf. Jer. 6.1 and Judg.
6.34; 7.16ff.) but it was also used to call together the congregation
for the cult (cf. Ps. 81.4 and Joel 2.15). Within the cult, it also seems
to have announced the epiphany of Yahweh (cf. Ex. 19.16, 19; also
II Sam. 6.15 and Ps. 47.6). In the conception of the sounding of the
horn on the day of Yahweh, the first and the last of the above
occasions are combined (cf. 18.3; Zech. 9.14; Joel 2.1; IV Esdras
6.23 and Ps. Sol. 8.1ff.). As the horn became the sign of the onset of
the last day which was to transform the destiny of the world and of
mankind, other expectations from the complex of ideas belonging to
this day came to be associated with its sounding. The various stages
of the final drama were introduced by the sounding of a trumpet (cf.
Rev. 8.2ff.; 11.15); or else it was the particular sign for the resurrection of the dead (cf. I Cor. 15.52; I Thess. 4.16). Here, as in Matt.
24.31, the sounding of the eschatological horn also takes on the
significance of a call to a cultic assembly. When it sounds the lost
tribes of Israel, which were once deported to Assyria (cf. II Kings
17.5), as well as those driven out to Egypt (cf. Jer. 42ff. and Isa.
19.16ff.), will set out on a pilgrimage to Jerusalem to worship there

[a] Delitzsch held that it referred to the resurrection of the dead of Israel.
[b] Rudolph, p. 52.

on the mountain of Yahweh's temple. The verses look forward not only to the return of the *gōlā*, the Judaean diaspora in Mesopotamia (cf. Isa. 40.9ff.; 49.22ff.; 60.4; Ezek. 20.40ff.; 34.11ff.; Bar. 4.36ff.; 5.5f.; Eth. Enoch 57; Ps. Sol. 11.1ff.), but also to the return of the former Israelite population of the northern kingdom (Jer. 31.7ff., cf. Micah 4.6ff.; Zeph. 3.19f.; Jer. 31.15ff., 20ff.; IV Esdras 13.39ff.). They express the hope, then, of the return and reconstitution of the whole of the people of God which was once divided into a northern and a southern kingdom (cf. Ezek. 32.15ff.; Zech. 10.6ff.; Hos. 11.10f.; Isa. 11.11f., 16). The circumstances of the time explain the simultaneous inclusion of Egypt and Assyria (Syria), the two world powers whose interests overlapped in Palestine, the Ptolemies in the south and Seleucids in the north-east (cf. also 19.23ff.). This justifies the assumption that the diaspora in these two kingdoms stands for all the scattered Israelites. The tacit assumption that they have no greater wish than to return to their homeland (cf. Ps. 137) shows the Palestinian point of view of the writer, which has been justified by the pogroms of history. Whereas in 24.23 the elders stood before God, in 27.13 it will be the whole people of God drawn together from the whole world. This provides a fine conclusion to whole Apocalypse of Isaiah (cf. 45.25), but it is a hope which needs to be supplemented by Rev. 7.9ff. (cf. also Isa. 19.24f.).

CHAPTERS 28–32

The Eschatological Struggle for Jerusalem

The composition which we possess in chs. 28–32 takes its present form from the theme of the eschatological struggle for Jerusalem, the climax and turning point of the eschatological drama. But it is not possible to subdivide it with certainty.

The basic material which it contains is a collection of sayings of Isaiah from the period of the revolt of Judah against Assyria in the year 703–701. This collection was put into its original form at the earliest between 597 and 587, and possibly not until after the conquest of Jerusalem in 587. It consists of 28.7–12; 28.14–18; 29.9–10; 29.13–14; 29. 15–16; 30.1–5; 30.6–7, 8; 30.(8) 9–17 and 31.1–3. 28.7–12 must have formed its beginning and 30.(8)9–17 its conclusion. The collection may be ascribed to a school of disciples of Isaiah, as an indication of its connections with the thought and preaching of the prophet. 28.7–12 has at the very least undergone redaction by the members of the school, while 28.16–17 and 30.(8) 9–17 are entirely their work. Only further study can show whether the short oracles 29.9f., 13f. and 15f. were also composed on the occasion when the collection was written down. The preference displayed in them, as in 30.1ff. and 31.1ff., for sharp antitheses suggests that they should be ascribed to Isaiah, who in the decisive years of his ministry consistently pointed to the ruinous effect of a policy and an attitude which trusted in the support of Egypt instead of in Yahweh. The date of 31.1ff. seems to fall between 30.1ff. and 30.6f.(8), since 30.6f. seems to refer to an embassy which set out to Egypt later than that mentioned in 30.1ff. and 31.1ff. Although 30.1ff. and 31.1ff. are related, this does not exclude the possibility that 31.1ff., with its much more general statements, was not first composed by a redactor. He differs from Isaiah in expressing the positive demand which underlies its proclamation of judgment, and in making explicit the rejection of this demand by the people, in order to state unequivocally their responsibility for the catastrophe (cf. 28.12 and 30.15). The sayings concerning rest (28.12) and return (30.15) seem to show him as a forerunner of the Deuteronomic movement. Isaiah had an acute sense of the contradiction between a formal obedience limited to the cult and the practical atheism demonstrated by the response to the approaching danger from Assyria (cf. 28.14ff.; 29.13f., 15f. and 30.2). He unceasingly stresses that the nation will be faced with a terrifying awakening from its dreams (cf. particularly 29.9f.). As is shown by the saying in 22.1–4, 12–14, which has been preserved outside the collection and which was composed after the Assyrian troops had withdrawn from Jerusalem, the prophet persisted in his proclamation of judgment even after the capitulation had taken place.[a]

Not only because we assume that the prophet's preaching was coherent (arguments based upon the situation at any particular time may be advanced against this assumption) but also for reasons based upon the history of religion and the psychological and sociological background, in this commentary we regard 29.1–18; 30.27–33 and 31.4–9 as deriving either not at all or only in part from Isaiah. From the point of view of tradition history, they derive from the myth of the battle of the nations and look forward to the salvation of Jerusalem by Yahweh himself at the last moment, by non-military means. Thus they already border on apocalyptic, in so far as they do not already fall into this category. From a psychological point of view the mixture and alternation of prophecies of judgment and of salvation is hardly conceivable in the concrete situation of the years 703–701. Apart from the fact that they would have represented a remarkable vacillation in the prophet's preaching, a people which still played an active part in its own history would rightly have dismissed them. It is one thing to warn against a policy of alliances and to proclaim its consequences, and another thing to prophesy that a hostile army will be defeated by a thunderstorm. The former is a matter of history, and the latter of later speculation; and we shall deal with its theological significance when we come to it.

29.1ff.; 30.27ff. and 31.4ff. hardly seem to belong to the oldest eschatological additions to the collection, which apparently begin with 28.1–4, 7a, 13, 19–22. The prose additions in 28.5–6; 29.11–12; 30.22 and 31.6, which are reminiscent at least of 17.7f., breathe the same spirit. The prophecies of salvation in 29.17–24 and 30.19–26 should be regarded as relatively recent compositions, which may be as late as the first half of the second century BC. The short apocalypse

[a] How far the same redaction can be demonstrated to be present in chs. 1–12 remains to be seen.

in 32.9–20 seems to be related to them. Its first half has kept commentators busy for a long time, so that it has come to be regarded by them as the prophet's last word.

Finally, we must mention 28.23–29 and 32.1–8, both of which display the outlook of the wisdom schools. 32.1–5(8) looks forward to the time of salvation, whereas 28.23–29 tries to give an explanation of the fact that God acts differently in different periods. The short didactic passage perhaps has in mind the difference between the prophecies of judgment and of salvation in the whole composition, and attempts to make it acceptable to the reader.

Chapter 28.1–4

Against the Crown of Ephraim

1 Woe to the proud crown
    of the drunkards of Ephraim,
and to the fading flower
    of its glorious beauty,
which is on the head ⟨   ⟩ᵃ
    of those struck by the wine.
2 Behold, a strong
    and mighty one of Yahweh
like a storm of hail,
    a destroying tempest,
like a torrent of waters,
    mighty, overflowing
he will cast down to the earth
    with violence.
3 Trodden under foot will be
    the splendid ⟨crowns⟩ᵇ
of the drunkards of Ephraim.

ᵃ 'The rich valley' is excluded not only by syntax, but also as a gloss deriving from v. 4a, cf. G-K, § 128c.

ᵇ Cf. *BH*; it is possible that the plural should also be read in v. 1a. But cf. *BHS ad loc.*

4 Then the fading flower[a]
   of its glorious beauty,
   which is on the head
   of the rich valley,
   will be like the early fig[b] before the summer:
   whoever sees it,[c]
   as soon as it is in his hand, he eats it up.[d]

Modern commentators are unanimous in relating this prophecy of warning, taking the form of a stylized proclamation of woe, to the city of Samaria, and in attributing it to Isaiah. Donner declares, 'It is beyond all doubt that the oracle derives from the period between 733/32 and 722. It probably falls in the period around 724, when king Hoshea of Ephraim began to offer resistance to Assyria; but we cannot be completely certain about this.' He sums up the prevailing view very accurately.[e] But this completely ignores an aspect of the prophecy which long ago caused Duhm to date it in the very earliest period of the prophet's ministry. This was the perfectly correct observation that Isaiah could have spoken in the mysterious terms of v. 2 only before any attack by the Assyrians had taken place. Now Tiglath-pileser III had already appeared in Syria between 743 and 740, and king Menahem of Israel had had to pay him, either in 738, or possibly as early as 742, a tribute which was exacted from the whole of the northern kingdom, whereas Isaiah certainly could not have been called before 742.[f] But the conclusion which Duhm drew from a correct observation leads in fact to the opposite conclusion: by the year in which Uzziah died (cf. 6.1) the danger from Assyria was already obvious in Jerusalem. A cryptic description of the enemies of the northern (or of the southern) kingdom would have been even in the earliest years of the prophet's ministry a pure frivolity such as we have no need to attribute to a prophet who lived in a period and a world of political upheaval. Thus we must conclude that it is impossible for the present passage to have been composed not only by Isaiah, but at any time before the exile. Rather, this prophecy of

[a] Cf. R. Meyer, *Hebräische Grammatik* II, Berlin [2]1955, § 97.6.
[b] Cf. *BH*.
[c] Cf. G-K, § 128w and § 144e.
[d] Cf. R. Meyer, *Hebräische Grammatik* II, Berlin [3]1969, § 84.2e.
[e] SVT 11, 1964, p. 77.
[f] Cf. most recently K. T. Andersen, 'Die Chronologie der Könige von Israel und Juda', *StTh* 23, 1969, pp. 95ff.

warning gives us an insight into the eschatological hopes of certain circles in Jerusalem who did not consider that the former capital of the northern kingdom and of the later province of Samaria ought to be omitted from the list of cities and nations who were destined to suffer the final chastisement. Since there are no clear criteria for dating the passage, we cannot even say whether the proto-apocalyptic poet had in mind the Samaria inhabited by the descendants of ancient Israel, or was already referring to the inhabitants of Shechem, which was rebuilt at the end of the fourth century, and the temple on Gerizim.[a] The custom of crowning practised by heavy drinkers very likely already betrays Hellenistic Greek influence.

A closer examination of the poem shows that from the artistic point of view it is not of the first rank. A reading of the first three verses gives the impression, albeit made somewhat uncertain by the obscurity of the text of v. 3,[b] that the poet is really thinking of the adornments of the drunkards, and that the destruction of these adornments is a metaphor for their own ruin. Verse 4, however, requires the identification of the adornments with Samaria or Gerizim, both of which tower over and crown a fruitful valley. The glossator of v. 1 intends the whole poem to be understood in this sense. Unless we regard v. 4 as an early addition, the fine image becomes overburdened, and seems contrived and artificial. But even if we do not take v. 4 into account, vv. 1-3 must be regarded as imperfect, since the comparison of the attack of the mighty one of Yahweh with a hailstorm and a cloudburst is not really appropriate to the preceding image of flowers which have already been cut and are fading. Nor can we overlook the fact that both the images in v. 4 conflict: the comparison of a city or a temple first with a fading flower, and then of the fading flower with an early fig, seems contrived and baroque.

[1] Perhaps inspired by Amos 6.1ff.[c] the proto-apocalyptic prophet utters his strange woe not against the drunkards of Ephraim but against their headdress. The strange affectation of the expression in v. 1aβb already suggests that the poet has another idea in mind which he keeps back at first; and this in fact he reveals in v. 4. To begin with, he is apparently portraying only a hard-drinking group of

[a] Cf. H. G. Kippenberg, *Garizim und Synagoge*, Berlin 1971, pp. 33ff. or the summary on pp. 57ff.

[b] Cf. above p. 236 note b.

[c] Cf. R. Fey, *Amos und Jesaja*, WMANT 12, 1963, p. 82.

men who according to the Greek custom of the symposium are each wearing a crown of flowers,[a] which begins to fade in the course of the evening. Another indication of the late hour is that the company is drunk, or, in the dramatic language used, struck by the wine. That they belong to the heartland of the former northern kingdom is shown by the reference to Ephraim (cf. 7.2ff., 17; 9.8, 20 – and also 11.13). The only reproach made against them lies in the reference to their complete drunkenness, which can be taken literally, in the sense of 28.7f., or in a metaphorical sense as in 29.9, referring to their complete confusion of belief and blindness to the signs of the times, or in a way which includes both possibilities. In view of the late dating suggested above a double meaning is particularly likely. The community which meets on Gerizim, in bad repute because of its Hellenistic drinking habits and under suspicion because of a special cult, calls down upon itself a prophecy of woe from a Jew who was firmly committed to Jerusalem as the place of the cult and was concerned to avoid all alien ways.[b]

[2] One who is 'strong' and 'mighty', under the command and with the authority of Yahweh, is to break in upon this festival gathering of Samaritans, unsuspecting in their 'drunkenness'.[c] Whether the poet meant by him a particular eschatological figure or thought of him merely as a representative of the eschatological nations who in their march on Jerusalem would also threaten the Samaritan hills and their principal city, is impossible to tell. The comparison of the

[a] Cf. S. Oppermann, *KP* III, col. 324f.

[b] In the east drunkenness is still regarded as a shame to a man so that he cannot allow himself to be seen in this condition publicly, a custom which like many others shows a sound feeling for respect and dignity. Even though not all traditional limits upon an individual's behaviour are meaningful, not all are meaningless or harmful. If the enlightened removal of abuses is not to leave psychological debris behind, there is room in the process of trial, in doubtful cases, for a prudent and cautious reserve and in every case for the maintenance of respect to oneself and others. Some taboos are due to prejudice, and others to long experience. Nietzsche knew why he wrote in *Thus Spake Zarathustra*: 'Thou wouldst wear no raiment before thy friend? It is in honour of thy friend that thou showest thyself to him as thou art? But he wisheth thee to the devil on that account! He who maketh no secret of himself shocketh: so much reason have ye to fear nakedness!' (*Complete Works*, vol. 11, Edinburgh and London 1909, p. 64).

We are not breaking a lance here for prudery or hypocrisy, but for an attitude which will not break down respect for oneself and for others – for even if this is ultimately based in man's acceptance by God through Christ, we are not gods.

[c] The terms are found in Amos 2.14 and 16.

enemy with mighty, overflowing waters seems to point to a connection with the expectation of the tempest of the nations against Zion,
since these themes occur in the same context elsewhere in the book of
Isaiah (cf. 17.12; 28.15; and also 8.5ff.). In any case the enemy will
burst in as unrestrained and irresistibly as a hailstorm over the city
and the valley, or like a mighty and overflowing torrent of water. In
terms of the original image, he ought only to throw to the ground the
crowns of the drinkers, and the new similes conflict with this. But it is
once again clear that the poet has something else in mind. **[3]** First of
all, however, the woe against the crown of the drunkards completed
in v. 3: the crown or crowns – the text is not quite in order at this
point – are trodden to the ground. **[4]** Without a single glance aside
at the fate of those who were wearing the crowns, which does not
seem to need any special description, the proto-apocalyptic prophet
moves on in v. 4 to the real purpose of his prophecy of warning, when
he foretells the rapid and indeed instantaneous annihilation of an
object which unfortunately for our curiosity is described only in
poetic terms. His contemporaries would have been able to identify it
without having to guess at the riddle, whereas we have to rely on
conjecture. We have a choice, depending upon our dating of the
oracle, between Samaria and Gerizim. Although the interaction of
the metaphors is aesthetically unsatisfactory, the fresh originality of
the final simile must be recognized. It is reminiscent of 17.5f., and
this is perhaps no accident. Before the summer figs which come from
the second flowering are harvested in August, the less numerous early
figs, particularly prized as being the first fruit of the year, are ready
to pick.[a] Anyone who finds them on a tree by the wayside plucks and
eats them straight away: and the poet expects that the end of the
adornments of Ephraim, Samaria or Gerizim will come just as
quickly.

[a] Cf. P. Volz, *Die biblischen Altertümer*, Stuttgart 1925, p. 382, Jer. 24.2, and
Aristophanes, *Knights*, 256ff.

CHAPTER 28.5-6

Justice and Courage for the Israel of the Time of Salvation

> 5 In that day Yahweh Sebaoth will be a beautiful crown and a glorious diadem to the remnant of his people; 6and a spirit of justice to him who sits in judgment, and strength ⟨to⟩ª those who turn back the battle to the gate.ᵇ

The repetition of the opening phrase and the transition to rhythmical prose suggest that vv. 5 and 6 should be considered separately. The proto-apocalyptic writer who speaks here is quite deliberately presenting a contrast to the previous woe against the 'crown of Ephraim' in 28.1–4. But his language in v. 5 is so mechanical that we are not sure that we can really tell what he has in mind: the opening words of the previous passage suggest that 'that day' is the day of the afflictions brought by the tempest of the nations. But v. 6 gives the impression that the phrase has no more than the general meaning of our word 'then'. Nevertheless, there is still a connection in time with the events of 28.1–4. Whereas in the tempest of the nations the 'crown of Ephraim' is to be destroyed, the almighty Yahweh Sebaothᶜ will by contrast be a glorious crown for the remnant of his people (cf. 4.2). In the future the dignity and honour of the remnant will depend upon the support of their God who will display his power in saving the remnant and in subsequently guaranteeing its internal and outward security. If we may look back to 7.11ff. – and this is where the exposition becomes uncertain – the remnant includes not only the inhabitants of Jerusalem and Judaea who have survived the tempest, but all those of the former people of the twelve tribes who have survived the ages and who have now been set free. This therefore includes the survivors of Ephraim, cf. 11.13. Thus the proto-apocalyptic writer supplements the image of 28.1–4, which his predecessor drew in purely negative terms, even though he no doubt followed 17.4ff. in estimating the numbers of the Ephraimites who would be saved as very few.

The prophecy in 1.27 that Zion shall be redeemed by justice will, according to the theologian writing here, become a reality in the

---

ª Cf. *BHS* and G-K, § 119hh.

ᵇ Cf. G-K, § 90l.

ᶜ See my commentary on 6.3, *Isaiah 1–12*, OTL 1972, p. 76, and 13.4.

time of salvation for the whole of the new Israel, because Yahweh himself will support, as the spirit of justice, him who sits in judgment. The object here, which by contrast to the next half verse is in the singular, can be regarded as a generalization applying to everyone who sits in judgment (cf. 32.1b) but this is not absolutely necessary. There is at least a possibility that the proto-apocalyptic writer was thinking of the righteous king of the time of salvation, who according to 11.1ff. would judge righteously under the direct influence of Yahweh. Just as Yahweh guarantees the internal security of the remnant, the Israel of the time of salvation, he also takes care of its external security, by being the spirit of strength to its warriors, so that they can turn back any future attack upon one of the cities of Judah, in so far as there will ever be any (cf. 9.6). This is a good example of the way in which the Hebrews emphasize the objective aspect, strength, whereas we would speak of the subjective aspect, courage. We can translate by saying that Yahweh gives courage to the new Israel to go on asserting itself in the present world. For in the expectation of the proto-apocalyptic writers, the new Israel will dwell upon an earth which, while it has been changed by the revelation of Yahweh, is still the same real world.

Chapter 28.7–13

Against the Drunken Scoffers

7   *These also*
         reel with wine
         and stagger with beer
     priest and prophet
         reel with beer
         they are confused with wine,
     they stagger with beer,
         they err in vision,
         they stumble in giving judgment.
8   For all tables
         are full of vomit,
         no place without filthiness.

9 'Whom will he teach knowledge
and to whom will he explain the message?
Those who are weaned from the milk,
those taken from the breast?

10 For (he says): Saw to Saw, Saw to Saw
Qaw to Qaw, Qaw to Qaw.
Boy, ⟨be careful⟩[a]
Boy, ⟨be careful⟩.'[a]

11 Nay, but by men of stuttering lips
and with an alien tongue,
he will speak to this people,

12 he, who has said to them,
This is rest;
let the weary rest;
and this is the place of repose;
yet they would[b] not hear.

13 *Therefore the word of Yahweh*
will be to them:
Saw to Saw, Saw to Saw
Qaw to Qaw, Qaw to Qaw
Boy, ⟨be careful⟩[a]
boy, ⟨be careful⟩[a]
and fall backward,
and be broken, and snared, and taken.

This prophecy of warning is so extraordinarily dramatic, and gives so natural an impression, that it has had little difficulty in retaining its place among the basic Isaianic material of the book. At the same time, the literary analysis of the prophecy has caused difficulty to almost every commentator. In the first place, it is clear that v. 7a is meant to provide a link between this prophecy of warning and the preceding one. Since the scene in fact plays no further part, in vv. 9ff., the view has even been put forward that vv. 7 and 8 form either in whole or in part a later literary transition to what follows.[c] It has even been suggested that the repetition of a prophecy formerly

[a] Following a proposal by G. R. Driver, *Semitic Writing from Pictograph to Alphabet.* The Schweich Lectures of the British Academy, 1944 London, ²1954, p. 90 note 1, *ṣīm*, and at the same time treat *zeʿīr* as masculine, cf. also Procksch, *ad loc.*
[b] For the form cf. G-K, § 231 and R. Meyer, *Hebräische Grammatik* I, Berlin ³1966, § 12.2.
[c] Cf. e.g. Marti and Duhm, *ad loc.*

uttered by Isaiah led to the scene described here.[a] The surprising
absence of the historical reference which it was assumed the prophet
was making has led to the consideration that the object of comparison
of v. 7a has probably not been preserved, and that the link with
28.1–4(6) is no more than a redactional device.[b] Finally, the odd fact
that vv. 9–13 contain no allusion to priest and prophet have led to the
view that it is v. 7b which should be excluded as a redactional
addition.[c] The original Isaianic material can best be isolated by
treating v. 7a as a redactional transition from the preceding passage,
v. 7b$a_2\beta$ as a later attempt to make the purpose of the reproach more
spiritual or more concrete, and excluding v. 13 as an artificial construction compiled from v. 10 and 8.15.[d] In view of v. 12 (cf. 30.15) it
can be supposed that the basic text received its present form as the
result of the redaction, perceptible in 30.8–17, of a prophecy composed by Isaiah in the period of the Assyrian crisis in the year 701.
When it was linked with 28.1ff., probably much later, the passage
found its way into a context which was eschatological in purpose, and
our exposition must conclude by taking this into account.

[7ba_1,8] Let us first of all go through the passage and comment
upon what we judge to be the basic Isaianic material. We shall then
go through it again and take into account the eschatological interpretation. If the connection between vv. 7ba_1,8 and 9ff. is regarded
as original, Isaiah must once have witnessed this disgusting scene,
which would have followed a sacrificial meal, and which showed
that there were good grounds for the regulation in Lev. 10.8f. that
priests should drink no wine or beer.[e] [9] Isaiah's antipathy, which
he had no doubt made known on previous occasions, may have been
expressed at the time by shouting at them, and the prophet may
have composed from the substance of his remarks the question and
answer dialogue which we find in vv. 9 and 10. This is a telling
characterization of persons who disqualify themselves by their own
behaviour while at the same time claiming to be those who truly
proclaim the will of God. They reject the idea that they need any
instruction about the true content of the knowledge which they

[a] Cf. Procksch, *ad loc.*
[b] With Eichrodt, *ad loc.*
[c] With Kissane, *ad loc.*
[d] Cf. also H. Donner, SVT 11, pp. 146ff.
[e] Cf. K. Elliger, HAT I, 14, 1966, p. 134 and p. 138.

impart as priests or the 'message', the revelation,[a] which is received from them as prophets. In short, they consider they have the right to take issue with Isaiah who is acting towards them as if he was teaching children. In Israel, the weaning of infants took place, as it still does among many peoples, much later than among ourselves, between the third and the fifth year of life (cf. II Macc. 7.27 and I Sam. 1.22ff.).[b]

[10] The significance of the words *ṣaw-lāṣāw*, *qaw-lāqāw* in v. 10 has been much discussed. At first they were usually treated as words with meaning, and *ṣaw* was regarded as an abbreviation of *miṣwā*, commandment, or of a conjectural *ṣāwā*, 'precept', while *qāw* was identified with the known word 'measuring line', so that the expression was taken as a mockery of what was assumed to be the constantly moralizing teaching of these prophets.[c] The solution to the puzzle is now sought in another direction, although by no means all commentators' yet agree. The words are taken as onomatopoeic sounds, imitating the speech or the sound of the rapid footsteps of the prophet incessantly following his calling.[d] On the basis of v. 11, the suggestion has been made that the words are a mocking imitation of the way Isaiah usually spoke.[e] Others, looking back to v. 9b, regard *ṣaw-lāṣāw*, *qaw-lāqāw* as the imitation of the meaningless words with which children are taught to walk.[f] The first interpretation mentioned here, which used to be very widely held, breaks down on the fact that there is no evidence for a metaphorical use of *qaw*, measuring line, in this sense (cf. 28.17; 37.11, 17) while a colloquial form *ṣaw* for *miṣwā* is just as much an invention as the noun *ṣāwā*. We do not know enough either to accept or to reject an interpretation which implies an individual infirmity on Isaiah's part.[g] In view of v. 11, therefore, there are two possibilities. The first is that of a vulgarism or colloquial term corresponding to our 'burble, burble'. An alternative and less artificial suggestion is that the words are an imitation of a teacher,

[a] Cf. 28.29; Jer. 49.14; Ezek. 21.12 and Obad. 1.

[b] Cf. F. Nötscher, *Biblische Altertumskunde*, Bonn 1940, p. 71.

[c] Cf. e.g. Delitzsch, Orelli, Feldmann, König, Fischer, Ziegler and Kissane, *ad loc.*

[d] Cf. Duhm, *ad loc.*

[e] Cf. I. P. Seierstad, *Die Offenbarungserlebnisse der Propheten*, Oslo 1946 (²1965) pp. 176f.

[f] Cf. Marti, *ad loc.*; and similarly Lindblom, *Prophecy in Ancient Israel*, Oxford 1962, p. 201.

[g] Following Seierstad, p. 176, and in disagreement with G. Hölscher, *Die Profeten*, Leipzig 1914, p. 35 and p. 149.

i.e. at that period, a wise man,[a] who is teaching his pupils the alphabet and is making them write down from dictation the letters which were later called *ṣādē* and *qōp*, with plenty of interjections and advice. Recent research has discovered that it is probable that the letters of the alphabet were originally not all known by the names which later became current, but were partly known only by a simple vocalization of the consonants – and the Hebrew alphabet has only consonants – such as still exists in the case of *wāw* and *tāw*.[b] This interpretation, therefore, is neither impossible of itself nor excluded by the context. One can imagine that the voice of a teacher repeating the letters over and over again to the boys who are writing them could sound ridiculous to someone who overheard them by chance, particularly if he heard only the sounds.

[11–12] This further prophecy of warning takes up the mocking comparison of the prophet who never preaches anything but disaster, and envisages that Yahweh will speak to the scoffers in Jerusalem through foreigners who speak a language unknown to the Jews (cf. 36.11f.), by whom Isaiah's contemporaries would understand, and were meant to understand, the Assyrians. The scoffers are contemptuously referred to as 'this people'.[c] It is interesting that Yahweh should be paraphrased by a reference back to his message. He had shown them the way to rest, a place and condition of undisturbed safety from their enemies (cf. Deut. 12.9f. and I Kings 8.56), and called upon their leaders to give his rest to the people who were worn out by the disturbances of recent decades. As in 30.15 the redactor makes Yahweh state explicitly that his message is rejected by the people and their leaders, in order to impress upon later readers that the catastrophe was a consequence which they had brought upon themselves by rejecting what Yahweh offered through the agency of the prophet. Thus v. 12 is a summary of Isaiah's preaching by a redactor looking back upon the past and working at the earliest between 597 and 587.

[7a] Going back to consider the composition as enlarged by the proto-apocalyptic redactor, we must turn first to the link in v. 7a

---

[a] Cf. H. J. Hermisson, *Studien zur israelitischen Spruchweisheit*, WMANT 28, 1968, 129ff.

[b] Cf. W. W. Hallo, *JBL* 77, 1958, pp. 337f. and G. R. Driver, *Semitic Writing*, Oxford and New York ²1954, pp. 89f. but also Bredenkamp, Procksch, Fohrer and S. Erlandsson, *The Burden of Babylon*, Lund 1970, pp. 64f.

[c] Cf. 8.6, 11, 12; 9.15; 28.14; 29.13f.

with the previous prophecy against Ephraim. Although he may have received approbation from many circles in Jerusalem when he prophesied the fall of Samaria or even of the temple upon Gerizim, with his eschatological message he seems to have encountered not merely rejection but mockery among some circles, which we ought most probably to identify with those associated with the temple priesthood.[a] This led him to place the prophecy of the warning, with its reason, against the scoffers immediately after the prophecy against the 'crown of Ephraim', especially since both spoke of drunkards. Anyone who agreed that it was right to foretell the fall of the crown of Ephraim ought at least to ask whether there were not reasons for believing that the same disaster would come upon Jerusalem. Anyone who from the Jewish point of view regarded the Samarians or the Samaritans as immoral and blinded, ought to consider whether the same judgment could not be passed upon Jerusalem. Since a suitable prophecy by Isaiah was available to him, it was now easy for him to reinterpret it; we need only to assume that the Greek practice of the symposium had meanwhile come into use among the upper classes of Jerusalem and even among the priesthood, in order to give a new meaning to v. 7, and also to understand how the original and the imputed meanings are intertwined. [7b$\alpha_2\beta$] Perhaps among the late cultic prophets an alcoholic technique of ecstasy was practised, so that the charge of being drunk on duty was doubly true.[b] We need only to suppose that both groups denied the eschatological message to understand that their decisions and divine oracles[c] were in the eyes of the proto-apocalyptic redactor evidence of their spiritual blindness, in the sense of 29.9ff. The priesthood who at this period formed the leadership of the nation may very well have conducted, with mocking superiority, disputes with the eschatological teachers. Thus the juxtaposition of mockery and judgment may have been very much in

---

[a] Cf. Plöger, *Theokratie und Eschatologie*, WMANT 2, 1959, pp. 132f. (ET, *Theocracy and Eschatology*, Oxford and Richmond, Va., 1968, pp. 113f.); and for the later disputes about the eschatological message within the priesthood, F. M. Cross, *The Ancient Library of Qumran and Modern Biblical Studies*, New York [2]1961, pp. 128f., and H. Stegemann, Die Entstehung der Qumrangemeinde, thesis, Bonn, 1971, pp. 198ff.

[b] Cf. Lindblom, pp. 58f.

[c] Cf. J. Begrich, 'Das priesterliche Heilsorakel' *ZAW* 52, 1934, pp. 81ff., reprinted *Ges. Studien*, ThB 21, 1964, pp. 217ff.; *Die priesterliche Tora*, BZAW 66, 1936, pp. 85ff., reprinted *Studien*, pp. 232ff.; and R. Rendtorff, *Die Gesetze in der Priesterschrift*, FRLANT 62, 1954 ([2]1963), pp. 34, 45, 66 and 77.

accordance with what the proto-apocalyptic redactor intended. **[13]** But he felt it important to leave no doubt that the rejection of his message would be punished in the same way, so that he repeated v. 10 and expanded it with words from 8.15.

CHAPTER 28.14–22

God's Strange Works

14   *Therefore*
     hear the word of Yahweh,
       you scoffers,
     You proverb-makers[a] of this people
       in Jerusalem!

15   Yes, you have said, we have made
       a treaty with death,
     and with Sheol
       we have a pact.[b]
     When the raging[a] ⟨flood rises⟩[c]
       it will not reach us;
     for we have made lies our refuge,
       and in falsehood we have taken shelter.

16   Therefore thus says the Lord Yahweh
     [d]Behold, I ⟨am laying⟩[e] on Zion ⟨   ⟩[f]
     a hard stone[g]
     a precious cornerstone as a foundation ⟨   ⟩[f]
      He who believes will not waver.[h]

[a] An alternative translation is given by Herrscher.

[b] For the unusual *ḥōzē* in v. 15 and *ḥazūt* in v. 18, cf. A. R. Johnson, *The Cultic Prophet in Ancient Israel*, Cardiff and Mystic, Conn., ²1962, p. 13 note 3. We follow the translation given in the ancient versions.

[c] Cf. v. 18.

[d] An early exilic redaction; cf. below.

[e] Cf. *BHS*, with 1Q Isa.

[f] Cf. *BHS*, with LXX and I Peter 2.6.

[g] Literally: *bohan* stone; that this is probably a slatey gneiss is suggested in *HAL* sub voce, together with the other suggested renderings.

[h] Cf. with Donner 1QS VIII. 7f., which reads 'This is the tested wall, the precious corner stone, its foundations will not shake nor move from their place.' Translation based on E. Lohse, *Die Texte von Qumran*, Darmstadt, 1964, p. 29.

17   *And I will make justice the line,*
         and righteousness the plummet;
      Then hail will sweep away the refuge of lies,
         and waters will overwhelm the shelter.
18   Then your treaty with death will be annulled,[a]
         and your pact[b] with Sheol will not stand;
      when the flood rises
         you will be beaten down by it.
19   *As often as it rises*
         it will take you.
      When it rises morning by morning,
         by day and by night;
      and it will be sheer terror
         to understand[c] the message[d]
20   *For: the bed is too short to stretch oneself*
         and the covering too narrow ⟨to wrap oneself.⟩[e]
21   *Far as on Mount Perazim*
         Yahweh will rise up;
      as in the valley of Gibeon he will thunder,
         to do his deed
         strange is his deed!
         And to work his work
         alien is his work!
22   *Now therefore do not scoff,*
      lest your bonds be made strong.
      For that destruction is decreed[f]
      upon the whole earth,
         I have heard from ⟨   ⟩[g] Yahweh Sebaoth.

It is certain that in its present form 28.14–22 is meant to be understood as a unity. But it is extremely doubtful whether the passage was
a unity originally. The oracle can be divided into vv. 14–15, a
prophecy of reproach, and vv. 16–22, a prophecy of warning. The
prophet's reproach is followed by a divine warning. But we must not
overlook the fact that the prophecy of warning really ends with v. 18,

---

   [a] The reading *wtpr*, which is often proposed, cf. also 8.10, is excluded for reasons
of verbal syntax, because in this position it would have a preterite sense.
   [b] See above, p. 248 note b.
   [c] Another possible translation: 'To interpret'.
   [d] Cf. 28.8 and 53.1.
   [e] Cf. *BHS*, with LXX and I Peter 2.6.
   [f] Literally, 'Destruction and decision'.
   [g] Cf. *BHS*, with 1 Q Isa.

while v. 19 is an addition. Verses 20 and 21 have no place in the section in which Yahweh is the speaker. Verse 22 concludes with a warning which seems to be based on the idea of a world-wide destruction. Finally, it has often been noted that the saying concerning the cornerstone fits remarkably loosely into its context. The theme of a promise in v. 16 is surprising, and there is also a tension between the already existing building of lies and the building which is yet to be set up upon Zion.[a] Perhaps the most likely explanation of the growth of the passage is to see it as taking place in three main stages. The first stage was the prophecy by Isaiah to be found in vv. 14–15 and 16aα, 17b–18. To this the redactor who can be seen at work particularly in 30.8–17, and perhaps lived before the exile, added vv. 16aβ, b and 17a. Finally, the passage was reinterpreted in an eschatological sense by the addition of vv. 20–22. It is no longer possible to tell whether v. 19 was inserted at the same time or separately.

[14–15, 16aα, 17b, 18] *The pact with death.* The word *lākēn*,therefore, is used to link this later prophecy of warning, with its reason, to 28.7ff., with which it has in common the idea of scoffing. Isaiah addresses his demand to listen to the word of Yahweh to a group (cf. 1.10; Hos. 4.1; Isa. 66.5)[b] whom he describes as 'scoffers' (cf. Prov. 29.8)[c] and also as 'proverb-makers of this people'. Proverb 21.24 defines the scoffer as the man who is arrogant because of his pride and who acts accordingly (cf. also 29.20). 'Proverb-makers' are people who make a *māšāl*, a statement which draws together two things because of their similarity. This is something that wise men do with the serious purpose in giving moral and religious instruction to their hearers (cf. Prov. 1.5) but which can also be done to bring contempt on persons whom one dislikes or to convince people (cf. 14.4 and Ezek. 22).[d] The parallel with the 'scoffers' shows that we have here the second use, that of expressing contempt. Those who are addressed are clearly the spokesmen of a larger group to whom Isaiah

---

[a] Cf. Procksch and Scott, *ad loc.*, R. Fey, *Amos und Jesaja*, WMANT 12, 1963, p. 120; S. Herrmann, *Die prophetischen Heilserwartungen im Alten Testament*, BWANT 85, 1965, p. 144 and B. S. Childs, *Isaiah and the Assyrian Crisis*, StBTh II. 3, 1967, p. 30.

[b] Cf. also Jer. 2.4; 5.21; 7.2; 17.20; 31.9 etc.; also II Kings 18.28.

[c] Cf. also Prov. 1.22.

[d] Cf. A. R. Johnson, in *Wisdom in Israel and the Ancient Near East*: presented to H. H. Rowley, SVT 3, 1955, pp. 162ff. and most recently W. McKane, *Proverbs*, OTL, 1970, pp. 22ff.

has an antipathy, so that he speaks of them as 'this people'.[a] The last word of the address shows that the dispute is taking place in Jerusalem.[b]

Great care is needed in evaluating v. 15. Like 30.10f., it contains not an idea actually uttered by Isaiah's opponents, but one which Isaiah attributes to them to characterize their attitude. In face of an imminent danger they believe that they are potentially immortal. As in Ps. 49.15; Job 18.13 and Isa. 5.14 death and the underworld are almost personified beings,[c] just as *mōt*, death, was in fact a Canaanite god.[d] We need not necessarily assume that religious or magical measures were taken against the possibility of death. The passage should be interpreted more cautiously in a very general and metaphorical sense:[e] the scoffers are behaving as though they have made a pact with death and the underworld; as though both had assured them that they would not bring them into their power; as though they were immortal, though of course only for a time. Any contemporary listener would at once have understood this as a challenge to the God from whom man is unable to conceal himself or find refuge even in the underworld (cf. Ps. 139.8; Amos 9.2). In Isaiah's view, these opponents are claiming potential immortality in the face of a danger which he compares to a flood; they regard lies and falsehood as giving them protection against it. The waters, the raging, *šṭp*, overflowing or rising, *'br*, flood are really, as can be seen from a glance at the history of this theme, the waters of death and the underworld (cf. Ps. 124.4; 18.5ff.; 63.3, 16: Job 38.16f.).[f] Thus it is clear once again that this arrogant people are imagining themselves safe from premature death. The idea of being safe from death altogether lies outside the realism of Old Testament anthropology. The two exceptions, Enoch and Elijah (cf. Gen. 5.24 and II Kings 2.11f.), are meant at best to remind men that they themselves are only ordinary persons, subject to death. Lies and falsehood represent an attitude which is

[a] Cf. 6.10; 8.6, 11, 12; 9.15; 29.13f. Cf. also Jer. 6.19; 7.16; 8.5; 13.10; 14.11, etc.

[b] For this expression cf. Ezra 1.3ff.; Neh. 11.3 and I Chron. 14.4.

[c] Cf. also H. J. Kraus, BK, 15.1, 1960, or Ps. 49, 15 and F. Horst, BK 16. 1, 1968, or Job 18.13.

[d] Cf. H. Gese, *Die Religionen Altsyriens*, RM 10. 2, 1970, pp. 135f.

[e] For the discussion of the translation of *berīt* as 'treaty' cf. most recently E. Kutsch, *ThQ* 150, 1970, pp. 299ff. where practical summaries of the different possible ways of making a contract are given.

[f] Cf. also above, p. 35 note a.

contrary to the objective order and therefore untrue, and as such is characteristic of the godless person who is subject to judgment (cf. Ps. 4.3; 7.15; 27.12; 31.19). Since man has to seek refuge in Yahweh (cf. Ps. 46.2; 61.4; 7.2; 11.1; 25.20; 31.2; 71.1; 141.8; 144.2),[a] any other refuge which man tries to find is necessarily a lie. Thus the prophet's charge against his opponents is reduced to their reliance in the face of imminent danger not upon God but upon some human aid. By so doing they are acting as if they were immortal. Unless the contemporary setting of this prophecy by Isaiah was some chance occasion, we may assume that it belongs in the situation of the years 703–701, and that its background is in fact Hezekiah's policy of alliances, which had probably just been initiated. Isaiah rejects it, because in his eyes it expresses the fact that the people were seeking help not from Yahweh but from earthly forces. By the rejection of his warnings and threats about the danger from Assyria, which is described here as a flood, the advocates of this policy were behaving as if they were potentially immortal, and did not realize that by their godless actions they were bringing upon themselves the danger from which they imagined they were seeking refuge.

As a result of the reduction responsible for the interpolation of vv. 16aβb and 17a, the prophecy of warning which follows the reproach may have been corrupted at the beginning of v. 17b perhaps by more than the introduction of the word w^e ('and' or 'then'), but the sense is still clear: Yahweh will immediately make clear that the falsely chosen earthly refuge does not contain what it promises. Hail, which we find elsewhere as the instrument of the eschatological judgment (cf. 28.2; 30.30 and 32.19), will sweep away the false refuge, which by implication is very fragile, and waters will overwhelm the shelter. Thus v. 18 explicitly states that the pact with death and the underworld will be of no use when the flood, or to abandon the metaphor, the Assyrian army, sweeps over the land and claims its victims.[b] The content of the prophecy of warning is a simple reversal of the statements in the reproach, giving the whole passage an almost chiastic structure.

[16aβb, 17a] *The cornerstone*. The beginning of the famous prophecy of the cornerstone faces the commentator with a problem. Since the verbal construction occurring in the traditional Hebrew text at the beginning of the words spoken by God seems syntactically impossible,

---

[a] Cf. also 30.2; 31.1 and 30.12.
[b] Cf. 5.5; 7.25; 10.6 and 28.3.

it must be amended to a more normal form, in which 'Here I am' or 'Behold, I . . .' is followed by a participle. However, the tense remains vague; in Hebrew in general it can only ever be determined from the context. The interpretations of the cornerstone is inseparable from a decision about the tense in this passage. The many commentators who have left unamended the traditional verbal form following 'Behold, I . . .' and have treated the perfect tense as referring to the past (according to present-day understanding this is not necessarily so of a perfect in this position)[a] have produced almost as many attempts to interpret the cornerstone. Thus it has been identified with the law of Yahweh revealed upon Zion,[b] the Temple upon Zion as the refuge of those faithful to Yahweh,[c] the archetypal monarchy set up in the person of David,[d] the city of Jerusalem on its hill,[e] the saving work begun by Yahweh on Zion,[f] Yahweh's relationship to his people,[g] and even with the true community of believers already founded by God.[h] On the other hand, those who have emended the verb into a participle and understood it in a future sense have interpreted the statement as referring to Zion as the righteous foundation by Yahweh,[i] to the Messiah as the foundation stone of a temple not built with hands,[j] faith,[k] the remnant of believers,[l] or very precisely to the statement that 'He who believes will not waver', as Yahweh's promise.[m]

[a] The problem arises from the fact that a perfect at the beginning of the sentence can have a future or durative meaning in circumstances other than what is called the consecutive construction, and so corresponds in function to the 'imperfect'.

[b] Eichhorn.

[c] Ewald.

[d] Delitzsch.

[e] Knobel-Diestel. E. Rowland, Die Bedeutung der Erwählungstraditionen Israels für die Eschatologie der alttestamentlichen Propheten, thesis, Heidelberg 1956, p. 151, takes it to refer to the holy rock upon Zion.

[f] Feldmann.

[g] Duhm.

[h] Eichrodt.

[i] Childs, p. 67.

[j] Procksch and Scott.

[k] Marti, Fohrer, who takes the participle in a preterite sense, and also Kissane, who retains the reading found in M.

[l] Donner, cf. also Guthe and H. Schmidt, ad loc., and also F. Giesebrecht, Beiträge zur Jesajakritik, Göttingen 1890, p. 67, who emphasizes that v. 16 occurs in a statement of condemnation and mentions the possibility of a remnant 'only once in passing and basically in contrast to the defiant arrogance of the present time'.

[m] König, ad loc.

It is immediately obvious that a foundation, and particularly a cornerstone, must consist of strong, resistant material, because it has to bear the weight of the building. The durability of its building depends upon a firm foundation.[a] Before we consider the meaning in this context of the statement 'He who believes will not waver', let us consider the train of thought which continues to v. 17a. In v. 17a, in accordance with the further metaphor taken from building, we would expect the testing of the building begun in v. 17. The measuring line and plumb are used to check an uncompleted new building,[b] but are also used to find out whether an old building is fit for demolition (cf. II Kings 21.13; Amos 7.7; Isa. 34.11). In plain terms, this means that justice and righteousness are to be the standard which Yahweh will apply in his future acts in history. That it will be impossible for those who arrogantly despise God to endure in the judgment follows as a matter of course, and is explicitly stated in the continuation which forms part of the original prophecy. Verse 16, however, points to the alternative which exists, of holding firm and unshaken to Yahweh, trusting in him and so avoiding the judgment (cf. 7.9). Thus the cornerstone is formally speaking the promise, but in practice the faith which gives a refuge as safe as the foundation stones which neither hail nor floods can damage.[c] Very much in the spirit of the great prophet, the redactor contrasts the unsuccessful policy which had led the kingdom of Judah to catastrophe with the faith which is the alternative, and which could have protected the country from catastrophe. Perhaps it is not enough to say merely that it could have done. Perhaps the drama was not yet over, and the prophet's disciple still saw a chance. The ultimate purpose of his addition, as of his redaction in 28.7ff. and the longer addition in 30.8ff., is that of posing the alternative which lay in the background of Isaiah's prophecies of judgment.

[19] It is of little importance whether v. 19 forms a separate *eschatological redaction* or is from the same hand as gave us the following

[a] For the problem of the cornerstone cf. L. Köhler, *ThZ* 3, 1947, pp. 390ff.; J. Lindblom, in *Interpretationes . . . S. Mowinckel*, Oslo 1955, pp. 123ff. and K. Galling, in *Verbannung und Heimkehr. Festschrift W. Rudolph*, Tübingen 1961, pp. 72f., whom we follow in understanding the stones in a collective sense as a structure.

[b] Cf. Job 38.5 and Ezek. 47.3.

[c] For the Old Testament concept of faith cf. also R. Smend, 'Zur Geschichte von *h'myn*', *Hebräische Wortforschung. Festschrift W. Baumgartner*, SVT 16, 1967, pp. 284ff., though his evaluation of the occurrences in the Book of Isaiah, based upon literary criticism, is not followed here.

addition. In order to understand it we must remember how simple it must have been to interpret the flood mentioned in vv. 15 and 17f. as a symbol for the nations who would one day surge against Jerusalem (cf. 17.12ff.).[a] By his own reference to their ceaseless onrush and the terror brought by the eschatological ministry of prophecy, which would have nothing but disaster to proclaim, he emphasizes the prophecy in the previous verses of the threat that is coming to Jerusalem. [20] In v. 20 he foretells that people will be completely without protection. [21] Without drawing back the veil from his eschatological expectations and describing the dangers directly, he concludes by explaining why what is to come upon the scoffers will be irresistible, recalling two acts of Yahweh on behalf of his people from the early days of Israel's history, the annihilating defeat of the Philistines on Mount Perazim (cf. II Sam. 5.17ff.; I Chron. 14.8ff.)[b] and the destruction of the Canaanite kings in the battle at Gibeon, actually brought about by a heavenly intervention (cf. Josh. 10.9ff.).[c] This time, however, Yahweh will do exactly the opposite. He will not relieve Jerusalem and Judah from the Philistines, but will let the nations storm against it and besiege it, fighting from heaven with a hailstorm against his own city. Here too, the proto-apocalyptic writer refrains from using concrete terms and makes do with the assertion that Yahweh will here bring about his strange work, his *opus alienum*. This is meant to impress upon those who hear the prophecy that in the future Yahweh will act mightily as in the past, but in a strange and alien way, apparently forgetting his former relationship to this people and this city. Verse 16 implies that this judgment will not be his final act. But this is not the concern of the person who with his eschatological message found himself exposed to the mockery of his contemporaries, as Isaiah had been with his message of faith. [22] Thus he concludes with an exhortation, accompanied by a reason, to scoff no longer in order not to bring about an even greater involvement with doom. For he is certain, either through his study of scripture or as the result of a direct revelation, that Yahweh has decided to afflict and annihilate not only

[a] For the beginning of v. 19 cf. also II Kings 4.8. For the later rabbinic conception of the holy rock in Jerusalem as the central point of the earth where it was washed by the primaeval ocean, and the place of access to it, cf. J. Jeremias, *Golgotha*, Angelos-Beiheft 1, Leipzig 1926, p. 67 and pp. 58ff.

[b] Cf. H. W. Hertzberg, ATD 10, ²1960, pp. 222ff.; ET *I and II Samuel*, OTL, pp. 272ff.

[c] Cf. H. W. Hertzberg, ATD 9, ²1959, pp. 71ff.

Jerusalem but the whole earth (cf. 24.1ff.). Whether by bonds he means the ropes that bind a prisoner or someone being led to execution (cf. 52.2; Ps. 2.3) or those of a draught animal tied to the yoke or being led to slaughter (cf. Jer. 2.20) is uncertain, but of no real importance for understanding the passage. Someone who in the face of a coming catastrophe could offer an exhortation and was convinced that its severity could still be influenced by one's own behaviour was perhaps also aware that Zion could provide protection for those who believed.

The New Testament writers, headed by the apostle Paul, emphasized by their use of 28.16 (cf. Rom. 9.33; 10.11; I Peter 2.4ff. and I Tim. 1.16)[a] that salvation or damnation depends upon the faith which we have in God through Christ.[b] Since in Rom. 9.33 Paul also brings in Isa. 8.14, it is quite likely that this composite quotation was available to him in a Jewish florilegium, a selection of Messianic prophecies. When the believer examines his faith in Christ, he says that it is also and ultimately a faith in God who as the basis and unfathomable ground of the world remains our Lord and our hope. The disciple of Isaiah who, following his master, responded to doubting mockery with his message of trust in the faith of God, shows that we cannot understand the distinction between the Old and the New Testament simply as one between the law and the gospel. Both teach a new obedience, and neither of the prophets who speak in these passages think of salvation without obedience. But they are aware that the roots of obedience and salvation lie in trust, in the constant clinging to Yahweh which we call faith.

We would recall that behind v. 21 lies Luther's concept of the *opus alienum Dei*, God's alien, death-dealing work, behind which is concealed his true life-giving work. The formula in the Defence of the Augsburg Confession repeats his teaching and refers to this verse: *Alienum opus Dei vocat, cum terret, quia Dei proprium opus est vivificare et consolari.*[c] The view that God's judgments are part of his work of grace was shared by the proto-apocalyptic prophet in so far as he saw the judgment on Jerusalem in the framework of a wider eschato-

---

[a] Cf. J. Jeremias, *ThWBNT* IV, pp. 275ff.

[b] Cf. O. Michel, Meyerk IV, [4]1966, *ad loc.*

[c] 'He says: God will terrify, although the same is God's work; for God's proper work is to make alive. Other works, such as terrifying and killing, are not God's proper work.' Quoted from *Bekenntnisschriften der ev.–luth. Kirche*, pub. by the Deutscher Ev. Kirchenausschuss, Berlin 1930, p. 261.

logical conception which is not developed here, as the necessary preliminary to the conquest of the nations who oppressed Jerusalem and to the glorification of the liberated city upon an earth which is at peace. But the idea that God kills only to make alive is not worked out on such a fundamental level here as in Paul and Luther. In order to understand this principle, one must first recognize something which can be found in the Old Testament, but is taken completely seriously only by the New Testament, that in the eyes of God we are all fallen men, so that there is no one who does good, not even one (cf. Ps. 14.3 with Rom. 3.10ff.). In the 'nevertheless' of the gospel there is a power which can make the life which men live together more tolerable in a world which is growing smaller, and necessarily exposes us to greater pressures; but in an age dominated on the one hand by an enthusiasm for action and change and on the other hand by an Utopian dream of freedom, the presence of this power is overlooked. In a world which is growing smaller the pressure to achieve grows no less. But it would be made more tolerable by the knowledge that one belongs to the fellowship of those whose sins are forgiven. Only when God is lost can the freedom and joy of the children of God in this world be lost. Trust in God is something more and something greater than flight from the world and boredom with the world, but more too than mere delight in the world. If God is behind everything that terrifies us, in order to carry out his strange work and call us to him, the fear and resignation of men justifies the God who desires to be our God.

CHAPTER 28.23–29

Everything in Due Time

23 Give ear, and hear my voice;
   hearken, and hear my speech.
24 Does he who ploughs ⟨   ⟩a for sowing plough all day?
   Does he continually break and harrow his ground?
25 When he has levelled its surface,
   does he not scatter black cummin and sow plain cummin,
and set wheat, millet and barley ⟨   ⟩a
   and emmer at its edge?

a Cf. *BHS*.

26   For he instructs him aright,
        his God teaches him.

27   ⟨   ⟩ᵃ Black cummin is not threshed with a threshing
        sledge,
        nor is ⟨the wheel⟩ᵇ rolled over plain cummin;
        but black cummin is beaten out with a stick,
        *and plain cummin with a rod.*ᶜ

28   Yes,ᵈ bread grainᵉ is pounded,
        it is not threshed continually;ᶠ
        when the cart wheel is driven over it
        ⟨it is broken up⟩ᵍ but not crushed.ʰ

29   This also comes
        from Yahweh *Sebaoth,*ⁱ
        he is wonderful in counsel,
        and gives great success.

In the middle of great prophecies about the fate of Jerusalem and
indeed of the whole earth, we suddenly find this artistically constructed wisdom poem of two stanzas.ʲ Its purpose is ostensibly only
to inform us how marvellously Yahweh instructs the farmer, so that
he can carry out all his activities in the right order and with the
appropriate tools. If this didactic poem had been preserved in the
framework of a collection of proverbs or some other category of
wisdom writing, no one would have thought to look for any hidden

ᵃ Delete the introductory *kī* on metrical grounds.

ᵇ Delete *ʿagālā* on metrical grounds and read *weʾōpān.*

ᶜ V. 27b is an interpretive comment which is factually correct, but disrupts the
structure of the stanza.

ᵈ Move the *kī* to the beginning of the verse on metrical grounds.

ᵉ For the significance of *leḥem* cf. 30.23; Gen. 41.54 and Ps. 104.14.

ᶠ For the form cf. B-L § 56u″, p. 402.

ᵍ Cf. *BHS.*

ʰ Delete the *māqqēp.*

ⁱ For metrical reasons 'Sebaoth' is clearly secondary.

ʲ The metrical structure of the poem has evidently been disrupted by later
additions, but is still so clearly recognizable that one may venture a reconstruction.
Whereas the opening formula has a separate 3+3 metre, is followed in v. 24 by a
4+3 metre, in v. 25a by 3+4 metre, in v. 25b 2+2+2 and in v. 26, 2+2. In the
second stanza the natural lack of an opening formula results in the odd number of
lines at the beginning being compensated by the addition of a couplet at the end.
Once the emendations proposed above are taken into account, the body of the
stanza shows a remarkable similarity to the first stanza, with 4+3 in v. 27a, 3+4
in v. 28a, 2+2+2 in v. 28b and finally 2+2 in v. 29a, which is followed in v. 29b
by the compensating couplet, 2+2.

sense going beyond its surface meaning[a] or of regarding it as a parable.[b] But unless we are to assume that the redactor, responsible for the interpolation of the poem, as the prophet himself, had completely overlooked when he did so the prophetic nature of the Isaiah roll, we must look for good or ill for a hidden sense which can be deduced only from relationship of the passage to the context.

[23] The introductory formula, which has not inaccurately been described here as a 'request to listen at the beginning of instruction'[c] makes it clear that the poem cannot have been uttered by Isaiah in the course of his oral preaching before it was introduced into its present position. If we look for similar opening formulae, meant to attract the attention of hearers, such as we find from wisdom teachers,[d] ancient singers[e] and prophets,[f] we note that without exception they name the audience they have in mind. The fact that here those addressed are not named can be regarded as an indication that the original setting of this passage was a literary one.[g] It remains an open question, however, whether the poem was composed by the redactor for its present position, or taken from a larger didactic poem which has not been preserved. In view of the interpretative function of the poem in its present context we can no longer accept that it was composed by Isaiah. Readers or listeners who have by now come to have doubts about the content of the Isaiah roll, or who may be led to doubt in the course of the coming chapters, are startled out of their thoughts, so that they can then read or listen on in the light of the instruction given to them.

[24] To begin with, we must ignore the question of the hidden meaning, in order to understand the surface meaning. The wisdom teacher begins with a rhetorical question, didactic in intent, to which the answer is of course a negative one: no ploughman ploughs on continuously without purpose or understanding. Everyone of the tasks mentioned is carried out for a particular purpose, and only until that purpose is achieved. The ploughing in v. 24a and 24b is divided

---

[a] Cf. G. von Rad, *Theologie* II, Munich [1]1957, p. 174 note 19; ET *Old Testament Theology* II, London and New York 1965, pp. 163f. note 21.

[b] Cf. E. König, *Stilistik, Rhetorik, Poetik*, Leipzig 1900, pp. 89, 14ff.

[c] H. W. Wolff, BK 14, 1, 1961, p. 123.

[d] Cf. Prov. 4.1; 7.24; Ps. 49.2; Job 33.1 and 34.1.

[e] Cf. Gen. 4.24 and Judg. 5.3.

[f] Cf. Hos. 5.1 and Isa. 1.10.

[g] Cf. also Jer. 13.15–17. I owe this observation to Pastor Hartmut Bobbe of Leer, East Frisia.

into the rough preliminary ploughing or breaking up of the hard ground (*pth*) and the secondary ploughing in order to crumble the sods (*śdd*).[a]

[25] The wisdom teacher begins a new example, making sure of assent to the statement which follows, and draws the practical conclusion from the preceding question. In this way he holds the attention of his actual or imaginary readers. When the ploughman has sufficiently prepared and harrowed his ground and finally levelled it again by ploughing it several times, he of course goes on from this work to that of sowing, and quite in accordance with his purpose, uses all kinds of seeds. The comparatively abundant seed of black cummin (*nigella sativa*) and ordinary cummin (*cuminum cyminum*),[b] used as a spice and on the surface of loaves is scattered carelessly, while the more valuable corn for bread is sown more carefully: the wheat (*triticum durum* or *aestivum*),[c] the sorghum or millet (*sorghum vulgare* or *panicum miliaceum*)[d] and barley (*hordeum vulgare*).[e] Finally, he also sows on the edge of the field the emmer (*triticum dicoccon*),[f] which obviously brought a much lower yield. [26] Thus according to his human understanding the farmer is acting quite rightly, carrying out his various tasks one after the other for the appropriate length of time and in the right order. When v. 26 states that the correctness of the procedure comes from direct instruction from God, it expresses an idea of order which is familiar in wisdom literature (cf. Job 39.13-17). It is unlikely, however, that there is any reference to the instruction of man by a god, in the myth of the primal age, about cultivation.[g]

[27-29] Not content with having once impressed upon us that actions carried out in the proper order are reasonable and in accordance with the will of God, the wise man repeats the lesson in an example contrasting with ploughing and sowing, that of the right way of dealing with the product. It would obviously be inappropriate to

[a] Cf. G. Dalman, *Arbeit und Sitte in Palästina* II, Gütersloh 1932, pp. 189f.

[b] Cf. Dalman, pp. 290f.; A. S. Kapelrud, *BHW* II, col. 1027.

[c] Cf. Dalman, pp. 243ff.; Kapelrud, *BHW* III, col. 2159; and also M. Hopf and G. Zachariae, 'Determination of Botanical and Zoological Remains from Ramat Maṭred and Arad', *IEJ* 21, 1971, p. 60.

[d] The originality and the meaning of *śōrā* are disputed. But cf. *KBL* sub voce, and on the matter, Dalman, pp. 258f. and p. 260.

[e] Cf. Dalman, pp. 251ff.; Hopf and Zachariae, pp. 6off., but also J. Feliks, *BHW* I, col. 554.

[f] Cf. Dalman, pp. 246ff. and Feliks, *BHW* III, col. 1830.

[g] Cf. Ecclus. 7.15; Diodorus I. 14f.; Vergil *Georgics* 121ff., cf. also 43ff.

use a threshing sledge or threshing cart for the various kinds of cummin, the seeds of which are so easily lost. The glossator quite correctly explains that for this only a stick should be used.[a] In v. 27a the proper tool is the main idea, whereas v. 28 returns once again to the right length of time for the task. It is of course the woman with the hand-mill who is responsible for the actual milling of the corn.[b] Thus the threshing cart drawn by oxen on the threshing floor is rolled over the corn spread out there only as long as is necessary to break up the ears,[c] and the grains are never allowed to be crushed and destroyed on the threshing floor. Once again, and in particularly solemn words, the wisdom teacher impresses upon us that the right choice of tools and the right time to use them is taught by Yahweh. What seems to us simply appropriate and natural, the result of rational observation, is regarded by him as the consequence of impressive advice given by God himself, which of its nature can only be followed by success.[d] Thus for the wisdom teacher God's ordering of the world includes not only the ordered course of the stars and the earth which he has established so magnificently, with the animals which feed upon its plants (cf. Ps. 104), but also the meaningful activity of man. He who has fashioned all hearts (Ps. 33.15) and has given man reason, guides him aright in his everyday life.

The attempt to identify the meaning of the poem as a parable will also make clear whether it was composed for its present position or previously existed independently in another context. In the first case the interpretation should present no complications, while in the second case there might well be difficulties. That the task is harder than one would suppose from the simple meaning of the poem will soon be seen. But before we look at the actual interpretations which are possible, we must lay down the principles of interpretation. In both stanzas the poem presents the single idea that someone who is instructed by God uses in his actions the right tools in the right succession and for the correct length of time. Consequently, the person who is being compared with the farmer must be someone

---

[a] Cf. G. Dalman, *Arbeit und Sitte* III, Gutersloh 1933, pp. 82ff., 92f. and pp. 113ff. or F. Nötscher, *Biblische Altertumskunde*, Bonn 1940, p. 179.

[b] For the understanding of v. 28aα cf. Fohrer, *ad loc.*; for the matter cf. Dalman, *Arbeit und Sitte*, III, pp. 208ff.; Nötscher, p. 210 or J. Rogge, *BHW* II, col. 1246f.

[c] Cf. Nötscher, p. 180.

[d] For *tūšiyyā* cf. G. Kuhn, *Beiträge zur Erklärung des salomonischen Spruchbuches*, BWANT 57, 1931, pp. 3f.

other than God.[a] Since both stanzas conclude with the same basic idea, we can also assume that we have a parable and not an allegory. We do not have to look for a secret and allusive enciphering of some situation, in which every individual feature of both stanzas can be interpreted, but for the basic attitude of an unnamed third person, exemplified by that of the farmer instructed by God. This seems to exclude any serious search for a theology of suffering developed by Isaiah, in which those who are noble have to suffer more in the historical process of purification than those who are less important, just as in the second stanza the best corn is dealt with more vigorously than smaller seeds.[b] Again, the conclusion from the succession of ploughing and sowing, threshing and gathering of the corn, that apparently destructive actions really have a constructive purpose, and God's acts of judgment have as their purpose the work of salvation,[c] is unlikely to be the correct interpretation. Nor can the poem be satisfactorily interpreted as merely a justification of change as such, on the supposition that Isaiah was defending himself against the charge that he had abandoned his original assessment of the Assyrians as the instrument of Yahweh's punishment and had come to be convinced that they would soon be destroyed.[d] But in the case of the two last mentioned interpretations we feel that while they may not represent the intention of Isaiah, they are close to that of the redactor, since they fit the change of ideas which takes place between ch. 28 and ch. 29.

Who or what has been so instructed by God as to act correctly in choosing his tools, and in using them for the right length of time, with consequent success? Are these words by Isaiah himself, or at least words preserved by the redactor as such, containing the same strange alternation between the preaching of judgment and of salvation as in the transition from 28.22 to 29.1ff., and again within 29.1–8? Is the wisdom teacher, then, giving us a theology of Isaiah's prophecy? Perhaps he meant to impress upon hearers or readers, surprised by this alternation, that the prophet was instructed by God, and proclaimed his warnings no longer than was necessary, going on to prophesy salvation, and that his prophecies accurately traced the course of history down to the withdrawal of Sennacherib in 701. And

[a] Fohrer, *ad loc.*, correctly.
[b] Cf. Procksch, *ad loc.*
[c] Cf. Eichrodt, *ad loc.*
[d] Cf. Fohrer, *ad loc.*

were these readers or hearers then to draw their own conclusions for
the future which faced them? Or is the link between the poem and
the book of Isaiah much looser, so that the wisdom teacher's words do
not fit completely into their new context. If this is so, we should forget
the farmer and consider only God, who himself does everything at the
proper time and – as implied by the context – does not continually
punish, but also saves and so achieves his purpose in history.

CHAPTER 29.1–8

The Affliction and Redemption of Zion

1 Woe, Ariel, Ariel,
   city[a] where David encamped!
   Add year to year!
   when the feasts run their round,[b]
2 I will distress Ariel,
   and there shall be moaning and lamentation,
   and she shall be to me like a sacrificial hearth.[c]
3 And I will encamp against you round about,[d]
   and will besiege you with outposts,
   and I will raise siegeworks against you.

4 Then cowering from the earth you shall speak,
   from low in the dust your words shall come;
   your voice shall be from the ground like a ghost,
   and your speech shall whisper out of the dust.
5 But the multitude of ⟨the strangers⟩[e] shall be like small dust,
   and the multitude of the ruthless like passing chaff.[f]

[a] For the construction cf. G-K, § 130d.
[b] A bold translation proposed by H. Donner, SVT 11, 1964, p. 154.
[c] Text: Ariel.
[d] M should be preferred here to LXX and to complete Hebrew manuscripts,
together with those who defend them: it presents the *lectio difficilior*, while LXX
and those who follow it are influenced by v. 1. The fact that *HAL*, p. 209, simply
adopts the conjecture and refuses to give a *dūr* II, shows to what a considerable
degree the study of words and exegesis are unfortunately involved in Hebrew
lexicography.
[e] Read *zārīm*. M is the result of a confusion of *m* with the *k* of old Hebrew script.
[f] For the division of the lines cf. *BHS*.

Then it will come about very suddenly,
6   ⟨you will be visited⟩ᵃ by Yahweh Seboath
with thunder and with earthquake and great noise,
    with whirlwind and tempest, and the flame of a devouring
    fire.
7   And like a dream, a vision in the night shall be
    the multitude of all the nations that fight against Ariel,
all that fight against herᵇ and besiege herᶜ
    and distress her.
8   As when a hungry man dreams he is eating
    and awakes, and his throat is empty,
or as when a thirsty man dreams he is drinking
    and awakes, ⟨   ⟩ᵈ and his throat is parched,
so it shall be for the multitude of all the nations
    that fight against Mount Zion.

The poem which we find in 29.1–8 can be divided without doing violence to its content into three stanzas of ten lines, vv. 1–3, 4–6 and 7–8, each forming a unity. Of course not all the lines are of the same value metrically. Commentators have even regarded v. 8 as prose. If we attempt to define the literary category of the poem, we are faced with difficulties. Should the definition be based upon its opening words or its conclusion? The 'woe' which begins v. 1 leads us to expect a prophecy of warning. But by v. 7, if not before, we have the beginning of a description of salvation, and indeed the change is already introduced by v. 5bβ. Only the ambiguity of the Hebrew verb in v. 6aα, which we translate 'visit', has prevented this realization, because it has been assumed that it should be interpreted here in a hostile sense. But after the city has already been besieged by an innumerable swarm of enemies, vv. 5bβ–16 taken in this sense would be too late. Since ultimately the poem must be interpreted as a whole, and therefore on the basis of its conclusion, it should be defined as a description of salvation. The distinctive movement within it, from threat to deliverance, derives from the complex of ideas associated with the battle of the nations for Jerusalem, in which as the nations attack the city of God they are to be defeated by Yahweh himself.ᵉ

ᵃ Cf. *BHS*.
ᵇ For the form cf. G-K, § 75qq.
ᶜ In the text as a substantive, 'her siegeworks'.
ᵈ Cf. *BHS*.
ᵉ For the discussion upon the age of the theme of the battle of the nations now cf. G. Wanke, *Die Zionstheologie der Korachiten*, BZAW 97, 1966, pp. 70ff.; H. M.

We must still ask, however, whether the poem was always of its present extent, and was always based upon this pattern. The suspicion that it contains later interpolations is aroused first of all by v. 4, the second half of which, introduced by 'And (it) shall be' adds nothing of substance to the first half, and by its introduction raises the suspicion that it may be secondary. Once our attention has been drawn to this phenomenon, we note, more easily by looking at the Hebrew text than at a translation, that this introductory phrase is found in the poem no less than seven times, in vv. 2ba, 2bβ, 4b, 5a, 5bβ, 7aα and 8aα, while in addition we have the 'So it shall be' in v. 8ba. Here we have one of the favourite opening phrases of interpolators and redactors, using the Hebrew verb *hyh*, to be, to become, to happen, forming a copula or demonstrative. If experimentally we delete this phrase from vv. 1–4, we have a prophecy of warning which foretells a future siege of Jerusalem, which is still free, and which is hidden in the pseudonym Ariel. But it is surprising that it does not go further than the faintheartedness of the besieged in v. 4a, though this feature does seem to point beyond itself to some kind of decisive event. It is natural to continue the experiment by making v. 6 follow v. 4a and understanding 'visit' in a hostile sense: the besieged city is given the final blow by Yahweh himself. This, however, produces two difficulties which ultimately make it impossible to include v. 6 in the prophecy of warning. In the first place, this now leaves v. 6aα without a line to form a parallel to it. Secondly, it seems strange that while the city is clearly besieged by earthly enemies, it is not conquered by them. Thus the question remains whether, because the short prophecy of warning now seen to consist of vv. 1, 2aα, 3 is preserved in the book of Isaiah, it should be regarded as an originally independent prophecy by Isaiah himself.

The assumption here would be that it was written at a time relatively free from troubles, in which the people of Jerusalem were obviously not expecting what the prophet was foretelling, a siege of the city. This might have been during the period following the defeat of the Philistine revolt and the last seven years of the reign of Sargon II (721–705), or the period following Hezekiah's defection from Sennacherib in 703 and before the latter's attack upon Syria in

Lutz, *Jahwe, Jerusalem und die Völker*, WMANT 27, 1968, pp. 213ff.; F. Stolz, *Strukturen und Figuren im Kult von Jerusalem*, BZAW 118, 1970, p. 88 note 69; and J. C. de Moor, *New Year with Canaanites and Israelites* I, KC 21, 1972, p. 8, but also pp. 26 and 28.

701. But there are a number of facts which argue against this view. First of all, the prophecy of warning contains no proper reproach. Verse 1b fulfills this function in a very unsatisfactory fashion: for why should the people of Jerusalem not celebrate the New Year festival? Isaiah himself would have given reasons for this which lay in the present and not in the future. Secondly, we do not really know the purpose of the allusion to David in v. 1aβ. Is it mere historical reminiscence, or is it meant to recall the fact that the city was once besieged and conquered by David, or is it even intended to recall that since David's time it had been the city of Yahweh (cf. II Sam. 5.6ff. and Ps. 132.13ff.)? And why does the poet choose the name Ariel? Was the meaning 'sacrificial hearth', which is assumed in v. 2bβ at least, intended from the first to recall that here the nations were to be sacrificed to Yahweh, as the later, much more apocalyptic poem 30.27ff. makes explicit? In fact the difficulties are too great to support the view that there is an Isaianic nucleus to this poem, which gives the impression of having been to some extent patched together, and casts an artificial obscurity over what it prophesies. With its unhistorical conception of deliverance it is of a piece with 30.27ff. and 31.4ff. But it is clearly so strongly influenced by 28.14ff. that it fails completely to suppress the idea of the afflictions to come in favour of the deliverance which will immediately follow them.

[1–3] *The future affliction of Jerusalem.* In mysterious terms, referring to an equally mysterious event, a poet thinking in apocalyptic terms begins his woe upon Ariel. He makes it clear himself that this means the city of Jerusalem, by describing Ariel as the city where David encamped. 'Encamped' means here perhaps nothing more than that David made it his dwelling place (cf. Neh. 11.30). It is virtually impossible to tell whether the poet's historical recollection had any other purpose than to interpret to his hearers or readers the code word Ariel, unless we follow two Hebrew manuscripts and the Septuagint in v. 3aα in comparing the future attack by Yahweh with the former attack by David. There have been many attempts to solve the riddle of the meaning of 'Ariel', though scholars have not yet reached agreement. There are no grounds for the suggestion that it was the ancient Canaanite name of Jerusalem, or a part of the city wall adorned with a lion gate.[a] We need not nowadays pause to consider the rendering 'lion of God'.[b] But the Mesha inscription

[a] The first view is that of Kissane, and the second of Procksch, *ad loc.*
[b] Cf. Procksch, *ad loc.*, but also E. Ullendorff in: D. W. Thomas, *Documents from*

from the ninth century, line 12,[a] and Ezek. 43.15f. both show that it refers to an altar hearth. It is not immediately clear, however, whether there lies behind it an originally Sumerian word which referred to the underworld and then to the temple as the mountain above the underworld,[b] or a genuine Semitic form derived from the root '*rh* 'burn', and meaning 'fire pit, altar hearth'.[c] Whether Jerusalem was in fact ever so called must remain undecided. The poet's delight in mysteries is sufficient explanation.

While the community is unsuspectingly celebrating its New Year festival, the poet knows the secret of the ages, but clearly not well enough to give exact details. But perhaps the poet's cryptic language is once again only his personal style. In any case, what he is saying is that in a few years at the most the prophecy which Yahweh has given him to utter will come about, and the altar hearth, or sacrificial hearth, of Jerusalem will be surrounded by a hostile army on Yahweh's command. When the poet foretells mourning and lamentation (cf. Lam. 2.5) he certainly has in mind the present attitude of the people of Jerusalem, who are not to pass unscathed through the great affliction (cf. 28.14ff.). But the question of course arises whether Yahweh intends to sacrifice only his own people upon the sacrificial hearth at Jerusalem, or whether the assertion that the city will become a sacrificial hearth is not already looking forward, in a way reminiscent of 30.33 and 31.9, to a future transformation and a quite different sacrifice.

[4-6] *Deliverance from the utmost distress.* First of all, however, the poet continues to portray the affliction of the besieged people of Jerusalem. In v. 4 he juxtaposes two different conceptions, the first that of a person who has fallen to the ground and begs his conqueror for mercy,[d] and the second that of a dead person who speaks out of

---

Old Testament Times, London, 1958, p. 198.

[a] Cf. *TGI*[2], pp. 51ff. or Donner and Röllig, *KAI* n. 181.

[b] W. von Soden, *AHW* I, p. 64, cf. also Fohrer, *ad loc.*

[c] S. Segert, *ArOr* 29, 1961, p. 240, in H. Donner and W. Röllig, *KAI* II, 1964, p. 51 or no. 32.3, cf. also p. 175 or no. 181.12.

[d] Commentators show some embarrassment. Procksch supposes that Jerusalem would crawl in the earth in order to avoid the danger. Unfortunately he did not go on to say how he conceived of this. Fischer thought that the siegeworks would be so high that the voice of the people of Jerusalem could only be heard in a muffled form from the depths. Kissane saw the juxtaposition of the two images as a prophecy of the complete destruction of the kingdom of Judah. Feldmann took the image of Jerusalem sunk to the earth and lying dying.

the earth like a ghost with a voice reduced to a whisper. This makes clear that the enemy attack which God himself has brought about will bring Jerusalem into the utmost distress and that, rescued to humility (cf. 2.9; 5.15, 20.33) the city will beg its God for deliverance.[a] Or the poet may be thinking only of a terrified and virtually inaudible whimpering. Neither would be remarkable, in view of the vast numbers of the enemy, like fine dust, outside its walls (cf. 17.12; 1.7 and 40.15) and their violent rulers, who themselves are innumerable as the chaff blown from the threshing floor by the wind (cf. 17.13; Hos. 13.3; Pss. 1.4; 35.5 and Isa. 13.11; 25.3ff.; 29.20). But it is odd that no more unambiguous expression for prayer has been used, so that the poet seems to be trying to portray solely the terrified collapse of the people of Jerusalem in the face of the utmost distress. In this way he provided the dark background for the bright picture of the wholly unexpected deliverance which is to be brought about by Yahweh's direct intervention in the form of a theophany in a storm. He shows his concern for his city[b] by making his thunder crash, his whirlwind roar and his thunderbolts come down upon the besiegers (cf. 30.27ff. and 31.8).[c]

[7-8] *It was like a dream.* If the people of Jerusalem, set free by Yahweh's miraculous direct intervention, look back upon the day of distress, they will imagine that they had only dreamt of a siege by an immense multitude of nations (cf. 17.14; Pss. 73.20 and 126.1). Before they have understood what is happening the danger will have been removed. The nations, on the other hand, will be like a hungry or thirsty person who satisfies his needs in a dream and then wakes up hungry or thirsty; their prey seemed as certain as anything could be, but Yahweh's intervention will have deprived them of the fruit of their campaign. In 30.27ff. and 31.4ff. the destruction of the enemy is portrayed, but the poet has not done so here; he certainly assumed that some of them would escape. He is not interested in their fate for its own sake. He mentions them only to impress upon his community how startling their deliverance will be.

[a] Fohrer, and similarly Eichrodt.
[b] For *pqd* in the niphal in a friendly sense, cf. Ecclus. 49.15.
[c] Cf. Ex. 19.18; Judg. 5.4; I Kings 19.11f.; Pss. 50.2f.; 18.8ff.; 29.3ff.; 68.8f.; Nahum 1.3ff.; Hab. 3.3ff. and John 2.2f. and 4.16.

CHAPTER 29.9–12

The Blinding

9 ⟨Look fixedly at each other⟩ᵃ and be stupified,
   ⟨Stare at each other and stare⟩ᵇ
   ⟨Be drunk⟩,ᵃ but not with wine;
   ⟨stagger⟩,ᵃ but not with strong drink!
10 For Yahweh has poured out upon you
   a spirit of deep sleep,
   and has closed your eyes, ⟨   ⟩ᶜ
   and covered your heads, ⟨   ⟩ᵈ

  11 *And the vision of all this has become to you like the words of a sealed book.*ᵃ *When men give it to one who can read, saying, 'Read this', he says, 'I cannot, for it is sealed.'* ¹²*And when they give the book to one who cannot read, saying, 'Read this,' he says, 'I cannot read.'*

The transition from verse to prose shows that we must distinguish vv. 11 and 12 from the short prophecy of warning in vv. 9 and 10. The two latter verses are clearly meant as a commentary upon the prophecy of warning, declaring that 'the vision of all this' will be completely incomprehensible to those who are addressed, as a result of Yahweh's action in rendering them insensible to it, and that it is bound to remain so because it is like a sealed book which can of course be understood neither by those who can read nor, needless to say, by those who cannot read in any case. We cannot understand the purpose of the addition until we realize what is meant by 'vision'. Perhaps it is going too far to regard the expression as referring to literally extraordinary prophetic apprehensions through visions; it is more likely to have the general meaning of 'revelation' (cf. 2.2, and also 1.1) without any particular emphasis upon the way the revelation is received. Vision is a more remarkable prophetic phenomenon than hearing or the imparting of a saying. Unless we are to give up the task of exposition altogether, we must interpret it for good or for

  ᵃ Cf. *BHS*. For the form in v. 9 cf. G-K, § 55g.
  ᵇ Cf. *BH*. M reads: 'Show yourself blinded (i.e. with your eyes plastered over) and be blinded!' and no doubt came about under the influence of v. 10 and a figurative understanding of v. 9.
  ᶜ 'The prophets' is a gloss, cf. 28.7.
  ᵈ 'The seers' is also a gloss. It is interesting that the interpolator did not mention the priests, cf. also 9.14 and Lam. 2.14.

ill as referring to the context with its eschatological statements. We can then conclude that the eschatological interpretation of the prophets was disputed. This interpretation saw the ancient prophecies against Jerusalem and Judah uttered by Isaiah in the eighth century and later written down as not having been fulfilled by the events of 701 and 587, and looked forward to a new threat to Jerusalem preceding the onset of the age of salvation. Since we cannot place an exact date upon the beginnings of the eschatological understanding of scripture in the post-exilic age, it is also impossible for us to place an exact date upon the addition in vv. 11f., particularly as resistance to eschatological expectations must have existed before the third century. We need only to think of the disappointment which must have followed the proclamation of the intense hopes of Zechariah (cf. Zech. 6.9–15),[a] or the failure of the anti-Persian disturbances, presumably provoked by eschatological expectations, which seemed to have begun at the beginning of the reign of Xerxes,[b] and the troubles which seemed to have taken place during the Phoenician revolt round about 340.[c] But the eschatological determinism of the addition suggests that it is late rather than early. The eschatological teacher who speaks here (cf. 30.20) regards it as hopeless to attempt to convince his opponents that his belief is true. Only when the monstrous event which radically alters history comes upon them will they recognize in terror the truth of this words – so we must reconstruct their connection with the two previous verses. Anyone writing such words is addressing on the one hand those who share his faith, and who are disturbed and tempted by the unbelief in their midst, in order to make comprehensible to them why a considerable number of people reject their eschatological faith. But he probably also had the subsidiary purpose of shaking the self-confidence of his opponents by startling paradoxes, and compelling them to listen again. As far as the concrete form of his expectations are concerned, the eschatological teacher may have been mistaken, but by contrast to his opponents, who presumably relied upon the devout practice of the cult, he was right in his belief that the future was wholly reserved to God and not unchangeably determined by the present power structure of the

[a] Cf. K. Elliger, ATD 25, ⁶1967, *ad loc.*
[b] Cf. O. Kaiser, 'Der Geknickte Rohrstab', in *Wort und Geschichte. Festschrift K. Elliger*, AOAT 18, 1972, p. 102.
[c] Cf. F. K. Kienitz, *Die politische Geschichte Ägyptens vom 7. bis zum 4. Jahrhundert vor der Zeitwende*, Berlin 1953, pp. 101f.

world. To those who hope, the world looks different. Thus it is people who hope who are best able to change the world. But a Christian who accepts this must remember that he is mortal, while the hope that has been offered to him is immortal.

The question that now has to be answered is to what we are to relate vv. 9 and 10. At first sight one would suppose that they simply related to the situation responsible for the addition, belonging to an earlier stage of the dispute about the truth of the eschatological message. In this case they would not of course have been composed by Isaiah. On the other hand, it is notable that both in the antithesis between 9a and 10b, and that within 9b itself, they show a relationship to the style of 30.1ff., 6ff.; 31.1ff. and also to that of 30.8–17 and 29.15f., and are also reminiscent of 28.7ff. Thus the view that they were composed by Isaiah should be given the benefit of the doubt, and they should be included in accordance with the tradition amongst the sayings from the period of the great revolt against Assyria in the years 703–701.[a] Their content should be understood as a reaction on the part of the prophet against the policy of alliance with Egypt carried out by the kingdom of Judah in spite of his prophecies of warning, a policy which assumed that there was not yet any direct danger to Jerusalem. The rulers of Jerusalem, who now regard the prophet extremely condescendingly, and when faced with his warnings and threats give each other knowing looks about such political ignorance, will soon be stupefied with horror (cf. Jer. 4.9; Hab. 1.5 and Ps. 48.6) and will look round in vain for help (cf. II Sam. 22.42; Isa. 41.10; 17.7; 31.1) and then will stagger around like drunk men (cf. 28.7; Jer. 25.27; Isa. 24.20 and Ps. 107.27), either because the enemy are pushing them in front of them as prisoners on their long journey, or because they have been struck and sink to the ground. There would still have been time to abandon the policy of opposing Assyria and so of returning to Yahweh, who has not, and has no intention of having, any part in it (cf. 30.1; 31.1); but it is clearly Yahweh himself who has poured upon them the spirit of deep sleep, an unconsciousness which excludes any awareness of themselves or of anyone else (cf. Gen. 2.21). Thus with eyes that see they do not see, and with ears that hear they do not hear (cf. 6.10), and as it were with a covering over their heads rush to their destruction. What from the human point of view must be judged as unwillingness (cf. 28.12 and 30.15) can also be judged from God's point

[a] But cf. also above, p. 235.

of view as stupefying and blinding. It is very easy to imagine a
prophecy of this kind being produced by the excitement of such a
situation and giving rise on reflection to a theology of God's hardening men's hearts such as we find in Isa. 6. The prophet in his prophecy
of judgment, with the strange reason given in it, may have intended
to persuade those who heard him to think again and seek reconciliation, or may only have been prophesying their obscure fate.[a] This,
together with the situation, which we cannot reconstruct in detail,
must remain one of the secrets of history.[b]

CHAPTER 29.13-14

Against Worshipping with the Lips Alone

13   And the Lord said:
      Because this people draw near[c] with their mouth
          and honour[d] me with their lips,
      while their hearts are far from me,
          and their fear of me is ⟨emptiness⟩,[e]
      a commandment of men learned by rote;
14   therefore, behold, I will ⟨again⟩[c]
          do marvellous things with this people,
      wonderful and marvellous;
      and the wisdom of their wise men shall perish,
          and the discernment of their discerning men shall be hid.

[a] The prophecy that God would blind people is interpreted as the most severe
form of the prophecy of judgment by J. M. Schmidt, 'Der Verstockungsauftrag
Jesajas', *VT* 21, 1971, p. 89.
[b] The fact that we usually read of a deep sleep falling upon men, cf. Gen. 2.21;
15.12; I Sam. 26.12; Prov. 19.15; Job 4.13 and 33.15, and that we do not seem to
hear of the pouring out of a spirit until Deutero-Isaiah, cf. Isa. 44.3; 19.14; 32.15;
Ezek. 39.29; Joel 3.1f.; Zech. 12.10; Eth. Enoch 62.2; Testament of Judah 24.2, is
not a certain argument against Isaianic authorship, since the idea of blinding or
the hardening of men's hearts led to a modification of the traditional expression.
[c] See *BHS*.
[d] The emendation of *BHS* may be adopted, but in view of a possibility of a
constructio ad sensum, cf. G-K, § 145b, and *yr'tm* which follows, it is perhaps better
not to do so. Cf. also Ps. 62.5.
[e] Read with LXX, cf. Matt. 15.8f., *wetōhū*.

Faith and religious practice can be maintained within a community only in fixed forms. That this always brings the danger of confusing form and content is not a recent insight, but was well known to the ancient world.[a] Thus even in Plato we find the statement with regard to cultic actions that 'for the undevout to go to great trouble with regard to the gods is in vain, but for all the devout it is very much to the point'.[b] The author of the present passage sees his people, from whom he disassociates himself to some extent by the emphatic use of the expression 'this people',[c] as following the perverted ways of a cultic piety[d] which for all their outward zeal is clearly a feigned worship to which their hearts are not committed,[e] which is not really directed towards God, and which, in spite of their assertions, does not fear him. If this were not so, they would be bound to take seriously, to seek and to obey the will of him to whom the heading very consciously refers as the Lord.[f] But this shows that their alleged fear of God is nothing more than the following of a standard set by men. This reproach in v. 13 gives the reason for the prophecy of warning which follows in v. 14, and which foretells that 'marvellous' things will be done again to 'this people', cf. also Deut. 28.58f. Since the final statement is that the wisdom of the wise and the discernment of the discerning men will be brought to nothing (cf. also Jer. 8.8f.) we must conclude that the coming act of God will run contrary to their present opinion and understanding, however much faith they put in it (cf. 5.21).

This faces us with the question of the situation underlying this prophecy of warning and its reason. Unlike 1.10ff., it does not state why its author, speaking in the name of his divine Lord, wishes to proclaim that his people's worship is feigned and does not come from the heart. Although the general terms in which it is worded has meant that the immediate relevance of the prophecy has survived the centuries (cf. also Matt. 15.8f.), it also makes it difficult to identify its contemporary occasion and setting. From the stylistic point of view the sharp antithesis in v. 13a and 13b, when compared with 29.9f.

[a] Cf. my comment on 1.10ff.; ET, *Isaiah 1–12*, OTL, 1972.
[b] *Laws* 717a.
[c] Cf. 6.10; 8.6, 11f.; 9.15; 28.11, 14 and Jer. 6.19; 7.16; 8.5, etc.
[d] For *ngš* as a technical term of the cult cf. e.g. Ex. 24.2; Num. 8.19; Jer. 30.21 and Ezek. 44.13.
[e] Cf. also Hos. 7.14; Isa. 51.7; and also Jer. 2.5; Ezek. 44.10 and Ps. 37.31.
[f] Cf. the formula of quotation in v. 13a with 10.12; 11.11; 21.1, 8, 16; 30.20, but also 9.7 and 16.

and 15f., as well as 30.1 and 31.3, suggests that Isaiah was the author.[a] This suggests that the specific disobedience of the people should be sought in Hezekiah's anti-Assyrian policy of the years 703–701, which is censured in other prophecies, and which looked for support from Egypt; in 30.1 and 31.1 Isaiah explicitly attacks the sending of an embassy to Egypt without previously consulting Yahweh. The wisdom of the wise and the discernment of the discerning men would accordingly refer in wholly concrete terms to the practical understanding claimed by the advisers of the king who were responsible for this foreign policy. Yahweh's future action will bring it to ruin. Note, however, that v. 14 prophesies a new action to which the poet applies the same word as is used to describe his original act of creation (cf. Ps. 89.6) and particularly his saving act when Israel was led out of Egypt (cf. Pss. 77.12, 15 and 78.11). For a miracle is an event which is out of the ordinary and therefore arouses astonishment. While Isaiah now looks forward to a new but similar act of God, he contrasts it with God's actions at the beginning: whereas the former had the effect of a miracle, people will be astonished at that which is to come,[b] because they will not have been expecting it (cf. also 28.21). In other words, whereas the politicians of Jerusalem are convinced that they are doing their best for their country with an anti-Assyrian policy which relies upon Egyptian help, they are in fact leading into a catastrophe, because they have actually changed their plan without consulting God's judgment. There is much which seems right to us men, not only in public life. Perhaps we should ask more often whether it is in accordance with God's will. This would in fact avoid many catastrophies.

CHAPTER 29.15–16

Atheism?

15   Woe to those who hid
        deep from Yahweh their counsel

---

[a] But cf. above p. 235.
[b] Cf. Fohrer, ad loc.

> so that their deeds were in the dark,
> and who thought 'Who sees us? Who knows us?'[a]
16 Your perversity![b]
> Shall the potter be regarded as the clay?
> Can the thing made say of its maker,
> 'He did not make me?'
> Or a pot say of its potter,
> 'He has no understanding?'

Like 29.9f. and 13f., vv. 15 and 16 are obscure. In formal terms they consist of a cry of woe, v. 15, followed by a cry of reproach in v. 16aα and three didactic questions. The train of thought in the cry of woe is clear; like the reproach which follows a prophecy of warning, the reason for the preceding cry of woe is given in v. 16. But the content of the cry of woe really needs no further justification, because substance of the accusation in fact lies in the characterization of those to whom the woe refers (cf. 5.8, 11f., 18f., 20, 21, 22f. and 10.1f.). Although the comment in v. 16 on the perverse attitude of those who have made their plan and hidden it from Yahweh is an acute one, it is superfluous, for what we want to see instead is a concrete explanation about who has made a secret plan and in what circumstances. It is natural that in this situation commentators should have tried to find enlightenment in the context, and have looked first of all to the prophecy of warning which immediately follows in 30.1ff. This begins with a proclamation of woe, and is an attack upon a Jewish request for help to Egypt. Have we here, then, a prophecy composed by Isaiah himself? Or is it at least possible that these verses, like vv. 9f. and 13f., deal with the problems of a later period? The idea of plans made in secret is found both in the lament of the individual (cf. Ps. 64.7) and in the collective lament (cf. Ps. 94.7). And both the evil-doers who persecute the devout man and the wicked men who offend against Israel carry out their acts unnoticed. Thus the poet in the psalms describes the former as asking, 'Who can see them (i.e. the snares they have laid)?' (cf. Ps. 64.6) and the latter as thinking, 'Yah(weh) does not see; and the God of Jacob does not perceive' (cf. Ps. 94.7). That God as the creator is as superior to man as the potter to the pot he has made is an idea used in Jer. 18.6 to explain a prophecy of judgment, and in Isa. 45.9 to introduce a

[a] In my view *wayyōmer* here does not allow any other tense, cf. also König and Feldmann, *ad loc.*

[b] Cf. G-K, § 147c.

disputation which is the basis for a prophecy of salvation. That God has made man like a potter out of clay is an idea which we find in wisdom poetry (cf. Job 10.9 and 33.6), and there is at least an allusion to Gen. 2.7, 19. The idea that a human being cannot hide his actions from Yahweh, nor keep items hidden from him, is an idea which we find in the psalms of lamentation (cf. Pss. 44.22; 94.11; 139.1ff.), in wisdom poetry (cf. Pss. 1.6; 37.18; Job 34.21f.) and also in prophetic writings (cf. Amos 9.3; Jer. 23.24). Thus we might be inclined to link the poem, in accordance with the use of the basic theme of v. 15 in the psalms of lamentation, and in view of 29.17–24, and particularly vv. 19ff., to measures taken at a late period by the ruling class in Jerusalem to oppress the devout, who regarded themselves as the humble and poor. But we must first remember that the prophecies of warning with which are reasons found in 30.1ff. and 31.1ff., and which take the stylized form of proclamations of woe, have clearly been influenced in a similar way by the language of the psalms of lamentation and similar poems. There too we find a sharp contrast between God and man, the will and power of God and human plans and earthly power. Since both these oracles are likely to have been composed by Isaiah, and cast light upon the prophet's preaching in the year 701, it seems sensible to ascribe the present proclamation of woe to Isaiah and to date it, together with 29.9f. and 29.13f., in the same period.[a] The plan conceived in secret and concealed from Yahweh was the decision to send an embassy to the Ethiopian Pharaoh Shabako with a request to send cavalry and chariots to drive out or provide a diversionary attack against the punitive campaign begun by Sennacherib against the rebels in the west (cf. 30.2 and 31.1).[b] By so doing, the ruling powers in Jerusalem were behaving towards Yahweh like scoundrels who had every reason to hide what they planned. It is obvious that a pot cannot dispute the potter's ability. Supposing it could speak it would have no right to make itself out to be cleverer than him who made it and determined its form and function. This is not the situation only of the rulers of Jerusalem, but of all men before God. If man supposes that he can ignore God in his actions and therefore call into question the reality of God, he is making a comparable error, because in objective terms there can be no godlessness. Anyone who supposes that there can be, will nevertheless come into conflict with God (cf. Ps. 14.1).

[a] But cf. also above p. 235.
[b] Cf. below pp. 283ff.

The story is told of the hasidic Rabbi Levi Isaac of Berdychev, that he broke down the resistance of a follower of the enlightenment who visited him by saying to him time and again, 'But perhaps it is true after all.' Finally he said, 'My son, the great Torah scholars with whom you debated wasted their words on you. When you left them you only laughed at what they had said. They could not set God and his kingdom on the table before you, and I cannot do either. But, my son, only think. Perhaps it is true! Perhaps it is true after all!'ª

CHAPTER 29.17–24

Salvation is Near!

17 Is it not yet a very little while
    until Lebanon shall be turned into a garden
    and Carmelᵇ shall be regarded as a forest?
18 In that day the deaf shall hear
    the words of scripture
    and (set free) from their gloom and darkness
    the eyes of the blind shall see.
19 The meek shall obtain
    fresh joy in Yahweh
    and the poor among men
    shall exult in the Holy One of Israel.
20 For the ruthless shall come to nought and the scoffer cease,
    and all who watch to do evil shall be cut off,
21 who make men sin in court,
    and lay a snare for him who reproves in the gate,
    and for no cause rebuff the righteous,
22 Therefore thus says Yahweh
    who redeemed Abraham,
        toᶜ the house of Jacob:

ª M. Buber, *Die Erzählungen der Chassidim*, Zurich 1949, pp. 363f.; ET Olga Marx, *Tales of the Hasidim; The Early Masters*, London, 1956, pp. 228f.

ᵇ Or fruitful field, garden.

ᶜ I agree with Ziegler that there is no justification for the attempt which is now almost universal, but is contrary to the received text, to read *'ēl*, God, instead of *'el*, 'to', and to translate 'says Yahweh, the God of the house of Jacob, who redeemed Israel. . . .'

'Jacob shall no more be ashamed,
    no more shall his face grow pale.
23 For when he sees ⟨   ⟩ᵃ the work of my hands, in his
    midst,
        they will sanctify my name;
    they will sanctify the Holy One of Jacob,
        and will stand in awe of the God of Israel.
24 And those who err in spirit will come to understanding,
        and those who murmur will accept instruction.'

A description of salvation which begins with an imminent transformation of nature and concludes with a transformation of society
(vv. 17–21) is followed by a statement in the person of God (vv.
22–24), which combines features of the prophecy of salvation and the
description of salvation, and in formal terms provides the reason for
the preceding statement. The promise as a whole gives us an insight
into the internal groupings of the Jewish community, as they were
seen by a devout scribe who believed in an eschatological theology of
history, at a time which cannot be earlier than the Hellenistic
period. He clearly feels solidarity with the group to which he refers as
the 'meek and poor'. Radically opposed to them is the group amongst
whom he includes the ruthless and the scoffers, who lead a life which
is godless and hostile to other people. Between these two groups
stands a third, which in the eyes of this devout Jew clearly lacks a true
understanding of the scripture. Taken as a whole, this passage makes
it quite clear of what such an understanding consists: an eschatological belief and hope that the course of history will soon bring a
transformation of everything upon earth by Yahweh himself. His
prophecy, bringing consolation and strengthening the belief in the
imminent onset of this transformation, is addressed to the group of
the meek and poor. That of the ruthless and scoffers is not accessible
to him, and he regards it as doomed to disaster, while that which is
'deaf and blind' will be instructed and converted by the events which
are prophesied, if not before. Since this group is mentioned twice, the
boundary between it and the devout is perhaps still fluid, and the poet
considers that what he has to say may still reach them. The intense
preoccupation with internal affairs makes it uncertain whether the
ruthless tyrants of v. 20 are foreign oppressors, or, perhaps more
likely, brutal rulers of his own people, as v. 21 seems to imply. Thus

ᵃ 'His children' is a gloss.

we are probably correct in dating this promise before the beginning of the conflicts between Judaism and the Seleucid kings Seleucus IV and Antiochus IV.[a] It is not possible, however, to be so certain about the earliest possible date. The particular importance of the poem lies in the way it links together the fear of God, justice and a salvation which takes in the whole of the earth, nature and society. As a result it holds more meaning for us today than the prophecies which are preoccupied with the destruction of the nations.

[17–21] *The time of salvation.* With the statement, put in the form of a question, that the great crisis in the course of the world is imminent (cf. 10.25 and 16.14), the learned scribe and theologian begins his description of salvation. He is clearly able to assume among his hearers and readers a knowledge of eschatological expectations, and even an agreement that they are shortly to be fulfilled (cf. 26.20; 29.5 and Mal. 3.1). He describes the imminent transformation of nature in words which are reminiscent of 32.15, which prophesy the transformation of the wilderness into an orchard and of the orchard into thick forest. Here the two mountains are examples of the change that will take place in nature as a whole, the increase everywhere of growth and fertility which will bring men better times. The Old Testament expectations of future fertility, like that of paradise, are distinguished from those of fairy tales by the fact that they associate the transformation of nature, which will then bestow its produce upon all men, with a change in men (cf. Ps. 72; Hos. 2.18ff.; Ezek. 36.26ff.; 47.6ff.; Isa. 11.1ff.). In the Old Testament righteousness and salvation cannot be separated. Thus for this poet the outward transformation of the world corresponds to an internal transformation of the Jewish community. [18] The deaf and the blind, those members of the Jewish cultic community who honour their God but reject the eschatological interpretation of the prophets (cf. 6.10; 28.13; 29.9f., 11f.; 42.18ff.) will no longer be able to overlook the true, i.e. the eschatological meaning of scripture, because events meanwhile will have justified it. It is clear from this passage not only that living prophecy had ceased and the scripture had taken its place, but also that the poet, with his anticipation of what was to come, was striving to be believed by the sceptics. [19] The meek and poor (cf. Deut. 12.3; Ecclus. 45.4; 14.30),[b] those whose whole hope has been and

---

[a] Cf. for the history of the period E. Bickermann, *Der Gott der Makkabäer*, Berlin 1937, pp. 66ff.

[b] Cf. also W. Grundmann, *ThWBNT* VIII, p. 6; *TDNT* VIII, p. 6.

has remained in God, will then be seized by exultant joy (cf. 41.16b, 17;35.10; 51.11) because the time of their sufferings will be over, and they will see what they have faithfully hoped for, the age in which there will no longer be any injustice, and in which the Holy One of Israel will be sanctified by his people. This title for God, characteristic of Isaiah, and of the book of Isaiah, makes the paradox of Old Testament faith most acute; as the Holy One, Yahweh is the God who is withdrawn and above the whole world, the God who of his nature is not the world (cf. 6.3). But as the Holy One of Israel he has at the same time intervened in the history of this people, and in so doing he has himself remained the Holy One and has demanded of his people that in every respect they should abstain from anything that could come between him and them. In other words, just because he is the Holy One, he is also their judge (cf. 10.16). While the devout will be able to rejoice in the Holy One of Israel, this entails the maintenance of his holiness by the destruction of his opponents. [20–21] Accordingly, the period in which the ruthless (cf. 13.11; 25.3ff.; 29.5), scoffers (cf. Prov. 21.24; 19.29; Ps. 1.1 and Prov. 3.34; 21.11) and all other people bent upon evil[a] could have continued their activities will lie in the past, and the enemies of the devout and of God will be destroyed. The example given of their wrongdoings is that of abuses in the courts, as the most obvious perversion of justice. The victims of this perversion are both those who try to give right decisions (cf. Amos 5; Job 32.12)[b] and those who are seeking their rights (cf. Isa. 10.2; 5.23; 3.15).

[22–24] *The nature of the time of salvation.* The word of God which forms the climax and conclusion of the promise begins with a solemn introduction recalling the history of salvation and proclaims comfort and hope to those who are tempted and suffering. Even now, in a period of the slavery, shame and internal dissension for his people, Yahweh is still the one who once 'redeemed' Abraham (cf. Pss. 46.5; 46.8, 12) and thereby set into motion the course of history which was to culminate in that of the people of Israel, the house of Jacob.[c] It is difficult to tell whether the poet had in mind only the biblical narratives in which Abraham was delivered, or also the extra-biblical traditions of his deliverance from the idolators in Mesopotamia (cf. 3.12 and Apoc. Abr. 8). The devout poet believed that in the name of

---

[a] Fof '*āwen*, 'evil' cf. R. Knierim, *THAT* I, col. 81ff.

[b] Cf. also W. Rudolph, KAT 13, 2, 1971, p. 198.

[c] Cf. 2.3, 5, 6; 10.20 and 14.1.

his God he could assure his community and those who heard and read the Isaiah roll that the time in which the people who had come down in history under the name of Jacob were objectively and subjectively made a mockery and put to shame is now past for ever (cf. also 19.9). When the people see what God does, not just anywhere but in their very midst (cf. 5.12; 2.7; Josh. 24.31 and Ex. 3.20), a decision for Yahweh will be taken once for all. The poet does not have to describe this great act at length here, because he is convinced that it is explained clearly enough in the Isaiah roll, and in any case it was not in dispute among his own community; Yahweh would judge Jerusalem by the flood of the nations and then smite the nations themselves, and the nations would then make pilgrimage to Zion. Those to whom God had revealed himself in his power would no longer abuse his name, but would honour it through their own words and actions. In so doing they would escape the judgment which hung over those who reviled him or brought contempt upon him by their claim to be members of his people. A direct line leads from Ex. 20.7 through Isa. 29.23 to the first petition of the Lord's Prayer (cf. Matt. 6.9 para.). Only someone who knew the power of God would take him seriously enough, treat him as the Holy One and keep due distance from him (cf. 8.12f.; 29.13) by being obedient to his will. Anyone who fears God and is in awe of him avoids him by doing his will. [24] Once again the poet turns to what is clearly his main concern, the true understanding of scripture, which of course after the fulfillment of all the sayings of the prophets would present no difficulties. Spiritual error and weary criticisms, which now crippled the congregations, would then be brought to an end. In an age which was apparently far from God, the poet, who was convinced that God has once acted in his people, was drawing the attention of his people to the future which would once again belong to their God. And it is regarded as very close.

The New Testament church, and particularly the established churches of the present day, contain similar groups with similar concerns. As long as they take God seriously, they will also look forward to the consummation of the world at his hands. We might say that as long as they take seriously God and the suffering of the world, they will look forward to a new world of righteousness. But how can they really look forward to the future power and glory of God if they do not take it seriously now, and so act in every respect with the aim neither of reviling his name nor of giving others cause to revile it. We do not know at what hour the clock stands in the history of the world (cf. Mark 13.32) but we ought to know where we stand ourselves.

CHAPTER 30.1–5

Refuge with Pharaoh

1 Woe to the rebellious children,
    saying of Yahweh,
who carry out a plan,
    but not mine;
and who pour a libation,[a]
    but without my spirit,
in order ⟨to add⟩[b]
    sin to sin
2 who set out to go down to Egypt,
    and did not ask for my counsel,
to take refuge[c] in the protection of Pharaoh,
    and to seek shelter in the shadow of Egypt!
3 *Therefore shall the protection of Pharaoh turn to your shame,*
    and the shelter in the shadow of Egypt to your humiliation,
4 For though his officials are at Zoan
    and his envoys reach Hanes,
every one ⟨who went was shamed⟩[b]
    through a people that does not profit them,[d]
that (brings) neither help nor profit,
    but shame and indeed disgrace.

30.1–5 takes the form of a proclamation of woe followed by a reason for it. The reason for the woes uttered in the first two verses is given in the three verses that follow. Since the content of v. 3 in part overlaps with v. 2 and in part with v. 5, we can regard it as a later explanatory exegesis, perhaps from a period in which the ancient

---

[a] The translation is hypothetical. We probably have here a figurative poetic term for the making of a pact, cf. *KBL* sub voce.
[b] Cf. *BHS*.
[c] Cf. G-K, § 72q.
[d] Cf. G-K, § 145b.

prophets of Isaiah had come to have new relevance.[a] We need not look far for the historical situation to which the prophecy refers. Even though one should not ignore the constant disagreements which arose between Persia and Egypt,[b] three periods are the most likely. (1) The years of the great revolt led by Hezekiah against the Assyrian emperor Sennacherib in 703–701. (2) The years of the fall of the Jehoiakim and particularly that of the overthrow of Zedekiah by Nebuchadnezzar, the great neo-Babylonian emperor, 601/600–697 and 589–587. (3) The latest possible time to which the activity of the redactors of the Isaiah roll seems to have extended, the period following the death of the Seleucid king Antiochus III, 187 BC, when some people in Jerusalem seem to have placed their hope in the Ptolemies who ruled in Egypt.[c] On the whole it is not likely that the introduction of the whole passage can be attributed to this last period, but at most that of some interpolations. It is very difficult to find conclusive arguments for deciding between one or other of the possibilities which remain. But since the legendary tradition concerning Isaiah assumes that he was active during the siege of Jerusalem in 701, and also seems to reflect a knowledge of Hezekiah's pro-Egyptian policy (cf. 36.6ff.), there is no real reason for not attributing the proclamation of woe to Isaiah himself, for the fact that it has been preserved is due to the continued relevance of its theme. To conclude this digression, we may perhaps also point to the intensity and force of its expression, which leaves no doubt about what is being said, and to this extent places both the commentator and the reader of the book in an unusually fortunate position.

When the great emperor Sennacherib began to close upon Jerusalem and the fortresses of Judah – if not before – Hezekiah sent a embassy to Pharaoh Shabako with a request for military assistance. Perhaps the diplomatic mission to Egypt which underlies this passage took place as early as the time when the news was abroad of the approach of the emperor and of his subjection not only of the cities of Phoenicia and some of the Philistine cities, but also Ammon, Moab, and Edom. In addition to what we learn from Sennacherib himself,

[a] Cf. also H. Donner, SVT 11, Leiden 1964, p. 132; though B. S. Childs, *Isaiah and the Assyrian Crisis*, StBTh II.3, 1967, p. 33, disagrees.

[b] Cf. O. Kaiser, in *Wort und Geschichte. Festschrift K. Elliger*, AOAT 18, 1972, pp. 99ff., and in *Wort, Lied und Gottesspruch. Festschrift J. Ziegler*, FzB 2, 1972, pp. 197ff.

[c] Cf. M. Hengel, *Judentum und Hellenismus*, WUNT 10, 1969, p. 17 and see above p. 235.

it is probable that not only the Philistine cities of Ashdod and Ekron but also Hezekiah urgently begged Pharaoh to intervene. But the Egyptian army that actually set out was defeated at Eltekeh. This seems to have sealed the fate of the allies.[a] One can imagine how closely the course of events was followed by all the people of Jerusalem, and that in view of the royal embassy which had left for Egypt, there was also an interest in public circles in Jerusalem in a prophetic oracle concerning the whole matter. Isaiah left no doubt that he condemned the official hopes, which may have been shared by wider circles, of Egyptian help. On the one hand the actual decision to send the embassy had been taken without consulting the prophet of Yahweh and therefore without an oracle from Yahweh having been sought (cf. 31.1b). Secondly, in Isaiah's view the history of the previous decades seems to have shown clearly what could be expected from Egyptian help; the last king of the northern kingdom of Israel, Hoshea, had relied upon the Egyptians for help during his rising against Shalmaneser V in 724 and had brought disaster upon his country.[b] In the course of the revolts which shook the Assyrian kingdom in the early years of the reign of Sargon II, Hanno of Gaza had entered into alliance with Egypt, and was nevertheless defeated with his Egyptian allies at Raphia in 720.[c] The revolt of the Philistine cities, which seems to have lasted from 713–711, and in which Ashdod tried at least to involve Hezekiah, failed quite miserably; not only did Shabako refuse to send the reinforcing army but actually handed over to Sargon the 'Ionian' who was at that time the ruler of Ashdod.[d] One must concede that Isaiah had a gift of cool political observation, as well as an equally firm belief in the zeal with which Yahweh watched over the obedience of his people and avenged every offence against his deity.

[1] Thus the mere fact that the Jews in their responsible ruling circles had behaved towards Yahweh as rebellious sons would have been sufficient to condemn their plans. In Old Testament times, as today, a rebellious son is for his parents one who resists their will and who does not obey them even when he is punished (Deut. 21.18). But in those days the parents had the right to have such a son stoned.

Cf. *AOT*[2], pp. 352ff.; *ANET*[2], pp. 287f.; *TGI*[2], pp. 67ff. and Y. Aharoni, *The Land of the Bible*, London 1966, pp. 336ff.

[b] Cf. H. Donner, pp. 64ff.

[c] Cf. Donner, pp. 106ff.

[d] Cf. above pp. 112f.

The relationship between father and son, assumed here, as in 1.2f., between Yahweh and Israel does not refer to any kind of consubstantiality between God and man (cf. Ps. 2.7)[a] nor to the relationship of protection and friendship so beautifully described in these terms in Isaiah 63.15f., but to unconditional authority and power over his son, obedience without question (cf. Deut. 32.5f., and Mal. 1. 6; 2.10. The form taken by their rebelliousness is that of having forged a plan[b] in which Yahweh had had no part, and which in the eyes of the prophet was bound to fail for this reason alone (cf. 8.10; Prov. 21.30; Ps. 33.11). The delegation sent to Egypt by Hezekiah seems to have had the purpose of concluding a formal defensive and offensive agreement with Shabako. Perhaps there is an indication of this in the expression 'to pour out a pouring', which has been explained in terms of the drink offering made when a treaty was concluded.[c] In a few intense words Isaiah states that the plan has not come from Yahweh, and that the treaty is neither in accordance with his will nor derives from him, cf. 34.16. When the prophet, speaking in the person of Yahweh himself, affirms that this has heaped sin upon sin, he is presumably thinking of the treaty made by Ahaz with Tiglathpileser ·during the war with Syria and Ephraim (cf. ch. 7f.) and the participation by Hezekiah in one form or another in the Philistine revolt led by Ashdod (cf. 20.1ff.).

[2] From the point of view of comparative religion, v. 2 is particularly interesting, because it shows that on the occasion of all acts by the ruler of the state an oracle was required to be sought from Yahweh, and that this was in fact largely done (cf. 32.2ff., II Kings 21.12ff. and Jer. 37.17ff.; 38.14ff.). This practice was in force more or less everywhere in antiquity and is certainly not peculiar to Israel. The Hebrew word used here, with a range of meaning including 'beg, entreat, ask' is an ancient technical term for seeking an oracle from Yahweh, e.g. in the holy war (cf. Josh. 9.14; Judg. 1.1; 20.18, 23, 26, I Sam. 13.41; 23.9ff.). An utterance by a prophet now seems to have replaced the oracle by lot which was the usual practice before the setting up of the monarchy.[d] The formula of request for an alliance

---

[a] Cf. A. Weiser, ATD 14/15, [7]1966, *ad loc.*, ET *The Psalms*, OTL, 1962, *ad loc.*

[b] For the connection between a decision and its carrying out, as is found in the Hebrew equivalent, cf. J. Pedersen, *Israel I–II*, Copenhagen and London, 1926 (1954), pp. 128ff.

[c] Cf. also the Greek σπονδὰς ποιεῖσθαι, meaning 'to conclude an agreement'.

[d] Cf. C. Westermann, *KuD* 6, 1960, pp. 9ff.

uses expressions from the language of the psalms, in order to emphasize how unnatural this behaviour is; for Yahweh is really the refuge of his people and his worshippers (cf. Pss. 90.1; 27.1; 31.3; 28.8; 43.2; 37.39; 52.9), and it is in his shadow that his people seek shelter (cf. Pss. 17.8; 91.1; 121.5; 38.8; 57.2; 63.8). What the people of Judah ought to look for from their God, they are seeking instead from men (cf. 31.3). **[4f.]** They can and ought to know what would be the real outcome of help from Egypt. Even when the Ethiopian Twenty-fifth Dynasty succeeded under Shabako in 715 in wiping out the short lived Saitic Dynasty[a] and bringing all Egypt under their control, so that his officials could come and go as far as Zoan, the Tanis of the Greeks and the present-day *ṣān el-ḥagar*, in the northern Delta,[b] and his envoys in Hanes, the Heracleopolis Magna of the ancient writers, and the present-day *aḥnās*, south of Memphis[c] and east of the present-day branch of the Nile known as *baḥr yusuf* and leading into the Fayyum,[d] Isaiah regards the damage done by a foreign policy based on Egypt as already demonstrated in the previous decades. He had no more faith in the larger kingdom of Shabako than in the Delta state of the Saitic Pharaohs. In brief, telling words he characterizes Egypt as a people that cannot profit anyone (cf. 30.6) and can offer no help (cf. 31.1) but brings shame upon those who rely upon it (cf. 36.6 and, for the opposite, cf. Pss. 44.8; 70.3; Isa. 1; 54.4; I Sam. 25.28).

[3] In order to emphasize the senselessness of this behaviour, a later writer interpolated v. 3, either with a specific historical occasion in mind, or for the purpose of the reading of the passage in Jewish worship; but he did not add any new ideas.[e]

Isaiah shows that trust in God and clear, sober political thought are not irreconcilable, and that the person who takes God into account in good and ill can assess reality. When a Christian is required to take political decisions there is no prophet whose oracle can confirm that his decisions are pleasing to God. If he really knows that his true citizenship is in heaven, looks to God for his salvation and yet acts at the same time as though his salvation depended upon his actions

[a] Cf. A. Gardiner, *Egypt of the Pharaohs*, Oxford and New York 1961, pp. 340ff., and E. Otto, *Agypten. Der Weg des Pharaonenreiches*, Stuttgart ³1958, p. 228.

[b] Cf. M. Krause, *BHW* III, col. 2244f.

[c] H. Donner, p. 134 gave us an interesting interpretation of v. 4 in this sense.

[d] Cf. *HAL* sub voce and H. Kees, *Ancient Egypt. A Cultural Geography*, ed. T. G. H. James, London 1961, pp. 212ff.

[e] For the doublet 'shame and disgrace' cf. also Ps. 109.29 and Jer. 3.25.

upon this earth (cf. Phil. 3.20; Zech. 12f.), he ought to be sufficiently
clear-headed to accord to the state what belongs to the state, to man
what belongs to man, and to God what belongs to God. But God is
above man and man is above the state, which derives its value solely
from the fact that it makes it possible for men who differ greatly from
each other to live together. And this generation, no less than those
which preceded it, needs forgiveness even in its political actions. If it
is aware of this, it will deal more humanely with political opponents.

CHAPTER 30.6–7

Vain Hopes

6   *An oracle on the beasts of the Negeb*[a]
    Through a land of trouble and anguish,
    of the lioness and ⟨growling⟩[b] lion
      the viper and the flying serpent,[c]
    they carry their riches on the backs of asses,
      and their treasures on the humps of camels,
    to a people that cannot profit,[d]
7 ⟨   ⟩[e] whose help[d] is worthless and empty,
    therefore I say to her:
    'Are they Rahab? – Sitting still!'[f]

[a] Duhm proposed to read *b^ešammot negeb*, 'in the deserts of the south', and to
repeat it as the opening words of the oracle which have been lost in error. But cf.
against this Dillmann-Kittel. K. D. Schunck, *ZAW* 78, 1966, p. 49 has recently
proposed the reading *b^ehēmōt*, hippopotamus.

[b] Read *nōhēm*. In view of the word *m^e'ōpēp*, there is no reason for completely
deleting *mhm*; I disagree here with Duhm *ad loc.* and Schunck, pp. 50f.

[c] Literally: *sārāp*.

[d] For the construction cf. G-K, § 145b.

[e] Cf. *BHS*.

[f] Among the numerous proposed emendations the following should be noted:
rahab haššamōt, Rahab of the deserts, i.e. a water monster in a dry place; *rahab
hammosbāt*, the silenced monster: *rohbāh mušbāt*, 'his noise ceases'; *rahab hammušābet*,
rahab led back; *rahab hayyōšebet*, Rahab which keeps silence, and *b^ehemōt negeb*,
hippopotamus of the south. In my view it is best to retain the received text like
Delitzsch, and, directly following H. Donner, SVT 11, 1964, p. 158, to attempt
to get a meaning from it.

In this saying there are a number of peculiarities which do not make its interpretation easier. From the purely formal point of view, we find for the first and last time in this section a title like those in chs. 13–23. Its similarity to the headings in chs. 21 and 22, which take up a keyword from the text that follows, is obvious. But in the form in which we possess it the heading we have here is not a keyword taken from the text, but an original phrase which quite rightly states that it also mentions all kinds of animals of the Negeb, the land of the south. It is also obvious that the heading forms part of a couplet; and is one of the ten lines of which the poem consists. This suggests that the original heading was either badly corrupted or had disappeared, so that a redactor composed a new opening in the form of the present heading or built it up from the fragments. When we look at the content, v. 7b at once raises the question of who is actually speaking, Yahweh, the prophet Isaiah, or someone else convinced of the importance and truth of his diagnosis, and perhaps even composing in writing. But since a human reflection as such cannot claim a place in a book of prophecy, and no statement can claim to be accepted by faith if someone other than Yahweh is assumed to be speaking, then Yahweh has to be presented as the speaker.[a] The formal category is that of a prophecy of warning. If we seek to define it more closely, the description in vv. 6b–7a provides only a momentary difficulty; once one accepts that it is Yahweh himself who is speaking, it is clearly a reproach, which combines with the warning in v. 7b to form a prophecy of warning with a reason. When Yahweh says that people are carrying their property to other people who cannot help them, while he is their true and only real helper, the reproach is implicit in the words. The form of the warning is admittedly also somewhat enigmatic. Whether the brevity of v. 6b can be explained by the fact that it was meant for an inscription, depends upon one's understanding of 30.8.[b] The present position of the oracle is possibly due to the redactor, and we must examine its original context. We recall that the desert which lay between Egypt and Palestine was thought of as inhabited by real and fantastic beasts which were a danger to man (cf. Deut. 14f.) and that Ps. 87.4 (cf. Isa. 51.9f.) certainly permits the identification of Rahab with Egypt. Thus the heading, which connects this oracle with a journey through the Negeb, is as appropriate as its position following 30.1–5 (cf. also 21.1). It refers to a journey to

a Cf. below on 31.8.
b Cf. below on 31.8.

Egypt which has not been approved by Yahweh, and will not obtain
the help which is sought from Egypt. The statement that those who
are being accused are carrying their goods to Egypt may suggest
simply that they are fleeing (cf. Jer. 26.20ff.; 41.16; 42.1ff.). But
since those who are going to Egypt are clearly looking for active help
and not merely for asylum. 'Their riches' and 'their treasures' are
perhaps not their own valuables, but simply those they are carrying
with them, in which case they will not be refugees, but an official
embassy. It is interesting that the author thinks of the route to Egypt
as peopled not only with real animals but also with imaginary beasts.
Unless we accept that the whole text is a product of scholarly ingenuity and therefore a very late composition which either hesitates
to name its true object or attempts to produce a particular affect of
mystery by artificial devices, it does not refer to a journey along the
coast road, but through the Arabah and then across the Sinai
Peninsular to Egypt. This hypothesis is favoured by the fact that the
episode with the fiery serpents (Num. 21.4ff.) is set somewhere near
the Red Sea, i.e. the Gulf of Aqaba (cf. Deut. 2.8).[a] On the boundary
of the world that they really knew, by a secret route threatened by
unknown dangers, envoys travel heavily laden to Egypt to get help
for their own country. On this interpretation there are no longer any
objections against associating this prophecy of warning with that
which immediately precedes it (30.1–5) and with the later prophecy
in 31.1; and attributing them to the same basic situation in the year
701 and to the prophet Isaiah. If our view of the route taken by the
embassy is correct it gives us some additional historical information;
when the *Via Maris*, the coast road,[b] was already closed and the
Assyrians had interrupted normal communications between Egypt
and Judaea, Hezekiah chose the less usual and more dangerous
alternative route across the Sinai Peninsular. Perhaps we may assume
from this that the battle of Eltekeh had already been fought and lost,
and the first and only attempt on the part of Egypt to bring relief
which is known to us from the sources[c] had already failed, when
Hezekiah tried again, summoning all the resources at his disposal, to
persuade Pharaoh Shabako to intervene on his behalf.

[a] But cf. Eichrodt *ad loc.*, though he has in mind an attempt to obtain help
addressed to Arabian tribes.
[b] For the route it followed cf. Y. Aharoni, *The Land of the Bible*, London 1966
and Philadelphia 1967, pp. 41ff.
[c] Cf. above p. 284.

[6–7] The prophet sees the difficulties of the distant caravans travelling through a country which was scarcely known and therefore doubly dangerous (cf. 8.22; Prov. 1.12)[a] and where one might possibly meet not only lions (cf. 5.29; Job 4.11; Prov. 9.12) and adders,[b] but also winged, poisonous snake-like creatures, dragons (cf. 14.29, but also 6.2). [6] He sees the donkeys and camels going heavily laden to these distant regions. Where are they going? To a people that profits nothing (cf. 30.5a; I Sam. 12.21; Prov. 10.2) whose help, literally translated, is a wind[c] and empty, from whom it had been impossible to expect anything (cf. 30.4 and 5a) and from whom there was still nothing to be expected. It is not stated that the ambassadors were sent from a people and a king whose God and protector was the Holy One of Israel (cf. 31.1b) but this is implicit in the background. The judgment is short and annihilating; Egypt will not rise up, as the terrifying dragon once did with its helpers in the past, but will remain seated and inactive (cf. Judg. 5.17; Jer. 8.14). The prospects of renewed and more effective help from Egypt are groundless, and all efforts and expenditure are in vain.

We know of the myth of Rahab only through a few allusions. In it Rahab seems to have personified the primeval sea which rebelled against the creator, but was nevertheless destroyed by Yahweh with its helpers, a battle which preceded the creation (cf. Job 9.13; 26.12 and Ps. 29.10). The second Isaiah, who prophesied during the exile – actually an unknown person who has been given this name by scholars because his words are preserved within the book of Isaiah, chs. 40–55 – drew a parallel between the drying up of the sea at the exodus of the Israelites from Egypt, and the conquest of Rahab before the creation.[d]

---

[a] The expression 'the day of distress', was common: cf. 37.3; Jer. 14.8; Obad. 12; Neh. 1.7; Hab. 3.16; Ps. 20.2; etc.; but the expression 'the time of distress' is found less often, cf. 33.2; Ps. 37.39; Dan. 12.1.

[b] According to I. Aharoni, *Osiris* 5, 1938, p. 474, it was an *echis colorata*.

[c] For *hebel* cf. R. Albertz, *THAT* I, col. 487ff.

[d] Cf. O. Kaiser, *Die mythische Bedeutung des Meeres in Ägypten, Ugarit und Israel*, BZAW 78, ²1962, pp. 140ff., esp. p. 144.

CHAPTER 30.8–17

The Great Alternative

8   And now, go, write it down ⟨   ⟩ᵃ
     and inscribe it in a book,
   that it may be for the time to come
     as a witnessᵇ for ever.
9   For they are a rebellious people,
     lying sons,
   sons who will not hear
     the instruction of Yahweh
10 who say to the seers,
     'See not',
   and to the visionaries, 'Prophesy not
     to us what is right;
   speak to us what suits us,ᶜ
     prophesy illusions,
11 leave the way,
     turn aside from the path,
   let us hear no more
     of the Holy One of Israel.'
12 Therefore
   thus says the Holy One of Israel:
   'Because you despise
     this word
   and trust in ⟨falsehood⟩ᵈ and error,ᵉ
     and rely on them;
13 therefore this guilt
     shall be to you
   like a break, sinking and bulging,
     in a high wall,
   in which suddenly, in an instant,
14   the crash comes,
     ⟨   ⟩ᵇ like the breaking of a potter's vessel
     which is smashed so ruthlessly

ᵃ 'On a table with them' is a later gloss.
ᵇ Cf. *BHS*.
ᶜ Literally, 'smooth things'.
ᵈ Cf. *BH*.
ᵉ Cf. below, p. 311 note a.

> that among its fragments
>   not a sherd is found
> with which to take fire from the hearth,
>   or to dip up water out of the pool.'

15 For:
> Thus said
>   the Lord Yahweh,
>   the Holy One of Israel,
> 'In returning and rest
>   you are saved;
> in quietness and in trust
>   is your strength.'
> And you would not,
>   but you said, 'No!

16 We will fly[a] upon horses',
>   therefore you shall flee,[b]
> 'and will ride upon swift steeds',
>   therefore your pursuers shall be swift.[c]

17 ⟨   ⟩[d]
> At the threat of five
>   you shall flee,
> till you are left
>   like a flagstaff on the top of a mountain,
>   like a signal on a hill.

In 30.8–17, the joins between vv. 8 and 9, 11 and 12, and 14 and 15 are clearly visible, and seem at first sight to indicate as usual that these sections have been combined by a later redactor. One might be inclined to read 30.8–11; 30.12–14, and 30.15–17 as originally independent units. Verse 8 contains a command to write an inscription which lacks a special introduction, so that we have to look for a connection with what precedes. The reproach contained in vv. 9–11 serves to provide the reason for the command given in v. 8. The fact that the prophecy of warning with a reason (vv. 12–14), possesses its own reproach in v. 12 argues against any connection with vv. 8–11. On the other hand it is clear that vv. 12–14 cannot have existed in isolation, because the 'word' mentioned in v. 12 must be sought

---

[a] Literally: 'flee'.

[b] For the form cf. R. Meyer, *Hebräische Grammatik* II, Berlin ³1969, § 63.5a.

[c] A play of words on the Hebrew *qal*, light, quick.

[d] 'A thousand shall flee at the threat of one' is a gloss in the sense of Deut. 32.20; Josh. 23.10 and Lev. 26.8.

somewhere outside these verses. It remains to be seen whether they refer to a saying of Yahweh preceding v. 8, the instruction from Yahweh mentioned in v.9ᵃ or the word of God quoted in v. 15. But this does not alter our view that vv. 12–14 are a literary formation. The prophecy of warning, with a reason, which follows could itself have derived from oral traditions. With its reference to a rejected oracle of Yahweh as a reason for the warning, it nevertheless calls for caution. The suspicion that it is once again a purely literary formation cannot be easily dismissed. The word of Yahweh is reminiscent of 28.12 and 16, and seems, like 28.12 itself, to be moving in the direction of the theology of the Deuteronomic prophets, although in substance it gives a correct interpretation of 30.1ff., 6f.; and 31.1ff. With its keyword 'horses', v. 16 is also reminiscent of 31.1, but one wonders whether the conception is the same in both cases, since 31.1 seems to be an Egyptian contingent (cf. 31.3) whereas here we have the impression that it is those who are accused who want to ride the horses. Verses 9–11 also seem to be explicable as a summary of the sayings of Isaiah contained in chs. 28–31. Verse 9 does refer back to 30.1, but the reproach made in vv. 10 and 11 has at best only a loose connection with 28.7ff., and is formulated in much more general terms here. The same generalizing tendency can be seen in v. 12. Thus the question which faces the commentator is whether in this passage we really hear the voice of Isaiah, looking back with great revulsion at the end of his activity in the year 701, gathering his sayings together and publishing them with this postscript, or whether what we have is a piece of prophetic theology which was looking back upon the catastrophe of the year 587 and interpreting it as a fulfilment of the words of Isaiah, or ought verses 13f. and 16f. to be located in the period between 597 and 587? In this case, it would be impossible to include 28.14ff. within the same cycle. The second hypothesis explains the distinctive features of 28.7ff., which was probably, if not composed, at least edited to serve as the opening passage of this collection. And it can resolve a good many of the doubts about the attributions of 29.9f., 13f., and 15f., though it is quite possible that redactors may have made a number of alterations or, as in the passage just mentioned, rewritten a section completely.

[8] *The command to write an inscription.* Verse 8 presents certain problems which are not immediately obvious from the translation. The Hebrew word *ḥqq*, translated as 'inscribe', merely means the

———
ᵃ Cf. Fohrer, *ad loc.*

engraving, incising, scratching or carving of an inscription into hard material such as stone and metal. And the word *seper*, translated as 'book', can also mean an inscription.[a] Thus the question is whether we have a figurative statement by a redactor or a concrete statement by the prophet. In the latter case the verse supplied by the tradition would have formed the starting point for the drawing up of the collection by later disciples. It would only have been a very short inscription, because of the practical difficulties for an unpractised person of carving a long inscription in hard material. This makes impossible the hypothesis that this· verse should be regarded as the divine command to the prophet to inscribe 28.1–30.17[b] or 30.8–31.9[c] himself. On the other hand it is worth asking whether Isaiah was commanded to inscribe the expression 'Are they Rahab? – Sitting still!' in 30.7bβ, in which case v. 8 would actually be an addendum to v. 7.[d] In its present context the verse forms a transition between the previous sayings of Isaiah and the postscript that follows, in which the purpose of the redactor is identical with that of the prophet, to bear witness after the disaster to his people to the prophet's message and at the same time to the guilt of the people and the unbroken power of God.

[9–11] *The rejection of the prophet's message.* Drawing upon 1.2,4 and 30.1 (cf. also Ezek. 2.5; 3.9; 12.3, etc.) the trustee or trustees of Isaiah's legacy accuse a nation which has shown itself disobedient to its God in the course of its history. All its members are described as sons of Yahweh; this does not refer to a physical worship of God, breaking down the barrier between God and man, but to the childlike obedience which they owe to their God.[e] When they are reproached for their lies, the reference is unlikely to be to their foreign policy, conducted with every kind of cunning, but according to the context to the refusal to obey the word of God (cf. also Prov. 30.9; Job 31.28). As in 1.10 and 8.16 the instruction of Yahweh means the prophet's message. The words placed in the mouths of the Judaeans in vv. 10–11 should be understood not as quotations, but as a description of their attitude by the redactor. Although the prophet's

[a] Cf. Job 19.23, and also *KAI*, no. 24.14f.; 222 C 17, but also Isa. 49.16 (though with the comment by Delitzsch *ad loc.*).

[b] Cf. e.g. Duhm, Marti, Guthe and Eichrodt, *ad loc.*

[c] Cf. Procksch, *ad loc.*

[d] The first possibility is supported by Delitzsch and H. Schmidt, *ad loc.*, and also by O. Kaiser, *Einleitung in das Alte Testament*, Gütersloh ²1970, p. 236.

[e] Cf. on 30.1.

disciple speaks not of prophets but of seers and visionaries, there is no distinction in practice (cf. I Sam. 9.9). The choice of words, however, gives preference to seeing over hearing, the purpose being to make immediately evident the senselessness and perversity of the attitude that is being reproached. Anyone who denies that the seer has seen his visions and reproduces their content is attacking the seer not only as a person, but above all as the instrument of God (cf. also Amos 2.11f.).[a] In the past the people have not really been interested in what Yahweh had wanted to reveal to them, but preferred to listen to what pleased and flattered them (cf. Micah 6ff., and for the phraseology Prov. 26.28, and Ps. 12.3f.). As a result they tempted the prophets to deny the commission given to them by Yahweh in favour of human wishes, and to depart from the path which Yahweh had shown them (cf. Job 23.10f. and Isa. 3.12). Just as, according to 5.19, there had been mocking questions about the fulfilment of the purpose of the 'Holy One of Israel', which it was assumed the prophet knew, so the people of Judah had always made it clear that they did not want to hear or know anything about the God who is above the whole world, whose power is nevertheless at work throughout the world and who destroys impure and unholy men when he encounters them, the Holy One of Israel. They ignored what it meant for him to have taken Israel under his protection, and this was found to lead to catastrophe.

[12–14] *The consequences of the rejection of the message.* Verse 12 now sums up in telling words what was set out in the previous verses. Yahweh himself speaks, accusing and passing judgment upon his people. Formally, 'this word' in v. 12 seems to refer to the instruction of Yahweh mentioned in v. 9. But in substance it seems, like v. 15, to sum up the whole message of the pre-exilic prophets. The rejection of the word of Yahweh (cf. 8.6) has been demonstrated in a pseudo-religious[b] confidence on the part of the people, which from the point of view of Yahweh and his words can only be condemned as perverted, false and in error (cf. for the wording Prov. 8.8 and 2.15, and for the substance v. 16). Verses 15f. sum up equally clearly the nature of this false confidence. The warning which follows shows how closely related guilt and the consequences of guilt are, *'āwōn*, guilt, as it were

[a] These verses are regarded as a deuteronomic redaction by H. W. Wolff, BK 14. 2, 1969, p. 172 and p. 207.

[b] For this problem at the present time cf. also C. H. Ratschow, *Von der Religion in der Gegenwart*, Kirche zwischen Planen und Hoffen 6, Kassel, 1972, pp. 18ff.

entails in itself the consequences of guilt. That what happens does not take place independently of Yahweh, but is set in motion by him, is assured by the fact that the statement is presented as uttered by Yahweh. The two similes, which are comprehensible without explanation, show how complete the judgment will be. We ought perhaps to add that in a period when there were no matches or lighters, people would rake through the ashes to find a glowing ember in order to light a new fire, and that in a country which was short of water they would be glad to make use of puddles.

[15–17] *The decision against Yahweh.* In this final prophecy of warning, with its reason, we learn at last what are the concrete alternatives, the way recommended to the people by the prophets and the way they have chosen instead. The ceremonious title given to God indicates the seriousness of the words which follow, once again spoken in the person of Yahweh. The recollection that the theologian who is speaking here was unlikely to have been compulsively inspired like one of the ancient prophets, but owed his message to devout reflection upon his faith, does not mean that we should be scandalized at his use of the device of speaking as Yahweh's messenger, any more than at a modern clergyman speaking in the name of God. Whether a statement is truly the word of God cannot be decided by the nature of the psychological process in which it comes into being in a person's mind, but by whether or not it corresponds with the will of God.[a]

The accusation begins with an affirmation of the help with which has been squandered, wilfully rejected – yet which, we may add, in view of the real purpose of the redactor, is still the only help available.[b] The phrases chosen are deliberately paradoxical, and assume that the reader or hearer tacitly recognizes Yahweh as the God of repentance (cf. 9.12),[c] the basis of confidence (cf. 30.12; 31.1),[d] of peaceful calm (cf. Eccles. 9.17)[e] and of the ability to wait in silence

---

[a] Although I have changed my view of the age of the covenant theology and some of the judgments of literary criticism assumed there, cf. my article 'Wort des Propheten und Wort Gottes' in: *Tradition and Situation. Festschrift A. Weiser,* Göttingen 1963, pp. 75ff.

[b] *yšʿ* (niphal) almost always means assistance in the face of enemies, cf. Deut. 33.29; Ps. 18.4; Jer. 17.14; 30.7 and Ps. 28.18.

[c] Cf. Hos. 6.1; Lam. 30.40; Deut. 30.8; II Kings 17.13; Jer. 3.14; 4.1; 15.19; 18.11; 25.5; 35.5; Hos. 12.7; 14.3 and Joel 2.13.

[d] Cf. the comment on 31.1.

[e] Fohrer's translation of *naḥat* as 'faithfulness to a contract' does not seem to me to be supported by the other examples of its occurrence, Prov. 29.9; Eccles. 4.6;

(cf. 7.4). The positive alternative which lies behind the prophecies of judgment by Isaiah and the pre-exilic prophets is described in a way which in substance is reminiscent of 7.9b. The post-prophetic sermon, which considers that it has been confirmed by the consequences of the policy actually followed by the kingdom of Judah, is intended to be a testimony, like v. 8, that this alternative was not only valid in the past but remains valid throughout the ages. Israel's denial had found unequivocal expression in that policy. It represented the rejection of the command of God underlying the prophet's preaching of judgment. By means of an allusion to 31.1ff., the purpose and the result are contrasted, revealing that the policy of strength which failed to consult the will of Yahweh was in fact a policy of weakness.[a] The extent to which the prophecy is also an attack upon the general human failing of megalomania is shown by the reference to the disgraceful flight from a handful of enemies. The contrast between the outcome and the arrogant purpose is sufficiently clear; all who remain, and will remain if the judgment is repeated, can be compared to a bare signal post on the hilltops (cf. 1.8).

When Christian faith gives to Caesar what is Caesar's, this post-prophetic sermon, briefly summing up the legacy of Isaiah, is a warning against too easy an answer to the question, whether it is also giving to God what is God's. On the other hand, when Christian faith gives to God what is God's, it has no right to give an easy answer to the other question, whether it has given to Caesar what is Caesar's (cf. Mark 12.13ff.). There is no way out of the obligation to be a citizen of two kingdoms.

CHAPTER 30.18

Blessed be those who Wait on Yahweh

18 Therefore Yahweh waits to be gracious to you;
    therefore he exalts[b] himself to show mercy to you.

6.5; Job 17.16 and 36.16, and in view of the parallelism here with *hašqēṭ* is unlikely.
    [a] Cf. also Hos. 14.3.
    [b] Against the widely accepted conjecture once again given in *HAL* sub voce *dmm*, now fortunately with a question mark, cf. Marti, *ad loc.*

> For Yahweh is a God of justice;
>> blessed be all those who wait for him.

When a devout redactor later interpolated this prophecy of salvation which follows in vv. 19-26 into the Isaiah roll, he either found v. 18 there already, as an addition to the great sermon on judgment and repentance which precedes it in vv. 8-17, and deriving from the liturgical reading of the passage; or else he composed it himself as a transitional passage. The logic underlying this short prophecy of salvation, concluding in a prayer for good fortune (or a beatitude, 'blessed are . . .'), is not immediately obvious to the present-day reader. If the introductory 'therefore' is not to be seen as a very unsuccessful attempt to connect the verse with the preceding passage,[a] we must suppose that the preacher of consolation who speaks here regarded the condition for God's help laid down in v. 15 as fulfilled within his community.[b] As a God of justice (cf. 28.17) he responds to the longing expectation of which he is the object (cf. 8.17) with his salvation, and it is matched by the way he waits himself for the moment in which he can come to his people in grace and mercy (cf. Pss. 77.10; 123.3; 102.14 and 103.13). That the moment of salvation is near was the conviction of the person who wrote the present verse. This was why he was able to wish good fortune to his waiting community.

CHAPTER 30.19-26

The Great Transformation

19   Yea, O people in Zion,
        who ⟨dwell⟩[c] at Jerusalem;
        you shall weep no more.

---

[a] Cf. Eichrodt *ad loc*. The various earlier attempts at a solution are given by Feldmann *ad loc*.

[b] Cf. Fohrer *ad loc*.

[c] Cf. *BHS*.

He will surely be gracious to you
   when you cry for help.[a]
When he hears you, he will answer you.

20   Then the Lord will give you
      food ⟨   ⟩[b] and drink,[b]
then your teacher
   will not have to hide any more.[c]
Then your eyes
   will see your teacher,

21   and your ears will hear
      behind you the cry:
'This is the way,
   that you are to walk in,
whether you turn to the right
   or turn to the left.'

22   Then ⟨you will⟩ defile your silver-covered graven images,
      and your gold-plated molten images.
You will scatter them as something unclean,
   you will say to them, 'Begone'.[d]

23   Then he will give rain for the seed
      with which you sow the ground,
then the grain, the produce of the ground
   will be fat and succulent.
Your cattle will graze[d]
   in that day
   in broad pastures;

24   and the oxen and asses
      that till the ground
will eat sour fodder
   which is put in
   with shovels and forks.

25   Then there will be
   on every lofty mountain
   and on every high hill
   channels which will bring water,

[a] Literally: 'according to the voice of your cry'.

[b] With Marti, delete ṣār and lāḥaṣ 'adversity' and 'affliction' as ill considered glosses; for although all the textual evidence is in their favour, unless they are deleted v. 20a makes no sense in its present context. 33.16 can be quoted in favour of deletion.

[c] 1Q Isa, cf. also LXX, reads the plural. M, with its preceding singular, does not make it essential to interpret the following plural as a plural of majesty referring to God, cf. G-K, § 145o.

[d] The breakdown of classical verbal syntax betrays the late character of the text.

> In the day of the great slaughter,
>   when the towers fall,
> 26 then the light of the moon
>   will be like the light of the sun
>   and the light of the sun
>   will be sevenfold ⟨   ⟩.[a]
> In that day Yahweh will bind up
>   the hurt of this people[b]
> and heal the wounds
>   inflicted on them.[c]

The new introduction in v. 27 makes clear where this description of salvation concludes, but it is not so easy to tell whether it begins with v. 18, or not until v. 19. In favour of the former view it can be pointed out that in late Judaism 'the intensity of the distress was a sure sign that redemption was at hand'.[d] In favour of the latter view, which to my knowledge was last put forward by Kittel and Procksch, there is the fact that it does not require the commentator to assume a second idea which is not expressed in the text itself. It can also be shown that v. 18 belongs organically to 30.15–17 as a later interpretation.[e] It is of course clear that the present passage assumes the existence of v. 18. The close connection between the content of this passage and that of 29.17–24 is obvious, though the allusion to the battle of the nations taking place before the gates of Jerusalem in v. 25b is clearer than the more general reference to Yahweh's action in 29.23a. Moreover, the passage differs from 29.17ff. in not taking up the idea of a judgment upon Israel itself. This may be because the writer's expectations took a different form, but may simply have been omitted because of the link established with v. 17 by means of v. 18. It is impossible to tell for certain whether this description of salvation was interpolated on one occasion or in several steps, for regular features in late writers include not only repeated fresh starts (cf. 29.1ff.) but also a tendency to jump from one theme to another (cf. 30.27ff.). But note that if our interpretation of v. 20 is correct, the

---

[a] 'As the light of seven days' is a gloss.

[b] Cf. G-K, § 114r.

[c] Cf. G-K, § 135m.

[d] Guthe, *ad loc.*

[e] Cf. also J. Vermeylen, *La composition littéraire du livre d'Isaïe*, I–XXXIX, Louvain 1970, p. 64: 'It is not impossible that v. 18 may be older than the verses that follow.' The difficulty of the usual division of the text can most clearly be seen in Feldmann's comment on 30.18.

ideas in it are carried on in vv. 23ff.; the obvious fresh start in v. 25a occurs too late following vv. 23ff., while both vv. 25b–26a and 26b can both be regarded as later additions. Finally, it may be asked whether v. 22 is still necessary following vv. 20b–21, although it seeks to illustrate it by examples.

Verse 20b gives us a clear indication of the circles in which this description of salvation originated. As with the book of Daniel (cf. 11.23 and 12.3) they consisted of men who because of their eschatological knowledge had the position of teachers in their community,[a] but found no audience for their message outside the group of those devout believers who regarded themselves as the 'meek and poor' (cf. 29.19). By contrast with 29.17ff., the situation seems to have become so acute that they had to seek safety from persecutions. This description of salvation may therefore belong in the period of religious persecutions under Antiochus IV Epiphanes, the background being either the repression of conservative religious groups under the high priest Jason or the edict on religion put out by the king in the year 167.[b]

[19] In a form of address found only here, the eschatological teacher addresses the people of Jerusalem, assuring them that the time of weeping will shortly be over for them (cf. Lam. 1.2; Ps. 126, and also Isa. 25.8 and Rev. 7.17). But he seems to be convinced that the coming of the divine help and mercy depends upon themselves: when they address their lamentations[c] to Yahweh, he will not fail to hear them (cf. Pss. 50.15; 107.13, 19).[d]

[20f.] In view of the fact that vv. 23ff. speak explicitly of the renewed fruitfulness of the land, it is possible that 'bread' and 'water' ought perhaps to be understood here, as in 55.1f., in a figurative sense: when God answers the prayer of Jerusalem, he will give them[e] all they need for their outward and inner life (cf. also Amos 8.11f.).

[21] For inner life, and of course for outward life as well – it must be realized that this distinction is completely foreign to Israel – it is of fundamental importance that in the future the people walk in

[a] Cf. O. Plöger, KAT[2] 18, 1965, pp. 171f.
[b] Cf. M. Hengel, *Judentum und Hellenismus*, WUNT 10, 1969, pp. 503ff.
[c] For this expression cf. 65.19.
[d] Cf. also Ps. 4.2.
[e] For this expression cf. Josh. 1.13.

Yahweh's ways[a] and consequently do not call down his anger upon themselves again. The mere fact that in the time of salvation which was to follow the eschatological drama the teachers of the community who now proclaim it and are therefore persecuted will no longer have to hide (cf. 26.20) it to this theologian, who belongs to that group, a guarantee that the people will then be led aright. After their prophecy has been fulfilled, their views will be so firmly based that the community will listen unceasingly to their vigilant instruction,[b] which will keep them from deviating in any respect from a way of life pleasing to God.

[22] Verse 22 may be the interpolation of a later hand, emphasizing that the destruction of idols must be the first consequence of a way of life pleasing to God. As in 40.19f. (cf. also 41.7; 44.9ff. and 46.5ff.) the interpolator has in mind small bronze statuettes with a gold or silver covering.[c] The inner threat to the community which is clearly obvious in the prophecy, and which was expressed in private idolatry, may perhaps be associated with the hellenizing tendencies of the period (cf. 2.20f.). The things that were venerated more or less in secret will then be crushed to pieces (cf. Ex. 32.30) and scattered to the winds as things which defile their possessors[d] (cf. Lev. 15.33; 20.18).

[23–25a] As a consequence of this new obedience the land will come to enjoy a fruitfulness like that of paradise. Sufficient rain will fall, and at the right time, so that the corn flourishes (cf. Deut. 11.13ff.; 28.12, and also Ps. 72.16, and for the expression 'fat and succulent' also Ps. 92.15). How close the author is to life on the land is shown by the fact that he forgets neither the animals in the pasture nor those in the stall, though one cannot conclude with certainty that he had a particular love for animals. In an agrarian society it is necessary for a prosperous life that the animals too have plenty to eat

[a] For the figurative meaning of 'way', as 'way of life' cf. e.g. Prov. 1.15; Ps. 1.1; Jubilees 5.13; 4 Esdras 14.22; Matt. 7.13f. and John 14.16, with the comment of W. Michaelis, *ThWBNT* V, pp. 50ff.; *TDNT* V, pp. 50ff.

[b] Cf. also Ex. 18.20; Deut. 5.33; Jer. 7.23.

[c] As rightly recognized by K. Elliger, BK 11.1, 1970, pp. 74f. who gives as examples *ANEP* no. 481; 483; 484 and 497, and also *AOB²* no. 347. The usual interpretation of it as an idol consisting of a wooden centre with a metal cover is still found in H. D. Preuss, *Verspottung fremder Religionen im Alten Testament*, BWANT 92, 1971, pp. 194f.

[d] 'Begone' following Ziegler, is translated by others as 'dirt, filth' or the like, which is equally possible on the basis of the consonant text.

and are so able to provide wool and meat in abundance, or work as draught animals or beasts of burden. There will then be so much fodder available that it will be possible to throw in the food to the draught oxen and pack asses which are in the stalls, with winnowing shovels and forks, tools which are really meant for dealing with the sheaves or the grain.[a] The teacher who gives us this verse seems to have been so much of an expert, as Lutheran country pastors once were, that he could name the best mixed fodder, with sorrel added.[b] We need not decide whether it is he or a colleague who speaks in v. 25a, but in any case the author of this sentence has remembered that complete fruitfulness independent of the rainy seasons can only be achieved with adequate artificial irrigation, and has therefore added the idea that upon every mountain and hill (cf. 40.4) there will not only be water channels (cf. Pss. 1.3; 46.5) but also water (cf. Isa. 41.8; 44.4; Ezek. 47). Whether or not one finds the agricultural practicality of these hopes attractive depends upon one's own point of view. In my view they seem to deserve sympathy precisely because they do not wander into the realm of fantasy. This close connection between human righteousness and the fruitfulness of the land is in this form an alien idea to the modern age. But we should not automatically assume that it is therefore false.[c]

[25b–26] Verses 25b and 26a introduce another idea which can be shown to occur in apocalyptic in two forms. According to one, the stars will be superfluous in the period of salvation, because God himself will uninterruptedly illuminate the world and particularly the holy city (cf. 60.19; 24.23; Joel 3.4; Rev. 21.22ff.; 22.5 and Isa. 4.5). According to the other idea, the light of the sun and the moon will be so increased that at night it will be as bright as day, and during the day much brighter than at the present (cf. Jub. 1.29 and 19.25). This sevenfold increase in the strength of the light is also expected in Eth. Enoch 91.16.[d] If anyone should ask when all this is to happen, the answer is, on the day of the great slaughter (cf. Ezek. 26.15; Jer. 12.3) in which Yahweh will rise up against all pride and loftiness and will therefore also bring down the towers of the fortresses of this earth (cf.

[a] Cf. Galling BRL, col. 139.
[b] Cf. L. Köhler, ZAW 40, 1922, p. 17.
[c] Cf. O. Kaiser, 'Dike und Sedaqa', NZSTh 7, 1965, pp. 251ff.
[d] The terms the 'white one' for the moon and the 'hot one' for the sun occur also in S. of Sol. 6.10 and Isa. 24.23. For the different apocalyptic conceptions, cf. P. Volz, Jüdische Eschatologie von Daniel bis Akiba, Tübingen 1903, p. 298.

2.12ff. and particularly 2.15). But in order that devout readers should not be afraid of this day, there is a concluding reminder that it will bring the fulfilment of the longings of all the centuries. For it is the day in which Yahweh will bind up the wound which was made, as it were, by the surrender of Jerusalem, its king and its temple in 587 (cf. Lam. 2.11; 3.48; Jer. 6.14; 8.11) and the day in which he will heal the blows received at that time (cf. 1.6f.; Ezek. 34.16 and Hos. 6.1).

CHAPTER 30.27–33

Yahweh's Feast

27 Behold, the name of Yahweh
   comes from far,
burning is his anger,
   mighty the rising,
his lips are full of indignation,
   and his tongue is like a devouring fire;
28 his breath is like an overflowing stream
   that reaches up to the neck;
to turn the nations with the bridle of destruction,
   ⟨and to place⟩ᵃ on the jaws of the people a halter that
     leads astray.

29 You shall sing a song
   as in the night when a feast is celebrated,
and your hearts will rejoice
   like those who go along with flutes
to go to the mountain of Yahweh,
   to the rock of Israel.
30 Then Yahweh will sound
   his majestic voice
and show the descending blows
   of his arm
in thundering anger
   and flame of devouring fire,

ᵃ Read *ūleśim*, which has no doubt been omitted behind the similar *sw'*, cf. also Kissane, *ad loc.*

cloudburst and tempest
and hailstones.
31 Yes, before the voice of Yahweh
the Assyrians will be terror-stricken,
who strike with the rod.

32 And it will come about:
Every stroke of the staff
will ⟨strike them⟩ᵃ
which Yahweh
⟨lays⟩ᵃ upon them.
With timbrels and lyres
and ⟨sacred dances⟩ᵃ
he will fight against ⟨them⟩.ᵃ
33 For ⟨the Topheth⟩ᵇ
is long prepared.
⟨Is⟩ it ⟨indeed⟩ᵇ for ⟨Moloch⟩?ᶜ
Its pyre is set up,
⟨deep and wide⟩,ᵃ
⟨straw⟩ᵈ and wood in abundance.
The breath of Yahweh
like a stream of brimstone,
kindles it.

This description of salvation, which is impressive not only on a first reading, presents some difficulties of text and content. Not only is the question in v. 33 clearly a later interpolation, but vv. 31b and 32a also arouse the suspicion that they may be secondary. Verse 29 also seems to break the connection between vv. 28 and 30, while at a first glance v. 32b seems to be a continuation of v. 29. But a number of observations militate against undertaking changes in the order of the text and extensive alterations in the wording as we possess it. The remarkable change of imagery between v. 28a and v. 28b shows that we are faced with the product of an uneasy mind. Perhaps the task of literary criticism will be made easier for us if we remember the author's delight in quoting from the book of Isaiah: when he speaks in v. 28a of a raging stream 'dividing' up to the neck, he is no doubt recalling 8.8, which speaks of a stream which flows over Judah and reaches to

---

ᵃ Cf. *BHS*.
ᵇ Read *tōpet*. Take the *h* with *gam* and read *hᵃgam*.
ᶜ Cf. below *ad loc.*
ᵈ Read *qaš*.

the neck. Whereas this overflowing stream is also an element in the proclamation of judgment in 28.2 and 28.15, here it forms part of the promise. There is a further antithesis in the relationship between the themes in 31.4a and v. 31a in this passage: in the former the lion is not frightened by the band of shepherds gathered together against him, and Yahweh will not leave his own property to its enemies, while here the Assyrians who have advanced up to the city of God will be terrified by Yahweh's voice.

In 10.24 Assyria is described as he 'who smites you with a rod'. Since in the present context, in v. 32, it is clearly Yahweh who is striking Assyria, v. 31b has always caused difficulties, for in this verse 'who strike with the rod' can best be taken of Assyria, while the first part of the sentence affirms its destruction. Once we realize that the purpose of the quotation is to emphasize the reversal, there is no need for any amendment. The demonstration of these quotations, or to use a more cautious term, connections between the language and ideas of the present text and others in the book of Isaiah, resolves the problem of its authorship in at least one respect: this description of salvation is not by Isaiah himself.[a] Although the date of 8.5ff. may need further consideration, it is at least certain that 10.24ff.; 28.1ff., 14ff. and 31.4ff. were not composed by the eighth-century prophet. In 10.24 and 31.8 Assyria most probably means the Seleucid kingdom, as in 19.23. Thus we are right in assuming that the present description of salvation is, like 31.4ff., not based on a genuine historical event, and comes from a redactor who, in view of the conceptions he holds, may perhaps already be regarded as an apocalyptic thinker. In support of this late dating we would point out that there is no evidence for the use of the tradition of the theophany in promises before Deutero-Isaiah, that is, before the time of the exile.[b]

[27–28] *The judge of the nations comes!* Although the present poem does not say so explicitly, it is certain that the scene which the apocalyptic writer presents is located at Jerusalem, against which the nations are raging under the leadership of 'Assyria'. But as we already know from 17.12ff. and 29.1ff., Yahweh's help is closest when the

[a] Most recently, H. Donner, *Israel unter den Völkern*, SVT 11, 1964, p. 164. The lengthiest discussion of the question of authenticity, which comes to a negative conclusion, is still to be found in T. K. Cheyne, *Introduction to the Book of Isaiah*, London 1895, pp. 199ff.

[b] Cf. also B. S. Childs, *Isaiah and the Assyrian Crisis*, StBSt II. 3, 1967, pp. 49f.

distress is greatest. In a miraculous way he intervenes to reverse the fate of his own city of God. Of course the late author cannot conceive that Yahweh, who is transcendent over the whole world, can come to earth himself to perform his work there. Consequently he makes use of a conception developed in the circle of Deuteronomic theologians, in which the name of Yahweh represents his presence upon earth.[a] But apart from this, the author's mind is full of the ancient conceptions of the theophany of Yahweh, and the only surprising thing is how literally he uses them to portray his future hopes. Just as in texts handed down from ancient times Yahweh came in the storm from his mountain of God, either from Sinai or from the mountainous country of Seir (cf. Judg. 5.4 and Deut. 33.2, and also Isa. 2.12), his 'name', which now takes his place, will come down from afar, from the mountain of God or from heaven in a mighty thunderstorm, with sheet lightning which could be seen as his burning anger, forked lightning as his tongues, and thunder which could be heard as his voice cursing his enemies (cf. Ps. 18.9ff.; 29.3ff.; 50.2ff.; Nahum 1.3ff. and Hab. 3.3ff.). The breath of the mighty approaching God, or of his hypostasis, is then compared with a raging torrent which suddenly rises up to the neck of the traveller (cf. 8.8). Here the poet seems to have in mind the powerful cloudbursts which in those latitudes can suddenly transform a dry stream bed into a raging torrent (cf. Judg. 5.4, 21; Ps. 18.12ff.). If we look for an organic connection between the metaphor which follows and what precedes it, we must imagine the powerful rushing waters carrying the assembled nations away from Jerusalem and therefore following a course which leads them directly to their ruin. From the poetic point of view the transition from the description of the 'name' which approaches in the storm to a metaphor which presents him as a servant on a farm or in an army who places a bridle and halter on a rebellious horse, donkey or mule,[b] in order to subdue it to his will (cf. Ps. 32.9) is an abrupt one. When Yahweh treats the nations in this way, he is not guiding them along his straight path, but deceitfully into their certain ruin (cf. 19.14, 16 and 37.29).

[29–30] *The rejoicing at Yahweh's intervention.* What seems at the first reading of the text to be awkwardness or the consequence of later confusion appears on further examination to be a deliberate

---

[a] Cf. Deut. 4.36 with 12.11; II Sam. 7.13; I Kings 8.17 and Isa. 59.19; Ps. 54.3, 8f. and H. Bietenhard, *ThWBNT* V, pp. 255ff.; *TDNT* V, pp. 256ff.

[b] Cf. F. Nötscher, *Biblische Altertumskunde*, Bonn 1940, p. 176.

artifice. Before the poet returns from his metaphorical description of
the divine purpose to the description of God attacking in the storm,
he addresses his hearers or readers to assure them that this coming of
Yahweh will be a joyful event for them, and that they themselves will
not be punished by the judgment of their God. When Yahweh attacks
the besiegers, what happens in the besieged city will be like the night
preceding a festival, when the pilgrims go up to the temple to the
sounding of flutes, and songs. Up to the present day, the usual view
has been that this passage refers to the night celebration of the
Passover, which preceded the Massoth festival, the festival of un-
leavened bread (cf. Ex. 23.15; Deut. 16.6f. and Matt. 26.30).[a] But
the objection has long ago been made that the Passover, a separate
sacrificial feast, could not be understood as the inaugural ceremony
of the Massoth festival that followed.[b] Thus we must think either of
the New Year festival (cf. 29.1) or the feast of Tabernacles, which in
post-exilic times had become separated from it (cf. I Kings 8.2;
Neh. 8.1; Lev. 23.24 and 34).[c] The tradition of the Israelite New Year
festival, the roots of which went far back into Canaanite religion, is
certainly the origin of the idea of the conquest in the night of the
nations who had gathered together against Zion; although the time
it was supposed to take place is barely evident from the reference to
the joy of the festival night (cf. Pss. 46.6; 47; 122 and Zech. 14.16).
The festival procession proceeded to Zion, here described as the
mountain of Yahweh, with its temple (cf. Ps. 2.6; Isa. 11.9 and 2.2).
The parallelism suggests that the 'rock of Israel' is the holy rock of the
temple site, on which the altar of burnt offerings stood, and which was
regarded in Judaism as the stone which kept the primaeval sea locked
up.[d] But since the 'rock of Israel' was familiar as a divine title (cf.
II Sam. 23.3; Isa. 17.10 and Gen. 49.24) it probably had its traditional meaning here too, and refers to the God in whose honour the
festival procession was held, Yahweh, the God in whom Israel could
trust. He – the hypostasis of the name has obviously been displaced
by the power of the image – will descend upon the enemy with his
thundering voice and the descending blow of his arm, his lightnings,
upon the enemy (cf. Pss. 29.3f.; 50.3; 98.1; 89.11; 77.16; Isa. 33.2;

[a] Cf. e.g. Kissane, ad loc.
[b] Cf. Duhm, ad loc.
[c] For the problem of the Israelite New Year feast cf. recently J. C. de Moor,
New Year with Canaanites and Israelites I–II, Kamper Cahiers 21/22, Kampen 1972.
[d] Cf. J. Jeremias, Golgotha, Angelos-Beiheft 1, Leipzig 1926, pp. 65ff.

52.10; Ex. 6.6. and Ps. 136.12. There is no doubt that the apocalyptic author thinks of the destruction of the enemy as directly caused by God acting in the storm. Just as during Deborah's battle the Kishon had risen furiously as a result of a storm and at least cut off the enemy's path (cf. Judg. 5.20f.), and as in the battle at Gibeon hail had killed the Amorites (cf. Josh. 10.11 and Isa. 28.21), so Yahweh would destroy the enemy gathered before the gates of Jerusalem by a gigantic storm. The supernatural aspect of the conception lies in the fact that the storm is to affect only the enemy, but not the people of Jerusalem.

'Assyria', the world power hostile to God which was embodied in the Seleucid kingdom, and the world of the nations which has gathered together to attack Jerusalem, will be so terrified by the very voice of God in the thunder that it will be unable to think of resisting or attacking. If the nations are unable to influence God by the noise they make while he attacks, there can be no doubt that they will have to give way to his voice, however dangerous and powerful they may seem (cf. 31.4 and 10.24).

[32–33] *The final destruction of the enemy.* When Yahweh then strikes with the rod of his own lightning, every blow will tell, and there will be no escape for 'Assyria'. But in the city they will begin to play the drums and the lyre, probably not to begin the song and dance of victory in praise of Yahweh (cf. Ex. 15.20; Judg. 11.34; I Sam. 18.6f.; Pss. 150.4; 68.25ff.; Pss. 46 and 48) but in order to consecrate the enemy like a sacrifice for slaughter.[a] For while God fights with them and naturally completely conquers them, as in ancient times, which stood condemned in the Deuteronomic history and the post-exilic laws, there would be prepared in the valley of Hinnom, in the deep valley to the west and south of the city,[b] the Topheth, the place of burning (cf. II Kings 23.10; Jer. 7.31f.; 19.6, 11ff.; 32.35 and Lev. 18.21; 20.2ff.; Deut. 12.31; 18.10). At one time abominable sacrifices of children had been offered there to Molech (Moloch) (cf. I Kings 11.7; II Kings 16.3; 17.31, and also II Kings 3.27). Now those who have been struck by Yahweh's lightnings will be burnt up there in an immense pit, filled with straw and wood (cf. Ezek. 16.21 and 39.11ff.), and it is Yahweh who will add the final stroke by

[a] Cf. e.g. Lev. 7.30; Deut. 35.22; 38.24 and Num. 8.11 and for the basic meaning of the word *tᵉnūpā* cf. also G. R. Driver, *JSS* 1, 1956, pp. 97ff., according to whom it should be translated 'contribution'.

[b] Cf. H. Kosmala, *BHW*, col. 723.

lighting the funeral pyre with his breath, which is now fiery, and with his lightnings like a burning stream of brimstone (cf. 66.24 and Eth. Enoch 26f.; 90.26f.).[a]

Into this context a later reader has inserted the almost heretical question whether the mighty sacrifice was once again meant for Molech (Moloch). The divine name Molech has a strange history. Behind it lie both the ancient Phoenician and Punic term for a sacrifice, *molk*, and a royal deity (*melek*). When the Israelites learned of the abominable sacrificial practice of the Phoenicians, they probably confused the term for the sacrifice with the familiar king-god.[b] Originally, they probably spoke of a sacrifice for the 'king' (*melek*), but in the course of Jewish history the practice grew up of pronouncing the word with the vowels of the Hebrew word 'abomination', *bošet*, as *molek*. – This interjection clearly presented immediate difficulties, since Yahweh could hardly offer sacrifice to an idol. Thus the word *molek* was vocalized once again as *melek*, so that the question then simply seemed to be whether the Assyrian king would go down into the Topheth.

One may marvel at the courageous faith which, in what seems to us an almost childish way, looks forward to the end of the powerful enemy before the gates of Jerusalem. But the content of these expectations shows how deep a gulf there must have been between Judaism and Hellenism for this apocalyptic thinker, since he desired nothing but death and destruction for the Hellenistic power. That differences of faith divide men and nations is unfortunately something that does not just belong to the past but also to the present. The assurance of Christian faith should be demonstrated in seeking only the good of those who have a different faith. Anyone who does not only have this in mind, but actually seeks to live it out, will recall John 8.7.

[a] Cf. W. Bousset and H. Gressmann, *Die Religion des Judentums im späthellenistischen Zeitalter*, HNT 21, 1926, p. 286 and P. Volz, *Jüdische Eschatologie von Daniel bis Akiba*, Tübingen and Leipzig 1903, pp. 288ff.

[b] Cf. for this view R. de Vaux, *Studies in Old Testament Sacrifice*, Cardiff 1964, pp. 89f., and also the whole material, pp. 73ff.

CHAPTER 31.1–3

Help from Egypt?

1 Woe to those who go down to Egypt for help
     and rely on horses,
   who trust[a] in chariots because they are many
     and in horsemen because they are very numerous.[b]
   But they did not look to the Holy One of Israel
     or consult Yahweh.
2 And yet he is wise and brought disaster,
     and did not call back his words,
   He will[c] arise against the house of the evildoers,
     and against the help of those who work iniquity.
3 For the Egyptians are men, and not God;
     and their horses are flesh, and not spirit.
   When Yahweh stretches out his hand,
     the helper will stumble, and he who is helped will fall,
     and they will all perish together.[d]

The formal category of this prophecy of woe is best described as a
prophecy of warning with a reason, in which v. 1 forms the reproach
and vv. 2 and 3 the prophecy of warning. It shares with 30.1ff. its
intensity of expression, and shows like that prophecy, and in part
with the same intention, links with the language of the cult and the
psalms. In addition it displays clear connections with the rest of the
Isaianic material.[e] Thus we can scarcely be wrong in attributing
31.3–3 to the prophet Isaiah, dating it in the year 701, and ignoring
the similar situations in the years 589–587, 486–484, 362–360,
349–343 and 188.[f] The fact that in v. 2a Isaiah was able to point to

---

[a] The difficulties of the verbal syntax in the verse are sometimes ignored in the
literature in an astonishingly casual way. It is to Feldmann's credit that he
acknowledges them. *bṭḥ* is what is known as a stative verb, and as such has a
syntax of its own: as a shortened imperfect at the beginning of a sentence it is to
be taken in the sense of a depunctualized *ḥameṭ* in a stative sense (verbal com-
munication from O. Rössler, of Marburg).

[b] Once again, a stative.

[c] *weqām* ought to be interpreted as prophetic perfect, cf. LXX and Vg.

[d] For the form cf. R. Meyer, *Hebräische Grammatik* II, Berlin ³1969, pp. 100f.

[e] Cf. v. 1 with 30.1; 10.3; 20.6; 30.12 and 16; v. 2 with 2.9, 14; 9.7ff.; v. 3 with
9.11, 16, 20; 5.25; 3.8; 8.18; 28.13.

[f] Cf. above p. 283, and also M. Noth, *Geschichte Israels*, Göttingen ³1956, pp.

misfortunes which had already come about and were in accordance
with his previous preaching (cf. 29.15f.; 30.1ff.) leads to the conclusion either that in the meantime the army of the Assyrian emperor
Sennacherib had penetrated at least as far as the Philistine plain, or
else that we have here a variant upon 30.1ff. which goes back to the
early exilic redactor whose work we find particularly in 30.(8)9–17.
It is not clear whether the battle of Eltekeh, which the Egyptians
lost, had in the former case already taken place. Assuming that
Isaiah is the author, the prophecy must be dated before 30.6f.[a] It is
possible that this oracle was placed at the conclusion of the prophet's
sayings from the year 701 only because it summed up once again in a
telling form the objections Isaiah made in the name of his God to the
pro-Egyptian policy of the kingdom of Judah.

[1] The fault that Isaiah found in this policy, which had sought
from the Ethiopian Pharaoh Shabako a corps of cavalry and a contingent of chariots for a more effective defence against the Assyrian
danger,[b] is shown by the choice of verbs in v. 1abα which effectively
prepares the way for the antithisis in v. bβ. It was of course normal to
speak of going down to Egypt, in view of the route from the mountains
of Judah to the Nile (cf. Gen. 43.15; Deut. 26.5 and the Lachish
ostrakon III. 14).[c] But has a human being the right to rely upon his
own plans and the cavalry of his allies and seek support from them,
instead of from Yahweh (cf. Prov. 3.5; Isa. 30.12; Miach 3.11; and
also Isa. 50.10; 10.20)? When a devout person is in distress he con-
fesses by his prayer of petition that he trusts Yahweh (cf. for example
Pss. 13.6; 21.8; 22.5f.; 25.2; 31.7, 15; 52.10). May a nation trust in
chariots and carts, in the heavy weapons of his allies (cf. Hos. 10.13)[d]
instead of trusting in Yahweh's help (cf. Ps. 118.8f. and Jer. 17.5ff.)?
Must not Jerusalem look for help in the first place to its God (cf. II
Sam. 22.42) who is far above the world and yet has protected Israel,

---

256ff.; ET *History of Israel*, London and New York ²1960, pp. 257ff., esp. p. 267;
O. Kaiser, 'Der geknickte Rohrstab' in *Wort und Geschichte. Festschrift K. Elliger*,
AOAT 18, 1972, pp. 101f. and especially n. 24; 'Zwischen den Fronten', *Wort,
Lied und Gottesspruch. Festschrift J. Ziegler*, FzB 2, 1972, pp. 201ff.; F. K. Kienitz,
Die politische Geschichte Ägyptens vom. 7. bis zum 4. Jahrhundert, Berlin 1953, pp. 101f.
and M. Hengel, *Judentum und Hellenismus*, WUNT 10, 1969, p. 17.

[a] Cf. above p. 234 and p. 289.

[b] Cf. above pp. 283f.

[c] *KAI* no. 193; *ANET²*, p. 322; *TGI²*, pp. 75f.

[d] Cf. H. W. Wolff, *ad loc.*; W. Rudolph, *ad loc.* disagrees.

the God who is the Holy One of Israel (cf. 17.7)? And can Yahweh tolerate his own people taking decisions in this critical moment without asking him whether their plans have his approval (cf. 30.2)?[a]

[2] Ought not the rulers in Jerusalem to have remembered that Yahweh is wise (cf. Job 9.4; Eccles. 1.1; 15.18) and understands his own affairs as well as the ambassadors who have set off for Egypt and the court at whose bidding they have departed, and indeed perhaps the war party among the people? This has already been shown by the fact that in the meantime he has begun to bring about the misfortunes prophesied by Isaiah.[b] Quite clearly, then, he has not taken back his word once it has been proclaimed, and it therefore remains in force. Consequently, further misfortune is to be expected (cf. 9.7ff.; Jer. 39.16; 44.29; Ezek. 12.28; Isa. 40.8; 44.26; 55.10f.). Isaiah expresses quite clearly the fact that a word can nevertheless not have independent life apart from its author, when he foretells that Yahweh himself will rise up and bring to nothing the 'house of the evildoers' (cf. 1.4) and the help of those who do wickedness.[c]

[3] Thus the people of Judah have not only made a mistake in their choice of means to avert the danger that hangs over them, but have also brought guilt upon themselves (cf. 30.1b). This is shown by the unique intensity of the double antithesis between the Egyptians as men and what God is (cf. Hos. 11.9 and Ezek. 28.2, 9) and between their forces as mere flesh which without the breath of life sent from God crumbles to death, and God's $r\bar{u}^a\dot{h}$, his breath or spirit, which makes all life possible (cf. Ps. 78.39; 39.6, 12; 62.10; 103.14ff.; 104.29f.; Job 27.3; 34.1f. and Eccles. 12.7).[d] When Isaiah speaks here of '$\bar{e}l$, God, he is by no means assuming in his use of the generic term[e] that there are other gods beside the Holy One of Israel. If he were, the antithesis would lose its point. Man does not exist without the God who has created him (cf. Gen. 2.7; Pss. 8.5ff.; 144.3) nor

---

[a] For *drš*, 'inquire of' as a technical term for consulting God through an oracle technique or a prophet, cf. Gen. 25.22; I Kings 14.1ff.; II Kings 8.8ff.; 22.13ff. and the comments of C. Westermann, *KuD*, 6, 1960, pp. 17ff.

[b] Cf. 29.15f.; 30.1ff. and, in so far as it is older, also 30.6f. For the formula cf. e.g. Josh. 23.15; I Kings 9.9; II Kings 22.16; Jer. 6.19; 19.3; Job. 42.11 and *passim*; the small difference should be noted, that the deuteronomic set phrase uses *hārā'ā*, but Isaiah speaks only of *rā'*.

[c] Cf. K. H. Bernhardt, *ThWAT* I, col. 158f.

[d] Cf. A. R. Johnson, *The One and the Many in the Israelite Conception of God*, Cardiff ²1961, pp. 13ff. and especially p. 16.

[e] Cf. F. M. Cross, *ThWAT* I, col. 278.

animals without the God who has formed them and who has given them their breath as he has to man (cf. Gen. 2.18ff.; Ps. 104.29ff.). Thus there is no escape from Yahweh's hands stretched out to punish (cf. 9.11, 16, 20; 5.25). The helper and he who allows himself to be helped, Egypt and Judah, will stumble and fall (cf. 3.8; 8.15; Ps. 27.2) and perish (cf. 1.28).

The Egyptian army was defeated at Eltekeh. We know of no other army from the sources which we possess. Hezekiah was besieged in Jerusalem and as one fortress after another outside Jerusalem fell, he was forced to surrender.[a]

The confusion of creature and creator was not limited to the days of Isaiah or of the Old Testament, and certainly appears in the history of nations and states in a particularly clear form, to such an extent that it can be regarded as the temptation to obtain peace and prosperity by improper means – when violence and cunning have possessed, if possessed is the right word, greater importance than the moral law; and when even trust in God has frequently served, if served is the right word, merely the purposes of violence. What takes place on a grand scale is a reflection of what takes place with the individual. Thus it is useless to become incensed at the course the world is taking or even to make the blind decision, in ignorance of what is really at issue, to fight with violence against violence. On the other hand everyone must first wrestle with himself and therefore with his God in such a way that God conquers and he is defeated. When this happens, mankind will have become more peaceful in at least one case. For whether or not we can maintain peace and further it depends upon whether we are able to let God be God, man be man and the world be the world.

CHAPTER 31.4–9

The Deliverance of Zion

4   For thus Yahweh said to me,
     As a lion or a young lion
        growls over his prey,

---

[a] Cf. the passages mentioned above, p. 284 note a.

> and when a band of shepherds
> is called forth against him,
> is not terrified by their shouting
> or daunted at their noise,
> so Yahweh Sebaoth will come down
> to fight upon Mount Zion and upon its hill.

> 5 Like fluttering birds
> so Yahweh Sebaoth will protect Jerusalem;
> he will protect and deliver it,
> he will spare and rescue it.[a]

6[b] *Turn to him from whom you have deeply revolted, O people of Israel.* [7]*For in that day every one shall cast away his idols of silver and his idols of gold, which your hands have sinfully made for you.*

> 8 And Assyria shall fall
> by a sword, not of man;
> and a sword, not of man,
> shall devour him;
> *then he shall flee from the sword,*
> *and his young men shall be put to forced labour.*
> 9 *His rock shall pass away in terror,*
> *and his officers desert the standard in panic,*
> Saying of Yahweh, whose fire is in Zion,
> and whose furnace is in Jerusalem.

There is disagreement not only about the content of 31.4–9, but also about its literary criticism. It is generally accepted that vv. 6 and 7, which can be distinguished from their context by the obvious fact that they are in prose, and also vv. 8a and 9a at least, which to some extent conflict with 8a, are secondary additions. But from this point on commentators begin to disagree. Although it is clear that v. 5, together with v. 8a and perhaps also v. 9b, refer to the future deliverance of Jerusalem from the Assyrians by Yahweh himself, the meaning of v. 4, and whether or not it originally formed part of the prophecy of salvation which follows, is disputed. If the simile of God claiming his prey like a lion is regarded as a warning addressed to Jerusalem, then v. 4 must be regarded as separate from the prophecy of salvation which follows. On the other hand, if v. 4 itself is a prophecy of salvation, then with the original substance of what follows it forms a single prophecy of salvation. Thus the decisive question concerning the content and the literary criticism of the

---

[a] Cf. G-K, § 113t.   [b] A prose addition, cf. below.

present text is: What is the meaning of the simile of the lion in v. 4?

[4] The first argument in favour of taking the verses as a warning is that the Hebrew expression translated here 'fight upon' can as well mean 'fight against', and occurs in this hostile sense in 29.7f.; Num. 31.7 and Zech. 14.12. If this translation is regarded as convincing, then the shepherds must be seen as the Judaeans and their allies the Egyptians, who are unable to avert the disaster which the threat from Assyria is bringing upon Jerusalem (cf. 31.3). In this case, the verse – of course without its introduction – can be attributed to the prophet Isaiah, who would have uttered these prophecies against the coalition organized by Hezekiah, during the years between the advance of Sennacherib and his attack upon the capital of Judah. But it is clear that this argument does not carry as much force as might appear at first sight. On the one hand, there can be no doubt that it is perfectly possible to translate the Hebrew expression in question by 'fight against'.[a] On the other hand, the even balance of the simile is the decisive argument for taking the verse as a prophecy of salvation. The simile is that of a lion defending his prey, which he regards as it were as his own property, against the attempts of shepherds to take it back from him. In other words, the lion will not allow anyone to steal from him what belongs to him. This behaviour is compared to Yahweh's descent from heaven to fight upon the hill of Zion (cf. 10.32); thus what Yahweh does and the behaviour of the lion correspond. In other words, Yahweh does not allow anyone to steal from him what belongs to him. Jerusalem belongs to him because he has chosen it (cf. Ps. 132.13f.) and therefore he will not allow it to fall into the hands of the attackers, whom we at once recognize as 'Assyria' though without thereby fixing the date (cf. v. 8a). The tension between v. 4a and v. 4b does not require us to assume that the mixed imagery of the lion and the bird results from a late addition.[b] Rather, it points to a poet who was firmly set upon his purpose but was not so consistent in carrying it out. His simile may or may not have been inspired by 5.29, but there is nothing against the conclusion that in the book of Isaiah the image of a lion defending its prey is used in different senses, as it is in the *Iliad*, cf. XII. 298ff. and XVIII. 161.

In the introduction to v. 4 the poet is claiming that he speaks with

---

[a] As a 'control experiment' one may work out how 'fight upon' would have sounded in Hebrew.

[b] Cf. most recently Eichrodt, *ad loc.*

the authority of Yahweh and finds no difficulty in the fact that his own words speak of Yahweh in the third person. His 'for' is defensible only at first sight. His own promise is clearly meant to give a reassurance, by contrast to the expectations condemned in 31.1–3, that hope placed in Yahweh will not be disappointed. He contrasts the deliverance vainly expected from Egypt, that is, from men, with one which will be brought about not by men (v. 8a).

[5] It must be admitted that the poet also shows a certain awkwardness in his choice of images at the beginning of v. 5, for a flock of fluttering birds does not accord well with the one protecting God, Yahweh. This has led to the suggestion that something has been lost from the text, and that the sentence once read, 'like fluttering birds the nations will be scattered'. The verse would then in fact continue without any awkwardness. But since v. 4 has already shown some uncertainty in the link between images and their content, such an emendation is perhaps better avoided. The poet is telling us that Yahweh will protect Zion in the same way as birds fluttering backwards and forwards above their nests defend their brood (cf. Deut. 32.11 and Ps. 91). Here as in the previous verse the poet deliberately chooses the full divine title with which Yahweh is described as the Lord of all heavenly and earthly powers;[a] not only because of its sonority, but also to remind the reader which God it is who will carry out this incredible promise. In order to arouse confidence in the future saving action of this God on behalf of his city, the poet alludes to the former saving act of Yahweh in Egypt, when he killed the firstborn of the Egyptians but spared those of Israel (cf. Ex. 13.23, 27).

[8a] Whereas the people of Judah once hoped in vain for the liberation of Jerusalem from the Assyrians by the Egyptians, that is, by men (cf. 31.3), when a last 'Assyria' makes its final attack (cf. 10.24ff.), it will be destroyed by sword of one who is 'not man'. Whether the poet meant by this Yahweh himself and was therefore thinking as in 29.5f. 30.27ff. of a mighty theophany in a storm (cf. also Ex. 12.29ff.) or an angel carrying out Yahweh's judgment in a mysterious way and perhaps by means of a plague (cf. 37.36ff.), is something that is impossible to tell. What matters to the poem is the fact, and not the way it will happen. [9b] If v. 9b was composed by the poet himself and not by the redactor who gave us v. 8b and v. 9a, he was following 30.33 in describing how the defeated would be burnt on a huge mound of wood and a funeral

[a] Cf. my comments on 6.3 (ET *Isaiah 1–12*, OTL, 1972, *ad loc.*) and 13.4.

pyre, and no doubt regarded this as the act of God himself in his self-revelation. The unusual mention of the fire and the oven should be taken in the sense of Gen. 15.17 as an allusive description of the God who is present in the fire, the hearth signifying the place in which the enemy are destroyed and burnt up.

We have tacitly assumed during our exposition that the description of salvation was composed by a late poet who may perhaps even be regarded as an apocalyptic thinker. The decisive reason for this view lies not so much in his lack of poetic skill, but rather in his technique of allusion, and above all the content of his statement: the expectation of a direct intervention of Yahweh, transcending all historical reality, in the course of history is something which in our view cannot be attributed to a prophet who was one of a people still able to play an active part in history. The prophets believed that Yahweh acted through real forces of nature and history, working through realities, through droughts and earthquakes which afflicted a country or a city, and through nations whom he forced to carry out his will. What is expected here goes beyond these limits. The tradition that lies behind and influences this apocalyptic writer is the legendary story of the deliverance of Jerusalem in 701, cf. 36f.; and of course he is also influenced by the conceptions of the last attack upon Zion, and its final liberation, which were developed in the process of coming to terms with the exile and with prophetic and cultic traditions. In a period in which the changing fortunes of the great powers in their struggle to control Syria and Palestine, and to achieve world domination, had long shown that there was no real chance of the recovery of independence and freedom by the tiny Jewish nation, their hopes were directed in an astonishing way towards their God, who was capable of what seemed impossible to men. Just as it had received its very existence from him, so it would finally receive everlasting deliverance, when the forces of this earth hostile to God rose up against the city of God in the guise of 'Assyria', perhaps already a term for the Seleucid kingdom.

[8b, 9a] A reader, probably not much later, felt that the details of the attackers' fate were not made sufficiently clear. Regardless of the contradiction with v. 8a, he sought to affirm that the young men among the enemy would not be destroyed, but would have to carry out forced labour for those who had been set free. Before giving way to indignation at such a hope, one must remember that in the ancient world defeated nations, including the Jews (cf. Ex. 1.1ff.),

invariably suffered this fate. This promise of a reversal of the relationship between lords and masters is embedded in an account of the flight of the hostile army and its princes and the death of its king, here described as its rock,[a] which would result from terror at the mighty manifestation of God.

[6–7] The same hand that is responsible for 30.22 (cf. also 17.8; 2.20 and 27.9) may also be responsible for the interpolation of vv. 6 and 7. The intention is to affirm that the mighty and redeeming manifestations of Yahweh and the conversion of Israel, its relinquishing of all idolatry, are related. According to the received text v. 6 begins with a call for conversion. But the continuation suggests that this text may not be original, and the suggestion that the demand should be emended to a prophecy, 'then you will turn to him . . .', may well be correct. The redactor clearly does not regard the Israel of his time as the ideal community of believers which it ought to be, but knows that among its members there is profound apostasy (cf. Hos. 9.9) expressed in the secret possession of gold and silver domestic idols. When God appears to man in person, he does not merely hear about him, but becomes certain of his mighty presence; false belief and superstition are automatically rejected, and man puts away from himself what has hitherto separated him from God.

The person who turned the affirmation at the beginning of v. 6 into a command, and must also have altered v. 7b accordingly, intended to encourage the community not to wait until the hour of the judgment upon the nations to purify itself – perhaps because he knew that God's judgment ultimately falls impartially upon all nations.

[a] The identification of the rock with the king is, however, not certain. At best the parallelism is in favour of it. Fohrer tries to make it easier by emending to 'his heroes will be driven out by horror'. For the identification of the rock with the god Assur, who in Assyrian text is in fact called 'great mountain', cf. Kissane, *ad loc.* His own interpretation, which identifies the rock with the capital city Assur, is of course completely hypothetical.

CHAPTER 32.1-8

In the Kingdom of Righteousness

1 When[a] a king reigns in righteousness,
   and ⟨   ⟩[b] princes rule in justice,
2 each will be like a hiding-place from the wind,
   a covert from the tempest,
   like streams of water in a dry place,
   like the shade of a great rock in a parched land.
3 Then the eyes of those who see ⟨will not be closed⟩[c]
   and the ears of those who hear will hearken.
4 The heart of the rash will have good judgment
   and the tongue of the stammerers will speak readily.
5 The fool will no more be called noble,
   nor the knave said to be honorable.
6 For the fool speaks folly,
   and his heart plots[d] wickedness,
   so that he acts perversely
   and talks stupidly about Yahweh,
   so that he leaves the craving of the hungry unsatisfied,
   and deprives the thirsty of drink.
7 The weapons of the wicked[e] are evil;
   he devises abnominable deeds
   to ruin the poor with lying words,
   even when the plea of the needy[f] is right.[g]
8 But he who is noble devises noble things,
   and by noble things he stands.

Two things will be obvious to an attentive reader of this passage. First, its language and conceptions have remained virtually un-influenced by the prophetic tradition, and are those of the wisdom schools. Secondly, it is intended in spite of this to be understood in relation to its context as a prophecy of the change in society in the time of salvation which is to come. But the pressure of the charac-teristic conceptions of wisdom are such that one rightly hesitates to

[a] For the construction cf. G-K, § 159w and Prov. 11.31 and 24.12f.
[b] Cf. G-K, § 143e and *BHS*.
[c] Cf. *BHS* 29.9 and 6.10.
[d] Cf. *BHS* and LXX[L] and Tg.
[e] The alliteration is in imitation of the Hebrew.
[f] The singular of M should be retained as the more difficult reading.
[g] For the construction cf. Delitzsch, *ad loc.*

describe it as a Messianic text. It can be said, however, that its present purpose is to bear witness to the righteous government and devout citizenship in the Messianic age.[a] For the following 31.4-9, which speak of the deliverance of Zion from the utmost distress by Yahweh's personal intervention, the reader is bound to relate the wisdom discourse which follows, regardless of its proper character, to the age of salvation which follows the destruction of the enemy. The wisdom teacher speaks in very general terms of the consequences of just government by the king and his officials, 32.1-5, and of the difference between the fool and him who is noble. But in an age of unrighteous government, or when perhaps there was no king at all, his words would be bound to sound a Messianic note to Jewish readers. Moreover, there is no lack of connections between their content and that of the preceding prophecies: v. 3 provides an antithesis, by way of 29.9f., to 6.9f., while v. 6 once again provides an antithesis to 9.16αβγ, so emphasizing the difference between the time of disobedience and judgment, in which men's hearts are hardened, and the future age of salvation in which men are open to the word and the will of God. Thus whereas some parts of this passage may have a history of their own before the time of their incorporation into the book of Isaiah, in its final form it was certainly meant for its present position. As in the case of 28.23-29, we have before us a redaction of the book of Isaiah by wisdom thinkers.

This wisdom prophecy, as we can now describe this passage, clearly falls into two stanzas, each of six couplets: 32.1-5 and 6-8. The logical coherence of the first stanza is clear, for it portrays the consequences of a righteous rule which transforms the circumstances of the whole population. But the connection between the first and second stanzas is not so clear. It is apparently a digression on the part of the wisdom teacher, in which, in the familiar manner of the wisdom schools, he instructs his reader in the difference between the fool and him who is noble. But the effect is to complete the portrait of the age of salvation: v. 5 clearly shows that all the godless and anti-social activities of the 'fools' will then come to an end. – From the formal point of view vv. 1f., 6, 7 and 8 can be described as maxims. We may be correct in thinking that the proverbs in v. 1f. and v. 6a, together with v. 8, were drawn by the wisdom teacher from tradition.

[1-2] In spite of the artificial similes with which, if we are correct,

[a] Cf. the title which Marti gives the passage. For this topic cf. also S. Mowinckel, *He That Cometh*, Oxford and New York 1956, p. 17.

the wisdom schools were already describing the protective function
of just government, their sense of reality is displayed in the fact that
they consider, as necessary conditions for such government, not only
the king, but also his princes, his officials (cf. I Kings 4.2; 20.15;
II Kings 24.12; Hos. 7.3; 8.4; Jer. 39.3). In this way they introduce a
realistic feature into the portrait of the Messianic age. According to
the conceptions of this wisdom redactor, kings in the Messianic age
will be real kings in a real kingdom, and so will not be able to do
without officials who rule righteously like himself. This undoubtedly
means in particular giving just judgment in court (cf. also 22.20ff.),
for in a vast kingdom stretching from one sea to the other and including the whole inhabitants of the world (cf. Ps. 72.8ff.)[a] the king will
naturally be unable to decide all the cases that occur himself. Indeed,
the kings of Judah were not able to do this.[b] From the very first wisdom had been concerned with the importance of justice for a king's
rule, as we learn from Prov. 16.10; 20.8, 26, and especially from 20.28;
29.4, 14 and 31.4f.; cf. also 25.5. Thus if kings and royal officials ever
truly rule according to justice and righteousness, and so give everyone his due, they will form a strong bulwark for all their subjects
against any attempt to do violence. In the language of imagery,
then, they are as it were a roof against the summer thunderstorms
and the winter squalls of rain (cf. also 4.6 and 25.4). The way in
which they also positively improve the life of their subjects is shown
by the two concluding metaphors, which compare them to the
irrigation channels in a dry country (cf. Ps. 1.3 and Isa. 44.4) and to
the shadow of a huge rock which prevents the ground from becoming
dried out, and gives men protection from the heat of the day (cf. 4.6;
25.4, and Job 7.2, as well as Hesiod, *Works and Days*, 589 and Virgil,
Georgics III.145).

[a] For the problem cf. also W. Thiel, 'Der Weltherrschaftsanspruch des judäischen
Königs nach Psalm 2', *Theologische Versuche* 3, Berlin 1971, pp. 53ff. and especially
pp. 57ff.

[b] For judging as a function of the king cf. I Sam. 8.20; II Sam. 8.15; I Kings
3.9; 10.9, for the institution of judges in the southern kingdom II Chron. 19.4ff.
and the comments of R. de Vaux, *Institutions de l'Ancien Testament* I, Paris, 1958,
pp. 236ff.; ET *Ancient Israel. Its Life and Institutions*, London and New York 1961,
pp. 150ff. II Sam. 23.3ff. is similar in substance to the present oracle. For the
connections between the Old Testament ideal of kingship and justice and the
corresponding ideas in the ancient near East, cf. my comments on 9.5 and 11.4
(*Isaiah 1–12*, OTL, 1972, *ad loc.*); O. Kaiser, *Der Konigliche Knecht* FRLANT 70,
²1962, pp. 24ff.

[3] Verse 3 seems to speak not only of the king's subjects, but also of the king himself and his assistants. In the age of salvation none of them will any longer be inaccessible to God's claims and will consequently regard everything that happens from God's point of view, and will likewise understand the meaning of all the words which he has once uttered and now repeats, and will act accordingly. The time of disobedience and the hardening of hearts, two sides of the same human attitude, will then be past (cf. 6.9f.; 29.9f.; 30.10f. and 29.18 and 24).[a] [4] The heart, the centre of the functions of knowledge and will,[b] of those who once acted rashly,[c] reached false conclusions and carried out false acts, will now be calm and will consequently fulfil its function aright. Free of all haste and upheaval, and no longer subject to fear of each other, human beings will have insight into what is taking place round about them and what they are required to do about it. Similarly, people who feel themselves oppressed and therefore stutter will be able to speak freely and without stumbling. The kingdom of righteousness is also the kingdom of prudence and freedom. [5] This will bring the end of the age in which people who take seriously neither God nor their neighbour, and consequently show that they are fools, (cf. Ps. 14.1) are described as noble, and given a title, voluntarily or under compulsion, which really describes the person who devotes his surplus goods to the benefit of society, his guests, his friends and the poor, i.e. the generous man (cf. Prov. 19.6).[d]

[6] The wisdom teacher now makes clear to us what it is from which mankind is set free when everyone once again acts and is treated according to his true value. Taking up an ancient maxim concerning the difference between the fool and the noble man, he outlines a picture of the fool. The fool speaks – perhaps we ought to translate: thinks – foolishness. His thoughts and plans belong to what does not form part of the sphere of prosperity and peace, *šālōm*, has no part in goodness and can therefore only bring about wickedness, *'āwen*.[e] If a man's heart is devoted to wickedness, then his actions cannot but bring about wickedness: the fool acts contrary to all order

[a] Cf. also Jer. 7.24, 26; 11.8; 17.23; 34.14; 44.5; 31.33f. – for the equivalent of hearing and obeying cf. Ps. 18.45; and also Prov. 15.31 and 25.13; but also Isa. 50.4f. and Job 33.16.

[b] For *lēb*, heart, now cf. F. Stolz, *THAT* I, col. 81ff.

[c] For this expression cf. also 35.4.

[d] Cf. S. Nyberg, *Beduinentum und Jahwismus*, Lund, 1946, pp. 132ff.

[e] For this term cf. R. Knierim, *THAT* I, col. 81ff.

which is righteous and in accordance with the will of God, and perverts it.[a] When he speaks of Yahweh, what he says is confused and confusing, perverse and untrue, because he does not take him seriously, and indeed perhaps denies him in his words as he does in his own acts, or even dares to question that he guides and controls the actions of men (cf. 9.16; 5.18f., 20; 29.15f.; 30.2, 9ff.; 31.1, and Ps. 14.1 again). Logically, then, he also ignores the claims of his neighbour by not fulfilling even the most immediate duty of feeding the hungry and giving drink to the thirsty (cf. Isa. 58.7; Ezek. 18.16; Job 22.7; Prov. 25.21f.; Ps. 107.9 and Matt. 25.35ff.). [7] Just as bad is the wicked man[b] who does things in secret which are bound to arouse disgust,[c] such as depriving the poor and the dependent of their rights in court by obtaining their condemnation through his lies, even though their innocence has been demonstrated (cf. Prov. 7.15). [8] The behaviour of the fool and the knave, which is now thought of as noble and distinguished, because society has been perverted by godlessness and the resultant unrighteousness, is finally contrasted by the wisdom teacher with the image of the noble man, whose purposes and actions are rigidly in accordance with the ideal of a readiness to serve and help, by which true nobility is known.

It should by now be clear that this prophecy is not by Isaiah.[d] This conclusion of literary criticism, however, makes no difference to the attention that should be paid to this wisdom teacher, who associates the kingdom of righteousness and peace with the obedience of ruler and subject to the ordinance and will of God, an obedience demonstrated in righteousness, truthfulness and a willingness to serve and help. Perhaps in an age in which there are such loud and frequent complaints, some justified and some not, about oppressive rule and the restrictions and the lack of freedom which this brings, we need to be reminded that there can only be freedom for everyone when all regard themselves as to the same degree under an obligation. And perhaps in this context the words of the Bible are not as old fashioned as many people think, when they draw men's attention first to God and then to each other.

---

[a] For the term *ḥnp* cf. Knierim, *THAT* I, col. 597ff.

[b] The Hebrew word is a hapax legomenon.

[c] *zimmā* often refers to a sexual transgression, cf. e.g. Lev. 18.17; Job 31.11. As a term for the activity of a sinner it is found e.g. in Ps. 26.9f. and of the godless in Prov. 21.27.

[d] For a lengthy discussion cf. Cheyne, *Introduction*, pp. 172ff.

CHAPTER 32.9–14

To the Women

9   *Rise up*,[a] you women who are at ease,
      hear my voice;
   you complacent daughters,
      give ear to my speech.

10 In little more than a year
      you will shudder, you complacent women;
   for the vintage will fail,
      the fruit harvest[b] will not come.

11 Tremble,[c] you women who are at ease,
      shudder,[d] you complacent ones;
   strip[d] and make[d] yourselves bare,
      and gird[d] your loins.

12 *Beating upon your breasts*[e]
      for the pleasant fields,
      for the fruitful vine,

13 for the soil of my people
      growing up in thorns, *briars*,
   yea, for all the joyous houses
      in the joyful city.

14 For the palace will be forsaken,
      the tumult of the city still;
   the hill[f] and the watchtower[g]
      will become as dens[h] for ever,
   a joy of wild asses,
      a pasture of flocks.[i]

[a] But cf. *BHS*.

[b] For the expression and the topic cf. Ex. 23.16; 34.22.

[c] Imp. masc. pl.

[d] For the aramaicizing imperatives cf. G-K, § 48i and B-L, p. 305, § 41g.

[e] Part. masc. pl. Unless the emendation of *BHS* is to be followed, this must be an unskilful gloss.

[f] Actually: Ophel, cf. Micah 4.8; Neh. 3.26f.; II Chron. 27.3; 33.14 and the comment of G. Sauer, *BHW* II, col. 1352.

[g] Cf. *HAL* sub voce bahan.

[h] But it is also possible to assume with *KBL* a *me͑ārā* II, 'bare field' so that the asses mentioned next can gambol on the open field.

[i] There is possibility here, merely by changing the punctuation, of providing a doublet to the wild asses, cf. *KBL* sub voce ͑*arād*, so providing a fine parallelism, though this conflicts even with the tradition of the ancient versions.

The question whether 32.9–14 (20) are a poem by Isaiah or a later oracle composed for the present context has been discussed by Old Testament scholars for almost a hundred years.[a]

In order to display the problems of the received text, in the translation above we have refused to offer a completely tidy text by means of various orthographical changes and some deletions which are implied by the dominating 2+2 metre. Thus a glance at the footnotes to vv. 11 and 12 will make clear the uncertainty of the syntax in the imperatives. If we do not treat v. 12a as a later gloss, or as severely corrupted by the negligence of a copyist, the phenomenon extends to this half verse. In v. 13 we are surprised to find the two words 'thorns, briars' without a conjunction, particularly as they can both be translated by the same word. But of course a reader could well have explained the less common word which occurs first in the Hebrew text by the second word, which occurs elsewhere in the book of Isaiah, though coupled with a different word.[b] Anyone looking at the original will also remark upon the second line in v. 14b and will wonder whether the word be^cad, 'as', very unusual in this application, ought to be deleted, and whether the same is true of the expression 'for ever', which some scholars find conveniently supports their dating, while to others it is an embarrassment. If because of the metre we delete v. 12a and regard the opening of v. 11 as possible, if not stricly grammatical,[c] and also delete 'rise' in v. 9a, we have a poem which outwardly appears to present no complications, though we must always remember that it contains imperatives in an Aramaic form.

If we try to define the literary category of the poem we must with some uncertainty regard it as a prophecy of warning without a reason, i.e. lacking a reproach. But we must not overlook the fact that the women addressed here as at ease and complacent are being implicitly reproached for what is in store. Of course excellent additional arguments can be found in other texts, such as 3.16ff. (cf. also Amos 6.1ff.), or from a comparison with v. 10 and v. 14, for the view that the women addressed are concerned only with festivities

[a] Cf. B. Stade, *ZAW* 4, pp. 266ff.; T. K. Cheyne, *Introduction to the Book of Isaiah*, London 1895, pp. 176ff., and especially pp. 178f.: Guthe and Marti, *ad loc.* For the present view, J. Vermeylen, *La composition littéraire du livre d'Isaïe, I–XXXIX*, Louvain 1970, p. 67, tells us: 'this pericope is usually attributed to Isaiah'.

[b] Cf. 5.6; 7.23ff.; 27.4.

[c] Cf. G-K, § 145t, but also W. Wright, *A Grammar of the Arabic Language*, revised ed. W. Robertson Smith and M. J. de Goeje II³, Cambridge, 1898 (1955), § 148.

such as were associated with the harvest, and by contrast to the poor lived in magnificent palaces. But since a passage within a prophetic text must be interpreted in the first instance and in the main on the basis of what it contains itself, these arguments must be regarded as imagination, something which a commentator must possess, but which he must not allow to swamp his text. In other words, we can only tell from the text that the women have no inkling of the events foretold, which of course they will not find enjoyable. It is this that makes it possible for the speaker to instruct them about what is to happen. That the women live in Jerusalem can be taken as reasonably certain from v. 14; that they themselves belonged to the people of Yahweh follows indirectly from the use of the expression 'my people' in v. 13, although we cannot be sure whether the ideal speaker is to be identified with Yahweh or with a human being. We could only be certain who the speaker was if we could establish that this prophecy of warning was closely related to the description of salvation which follows. There, according to v. 15a, the speaker is a human being, though it is noteworthy that he too speaks in v. 18 of 'my people'.[a]

As far as the authorship of the oracle is concerned, it can best be thought of as proclaimed on one of the squares by the city gates of Jerusalem or in the outer court of the temple. Certainly the attention of the women is artificially attracted by what is usually known nowadays as a 'didactic opening formula' (cf. 28.23, and especially Gen. 4.23).[b] Again, if the announcement that followed was taken seriously and not regarded as the utterance of a madman, it would have terrified them, but no more than any other gloomy prophecy about the future. It is of course possible to reintroduce the person of Isaiah, and assume that he was the prophet, and was known to the women listening to him, with all his great moral claims and religious views. In this case the oracle would have a religious meaning, drawing together the nation, its destiny and God himself. But the implications of this must be realized. The text itself makes no mention of such matters, and must be understood on the basis of what it contains itself, otherwise there is no end to the possible interpretations. In this case it cannot be regarded as composed by Isaiah, because a religious significance can be attributed to it only as a result of its position between 32.1–8 and 32.15ff.

[a] Cf. 5.13 and 22.4, where the prophet uses the term, with 1.3; 3.12, 15; 10.2, 24, where it is spoken by Yahweh.
[b] Cf. above p. 259.

Verses 1ff. make it clear that at the present time the age of the righteous king has not yet begun. Verses 15ff. look forward to the coming age of righteousness, bringing with it a condition of total salvation which includes nature. According to v. 15a it is to bring to an end the period of distress proclaimed in 32.9–14. As far as the content is concerned, it is clear that 32.1–8 can stand on its own, whereas 32.15ff. assumes the present passage, but also displays certain thematic links with 32.1ff. In other words, 32.9ff. were certainly included in the Isaiah roll later than 32.1ff. As the Aramaisms show, they are composed by a Jew who himself already seems to have spoken Aramaic, living at a period later than that of 24.7ff., which he tacitly reinterprets in order to give the necessary dark background to his prophecy of salvation. We are now faced with the problem of interpreting 32.9–14. Was the scribe who wrote the poem taking on himself the mantle of Isaiah in order to encourage his own community to believe that the time of salvation was imminent, by means of a *vaticinium ex eventu*, a prophecy of judgment looking back upon events that took place long ago? In particular, was he attempting in v. 14 to recall the destruction of Jerusalem in 587 (cf. Jer. 52.12f.; Micah 3.12 and 4.7)? *le⁽ōlām*, 'for ever', could indeed be regarded as a period which from the fictional date of the prophecy was incalculable. This would mean, oddly enough, that the apocalyptic author of the present passage did not share the view that Jerusalem faced a further visitation, a view constantly repeated from ch. 28 on; but this would make the mention of the time of the visitation in v. 10a superfluous. The fact that his prophecy shows similarities to 24.7ff., the content of which he tacitly makes even more gloomy, rules out this possibility. Instead, the connection between 29.1 and 32.10 suggests that the prophecy contains a seriously intended threat of a new siege and destruction of Jerusalem, such as is also assumed in Zech. 14.1f. We can hardly suppose that it expresses the conviction that the city will now be destroyed for ever, but must accept that 32.15ff. is by the same hand, and was originally meant to form the sequel to this prophecy of warning. That there is a formal unity, with a single speaker, is made more likely by the occurrence of 'my people' in v. 13 and v. 18, while the unity of content is most clearly seen by an exegesis of 32.9ff. which takes into account its stylistic devices and the purpose behind them. These considerations may seem complex, and they are certainly not simple. They are perhaps at first sight not obvious at all to a reader who has no experience of dating prophetic texts. How much easier it would be both for the reader and the commentator to imagine the prophet Isaiah among the daughters of his people, adorned and made up for a festival, and putting disturbing questions to women in whose lives the festivals formed the climax, and little else of note happened. This would present a vivid scene and would avoid our spending a lot of time on wide-ranging discussions. But it is perfectly possible for a book of Isaiah's prophecies which was transcribed in the course of centuries, and to which additions have demonstrably been made, to have received additions and interpolations where at first sight we should have least expected them. To identify them is to cast a little more light upon the religious history of Israel and Judaism, and to obtain a slightly clearer portrait of the prophet Isaiah by removing what has later come to overlay it. Perhaps both these tasks are worth the trouble of enquiry, thought and an attempt to understand the ideas of ancient writers – if it is true that the God of Israel, the God of Isaiah, the God of the men who wrote down his words and added their own words and sometimes those of others, is also the God of Jesus and is still our God.

[9] In a way reminiscent of Gen. 4.23, and in content, of Jer. 9.19, and similar too to what we find in the book of Isaiah in 28.23, the women and daughters of Jerusalem, who are described as in Amos 6.1 as at ease and complacent, are started out of their calm. They are called upon by someone who seeks, like a singer or a wisdom teacher, to attract their attention in order to tell them of a great misfortune which is to fall upon each and every one of them. [10] Within a period which cannot be exactly foretold, but which is to be fairly short,[a] their calm complacency will come to an end and they will shake with terror – because the wine and fruit harvests cannot take place, the agricultural year will bring nothing. Bearing in mind the great joy of this harvest time (cf. 16.10) and particularly that of the women (cf. Judg. 21.20f.; Deut. 16.13ff.)[b] one must agree that the poet has succeeded with great skill in confining considerable force of expression with oracular obscurity. The latter characteristic is found not only in the indication of time given at the beginning of v. 10

[a] The reference is clearly to the time when this begins, and not to the length of time for which they would tremble. 'Days to a year' can be understood either as 'in little more than a year' or, relating it to the use of *yāmīm*, 'days' with the meaning 'year', cf. Judg. 17.10; I Sam. 27.7 and Isa. 29.1 in the sense of 'in a few years'.

[b] Cf. F. Nötscher, *Biblische Altertumskunde*, Bonn 1940, pp. 182ff. and p. 186.

(cf. also 29.1) but also in the foretelling of the event which is to cause
the women's terror. For it remains completely obscure why the fruit
harvest will not or cannot take place. Of course one can assume from
vv. 13f. that it is acts of war which have led to the devastation of the
fields and gardens (cf. Jer. 6.6; Deut. 20.19f.)[a] and this is certainly
the poet's intention; but if these verses too are more closely examined,
we see that there again the cause is ultimately obscure. For all that is
really clear is that the fields and the city will be deserted. Thorns
and briars will grow upon deserted fields. Wild animals will roam.
Only if we were to translate $me^c\bar{a}r\bar{o}t$ by 'bare fields' would the passage
speak unequivocally of a violent destruction of the city. But here
again the way in which this is to happen is not mentioned, but left to
the reader to guess. The reader is obviously meant to think not of the
combined effect of all kinds of natural catastrophes, but of a military
attack upon the whole country. The keyword 'joy', which occurs in
vv. 13 and 14, shows that in the reason given in v. 10 for the terror of
the women, the poet is foretelling the end of joy. But in view of the
range of the catastrophe which is prophesied, this introductory
feature produces an effect which in spite of 24.11 and Lam. 5.15 is
somewhat strange and unrealistic. The troubles faced by the people
of a city which has suffered a comparable fate are shown by Lam.
1.11; 2.9–12, 20f.; 4.2–5, 7f., 10 and by 5.15 when seen against the
background provided by 5.8ff.

[11] Verse 11 is a very good example of the way in which the
Hebrews had to describe bodily reactions when they were referring to
emotions. Here we have a description of putting on mourning
garments. The stripping naked probably does not refer to taking off
everyday garments (cf. Gen. 37.29; II Sam. 1.11), much less to
taking off all one's clothes. More likely it means a baring of the breast
such as seems to be portrayed in the case of the mourning women on
the coffin of King Ahiram of Byblos[b] and has been observed even in
this century among Bedouin women.[c] That the bared breast was
struck is shown by v. 12a, which we suspect may be an addition. The
typical mourning garment was the sack, a coarse garment of hair
which the mourners wrapped round their loins (cf. II Sam. 3.31;

---

[a] Cf. also what Tiglathpilesar III tells in his annals of the cutting down of the
fruit trees before Damascus, AOT^2, p. 346.

[b] Cf. AOB^2, fig. 665.

[c] Cf. A. Musil, *The Manners and Customs of the Rwala Bedouins*, New York 1928,
p. 671.

Isa. 15.3 and 22.12).[a] **[12–14]** The poet calls the women to mourn
not for the death of their relatives, parents, brothers, husbands and
children, but for the fields which produced the precious and plentiful
harvest (cf. also Amos 5.11) and the vines (cf. 7.23; 16.9) and for the
whole country of the nation to which he himself belongs and which
he can therefore describe as 'my people' (cf. v. 18, and also 5.13;
22.4; Gen. 23.11). There thorns and briars will now flourish because
they will no longer be cultivated (cf. Gen. 3.18; Hos. 10.18; Isa. 5.6;
7.23ff.; 27.4). But there is cause for mourning not only in the fields
and gardens, but also in the city itself, in the contrast between its
former joyful noise and activity (cf. 24.8ff.; 5.11ff.; 22.2) and its
present abandonment. It is not only the palaces (cf. Jer. 6.5; 9.20 and
17.27) but the whole city which is deserted; on its ridge with its
great tower, rising between the temple hill and the city of David to
the south-east of it (cf. Neh. 3.27), the wild asses will take their
pleasure (cf. Job 39.5ff.) and the flocks will pasture (cf. 17.2; Zeph.
2.14; and also Isa. 13.21f.; 34.11ff.).

While the poet faces his hearers or readers (ultimately the fact that
the poem is addressed to women in particular must be taken as a
purely artificial device, intended to permit a more impressive
description of the mourning that was to come than if the imaginary
audience had been composed of men) he sets out to arouse appre-
hension only in order to make even greater the relief given by the
prophecy of salvation which follows.

CHAPTER 32.15–20

The Gifts of the Spirit

15 Until the Spirit from the height
      is poured upon us
    and the wilderness becomes a fruitful field,
      and ⟨the fruitful field⟩[b] is deemed a forest.

---

[a] But cf. also the bundle of clothes on the hips of the lamenting women on the
Ahiram sarcophagus, which has been interpreted as the sack, or as the upper part
of their clothing pulled down.
[b] Cf. *BHS*.

16   Then justice will dwell in the wilderness
        and righteousness abide in the fruitful field.
17   And the effect of righteousness will be peace,
        and the result of righteousness,[a] quietness and trust for ever.
18   My people will abide in a peaceful pasture
        in secure dwellings, and in quiet resting places.
19   And it will hail[b] when the forest falls,
        and the city will be utterly laid low.
20   Happy are you who sow beside all waters,
        who let the feet of the ox and the ass range free.

The opening words show that this description of salvation is not
regarded as a unity on its own but is meant to be interpreted in a
close relationship with the prophecy of warning in 30.9–14. When
we studied that oracle, we saw that both were probably interpolated
into the Isaiah roll by the same hand. They are the work of a scribe
who wished to encourage his community to look beyond the distress
of the imminent final age to the time of salvation which would follow,
when the Spirit of God would transform this earth into a paradise
and would finally teach men to live together in righteousness and in
peace, thus bringing an end to the sufferings of Israel in history. The
agricultural realism of his hopes is immediately evident in the
concluding verse, which makes clear both that the age of salvation
will be a time of fruitfulness, of the righteousness of peace, but will
nevertheless be a reality in which work itself continues. The scriptural
learning displayed in this description of salvation is shown by the
way it constantly borrows the very words of other prophecies of
salvation, particularly from the book of Isaiah. The last verse, however, brings a comparatively original feature. The only doubt about
the unity of the oracle arises from the fact that v. 19 seems to come
somewhat awkwardly between vv. 18 and 20, for it describes an
event which chronologically ought to come between v. 14 and v. 15.
It has been suggested that it is a marginal gloss upon v. 14 which was
later incorporated into the text at the wrong place,[c] or, more
probably, a later interpolation.[d] But we cannot be sure that the scribe
did not intend to supply a contrast to the future salvation of his

[a] In so late a text one should be cautious in making emendations.

[b] The more difficult reading, which is also found in 1Q Isa is also supported by the
fact that it is a hapax legomenon.

[c] Duhm and Marti.

[d] Fohrer.

nation, and to make clear why in future it would be safe, by referring
to the fall of the world power that was to take place at the beginning
of the age of salvation. In this way he completes the picture drawn
in his short apocalypse, 32.9–20. Consequently, the emendations of
literary criticism are best avoided here. The dependence or relationship of this apocalypse to texts such as 29.17ff.; 30.19ff. makes it
sufficiently clear that it was composed in a late post-exilic Hellenistic
period. The experience of post-exilic Judaism underlying it, that we
men cannot bring about our own salvation, but are dependent upon
the Spirit of God who brings salvation about, ought not to be dismissed without further thought at a period in which even Christians
are dominated by confidence in man's technical ability to control the
future and to improve the world by education. Precisely because this
text does not in the end exclude human activity it leads us to consider the difference between the future of our salvation which is in the
hands of God, and the possible improvements in human society which
we are called upon to make. One must of course remember that we
are not only imperfect and prey to evil, but also mortal. The apostle's
statement that the wages of sin is death presents us with some
difficulties, but we may perhaps realize that the fear expressed in our
inability to achieve peace and righteousness is the consequence of sin,
and is a fear of death. If we understand this, we can assume the
question of how a better and more just world is to be achieved by
pointing to our hope in God, who is not the God of the dead but of the
living (cf. Mark 12.17), or by another question, whether we are able
to join in the rejoicing of I Cor. 15.55ff. which brings us face to face
once again with the mystery of the Spirit.

[15] The transformation in the history of Israel, after the distress
of the last tribulation of Jerusalem (cf. 32.9ff.), is brought about by
the Spirit from the height, who will be poured out upon us, that is,
upon the community with whom the scribe regards himself as one.
mārōm, the high place, usually means the high place in the absolute
sense, heaven (cf. 40.26; 24.21), and refers particularly to heaven as
the dwelling place of God (cf. II Sam. 22.17; Ps. 144.7; Jer. 25.30;
Isa. 57.15; 33.5; 38.14). The description of Zion as the 'high place',
the place of the manifestation of Yahweh, seems to be secondary
(cf. Jer. 31.12). The custom of speaking of God as the God of the
height, or in the height (cf. Micah. 6.6; Ps. 93.4; Luke 2.14), led to
the possibility of speaking of Yahweh or of God figuratively as 'the
height' (Ps. 75.6; Isa. 58.4). Thus in the present passage the Spirit

coming from the height is the Spirit poured out by God, a conception which by way of Joel 3.1 has found its way into the New Testament narrative of Pentecost (cf. Acts. 2.1ff., 15ff.). The Spirit of God is not only nor even primarily an intellectual phenomenon, but one intimately linked with life (cf. Ps. 104.29f.; Isa. 31.3). Because it is the characteristic life force of God, which according to early conceptions was manifested in breath, and as such is also his will (cf. 30.1), purpose and understanding (cf. Ps. 139.7),[a] its effects are correspondingly wide-ranging, and extend from the bestowal of life itself (cf. Ps. 104.29f.) to the faculties of knowledge, will and activity (cf. 11.1ff.; Judg. 3.10) and include even the gift of prophecy (cf. Num. 11.24ff.). In so far as it is beyond the control of man, as of every creature, and yet seeks to be acknowledged by him in its dignity and purpose, it is known as the Holy Spirit, a term which in the Old Testament we find only in Ps. 51.13 and Isa. 63.10. The pouring out of the Spirit, an imparting of divine power which no opposing force can resist, is therefore a characteristic of the age of salvation. It brings about a miraculous increase in the vital force of Israel (cf. 44.3f.) and bestows upon the people of God either obedience, without which there can be no salvation (cf. Ezek. 36.26f., and also Ezek. 39.29), or else a direct relationship to God such as the prophets possess (cf. Joel 3.1f.).[b] The scribe and apocalyptic thinker who writes here looks forward to almost all this. He foresees the replacement of the devastation of the fields in the final age (cf. 32.12f.; 10.18) by an increase in fruitfulness which was hitherto unknown, but which was already expected by the second Isaiah. As a result of this the deserts would be transformed into orchards and the orchards to forests (cf. in the first place the almost literal parallel in 29.17 and secondly 41.18; 43.20; 35.1f., 6f., as well as Joel 2.22ff.).

[16–18] Verse 16 may be intended simply to emphasize that there will be no end to the new fruitfulness, since for Old Testament thought fruitfulness and the righteousness of men are linked (cf. Ps. 72; Isa. 11.1–9). In this concept justice and righteousness seem almost to be independent saving forces (cf. 45.8 and Ps. 85.12). But the ideas assumed and taken for granted as the basis of the present passage show, and the continuation in v. 17 confirms, that here a complete correspondence is intended between fruitfulness and righteousness. If the author did not have in mind the events brought about by the

---

[a] The fact that *rūᵃḥ*, spirit, can also stand for 'I' is shown by Gen. 6.3.
[b] Cf. A. Weiser, ATD 24, ⁵1967, and H. W. Wolff, BK 14. 2, 1969, *ad loc.*

pouring out of the one Spirit of God, one would be tempted to regard
v. 16 as the reason for the promise in v. 15b, and to see the new
fruitfulness as the consequence of the new righteousness. But the
scribe sees things the other way round; he thinks first of the new
possibility of life bestowed by God and then of the new human society
set up in the midst of a transformed nature, a society now characterized by righteousness. Only then does he turn to consider, in v. 17,
the effects of righteousness, consisting of the free and untroubled
existence and unhindered progress of men, animals and fields, in
all-embracing peace and prosperity, šālōm, and secondly in the quiet
confidence of men towards their God (cf. 30.15) and security in the
relationship between men and their fellow men, men and animals,
and animals and other animals (cf. Ezek. 34.25ff.; Deut. 33.28 and
Isa. 11.1–9). Thus Israel, referred to here as in v. 13 as 'my people',
will in the end be able to dwell in peace, unconcern and security, a
situation which in the period before the beginning of the final threat to
Jerusalem and the Holy Land could only be imagined as a present
reality if one deceived oneself (cf. 32.9ff., and for individual expressions also 33.20; 60.21 and 28.12).

[19] Verse 19 has caused commentators much bewilderment,
because it consists entirely of allusions.[a] It has actually been proposed
to relate it to the events prophesied in vv. 13f. and to see the forest as
the wildness, haughtiness and pride displayed in Judaea; together
with Jerusalem these will be annihilated in the imminent divine
judgment.[b] The poet or glossator would in this case be repeating
indirectly the ideas of 1.21–26. But was such an emphasis necessary
following vv. 16 and 17? More recently, v. 19 has been regarded as a
very general antithesis to the statements in the two previous verses:
although forests fall and cities decline, Judah will nevertheless be
protected henceforth from natural catastrophes and from enemies.[c]
The verse would then be a further emphasis upon what is stated in
vv. 17f. But it is questionable whether the apocalyptic author thought
that in the age of salvation there would be peace in Judaea but
further upheaval elsewhere in nature and in history. There is nothing
in his poem to suggest this. Thus we must retain the interpretation
suggested long ago, that the forest destroyed by the hail is in fact the
enemy army, which has overwhelmed the city of God (cf. 10.33f., 18;

[a] Cf. Feldmann, pp. 384f.
[b] Cf. Dillmann-Kittel, ad loc.
[c] Kissane, ad loc.

30.30) while the city itself is the world capital which is the source of all hostility towards the people of God and the city of God (cf. 25.1ff.; 27.10). Behind this lies the conception of Yahweh's mighty theophany of judgment, as is shown by the reminiscences of 2.12ff. As long as the world power, or, as we can put it, the world powers triumph, there can be no hope of the peace to which the apocalyptic author and his community look forward, and not they alone, but all men.

[20] The devout author concludes his promise by wishing good fortune (cf. 30.18) to his community, who he is clearly convinced will experience the beginning of the age of salvation – or rather, in view of vv. 9ff., some of them will. In an image which is instantly clear to a farmer he gives yet another picture the age of salvation, when the seed will grow in such profusion beside the waters which now flow abundantly (cf. 30.23ff.) that the draught animals which would otherwise have been fed in their stalls can be allowed to walk across the fields and pasture there, an idea which is clearly meant to go beyond 30.24.

CHAPTER 33.1–24

The Inauguration of the Kingdom

1 Woe to you, destroyer, who yourself have not been destroyed;
     you treacherous one, ⟨with whom⟩[a] none has dealt
          treacherously!
   When you have completed[b] destroying[c] you will be
          destroyed;[d]
   and when you have ⟨concluded⟩[e] dealing treacherously,[c]
     you will be dealt with treacherously.

---

a Cf. *BHS*.
b For the form cf. G-K, § 53v or B-L, § 58p′ p. 439.
c For the construction cf. G-K, § 120b.
d For the form cf. G-K, § 53u or B-L, § 38m′ p. 286.
e With B-L, § 59e p. 442 *kanᵉlōtᵉkā* and cf. Ges. – Buhl [17] sub voce *nlh*.

2   Yahweh, be gracious to us; we wait for thee.
    Be ⟨our⟩ᵃ arm every morning,
    our salvation in the time of trouble.

3   At the thunderous noise peoples flee,
    at thy cryᵇ nations are scattered;ᶜ

4   and ⟨spoil⟩ is gathered ⟨as⟩ᵃ the locust gathers;
    as the grasshopper leaps men leap upon it.ᵈ

5   Yahweh is exalted, for he dwells in the height,
    he will fill Zion with justice and righteousness;

6   and your times will be stable,
    abundance of salvation, wisdom, and knowledge;
    the fear of Yahweh is ⟨your⟩ᵉ treasure.

7   Behold the ⟨warriors⟩ᶠ cry without;
    the envoys of peace weep bitterly.

8   The highways lie waste, no one travelsᵍ
    He breaks the treaty, despises ⟨the witnesses⟩,ᵃ
    has no regard for man.

9   The earth ⟨dries up⟩ᵃ and languishes;
    Lebanon is confounded and withers away;
    Sharon is like a desert;
    and Bashan and Carmel stand bare.

10 Now I will arise, says Yahweh,
    now I will lift myself up,ʰ now I will be exalted.

11 You conceive hay, you bring forth stubble;
    ⟨a wind like a fire⟩ᵃ will consume you.

12 And the peoples will be burned to lime,
    like thorns cut down, they will be burned in the fire.

ᵃ Cf. *BHS*.

ᵇ Read *mērimmātīkā*, cf. *BHS* and C. Bezold, *Babylonisch-Assyrisches Glossar*, ed. A. Götze, Heidelberg 1926, p. 256, sub voce *remmatu*.

ᶜ For the different possible ways of interpreting this form cf. G-K, § 67dd.

ᵈ The expression has been simplified. For the form taken by *maššaq*, cf. B-L, § 61k, p. 491.

ᵉ Read *'ōṣār°kā*.

ᶠ The ancient versions have restored the text as well as they could, 1QIsa, apparently like Aq, Sym and Th, reads *'ērā'*'ēlām, 'I will appear to them'. Since Cheyne, *Introduction*, p. 107, but cf. before him Delitzsch *ad loc.*, an allusion has usually been thought to exist to 29.1, giving the reading 'men of Ariel', followed by *šālēm*, 'Salem', and this is followed most recently by Fohrer, whereas Eichrodt reads simply Ariel. Delitzsch, followed recently by B. Mazar, *VT* 13, 1963, p. 316, note 2 referred to II Sam. 23.20; I Chron. 11.22 and translated 'warriors'. – Read a simple plural with *BHS*.

ᵍ Literally: 'The wayfarer ceases'.

ʰ For the form of M, which corresponds to that of 1QIsa, cf. B-L, § 56u″ p. 405.

13   Those who are far off ⟨will hear⟩ᵃ what I have done
       and those who are near, ⟨will acknowledge⟩ᵃ my might.

14   The sinners in Zion shudder,
       trembling has seized the godless.
     Who among us can dwell with the devouring fire?
     Who among us can dwell with everlasting burnings?
15   He who walks righteously and speaks uprightly;
       he who despises the gain of oppressions,
     who shakes his hands, not to take a bribe,
       who stops his earsᵇ from hearing of bloodshed,
       and shuts his eyes from looking upon evil.
16   He will dwell on the heights;
       his place of defense will be the fortresses of rocks;
       his bread will be given him, his water will be sure.

17   Your eyes will see the king in his beauty
       they will behold a land that stretches afar.ᶜ
18   Your mind will muse on the terror.
     Where is he who counted, where is he who weighed?
     *Where is he who counted the towers?*ᵈ
19   You will see no more the insolent people,
       the people of an obscure and incomprehensible speech,
       stammering in a tongue that cannot be understood.

20   Look upon Zion, the city of our appointed feasts!
       Your eyes will see Jerusalem,
       a quiet habitation, an immovable tent
     whose stakes will never be plucked up,
       nor will any of its cords be broken.

ᵃ Cf. *BHS.*   ᵇ Singular in the text.

ᶜ This verse has been found difficult by commentators. Following Marti, and with him H. Gunkel, 'Jesaja 33, eine prophetische Liturgie', *ZAW* 42, 1924, p. 179, and recently Fohrer, it is usual to read *miklal yopī*, a consummation of beauty, and since *'ereṣ marḥaqqīm*, elsewhere means a distant country, to read in accordance with the context *'ereṣ maḥᵃmaddīm*, the land of precious things. At the same time it is pointed out that there is no mention of a king until v. 22, and beside him there seems to be no place for a human, whereas to speak of the divine king here would be from the poetic point of view an unskilful anticipation. As it is not impossible that we have here the result of a later redaction, I retain the received text in M.

ᵈ Here again there are many conjectures, cf. Duhm, *ad loc.*, who proposes *'ē ṭipsār 'et-hamminzārīm*, 'where is the prefect with the taxpayers', cf. Neh. 3.17 or Gunkel, who proposes *mᵉgādīm*, the best products of the land, cf. e.g. Deut. 33.13ff., but I follow Fohrer in supposing that we have here a secondary gloss, which of course looks back to 22.10.

21   For ⟨there will be a glorious name⟩ᵃ for us,
    a ⟨source⟩ᵇ of broad streams,
  where no galley with oars can go,
    nor stately ship can pass.

22   For Yahweh is our judge, Yahweh is our ruler,
  Yahweh is our king; he will save us.

23   ⟨His⟩ᶜ rigging hangs loose; it cannot hold the
    mast firm,
    or keep the sail spread out.
  Then ⟨the blind will divide⟩ᶜ spoil in abundance,
    the lame will take booty.
  And no inhabitant will say, I am sick;
    the people who dwell there will be forgiven their iniquity.

The reader who approaches this chapter for the first time without any experience of reading the Psalms and the eschatological redactions of the prophetic books may well take in the main outlines of its content. He will understand that it speaks of a powerful enemy who has risen up against Jerusalem, and of the ultimate destruction of that enemy, to be followed by the glorification of Jerusalem. But he will nevertheless be confused by the changing aspects and speakers, and will be irritated by the partial obscurity which is found in some of the statements. But even an experienced reader, well acquainted with the Old Testament, will find constant difficulties, and will wonder whether he has understood correctly what he has read, whether the received text is reliable and whether individual themes have been accurately interpreted. The prophecy begins with a proclamation of woe in v. 1. But the person at whom the warning is directed is described in such general terms that all we learn of him in the whole passage is that he is now terrible and will fall in the future. We will see later that here the poet has given us as it were the *leitmotif* and theme for the rest of the poem. Verse 2 brings a change of direction, and the poet addresses Yahweh in the name of his community. It can easily be demonstrated that he is drawing here upon the tradition of the collective lamentation, the lamentation of the people.ᵈ A short petition derived from

   ᵃ With Marti, Guthe, etc., delete *'im*, and instead of *šām*, there, read *šem*, name; and instead of *yhwh* read *yihᵉyē*.
   ᵇ With Marti, who is followed by most subsequent commentators, read *mᵉqōr*, instead of *mᵉqōm*, place, and delete the word *nᵉhārīm*, streams, which follows as an interpretative gloss upon the next word, *yᵉ'ōrīm*, which means 'the Nile'.
   ᶜ Cf. *BHS*.
   ᵈ Cf. Gunkel, *ZAW* 42, pp. 190ff. – The link with the conceptual world of the

Ps. 123.3 is followed by a brief expression of trust and the petition proper. It is obvious that the distress from which Yahweh is to deliver the people is caused by the destroyer in the previous verse. Verse 3 occupies an unusual intermediate position between a profession of confidence and an answer to the lamentation: Yahweh is addressed as in the profession of confidence, but in substance the statement is addressed to the petitioners, the community, for whose consolation the whole poem is intended.ᵃ Without any further digression, there-fore, v. 4 goes on to a description of salvation which is followed in v. 5 with a prophecy of salvation, introduced by divine predicates in the style of a hymn, and continued in v. 6. Verse 6 also brings the intro-duction of wisdom material into the poem.

In v. 7 the setting changes, and we are brought back from the future of well-being and prosperity into the miseries of the present day, described in lamentable terms down to v. 9. This gives us an impressionistic picture, picking out individual features, of the activity of the destroyer from whom the poet begged, affirmed and promised deliverance by God, with and on behalf of his community. In v. 10, Yahweh himself speaks, giving an oracle of salvation which extends to the end of v. 13.

Following the opening statement that he will now intervene – the introductory words are taken from Ps. 12.6 – he speaks in v. 11 to unknown persons whom we can associate with the activity of the destroyer, and who represent many nations (cf. v. 3 and v. 12). God promises the total destruction of his enemies and, in v. 13, the resultant revelation of his power throughout the world. This gives us as it were the keyword, the substance of which is taken up in vv. 14–16: even for the people of God the revelation of the full power and strength of God raises problems, because this people consists not only of the devout but also of sinners. The return of the victorious God to Zion (cf. Pss. 24 and 50.1ff.), his epiphany which is to take place in burning fire, signifies the end of everyone who approaches Zion un-worthily. Thus in v. 14b we hear the chorus of the pilgrims demand-ing admission at the entry to the Temple, and in vv. 15 and 16 the entry *tōrāh* is pronounced (cf. Pss. 15 and 24.3ff.). Of course the reader must not overlook the fact that the scene takes place in the

---

enthronement psalms has been shown by S. Mowinckel, *Psalmenstudien* II, Kristiania 1922, pp. 235ff.

ᵃ Cf. Weiser, ATD 14/15, pp. 44ff.; ET *The Psalms*, OTL, 1962, pp. 84f.

future, and therefore possesses a didactic and exhortatory character in its present application. The poet's community are now to live in such a way that in the future they will have access to Zion and to their God, and therefore to the salvation which he has brought about and will not be judged.[a] In three separate statements the poet portrays the coming glory of Jerusalem after its liberation, and emphasizes that the power before which his community trembles will in fact be conquered by God's help and that we men have consequently cause to tremble before God but not before men. In the description of salvation in vv. 17–18, as well as at the beginning of the following vv. 20–21, the community is addressed in the second person singular, which in v. 21 changes to the first person plural, without causing any difficulty to the reader; the description of salvation once again takes upon features of a profession of confidence, into which it develops in v. 22, by way of providing a reason and basis for the description. The final stanza in vv. 23 and 24 is to our taste an anticlimax after v. 22. This does not of course mean that it is secondary. It should rather be regarded as an intentional development of the theme of spoil in v. 4, which now by association presents an opportunity to proclaim that the beginning of the age of salvation will bring with it the end of all disease. This in its turn assumes that wickedness is forgiven. Thus the naïve dramatic trait of a promise of spoil is once again incorporated into a religious theme in the narrower sense, adding a profound underlying note to the poem.

It is certain that in the background of the poem is formed by the oracle of salvation given as an answer to a lamentation. Similarly the entry *tōrāh* and the connection which it probably possessed with the ideas of wisdom teaching has influenced the poem. And yet, as is shown by the impossibility of ascribing vv. 2–6 and 20–22 unequivocally and convincingly to two different choirs, the passage is not a true liturgy, with a set alternation between individual voices and choruses, but a short apocalypse which makes free use of the traditional form, and which reveals its late composition by its learned use of scripture, which is not limited to direct quotations but extends to an adroit application of the set themes of various categories of psalm. It is difficult to fix the exact date, since we cannot tell whether the destroyer who broke agreements is an ideal or a real figure. In view of the fact that v. 14a seems to refer to a group within Judaism, by

---

[a] Cf. also Weiser, ATD 14/15, p. 21 and pp. 30ff.; ET pp. 47 and 64f.

contrast to the whole community in v. 2 and v. 22, and because of the use of scripture quotations, the most likely date is in the Hellenistic period, although it is uncertain whether v. 18b refers to the tribute collectors of the Ptolemies or of the Seleucids.[a]

[1] *The violence and the fall of the tyrant*. This proclamation of woe places us in the final age of a history which has consisted of conflict between the nations and their hostility to Yahweh and his people, and proclaims the end of the destroyer. As we see from Hab. 2.5, and also from Isa. 16.4a and 21.2,[b] the term refers to the leader of the nations who at that time will rage over the earth, destroying and annihilating, and will finally storm against the city of God itself. Thus he corresponds exactly to the figure of Gog from the land of Magog in Ezek. 38f. As in 21.2 he is also called the 'false one', because no agreements can be made with him (cf. v. 8b) and no reliable relations can be established with him (cf. 24.16).[a] An unconquered enemy whom no nation of the earth has succeeded in outwitting will conclude his work of destruction by casting to the ground the entire known world of the nations in an uninterrupted series of victories, and will then fall himself. The mysterious paraphrase of what is to happen in the future indicates that these events will be monstrous and will be far beyond the normal measure of historical events. Throughout the poem the name of the enemy is not given. The pseudonym tells us all that needs to be told about him. That he will meet his end before Jerusalem will be understood by everyone who is familiar with the conceptions of the tempest of the nations against Zion, and its marvellous deliverance, and this includes the reader or hearer of the book of Isaiah, who will recall 17.12ff., 29.1ff.; 30.27ff. and perhaps even 32.9ff., not to speak of Hab. 2.5ff. or even Ezek. 38f.

[2–6] *Yahweh's help*. The attention is naturally drawn from the future affliction to the God who can and will help when it is taking place, to Yahweh, who is addressed in words taken from Ps. 123.3 (cf. Pss. 4.2; 6.3; 31.10) and in whom confidence is once again expressed in words reminiscent of the Psalms (cf. Pss. 25.21; 25.5; 33.22; 39.8 and Isa. 25.9; 26.8). When the apocalyptic poet begs him on behalf of the community to be their arm every morning, we

---

[a] Cf. e.g. Marti, *ad loc.*

[b] The title is given in Jer. 25.36; 47.4 and 51.55f. to Yahweh as the executor of the eschatological judgment.

[c] Cf. also Judg. 9.23; I Sam. 14.33; Hos. 5.7; 6.7; Mal. 2.10; Ps. 78.57 and 119.158.

quickly perceive that the early morning is the time when battle begins. We recall that the waves of the enemy are to dash morning after morning against Jerusalem (cf. 28.19) and that in the end Yahweh is to destroy the hostile enemy before daybreak in front of the gates of Jerusalem (cf. 27.14; Ps. 46.6 and also Isa. 29.7ff.).[a] Since the people of Judah have no effective army of their own, they are entirely dependent upon the help of God, who will place at their disposal his arm in battle. Thus at the very end of the Old Testament we find Yahweh once again as the warrior who fights for his people (cf. Ex. 14.14) and for his arm (Ps. 89.14; Isa. 40.10; 51.5, 9; and 52.10). The psalmist had already praised him for his daily help (cf. Ps. 68.20) while a prayer from wisdom circles testifies that he will not let the righteous be put to shame in the time of distress (cf. Ps. 37.19, 39; and also Jer. 14.8; 15.11). The poet speaks mysteriously of the flight[b] of the nations before the thunderous noise. It is obvious that this time the noise does not proceed from the nations (cf. 17.12; 13.4; Ezek. 23.42) but from Yahweh (cf. Dan. 10.6), because the poet goes on to proclaim the future deliverance, strengthening by his demonstration of trust the link between God and his people. That Yahweh's cry consists of his voice in the thunder can be concluded from the tradition (cf. also 17.13; 29.6; 30.30).[c] If the poet is thinking in realistic terms of the rich spoil on which the people of Jerusalem could cast themselves like grasshoppers and locusts on meadowland, this would be quite in accordance with the feelings of a nation which had been under subjection for centuries and yet was still full of a living inner hope (cf. Ps. 76.6; Hab. 2.8; Ezek. 39.10; Isa. 53.12). Verse 1 does not rule out the possibility that the apocalyptic author followed Zech. 14.1 and Isa. 32.9ff. (cf. also Ezek. 38.12f. and Isa. 10.6) in expecting that his own people would be plundered first, and therefore looked forward to a change in circumstances such as is described in v. 1. The fact that he chose a plague of locusts as his metaphor must be primarily due to his own personal experience of such a plague, but also to its power to indicate complete helplessness (cf. not only Amos 7.1f. but also Joel 1.1ff.). By contrast to the teeming throng conjured up by v. 4, the epithets attributed to

[a] Cf. J. Ziegler, 'Gottes Hilfe am Morgen' in *Alttestamentliche Studien. Festschrift F. Nötscher*, BBB1, 1950, pp. 281ff. and F. Stolz, *Strukturen und Figuren im Kult von Jerusalem*, BZAW 118, 1970, pp. 214f.

[b] Cf. Ps. 68.2, 13.

[c] Cf. above, p. 88 note b.

Yahweh, in the style of a hymn, which begin v. 5, emphasize his transcendence over the world by stressing his actual height above the earth (cf. 2.11, 17 and 32.15). By an allusion to 1.21 the poet assures us that this God, who stands above all earthly intrigues, will once again make Jerusalem the dwelling place of justice and righteousness and therefore of all-embracing salvation.

Verse 6a presents a rather odd ʹappearance between vv. 5 and 6b, and in addition lacks any parallel in the Old Testament, but it cannot with certainty be explained as a later interpolation. For devout Israelites stable times could of course only be times which are in Yahweh's hands (cf. Ps. 31.16). Verse 5b sounds like a maxim borrowed from a different context of wisdom teaching. It describes wisdom and knowledge (cf. Eccles. 1.16; 2.21 and also Isa. 47.10) which are defined wholly in the sense of Prov. 1.4 as the fear of Yahweh, as the treasure of salvation, of divine help (cf. Ps. 74.12 and Prov. 15.6). In this way the apocalyptic poet gives an assurance that God will not only annihilate the destroyer in the end but will also henceforth grant his people a blessed future sustained by their fear of God. The dramatic expectation of spoil is surpassed by that of a life in righteousness and the fear of Yahweh in the new Jerusalem. The intrinsic connection between the two can be seen from a study of 11.1ff.

[7–9] *The rule of the tyrant.* The three verses that follow describe in a few bold strokes what will take place in the country as the destroyer advances. In this way they look back behind the promise of divine help to the figure of the destroyer in v. 1. Although the situation is not indicated, we are surely correct in seeing v. 7 through the eyes of an inhabitant of Jerusalem who was expecting the tempest of the army of the nations to descend (cf. also 10.27bff.).[a] The parallel between the warriors and the envoys of peace (cf. also 52.7) and the indication that the former are crying and the latter weeping bitterly outside, i.e. no doubt as in II Chron. 33.15f. before the walls,[b] suggests that a single event is being described. We can perhaps assume that the poet is thinking of a lost battle and of the failure of the peace negotiations offered immediately afterwards: the victor does not want peace, but unconditional surrender. The cries of the fled warriors and of the

---

[a] It is necessary to enquire whether this text is really to be explained on the basis of Isaiah's period, or should not be regarded an eschatological itinerary of the enemy.

[b] Cf. in addition Matt. 26.75.

negotiators sent in vain indicate to the inhabitants what is awaiting them. The advance of the destroyer with his army of nations has already brought all travel to a standstill, because no one dares to go out on the highway (cf. Judg. 5.6; Jer. 6.25 and also Jer. 9.9, 12; Zech. 7.14). The further statement in v. 8 that the destroyer breaks treaties (cf. I Kings 15.19; II Chron. 16.23; Ezek. 17.15ff.)[a] and rejects the witnesses to it (cf. Jer. 32.10, 25, 44; Isa. 8.2; Josh. 24.22f.) does not assume that any kind of treaty relationship existed between him and the people of Jerusalem. Verse 7a even suggests that this was not the case. What we have is probably a characterization of the man which is meant to make clear the hopeless situation of Jerusalem: this is the kind of man he is! No one can make a treaty with him, because he breaks it, rejects the statement of the witnesses who were present when the treaty was made and in any case holds people in contempt.[b]

We need only mention in passing that v. 9 gives us no indication of the time of year when the attack took place; because of the falling leaves older interpreters took it that it was in the autumn.[c] It remains of course open to question whether the drought that had broken out upon the earth, the drying up of the woods and meadows, should be regarded as nature's response to the violence of the destroyer or as the consequence of his attack, the latter apparently being assumed in Hab. 2.17 (cf. also Nahum 1.4; Joel 1.12; Isa. 24.7, 4; Jer. 14.1; 23.10; Hos. 4.3; Amos 1.2 and Jer. 4.28; 12.4). The listing of the areas of Palestine affected, first Lebanon in the north and then the plain of Sharon in the centre of the west coast south of Carmel,[d] and finally the land of Bashan east of the Jordon, famed for its patures,[e] and finally Carmel itself[f] (cf. also Nahum 1.4) is also unusual. It is probably once again a hidden allusion to the theme of the enemy from the north (cf. Jer. 1.13ff.; 4.6; 6.1, 22; 10.22; 13.10; Isa. 14.31)[g] but also gives us an impression of the scale of the enemy advance, extending across the whole country (cf. 8.8).

[a] The parallel statements concerning the covenant with Yahweh are not relevant here, cf. e.g. Gen. 17.14; Deut. 31.16, 20; Jer. 11.10; Ezek. 16.59 and Zech. 11.10.

[b] For ḥšb cf. also W. Schottroff, *THAT* I, col. 644.

[c] This is also the view of Delitzsch.

[d] Cf. K. Elliger, *BHW* III, col. 1673f.

[e] Cf. e.g. Deut. 32.14; Amos 4.1; Ezek. 39.18 and H. J. Boecker, *BHW* I, col. 203f.

[f] Cf. G. Sauer, *BHW* II, col. 934f.

[g] Cf. also above, pp. 54f.

[10–13] *Yahweh's intervention.* In the face of the most acute distress, and the irresistible and incessant onrush of the army of the nations against Jerusalem (cf. v. 2f.), Yahweh considers that the moment for his intervention has come (cf. Ps. 12.6; Deut. 10.35; Pss. 68.2; 3.8; and also Pss. 94.2 and 7.7). In the interests of the image that follows, the vanity of the enemy's purpose is compared to a pregnancy and birth of hay (cf. 5.24) and straw (cf. also 26.17f.). The enemy army delivers itself up with its leaders to its ruin, thus as it were providing the material with which it is burnt (cf. also 5.24; Joel 2.5; Nahum 1.10 and Isa. 30.33). In the context of an address by God there is no question as to who will bring this about. It is naturally Yahweh's fiery breath and his lightnings flashing down upon the attackers (cf. 29.6 and 30.27, 30, 33). When they are burnt to lime, no remnant of them remains in its original setting; the souls of the dead find no dwelling place which holds them together and they therefore dissolve and are brought to an immediate and total end (cf. Amos 2.1 and Isa. 14.18ff.).[a] That this means a complete annihilation of the attackers is also shown by the final comparison with thorn branches cut off and thrown into the fire (cf. Ps. 118.12; Isa. 9.17 and, for the idea, Jer. 51.58). That so mighty an event as the destruction of the nations advancing under the leadership of the destroyer cannot remain hidden, but is bound to reveal the power of Yahweh to the whole of mankind, can be taken for granted, but, as the conclusion of the divine oracle of warning addressed to the nations, it is explicitly stated by Yahweh (cf. Jer. 7.12; Ezek. 39.21), the terms 'far off' and 'near' standing for all mankind. By using the common pair of concepts 'the near and the far' in reverse order,[b] the poet is preparing the way for the following stanza.

[14–16] *The conditions of participation in salvation.* It is the people of Jerusalem, as those most directly affected, upon whom the mighty act of God makes the most powerful impression. Inevitably all those who have no longer observed the divine will will seriously be afraid and will ask trembling (cf. Pss. 15.1; 48.7) what will become of them. The God who has destroyed the enemy with his fire is now present in Jerusalem and is a devouring fire (cf. Deut. 4.24; 9.3, and also Ps. 50.3; Ex. 19.18; I Kings 19.12). This was no doubt conceived by the

---

[a] Cf. R. de Vaux, *Institutions* I, Paris 1958, p. 94; ET *Ancient Israel. Its Life and Institutions*, London and New York 1961, p. 56; H. W. Wolff, BK 14.2, *ad loc.*, disagrees, but is not convincing. On this topic see also above, p. 41.

[b] Cf. Deut. 13.8; Jer. 25.26; Dan. 9.7 and Esth. 9.20.

apocalyptic poet in a similar way to Ezek. 43.2ff. Their questions, which coincide with the words of those who seek access into the sanctuary (cf. Pss. 15.1; 24.3), find an answer which points not to all kinds of cultic demands but to the social loyalty which stands at the heart of all Old Testament religion, that of righteousness (cf. Ps. 15.2a; Prov. 10.9; 14.2). This is displayed in truthful utterances (cf. Ps. 15.2b; Prov. 23.16; Isa. 26.7), the renunciation of profit from oppression (cf. Lev. 19.13; 5.21ff. Ex. 18.21; Micah 2.2; Hab. 2.9 and Ezek. 22.27), the rejection of bribes in legal actions (cf. Ps. 15.5b; Ex. 23.8; Deut. 10.17; 16.19; 27.25; Prov. 17.23ff.; Isa. 1.23; 5.23) and also, of course, a refusal to take part in any plans for murder (cf. Prov. 21.13; IQH VII. 3; Isa. 1.15)[a] and the avoidance of evil in general (cf. IQH VII. 2f. and also Isa. 29.10; Ps. 119.37 and Hab. 1.3). For the righteous there are as it were fortresses in the rock on high mountains, in which he is protected from all troubles (cf. Pss. 144.2; 9.10; 46.8, 12; 59.10 and 94.22, and in which he will lack neither food nor drink (cf. 30.20; Pss. 111.5; 145.15f.; 65.10; 30.25 and Deut. 28.3ff.; 30.9f.; Lev. 26.3ff.). It is hard to tell how far the poet was thinking of actual life in the liberated Jerusalem with its new supplies of water, and how far his generalizing expressions led him and his ideas into abstractions.

[17–19] *The ruler of the age of salvation.* Ignoring the question of whether v. 17 is original, we are still faced with the difficult decision whether the vision of the king foretold at the beginning of the description of salvation which opens with this verse is a divine manifestation or a vision of the Messiah. In support of the latter possibility one can refer to Ps. 45.3ff. with its description of the beauty of the young king, and also to the principle that anyone who sees God dies (cf. Ex. 33.20; Isa. 6.5). On the other hand the emphatic praise of God as King in v. 22 argues against this interpretation. We should also draw attention to IV Esdras 7.98; Matt. 5.8 and Rev. 6.16,[b] and also to Pss. 11.7; 42.3, with their allusions to a vision of God in the cult. Moreover, the identification of the king with God provides a link with the ideas of v. 14ff.; in the 'devouring fire' the righteous are to survive and have therefore a right to see the God who has brought them salvation and life. When the poet refers once again to the country which stretches far in both directions, he is probably

---

[a] G. Gerleman, *THAT* I, col. 450 is wrong when he denies that there is a biblical background to 1QH VII.3.

[b] E. Lohmeyer, MeyerK, 1956, on Matt. 5.8.

thinking of its transformation, and the disappearance of the mountains which hinder travel and cultivation. With a reference to the terror which will seize the redeemed when they look back upon their former afflictions, the poet is attempting to make their present misery and future distress more tolerable: someone who knows how bright the morning will be can well endure a dark night! Verse 18b refers to the foreign ruler whose tribute is counted and weighed by scribes (cf. II Kings 18.14ff.)[a] but who, according to v. 8, is utterly unreliable; but it may also refer to a tax collector of the Hellenistic rulers,[b] though of course these two possibilities need not necessarily be mutually exclusive. But the people of Jerusalem will be set free by eventual disappearance of the people who, as in 28.11, speak as though they were stammering, obscurely and incomprehensibly (cf. Ezek. 3.5f.).[c] There is scarcely anything more uncanny and at the same time more likely to give rise to constant embarrassment than an occupying force whose language the people do not understand. We do not know whether the poet is merely thinking of a Greek-speaking people, or rather of some imaginary entity, even though there is something to be said for the idea that the conception of such figures as Gog from Magog and the destroyer were connected with the rise of Alexander the Great.

[20–22] *Salvation in the age of salvation.* The poet turns from the still terrifying conception of the foreign nation to a brighter picture, that of the new Jerusalem which will never again be in danger, the place of pilgrimage for those who together with its inhabitants celebrate the festivals (cf. 4.5). He promises that his community will see this (cf. Ps. 128.5). Was he contrasting the eternal sanctuary with the portable sanctuary of the time in the wilderness (cf. Ex. 26.1ff., 38.9ff.) or was he rather using an image from the life of shepherds? In view of the continuation, the latter possibility seems more likely. Just as the shepherd who has found a protected and well-watered pasture of adequate size no longer has to wander and search, so in the future all the people in Jerusalem will find a permanent residence and means of subsistence in a liberated and marvellously transformed country. This city, which was not without water supplies but was certainly not abundantly watered, will then be famous for its new spring which feeds abundant water into whole rivers, a conception which is

---

[a] Cf. Dillmann-Kittel, *ad loc.*

[b] Cf. M. Hengel, *Judentum und Hellenismus*, WUNT 10, 1969, pp. 32ff.

[c] For *šmᶜ* with the meaning 'understand' cf. Gen. 11.7; 42.23.

developed in greater detail in Ezek. 47. The idea that the rivers which originate here could become a new source of danger is explicitly rejected: they are unnavigable. This very idea shows that we are in a time of highly developed maritime trade, which had received fresh encouragement from the founding of Alexandria and Seleucia Pieria, in addition to the ancient Phoenician ports. That there will be no dangers for the liberated city of Jerusalem and the liberated people of God is emphasized by the concluding confession of praise, which can be compared with Judg. 8.23; Pss. 89.19 and 25.9.

[23–24] *The spoil and the salvation of the age of salvation.* It was either the apocalyptic author of the rest of the passage or a later redactor who added these verses, taking up the theme of spoil first mentioned in v. 4 and developing it in a new and fantastic direction. He clearly supposes that from time to time a ship would sail up the river into the territory of Judah. Then it would become as it were enchanted, and would lose its ability to sail, so that it could be plundered with all its treasures.[a] The blind and the lame (cf. Sam. 5.8) would need to do no more than reach out. It is reminiscent of the old mercenaries' song, *Das wird ein lustig Leben bei uns im Lager geben* ('Life in the camp will be fine for us'). If we are somewhat shocked at the shamelessness of this hope, we are surprised once again to learn that there will no longer be anyone lame or blind in the literal sense, a hope with which anyone who has passed through the streets of an Eastern city, with its blind and crippled persons, will sympathize. For now all the inhabitants of Zion will be healthy (cf. 35.5f.), a consequence of the foregiveness of their wickedness. This completes the picture of a city which is waiting for its wanderers to return home – perhaps it is they who are addressed in v. 17 and 20 – in which righteousness rules, in which there is no one sick or frail, whose springs feed mighty rivers, around which the land spreads away into the distance, and over which, with its people, Yahweh himself rules as king (cf. Ps. 24; 47; 76; 96; and also Rev. 21.9–22.5). Anyone who desires more righteousness, less sickness and more fruitfulness upon this earth must himself be more righteous, bind up wounds, heal sickness and cultivate waste places. Whether this will be successful, and whether we shall thereby become really more human, no doubt still depends upon whether we regard the fear

---

[a] For the details of the description of the ship cf. Ezek. 27.1ff. On the subject in general, cf. also the modern parallels in cargo cults and the comments of E. Dammann, *Grundriss der Religionsgeschichte*, Stuttgart 1972, pp. 109ff.

of God as the beginning of wisdom and measure our own conscience against the entry *tōrāh*. That everything which we achieve remains ultimately fragmentary will ensure that in looking for the earthly Jerusalem we do not entirely forget the heavenly.

CHAPTERS 34–35

The End of Edom and the Redemption of Zion

CHAPTER 34.1–17

The Judgment upon Edom

1 Draw near, O nations, to hear,
    and hearken, O peoples!
Let the earth listen, and all that fills it;
    the world, and all that springs from it.

2 For Yahweh is enraged against all the nations,
    and furious against all their host,
he has doomed them, has given them over for slaughter.

3 Their slain shall be cast out,
    and their corpses – their stench shall rise;
the mountains shall dissolve with their blood,

4   and all ⟨hills⟩ᵃ shall rot away.
And the skies shall roll up like a book,
    and all their host shall wither,
as leaves fall from the vine,
    like leaves falling from the fig tree.

5 For in heaven the sword ⟨of Yahweh⟩ᵇ ⟨swings⟩ᶜ
    behold, it descends for judgment upon Edom,
upon the people ⟨he⟩ᵇ doomed.

6 Yahweh's sword is sated with blood,
    it is gorged with fat,
with the blood of lambs and goats,
    with the fat of the kidneys of rams.
For Yahweh has a sacrifice in Bozrah,
    a great slaughter in the land of Edom.

7 Wild oxen shall fall with them,
    and young steers with the strong ones.ᵈ

ᵃ Read *gᵉbāʿōt* with Ziegler.
ᵇ Cf. *BHS*.
ᶜ Read *dāʾᵃtā*, once again with Ziegler; cf. Deut. 28.49; Jer. 48.40 and 49.22.
ᵈ It is of course bulls which are meant.

Their land ⟨shall be soaked⟩[a] with blood,
    and their soil manured with fat.

8   For Yahweh has a day of vengeance,
    a year of recompense for the quarrel of Zion.

9   And her streams shall be turned into pitch,
    and her soil into brimstone;
  her land shall become
    burning pitch.

10   Night and day it shall not be quenched;
    its smoke shall go up for ever.
  From generation to generation it shall lie waste;
    none shall pass through it for ever and ever.

11   But the owl and the bustard shall possess it,[b]
    the hornbill[c] and the raven shall dwell in it.
  He shall stretch the line of waste over it,
    and the plummet of chaos.[d]

12   ....
    ....and its nobles.[e]
  There no kingdom shall be acclaimed,
    and all its princes shall come to nothing.

13   Thorns shall grow over its palaces,
    nettles and thistles in its fortresses.
  It shall be the haunt of jackals,
    and abode[f] for the daughters of the desert.[g]

14   And devils shall meet with hyenas,
    the hairy one shall cry to his fellow;
  yea, there shall *Lilith* a light,
    and find for herself a resting place.

15   There shall the viper nest ⟨   ⟩[h]
    and lay[i] and leave[j] ⟨her eggs⟩[a]

[a] Cf. *BHS*.

[b] The identification of animals and plants is largely conjectural.

[c] Cf. H. Wehr, *Arabisches Wörterbuch*, Wiesbaden 1958, p. 854, *sub voce nussāf*.

[d] It is the stones for casting lots which are meant. For 'waste' the original has *tōhū* and for 'chaos' *bōhū*.

[e] If the word is not a marginal gloss on 'princes' which is incorporated into the text in the wrong place, there is a gap in the text.

[f] *ḥṣyr* can be regarded as a parallel form of *ḥāṣēr*, which makes an emendation unnecessary.

[g] Ostriches are meant.

[h] It seems to me risky to translate *wtmlṭ* as 'laid', and the word should be deleted.

[i] It does not seem possible to derive from the basic meaning of the verb *bqʿ*, 'divide' the meaning 'hatch'.

[j] Cf. the Arabic *daraja*, to leave the nest.

yea, there shall the kites be gathered,
none ⟨shall miss⟩ᵃ her mate.

16 Seek and read from the book of Yahweh:
Not one of these is missing. ⟨   ⟩ᵃ
For the mouthᵇ has commanded,
and his Spirit has gathered them.

17 He has cast the lot for them,
his hand has portioned it out to them with the line;
they shall possess it for ever,
from generation to generation they shall dwell in it.

Just as the concluding redaction of the book of Isaiah placed the
Apocalypse in chs. 24–27 after the oracles against the nations handed
down in chs. 13–23, in order to turn the attention from individual
events to the whole drama which would ultimately bring Israel
salvation, here again an independent short apocalypse has been
inserted after chs. 28–32. The prophecies in those chapters, at least
in the stage of the tradition in which we possess them, are concerned
with the final fate of Jerusalem. This apocalypse gives an explicit
assurance that Yahweh's final judgment will also fall upon Edom,
which it is clear was particularly hated, and will be followed by the
return of the redeemed to Zion. The dependence which can be
observed in the prophecy of salvation upon Deutero-Isaianic
promises from the late exilic period, preserved in chs. 40–55, has
repeatedly led to the view that we have in the case of both chapters a
composition which was originally also by Deutero-Isaiah.ᶜ But a close
study of the related material and the whole conception shows that we
have here an apocalyptic composition from the post-exilic period.
Indeed to judge by its allusions to the cosmic catastrophe associated
with the final judgment, and its tendency towards a religion based on
the letter of the scripture (cf. 34.4 and 16), it may even be from the
late post-exilic period. 36.16 show clearly the role which the prophetic
book had come to have by this time. It is also clear that this short
apocalypse was presumably composed directly in order to be inserted
in the Isaiah roll. We do not have sufficient knowledge of history of

ᵃ Cf. *BHS*.

ᵇ Of course the mouth of Yahweh.

ᶜ Recently, M. Pope, 'Isaiah 34 in Relation to Isaiah 35, 40–66', *JBL* 71, 1952,
pp. 235ff. but cf. for a different view O. Eissfeldt, *Einleitung in das Alte Testament*,
Tübingen, ³1964, pp. 440f.; ET *The Old Testament: an Introduction*, Oxford and New
York 1965, pp. 327ff.; and once again K. Elliger, *Deuterojesaja in seinem Verhältnis zu
Tritojesaja*, BWANT 63, 1933, pp. 272ff.

Edom to be able to date it exactly. Just as Babylon played the role of the world power hostile to God and his people, Edom played both in the exilic and post-exilic period the role of the wicked neighbour, as we can tell from the prophecies of warning directed against it (cf. Lam. 4.21f.; Ps. 137.7; Obad. 11; Jer. 49.7ff.; Ezek. 25.12ff.; 35.1ff.; 32.29; Joel 4.19; Mal. 1.2ff. and Isa. 63.1ff., and also Amos 1.11f.). Thus the Edomites seem not only to have taken part in one of the first punitive measures of Nebuchadnezzar against Jerusalem and Judah (cf. II Kings 24.1) and ultimately in the destruction and plundering of Jerusalem, but also to have taken advantage of the weakness of Judah in order to extend their own territory, presumably under the pressure of Arabian tribes upon them, into the area of southern Judah up to and including Hebron (cf. III Esdras 4.50; Ezek. 35.10; I Macc. 5.65 and Josephus, *Ant.* XII. 353).[a] But it must be remembered that here the Nabataeans later took over the heritage of the Edomites and occupied their tribal lands (cf. Strabo XVI. 2.34). The conquest of Edom proper by the Nabataeans,[b] which took place at the latest by the end of the fifth century, no more gives us an indication of the date of composition of this apocalypse than does, for example, the mention of the Assyrians in 19.25ff. in the case of that oracle. For we must obviously assume that in Judaism the ancient names of nations and countries continued to be used even after the fall of these nations and the settlement of the countries by others. Thus it must remain uncertain whether the poet desired the fall of Edom, as the seat of the Nabataeans, for concrete reasons unknown to us, or whether he had in mind the Idumaeans of his time and the ancient land of Edom as a unity. Detailed studies of the poem have shown that the poet's passion led here to a remarkable formal expression, though not associated with the highest degree of clarity of thought.[c] Anyone who can read the Hebrew text will be aware both of the paronomasia, the intentional play on the sound of the words chosen in vv. 3b, 4a, 4b, 6b, 7b and 8a, and of the parallel openings in vv. 2, (5), 6b and 8; 12a, 14b and 15b. The basic metre used seems to be that of the funeral lament (3+2). It is impossible to tell how far the variations from this are due to later glosses and how far to an

---

[a] Cf. recently J. R. Bartlett, 'The Rise and Fall of the Kingdom of Edom', *PEQ* 104, 1972, pp. 32f., but also Y. Aharoni, *The Land of the Bible*, London 1966, and Philadelphia 1967, pp. 360ff.

[b] Cf. Bartlett, pp. 35f.

[c] J. Muilenburg, 'The Literary Character of Isaiah 34', *JBL* 59, 1940, pp. 339ff.

inadequate control of the form. There is perhaps no need to emphasize that powerful and artistic Hebrew poetry did not die out with the exile. Poetic skill is certainly no argument for an early date.

In considering the content, the present-day reader will find the prophecy of the return to Zion the most attractive, while the conceptions of the great festival of slaughter which Yahweh sets up for the Edomites, who in the Old Testament itself are really regarded as a brother nation of the Israelites (cf. Deut. 23.8) will be somewhat repulsive. A modern sociologist would perhaps categorize it among the poetry of the oppressed. Oppression often produces fine expressions of longing, but also literature which takes its tone solely from the glow of vengeful passion. It should be noted that the poet places his hope in God and not in his people's sword. The reader must perhaps ask the fundamental question whether the God who is love (I John 4.8) can be reconciled at all by us men with the catastrophes of history. In answering this question, we must note that what we are told of the love of God is binding on us only in conjunction with what we are told of the wrath of God. Secondly, however, as human beings *in* history, we are subject to God and not on the same level as he is. When we take part in events, or consider the events of the past as historians, we often believe that we can tell how the arrogance of a nation has ultimately led to its fall. But there are many contrary examples of a weak and tiny people being brutally extinguished by a stronger. In the disasters of history, as in our failures with regard to each other, we human beings are cast upon the God whom we need. But when we come to know him, we should beg not for the annihilation of our enemies, but for their enlightenment and their conversion (cf. Luke 23.34). This poem should not be regarded as a reason to consider oneself superior to a nation which saw God as its avenger and should not be sought by those who in their own history have imagined that they had to act as avengers towards this nation and so brought shame and death to innumerable people. Anyone who is weak must trust in God in all his difficulties. Anyone who thinks he is strong must remember that his strength and superiority may tempt others to beg in the words of Ps. 94.1 for the manifestation of the God to whom vengeance belongs.

[1–4] *The judgment of the world is at hand.* At first sight one might imagine here that a singer (cf. Gen. 4.23) or a wisdom teacher (cf. 28.23) was calling a world-wide audience to listen to him. But a comparison with similar calls in Deutero-Isaiah shows that the poet has in mind the summoning of the peoples and nations to judgment, for them to hear the pronouncement of sentence (cf. 41.1; 43.8f.; 41.21f.; 45.20; 1.10; Micah 1.2a and also 48.16). The earth and the plants which spring from it (cf. 42.5; Gen. 1.11f.) may be called upon as witnesses (cf. 1.2; Micah 1.2a; 6.2, cf. Deut. 32.1) or, on the basis of vv. 3f., as also subject to the judgment. Verse 1b is particularly reminiscent of Ps. 24.1. The nations of the earth, the earth and the beings which live upon it are to know that Yahweh has resolved to annihilate all the nations and their armies, because he is enraged at them (cf. Zech. 1.15). Why this is so is not at first made clear, and can only be concluded later from the analogy of the reason given for the judgment against Edom in v. 8. The proclamation that a ban has been placed on them entails their extermination. To place a ban upon a hostile army and its property is one of the practices of the war of Yahweh which to us seem primitive, but which was perhaps still possible at this time (cf. Deut. 20.16f.; 7.1f.; Josh. 11.21f.; 7; Micah 4.13; Jer. 50.26; 51.3; Isa. 37.11).[a] The proclamation of a ban before a battle means that the people condemned and their property are stated to be irreconcilable with one's own people and their possessions. Both are simultaneously assigned to the deity, which may not be injured by the alien substance.[b] When we recall that we do not like having things around us which remind us of people we do not like, or of misfortunes associated with them, we are on the right lines. The consequence of Yahweh's anger will accordingly be the total annihilation of the nations (cf. also Lam. 2.21; Jer. 48.15). The poet begins to work out the image of the huge mountain of corpses[c] (cf. also Ezek. 39) which under the southern sun gives off a filthy stench and from which innumerable streams of blood cause the mountains and hills to grow soft and melt away. According to ancient tradition this was to happen when Yahweh himself appeared (cf. Ps. 97.5; Micah 1.4). When he goes on to foretell that the firmament of heaven (cf. Gen. 1.6f.) will be rolled up like a scroll (cf. 51.6; 24.18, 21ff.) he loses track of his image. For he goes on to speak not of the heavenly ocean which would then pour down upon the earth (cf. Gen. 7.11; Isa. 24.18) but of the stars and constellations, the host of heaven (cf.

---

[a] Cf. G. von Rad, *Der Heilige Krieg im alten Israel*, Göttingen ²1952, pp. 13f.

[b] Cf. J. Pedersen, Israel, *Its Life and Culture*, III–IV, London and Copenhagen 1940 (1953), pp. 29ff. and pp. 331f.

[c] For *ḥll* and *pgr* together cf. Nahum. 3.3; for the rising of the stench, Amos 10; Joel 2.20.

40.26), breaking loose and falling like faded leaves to the earth. He has skilfully prepared the way for the movement which takes place in 4.5 from heaven to earth but he displays a lack of logic with regard to his further conceptions. Since he still needs the destroyed and devastated land of Edom to provide a contrast to the magnificent Holy Way, surrounded by watercourses and flowers, for the returning exiles, and clearly assumes that the geographical circumstances of the earth will continue to exist, he has not worked out final consequences of the destruction of the firmament and of the stars, but has really used it only as an image for the cosmic terrors associated with the day of Yahweh (cf. 13.9f.). Similarly he has tolerated the tension between vv. 8f. and 10–15, and has ignored the significance of individual features in favour of a picture of concentrated threats.[a] The conception of the end of the world can only logically be accepted in association with that of a new heaven and a new earth (cf. Rev. 21.1). This idea, which is probably of Iranian origin, was not yet wholly accepted by the poet who writes here.

[5–8] *Yahweh's sacrificial feast.* The image of the falling host of the stars is now replaced by another no less impressive image. In the sky, which is now as black as night, there appears a sword which strikes down unerringly upon the hated neighbouring people of Edom. There is apparently no thought of any human intermediary of God's judgment. The background is formed not only by the conception of Yahweh as a warrior whose bow was identified with the rainbow (cf. Gen. 9.13ff.) but also by that of his mysterious onslaught, originally associated with the theophany in the stars, against the nations gathered together before Jerusalem (cf. 31.8).[b] The way in which the divine intervention takes place remains obscure. What happens is mirrored for us in the events at the great sacrificial feast, in which lambs, goats, rams, the wild oxen feared because of their sharp horns,[c] steers and bulls[d] are sacrificed, so that the place of sacrifice is ultimately soaked with blood and manured with fat.[e] When the poet speaks of a *zebaḥ*, a sacrifice in which an animal is killed, followed by a ritual meal, he completely ignores the aspect of

[a] Cf. also H. M. Lutz, *Jahwe, Jerusalem und die Völker*, WMANT 27, 1963, pp. 20f.
[b] For the reward of Yahweh, cf. Jer. 12.12; 47.6; Ezek. 21.13ff. Isa. 27.1.
[c] Cf. Num. 32.22; 24.8; Deut. 33.17 and Ps. 92.11.
[d] For *'byrym* with the meaning 'bulls' cf. Pss. 50.13; 68.31.
[e] For the conception of the destruction of enemies as a sacrifice cf. Ezek. 39.17ff.; Jer. 46.10; and also Isa. 29.2; 30.32f.

the meal, unlike Ezek. 39.17ff. He may have chosen the expression because at a sacrificial feast of that kind more animals were sacrificed than at an *ʿōlā*, an honorific burnt sacrifice.[a] The place of the festival is given in v. 7 as Bozra, the present-day *el-buṣēra*, some 35 km: south-south-east of the Dead Sea,[b] which must not be confused with the more recent Nabataean city of the same name in the Hauran, south-east of Damascus. The capital stands in parallel to and represents the whole country (cf. 63.1, and also Gen. 36.33; 1.12; Jer. 49.13, 22). What the reader has long been expecting, at least since the words 'for judgment' in v. 5, is finally spoken at the conclusion of the stanza: the mighty judgment upon the nations, and particularly the fearful feast of slaughter by Yahweh, ending with the destruction of Edom, is his revenge[c] for what they have all done to Zion (cf. II Kings 24.1; Amos 1.11f.; Ezek. 5.12). Whereas the first stanza delineated the universal framework of the events of the final age, the second and third stanzas are concerned only with the fate of the hated brother and neighbouring nation[d].

[**9-15**] *The eternal devastation of Edom.* It is not impossible that the poet knew of the volcanic areas of the *harrat er-rahā* or the *harrat el-ʿuweiriz* in the northern Hejaz,[e] but is not of great importance for the understanding of the text. It is clear enough that he thought of the end of Edom in a similar way to the destruction of Sodom and Gomorrah (cf. Gen. 19.24ff.; Deut. 29.2; Isa. 13.19, and also Ps. 11.6). Whereas the apocalyptic author of 30.33 was still using the stream of brimstone as a simile, for the present author it has – temporarily! – become a reality: the streams of the country are turned into pitch and the ground to sulphur. And the country at once bursts into flames like a torch of pitch. Like the sacrificial fire (cf. Lev. 6.5f.) or the fire of an active volcano, the fire of Edom will not go out, but will go up to heaven for ever. It is natural that such a country should as far as possible be avoided by travellers (cf. Jer. 9.9; Ezek. 14.15; 33.28). Unfortunately the poet cannot rest content and makes what he has already said meaningless by introducing into the

---

[a] For the two sacrificial terms cf. R. de Vaux, *Studies in Old Testament Sacrifice*, Cardiff 1964, p. 37.

[b] Cf. also E. Jenni, *BHW* I, col. 269.

[c] For the day of vengeance cf. 63.4; 61.2; and also Jer. 46.10; 51.6; Deut. 32.35; Jer. 46.21; Ps. 149.7.

[d] For the second stanza cf. Isa. 63.1ff.

[e] H. von. Wissmann in M. Neumann van Padang, *Catalogue of the Active Volcanoes and Solfatara Fields of Arabia and the Indian Ocean*, Rome 1963, p. 6.

country not only all sorts of plants,[a] but also by making it the dwelling place of an army of particularly unclean and unpleasant animals and demons (cf. 13.21f.).[b] These include the much feared Lilith, originally an ancient Mesopotamian female demon which, probably because of a false etymology, had ultimately become a night-spectre.[c] An unknown person tried to protect himself against this demon with an amulet found in the Syrian Arslan Tash,[d] while the Talmud says of it that one ought not to sleep alone in the house in order not to be seized by Lilith.[e] On the other hand, when we read of owls and bustards, jackals and hyenas, poisonous snakes and kites, it needs little imagination to realize how terrible and frightening the place was meant to be, and to take it for granted that it was no longer possible for a new kingdom to come into being there, because Yahweh had reduced the country for ever to a place just like chaos, to a real *tōhū-wābōhū* (cf. Gen. 1.2),[f] dominated by eternal fire and by plants hostile to men and animals.

[16–17] *The testimony of scripture.* In order to emphasize that his prophecy of judgment would certainly be fulfilled, and to silence any doubts on the part of his readers or hearers, the poet anticipates the future, in which it will be possible to read through the book of Isaiah and confirm[g] that everything has been fulfilled which was prophesied here: just as no star is missing when Yahweh commands it (cf. 40.26b) and what his mouth has spoken comes about with certainty (cf. 40.5b), so too all these animals will have seized possession of Edom, because Yahweh has commanded them thither, has gathered them there (cf. Ezek. 39.17) and has as it were apportioned the land to them by lot (cf. Josh. 18.6ff., Obad. 11; Joel 4.3) and measured it out for them. Thus it will always be possible to tell that Yahweh

[a] The spiny burnet, *Poterium spinosum*, is a shrub which usually grows almost two feet high, its leaves falling in summer, and its flowers being similar to the euphorbias found in central Europe in winter, and somewhat similar to those of the Christ's thorn. But the foliage is lighter and more luxuriant. Cf. O. Polunin and A. Huxley, *Flowers of the Mediterranean*, London 1965, p. 85 and fig. 48.

[b] Cf. the comment on 13.21f.

[c] Cf. B. Meissner, *Babylonien und Assyrien* II, Heidelberg 1925, p. 201 and recently, with an up to date bibliography, R. Patai, *The Hebrew Goddess*, London and New York 1967, p. 209, or T. H. Gaster, *Myth, Legend, and Custom in the Old Testament*, New York 1969, pp. 578ff.

[d] Cf. *ANET*[3], p. 658.

[e] b. Sab. 151b, L. Goldschmidt, *Der Babylonische Talmud* I, Berlin 1964, p. 921.

[f] Cf. G. von Rad, ATD 2/4, [9]1972, pp. 30f.; ET *Genesis*, OTL, 1961, pp. 47f.

[g] Cf. John 5.39.

has given Edom to the wild beasts for all time as a dwelling place (cf. 13.20; Jer. 50.39). The full extent of the many allusions to other biblical passages in this poem can be seen only by working through the Hebrew text. It should be noted that there are particular similarities to 63.1ff. Perhaps this much more vivid poem inspired the present apocalyptic author to produce his own oracle. Finally, we note that the day of vengeance in v. 8 is none other than the day of Yahweh mentioned in 13.9. The fact that the cosmological conceptions have become more mythological than in 13.10f., while confidence that the earth itself is capable of salvation has grown less, is evidence that the present oracle is more recent than the Babylon poem in ch. 13.

CHAPTER 35.1–10

The Journey of the Redeemed to Zion

1 ⟨Let⟩ᵃ the wilderness and the dry land ⟨be glad⟩ᵃ
   Let the desert rejoice and blossom;
like asphodels 2 let it blossom abundantly,
   and rejoice with joy and singing,
for the glory of Lebanon shall be given to it,
   the majesty of Carmel and Sharon.
They themselves shall see the glory of Yahweh,
   the majesty of our God.
3 Strengthen the weak hands,
   and make firm the feeble knees.
4 Say to those who are of a fearful heart.
   Be brave, fear not!
Behold, your God!
   Vengeance comes,
the recompense of God!
   He will come and save you.ᵇ
5 Then the eyes of the blind shall be opened,
   and the ears of the deaf unstopped;

ᵃ The *m* should be deleted with B-L, § 56u″, p. 405, as a dittography of the *m* of *midbār* which next follows.

ᵇ For the form cf. B-L, § 55c, p. 384.

6   then shall the lame man leap like a hart,
     and the tongue of the dumb sing for joy.
  Yes, waters shall break forth in the wilderness,
     and ⟨flowing⟩ᵃ streams in the desert;

7   the burning sand shall become a pool,
     and the thirsty ground springs of water;
  the haunt where jackals ⟨rested⟩ᵇ
     shall become a placeᶜ for reeds and rushes.ᵈ

8   And a ⟨pure⟩ᶜ highway shall be there, ⟨   ⟩ᵃ
     and ⟨it⟩ᵃ shall be called the Holy Way;
  the unclean shall not pass over it,
     ⟨and the fool will not go on that way.⟩ᶠ

9   No lion shall be there,
     nor shall any ravenous beast come up on it;
  but the redeemed shall walk there.

10   and the ransomed shall return,
  and come to Zion with singing,
     everlasting joy will be upon their heads;
  they shall obtain joy and gladness,
     and sorrow and sighing shall flee away.

Against the gloomy background of ch. 34, with its proclamation of the destruction of mankind, the collapse of the cosmic order and the extermination of the Edomites in the course of Yahweh's bloody sacrificial feast, the marks of which are stamped upon the land for ever, the apocalyptic poet now gives us a glowing picture of the future transformation of the wilderness into a richly watered, thickly forested country, through which a holy highway leads to Zion as a processional way on which the redeemed return home rejoicing. The only explicit link with the content of ch. 34 is found in the prophecy of the coming of God with vengeance in v. 4 (cf. 34.8). Although the poet tries to conceal the true purpose of his promise as long as possible in a mysterious twilight – we do not learn until vv. 9b and 10 the real subject of his prophecy – his contemporaries must have

---

ᵃ Cf. *BHS*.

ᵇ Read *rābeṣā* and cf. G-K, § 145k.

ᶜ *ḥāṣīr* should be regarded as a parallel form of *ḥāṣēr*.

ᵈ Literally: papyrus. Cf. also 19.6.

ᵉ The addition in LXX is uncertain.

ᶠ V. 8b is seriously corrupt. 'And it is for them a wayfarer and the fools shall not err.' I take as original *weʾewīl lōʾ hālak derek* from which the present text has arisen through various additions.

perceived his purpose as quickly as a modern reader familiar with the Bible: behind the opening sentences the themes from the prophecy of Deutero-Isaiah are clearly recognizable and show for whom the desert is being so magnificently adorned. There are undertones and allusions from the Psalms and the so-called Trito-Isaianic collection (Isa. 55–56), which also serve to ensure that the reader remains in a familiar conceptual world. But characteristic changes and developments in these things leave no doubt that this chapter is not a corrupted prophecy of Deutero-Isaiah, but a later imitation, probably separated from its original by centuries. Whereas in ch. 34 the judgment of the world is locally concentrated on the tiny nation of Edom (cf. ch. 47 for the opposite), which shows that Babylon was no longer a real enemy, v. 6 makes it clear that v. 5 goes beyond 42.7, as well as 42.18 and 43.8, and unlike 29.18 and 32.3 has in mind the actual healing of human ailments in the time of salvation. The prophecy is also understood in this sense in the New Testament, in Matt. 11.15 and Luke 7.22. The prophecy is neither of the liberation of captives nor of the conversion and instruction of those who have strayed, but is about bodily restoration. And now that the neo-Babylonian kingdom had long vanished from the stage of world history, who should look forward to redemption and liberation more than, in the first instance, the people of Jerusalem and the Judaeans themselves, in the hope of returning from the sidelines to the centre of history, and secondly the world-wide Judaism of the diaspora, which on the whole would probably have been content with a pilgrim way to Jerusalem which guaranteed a safe journey and return. The diaspora too could also expect to gain from such an eschatological transformation, in being liberated by it from its isolated situation among the nations imposed by its faith, which led to constant persecutions. Thus vv. 8f. may have had in mind not only, like 40.3, a highway for the future return home of the prisoners of Babylon, now the eastern diaspora, but also of a processional way meant for permanent use and reserved solely for those who are pure, i.e. principally at least for the Jews, who even as small groups of pilgrims would not need to fear the wild beasts. As in ch. 34 the poet makes artistic use of paronomasia (cf. vv. 2, 5 and 10) and of emphatic opening phrases (cf. vv. 5 and 6) with their 'then' and vv. 8 and 9 with their three-fold 'there'. If it was certain that the apocalyptic poet had composed v. 10 himself and not borrowed it from Deutero-Isaianic material, a problem concerning which the views of scholars still differ, we could owe to him two lines which Brahms, in his *German Requiem*, interpreted as a valid symbol of Christian hope.

[1–6a] *The gifts of the coming God.* Deutero-Isaiah contains more than one prophecy of joy and of the transformation of the desert into a well-watered forest, with which he associated the conception that the first exodus and journey through the desert from Egypt to Canaan would be surpassed by the second journey from Babylon to Jerusalem. The present apocalyptic author also prophesies the joy which will come upon the desert and the wilderness (cf. 42.11; Ps. 107.35; Isa. 41.19; and also 51.3) when it is set free from its fruitless existence. Like the proverbially well-forested Labanon (cf. Ps. 72.16; Isa. 60.13; 29.17) and the richly wooded Mount Carmel with its southwards slopes running down to the plain of Sharon, which was also once thickly forested[a] (cf. 29.17; 32.15), the desert will now itself be covered with trees, and with flowers like the asphodel[b] (cf. also S. of S. 2.1).

It is not immediately clear who are to see Yahweh's glory. The first obvious suggestion, that it is the desert and wilderness as the scene of the manifestation of the glory of Yahweh going before his liberated people to Zion (cf. 40.3–5 and 10–11),[c] does not stand up to examination: Since v. 2aβ has already referred in the words 'to it' (fem. sing.) to the transformed land, the masculine plural which now follows, 'they themselves', must be understood as looking forward: the Jews who are now fainthearted and doubt God's power and its ultimate revelation will nevertheless see what is promised to all men in 40.5, the revelation of the God whom the apocalyptic poet, identifying himself with his hearers, can describe as 'our God' (cf. e.g. 40.3).

Verses 3 and 4 attempt a reconstruction of 40.1f. One can conclude from that passage that here too it is God who gives the command and instructs his messengers. The instruction to the messengers in v. 3 goes back to Job 4.3f. Verse 4 is reminiscent of 40.9bβγ; 40.2 and also 32.4, although in the last passage the idea of the rapidly beating heart has quite a different purpose. The introduction to the promise of salvation, with its call to be brave and not to fear, does not possess

[a] Cf. also 29.17; 33.9; 65.10; S. of S. 2.1; for Karmel cf. G. Sauer, *BHW* II, col. 934f. and for the plain of Sharon, cf. K. Elliger, *BHW* III, col. 1673f.

[b] For the asphodel, of which the following varieties can be found in Palestine: *Asphodelus microcarpus Salzm. and Vin.*, (*A. ramosus L.*), *Asphodelus fistulosus L.* and the yellow flowering *Asphodelus lutea* (*L.*) *Rehb.*, cf. O. Polunin and A. Huxley, *Flowers of the Mediterranean*, London 1965, pp. 208f. with figs. 233, 238 and 235.

[c] Cf. Delitzsch and Dillmann-Kittel, *ad loc.*

any such direct parallel in Deutero-Isaiah, but seems to be reminiscent of Deut. 31.6; 10.25 and II Chron. 32.7. On the other hand 'fear not', either on its own or coupled with a different expression, is not uncommon in Deutero-Isaiah (cf. e.g. 40.9; 41.10; 41.14; 43.1).[a] 'Behold your God!' is a quotation from 40.9, while 'vengeance comes' is reminiscent of 43.8a. In this way the previous prophecy against Edom is explicitly linked with this prophecy of salvation. The word *yābō*, 'he will come', may be a kind of keyword recalling 40.10, and should also be compared with 59.18; 66.6.[b] As in the previous prophecy of warning, the choice of words in this promise contains numerous allusions which are often clear only in the original.

With v. 5 the instruction to the messengers, with its promise of salvation, seems to be concluded, and the apocalyptic author is once again speaking in his own person. We have referred to the introduction to the new significance given to the individual expressions in their present combination. In 42.7 and Ps. 146.8 the blind may be regarded, under the influence of the previous verse, as the prisoners set free from their prisons, and when the idea is extended to the deaf, we may follow 42.18f.; 43.8 (cf. 29.18; 32.3) in regarding them as Jews set free by virtue of the revelation of Yahweh in a new historical act from their error and scepticism with regard to the eschatological message. But v. 6 gives a realistic turn to these ideas, to some extent influenced by 32.4 and 33.23. It is to the poet's credit that v. 6 has nevertheless something new and original to say, although it is ultimately not quite clear how he really meant these two verses to be interpreted; whether he was thinking only of bodily healing, or also of a liberation from prison, and from the prison of spiritual blindness. There is rejoicing at the beginning and rejoicing at the end of the first train of thought. It is not implicitly stated that this is joy in Yahweh, but by analogy with 42.10–13 this may be assumed.

[6b–10] *The return of the redeemed.* Once again the poet directs our attention into the desert in order to give an explicit assurance that it will be full of water, full of springs, pools and streams, and has therefore lost its terrors for the traveller. Behind v. 6b*a* we can recognize 42.20 and 48.21 (cf. Ex. 17.6 and Ps. 78.20) while behind v. 7a lie 41.18 (cf. Ps. 107.35) and 49.10 (cf. Ps. 107.33). In describing the den of jackals as having been transformed into a place overgrown with

---

[a] Cf. C. Westermann, ATD 19, 1966, pp. 6of.; ET *Isaiah 40–66*, OTL, 1969, p. 71.

[b] Cf. also Ps. 137.8; Zech. 9.16 and also Isa. 43.3.

reeds and papyrus, and therefore wet, v. 7b is reminiscent of 43.20, but there is also a contrast, presumably intended by the poet, with 34.13: whereas Edom has become the meeting place of jackals, the former desert has been changed into a well-watered countryside. Here the character of the inhospitable terrain, hostile to man, has been so changed that the hearer does not immediately object when he is told that in the future there will be a highway here (cf. 40.3; and also 43.19; 49.11 ; 62.10; 19.23 and 11.16). As a variation on 62.12a, where the redeemed are called a holy nation, the apocalyptic poet states that this highway will be called Holy Way, and will therefore lead to the sanctuary. But at first he does not mention where it leads, in order to prepare gradually the idea of the pilgrims returning home along this highway and travelling towards Zion. No impure person, no one excluded from the cult, or whether a Jew or a non-Jew, may use this highway, and no fool who has perverse views about the actions of God (cf. Job 5.2ff.; Prov. 10.21) may use it. These restrictions make it more and more certain where the highway leads to. But there must first be an answer to the objections of fearful or cautious minds, that the journey of pilgrims along this highway, in spite of its streams of water, pools and springs, would be much too dangerous because of the lions and other beasts of prey. The poet assures them that these animals will not be found there. He considers it superfluous to explain why this will be so, either because he has not thought about it or because he did not know, or because he took it for granted that it was within God's power (cf. also 11.6ff., 9).

Now at last he can lift the veil and make known the true purpose of all the preparations: along this highway will travel the redeemed of Yahweh (cf. 51.10bβ),[a] those who have been set free by his coming and by his revenge upon the nations (cf. 40.10f.; 43.5f.; 48.20; 49.22f.; 62.10ff.) and come to Zion rejoicing (cf. Ps. 105.43). Instead of the cloak which covers the face of those who mourn (cf. II Sam. 19.5 and Isa. 25.7f.) there is now joy upon their heads, a joy which can never be taken from them (cf. 61.7bβ). 51.11 certainly interrupts the context between v. 10 and v. 12, and is much too soon in taking up the keyword of the ransomed in the exodus from Egypt, and affirming the promise. Whether the verse was transferred there from 35.10 by a redactor[b] or, deriving from a disarranged Deutero-Isaianic context,

[a] Cf. also J. J. Stamm, *THAT* I, col. 387ff.

[b] Cf. K. Elliger, *Deuterojesaja in seinem Verhältnis zu Tritojesaja*, BWANT 63, 1933, pp. 206f.

was interpolated there and then was taken up by the present apocalyptic poet as the climax and conclusion of his promise,[a] is difficult
to tell. However, the borrowing of 51.11aβ in 61.7bβ is an argument
in favour of the second possibility. In this case the apocalyptic poet
would have created by means of his own sermon on salvation a
suitable framework for the isolated prophecy of salvation by the
second Isaiah.

[a] Cf. C. Westermann, ATD 19, p. 196; ET *Isaiah 40–66*, p. 243.

CHAPTERS 36–39

THE ISAIAH STORIES

In chs. 36–39 we possess more or less popular narratives in which, apart from the concluding story in ch. 39, the prophet Isaiah appears as the intermediary of divine messages of salvation, and indeed as a healer, together with King Hezekiah, who is portrayed as an example of piety and confidence in God. The fact that the whole block of tradition is almost literally identical to II Kings 18.13, 17–20.19 (cf. also II Chron. 32.1, 9–26)[a] makes it necessary to decide in which of the two books of the Bible the narratives were originally handed down. Since II Kings 18.13, with its parallel Isa. 36.1, clearly belongs to the annalistic passage II Kings 18.13–16, which has not been included in the book of Isaiah, it seems obvious that it is the book of Kings which has the priority.[b] Thus the task of explaining the growth of the traditions which have been assembled in the passage is ultimately a matter for a commentary on the book of Kings, although in what follows it cannot be entirely abandoned.[c] But the circumstance that the passage tells of the prophet Isaiah, the son of Amoz, led, presumably by analogy to the establishment, at what seems to have been an earlier date, of the narrative tradition about Jeremiah in the book which bears his name, to the natural wish to include these narratives in the book of Isaiah, so that the whole tradition associated with the name of the prophet and regarded as canonical was now united in a single book.[d] It is possible that by the date of their incorporation chs. 40ff. already formed part of the Isaiah roll, so that ch. 39 with its allusions to the Babylonian exile provided a transition to the prophecies of salvation of the anonymous prophet of the exile

[a] Cf. K. Galling, ATD 12, 1954, *ad loc.*

[b] Cf. O. Kaiser, *ZAW* 81, 1969, pp. 305ff.

[c] Cf. E. Würthwein, ATD 11, shortly to be published.

[d] For the late pseudepigraphic narrative of the martyrdom of the prophet Isaiah cf. L. Rost, *Einleitung in die alttestamentlichen Apokryphen und Pseudepigraphen einschliesslich der grossen Qumran-Handschriften*, Heidelberg 1971, pp. 112ff., or A. Weiser, *Einleitung in das Alte Testament*, Göttingen ⁶1966, pp. 364ff.; ET *Introduction to the Old Testament*, London and New York 1961, pp. 418ff.

whom we call the second Isaiah, Deutero-Isaiah. Since this story was clearly written some time after the events of the year 597 and 587(86)[a] and indeed should probably be dated after the exile,[b] we possess in it a *terminus a quo*, an absolute upper limit, for the incorporation of the narratives into the book of Isaiah, which must accordingly be regarded as post-exilic. Whereas chs. 36–37 can be regarded as containing a basic narrative which can probably be dated before the exile,[c] in its present form this narrative complex also displays features which can be attributed to its post-exilic redaction. The same is true of ch. 38. When we remember that the narratives must already have grown together we should hesitate to place their adoption into the book of Isaiah in the early post-exilic period, and should prefer instead a late post-exilic date.

We cannot overlook the fact that the narratives which we possess are only loosely connected. The story of Hezekiah's illness and healing, later expanded within the book of Isaiah by the Psalm of Hezekiah (38.9–29), together with the miracle of the sun, is only loosely connected with what precedes by 38.1. The same can be said of the following narrative of the visit of an embassy from the Babylonian King Merodach-Baladan to Hezekiah, with the consequences foretold by the prophet in 39.1. This is the only narrative which contains any recollection of the fact that Isaiah preached as a prophet of doom, but reveals a historical horizon wider than that which was accessible to the prophet. We should note that the portrait of Isaiah as a prophet of salvation in the year 701, as portrayed in chs. 36–37, cannot be reconciled with the picture of his activity presented in our preceding commentary. Here the attitude adopted by King Hezekiah was one of complete trust in Yahweh, something which according to Isaiah's prophecies in 30.1ff., 6f. and 31.1ff. (cf. also 30.7ff.) the policy of Judah lacked. Nevertheless, the theology of the prophet and that of these prophetic narratives agree in holding that the confidence that a man places in Yahweh will not be put to shame. It must be noted that a Christian can adopt this doctrine only with the double caution expressed in Matt. 10.24 and John 21.22, even though Christian faith also has a promise which is meant to display its power even in this life (cf. e.g. Mark 10.28ff.).

[a] We should explicitly mention the dating of the destruction of Jerusalem in the year 586 by A. Malamat, 'The Last Kings of Judah and the Fall of Jerusalem', *IEJ* 18, 1968, pp. 137ff.

[b] Cf. below p. 410.   [c] Cf. below pp. 384f.

CHAPTERS 36.1–37.38

The Deliverance of Jerusalem from Sennacherib[a]

36.1 In the fourteenth year of King Hezekiah, Sennacherib king of Assyria came up against all the fortified cities of Judah and took them. [2]And the king of Assyria sent Rabshakeh from Lachish to King Hezekiah at Jerusalem with a great army.[b] And he stood by the conduit of the upper pool on the highway to the fullers field. [3]And there came[c] out to him Eliakim the son of Hilkiah, who was over the household,[d] and Shebna the secretary[d] and Joah the son of Asaph, the chancellor.[d] [4]And Rabshakeh said to them 'Say to Hezekiah, "Thus says the great king, the king of Assyria: On what do you rest this confidence[e] of yours? [5]⟨Do you think⟩[f] that mere words are strategy and power for war? On whom do you now rely, that you have rebelled against me? [6]Behold, you are relying on Egypt, that broken reed of a staff, which will pierce the hand of any man who leans on it. Such is Pharaoh king of Egypt to all who rely on him. [7]But if you[g] say to me, 'We rely on Yahweh our God', is it not he whose high places and altars Hezekiah has removed, saying to Judah and to Jerusalem, you shall worship before this altar?[h] [8]Come now, make a wager with my master the king ⟨　　⟩[i]: I will give you two thousand horses, if you are able on your part to set riders upon them. [9]How then can you repulse (even) one ⟨　　⟩[j] among the least of my master's servants. For you rely on Egypt[k] for chariots and for horsemen. [10]Moreover, is it without Yahweh that I have come up against this

---

[a] The task of textual criticism does not consist here in the restoration of the original text of II Kings 18.13, 17–19.37, but in that of the text borrowed from there and altered on its insertion in the book of Isaiah. For the problems of literary criticism posed by the parallel texts, and the textual criticism of 36.1–37.7a, cf. also O. Kaiser, 'Die Verkündigung des Propheten Jesaja im Jahre 701', I, 1, ZAW 81, 1969, pp. 304ff.

[b] For the form cf. G-K, § 128w note.

[c] Cf. G-K, § 146f.

[d] For the titles cf. the exposition.

[e] Literally: 'What is this confidence, with which you confide?'

[f] Cf. BHS.

[g] The 2nd sing., by contrast with the 2nd pl. of I Kings 18.22 and some of the witnesses to the text, represents an awkward and, as the continuation shows, a superficial attempt to harmonize the context on the part of the Isaianic redactor.

[h] I Kings 18.22 adds: 'in Jerusalem'.

[i] Cf. BHS, and cf. Kaiser, p. 309.

[j] Cf. BHS.

[k] The abruptness of the opening words has rightly been emphasized by A. Sanda, Die Bücher der Könige, EH 9. 2, 1912, p. 256.

land[a] to destroy it? Yahweh said to me, Go up against this land, and destroy it." '

11 Then Eliakim, Shebna, and Joah said[b] to Rabshakeh, 'Pray speak to your servants in Aramaic, for we understand it. But do not speak to us in the language of Judah within the hearing of the people who are on the wall.' [12]But Rabshakeh said, 'Has my master sent me to speak these words to your master and to you, and not to the men sitting on the wall, (who are doomed) with you to eat their own dung[c] and drink their own ⟨urine⟩?'[d] [13]Then Rabshakeh stood and called out in a loud voice in the language of Judah: 'Hear the words of the great king, the king of Assyria! [14]Thus says the king: "Do not let Hezekiah deceive you, for he will not be able to deliver you. [15]Do not let Hezekiah make you have confidence in Yahweh by saying, 'Yahweh will surely deliver us; this city will not be given into the hand of the king of Assyria.' [16]Do not listen to Hezekiah; for thus says the king ⟨   ⟩:[e] Make a blessing[f] with me and come out to me; then every one of you will eat of his own vine, and every one of his own fig tree, and every one of you will drink the water of his own cistern; [17]until I come and take you away to a land like your own land, a land of grain and wine, a land of bread and vineyards. [18]Beware lest Hezekiah mislead you by saying, 'Yahweh will deliver us.' Has any of the gods of the nations delivered his land out of the hand of the king of Assyria? [19]Where are the gods of Hamath and Arpad? Where are the gods of Sepharvaim? Have they delivered Samaria out of my hand? [20]Who among all the gods of these countries have delivered their countries out of my hand, that Yahweh should deliver Jerusalem out of my hand?" ' [21]But they were silent and answered him not a word, for the king's command was, 'On no account answer him.'[g]

22 Then Eliakim the son of Hilkiah, who was over the household, and Shebna the secretary, and Joah the son of Asaph, the chancellor, came to Hezekiah with their clothes rent, and told him the word of Rabshakeh.

37.1 When King Hezekiah heard it, he rent his clothes, and covered himself with the sack, and went into the house of Yahweh. [2]And he sent Eliakin, who was over the household, and Shebna the secretary, and the senior priests, clothed with the sack, to the prophet Isaiah the son of

---

[a] II Kings 18.25: 'against this place'.
[b] Cf. G-K, § 146f.
[c] For the form cf. B-L, § 72x', p. 583.
[d] For the qere cf. *BH*, which is still indispensable.
[e] Cf. *BHS*, with v. 8.
[f] Cf. the exposition.
[g] The translation attempts to give expression to the imperative imperfect with the negative *lō'*, which is a sign of an apodeictic command. Cf. also (G. Beer and) R. Meyer, *Hebräische Grammatik* II, Berlin ²1955, § 100e, p. 123.

Amoz. [3]They said to him, 'Thus says Hezekiah, "This day is a day of distress, of rebuke, and of disgrace.

Children have come to the birth,
and there is no strength to bring them forth.

[4]It may be that your God heard the word of Rabshakeh, whom his master the king of Assyria has sent to mock the living God, and will rebuke the words which Yahweh your God has heard; therefore lift up your prayer for the remnant that is left." '

5 When the servants of King Hezekiah came to Isaiah, [6]Isaiah said to them, 'Say to your master,[a] "Thus says Yahweh: Do not be afraid because of the words that you have heard, with which the young men of the king of Assyria have reviled me. [7]Behold, I will put a spirit in him, so that he shall hear a rumour, and return to his own land; and I will make him fall by the sword in his own land." '

8 Rabshakeh returned, and found the king of Assyria fighting against Libnah; for he had heard that the king had left Lachish. [9]Now the king heard concerning Tirhakah king of Ethiopia. 'He has set out to fight against you.' And when he heard (it)[b] he sent messengers to Hezekiah, saying, [10]'Thus shall you speak[a] to Hezekiah king of Judah: "Do not let your God in whom you have confidence deceive you by promising that Jerusalem will not be given into the hand of the king of Assyria. [11]Behold, you have heard what the kings of Assyria have done to all lands, destroying them utterly. And shall you be delivered? [12]Have the gods of the nations delivered them, the nations which my fathers destroyed, Gozen, Haran, Rezeph, and the people of Eden [and those][c] who were in Telassar? [13]Where are the king of Hamath, the king of Arpad, the king of Lair,[d] Sepharvaim, Hena, and Ivvah?" '

14 When Hezekiah received the letter[e] from the hand of the messengers, and read it, he went up to the house of Yahweh and spread[f] it before Yahweh. [15]And Hezekiah prayed to Yahweh: [16]Yahweh Sebaoth God of Israel, who art throned above the cherubim, thou art the God, thou alone, of all the kingdoms of the earth; thou hast made heaven and earth. [17]Incline thy ear, Yahweh, and hear; open thy eyes Yahweh, and see; and hear all the words of Sennacherib, which he has sent to mock the living God. [18]Of a truth, Yahweh, the kings of Assyria

[a] For the form cf. R. Meyer, *Hebräische Grammatik* II, Berlin [3]1969, § 63, 5a, pp. 100f.

[b] II Kings 19.9: 'and he turned and'. – 1QIsa and LXX read: *wayyišma' wayyāšob*. Cf. also Kaiser, p. 305.

[c] The 'and' inserted by LXX[L] is correct in its meaning, but gives the impression of being a later correction. Cf. also J. Gray, *I and II Kings*, OTL, [2]1970, p. 686, n.

[d] Or 'for the city'. For Dussaud's proposal to read *la'aš*, cf. Gray, p. 688.

[e] For the plural cf. G-K § 124b, n. 1.

[f] I.e. the letter. The suffix is a *constructio ad sensum*. But cf. II Kings 19.14.

have laid waste ⟨all the nations and their lands⟩ᵃ ¹⁹and have cast their gods into the fire; for they were no gods, but the work of men's hands, wood and stone; therefore they were destroyed. ²⁰So now, Yahweh our God, save us from his hand, that all the kingdoms of the earth may know that thou Yahweh alone art ⟨God⟩.'ᵇ ²¹Then Isaiah son of Amoz sent to Hezekiah, saying, 'Thus says Yahweh, the God of Israel: Because you have prayed to me concerning Sennacherib king of Assyria, ⟨I have heard⟩.'ᵇ

22 *This is the word which Yahweh has spoken concerning him:*
    'She despises you, she scorns you –
        the virgin daughter of Zion;
    she wags her head behind you –
        the daughter of Jerusalem.

23 *Whom have you mocked and reviled?*
        Against whom have you raised your voice
    and haughtily lifted your eyes?
        Against the Holy One of Israel?

24 *By your servants you have mocked my Lord,*
        and you have said, with my many chariots
    I have gone up to the heights of the mountains,
        to the far recesses of Lebanon;
    ⟨I felled⟩ᵇ its tallest cedars,
        its choicest cypresses;
    ⟨I come⟩ᵇ to its remotest height,
        its forest-like orchards.

25 *I myself dug and drank*
        ⟨strange⟩ᵇ waters,
    and ⟨   ⟩ I dried upᵇ with the sole of my foot,
        all the streams of Masor.ᶜ

26 *Have you not heard? Long ago*
        I determined it,
    ⟨I planned it⟩ᵇ from days of old
        ⟨and⟩ᵇ now I bring it to pass,
    ⟨that you had to⟩ᵇ make fortified cities
        crash into heaps of ruins.

27 *Their inhabitants shorn of strength,*
        were dismayed and confounded,

ᵃ II Kings 19.17, which contrary to the principle laid down above p. 369 note a I prefer here. The Isaianic redactor reads: 'all lands and their land', and with the last word clearly has in mind the Assyrians.
  ᵇ Cf. *BHS.*
  ᶜ Cf. p. 98 note b, on 19.6.

and became like plants of the field
and like tender grass,
like grass on the house tops, that dries out[a]
⟨before the east wind.⟩[b]

28 *⟨Your rising up⟩ and your sitting down are ⟨before me⟩*[c]
and I know your going out and coming in, ⟨   ⟩[d]

29 *Because you have raged against me and ⟨your raging⟩*[e]
has come to my ears,
I will put my hook in your nose
and my bit in your mouth,
and I will turn you back on the way
by which you came.

30 *And this shall be the sign for you:*
One year they will eat the second growth,
and next year what grows from it.
But in the third year
sow and harvest,
and plant vineyards
and eat their fruit!

31 *And what has escaped of the house of Judah,*
and what is left,
shall once again take root downward,
and bear fruit upward.

32 *For out of Jerusalem shall go forth a remnant*
and out of Mount Zion some survivors.
The zeal of Yahweh Sebaoth
will accomplish this.

33 Therefore thus says Yahweh Sebaoth concerning the king
of Assyria:
He shall not come into this city,
or shoot an arrow there,
or come before it with a shield,
or cast up a siege-mound ⟨against it⟩.[e]

34 By the way he came,
by the same way he shall return,
but he shall not come into this city.
Saying of Yahweh Sebaoth.

---

[a] Read with 1QIsa *hanniŝdāp*.

[b] Read with 1QIsa *qādīm*.

[c] Read *l^{e}pānay* and with 1QIsa *qūm^{e}kā*, cf. Gray, p. 689, note k, on II Kings 19.26.

[d] Follow Gray, p. 690, note a, in deleting *w^e'ēt hitraggez^{e}kā 'ēlāy* which is a result of a dittography of v. 29aa.

[e] Cf. *BHS*.

35   For I will defend this city to save it,
            for my own sake and for the sake of my servant David.'

36 And the angel[a] of Yahweh went forth and slew a hundred and
eighty-five thousand in the camp of the Assyrians; and when men arose
early in the morning, behold, these were all dead bodies. [37]Then
Sennacherib king of Assyria set out and went and turned round and
dwelt at Nineveh. [38]And as he was worshipping in the house of Nisroch
his god, Adrammelech and Sharezer, his sons, slew him with the sword,
and escaped into the land of Ararat. And Esarhaddon his son reigned in
his stead.

Chapters 36 and 37 seem to present us with a continuous narrative
from the period of the danger from Assyria in the year 701, in which
Isaiah gave the devout King Hezekiah a prophecy of the withdrawal
and death of his mighty enemy. At that time, we are told, the
Emperor Sennacherib had first sent his Rabshakeh from Lachish
with a powerful force to Hezekiah at Jerusalem, in order to show him
how senseless his resistance was. When the Assyrian dignitary had to
withdraw with his task unfulfilled, in spite of his additional appeal to
the men on the wall, he found his master by this time before Libnah;
for the news that Tirhakah had set out against him and brought him
there. Sennacherib had once again tried to persuade Hezekiah to
submit by sending him a letter. On both occasions Isaiah prophesied
to the king, whose confidence in Yahweh remained unshakeable, that
the plans of the emperor would fail, and even that he would come to
a violent end without the city even being besieged. And this, we are
told, is what happened; the angel of Yahweh killed 185,000 men in
the Assyrian camp. Then the emperor returned to Nineveh, where he
was ultimately murdered by his own sons. The confidence which
Hezekiah placed in his God and the words of the prophet Isaiah had
been brilliantly confirmed!

The historical problem. Before we turn to literary criticism, however,
we must deal with the objections of the historian to this account,
which are based upon II Kings 18.13–16 and the annals of Sennacherib. According to the biblical record Hezekiah offered to the
emperor who was at Lachish – one must assume that in the meantime the city had been taken[b] – his subjection, and all the tribute he
asked, in order to avoid further punishment. This tribute he paid by
handing over the treasures of the temple and the palace. According

[a] II Kings 19.35 inserts 'It came about in the same night'.
[b] Cf. R. D. Barnett, 'The Siege of Lachish', *IEJ* 8, 1958, pp. 161ff.

to the annals Sennacherib besieged and conquered forty-six of Hezekiah's fortified cities, captured and deported more than 200,000 people, invested Jerusalem and finally did not only receive an immense tribute from Hezekiah, but also considerably reduced his kingdom. He also boasts that on the same campaign he defeated a king of Ethiopia, who is not named, at Eltekeh.[a] Egyptologists can add to this information the fact that in the year 701 Tirhakah was not king, and, in view of his youth, was probably not in a position to be in command of the Egyptian army. He did not ascend the throne until the year 690/89.[b] The Old Testament scholar can also add that the present narrative can be scarcely be dated during a later campaign by Sennacherib, because Hezekiah died at the latest in 697/96.[c] Finally, the Assyriologist can point out that we know that Sennacherib undertook his last campaign against Babylon in 689 and was not murdered until 681,[d] so that we cannot speculate about a possible incident underlying the present narrative in this respect. – Thus there can be no question of any miraculous deliverance of Jerusalem in the year 701. The city, however, was not conquered then, because Hezekiah submitted in good time and was able to purchase his freedom by his tribute. This narrative, taken from II Kings 18.13, 17–19.37, must be contrasted with the historical facts if we are to understand its purpose clearly. The attempt, on the basis of its position in the book of Kings following the mention of Hezekiah's capitulation in II Kings 18.14ff. and the rise of the Ethiopian Pharaoh Tirhakah, to relate it to a hypothetical later but (fortunately!) unknown campaign of Sennacherib is simply an attempt to avoid the admission required of the historian that here we have a legendary tradition.[e]

[a] Cf. *AOT*[2], pp. 352ff.; *AR* II, § 239ff.; *ANET*[2], pp. 287ff. and *TGI*[2], pp. 67ff.

[b] Cf. J. M. A. Janssen, 'Que sait-on actuellement du Pharaon Taharqa?', *Bib* 34, 1953, pp. 23ff. For the possibility of a confusion with the unsuccessful first campaign of Esarhaddon against Egypt cf. S. Smith, 'Sennacherib and Esarhaddon' in CAH III, Cambridge [2]1929 (1960), p. 74.

[c] Cf. K. T. Andersen, 'Die Chronologie der Könige von Israel und Juda', *StTh* 23, 1969, pp. 100ff.

[d] Cf. H. Schmökel, *Geschichte des alten Vorderasiens*, HO II.3, 1957, p. 274, and also still B. Meissner, *Neue Nachrichten über die Ermordung Sanheribs*, SAB 1932, pp. 250ff.

[e] Cf. what E. Schrader, *Die Keilinschriften und das Alte Testament*, edd. H. Zimmern and H. Winckler, Berlin [3]1902, p. 273, suggests in favour of a second campaign of Sennacherib; but against this cf. the recent article by W. W. Hallo, *BA* 23, 1960, pp. 57ff.

37.21-35. Although it is the task of a commentator on the books of Kings to explain the way this composition came to have its present form,[a] we must give some indication why the chapter is not treated as a unity in the exposition that follows, which in view of the priority of the book of Kings is necessarily a short one. In going through the translation, it can be presumed that the reader has already had his own ideas on this subject or has found difficulty in certain passages and is consequently to some extent prepared for the following considerations. Thus he may have noted that 37.21-35 prophesies twice that the Assyrian king will return home by the same way that he came (cf. v. 29 and v. 34). Since the introduction in v. 21 leads us to expect a word of God addressed to Hezekiah and speaking of Sennacherib in the third person, the poetic oracle in vv. 22-29, addressed to the king of Assyria himself, must in spite of its vigour be regarded as a secondary interpolation. Moreover, the prophecy addressed to Hezekiah in vv. 30-32 can clearly be seen from its opening words and its form to be related to vv. 22-29. Thus the continuation of v. 21 must be sought in vv. 33-35.[b]

37.7 and 37.33-38. When we turn to the two other oracles in these verses, we note first that both look forward to the return of the emperor to Assyria. The first makes the more precise statement that Yahweh had put a spirit into him so that he would hear a rumour, return to his own country and there fall by the sword. The second emphasizes that Jerusalem will neither be threatened nor besieged, because the emperor will leave the country by the same route, before he has reached it. The reason for his departure is not mentioned. There is no reference to the first oracle in the second. Similarly, everyone in the second episode acts as if they had no knowledge of the first. When Hezekiah reads the letter he shows no recollection that Isaiah has already prophesied to him the withdrawal and death of the emperor. In 37.2ff. he comes to the prophet with his courtiers to ask him to intercede, whereas in 37.14ff. he takes matters into his own hands. Thus when Hezekiah's prayer is nevertheless answered through the vehicle of the prophet, the reader can perceive the direct link between God and his ambassador on earth. Thus we are inclined to suspect that this single narrative, consisting of two episodes and a conclusion, has been compiled from two separate narratives which

[a] Cf. E. Würthwein, ATD 11, to be published shortly.
[b] Cf. B. Stade, ZAW 6, 1886, pp. 177f.

were parallel in content. We must accordingly look for the original conclusion of each.

37.36–38. If we examine 37.36–38 on this assumption, it is immediately clear, and has long been recognized, that at least v. 37b and certainly v. 38 refer to 37.7 and provide the conclusion of the first narrative. Similarly, v. 36, recording an astounding event which makes the king incapable of action and therefore forces him to depart, belongs to the second narrative and its prophecy, and indeed fulfils in exemplary fashion v. 20, the reason which Hezekiah adduces in his prayer; for such an event could not have remained concealed. And since we find two mentions of Sennacherib's return in v. 37a – otherwise 'he turned round' would have preceded 'and he went', which is organically linked here with 'and he set out'[a] – we can regard v. 37aα as belonging to the first narrative, which is continued in v. 37b, and v. 37aβ to the second.[b]

37.8–9. Special attention must next be paid to the join between the two narratives. The content shows that this lies in vv. 8 and 9. But where exactly the boundary is to be drawn remains a matter of controversy. Ought v. 8 and v. 9a, together with the words 'and he turned round' taken from II Kings 19.19[c] to be treated as part of the first narrative, which would consequently still include the information that Sennacherib had moved on?[d] Or ought we to regard the mention of this in v. 8aβb as a literary transition between the first narrative, which assumes that Sennacherib is in Lachish, and the second, which took it that he was in Libnah?[e] Whichever view one adopts, the assumption is that the news of Tirhakah's advance is identical with the rumour mentioned in the prophecy in v. 7, so that Sennacherib was made to break off his campaign solely by the news that the Pharaoh was setting out against him. This, however, cannot be reconciled either with the actual relative strength of Egypt and Assyria in the eighth century, nor with the arguments in 36.6. The experiences of Judah in the final revolt also argue against any such overestimation of Egypt (cf. Jer. 37.5ff.; 34.21f.). If 36.6 could be

[a] Cf. Ex. 14.19 with I Sam. 23.28.

[b] But cf. B. S. Childs, *Isaiah and the Assyrian Crisis*, StBTh II. 3, 1967, pp. 75f., who, following Duhm, deletes 37.33 and concludes the second narrative with 37.35.

[c] Cf. above, p. 371 note b.

[d] Stade, p. 174; Dillmann-Kittel and Fohrer, *ad loc.*

[e] Duhm and Marti, *ad loc.*; cf. also J. Meinhold, *Die Jesajaerzählungen*, Göttingen 1898, p. 71 and Procksch, *ad loc.*

shown to be secondary and this widespread view were correct, 37.7 would have to be attributed to circles which maintained an extreme form of prophecy of salvation, which had learnt nothing even from the Egyptian defeat at Carchemish in 605,[a] had come to live in an irresponsible world of fantasy (cf. Jer. 28) and consequently shared in the blame for the final collapse of the kingdom of the line of David. Alternatively, we would have to look as far as the fourth century, when the Persians first thought of reconquering rebel Egypt[b] and were beaten back at least three times.[c] In this case the events of the year 701 would then have presented such a contrast to the events of the years 589/87 that the Egyptian defeat would have been transformed into a victory. This explanation, however, would fail to explain why so late a narrator used information such as is preserved in 37.38, not to speak of the names of Sennacherib and Tirhakah. In view of this detail, the beginning of the formation of this tradition must lie close to the events narrated, even though it did not end there. Thus it must be regarded as at least possible that the first narrative included a scene referring to Tirhakah as a delaying element, increasing the tension, in order perhaps to present the emperor as suddenly departing, after a victory over Pharaoh, and on the basis of a rumour about difficulties in other parts of his empire, either to Assyria itself or to Babylonia. Such a story would have illustrated the principle that God's help is closest when the danger is greatest.[d] In view of 37.36 it is clear that these elements had to disappear when the two narratives were combined: Yahweh's destroying angel could not tolerate any competition. But the fragmentary first narrative now gives the impression that Sennacherib was a coward who removed himself as soon as there was even a rumour of Tirhakah's advance, while in the form in which we possess it, combined with the second narrative, it gives an adequate reason for Sennacherib to make fresh contact with Hezekiah: anyone who has to face a new enemy settles accounts with his old enemies. Thus we must agree that the redactor has done his work very skilfully. Looking back, then, it seems al-

---

[a] Cf. Jer. 46.2 and A. Weiser, ATD 20/21, ⁵1966, p. 382.

[b] Cf. O. Kaiser, 'Der geknickte Rohrstab', in *Wort und Geschichte. Festschrift K. Elliger*, AOAT 18, 1972, p. 106.

[c] Cf. O. Kaiser, 'Zwischen den Fronten', *Wort, Lied und Gottesspruch. Festschrift J. Ziegler*, FzB 2, 1972, pp. 200f., and F. K. Kienitz, *Die politische Geschichte Ägyptens vom 7. bis zum 4. Jahrhundert*, Berlin 1953, pp. 100f.

[d] Cf. A. Sanda, *Die Bücher der Könige*, EH 9. 2, 1912, pp. 265f.

together more probable that vv. 8 and 9a as a whole should be attributed to the first narrative. In support of this view, it should also be pointed out that the second narrative contains no mention of place names which are directly concerned with the action. If it is true that the event described in 37.36 was in the mind of the narrator a blow against the army left by the Rabshakeh before the gates of Jerusalem (cf. 36.2a), and the failure to mention the army in 37.8, and if this impression is not due merely to the combination of the two narratives,[a] then the second narrative must have assumed the existence of the first.

36.4–10. When we look at the tensions which still exist within the separate narratives which we have so identified, to see what they tell us about their composition, we find our first difficulty in the message of the emperor to Hezekiah, which in 36.4–10 is conveyed by the Rabshakeh. An analysis of it faces us once again with a puzzle. On the one hand the speech deliberately twice repeats the question asked in v. 4b, as to whether there were adequate grounds for Hezekiah's confidence and therefore for his rebellion against the emperor. Can you rely upon yourself, v. 5 and vv. 8–9a, upon Egypt, v. 6 and v. 9b, or upon Yahweh, v. 7 and v. 10? On the other hand the speech contains such obvious tensions that it is difficult to accept that it was originally a unit. Verse 4aβbα lead us to expect a message from Sennacherib to Hezekiah, words in which Sennacherib would be the real speaker and Hezekiah the listener. But in spite of the attempt by the Qumran Isaiah text to remove the difficulty at the beginning of v. 7a (cf. II Kings 18.22), v. 7b fails to play this part, for it speaks not to Hezekiah but about him. On the other hand vv. 8 and 9 overlook the fact that it is Sennacherib who is speaking, for they too speak naïvely about him. Even if we allow that an intermediary would have a certain freedom in the choice of his words in so delicate a matter,[b] there is no justification for these contradictions in terms of the literary category. A study of the content also reveals a further tension: there is no ultimatum or other demand for surrender appropriate to the situation, such as one would expect; and there are also unambiguous allusions to other biblical passages. Thus the reader will observe that Isaiah's prophecy in 31.1b is reflected in v. 9b, and 30.4ff. in v. 6, at least as far as the content is concerned.

---

[a] Fohrer, ad loc.
[b] Cf. Childs, pp. 8of. with the Nimrud letter, ND. 2632 in H. W. F. Saggs, Iraq 17, 1955, pp. 23f.

Similarly, it is obvious that v. 7 reflects an interpretation of Hezekiah's reform of the cult in II Kings 18.4, in the light of II Kings 23.8ff. and Deut. 12.2ff., while v. 10 is reminiscent of 10.5ff. and e.g. Jer. 27.6ff., and ultimately even of II Chron. 35.21.[a] The keyword of this speech is *bṭḥ*, to have confidence, trust. It occurs no less than seven times, while in the speech that followed to the men on the city wall it is replaced by *nṣl*, deliver, which appears nine times. This clearly shows the purpose of the narrative. It gives an example of the principle that anyone who has confidence in Yahweh will be delivered by him. When we ask who is responsible for the speech in its present form we should note that this confidence in God plays a part in the characterization of Hezekiah in the Deuteronomic history (II Kings 18.5). There can be no doubt that it is the work of a man influenced by the theology of Deuteronomy or of the Deuteronomic school.[b]

36.1–21. While it is certain that in its present form the whole narrative is the result of deliberate theological reflection,[c] we may still ask whether the tensions that can be observed in it are due to the stages in its growth. A useful starting point in our search for its oldest ascertainable basis is the change from discourse in the name of Sennacherib to the mention of him in the third person. The change to the latter occurs between vv. 8 and 9, and in the other direction between vv. 1–4a*α* and 5b. The Rabshakeh, one of the emperor's highest officers, if not the commander-in-chief in the field,[d] was sent by him to Jerusalem. He addresses the envoys of Hezekiah, who themselves represent the chief ministers of the government,[e] and

---

a The comparison with II Chron. does not assume any literary dependency.

b Cf. E. Würthwein, ATD 11, shortly to be published, and for the time being O. Kaiser, *Einleitung in das Alte Testament*, Gütersloh ²1970, pp. 138ff.

c Cf. also Childs, p. 85.

d If we follow the derivation of H. Zimmern, *ZDMG* 53, 1899, pp. 116ff., the title should be translated 'head cup-bearer'. This is the explanation of Opitz, RLA I, p. 461: 'originally the chief amongst the beer bearers, the *šāqū* . . . he was later like the turtan an army commander (cf. also II Kings 18.17) and governor.' But cf. also C. Bezold, *Babylonisch-Assyrisches Glossar*, Heidelberg 1926, p. 283, sub voce *šāqū*, where the meaning 'officer (?)' is given, with the comment of E. Schrader, *Die Keilinschriften und das Alte Testament*, Giessen, 1872, pp. 199f., and for his military function also W. Manitius, *ZA* 24, 1910, pp. 199ff. According to Opitz, *loc. cit.*, p. 461, the rank of the Rabshakeh was immediately below that of the turtan and equal to that of the *nāgir ēkalli*.

e The *ʾašer-ʿal-habbayit*, palace chamberlain or guardian of the royal domain, was responsible for maintaining the king, and his household, and the maintenance

begins to argue as a negotiator, with the aim of showing the king how useless his resistance is. This gives us a coherent text, wholly un-theological, which can be linked with the second and third scenes with no further difficulty. The second scene, in vv. 11–12, itself raises no problems. We can accept that a negotiator should suddenly assert that he is sent not to speak to Hezekiah or his envoys, but to the people on the wall, and we can assume that the basic narrative included a version of this. In the first scene we omitted everything associated with the keyword 'confidence', and we propose to treat in the same way the sentences in which the word 'deliver' or some other theological theme plays a part. Verse 13 is indispensible to the scene, and the same is true of its antithesis in v. 16a, as well as vv. 16b and 17. This gives us two vivid scenes, free of all theological reflection. Because of the unrestrained language of the Assyrian, the Judaean negotiators are worried that their compatriots on the wall will understand his words, and consequently propose that he should change from Hebrew to Aramaic.ᵃ It is their intervention that first

---

of the standing army, as well as the administration of the royal domain. According to Isa. 22.20 he had in the end practically become vizier. The *sōpēr* or scribe was the head of the royal chancellery and therefore, in one person, minister responsible for internal affairs, the court and foreign affairs. If his different functions had to be summed up in a single expression, he may be described as secretary of state. The *mazkīr* had the task of reminding the kings of current matters. In modern terms, he can be described as spokesman of the privy council and secretary of state. In rank he was always lower than the *sōpēr*, the scribe, and the *'ašer-'al-habbayit*, 'he who is over the house'. Whereas J. Begrich, 'Sofer and Mazkir', *ZAW* 58, 1940/41, pp. 1ff., *Gesammelte Studien zum Alten Testament*, ThB 21, 1964, pp. 67ff., derives both offices mentioned in the title of his article from Egyptian court offices, H. Graf Reventlow, 'Das Amt des Mazkir', *ThZ* 15, 1959, pp. 161ff., sought to show that the office named in his title was a function of the amphictyony. For the offices cf. also above on 22.15ff., together with the references given on p. 150, notes b and c.

ᵃ Here it should be noted in the first place that the expression 'Hebrew' for the language is not found in the Old Testament, cf. apart from II Kings 18.26 (para. Isa. 36.11 and II Chron. 32.18) also Neh. 13.24. As E. Ullendorff, 'The Know-ledge of Languages in the Old Testament', *BJRL* 44.2, 1962, p. 475, has noted, the Judean negotiators emphasized their ability to understand Aramaic as some-thing out of the ordinary, whereas they simply assume that the Assyrians under-stood this language. That Aramaic and 'Jewish' were not regarded as mutually comprehensible is also shown by Neh. 8.8, cf. W. Rudolph, HAT I. 20, 1949, *ad loc.* As early as the middle of the seventh century BC an ostracon from Assur shows that there was correspondence between Assyrian officers in Aramaic, cf. C. Brockelmann, HO III, 1954, p. 137.

suggested to their skilful opponent the idea, on which he immediately
acts, of addressing the people directly, calling on them to abandon
the city and make peace with the emperor.[a] He presents a tempting
picture to the people of Jerusalem, cut off from their fields and gardens
by the powerful Assyrian army, and with considerable subtlety he
describes even deportation as a comparatively pleasant affair – and
indeed in the eyes of the Assyrians it could not be the fearful thing
that it was to the people of Jerusalem and Judah.[b] Verse 21 concludes the scene and shows the failure of the Rabshakeh's efforts. He
returned to his royal master, as 37.8 also states, though in view of the
terse language of 37.8 and the sudden interruption of the story in v.
9, we cannot tell whether this was with or without his army. The way
the story has been told so far leads us to expect a sudden turning of
the tables, though it remains uncertain whether the original version
contained the account of Hezekiah's deputation to the prophet and
the resultant oracle of salvation.

36.22–37.9a. A critical examination of this section reveals three
facts. Firstly, Hezekiah's visit to the temple in 37.1bβ, unlike that in
37.14, is not followed by a prayer. Secondly, Joah is replaced, in the
deputation sent to Isaiah, by the senior priest. Thirdly, the carrying
out of their task is described in vv. 3f. before the announcement in
v. 5 that they have reached the prophet. Hezekiah's visit to the
temple (a journey from his palace to the temple precinct immediately
adjoining it)[c] can be explained by the purpose of including the
priests in the delegation; their importance is emphasized by the fact
that he does not use any intermediary. But the replacement of Joah
is remarkable. In II Kings 22.12 and 14 five people altogether are sent
by king Josiah to the prophetess Huldah, the deputation being
headed by the priest Hilkiah. It is unlikely that the presence of the
priest led to the replacement of the last member of the group. Thus
we may suspect that originally the narrative told only of the sending
of the senior priests, and that the other names, which in fact recur in
22.15 and 20, were later added because they were better known.

[a] 'Make a blessing with me' is best regarded as a euphemism for the submission
which is being demanded. Gray, p. 683, in my view ignores the text when he sees
here a demand that those who are addressed should acknowledge the salvation
revealed in Sennacherib's victorious campaign.

[b] Cf. the Nimrud letters ND. 2643 and 2725, published by H. W. F. Saggs, *Iraq*
18, 1956, pp. 41ff. which bears witness to the care officially shown by Assyria for
deported Aramaeans.

[c] Cf. the site plan in Galling, *BRL*, col. 411f.

Thus 37.2, like 36.12, suggests that the episodes were originally independent. If we continue our analysis on our previous principle of excluding statements which add a theological content, it is an open question whether the tearing of clothes and the wearing of penitential dress (cf. 36.22; 37.1f.) are meant to emphasize the distress and the humble attitude of the petitioners (cf. 22.12; 32.11; Josh. 7.6; Micah 1.8 and Jer. 4.8) or to portray them as devout persons who have heard a blasphemy (cf. Matt. 26.65). The vivid style of the underlying narrative as we have so far identified it suggests that the first possibility is more probable. Thus 36.22; 37.1, 2 (without Eliakim and Shebna), 3 (and perhaps also v. 4aα without 'to mock the living God') and certainly v. 6a, together with 'thus says Yahweh' and v.7 can be regarded as belonging to the basic narrative which then continued with 37.37 and 38.

37.9b–21, 36. We break off our exposition at this point, because an examination of the redactions is more meaningful in the context of the analysis of the book of Kings. 36.7, which takes insufficient account of the context, seems to me to imply that the redaction took place in several stages. If we look briefly at 37.9bff., it seems of particular significance that Sennacherib's message in v. 10 takes up the theme of trust, and in vv. 11 and 12 that of deliverance, both occurring in the same order as in ch. 36. Finally, the correspondence between 37.4aα and 37.17bβ should not be overlooked, and neither should that between 36.19 and 37.13, or between 38.18, 20 and 37.12. Are we to accept that when the second narrative was combined with the first, the first was thoroughly revised, or can we take it that the second narrative was composed simultaneously with the redaction of the first? The exaggerated role of the prophet, who without any human intermediary learns that an answer has to be given to Hezekiah's prayer, suggests the latter. In fact with regard to v. 36 it is very uncertain whether the narrator had at his disposal any reminiscence of the decimation of the Assyrian army by a plague,[a] and in spite of the curious narrative in Herodotus II. 141[b] it is very doubtful. But a glance at II Sam. 24.17 and Isa. 31.8 suggests that we should at least

---

[a] The attempt by H. Haag, 'La campagne de Sennachérib contre Jerusalem en 701', *RB* 58, 1951, pp. 358f., to see here a figurative expression for the Assyrian losses in the battle against the Egyptians as an act of Yahweh breaks down on the wording of the text.

[b] It is instructive that the attempt has been made in the other direction, to relate Herodotus' narrative, referring to the present passage, with the plague, for which the mice in Herodotus may be thought of as evidence.

be cautious. Theological reflection and a predeliction of the extraordinary, for miracles, obviously increased with the passage of
centuries, or was increasingly taken over from popular oral tradition
by the written tradition.

The historical background. Our suggestions concerning the growth of
the narrative, however, do not relieve us of the task of discussing
their relationship to history. The fact that according to the Assyrian
annals Hezekiah sent tribute to Nineveh, together with a delegation
to pay homage,[a] can be argued in favour of the view that Sennacherib found it necessary to withdraw very suddenly, and that only
this permitted a capitulation which guaranteed the survival of the
Davidic kingdom. A chance of survival, achieved as it were in the last
moment and in spite of the siege of Jerusalem (which is suppressed in
the present narrative), also explains the rejoicing of the people of
Jerusalem and the population of the countryside, who were crammed
together into the city, when the Assyrian troops withdrew, as is
assumed in 22.1ff., 12ff. When we recollect this passage, of course, it
becomes evident that the Isaiah whom we encounter in the present
narrative is a later creation. He himself had attacked the alliance with
Egypt in his preaching to the very last moment, maintained his
prophecy of doom in the face of the behaviour of the government in
Jerusalem, and did not abandon it even after the Assyrians had withdrawn.[b] But we can understand how in popular recollection the king
and the prophet, both of whom were regarded as devout, later grew
closer together, and the avoidance of the ultimate catastrophe came
to be seen as a deliverance by Yahweh attributed either to the king's
prayers or the prophet's, and of course basically to the fact that
Yahweh heard the prayer. The names and locations given in 36.1–3,
8–9a are certainly not to be regarded simply as historical.[c] But they
assume some recollection, even though it is vague, of the year 701 and
of the first half of the following century. The no less detailed recollection in 37.38 of what took place at the Assyrian court,[d] and the
fact that it is brought forward to the year 701, shows that in its oral

[a] Cf. the references in p. 375 note a.
[b] Cf. also S. H. Blank, *Prophetic Faith in Isaiah*, London 1958, and Detroit 1967,
pp. 9ff. and especially p. 11: 'If Isaiah was of the same mind still in 22.1b–14,
which, although it stands in a preceding chapter, is later than 31.1–4 – if he was of
the same mind still after Sennacherib withdrew, it is wholly improbable that
between times he held such a different view as chs. 36 to 39 contain.'
[c] Cf. above, pp. 377f.
[d] Cf. below, p. 391.

form at least the underlying narrative must go back to late pre-exilic times. On the other hand the assertion of monotheist faith in 37.17 and 19b show that the second narrative, and the redaction in a theological direction of the former narrative, must be dated in post-exilic times. Against the background of the experiences which led to the disaster to the kingdom of Judah in 587, the survival of Jerusalem in 701 became more than ever the outstanding example of the way in which a nation and a king which trusted in Yahweh would not be put to shame. The assessment of events and of the persons who took part in them changed as they became more remote. The faith of a later generation recognized that the survival of their forefathers was an act of grace, and their forefathers themselves are transfigured into archetypes of the confidence which the narrator knew was an effective force in his daily life.

[36.1–37.9a, 37aαb, 38] *Man's confidence and the help of God.*

[36.1–10] The exposition of the narrative places us in the year 701, when Hezekiah and his allies felt the punitive blows of the emperor against whom they had rebelled in 703. After Sennacherib had defeated Merodach-Baladan, the usurper of the Babylonian kingdom, which was united with the Assyrian kingdom in a personal union, and had then made the eastern frontier safe by a preventive campaign against a possible attack from Elam,[a] he turned to suppress the rebels in the west, where his mere arrival was sufficient to bring most of them to recognize his supremacy. In the south of Palestine, only the Philistine states of Ashkelon and Ekron, together with the kingdom of Judah, offered resistance, relying upon Egyptian help.[b] The Egyptian army which actually set out was defeated at Elthekeh,[c] so that the cities of the allies, who were still in a state of revolt and probably still hoped despairingly for fresh Egyptian support, were open to the conqueror's attack. He subdued one fortress after another. When he was besieging Lachish, which protected the quickest way from Egypt into the mountain country of Judah, or had already conquered it, he sent the Rabshakeh, his second highest military leader, whose title is treated by our narrator as a proper name, to Jerusalem with considerable army. Since the story is not concerned with military measures, or else details given later in it were suppressed in favour of

---

[a] Cf. below p. 409 and also S. Smith, 'Sennacherib and Esarhaddon', in CAH III, Cambridge, 1960 ([2]1929), and p. 70.

[b] Cf. also the comment upon 30.1ff., 6f., and 31.1ff.

[c] For this identification cf. K. Elliger, *BHW* I, col. 443.

37.33, the reader receives the impression that the detachment was merely the military escort of this high ranking officer. In fact, assuming that there is a historical kernel to these elements of the narrative, it must have formed the army which was intended to besiege the enemy capital. In a place which is also mentioned in 7.3, probably to the north or north-west of the city, where the terrain outside the walls is not more or less precipitous as on the east, south and west,[a] the general established his position. A message delivered in the name of the emperor and addressed to Hezekiah, who logically is not given the title of king, points out to the Judaean delegation[b] that in the eyes of the Assyrians any further resistance is pointless, or, in the theological language of the narrative, that further confidence is senseless. Even if someone placed two thousand horses at their king's disposal, he would not possess the troops to mount them. Behind this statement lies the fact that as early as the ninth century the Assyrians had introduced cavalry, whereas Israel and Judah do not seem to have possessed it.[c] Thus in his opponent's eyes – as unfortunately in reality – the only hope remaining to Hezekiah, who did not possess sufficient forces himself, lay in the arrival of a force of Egyptian chariots, and therefore in a helper whose value the narrator compares, in accordance with his people's experience, to that of a reed used as a staff which has an (unnoticed) crack in it, breaks off when one leans on it and pierces the hand (cf. Ezek. 29.6f.).[d] We must assume that the contemporary reader, living in a nation which had lost control of its history, would be impatiently expecting, in view of the constant repetition of the word *bṭḥ*, confidence, a mention of confidence in Yahweh, in order to appreciate the intrinsic tension which the present narrative possessed for those who first heard it. It can be imagined that the arguments in v. 7 were so fundamental in their misunderstanding, and so stupid that a Jewish reader would shake his head or interject (cf. also Jer. 44.16ff.). For the reform based upon Deut. 12 (cf. II Kings 23) was in fact a demonstration of piety demanded by Yahweh himself, an act of obedience which could look

---

[a] Cf. my comment on 7.3 (*Isaiah 1–12, ad loc*) and also J. Simons, *Jerusalem in the Old Testament*, Leiden 1953, pp. 334ff., and H. Donner, *Israel unter den Völkern*, SVT 11, 1964, pp. 1of.

[b] For its composition cf. above, p. 381 note a.

[c] Cf. J. Wiesner, *Fahren und Reiten in Alteuropa und im Alten Orient*, AO 38. 2–4, 1939, pp. 70f.; Galling, *BRL*, col. 425 and A. E. Rüthy, *BHW* III, col. 1584f.

[d] For the priority of the present passage cf. W. Zimmerli, BK 13.2, 1969, p. 710, and *Ezechiel*, BSt 62, 1972, p. 93.

forward to Yahweh's blessing and assistance. Here the narrator adopts a non-Jewish standpoint, and indicates the astonishment with which non-Jews at that time and later must have regarded the concentration of sacrifice upon the Temple of Jerusalem which was characteristic of post-exilic Judaism. On the other hand, v. 10 is based upon an idea which derived from the preaching of judgment by the prophets (cf. 10.5ff.). A knowledge of the latter passage, and its application in an anti-Judaean sense, however, is unlikely before the sixth century (cf. Jer. 40.1ff.). The Assyrian kings conducted their wars in the service of their God Assur. Thus Sennacherib states that at Elthekeh he fought trusting in his lord Assur and achieved victory against the army of Egypt and Palestine.[a] Thus this verse too appeals to the hearers of the narrative who knew that an enemy could do nothing against an Israel which had honest confidence in its God. Thus with the first speech of the Rabshakeh the narrative asks whom man should trust in extremity, himself, the help of other people or God. It presents the mighty emperor as denying that there is any possibility of deliverance from him and as arrogantly claiming that he is carrying out his war of subjection in the name of God.

[36.11–21] The anxious request of the Judaean delegation, that because of the people on the wall further discussions should be conducted in the diplomatic language, Aramaic, which they did not understand,[b] had the very opposite result, for it suggested to the Rabshakeh the idea of addressing the people directly. It is obvious from the situation that these included not only the people of Jerusalem but also the inhabitants of the surrounding villages at least, and this is confirmed by the mention of the cisterns at the end of v. 16. Thus it is clear, though it is not stated, that there was actually a siege taking place. The Rabshakeh's answer in v. 12 goes beyond what the situation required, and also beyond the authority of a negotiator. It should be noted that it skilfully attempts to drive a wedge between the government and the people by assuming a conflict of interests, and accordingly points out that the besieged people will ultimately have to eat their own excrement from hunger (cf. Lam. 2.11f.; 19ff.; Ezek. 4.16f. and also Thucydides II.52f.).

At once the Rabshakeh solemnly and loudly addresses the people on the wall, to impress upon them that neither Hezekiah nor, as the king might have persuaded them, Yahweh could save them. All they

[a] Cf. the references given above, p. 375 note a.
[b] Cf. above p. 381 note a.

need to do is make a blessing with him,[a] and then their land with all
its sources of nourishment would be at their disposal (cf. also Micah
4.4) until – and then we see what he really has in mind – the emperor
deports them into another marvellous country (cf. Deut. 33.28).[b] The
emperor shows a quite touching concern that the besieged people
should not be misled by Hezekiah's promise that Yahweh would help
them. The series of Assyrian victories, he says, have shown what can
be expected from the help of the gods, for the kingdoms of Hamath on
the Orontes, of Arpad further north, and of Sepharvaim, which may
have lain further to the north-east,[c] had been turned into Assyrian
provinces either by Sargon in 720, or by Tiglath-pileser (cf. also 10.9;
II Kings 17.24). The pointed mention of the capital of the northern
kingdom of Israel, Samaria (cf. also 10.11), makes threateningly
clear that Yahweh cannot be expected to help Jerusalem. It should
be noted that this argument would be quite unconvincing to Jewish
hearers; for in the first place Yahweh could not be compared with
other gods at all (cf. Ex. 15.11 and Isa. 37.16, 20), and secondly, the
Samarians and the whole of the northern kingdom with them had
only received the punishment they deserved from the hand of Yahweh,
and in the eyes of Judaism their fall was in fact a demonstration of the
power of Yahweh (cf. II Kings 17.7ff.; Amos 5.27 and Hos. 4.16ff.).
The people on the wall preserve a disciplined silence, no doubt
differing in this from those who first heard the story told, and obeyed
the king's command. Note that not everyone who distrusts the existing system of government is concerned for the true good of the
governed. In history, benevolent rulers have often been driven out
and exchanged for more severe rulers. Of course the reverse proposi-
tion cannot be maintained without qualification. Thus Christians are
faced with the question of the standard to adopt. Perhaps two
maxims make a decision easier: follow no one who forgets the world
for God's sake, and follow no one who forgets God for the world's
sake. Follow no one who promises the kingdom of God in the future
and sacrifices men for it as mere instruments; for in the kingdom of
God the ends never justify unjustified means. In other words, the

---

[a] The meaning of this expression, which occurs only here, is disputed. Some
commentators explain it as a friendly attitude recognizable in the greeting, while
others associate it with the formula of blessing and curse associated with a treaty.

[b] In greater detail, II Kings 18.32. For the deportation of the population of the
northern kingdom by the Assyrians, cf. II Kings 17.6.

[c] Cf. K. Elliger, *BHW* I, col. 131; II, col. 629g. and G. Sauer, III, col. 1772.

kingdom of God is experienced only where it is awaited and where at the same time its law is kept. That life on this earth must be ordered, and that the state must always use compulsion, is another matter. The kingdom of love and the kingdom of order are only identical in a qualified sense. Perhaps it is only because a Christian has reservations based upon eschatology that makes ordered life tolerable to him.

[36.22–37.7] The Judaean delegation return at once to their king. Because they have been given no opportunity for an honourable capitulation and have also heard the name of Yahweh blasphemed,[a] they tear their clothes. When they bring him their report, the king is deeply moved by the news, likewise tears his clothes and puts on the sack, the penitential garment.[b] He then goes to the Temple. It may be that the narrator regarded it as so obvious that Hezekiah would pray to Yahweh there that he assumed that it could be omitted; but cf. 37.15ff. In this context, however, the humility of the king should be recognized; he does not send for the senior priests, but goes to them. It is no accident that there is no mention of a high priest. This corresponds to the situation before the exile, when this office was unknown, even though in every sanctuary there must have been a chief priest (cf. II Kings 25.18).[c] The sending of the second delegation, composed in this way, to the prophet Isaiah emphasizes the priority of the spiritual Israel over the secular, and also of the prophets over the priests; in their quality as links between God and the people, the prophets seem to be almost above the king. Small features like this can usually be taken to imply that the narrative arose in a circle which can be cautiously described as favourable to the prophets. In accordance with the situation, the delegation also wore penitential garments.[d]

In 37.3 the message is introduced by a statement which is meant to describe the situation as exceedingly dangerous, if not without hope. A mother who cannot bring a birth to its conclusion is, without medical help, doomed to die and at best in extreme danger. Verse 4aα shows how God is taken completely seriously; the possibility that Yahweh was present at the scene outside the city as a silent witness is explicitly made prominent, so that the request to Isaiah to pray to him is seen as almost an additional act of respect to the divine

[a] Cf. above, p. 383.
[b] Cf. the comment on 15.2f.
[c] Cf. K. Koch, *BHW* II, col. 737ff.
[d] Cf. above, p. 383.

sovereign ruler, who is consciously described, by contrast to the gods of the nations, as the living God (cf. Pss. 42.3; 84.3; Jer. 5.2; 10.10; 23.36; Josh. 3.10; Dan. 6.27 and Matt. 16.16 and 26.63).

Verse 5 makes it somewhat doubtful whether the words of the deputation were necessary at all; because it gives the impression that the prophet was already in the picture and possessed Yahweh's answer, a prophecy of salvation to which a reason is added, belonging to the tradition of the cultic oracle of salvation which is particularly evident in Deutero-Isaiah (cf. e.g. 40.9; 41.14; 43.1).[a] The expression 'the young men of the king of Assyria' may refer to the Assyrian delegation, which according to II Kings 18.17 consisted of several members, or may already be influenced by v. 9b. It must be realized that the punishment for blasphemy against Yahweh was death (cf. Num. 15.30; Matt. 26.65) in order to realize that the link between vv. 6 and 7 is not merely superficial. Verse 7 influences the whole narrative down to 37.36. The fact that the sudden withdrawal of Sennacherib was attributed to a rumour which he had heard under the influence of a special spirit given to him by Yahweh (cf. I Kings 22.19ff.)[b] shows that in the narrator's view there was no objective reason for his sudden withdrawal. According to 36.2 and 13, it was not the Rabshakeh but his royal master who was called to account and came under the judgment of God for his arrogance (cf. 10.5ff.).

[37.8–9a] With 37.8 the text loses its clarity. Let us first recall that the Rabshakeh returned to his royal master, who in the meantime – presumably after the conquest of Lachish – had turned to attack Libnah.[c] Whether the Rabshakeh left his army or returned with it must unfortunately be a matter of conjecture, in view of the brevity of the passage and the break in its continuity. Verse 9 gives fresh ground for conjecture. The present text, which in my view has been pieced together in a garbled fashion from an older text, gives the impression that the rumour that Tirhakah was setting out caused the withdrawal, whereas originally v. 9a probably began a new episode which had no connection with 37.36, and was therefore suppressed in the process of redaction.[d] This is all the more unfortunate, in that

---

[a] Cf. C. Westermann, ATD 19, 1966, pp. 13ff.; *Isaiah 40–66*, OTL, 1969, pp. 11ff.

[b] Cf. E. Würthwein, 'Zur Komposition von I Reg 22.1–38' in *Das ferne und nahe Wort. Festschrift L. Rost*, BZAW 105, 1967, pp. 245ff.

[c] For the identification with *tell bornāṭ*, cf. K. Elliger, *BHW* II, col. 1081.

[d] Cf. above, p. 378.

it may have deprived us of the only possibility of checking the narrative of the emperor, which goes beyond II Kings 18.13ff. Thus it is not possible to tell how far the annals of Sennacherib maintain the chronological order. But since the narrative in its present form is intended to show that the hope which men place in Yahweh will not be put to shame, we have a theological consolation for our loss.

[37.37aab–38] When the king returned to Nineveh, however, he met the fate prophesied for him in our narrative in the form of a *vaticinium ex eventu* in v. 7: he was murdered, not, moreover, in a place, in circumstances and by people who were a matter of indifference, but as he was praying in the temple and by his own sons. The two cuneiform texts which refer to this event, the annals of his grandson Asshurbanipal and the Babylonian chronicle,[a] cannot be wholly reconciled with the present narrative. The annals of Asshurbanipal show that the king was killed by several persons. The fact that they seemed to have used the statues of protective deities as their instruments may confirm the biblical narrative that he was murdered in the temple, although it has not so far been possible to interpret the name of a god Nisroch given in v. 38. The Babylonian chronicle suggests that the deed was done by one of his sons, but similarly mentions no names, while in the biblical narrative it is questionable whether they are given correctly or completely.[b] Since the cuneiform sources leave us so much at a loss, the suspicion arises that influential circles close to his successor Esarhaddon may actually have been involved in the matter.[c] It is significant that vengeance was first exacted by his grandson.

But the main purpose of vv. 37 and 38 is not to give us historical information, but to provide a contrast to 37.2ff. and against the background of 36.4ff., 13ff.: whereas the prayer to Yahweh, the living God, was heard, Sennacherib was murdered in the temple as he prayed. This demonstrates who is the living God and who are the lifeless idols of the nations (cf. also 37.3ff.). The fact that the emperor also fell by the hand of his sons, while they had to flee in to the land of Ararat, the *urarṭu* of the cuneiform sources,[d] emphasizes for the ancient

[a] *AR* II, § 795f.; *ANET*[2], p. 288 and *TGI*[2], p. 69.

[b] For Nisroch, cf. R. Borger, *BHW* II, col. 1316; on Adrammelech, R. Borger, *BHW* I, col. 28 and on Sharezer C. A. Keller, *BHW* III, col. 1671, and also Montgomery-Gehman and Gray on II Kings 19.37.

[c] Cf. R. Borger, *BHW* I, col. 134f.

[d] Cf. O. Bückmann, *BHW* I, col. 120f., and also M. Riemschneider, *Das Reich am Ararat*, Leipzig and Stuttgart 1965.

reader, and one would hope for the modern reader also, the horrible and unnatural nature of his end (cf. 46.10; Deut. 21.18ff.) as well as the first steps in the collapse of the Assyrian kingdom.

[37.9b–21, 33–36, 37a] *Yahweh's help and the impotence of the gods.* In the present context the sending of a second message from the emperor to Hezekiah is to be regarded as a direct consequence of the news that an Egyptian army was setting out under the Ethiopian Pharaoh Tirhakah.[a] There is a contradiction between v. 10 and v. 14, in so far as v. 10 seems to assume a verbal message, whereas v. 14 seems to tell only of the handing over of a letter which has not previously been mentioned. It may be that this contradiction arises solely from the carelessness of the narrator who assumed the natural custom of conveying a message both verbally and in writing, and consequently did not consider it necessary to describe an incident of no importance for the rest of the story. In content, what is told to the messengers in vv. 10–13 is entirely the product of the theological concern of the narrator to bring to the fore the contrast between confidence in Yahweh and confidence in the gods. He achieves his purpose by making the emperor explicitly deny this distinction by means of an appeal to history. From his point of view there is no difference between Yahweh and the gods of the many countries whom his forefathers have incorporated in the Assyrian empire. The gods of the country of Gozan, far to the north-west on the river Habor (cf. II Kings 17.6; I Chron. 5.26),[b] of the caravan crossroads of Haran to the west of it,[c] of Rezeph, which may perhaps have lain between the Jevel Sinjar and the Tigris,[d] or of the Beth Adini,[e] which lay on both sides of the middle Euphrates, with its capital Til Barsip,[f] and Yahweh were all one and the same in his eyes. When we go on to the names listed in v. 13, some of which are already familiar from 36.19, we involuntarily ask whether the narrator associated with them with any concrete idea or was simply delighting in the exotic sound of the names. Hamath on the Orontes is followed by the North Syrian Arpad, by *lāʿir*,[g] which perhaps lay on the Elamite border, by

[a] Cf. above p. 374 and p. 377.
[b] Cf. M. A. Beek, *BHW* I, p. 585.
[c] Cf. M. A. Beek, *BHW* II, p. 647.
[d] Cf. Gray (2nd edition) on II Kings 19.12, pp. 687f., but also R. Knippenberg, *BHW* III, col. 1595.
[e] Cf. Honigmann, *RLA* II, pp. 33f.
[f] The biblical Tilassar may be a bowdlerised form of this name.
[g] Cf. A. Sarowsky, *ZAW* 32, 1912, p. 146.

Sepharvaim, which we know from 36.19, and finally by *hēnaʿ*,[a] which may have lain on the middle Euphrates, and *ʿiwwā*,[b] which cannot be identified with certainty. Thus the confidence placed in Yahweh seems to be deceptive (cf. v. 10) and the deliverance of Jerusalem impossible (vv. 11 and 12).

[37.14–20] In dramatic terms which would be appropriate to the underlying basis of the first narrative,[c] v. 14 describes the reaction of the king when he received the letter from the hands of the messengers, read it and convinced himself that the message which he had already received verbally was correct. He went to the Temple in order to spread out the letter 'before Yahweh'. Although Yahweh is the creator of heaven and earth (v. 16) yet his house is in a special sense the place of his presence and of dealings between him and men. The behaviour of the king is basically within the framework of what we know from ancient Mesopotamia about 'letters of God', letters which, for example, were read out and deposited in the Temple after a victorious campaign, so that the gods to whom they were addressed could take note of them.[d]

In his prayer Hezekiah addresses his God solemnly with the title 'Yahweh of hosts' which we find for the first time in I Sam. 4.4 in connection with the ark, and which is expanded here by the phrase 'God of Israel'. Yahweh of hosts is seated above the cherubim, and the title recalls his cosmic omnipotence, embracing heaven and earth. It is against this background that the real meaning of the profession of monotheist faith that follows is to be understood. The basis of his absolute rule over the kingdoms of the earth is the fact that he is the creator of heaven and earth. Verse 17 urgently begs God to take note of the arrogant mockery of Sennacherib. The request to look is preceded by a request to hear, which tacitly assumes that the letter has been read out. In order to keep to the fore the true theme, the distinction between Yahweh, the living God (cf. 37.4), and the gods of the nations, the king confirms in vv. 18 and 19 the succession of victories by the Assyrian kings, with the destruction of the gods of the conquered nations, as an introduction to the statement that they are nothing. According to post-exilic religious polemic this was

[a] Cf. *KBL* sub voce.
[b] Cf. *KBL* sub voce.
[c] Cf. above, pp. 382f.
[d] Cf. R. Borger, *RLA* III, pp. 575f. and A. Leo Oppenheim, 'The City of Assur in 714 B.C.', *JNES* 19, 1960, pp. 133ff. and especially pp. 144f.

demonstrated by the very fact that their images were manufactured,[a] a theme which has been rightly recognized as displaying a spirit of enlightenment.[b] Finally, when the king begs for deliverance in v. 20, he expects as a result of this the acknowledgement of the exclusive deity of Yahweh by all the kingdoms of the earth (cf. 45.2f.; Phil. 2.9f.; Rev. 11.15; 12.10).[c] Here the narrator was either unaware that he was bound to provoke the question why the kingdoms of the earth had not recognized the exclusive deity of Yahweh in spite of the deliverance of Jerusalem in 701, and still did not acknowledge it, or else he and his community agreed that the events of this year were an archetype of the tempest of the nations against the city of God in the final age and of the conversion of the nations which would follow it, so that what had not yet been fulfilled was turned into an eschatological prophecy (cf. 14.24ff.; 17.12ff.; 29.1ff.; 30.27ff.; 32.9ff., and also 25.6f.; 2.2ff.).

[37.21, 33–35] While the spreading out of the letter in the Temple might suggest a limitation of Yahweh conflicting with the profession of faith which follows, v. 21 corrects this by showing the prophet conveying the divine answer to Hezekiah without being asked. This makes it obvious that while Yahweh heard the prayer uttered in the Temple, he was in direct contact with his prophet, without limitations of space, and likewise had towards the world a direct relationship subject only to his will. That a prophet could go directly to his king was outside the conceptual world of the late author. Commanded by Yahweh, the God who seeks to be revealed in what happens to Israel, he assures the king that his prayer has been heard, that Jerusalem will remain inviolate, neither attacked nor besieged, and that Sennacherib will withdraw. It is not certain that v. 34 is a later addition to the oracle, taking up v. 29. Verse 36 assumes the death of most but all of the Assyrians. If the emperor had been one of those who had died, the narrator would not have hesitated to tell us so explicitly. The fact that v. 34b alludes to the beginning of the oracle in v. 33a may be intentional, in order to emphasize something which concerned the hearers regardless of the

---

[a] Cf. e.g. 40.19f.; 41.6f.; 44.9ff.; 45.16f.; Wisd. 13f.; Jub. 11.12, 20 and the Letter of Jeremiah.

[b] Westermann, ATD 19, 1966, p. 122; ET *Isaiah 40–66*, OTL, 1969, pp. 149ff.

[c] For the contrast with II Kings 19.19 cf. W. Zimmerli, 'Erkenntnis Gottes nach dem Buche Ezechiel', in *Gottes Offenbarung*, ThB 19, 1963, p. 104, note 90.

occasion, that Zion was inviolate. On the other hand, v. 35 explicitly takes up 31.5, the Deutero-Isaianic 'for my own sake' (cf. 43.25; 48.9; 55.5) and the Deuteronomic 'for the sake of my servant David' (cf. I Kings 11.13, 34; 15.4 and II Kings 8.9). This shows that it is redactional, as might already have been concluded from the fact that no continuation of the oracle was to be expected after the concluding formula at the end of v. 34: the honour of Yahweh and the word which he once gave to David is at stake in the fate of Jerusalem (cf. II Sam. 7 and Ps. 132.13ff.).

[37.36, 37aβ] The fulfilment of the prophet's oracle takes place in a wholly unexpected way: At night[a] the angel of Yahweh, who represents Yahweh in direct interventions on earth and so mediates between heaven and earth, goes forth to slay an immense number of those who were in the camp of the Assyrians, as he has once done to the first-born of Egypt (cf. Ex. 12.29). The assumption that the instrument of death was a plague is basically an inadmissable rationalization of the miracle. It should be noted that the number given is far beyond what was possible at that time.[b] We are not told where the miracle took place, and ought not perhaps to ask. But it is not impossible that the narrative had in mind the destruction of the enemy before the gates of Jerusalem, the inhabitants of which would in the morning bear joyful testimony to the terror of the night (cf. Ps. 46.9f.; 76.4 and Isa. 31.8) and would have nothing more to fear from Sennacherib who had now returned to Nineveh without having achieved his purpose.

[37.22-32] *The tyrant's withdrawal and the deliverance of Zion.* 37.22-32 is an extended oracle which has been interpolated later, though it is already found in the book of Kings. Verses 22-29 are addressed to Sennacherib and vv. 30-32 to Hezekiah. In vv. 23 and 24, 26 and 27 there are quite clear allusions to the context for which it must have been composed. Sennacherib – or whoever his name stood for at that moment – may have been very proud of his own power and strength. But Jerusalem, the daughter of Zion, the Zion to whom the promise was made, shakes her head behind him in contempt (cf. Ps.

---

[a] Cf. also the extra words at the beginning of the verse in II Kings 19.35.

[b] Cf. the discussion by W. W. Tarn on the strength of troops in the period of Alexander and the Diadochi in *Macedon 401–301 BC*, CAH VI, [3]1953 (1964), p. 367. For the number given by Sennacherib of those deported from Judah, however, cf. A. Ungnad, *ZAW* 59, 1942/43, pp. 199ff. who supports the reading 2150.

22.8; 44.15; Lam. 2.15; Job 16.4; Jer. 18.16 and Mark 15.29). According to v. 24 the arrogance of the emperor is expressed above all in his penetrating to the thickly wooded peaks of Lebanon, where the Mesopotamian overlords were already accustomed to satisfy their need for building timber (cf. 14.8). But there may also be an allusion to the idea consciously held by these beings that they entered into the garden of God (Ezek. 28.13). This was thought of, according to Gen. 2.8f. and Ezek. 31.8f., as a wooded garden. The fact that the poet attributes to Sennacherib, contrary to historical probability, the boast of having dried up the waters of Masor, the waters of Egypt (cf. 19.6), may be due either to his inability to distinguish between the reign of Sennacherib and that of his successors or to his desire to attribute to him a claim which placed him in direct competition with the actions of God and so unmasked his pride (cf. 51.10). On the other hand, v. 26 reminds the emperor that all his successes derive from plans made by Yahweh long ago, a conception which clearly shows the influence of later reflection.[a] Verse 27 described in metaphorical terms the sad fate of the inhabitants of cities which Sennacherib had conquered. Here the observation that the grass which grew on the flat roofs with their lagging of clay was the first to succumb to the burning east wind is quite original (cf. 40.6f. and Ps. 90.5f.). But whatever the emperor chooses to do or to permit, he cannot escape the control of Yahweh. When Yahweh considers the time has come he will lead him back like a wild animal (cf. Ezek. 19.4) or like a prisoner of war (cf. Ezek. 38.4)[b] to the place from which he came.

In v. 30 the oracle refers in the context to Hezekiah, but in fact to the eschatological Jerusalem and its mission. The sign promised in v. 30 lies in the future. It is apparently a considered estimate that the people of Jerusalem who are threatened by the Assyrians will be unable to gather in the harvest during the current year nor to plough the fields for sowing in the following year, so that the year after they will be dependent upon the second growth, and normal economic life will not return until the third year. But vv. 31 and 32 suggest that the sign may be allegorical in meaning, relating to the eschatological function of the remnant, which will have survived the tempest of the nations in the final days of a history full of struggle and conflict, and

[a] The fact that v. 26 is Deutero-Isaianic in its language is shown by comparison with 40.28; 45.24; 44.7 and 46.9.
[b] Gray, p. 691, but cf. Zimmerli, ad loc.

it is consequently destined to be the nucleus of a new Israel, an Israel to which the nations will make pilgrimage and which will rule the earth. The oracle of salvation concludes with a quotation from 9.6, naming as the basis of Israel's hope the zeal of Yahweh for his honour in the sight of the world. For once God is committed to the destiny of Israel, he cannot abandon it, for the sake of his own name. It is not impossible that vv. 30–32 are more recent than vv. 22–29.

CHAPTER 38.1–22

The Sickness and Healing of Hezekiah

1 In those days Hezekiah became sick and was at the point of death. And Isaiah the prophet the son of Amoz came to him, and said to him, 'Thus says Yahweh: Set your house in order; for you shall die, you shall not recover.' ²Then Hezekiah turned his face to the wall, and prayed to Yahweh, ³and said, 'Remember now, O Yahweh, I beseech thee, how I have walked before thee in faithfulness and with a whole heart, and have done what is good in thy sight.' And Hezekiah wept bitterly. ⁴Then the word of Yahweh came to Isaiah: ⁵'Go and say to Hezekiah, Thus says Yahweh, the God of David your father: I have heard your prayer, I have seen your tears; behold, I will add fifteen years to your life. ⁶I will deliver you and this cityª out of the hand of the king of Assyria, and defend this city.ᵇ

7 This is the sign to you from Yahweh, that Yahweh will do this

ª Contrary to J. Gray, *I and II Kings*, OTL, ²1970, p. 697, note c on II Kings 20.6 'and this city' can hardly be a dittography. The problem here is not one of textual but of literary criticism. Cf. 37.35a para. with II Kings 19.34a.

ᵇ The Isaianic redactor placed the story of Hezekiah's healing by the application of a cake of figs behind the sign (and behind the Psalm of Hezekiah which was interpolated later), cf. 20.7 with Isa. 38.21. But in so doing he also separated the introduction to the narrative of the sign from its context, shortened it and placed it at the end, cf. II Kings 20.8 with Isa. 38.22. Here his concern was clearly that of giving, in a form as unexceptionable and exemplary as possible, a portrait of a devout king. The suppression of II Kings 20.9f. serves the same purpose. On the other hand the increase in the powers attributed to the prophet can be noticed in the change in 38.8 by contrast to II Kings 20.11.

thing that he has promised: ⁸Behold, I will make the shadow on the
steps, which ⟨the sun⟩ᵃ has descended on the steps to ⟨the balcony⟩ᵃ of
Ahaz go back in the sun ten steps.' Then the sun turned back ten steps
on the steps on which it had gone down.

9 ⟨An atoning poem⟩ᵇ of Hezekiah king of Judah, after he had been
sick and had recovered from his sickness;

10   I said, In the ⟨misery⟩ᶜ
      of my days I must depart;
     I am consigned to the gates of the underworld
      for the rest of my years.

11   I said, I shall not see ⟨Yahweh⟩ᵃ
      in the land of the living;
     I shall look upon man no more
      among the inhabitants of the world.ᵈ

12   My dwelling is plucked up and removed from over meᵉ
      like ⟨the shepherd's⟩ᵃ tent;
     like a weaver ⟨thou dost roll up⟩ᶠ my life;
      ⟨thou dost cut⟩ᶠ me off from the thrum;
     from day to night thou dost abandon me,ᵍ

13   ⟨I cry for help⟩ᵃ until morning;
      like a lion he breaks
     all my bones ⟨   ⟩ᵃ

14   Like a swallow ⟨   ⟩ᵃ I squeal,
      I moan like a dove.
     My eyes ⟨languish⟩ʰ for the height,
      ⟨   ⟩ᵃ I am oppressed; be thou my security!

15   But what can I say ⟨and speak to him⟩?ᵃ
      For he himself has done it.¹

ᵃ Cf. *BHS*.

ᵇ The emendation of *miktāb*, 'writing, inscription' into *miktām*, probably 'psalm
of atonement' is based upon the headings to Ps. 16 and Pss. 56–60, cf. also LXX.

ᶜ Read *bᵉdōm*, from *dmm* II, lament.

ᵈ For *ḥedel* = *ḥeled*, cf. D. W. Thomas, SVT 4, 1957, pp. 11ff. and *HAL* p. 281
and p. 303 sub vocibus.

ᵉ J. Begrich, *Der Psalm des Hiskia*, FRLANT 42, 1926, p. 27, would read *wᵉnāgal*,
from *gll*, 'and rode up' and delete *minnī*. But against this, cf. already Dillmann-
Kittel, *ad loc.*

ᶠ Read *qippadtā* and *tᵉbaṣṣᵉʿēnī*, cf. Begrich, pp. 29f.

ᵍ Cf. the *šᵉlēm* of the Targum, M. Jastrow, *Dictionary* II, p. 1586, Eissfeldt, *ad loc.*
and Begrich, p. 33.

ʰ Read *kālū* with Begrich, p. 38.

¹ The comparison with Ps. 39.10 shows that contrary to Begrich, p. 41, the
lamentation has not yet passed to the song of thanksgiving.

⟨Lord⟩, my years ⟨fade away⟩[a]
⟨in the bitterness⟩[b] of my soul.

16 ⟨I thought, I must depart and be gone,⟩[c]
my spirit ⟨is destroyed⟩[d]
⟨Thou hast healed me and cured me,⟩[e]

17 ⟨   ⟩[f] my bitterness was turned to well-being.⟨   ⟩[g]
⟨   ⟩[h] Thou ⟨hast held back⟩[i] my soul
from the pit of destruction,
for thou hast cast all my sins
behind thy back.

18 For the underworld does not thank thee,
nor death praise thee;
those who go down to the pit do not hope
for thy faithfulness.

19 Only he who lives[j] thanks thee,
as I do this day;
the father makes known to the children
how faithful thou art.[k]

20 Yahweh ⟨was pleased⟩[l] to save us.
Then let us play stringed instruments[m]
all the days of our life,
at the house of Yahweh.

21 Now Isaiah said, Let them take a cake of figs, and apply (it) to the boil, that he may recover. [22]And Hezekiah said, What is the sign that I may go up (again) to the house of Yahweh?

[a] Read *'ᵃdōnāy kālū*, cf. Ps. 31.11. Vv. 15b and 16ab are so corrupted in the received text that any attempt at a reconstruction can ultimately only be a demonstration of its author's knowledge of the themes of the psalm of lamentation and his ability and his skill in the technique of Hebrew verse. With these reservations the following new proposals are made; they make use of the existing consonant text as far as possible, but assume that this too has been corrupted.

[b] Read *bᵉmar*, cf. Ezek. 27.31; Job 7.11; 10.1.

[c] Read *'āmartī 'ēlēk wᵉ'ēnennī*, cf. Ps. 39.14.

[d] Read *ḥubbālā*, cf. Job. 17.1.

[e] Read *wattaḥᵃlīmēnī watᵉḥayyēnī*.

[f] Delete *hinnē* as a dittography of *wᵉhaḥᵃyēnī*.

[g] Delete the second *mar* as a dittography.

[h] Perhaps read simply *'attā*.

[i] Read *ḥāśaktā*, cf. Ps. 78.50.

[j] Literally: 'the living, the living. . . .'

[k] Read *'ēt-'ᵃmittekā*, literally 'thy faithfulness'.

[l] With Begrich, p. 50, insert *hō'īl*.

[m] For the form cf. B-L, supplement p. I on p. 203.

Two passages here present a problem to the reader who is not looking for conflicts and gaps in the tradition, but is accustomed to read
the stories of the bible purely for his own edification: the Psalm of
Hezekiah introduced by v. 9 and reproduced in vv. 10–20, and still
more the two concluding verses, 21 and 22. For while he may be
prepared to accept that within the narrative the prayer is given in v. 3
in an abbreviated form and afterwards at length, there is no such
explanation for vv. 21 and 22. If Yahweh himself intends to prolong
the life of the sick king Hezekiah of Judah by fifteen years (cf. v. 5)
the prophet's manipulation with the cake of figs comes somewhat
late; it looks as though the prophet is trying to lend his God a helping
hand. Finally, v. 22 must appear completely meaningless, unless we
decide to translate it: 'Then Hezekiah said, What a sign for me to go
up (once again) to the house of Yahweh!' Perhaps this is the correct
translation. But the astonished and curious reader will in the meantime have turned to II Kings 20.1–11 and discovered that v. 22 in the
present chapter is there found in a quite different context, in v.8, and
must be translated as we have done above. It is also stated there that
the king is asking for a sign for the healing which Yahweh has
promised. If the two texts are further compared, it appears that v. 22b
in fact goes back to the similar promise in II Kings 20.5bβ, according
to which the king is allowed to return to the temple on the third day,
a feature which the redactor who was responsible for transferring the
Isaiah stories from the book of Kings to the book of Isaiah has
suppressed, cf. v. 5b with 20.5b and 6a. Thus we have here a shortened version of the narrative from the book of Kings. It is perhaps
possible that vv. 8–11 were added to the narrative in the book of
Kings after it had been transferred to the book of Isaiah.[a] But it is
more probable that the redactor abbreviated it in order to protect the
king against any suspicion of an impious challenge to God.[b]

[1–8, 21–22] *The miracle of the sun.* The question of the previous
history of the story which appears here in the shortened form, and in
the longer form in II Kings, can satisfactorily be left to a commentary

---

[a] In disagreement with B. Stade, *ZAW* 6, 1886, p. 184, with A. Šanda, *Die
Bücher der Könige*, EH 9.2, 1912, p. 304.

[b] Cf. above p. 397 note b. II Kings 20.4a is lacking in front of v. 4; v. 5b there corresponds to 6a, but omits 20.5b; v. 6 does not include 20.6b; 20.8 is reproduced in a
characteristically shortened form, and, cf. the comment, is reinterpreted in v. 22;
20.9a is found in v. 7; 20.10 and 11a are omitted, which necessitated the recasting
of v. 8, and the indications of place in 20.9 must have been lost later. Small
deviations are not discussed here.

on that book.[a] A few observations, however, may make the passage easier for the puzzled reader. – As we have suggested, there is some tension between the healing of the sick king by the prophet and the answer to his prayer by Yahweh with the promise of further years of life, and it is at least permissible to ask whether the stories have always belonged together or were not first combined when they were written down. [1, 21] For example, if we read v. 1, break off after 'and said to him' and immediately go on to v. 21 without the introduction, we have a very short but coherent episode which lacks only an account of the success of the treatment. A glance at II Kings 20.7 shows that this can easily be found in the received text. There the insertion of a single different vowel sign and the addition of a dot as the sign of a doubled consonant has turned 'he may recover' into 'he recovered'. Thus we conjecture that the story once told how the prophet Isaiah came to king Hezekiah, who was fatally ill, and healed him by the application of figs to his body. Notwithstanding accounts of the medical use of figs in antiquity, we must assume that the healing by the prophet seemed miraculous to his contemporaries,[b] or that his superior abilities were displayed by the very fact that he – and of course he alone – knew how to cure this potentially fatal disease. In the second case, even the relative familiarity of the procedure may have given those who heard of it a feeling that the prophet knew the right means to use, while the doctors had obviously failed. Thus we can imagine the tradition being narrated in prophetic circles in Jerusalem, in which certain practices of popular medicine were in use. Whether the prophet whom we know from his recorded words had provided any grounds for the formation of such a tradition by what he did or permitted cannot be proved, and is on the whole unlikely.

[2–5, 7–8] With a more practised eye, we now discover that the story of the miraculous sign also has a previous history of its own. Unless the person responsible for transcribing it, or his informant, has succeeded suppressing completely the origin of the demand for the sign, we must think once again, for good or for ill, of an illness of the king. During its course the prophet comes to Hezekiah to prophesy to him that his end is near. But on hearing the king's prayer, Yahweh

[a] Cf. E. Würthwein, ATD 11, shortly to be published.

[b] J. Meinhold, *Die Jesajaerzählungen*, Göttingen 1898, p. 11. Apart from the reference to Pliny, *Nat. Hist.* XXIII.7, J. A. Montgomery and H. S. Gehman, *The Book of Kings*, ICC, 1951, p. 512, refer to *CTA* 160.24 and J. Gray, *I and II Kings*, OTL, ²1970, p. 698 refers to *CTA* 161.33.

decides – it does not matter exactly how the passage originally read – to do differently (cf. II Kings 20.4), to convey to him the promise that he would be healed in three days, and consequently to take back the word which has just been uttered. The visit to the temple after three days no doubt refers simply to the making of a thank-offering as a sign of complete recovery in the meantime (cf. Ps. 107.17ff.). Perhaps, however, we ought to regard the story as it is recorded here as once again an independent and consequently a third story of the sickness and healing of Hezekiah. Sickness, the announcement of imminent death, prayer, the hearing of the prayer and the conveying of the word of life by the prophet are all clearly recognizable as the nucleus of all the narratives of the sick king, a nucleus which had as its only disadvantage that it was not sufficiently miraculous for the devout imagination of later times. The fact that the king emphasizes his piety in the prayer that is recorded is of course an unusual feature, suitable to the idealized Hezekiah of the Deuteronomic history, but theologically weak: would not Yahweh have known all this before he prophesied his death? And was there once some mention of a sin of Hezekiah which later editors felt they had to conceal? Or are these mere speculations? – If we follow the course indicated, the king is understandably irritated by the sudden change in what is foretold by the same prophet, so that he demands and actually receives a sign of confirmation. Faced by the prophet with a choice of having the shadow on the staircase leading to an upper storey built by his father Ahaz rise or fall, Hezekiah naïvely chooses, in accordance with what the hearers or original readers of the story would expect, the apprently more difficult alternative, for the shadow normally falls (cf. II Kings 20.9f.).[a] Nevertheless, it rises. The king knows that he will be cured – and so do the hearers! To attempt to give a scientific explanation of this legend is simply to destroy it. An eclipse of the sun, moreover, would not have brought about the event which is described.[b] No, the essence of the story is what seems impossible to

[a] Y. Tadin, *maʿalōt ʾāḥāz* (The Dial of Ahaz), *Eretz-Israel* 5, *Festschrift B. Mazar*, Jerusalem 1958, pp. 91ff. with figs. 1–6 and the English summary pp. 89f. points to the possibility of also interpreting the staircase as a sundial, with the necessary references.

[b] Gray, p. 699, refers to an eclipse of the sun on the 11 January 689, although he does not make use of it in his interpretation. His attempt on pp. 699f. to assume a historical nucleus to the narrative, according to which Isaiah emphasized to the king that his oracle should be believed by pointing to the impossibility of the

men in their everyday life, but what the pious imagination and a faith reflecting profoundly upon the power of God nevertheless regards as possible, a miracle. For the pious imagination, a possibility on principle becomes a reality. The fact that the prophet can move God to an extraordinary act (cf. II Kings 20.11) brings his respect and admiration. The redaction of the narrative which we possess, of course, brings back the act entirely under the control of God, and makes the prophet once again nothing more than a messenger. The promise in v. 5 that the king's life will be prolonged by fifteen years (cf. II Kings 20.6) must remain a matter of dispute, because it involves the debate upon the chronology of the kingdom of Judah in the second half of the eighth century. If the statement in II Kings 18.2, that Hezekiah reigned for twenty-nine years, is regarded as original, the promise must be regarded as a consequence of the inclusion of the story at the beginning of v. 1 among the events of the year 701, or of the fourteenth year of the king's reign (cf. II Kings 18.13; Isa. 36.1). But the reverse argument may apply. [6] There is nothing in the content of the story which shows any connection with the danger from the Assyrians. Verse 6 (cf. II Kings 20.6b, and also II Kings 19.34, with Isa. 37.35) makes this connection very loosely. Once the fifteen years had become established in the story – in which case they would form part of the version describing the king's illness and the demand for a sign – it would be possible, taking into account II Kings 18.13 (or Isa. 36.1), and after the whole of the present narrative had been incorporated with that of the threat from the Assyrians (cf. Isa. 36 and 37 para.), to calculate and include the mention of a reign lasting twenty-nine years.[a] A difficult problem! But by pointing it out we have shown that the indication of time at the beginning of v. 1 and the promise in v. 6 have assisted the literary link with what precedes.

[9–20] *The Psalm of Hezekiah.* The song is not organically incorporated into the flow of the narrative, but is provided with a heading which in the present context produces a somewhat abrupt impression, and is similar to that of many of the psalms. This excludes the possibility that it was added by the same redactor of the Isaiah roll who was responsible for the incorporation of II Kings 18.14, 17.20–19. If

---

shadow moving back can be regarded as no more than the latest attempt to rationalize the miracle story.

[a] Cf. K. T. Andersen, StTh 23, 1969, p. 102.

vv. 21 and 22 were not added until later, an opinion which is not certain, although it is widely accepted, the redactor responsible for the interpolation of the psalm would not be guilty of having failed to choose the best position for it. The category of the song can be defined as that of an individual psalm of thanksgiving. Although it is possible to translate the introductory '*a*nī '*āmartī* or '*amārtī*, in vv. 10 and 11, by the present tense, the departures from the form of a psalm of lamentation suggests they should be understood as preterites. Thus in vv. 10–15, and 16abα, the person uttering the prayer looks back upon the distress he has undergone and then continues with the thanksgiving as such. In formal terms, we note that the song begins neither with the address to Yahweh which is usual in lamentations,[a] nor with an introduction in the form of a declaration of the purpose of the praise, or an address, such as is typical of the psalm of thanksgiving.[b] The lamentation which begins immediately after the retrospective comment in v. 10 describes the suffering as though it was still taking place. Yet by v. 17 there is an attempt to remove the illusion so produced. If the conjectural 'I thought' which we propose at the beginning of v. 16 is acceptable, this attempt occurs even earlier. Thus this psalm of thanksgiving is unique in its category, a fact which can be attributed either solely to its relatively late origin or also to the fact that it was intentionally composed for its present context. For the retrospective section portrays for us someone fatally ill (cf. v. 1) who regards himself entirely in terms of what is stated in v. 3, and does not seem to display any awareness of sin or guilt.

[10–15] Elsewhere in the poem the themes differ somewhat from their classical application. Thus in vv. 10f. the speaker emphasizes that he supposed his sufferings would inevitably lead to death. This obviously differs from the assertion of the petitioner in a lamentation, that he is already in the underworld.[c] The parallel with the situation in v. 1 is equally evident. That the underworld has gates was a conception which the Israelites presumably inherited from the Babylonians by way of the Canaanites.[d] What the terrors of death really

[a] Cf. H. Gunkel and J. Begrich, *Einleitung in die Psalmen*, HK II E, 1933, pp. 212ff.

[b] Cf. *ibid.*, pp. 267f. and Begrich, *Psalm des Hiskia*, pp. 53f.

[c] Cf. Ps. 42.8; 49.16; 55.5; 69.2f., 15f.; 71.20; 88.4ff. and 130.1.

[d] With A. Jeremias, *ATAO*[4], p. 684, Job. 38.17; Ps. 9.14; Matt. 16.18; III Macc. 5.51; Wisdom of Sol. 16.13 and also B. Meissner, *Babylonien und Assyrien* II, Heidelberg 1925, p. 144 and H. Kees, *Totenglaube und Jenseitsvorstellungen der alten Ägypter*, Berlin [2]1956, p. 289.

meant is shown by v. 11: a separation from Yahweh, whom the
devout encounter in his saving epiphany in the temple (cf. Pss. 17.15;
11.7; 27.4 and 13),[a] and separation from those who live upon this
earth.[b] Here man is understood as in the first instance a being who
needs a relationship with God and his neighbour, but for whom both
are limited to this life. In this the psalm is in agreement with modern
scepticism. The expected end of his life is described in v. 12 in two
very original metaphors, that of the striking of a Bedouin or shepherd's
tent[c] and that of the cutting off of the completed piece of cloth by the
weaver from the supporting threads known as the thrum.[d] In v. 12bβ
the prayer turns to describe the suffering which is expressed in the
cries of the petitioner throughout the day and night.[e] Unlike e.g.
Pss. 5.3; 18.7 or 28.2, it is not stated that these are addressed to
Yahweh. Thus the poet seems to have understood them as the
expression of a ceaseless pain, torturing the very marrow and the
bone, as we may say in view of v. 13aβ[f] and caused in his view by
none other than Yahweh himself.[g] The continuous crying is compared in v. 14, once again in a very original and observant image,
with the 'long drawn out· "eeee . . ." ' with which a swallow flits
through the air,[h] and the ceaseless murmuring of doves, which a city
dweller may have noticed at least in the main squares of large cities in
Italy, if he is out of contact with the countryside at home (cf. also
59.11).[i] Although the pain does not allow him to pray, in his suffering

[a] For the cultic theophany cf. A. Weiser, ATD 14/15, ⁷1966, pp. 49f. and pp.
24ff. ET *The Psalms*, OTL, 1962, pp. 57ff. and 29ff.

[b] For the distinctive nature of a lament for separation from men as such in this
passage cf. Begrich, *Psalm des Hiskia*, p. 56.

[c] Cf. G. Dalman, *Arbeit und Sitte in Palästina* VI, Gütersloh 1939, pp. 12ff.

[d] Cf. the lengthy discussion of Begrich, *Psalm des Hiskia*, pp. 30f. and also
Dalman, *Arbeit und Sitte* V, 1937, pp. 112ff. and p. 124.

[e] Cf. e.g. Pss. 6.7; 13.3 and 42.9.

[f] Cf. Pss. 6.3; 22.15; 32.3; 42.11; Jer. 20.9; Lam. 3.4 and Job 30.30

[g] In Pss. 7.3; 10.9; 17.12; 22.14, 22; 35.17 and 57.5 the lion is a symbol for the
enemy of the worshipper, from whom Yahweh is to save him; but here it is a
symbol of Yahweh as the cause of the illness. Thus we have no need to concern
ourselves with possible demonological themes underlying the simile.

[h] Hans Schmidt, in *Vom Alten Testament. Festschrift K. Marti*, BZAW 41, 1925,
p. 258, quoted by Begrich, *Psalm des Hiskia*, p. 37. Neither author nor translator
can find a better rendering for *ṣpṣp* than 'pfeifen' in German or 'pipe' in English,
but these are felt to be closer to what is meant than 'zwitschern' or 'twitter'.

[i] Cf. also Begrich, *Psalm des Hiskia*, p. 37.

he raises his eyes to the height where Yahweh dwells,[a] to beg with a wordless lament that Yahweh will intervene on his behalf, like a guarantor for a debtor who cannot pay.[b] As in the case of Job, he is smitten by God himself, and can only appeal to God against God (cf. Job 9.13ff. and 19.6ff.). The poet is well aware that this is the real difficulty for the petitioner, if he is to turn to God in his distress. What can he say to him who himself has caused his suffering, and is not just anyone, but is Yahweh himself? He is either not conscious of any sin or in fact, as the prototype of a truly devout king, has in the eyes of the poet no sins to confess (cf. v. 4) although he later mentions his forgiveness. Consequently he reminds God how short his suffering life is (cf. Pss. 31.11; 39.6f.; Job 7.7ff. and 9.20ff.) in order to arouse his mercy and move him to help. But this is also an expression of the belief that man has no claim to make upon God for happiness, but is dependent upon his grace, a truth which is much more obvious to all of us in theory than in practice, and which human beings may never apply against others.

[16–20] Verse 16 moves away from the consideration of the suffering to the account of the deliverance by Yahweh, which is no longer looked forward to. For Yahweh has given the sick man back his life and health, and turned his bitter suffering into well-being. The fact that the sick man does not have to go down into the grave, described here as elsewhere as the pit (cf. Job 33.18; Ps. 16.10; 30.10), is explicitly attributed to the forgiveness of his sins by Yahweh. He has as it were thrown them over his back, so that he is no longer provoked by the sight of them to send further sufferings (cf. Pss. 51.3ff. 11; 103.3f.). The reason given in v. 18 for Yahweh's intervention contains a device which can be found both in lamentations and psalms of thanksgiving (cf. Pss. 6.6; 30.10; 88.11f. and 115.17): the underworld, Sheol and death are actually personified. All who are subject to their rule behave as they do. At first sight the modern reader finds this argument strange, but it is not as naïve as it seems. It has in mind what essentially constitutes man's relationship to God from the human point of view, and demonstrates whether a human being allows his God to be God and therefore needs him. In waiting upon his faithfulness (cf. Pss. 104.27; 145.15; 30.10) as in the praise and thanksgiving which acknowledge his help, man lets God be his

[a] Cf. the comment on 32.15.

[b] For ʿošqā and ʿrb as technical legal terms cf. Begrich, *Psalm des Hiskia*, p. 38 and e.g. Prov. 14.32 and 11.15.

God by admitting his indebtedness to God for his own being and that of everything around him. Thus man fulfils his destiny in the praise of God.

Following this reason, the thought turns in v. 19 to the profession of the healed man who now thankfully declares that he has been delivered. He considers his children as the witnesses of the future and considers in them the future of God and his community (cf. Deut. 4.9; Ps. 45.18) while in the community which is drawn into his praise he takes the present into account (cf. Pss. 22.23, 26; 149.1). It is quite natural that they too should have reason to acknowledge Yahweh's help and thank him with songs and instrumental music, if the life of their king has been restored to them (cf. Ps. 144.9f.; 149.2f.). But the praise of the community no doubt looks beyond the present moment and the help experienced in it, to all the help that it has ever received from Yahweh and – if it remains associated with him through praise and hope – will continue to experience. To praise him for ever in his temple was not a burdensome duty for Israel. It was not a conception which manifested to them the supposedly ridiculous existence of a believer, who devotes his life to an illusion; on the contrary, it is the fulfilment of life and the greatest happiness (cf. Ps. 84.4, 11). This cannot be understood by anyone who does not know that the splendour of the world comes solely from the present and future of God. When the individual forgets his community and the community forgets how to praise God, the individual makes a problem of his faith and the church makes God a mere topic of discussion, and there is no salvation for either. Whatever they do or do not do, whatever they change or fail to change, they will not bring about salvation, will not build up the community and will certainly not consummate the kingdom of God. For all three exist only where people look to God to give and establish them. Whenever we look away from ourselves to God, we are set free, and a new beginning together is made possible. The hope of his presence beyond the failure which is revealed for everyone by death, if not before, gives the patience to wait and work in tranquillity even in an imperfect world full of imperfect people, the patience to tolerate and support one another instead of hating and ultimately destroying one another. The hope that nowadays is often laughed at, that even the dead praise God, the expectation of the eternal praise of God, may not be so naïve as many suppose and many would like to believe.

CHAPTER 39.1–8

Envoys from Babylon

1 At that time Merodach-baladan the son of Baladan, king of Babylon, sent envoys with letters and a present to Hezekiah, for he heard that he had been sick and had recovered. ²And Hezekiah welcomed them; and he showed themª his treasure house, the silver, the gold, the spices, the precious oil,ᵇ his whole winecellar,ᶜ all that was found in his storehouses. There was nothing in his house or in all his realm that Hezekiah did not show them. ³Then Isaiah the prophet came to King Hezekiah, and said to him, 'What did these men say? And when did they come to you?' Hezekiah said, 'They have come to me from a far country, from Babylon.' ⁴He said, 'What have they seen in your house?' Hezekiah answered, 'They have seen all that is in my house; there is nothing in my storehouses that I did not show them.' ⁵Then Isaiah said to Hezekiah,

6   'Hear the word of Yahweh Sebaoth;
    Behold, the days are coming,
      when all that is in your house,
  and that which your fathers have stored up
      till this day, shall be carried to Babylon;
      nothing shall be left, says the Lord,

7   And some of your own sons, who come ⟨out of your loins⟩ᵈ
      shall be taken away;
    and whom you will beget,
      they shall be eunuchs in the palace of the king of Babylon.'

⁸Then said Hezekiah to Isaiah, 'The word of Yahweh which you have spoken is good.' For he thought, There will be peace and security in my days.

This narrative is taken with only very slight changes from II Kings 20.12–19, and together with the stories about the prophet in the three preceding chapters was a later interpolation into the book of Isaiah. Its purpose shown in vv. 5–7. The plundering of the royal treasury of

---

ª I.e. those who brought the letters and present.

ᵇ II Kings 20.13 refers to perfume. The placing of the article before *šemen* has altered the meaning.

ᶜ Convincingly argued by M. Dahood, *Bib* 40, 1959, pp. 162ff., cf. Jer. 48.11. But it should be noted that most scholars assume that the word refers to the armoury.

ᵈ Read *mimmēʿēkā* with 1Q Isa.

Judah by Nebuchadnezzar and the deportation of the Davidic kings to Babylon are traced back to an episode in the life of king Hezekiah, and ultimately to a saying of Yahweh imparted through the prophet Isaiah. The connection with the immediately preceding narrative of the sickness and healing of the king is provided by the redator in v. 1b.[a] Similarly, the general indication of time at the beginning of the verse provides a loose link. The substance of the narrative is derived firstly from the historical recollection that an embassy from the Babylonian king Merodach-baladan, the Marduk-aplu-idinna of the cuneiform texts, once came to Jerusalem with presents. The enterprising prince of *bīt yakin*, who belonged to the Aramaean tribes of southern Babylonia, succeeded in 721–710 and again in 703, though only for nine months, in ascending the royal throne of Babylon. He established himself with the aid of Elamite military assistance, which he bought with rich presents. After he had been driven out of *bīt yakin* by Sennacherib in the year 700, he withdrew to the Elamite *nagītu*, where he seems to have died in 694.[b] It is quite possible that with the support of the Arabs Marduk-aplu-idinna may have sent an embassy to Jerusalem by the southern route, avoiding the highway which ascended the Euphrates and then led across the 'fertile crescent' to Syria. This may have happened either during the years of the Philistine revolt in 713–711, or again in the year 703, when a coalition was formed against Assyria in the west under the leadership of Hezekiah.[c] Perhaps the second date is the most likely; in this

---

[a] Cf. J. Gray, *I and II Kings*, OTL, [2]1970, p. 702.

[b] Cf. J. A. Brinkman, 'Merodach-Baladan II', in *Studies Presented to A. Leo Oppenheim*, Chicago 1964, pp. 6ff.; 'Elamite Military Aid to Merodach-Baladan', *JNES* 25, 1966, pp. 161ff., and finally M. Dietrich, *Die Aramäer Südbabyloniens in der Sargonidenzeit (700–648)*, AOAT 7, 1970, pp. 1ff. For those whose name was *Bēl-iddina*, cf. *ibid.*, p. 43. According to Brinkman, it cannot be demonstrated that Nabopolassar, the father of Nebuchadnezzar, belonged to the dynasty of Yakin, to which Merodach-Baladan belonged (*Studies*, p. 29). The name of the father of Merodach-Baladan is also uncertain. It is possible but not certain that it was Erība-Marduk, *ibid.*, p. 30. The fact that II Chron. 32.31, with II Kings 20.12ff. and Isa. 39 can hardly be treated as an independent source and is clearly tendentious (cf. W. Rudolph, HAT I.21, 1955, pp. 613ff.) makes it unnecessary to discuss these passages. Brinkman, *Studies*, p. 36, considers that a selective evaluation of this verse is adequate confirmation of the visit of the Babylonians to Hezekiah.

[c] The reason why 703 rather than 705 is given here is connected with the chronology of Sennacherib, who was certainly in Babylon in 705, but did not ascend the throne in Assur until 704. Cf. J. Levy, 'The Chronology of Sennacherib's Accession', *AnOr* 12, 1935, pp. 225ff.

case Hezekiah's conspiracies would have extended from the Ethiopian capital of Napata as far as the ancient Mesopotamian capital of Babylon. This already implies that it was more than a courtesy visit such as has been in both ancient and modern times customary among monarchs and rulers. However, the narrator has no longer any inkling of the true political circumstances. Secondly, it was historical knowledge that Hezekiah and Isaiah had been contemporaries. The source of this knowledge may have been the Isaiah narrative in chs. 36–38, but oral tradition is not excluded. Thirdly, what is prophesied in the story had certainly already taken place: Jerusalem had already been plundered by Nebuchadnezzar in 587 and the Davidic line had already been deported to Babylon. Indeed we must ask whether we are right in dating it no later than the exile. For, fourthly, we must consider whether it may not already refer to the service rendered by Judaean princes at the Persian court, which is implied by Ezra 3.2 (cf. I Chron. 3.17) and for which Neh. 2.1ff. is probably evidence.[a] For while the remarkable answer of Hezekiah, and his thoughts in v. 8, may be partly apotropaic in intention,[b] and partly the expression of a degree of submission to God and at the same time a certain egotism, v. 8 shows that the events of 587 and their subsequent effects were accepted with a certain indifference by the narrator and his hearers or readers. There is as little sign of a still lively sorrow than there is of eschatological exaggeration, although the story contains an attempt at the interpretation of Judah's fate.

In order to appreciate the distinctive attitude of mind it displays, we must follow the course of the narrative as straightforwardly as possible. An embassy comes from Babylon with a letter and gifts, in order – so the narrative now relates – to congratulate the king who had just been healed.[c] At this the king of the small state of Jerusalem must have felt honoured and must have been pleased, and in order to make some impression upon the ambassadors of one who (in the imagination of the narrator and his community!) was a mighty king, he takes him to his treasury, in order to show him his gold and silver, his spices and perfume,[d] or, without listing everything, to show him

---

[a] Cf. U. Kellermann, *Nehemia. Quellen, Überlieferung, Geschichte,* BZAW 102, 1967, pp. 154ff. and especially p. 157. Cf. also Dan. 1.3ff. and Esth. 2.5f.

[b] Gray, pp. 702f.

[c] For the exchange of embassies on the occasion of illnesses, cf. Tell El-Amarna tablet. 23.

[d] See above, p. 408 note b.

all he possessed! Should he not have done so? Had he any right to do so? When a modern hearer or reader remarks upon his ostentation, he is no longer aware of the offence to the deity which is implied by the king's behaviour, and which is not made completely explicit in the word of God which follows. That this was immediately obvious to the men of the ancient world can be seen from the conversations invented by Herodotus between Croesus and Solon and Amasis and Polycrates.[a] A man who boasts of his riches and his treasures provokes the 'envy of the gods', which in avenging this arrogance becomes something more than and different from human envy; it is the maintenance of the order which is damaged when someone proudly imagines that he can live by what is under his own control.[b] As a reminder of the Greek narrative of the tyrant of Samos and the Egyptian king, let us quote two stanzas from Schiller's 'Ring of Polycrates', in which the theme is expressed. When in the course of the dialogue the news of victory over the Cretan fleet is brought, Amasis says:

> These words the guest heard with horror:
> 'I ought to count you fortunate indeed!
> And yet,' he said, 'I tremble for your safety.
> I dread the envy of the gods;
> The unalloyed joy of life
> Is not given to any mortal.'

Learning from this that happiness must be mixed with sorrow if misfortune is not to strike, the tyrant throws his ring into the sea. But the cook immediately finds it in the fish:

> 'See, lord, the ring which you wore,
> I found it in the fish's belly.
> Oh, is your good fortune boundless?'

And what is the answer?

> Then the guest turned with a shudder;
> 'Here I can remain no longer,
> And you can no longer be my friend.
> The gods desire your ruin –
> I shall haste away lest I die with you.'
> So saying he quickly embarked.

[a] Herodotus I, 26ff. and III, 40ff.

[b] Cf. H. Lloyd-Jones, *The Justice of Zeus*, Sather Classical Lectures 41, Berkeley and London 1971, pp. 68ff.

That these ideas are found in the Old Testament is shown by the story of the tower of Babel (Gen. 11.1ff.) and particularly by the taunt song upon the king of Babylon in Isa. 14.4bff. But the divine side of history has its human aspect. Not only can we say that Yahweh punishes the arrogance of the king. We also note that the king's ambassadors become spies. Their report provoked the greed of their master. Thus the kings of Babylon did not rest until they had taken possession of the treasures of the royal house, its precious goods, and the most precious of all, his sons. Only in the later forms of apocalyptic are the acts of God and human acts seen as two spheres which, although they are related, are separate. Apart from this, faith interprets what takes place in the world as the act of God, because the splendour and the terrors of the world are the consequence of God's presence or absence, his closeness or distance.

Other details of the narrative are more incidental: the secret knowledge of the prophet assumed in v. 3, the overlooking of the first part of the question, which is of no importance for the rest of the narrative, in Hezekiah's answer in the same verse, and finally the carefully engineered correspondence between the act of the king and the consequences of his act in v. 4 (cf. v. 6) which gives the showing of his treasures almost the significance of a prophetic sign. But they should be noted, if the structure of the narrative is to be understood. By their very nature they add nothing to the portrait of the historical prophet Isaiah. Instead, they show us how the figure of this great man could still move later generations.